EMILIA

UPDA

Cambridge IGCSE™ and O Level

History

Option B:
The 20th Century

Third edition

Ben Walsh
Benjamin Harrison

Covers the revised Cambridge IGCSE™, IGCSE (9-1) and O Level syllabuses (0470/0977/2147) for examination from 2024

Endorsement indicates that a resource has passed Cambridge International's rigorous quality-assurance process and is suitable to support the delivery of a Cambridge International syllabus. However, endorsed resources are not the only suitable materials available to support teaching and learning, and are not essential to be used to achieve the qualification. Resource lists found on the Cambridge International website will include this resource and other endorsed resources. Any example answers to questions taken from past question papers, practice questions, accompanying marks and mark schemes included in this resource have been written by the authors and are for guidance only. They do not replicate examination papers. In examinations the way marks are awarded may be different. Any references to assessment and/or assessment preparation are the publisher's interpretation of the syllabus requirements. Examiners will not use endorsed resources as a source of material for any assessment set by Cambridge International. While the publishers have made every attempt to ensure that advice on the qualification and its assessment is accurate, the official syllabus, specimen assessment materials and any associated assessment guidance materials produced by the awarding body are the only authoritative source of information and should always be referred to for definitive guidance. Cambridge International recommends that teachers consider using a range of teaching and learning resources based on their own professional judgement of their students' needs. Cambridge International has not paid for the production of this resource, nor does Cambridge International receive any royalties from its sale. For more information about the endorsement process, please visit www.cambridgeinternational.org/endorsed-resources

Third-party websites and resources referred to in this publication have not been endorsed by Cambridge Assessment International Education.

Every effort has been made to trace all copyright holders, but if any have been inadvertently overlooked, the Publishers will be pleased to make the necessary arrangements at the first opportunity.

Although every effort has been made to ensure that website addresses are correct at time of going to press, Hodder Education cannot be held responsible for the content of any website mentioned in this book. It is sometimes possible to find a relocated web page by typing in the address of the home page for a website in the URL window of your browser.

The practice questions, accompanying marks and mark schemes included in this resource have been written by the authors and are an opportunity to practise exam skills and are a guideline only. They do not replicate examination papers. In examinations the way marks are awarded may be different. Any references to assessment and/or assessment preparation are the publisher's interpretation of the syllabus requirements and may not fully reflect the approach of Cambridge Assessment International Education.

Hachette UK's policy is to use papers that are natural, renewable and recyclable products and made from wood grown in well-managed forests and other controlled sources. The logging and manufacturing processes are expected to conform to the environmental regulations of the country of origin.

Orders: please contact Hachette UK Distribution, Hely Hutchinson Centre, Milton Road, Didcot, Oxfordshire, OX11 7HH. Telephone: +44 (0)1235 827827. Email education@hachette.co.uk Lines are open from 9 a.m. to 5 p.m., Monday to Friday. You can also order through our website: www.hoddereducation.co.uk

ISBN: 978 1 3983 7505 5

© Ben Walsh and Benjamin Harrison 2022

First published in 2022 by

Hodder Education,
An Hachette UK Company
Carmelite House
50 Victoria Embankment
London EC4Y 0DZ

www.hoddereducation.co.uk

Impression number   10 9 8 7 6 5 4 3 2 1

Year   2026   2025   2024   2023   2022

All rights reserved. Apart from any use permitted under UK copyright law, no part of this publication may be reproduced or transmitted in any form or by any means, electronic or mechanical, including photocopying and recording, or held within any information storage and retrieval system, without permission in writing from the publisher or under licence from the Copyright Licensing Agency Limited. Further details of such licences (for reprographic reproduction) may be obtained from the Copyright Licensing Agency Limited, www.cla.co.uk

Cover photo © phanasitti/stock.adobe.com

Illustrations by Aptara Inc.

Third edition typeset by Aptara Inc.

Produced by DZS Grafik, Printed in Bosnia & Herzegovina

A catalogue record for this title is available from the British Library.

Contents

How this book will help you to achieve your
best in Cambridge IGCSE™ and O Level History — iv

Photo acknowledgements — vi

SECTION 1 Core Content Option B

The 20th century: International Relations from 1919

Part 1 The Inter-War Years, 1919–39 — 2
1. Was the Treaty of Versailles fair? — 5
2. To what extent was the League of Nations a success? — 25
3. How far was Hitler's foreign policy to blame for the outbreak of war in Europe in 1939? — 55

Part 2 The Cold War, 1945–75 — 78
4. Who was to blame for the Cold War? — 81
5. How effectively did the USA contain the spread of communism? — 99
6. How secure was the USSR's control over eastern Europe, 1948–c.1989? — 127

Focus on: Structured Questions — 148
Focus on: Document Questions — 155

SECTION 2 Depth Studies

7. Russia, 1905–41 — 171
8. Germany, 1918–45 — 221
9. The USA, 1919–41 — 285

Focus on: Structured Questions — 338
Focus on: Alternative to Coursework — 343

Glossary — 356

Index — 363

How this book will help you to achieve your best in Cambridge IGCSE™/O Level History

It will help you to explore the Key Questions

The syllabus is issues based. The aim is for you to develop and support informed views about the past. This book reflects that structure and that aim.
- Each chapter is organised around a Key Question from the syllabus.
- Each Key Question is broken down into Focus Points which tackle the main issues within each Key Question.
- Each Focus Point is tackled through a Focus Task. If you tackle all the Focus Points, you will be in a strong position to form your own arguments and views in relation to the Key Question.

It will help you to learn the content

This book covers the Option B 20th century route through the Core Content plus three Depth Studies. You will need good knowledge of the main events and the detail. This book will help you acquire both.

The author text explains all the key content clearly. But it does not just drone on about one thing after another. It helps you understand and investigate issues and establish links and relationships between topics.

SOURCE 1

An American cartoon commenting on Stalin's take-over of eastern Europe. The bear represents the USSR.

It's full of brilliant **sources**. History is at its best when you can see what real people said, did, wrote, sang, watched on film, laughed about, cried over and got upset about. Sources can really help you to understand the story better and remember it because they help you to see the big concepts and ideas in terms of what they meant to individuals at the time.

The **Factfiles** (key events) and **Profiles** (key people) are packed with hard facts and examples to use in your own work to support your arguments.

Factfile

The League of Nations
- The League's home was in Geneva in Switzerland.

Think!

Think of a suitable headline for each of the six 'episodes' in the collapse of the USSR.

Many of the Focus Tasks deal with quite big issues that you will find easier if you have thought things through beforehand. So the **Think!** feature is designed to prepare you for the Focus Tasks. Sometimes they are literally steps en route to a Focus Task, as in Chapter 4; at other times they simply ask you to think about an issue that is particularly important for understanding the period better. **Activities** serve a similar purpose – get you thinking about what you are reading – but they usually invite a more creative response.

Revision Tip

Make sure you can remember at least two examples of agreement at Yalta and the one (main!) disagreement.

There are **Revision Tips**. If the content seems overwhelming to you and you just don't know where to start this gives you an achievable target – just a couple of key points on each topic to identify and remember. Think of it as a 'first aid' kit.

Keywords

Make sure you know what these terms mean and are able to define them confidently.

Keywords. Every topic has its own vocabulary. If you don't know what these words mean you won't be able to write about the subject. So for each chapter we have provided a keyword list. These are the kind of words or terms that could be used in sources or a question without any explanation so you need to be able to understand them and use them confidently. They are all defined in the **Glossary** on pages 354–60.

Chapter Summary

The collapse of international peace

Finally there is a content **Summary** at the end of every chapter or Key Question. This condenses all the content into a few points, which should help you to get your bearings in even the most complicated content.

It will help you to apply what you learn

The next big aim of this book is to help you to work with the content and think about it so that you are ready to apply what you learn. This is not an easy task. You will not suddenly develop this skill. You need to practise studying an issue, deciding what you think, and then selecting from all that you know the points that are really relevant to your argument.

> **FOCUS TASK 7.10**
>
> **How did the Bolsheviks consolidate their rule?**
> 1. Draw a timeline from 1917 to 1924, and mark on it the events of that period mentioned in the text.
> 2. Mark on the timeline:
>   a) one moment at which you think Bolshevik rule was most threatened
>   b) one moment at which you think it was most secure.
> 3. Write an explanation of how the Bolsheviks made their rule more secure. Mention the following:
>   - the power of the Red Army
>   - treatment of opposition
>   - War Communism
>   - the New Economic Policy
>   - the Treaty of Brest-Litovsk
>   - the victory in the Civil War
>   - the promise of a new society

The main way we help you with this is through the **Focus Tasks**.

The title is linked to a **Focus Point** or **Key Question** from the Cambridge IGCSE and O Level syllabus.

Often we ask you to create a comparative or a summary **chart or timeline**, as in this example. The completed chart will also be perfect for revision purposes.

They help you to **apply your knowledge**. One of the most important skills in history is the ability to select, organise and deploy (use) knowledge to answer a particular question.

The structure of the task helps you to **focus on what is important** and ignore what is not. There are bullet points or charts to help you to **organise** your thinking.

And remember, to help you further, most Focus Tasks have a linked **Revision Tip** that gives you a more basic target – just a couple of key points that you will be able to apply in your answers.

It helps you prepare for your examination

If you read all the text and tackle all the Focus Tasks in this book we are sure you would find you were well prepared for your exam. However, this book also provides you exam-focused guidance with example answers and commentaries for different types of question. So:

> **Focus on**

Focus on starts on page 148 (for the Core Content) and page 338 (for the Depth Studies). These pages provide you with guidance on the exam requirements and show you the kinds of questions you might be asked, although these are not past paper questions. We also analyse and comment on some sample answers. These are not answers by past candidates. We have written them to help you to see what a good answer might look like.

> **PRACTICE QUESTIONS**
> 1 (a) What were the Five-Year Plans? (4)

Practice Questions. At the end of every chapter we have written some practice questions. These are **not** from past papers. And in the 'Focus on' sections there are plenty more examples of structured essays and questions on prescribed topics with sources and information.

> **Source Analysis**
> Explain how and why Sources 11 and 12 differ in their interpretation of the Soviet intervention.

Source Analysis. Sources are an integral part of history. Historians use them to write history. We have used them to add colour and human detail to the stories of Modern World History. In Cambridge IGCSE and O Level History you will also use sources to examine an issue, when you will need to evaluate sources. So dotted throughout this book are Source Analysis questions that help you to evaluate sources – for example, thinking about their message, their purpose or their usefulness for a particular line of enquiry.

Photo credits

pp.1,2,78, 167 © Universal Images Group / Getty Images; p.4 © Punch Cartoon Library / TopFoto; p.6 © Hulton Archive/Getty Images; p.7 Image courtesy of Kent Cartoon Library © Solo Syndication; p.8 © Hulton Archive/Getty Images; p.9 © Hulton Archive/Getty Images; p.10 © Illustrated London News Ltd/Mary Evans; p.14 © Mary Evans Picture Library; p.15 © TopFoto.co.uk; p.16 © ullstein bild/TopFoto; p.17 © akg-images; p.18 Cartoon by Will Dyson published by Daily Herald on 13 May 1919, British Cartoon Library; p.19 © Topfoto; p.21 *l* © Graphik: Landesarchiv Berlin/N.N, *r* © Imagno / Hulton Archive / Getty Images; p.24 © United Nations Library Geneva; p.26 © Express Newspapers, London; p.27 *l* © Punch Cartoon Library / TopFoto; p.28 'Your Bridge, Jonathan. We Shan't quarrel about this…', The League of Nations Bridge, American cartoon reprinted in the British newspaper 'The Star', June 1919 (newsprint), American School, (20th century) / British Library, London, UK / © British Library Board. All Rights Reserved / Bridgeman Images; p.29 © Punch Cartoon Library / TopFoto; p.30 © United Nations Library Geneva; p.37 © Punch Cartoon Library / TopFoto; p.38 © Punch Cartoon Library / TopFoto; p.45 © Solo Syndication/Associated Newspapers Ltd.; p.47 © Solo Syndication/ Associated Newspapers Ltd.; p.49 © Punch Cartoon Library / TopFoto; p.50 © Bildarchiv Preussischer Kulturbesitz; p.51 © Punch Cartoon Library / TopFoto; p.54 © Solo Syndication/Associated Newspapers Ltd. Photo: John Frost Historical Newspapers; p.59 *t* © Photo 12 / Alamy Stock Photo, *b* Cartoon by David Low, the Evening Standard 18 January 1935 © Solo Syndication/Associated Newspapers Ltd. Photo: British Cartoon Archive; p.60 *l* © Bruce Alexander Russell, *r* © The Art Archive/ Shutterstock; p.61 © Punch Cartoon Library / TopFoto; p.62 © Ken Gibson / TopFoto; p.63 *l* © TopFoto; p.65 © Solo Syndication/Associated Newspapers Ltd.; p.67 © Popperfoto/Getty Images, *r* © TopFoto; p.68 © Punch Cartoon Library / TopFoto; p.69 © Alinari/TopFoto; p.70 © TopFoto; p.72 © GRANGER - Historical Picture Archvie / Alamy Stock Photo; p.80 © Granger / TopFoto; p.82 © Solo Syndication/Associated Newspapers Ltd.; p.87 © Photo 12/Universal Images Group/Getty Images; p.88 *l* © Solo Syndication/Associated Newspapers Ltd.; p.92 *l* © Hulton Archive/Stringer/Getty Images; p.101 © Solo Syndication/ Associated Newspapers Ltd.; p.102 © VintageCorner / Alamy Stock Photo; p.103 © Picture Post/Stringer/Getty Images; p.110 © Cartoon by Victor Weisz, London Evening Standard, 24 October 1962, Solo Syndication/Associated Newspapers Ltd./British Cartoon Archive; p.111 © Solo Syndication/Associated Newspapers Ltd.; p.114 © Malcolm Browne/AP/Shutterstock; p.119 © ullstein bild/ullstein bild via Getty Images; p.120 © CBS Photo Archive/Getty images; p.121 1967 Herblock Cartoon © The Herb Block Foundation; p.131 © Keystone/Hulton Archive/Getty Images; p.133 *t* © Keystone Press / Alamy Stock Photo, *b* © Josef Koudelka / Magnum Photos; p.136 *tl* © TopFoto, *tr* © Popperfoto/Getty Images, *bl* © Patrice Habans/Paris Match via Getty Images; p.138 © Keystone/Getty Images; p.140 © Paul Popper/ Popperfoto/Getty; p.143 © Pictorial Press Ltd / Alamy Stock Photo; p.145 *t* © Wojtek Laski/Getty Images, *b* © Atlantic Syndication/Andrews McMeel Syndication; p.157 © News of the World/NI Syndication; p.158 © Punch Cartoon Library / TopFoto; p.160 © Punch Cartoon Library / TopFoto; p.161 'Your Bridge, Jonathan. We Shan't quarrel about this…', The League of Nations Bridge, American cartoon reprinted in the British newspaper 'The Star', June 1919 (newsprint), American School, (20th century) / British Library, London, UK / © British Library Board. All Rights Reserved / Bridgeman Images; p.164 1967 Herblock Cartoon © The Herb Block Foundation; p.169 © Popperfoto/Getty Images; p.170 © David King Collection; p.173 © Illustrated London News; p.175 © David King Collection; p.177 © PhotoStock-Israel / Alamy Stock Photo; p.179 © Sovfoto/Universal Images Group/Shutterstock; p.181 © David King Collection; p.183 © Mary Evans Picture Library; p.189 Science History Images / Alamy Stock Photo; p.190 © Pictorial Press Ltd / Alamy Stock Photo; p.193 *l* © Library of Congress Prints and Photographs Division, LC-DIG-ggbain-30798, *r* © Illustrated London News; p.196 Poster depicting 'The Bolshevik Rule over the Cossack Villages', 1918–21 (colour litho), Russian School, (20th century) / British Library, London, UK / © British Library Board. All Rights Reserved / Bridgeman Images; p.197 © Bolshevik cartoon on the intervention of the USA, Britain and France in the Russian Civil War, 1919 (colour litho), Russian School, (20th century) / Private Collection / Peter Newark Military Pictures / The Bridgeman Art Library; p.198 © Topical Press Agency/Getty Images; p.201 © David King Collection; p.203 © Illustrated London News; p.208 © Topham Picturepoint/ TopFoto; p.209 Original materials held by University of Chicago Library Special Collections Research Center; p.212 *l* © Album / Alamy Stock Photo; p.213 *l* © David King Collection; p.216 Original materials held by University of Chicago Library Special Collections Research Center; p.220 © Shawshots / Alamy Stock Photo; p.229 © Graphik: Landesarchiv Berlin/N.N; p.230 *l* © Punch Cartoon Library / TopFoto, *r* © Ullsteinbild/ Topfoto; p.231 © World History Archive/Topfoto.co.uk; p.233 © Bettmann/Getty Images; p.235 © Hulton Archive/Getty Images; p.236 © Peter Newark Pictures/Bridgeman Images; p.238 (Rohm) © GRANGER - Historical Picture Archive / Alamy Stock Photo, (Goebbels) © Keystone-France/Gamma-Keystone via Getty Images, (Himmler) © Everett Collection Inc / Alamy Stock Photo, (Goering) © Vintage_ Space / Alamy Stock Photo, (Hess) © ullstein bild Dtl./Getty Images ; p.240 © David Crausby/Alamy; p.242 © Bridgeman Images; p.243 *b* © Hulton Archive/Getty Images; p.246 © TopFoto; p.248 © Photo 12/ Universal Images Group/Getty Images; p.252 *t* © Keystone / Stringer / Hulton Archive / Getty Images, *b* © Bridgeman Images; p.253 *t* © Ullsteinbild/Topfoto, *b* © Ullsteinbild/Topfoto; p.254 *tl* © Keystone/ Getty Images, *bl* © Topical Press Agency/Getty Images, *b* © Bridgeman Images; p.256 © war posters / Alamy; p.257 © Topham Picturepoint/ TopFoto; p.258 © Hulton-Deutsch Collection/CORBIS/Corbis via Getty Images; p.260 © Ullstein Bild/TopFoto; p.261 No source; p.265 © Bridgeman Images; p.266 © Ben Walsh; p.267 © Chronicle / Alamy Stock Photo; p.268 © Ullstein Bild/TopFoto; p.271 © Ralf Feltz / TopFoto; p.275 © Popperfoto/ Getty Images; p.276 © World History Archive / Alamy Stock Photo; p.277 © Photo 12 / Alamy Stock Photo; p.278 *l* © Corbis Historical via Getty Images, *r* © Heritage-Images / TopFoto; p.284 © Library of Congress Prints and Photographs Division; LC-DIG-fsa-8b29516; p.289 (Harding) © Niday Picture Library / Alamy Stock Photo, (Coolidge) © Everett Collection Inc / Alamy Stock Photo, (Hoover) © Stock Montage/Stock Montage/Getty Images, p.291 *r* © Everett Collection Historical / Alamy Stock Photo; p.293 © Peter Newark American Pictures / Bridgeman Images; p.294 © Bettman/Getty Images; p.296 © The Builder (colour litho) by Beneker, Gerrit Albertus (1882–1934), Private Collection/Peter Newark American Pictures/The Bridgeman Art Library; p.297 © Lordprice Collection / Alamy Stock Photo; p.299 *t* © Bettman/Getty Images, *b* © Bettman/Getty Images; p.300 © Corbis Historical/Getty Images; p.302 © San Francisco Examiner; p.304 © Mary Evans Picture Library; p.305 © Mary Evans Picture Library; p.306 © Bettman/Getty Images; p.307 © US National Archives, Rocky Mountains Division; p.309 *l* © 'Wanted … a little boy's plea', c. 1915 (engraving), American School, (20th Century), Private Collection/Peter Newark American Pictures/The Bridgeman Art Library, *r* © Culver Pictures; p.311 *t* © Bettman/Getty Images, *m* © Bettman/ Getty Images, *b* © Clive Weed, Judge, June 12, 1926—American Social History Project; p.312 © Underwood Archives/Getty Images; p.317 © Popperfoto/Getty Images; p.318 Charles Deering McCormick Library of Special Collections, Northwestern University Library, © John T. McCutcheon Jr.; p.319 © Car and farm machinery buried by dust and sand, Dallas, South Dakota, 1936 (b/w photo) by American Photographer (20th Century), Private Collection/Peter Newark American Pictures/The Bridgeman Art Library; p.320 *t* © Topfoto, *b* © Corbis Historical/Getty Images; p.322 © 'Smilette', Democrat Election Poster, 1932 (litho) by American School (20th Century), Private Collection/ Peter Newark American Pictures/The Bridgeman Art Library; p.325 *l* © Granger, NYC / TopFoto, *r* © The Granger Collection, NYC / TopFoto; p.328 © Library of Congress Prints and Photographs Division; LC-DIG-fsa-8b29516; p.329 © Photographs in the Carol M. Highsmith Archive, Library of Congress, Prints and Photographs Division; p.330 © The Granger Collection, NYC / TopFoto; p.331 *l* © Library of Congress Prints and Photographs Division, LC-USZ62-117121, *r* 'Boo-hoo the New Deal is ruining the Country', cartoon of the effects of Franklin Roosevelt's (1882-1945) economic policies, 1936 (litho), American School, (20th century) / Private Collection / Peter Newark American Pictures / Bridgeman Images; p.332 *t* © Punch Cartoon Library / TopFoto, *b* Courtesy Franklin D. Roosevelt Library, Hyde Park, New York; p.333 Courtesy Franklin D. Roosevelt Library, Hyde Park, New York; p.335 © Bridgeman Images.

SECTION 1
Core Content

Option B The 20th century: International Relations from 1919

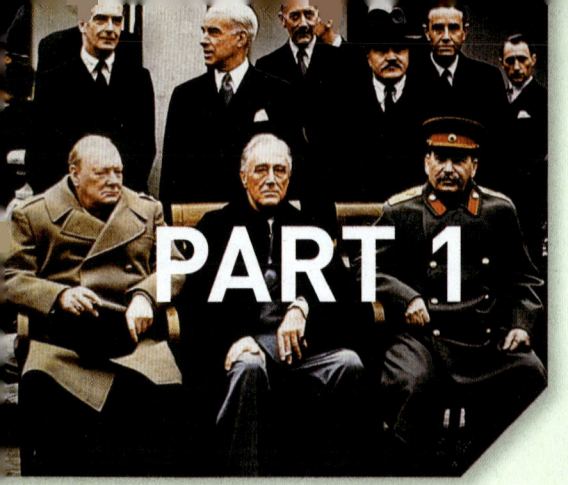

PART 1

The Inter-War Years, 1919–39

1918 | 1919 | 1920 | 1921 | 1922 | 1923 | 1924 | 1925 | 1926 | 1927 | 1928 | 1929

1918: The First World War

1919–1923: Post-war crises

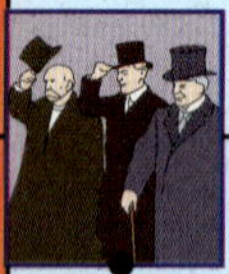

Jan–June 1919
The Paris Peace Conference: Allied leaders meet and draw up the Treaty of Versailles

Jan 1920
The League of Nations starts work. Its task is to sort out disputes between countries fairly

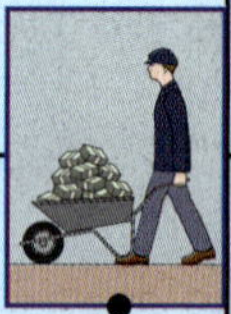

1923
Crisis in Germany as France invades the Ruhr and inflation makes money worthless

1924–1929: Improving international relations

1925
The Locarno Treaties: Germany appears to accept the Treaty of Versailles

1926
Germany joins the League of Nations

1928
The Kellogg–Briand Pact: most nations agree not to go to war to settle their disputes

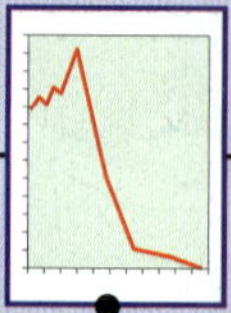

Oct 1929
The Wall Street Crash leads to a worldwide economic depression

Focus

Chapters 1–3 of this book cover a turbulent period of European history. After the trauma of the First World War, citizens of European countries were hoping for peace, prosperity and calm. Instead they got revolutions, economic depression, international disputes, dictatorships, and in the end a Second World War. How did this happen?

- In **Chapter 1** you will examine the Treaty of Versailles at the end of the First World War and consider whether it was fair on Germany. Some would say that the Treaty created problems for the future; others that it was the fairest it could have been given the very difficult situation after the First World War.
- The League of Nations was set up in 1920 to prevent war between countries. In **Chapter 2** you will evaluate its successes (it did have many) and its failures (which tend to be remembered rather more than the successes) and reach your own view on how we should remember the League – as a success or a failure or something between.
- Finally in **Chapter 3** you will examine the events of the 1930s which finally tipped Europe back into war. It is common to blame Hitler and his foreign policy for this slide to war but this chapter will help you to reach a balanced view that sees what other factors played a part.

The events in these chapters overlap in time. The timeline below gives you an overview of the main events you will be studying. It would be helpful if you made your own copy and added your own notes to it as you study.

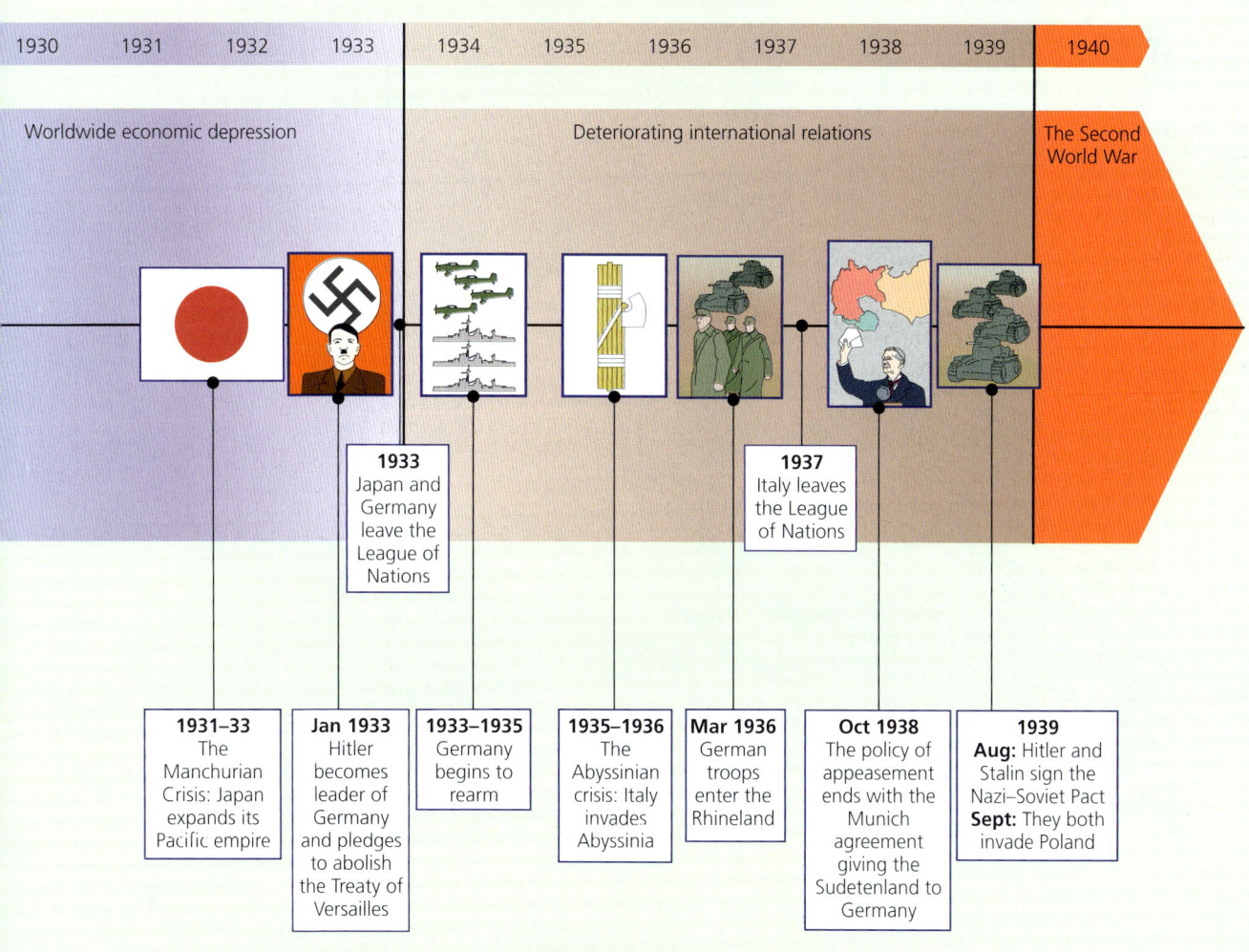

THE RECKONING.

Pan-German. "MONSTROUS, I CALL IT. WHY, IT'S FULLY A QUARTER OF WHAT *WE* SHOULD HAVE MADE *THEM* PAY, IF *WE'D* WON."

1 Was the Treaty of Versailles fair?

FOCUS POINTS
★ What were the motives and aims of the Big Three at Versailles?
★ Why did the victors not get everything they wanted?
★ What was the impact of the Treaty on Germany up to the end of 1923?
★ Could the Treaty be justified at the time?

However long or violent a war is, eventually the opposing sides must make peace. But because war is destructive and leaves a bitter legacy, the peacemaking after a long conflict can be the hardest job of all.

The people who had that role in 1919 had a particularly hard task. The First World War involved more countries, using more powerful weapons, causing greater casualties and physical destruction, than any war before it. The war had bankrupted some countries. It led to revolutions in others. There was bitterness and resentment.

In this post-war atmosphere almost everyone agreed that part of the job of the peacemakers was to avoid another war like it – but no one agreed how to do that.

Any treaty is a balancing act. The peacemakers have to keep the victors happy but ensure that the defeated country accepts the terms of the peace. Was it really possible to produce a treaty which all sides would have seen as fair? That's the key question you will have to think about in this chapter.

You are going to investigate what happened when these peacemakers got together to draw up the Treaty of Versailles.

You will focus on:
- what the peacemakers were hoping to achieve
- how they worked
- what they decided
- why they decided it.

Then you will reach conclusions about the key question – how 'fair' was the Treaty they came up with, which means thinking about:
- whether people at the time thought the Treaty was fair, and why or why not
- whether historians (with the benefit of hindsight) think it was fair.

This British cartoon was published in 1919 shortly after the terms of the Treaty of Versailles had been announced. A German man is holding the treaty terms which say how much Germany has to pay for the damage caused by the war.
1. Does he think the Treaty is fair? Why or why not?
2. Does the cartoonist think the Treaty is fair? Why or why not?
3. What is the message of this cartoon?

Profile

Woodrow Wilson
(President of the USA)

Background
- Born 1856.
- Became a university professor.
- First entered politics in 1910.
- Became President in 1912 and was re-elected in 1916.
- From 1914 to 1917 he concentrated on keeping the USA out of the war.
- Once the USA had joined the war in 1917, he drew up the Fourteen Points as the basis for ending the war fairly, so that future wars could be avoided.

Character
- An idealist and a reformer.
- As President, he had campaigned against corruption in politics and business. However, he had a poor record with regard to the rights of African Americans.
- He was obstinate. Once he made his mind up on an issue he was almost impossible to shift.

Aims of the Big Three: Wilson's viewpoint

High hopes for peace

Looking back it may seem that the peacemakers in 1919 had an impossible job. But that is not how people saw it at the time. There was great optimism. One of the main reasons for these high hopes was the American President Woodrow Wilson.

In 1918 Wilson made a speech outlining Fourteen Points (see Factfile), guidelines for a just and lasting peace treaty to end conflict.

When he arrived in Europe for the Paris Peace Conference, Wilson was seen almost as a saintly figure. Newspaper reports described wounded soldiers in Italy trying to kiss the hem of his cloak and in France peasant families kneeling to pray as his train passed by.

Wilson's ideas

How did Wilson think the peacemakers could build a better and more peaceful world?

- **Don't be too harsh on Germany.** Wilson did believe Germany should be punished. But he also believed that if Germany was treated harshly, some day it would recover and want revenge. He was also concerned that extremist groups, especially communists, might exploit resentment among the Germans and communists might even seize power in Germany as they had in Russia in 1917.
- **Strengthen democracy in defeated countries.** For Wilson democracy was a key to peace in Europe. If leaders in defeated nations had to listen to the views of their people and win their votes those people would not let their leaders cause another war.
- **Give self-determination to small countries that had once been part of the European empires.** He wanted the different peoples of eastern Europe (for example, Poles, Czechs and Slovaks) to rule themselves rather than be part of Austria–Hungary's empire.
- **International co-operation.** Wilson also believed that nations should co-operate to achieve world peace. This would be achieved through a 'League of Nations', Wilson's most important of the Fourteen Points.

You can see from these principles that Wilson was an idealist. However, he was not a politician who could be pushed around. For example, he refused to cancel the debts owed to the USA by Britain and its Allies so that he could put pressure on them to accept his ideas.

FOCUS TASK 1.1

What were the motives and aims of the Big Three at Versailles?

Using the information and sources on pages 6–9, fill out a chart like the one below summarising the aims of the three leaders at the Paris Peace Conference. Leave the fifth column blank. You will need it for a later task.

Leader	Country	Attitude towards Germany	Main aim(s) and motives	
Wilson				
Lloyd George				
Clemenceau				

Revision Tip

Your completed chart from the Focus Task should be perfect for revision on this topic. The basic requirement is to be sure you can name:
- each of the Big Three
- one priority for each of them at the peace talks
- two issues that they disagreed about.

SOURCE 1

THE MELTING POT.

A cartoon published in 1919 in an Australian newspaper.

Source Analysis
Study the main features of Source 1. Who is making the soup? Who is helping him? What are they adding to the mix? What is already in there?

Factfile

The Fourteen Points: a summary

1. No secret treaties.
2. Free access to the seas in peacetime or wartime.
3. Free trade between countries.
4. All countries to work towards disarmament.
5. Colonies to have a say in their own future.
6. German troops to leave Russia.
7. Independence for Belgium.
8. France to regain Alsace–Lorraine.
9. Frontier between Austria and Italy to be adjusted.
10. Self-determination for the peoples of eastern Europe (they should rule themselves and not be ruled by empires).
11. Serbia to have access to the sea.
12. Self-determination for the people in the Turkish empire.
13. Poland to become an independent state with access to the sea.
14. League of Nations to be set up.

Factfile

The Paris Peace Conference, 1919–20

- The Conference took place in the Palace of Versailles (a short distance from Paris).
- It lasted for twelve months.
- Thirty-two nations were supposed to be represented, but no one from the defeated countries was invited.
- Five treaties were drawn up at the Conference. The main one was the Treaty of Versailles, which dealt with Germany. The other treaties dealt with Germany's allies.
- All of the important decisions on the fate of Germany were taken by Clemenceau (Prime Minister of France), Lloyd George (Prime Minister of Britain) and Wilson (President of the USA) who together were known as 'The Big Three'.
- The Big Three were supported by a huge army of diplomats and expert advisers, but the Big Three often ignored their advice.

Profile

David Lloyd George
(Prime Minister of Britain)

Background
- Born 1863.
- First entered politics in 1890.
- He was a very able politician who became Prime Minister in 1916 and remained in power until 1922.

Character

A realist. As an experienced politician, he knew there would have to be compromise. Thus he occupied the middle ground between the views of Wilson and Clemenceau.

Did everyone share Wilson's viewpoint?

Not surprisingly, when Wilson talked about lasting peace and justice other leaders agreed with him. After all, who would want to stand up in public and say they were against a just and lasting peace?!

However, many were doubtful about Wilson's ideas for achieving it. For example, 'self-determination': it would be very difficult to give the peoples of eastern Europe the opportunity to rule themselves because they were scattered across many countries. Some people were bound to end up being ruled by people from another group with different customs and a different language. Some historians have pointed out that while Wilson talked a great deal about eastern and central Europe, he did not actually know very much about the area.

There were other concerns as well. So let's look at the aims and views of the other leaders at the Paris Peace Conference: David Lloyd George (from Britain) and Georges Clemenceau (from France).

Did Lloyd George agree with Wilson?

In public Lloyd George praised Wilson and his ideas. However, in private he was less positive. He complained to one of his officials that Wilson came to Paris like a missionary to rescue the Europeans with his little sermons and lectures.

He agreed with Wilson on many issues, particularly that Germany should be punished but not too harshly. He did not want Germany to seek revenge in the future and possibly start another war.

Like Wilson he was deeply concerned that a harsh treaty might lead to a communist revolution like the one in Russia in 1917. He also wanted Britain and Germany to begin trading with each other again. Before the war, Germany had been Britain's second largest trading partner. British people might not like it, but the fact was that trade with Germany meant jobs in Britain.

However, unlike Wilson, Lloyd George had the needs of the British empire in mind. He wanted Germany to lose its navy and its colonies because they threatened the British empire.

SOURCE 2

We want a peace which will be just, but not vindictive. We want a stern peace because the occasion demands it, but the severity must be designed, not for vengeance, but for justice. Above all, we want to protect the future against a repetition of the horrors of this war.

Lloyd George speaking to the House of Commons before the Peace Conference.

SOURCE 3

If I am elected, Germany is going to pay . . . I have personally no doubt we will get everything that you can squeeze out of a lemon, and a bit more. I propose that every bit of [German-owned] property, movable and immovable, in Allied and neutral countries, whether State property or private property, should be surrendered by the Germans.

Sir Eric Geddes, a government minister, speaking to a rally in the general election campaign, December 1918.

Source Analysis

1. In what ways are Sources 2 and 3 different?
2. Are there any ways in which they are similar?

Profile

Georges Clemenceau
(Prime Minister of France)

Background
- Born 1841 (he was aged 77 when the Paris Conference began).
- First entered French politics in 1871.
- Was Prime Minister of France from 1906 to 1909.
- From 1914 to 1917 he was very critical of the French war leaders. In November 1917 he was elected to lead France through the last year of the war.

Character
A hard, tough politician with a reputation for being uncompromising. He had seen his country invaded twice by the Germans, in 1870 and in 1914. He was determined not to allow such devastation ever again.

Pressures on Lloyd George

Lloyd George faced huge public pressures at home for a harsh treaty (see Source 2). People in Britain were not sympathetic to Germany in any way. They had suffered over 1 million casualties in the fighting, as well as food shortages and other hardships at home. They had been fed anti-German propaganda for four years. They had also seen how Germany had treated Russia in 1918 when Russia surrendered. Under the Treaty of Brest-Litovsk Germany had stripped Russia of 25 per cent of its population and huge areas of Russia's best agricultural land.

Lloyd George had just won the 1918 election in Britain by promising to 'make Germany pay', even though he realised the dangers of this course of action. So Lloyd George had to balance these pressures at home with his desire not to leave Germany wanting revenge.

Did Clemenceau agree with Wilson?

In public, Clemenceau of course agreed with Wilson's aim for a fair and lasting peace. However, he found Wilson very hard to work with. While he did not publicly criticise the Fourteen Points, Clemenceau once pointed out that even God had only needed Ten Commandments!

The major disagreement was over Germany. Clemenceau and other French leaders saw the Treaty as an opportunity to cripple Germany so that it could not attack France again.

Pressures on Clemenceau

France had suffered enormous damage to its land, industry, people – and self-confidence. Over two-thirds of the men who had served in the French army had been killed or wounded. The war affected almost an entire generation.

By comparison, Germany seemed to many French people as powerful and threatening as ever. German land and industry had not been as badly damaged as France's. France's population (around 40 million) was in decline compared to Germany's (around 75 million).

The French people wanted a treaty that would punish Germany and weaken it as much as possible. The French President (Poincaré) even wanted Germany broken up into a collection of smaller states, but Clemenceau knew that the British and Americans would not agree to this.

Clemenceau was a realist and knew he would probably be forced to compromise on some issues. However, he had to show he was aware of public opinion in France.

Think!
1. One of the ideas put forward at the Paris Conference was that Germany should lose some of its key industrial areas. How would you expect Lloyd George to react to a proposal like this? You could present your answer as a short speech by Lloyd George or in a paragraph of text.
2. Here are some extracts from the demands made by France before the Peace Conference started:
   a) German armed forces to be banned from the bank of the River Rhine (which bordered France).
   b) Germany to pay compensation for damage done by German forces in lands they occupied during the war.
   c) Germany's armed forces to be severely limited.

   Which of these terms do you think made it into the final Treaty? Give each term a percentage chance and keep a note of your guesses. You will find out if you were right later in the chapter.

How did the peacemaking process actually work?

In theory, the major issues like borders and reparations (compensation for war damage) were discussed in detail by all the delegates at the conference (see Source 4) – over 32 leaders with all their officials and advisers! As Source 5 shows, it quickly became impossible to consult everyone.

SOURCE 4

A painting showing the delegates at the Paris Peace Conference at work. It was made for the *Illustrated London News*, which was a very popular British newspaper aimed at a mass market. It was particularly well known for using paintings even after photography was well established. The paper's artists were given official access to the meetings of the Peace Conference to report and create illustrations. This image had the official approval of the Big Three.

Source Analysis

Study Source 4 carefully and then discuss these questions.
1 Why was this picture published?
2 What impression was it trying to give of the conference and the delegates?
3 After studying Source 4 and the other information in this section, do you think the impression is accurate? Make sure you can explain your view.
4 If you were using this image to introduce a documentary on the Treaty of Versailles, what main points would you make in the commentary that the viewer would hear?

SOURCE 5

'Wilson the Just' quickly disappointed expectations. Everything about him served to disillusion those he dealt with. All too soon the President was qualifying the Fourteen Points with 'Four Principles' and modifying them with 'Five Particulars'. Finding that one principle conflicted with another, he made compromising declarations about both. The Big Three abandoned Wilson's principle of open covenants openly arrived at, consulting others only when they needed expert advice. They were occasionally to be seen crawling round their maps on the hearth rug. Sometimes they agreed and, according to one British official 'were so pleased with themselves for doing so that they quite forgot to tell anyone what the agreement was'. Sometimes they almost came to blows. Lloyd George made rapid, quick fire points but they were ineffective against Clemenceau's granite obstinacy. Even Wilson's self-important confidence crashed against the rock of Clemenceau … Clemenceau was delighted when the American President fell ill. He suggested that Lloyd George should bribe Wilson's doctor to make the illness last.

Historian Piers Brendon writing in 2006.

It soon became clear it would be impossible to agree terms that everyone would agree about.

- **Clemenceau clashed with Wilson over many issues.** The USA had not suffered nearly as badly as France in the war. Clemenceau resented Wilson's more generous attitude to Germany. They disagreed over what to do about Germany's Rhineland and coalfields in the Saar. In the end, Wilson had to give way on these issues. In return, Clemenceau and Lloyd George did give Wilson what he wanted in eastern Europe, despite their reservations about his idea of self-determination. However, this mainly affected the peace treaties with the other defeated countries rather than the Treaty of Versailles.
- **Clemenceau also clashed with Lloyd George,** particularly over Lloyd George's desire not to treat Germany too harshly. For example, Clemenceau said that 'if the British are so anxious to appease Germany they should look overseas and make colonial, naval or commercial concessions'. Clemenceau felt that the British were quite happy to treat Germany fairly in Europe, where France rather than Britain was most under threat. However, they were less happy to allow Germany to keep its navy and colonies, which would be more of a threat to Britain.
- **Wilson and Lloyd George did not always agree either.** Lloyd George was particularly unhappy with point 2 of the Fourteen Points, allowing all nations access to the seas. Similarly, Wilson's views on people ruling themselves were threatening to the British government, for the British empire ruled millions of people all across the world from London.

ACTIVITY

Who said what about whom?

Here are some statements that were made by the Big Three at the Paris Peace Conference. Your task is to decide which leader made the statement and also whom he was talking about. You will need to be able to explain your answer.

a) 'He is too anxious to preserve his empire to want self-determination for colonies.'
b) 'His country has been ruling the waves for too long to accept the need for freedom of the seas.'
c) 'He wants to wreck a country which in a few years could be a valuable trading partner and a source of vital jobs.'
d) 'Freedom of the seas is all very well but who or what will protect my country's ships and trade?'
e) 'What does he know about colonies and how they should be ruled? He probably doesn't know where most of them are!'
f) 'How can I work with a man who thinks he is the first leader in 2000 years who knows anything about peace?'
g) 'If he is so anxious to make concessions to the Germans then they should look overseas and make naval or colonial concessions.'
h) 'He is stuck in the past. If he gets his way Germany will be left bitter and vengeful and there will be another war in a few years.'
i) 'He is very happy to give concessions to Germany in areas which do not threaten his country.'
j) 'If you carry on annoying me I am going to punch you!'
k) 'There are new, better ways of making a peace agreement. He should accept that all states should disarm.'
l) 'He must make concessions to the Germans, perhaps over the Rhineland or Alsace–Lorraine.'

The terms of the Treaty of Versailles

None of the Big Three was happy with the eventual terms of the Treaty. After months of negotiation, each of them had to compromise on some of their aims; otherwise there would never have been a treaty. The main terms can be divided into five areas.

1 War guilt	■ Article 231 of the Treaty was simple but was seen by the Germans as extremely harsh. Germany had to accept the blame for starting the war.
2 Reparations	■ The major powers agreed, without consulting Germany, that Germany had to pay reparations to the Allies for the damage caused by the war. The exact figure was not agreed until 1921 when it was set at £6,600 million (132 billion gold marks) – an enormous figure. If the terms of the payments had not later been changed under the Young Plan in 1929 (see page 38), Germany would not have finished paying this bill until 1984. ■ France also received the coal from the Saarland for fifteen years.
3 German territories and colonies	■ Germany's European borders were very extensive, and the section dealing with German territory in Europe was a complicated part of the Treaty. You can see the detail in Figure 6. The Treaty also forbade Germany to join together (ANSCHLUSS) with its former ally Austria.

FIGURE 6

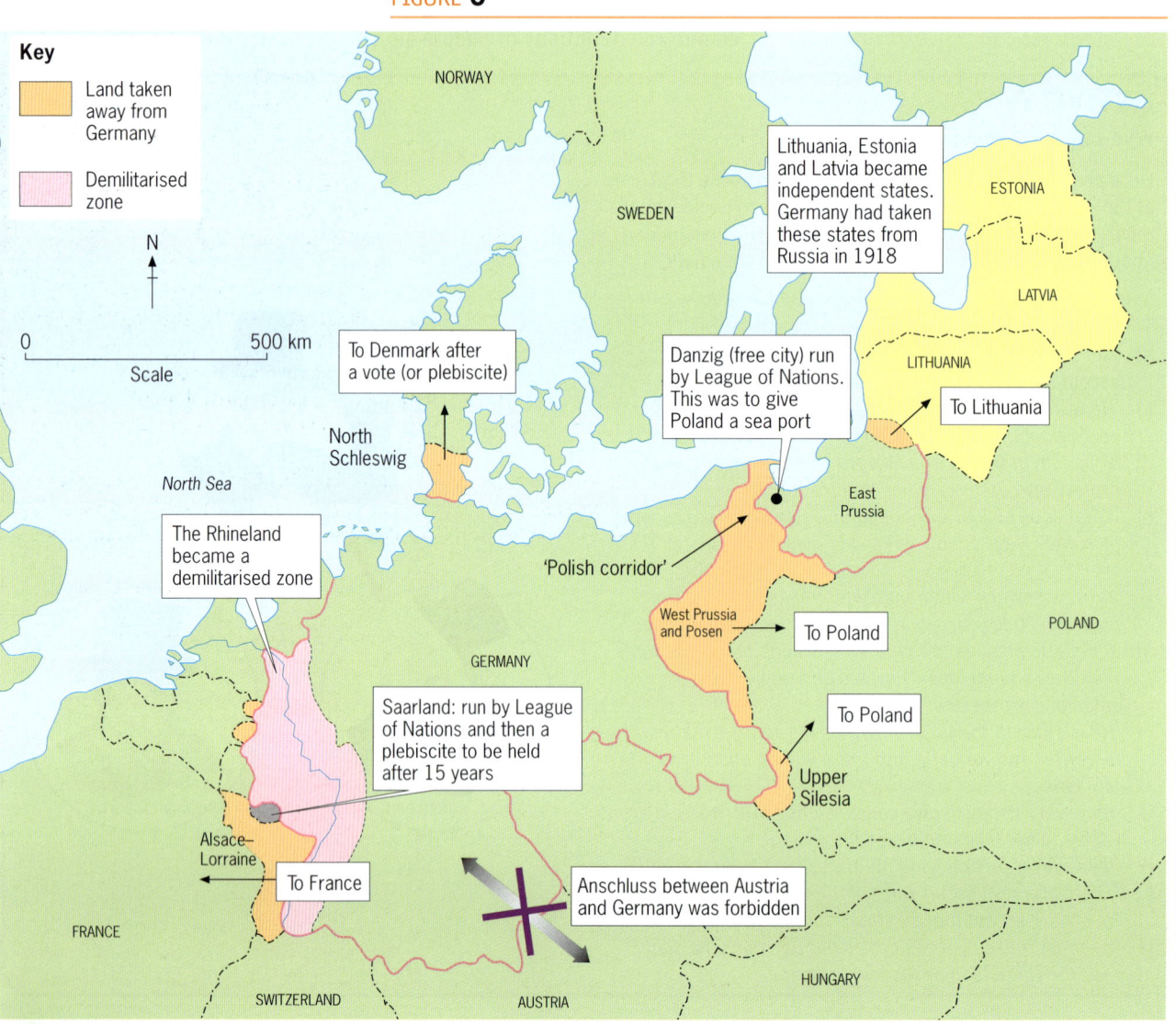

Map showing the impact of the Treaty of Versailles on the borders of Europe.

- Germany's overseas empire was taken away. It had been one of the causes of bad relations between Britain and Germany before the war. Former German colonies, such as Cameroon, became mandates controlled by the League of Nations, which effectively meant that France and Britain controlled them.

4 Germany's armed forces

The size and power of the German army was a major concern, especially for France. The Treaty therefore restricted German armed forces to a level well below what they had been before the war.
- The army was limited to 100,000 men.
- CONSCRIPTION was banned – soldiers had to be volunteers.
- Germany was not allowed armoured vehicles, submarines or aircraft.
- The navy could have only six battleships and 15,000 sailors.
- The Rhineland became a DEMILITARISED zone. This meant that no German troops were allowed into that area. The Rhineland was important because it was the border area between Germany and France (see Figure 6).

5 League of Nations

- Previous methods of keeping peace had failed and so the League of Nations was set up as an international 'police force'. (You will study the League in detail in Chapter 2.)
- Germany was not invited to join the League until it had shown that it was a peace-loving country.

Revision Tip

The more you know about the Treaty of Versailles, the more it will help you. Make sure you can remember one or two key points under each of these headings:
- Blame
- Reparations
- Arms
- Territory.

FOCUS TASK 1.2

Why did the victors not get everything they wanted?

1. Work in threes. Look back at the profiles of Wilson, Lloyd George and Clemenceau on pages 6, 8 and 9. Choose one each. Study the terms of the Treaty on these two pages. Think about:
   a) which terms of the Treaty would please your chosen leader and why
   b) which terms would displease him and why
   c) how far he seemed to have achieved his aims.
   Report your findings to your partners.
2. Look back at the chart you compiled on page 6. There should be a blank fifth column. Put the heading 'How they felt about the Treaty' and fill it in for each leader with a one-sentence summary.
3. a) Choose one of the following phrases to finish off this sentence:
   The victors did not get everything they wanted because . . .
   - Clemenceau bullied Wilson and Lloyd George into agreeing to a harsh treaty.
   - the leaders' aims were too different – they could not all have got what they wanted and someone was bound to be disappointed.
   - public opinion in their home countries affected the leaders' decisions.
   b) Write a paragraph to explain why you chose that phrase.
   c) Write two more paragraphs to explain whether there is evidence to support the other two.

FOCUS TASK 1.3

Was the Treaty of Versailles fair?

It is important to make up your own mind about this key question and be able to back up your view with evidence and arguments. So place yourself on this scale and write some sentences to explain your position. This is provisional. You will return to it again.

FAIR ←————————————————→ UNFAIR

German reactions to the Treaty of Versailles

The government that took Germany to war in 1914 had been overthrown in a revolution and the new democratic government in Germany was hoping for fair and equal treatment from the Allies. When the terms were announced on 7 May the Germans were horrified. Their reasons are summarised in the diagram opposite.

The new German government refused to sign the Treaty and the German navy sank its own ships in protest. At one point, it looked as though war might break out again. But what could the German leader Friedrich Ebert do? Germany would quickly be defeated if it tried to fight.

Reluctantly, Ebert agreed to accept the terms of the Treaty and it was signed on 28 June 1919.

SOURCE 7

THE TREATY IS ONLY A SCRAP OF PAPER! We will seek vengeance for the shame of 1919.

German newspaper *Deutsche Zeitung*, June 1919.

SOURCE 8

Cartoon from the German magazine *Simplicissimus*, June 1919. The caption in the magazine read: 'The Allies are burying Germany with the peace terms.'

Source Analysis

Study Source 8. If you did not know this source was German would you be able to work this out? Explain how.

German criticisms of the Treaty of Versailles

War guilt and reparations
Germany had to accept the blame for starting the war and therefore had to pay reparations.

- This 'war guilt' clause was particularly hated. Germans did not feel they had started the war. They felt at the very least that blame should be shared.
- They were bitter that Germany was expected to pay for all the damage caused by the war even though the German economy was severely weakened.

German territories
Germany certainly lost a lot of territory.
- 10 per cent of its land in Europe
- All of its overseas colonies
- 12.5 per cent of its population
- 16 per cent of its coalfields and almost half of its iron and steel industry.

This was a major blow to German pride, and to its economy. Both the Saar and Upper Silesia were important industrial areas.

Meanwhile, as Germany was losing colonies, the British and French were increasing their empires by taking control of German territories in Africa.

Disarmament
The German army was reduced to 100,000 men. It could have no air force, and only a tiny navy.

Germans felt these terms were very unfair. An army of 100,000 was very small for a country of Germany's size and the army was a symbol of German pride.

Also, despite Wilson's Fourteen Points calling for disarmament, none of the Allies were being asked or forced to disarm in the same way.

The Fourteen Points and the League of Nations
- To most Germans, the treatment of Germany was not in keeping with Wilson's Fourteen Points. For example, while self-determination was given to countries such as Estonia, Latvia and Lithuania, German-speaking peoples were being hived off into new countries such as Czechoslovakia to be ruled by non-Germans. *Anschluss* (union) with Austria was forbidden.
- Germany felt further insulted by not being invited to join the League of Nations.

Non-representation
Germans were angry that their government was not represented at the peace talks and that they were being forced to accept a harsh treaty without any choice or even comment. Germans did not feel they had lost the war so they should not have been treated as a defeated country.

SOURCE 9

A mass protest in Berlin in June 1919 against the Treaty of Versailles.

Consequences of the Treaty for Germany

The Treaty of Versailles had a profound effect on Germany for the next ten years and more. The Treaty was universally resented. The historian Zara Steiner argues that hatred of the Versailles Treaty was almost the only issue which all Germans in this period agreed on.

Many Germans viewed the signing of the Treaty as a betrayal and a humiliation. Right-wing groups referred to the Weimar politicians as the 'NOVEMBER CRIMINALS' who had stabbed Germany in the back at the end of the war. Territorial losses to France, Belgium, Denmark and Poland meant many ethnic Germans now lived in different countries, which led to social problems and even conflict. Also, the creation of the Polish Corridor had split East Prussia from the rest of Germany causing many German families to migrate back to mainland Germany. The military restrictions left German citizens feeling defenceless and demoralised as the German army had been a source of pride for many.

Political violence

Right-wing opponents of Ebert's government protested against the Treaty. In 1920, bands of ex-soldiers called FREIKORPS were ordered to disband by the government as their existence broke the military terms of the Treaty. Led by Wolfgang Kapp, an uprising began in March 1920 to overthrow Ebert and install a nationalist government. This rising, called the Kapp Putsch, was defeated by a GENERAL STRIKE by Berlin workers which paralysed essential services such as power and transport. It saved Ebert's government but it added to the chaos in Germany – and the bitterness of Germans towards the Treaty.

Although Kapp was defeated, political violence remained a constant threat. There were numerous political assassinations or attempted assassinations. In the summer of 1922 Germany's foreign minister Walther Rathenau was murdered by extremists. Then in November 1923 Adolf Hitler led an attempted rebellion in Munich, known as the Munich Putsch (see page 236). Hitler's rebellion was defeated but he was let off lightly when he was put on trial and it was clear many Germans shared his hatred of Versailles. Over the next ten years he exploited German resentment of the Treaty of Versailles to gain support for himself and his Nazi party.

Conflict in the Ruhr

Under the Treaty Germany agreed to pay £6,600 million in reparations to the Allies. The first instalment of £50 million was paid in 1921, but in 1922 nothing was paid. Ebert tried to negotiate concessions from the Allies, but the French ran out of patience. In 1923 French and Belgian soldiers entered the Ruhr region and simply took what was owed to them in the form of raw materials and goods. This was quite legal under the Treaty of Versailles.

The results of the occupation of the Ruhr were disastrous for Germany. The German government ordered the workers to go on strike so that they were not producing anything for the French to take. The French reacted harshly, killing over 100 workers and expelling over 100,000 protesters from the region. More importantly, the strike meant that Germany had no goods to trade, and no money to buy things with. Their response led, in turn, to hyperinflation (see page 17).

> **Source Analysis**
>
> Study Source 10. The artist had a difficult aim to achieve because he wanted to show the German worker as strong and determined but at the same time being threatened by the French troops. Do you think he has achieved this aim? Explain which elements of the poster led you to this conclusion.

SOURCE 10

A German poster from 1923 showing a German worker refusing to obey the French troops ordering him to work. The caption says 'No, you can't force me'.

There is much debate about the developments in the Ruhr. Most Germans believed that the crisis arose because the reparations were too high and Germany was virtually bankrupted. Many commentators at the time (including the British and French leaders) claimed that Germany was quite able to afford reparations: it just did not want to pay! Some historians argue that Germany stopped paying reparations in order to create a crisis and force the international community to revise the terms of the Treaty. The debate goes on, but there is no doubt that most Germans at the time believed the Treaty was responsible for the crisis and that the reparations were far too high.

Hyperinflation

The government solved the problem of not having enough money by simply printing extra money, but this caused a new problem – hyperinflation. The money was virtually worthless, so prices shot up. The price of goods could rise between joining the back of a queue in a shop and reaching the front (see page XXX)! Wages began to be paid daily instead of weekly.

Some Germans gained from this disaster. The government and big industrialists were able to pay off their huge debts in worthless marks. But others, especially pensioners, were practically left penniless. A prosperous middle-class family would find that their savings, which might have bought a house in 1921, by 1923 would not even buy a loaf of bread.

SOURCE 11

A German banknote of 1923 for one billion marks.

SOURCE 12

Billion mark notes were quickly handed on as though they burned one's fingers, for tomorrow one would no longer pay in notes but in bundles of notes ... One afternoon I rang Aunt Louise's bell. The door was opened merely a crack. From the dark came an odd broken voice: 'I've used 60 billion marks' worth of gas. My milk bill is 1 million. But all I have left is 2000 marks. I don't understand any more.'

Extract from *Convert to Freedom* by Eitel Dobert, published in 1941. Dobert was a writer and lecturer and joined the Nazi party in 1920.

Germany eventually recovered from this disaster, but it left a bitter memory. The bitterness was directed towards the Treaty of Versailles. It is no coincidence that when Germany faced economic problems again in 1929 many Germans believed Hitler's claims that the Treaty was to blame and they should support his plans to overturn it.

Summary

While the Treaty did cause some genuine problems for Germany the important thing to realise is that many Germans blamed it for other problems which had little to do with it. This resentment was then in turn exploited by extreme groups in Germany to gain power and influence for themselves.

Revision Tip

There were many problems Germany faced in the period 1919–23:
- social problems
- political violence, and
- hyperinflation.

Make sure you can explain how each one was linked to the Treaty of Versailles.

FOCUS TASK 1.4

What was the impact of the Treaty on Germany up to the end of 1923?

Summarise the impact of the Treaty on Germany under each of these headings:
a) Political impact
b) Economic impact
c) Social impact, e.g. morale

How was the Treaty seen at the time?

It was unfair!

Some said the Treaty was unfair!

None of the Big Three was happy with the Treaty (although for different reasons) and some of the diplomats who helped shape the Treaty were dissatisfied.

Some commentators at the time believed that the Treaty was unfair and unjust (see Source 13 for example).

Source 14 is probably the most famous cartoon produced about the Treaty of Versailles. The artist, Will Dyson, thought that the peacemakers were blind and selfish and as a result they produced a disastrous treaty that would cause another terrible war. It is a powerful cartoon. Because history proved it right (the cartoonist even gets the date of the Second World War almost right) this cartoon has been reproduced many times ever since, including in millions of school textbooks.

SOURCE 13

The historian, with every justification, will come to the conclusion that we were very stupid men . . . We arrived determined that a Peace of justice and wisdom should be negotiated; we left the conference conscious that the treaties imposed upon our enemies were neither just nor wise.

Harold Nicolson, a British official who attended the talks.

SOURCE 14

- Italy's leader Orlando (Italy).
- The Big Three: Lloyd George (Britain); Clemenceau (France); Wilson (USA).
- The Tiger is Clemenceau – he cannot see why the child is weeping.
- Cannon fodder – a reference to the millions of men mown down by guns in the First World War.
- The child is the class of 1940 – children like him will be the ones who will fight in a future war because of the Treaty.

A cartoon published in the socialist newspaper *The Daily Herald* in 1919.

Another powerful critic of the Treaty was a British economist, John Maynard Keynes. He wrote a very critical book called *The Economic Consequences of The Peace* published in 1919. This book was widely read and accepted and has influenced the way people have looked at the Treaty.

It is easy to think that everyone felt this way about the Treaty – but they did not!

It was fair!

SOURCE 15

The Germans have given in … They writhe [thrash] at the obligation imposed on them to confess their guilt … Some of the conditions, they affirm, are designed to deprive the German people of its honour … They thought little of the honour of the nations whose territories they defiled with their barbarous and inhuman warfare for more than three awful years.

British newspaper *The Times*, 24 June 1919.

SOURCE 17

Terms of Treaty Better Than Germany Deserves

WAR MAKERS MUST BE MADE TO SUFFER

Germany's chickens are coming home to roost, and she is making no end of a song about it. That was expected, but it will not help her much … If Germany had her deserts, indeed, there would be no Germany left to bear any burden at all; she would be wiped off the map of Europe … Stern justice would demand for Germany a punishment 10 times harder than any she will have to bear …

The feeling in this country is not that Germany is being too hardly dealt by, but that she is being let off too lightly.

From the British newspaper *The People*, May 1919.

Source Analysis

1. Study Source 16. On your own copy, analyse Source 16 the way we have analysed Source 14 on page 18.
2. What does Source 16 reveal about British opinions on the Treaty?

Others said the Treaty was fair!

At the time German complaints about the Treaty mostly fell on deaf ears. There were celebrations in Britain and France. If ordinary people in Britain had any reservations about the Treaty it was more likely to be that it was not harsh enough.

- Many people felt that the Germans were themselves operating a double standard. Their call for fairer treatment did not square with the harsh way they had treated Russia in the Treaty of Brest-Litovsk in 1918. Versailles was a much less harsh treaty than Brest-Litovsk. This is the comment being made in the cartoon on page 4.
- There was also the fact that Germany's economic problems, although real, were partly self-inflicted. Other states had raised taxes to pay for the war. The Kaiser's government had not done this. It had simply allowed debts to mount up because it had planned to pay Germany's war debts by extracting reparations from the defeated states.

SOURCE 16

PUNCH, OR THE LONDON CHARIVARI.—February 19, 1919.

GIVING HIM ROPE?

German Criminal (*to Allied Police*). "HERE, I SAY, STOP! YOU'RE HURTING ME! [*Aside*] IF I ONLY WHINE ENOUGH I MAY BE ABLE TO WRIGGLE OUT OF THIS YET."

A British cartoon published in 1919.

Did opinions change on whether the treaty could be justified?

Looking back at the Treaty from the present day we know that it helped to create the cruel Nazi regime in Germany and helped cause the Second World War.

As early as 1933–34 the British historian W.H. Dawson was arguing that the Versailles settlement was a major cause of the rise of Hitler's aggressive Nazi regime in Germany (see Source 19). And while many later historians disagreed with Dawson about the Treaty, they did agree that Hitler was able to exploit the way Germans felt about the Treaty (see Sources 18 and 20).

SOURCE 18

The Versailles Treaty was one of the most outrageous and predatory treaties in history. It was a blatant act of plunder perpetrated by a gang of robbers against a helpless, prostrate and bleeding Germany. Among its numerous provisions, it required Germany and its allies to accept full responsibility for causing the war and, under the terms of articles 231–248, to disarm, make substantial territorial concessions and pay reparations to the Entente powers.

An extract from an article on the website 'In Defence of Marxism', published in 2009. The title of the article was 'The Treaty of Versailles – the Peace to end all Peace'.

SOURCE 19

The rise of Hitler to power and the resurgence of militant nationalism throughout Germany is alarming. Hitler is certain to demand a reconsideration of the territorial provision in the Versailles settlement. These demands, in a country which was supposedly defeated and restrained indefinitely, serve as a warning to the powers who wish to defend peace and stability in Europe. They are also a reminder that nations tend to be slow to accept the truth of a given situation unless they are forced to. Germany's claims of unfair treatment under the settlement have been clarified and strengthened from year to year with the findings of impartial research by myself and other colleagues. No attempt was made by the victorious powers at Versailles to respect the rights and valid claims of Germany.

British historian W.H. Dawson writing in 1933.

SOURCE 20

Hitler used the Treaty of Versailles of 1919 to raise the European storms that Britain and France wanted to calm in the 1930s. Hitler's demands for the destruction of Versailles won him support at home and also allowed him to disguise his true ambitions to build a great empire from the German people and from foreign statesmen. Most Germans wished to change Versailles and so they supported Hitler. Even in Britain, Hitler's demands did not seem to be completely unacceptable. To the British, if Hitler's only purpose was to modify the Versailles settlement then it seemed reasonable to listen to him and give concessions. The grievances of Versailles provided Hitler with the means to appeal to German and foreign support for demands over territory and reparations. Indeed, to British observers the history of reparations came to be seen as the history of a grave and very large mistake.

British historian R.A.C. Parker writing in 1993.

Think!
Look back at your work in Focus Task 1.3 on page 13. Have you changed your views after reading the information and sources on pages 18–20?

We call this hindsight – when you look back at a historical event and judge it knowing its consequences. You would expect hindsight to affect historians' attitudes to the Treaty and it has – but maybe not exactly as you might expect.

Some historians side with critics of the Treaty and its makers. Others point out that the majority of people outside Germany thought that the Treaty was fair and that a more generous treaty would have been totally unacceptable to public opinion in Britain and France. They highlight that the peacemakers had a very difficult job balancing public opinion in their own countries with visions of a fairer future. Some say that the Treaty may have been the best that could be achieved in the circumstances.

SOURCE 21

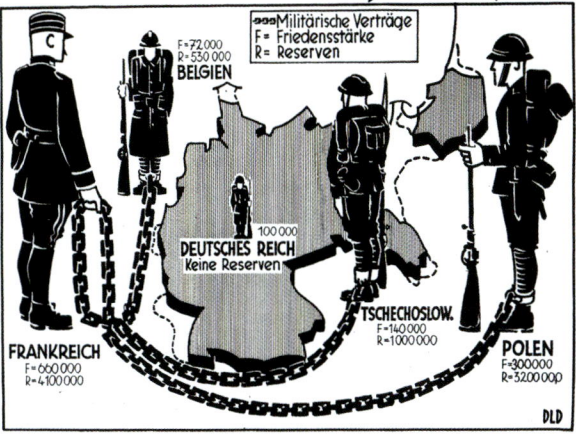

Nazi cartoon commenting on the military terms of the Versailles Treaty. The text reads: 'The Mammoth Military superiority of our neighbours'. The chain symbol = military treaties; F = peace time strength; R = reserves; the German Reich is surrounded by France, Belgium, Czechoslovakia and Poland (left to right).

SOURCE 22

A demonstration against the Treaty of Versailles in 1933. The march was organised by the Nazi Party. The banners read *'Day of Versailles, day of dishonour!'* and *'We would be free from Versailles!'*

Source Analysis
Study Sources 21 and 22. Explain how the authors of Sources 19 and 20 could have used these as evidence to support their ideas.

SOURCE 23

The Treaty of Versailles has been repeatedly pilloried [criticised], most famously in John Maynard Keynes' The Economic Consequences of the Peace, *published at the end of 1919 and still the argument underpinning too many current textbooks … The Treaty of Versailles was not excessively harsh. Germany was not destroyed. Nor was it reduced to a second rank power or permanently prevented from returning to great power status … With the disintegration of Austria-Hungary and the collapse of Tsarist Russia it left Germany in a stronger strategic position than before the war … The Versailles Treaty was, nonetheless, flawed. It failed to solve the problem of both punishing and conciliating a country that remained a great power despite the four years of fighting and a military defeat. It could hardly have been otherwise, given the very different aims of the peacemakers, not to speak of the many problems they faced, many of which lay beyond their competence or control.*

Historian Zara Steiner writing in 2004.

FOCUS TASK 1.5
Could the Treaty of Versailles be justified at the time?
1. Study Sources 18–24 carefully. Match one source to each of these headlines:
   - The best that could be achieved in the circumstances
   - They did what the people wanted
   - A death warrant for Europe
   - Betrayal.
2. For each source, decide whether you think it is a critical, positive or balanced view of the Treaty.

SOURCE 24

The peacemakers of 1919 made mistakes, of course. By their offhand treatment of the non-European world they stirred up resentments for which the West is still paying today. They took pains over the borders in Europe, even if they did not draw them to everyone's satisfaction, but in Africa they carried on the old practice of handing out territory to suit the imperialist powers. In the Middle East they threw together peoples, in Iraq most notably, who still have not managed to cohere into a civil society. [But] they could have done much worse. They tried, even cynical old Clemenceau, to build a better order. They could not foresee the future and they certainly could not control it. That was up to their successors. When war came in 1939, it was a result of twenty years of decisions taken or not taken, not of arrangements made in 1919.

Historian Margaret MacMillan writing in *Peacemakers*, 2001.

Factfile

Peace treaties for the other defeated countries

Germany had allies in the First World War – Austria–Hungary, Bulgaria and Turkey – known as the Central Powers. There were four other peace treaties imposed on them by the Allies:
- Austria: Treaty of St Germain, 1919
- Bulgaria: Treaty of Neuilly, 1919
- Hungary: Treaty of Trianon, 1920
- Turkey: Treaty of Sevres, 1920, later revised by the Treaty of Lausanne, 1923.

These treaties included many similar restrictions to the Treaty of Versailles and saw the empires of Austria–Hungary and Turkey broken up into new states.

FOCUS TASK 1.6

Was the Treaty of Versailles fair?

The key question for this topic is 'Was the Treaty of Versailles fair?' Use Sources 13–24 on pages 18–21 and your own knowledge to help you reach a judgement. You may want to also refer back to your answers for Focus Task 1.3 on page 13 before you start to complete the table.

Source	Does the source suggest the Treaty was fair or unfair?	Support from the source	Examples from my own knowledge

1. Write the number of the source you are examining in column 1. Use column 2 to decide whether the source suggests the Treaty was fair or unfair. Column 3 should be used to record some details from the source – a quote or a description of what you can see – that provide good evidence of your decision. You can then link this to your own knowledge in the final column.
2. Now reach your overall judgement: do you think the Treaty of Versailles was fair or not? Make sure you can give reasons to support your argument.

Keywords

Make sure you know what these terms mean and are able to define them confidently:
- Anschluss
- Big Three
- conscription
- co-operation
- demilitarised zone
- democracy
- disarmament
- Fourteen Points
- free trade
- Freikorps
- general strike
- hindsight
- hyperinflation
- idealist/realist
- Kapp Putsch
- League of Nations
- mandates
- November Criminals
- Paris Peace Conference
- public opinion
- reparations
- Rhineland
- right-wing
- Ruhr
- Saar
- secret treaties
- self-determination
- territories
- Treaty of Brest-Litovsk
- Treaty of Versailles
- war guilt
- Young Plan

Chapter Summary

Was the Treaty of Versailles fair?

1. The Paris Peace Conference was set up to sort out what would happen to the defeated countries after the First World War.
2. The Conference was dominated by 'The Big Three': Wilson, Clemenceau and Lloyd George representing the USA, France and Britain (the countries that won the war).
3. The Big Three did not agree on many things. In particular they disagreed on how to treat Germany, the League of Nations and Wilson's Fourteen Points.
4. The main terms of the Treaty of Versailles were that Germany should accept blame for starting the war, pay reparations, lose land (including industry and population) and colonies, and agree to disarm.
5. People in Germany were appalled by the Treaty, but Germany had no choice but to sign it.
6. Germany had many post-war problems such as attempted revolutions and hyperinflation, which they blamed on the Treaty, but the Treaty was not the sole reason for these problems.
7. The Treaty also set up a League of Nations whose role was to enforce the Treaty of Versailles and to help prevent another war.
8. Opinion on the Treaty of Versailles varied at the time: some people thought it was too lenient on Germany, others that it was too harsh and would lead to Germany wanting revenge.
9. The views on the Treaty would change over time with many seeing it as a cause of problems in Germany and a factor that led to another war in Europe.

PRACTICE QUESTIONS

Structured questions
1. (a) What were Germany's main territorial losses under the Treaty of Versailles? **[4]**
   (b) Why did Clemenceau and Lloyd George disagree about how to treat Germany at the Paris Peace Conference? **[6]**
   (c) 'The Treaty of Versailles was a fair settlement.' How far do you agree with this statement? Explain your answer. **[10]**

Document questions
1. Study Source 14 on page 18. What is the message of the cartoonist? Explain your answer using details of the source and your own knowledge. **[7]**
2. Study Sources 13 and 17 on pages 18 and 19. How far do these two sources agree? Explain your answer using details of the sources and your own knowledge. **(8)**
3. Study Source 15 on page 19. Does this source prove that the Versailles settlement was fair to Germany? Explain your answer using details of the source and your own knowledge. **[7]**
4. Study Sources 19 and 20 on page 20. How similar are these two sources? Explain your answer using details of the sources and your own knowledge. **(8)**
5. Study Sources 13–20 on pages 18–20. How far do these sources provide convincing evidence that the Treaty of Versailles was an unfair settlement for Germany? Use the sources to explain your answer. **(9)**

These are examples of the types of questions on this topic. There is more guidance on answering such questions on pages 148–67 but the key thing, always, is to answer the question rather than write everything you know.

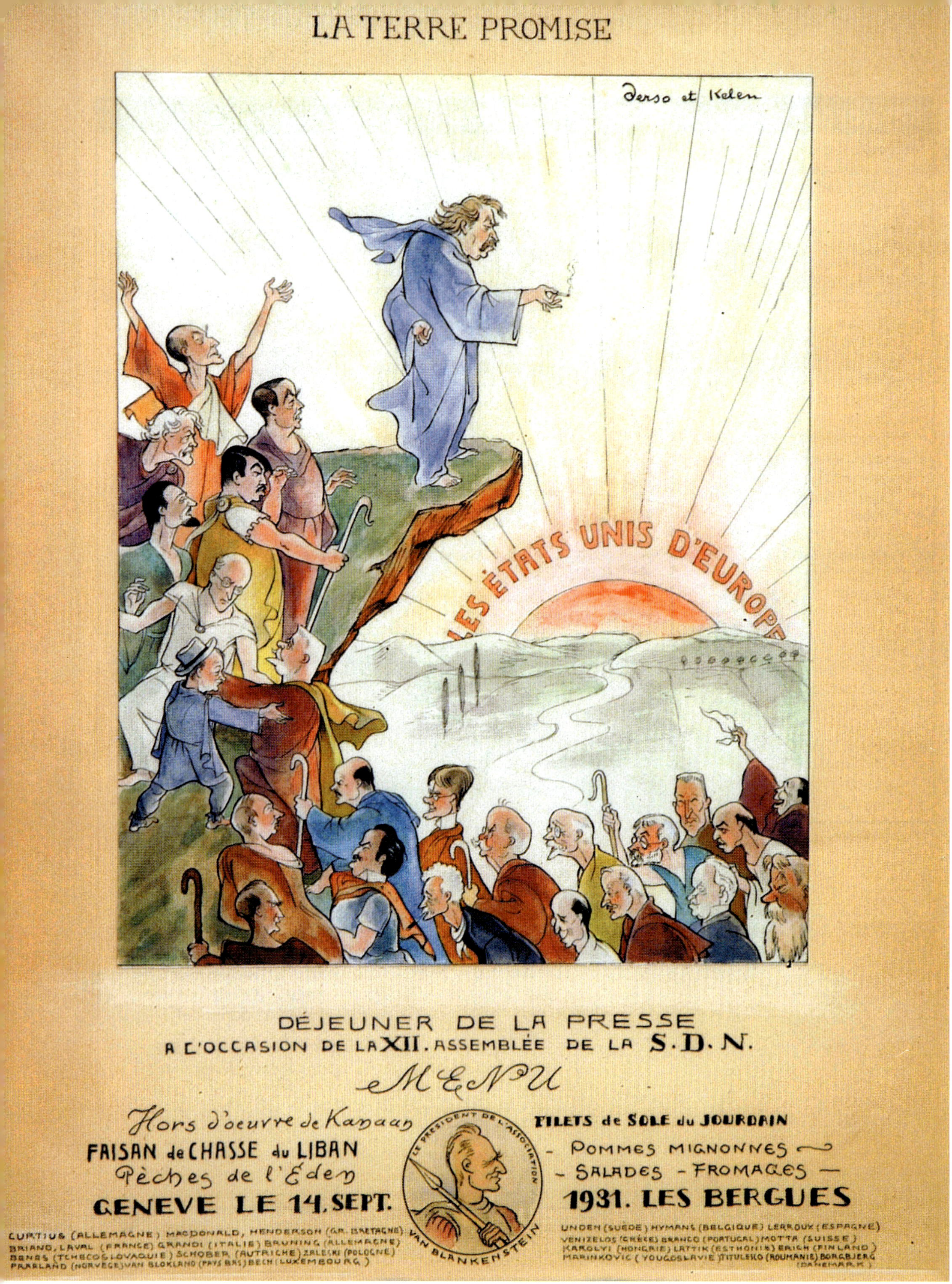

LA TERRE PROMISE

DÉJEUNER DE LA PRESSE
A L'OCCASION DE LA **XII** ASSEMBLÉE DE LA S.D.N.

Menu

Hors d'œuvre de Kanaan
FAISAN de CHASSE du LIBAN
Pêches de l'Éden
GENEVE LE 14. SEPT.

FILETS de SOLE du JOURDAIN
— POMMES MIGNONNES —
— SALADES — FROMAGES —
1931. LES BERGUES

CURTIUS (ALLEMAGNE) MACDONALD, HENDERSON (GR. BRETAGNE)
BRIAND, LAVAL (FRANCE) GRANDI (ITALIE) BRUNING (ALLEMAGNE)
BENES (TCHECOSLOVAQUIE) SCHOBER (AUTRICHE) ZALESKI (POLOGNE)
PRAARLAND (NORVEGE) VAN BLOKLAND (PAYS BAS) BECH (LUXEMBOURG)

UNDEN (SUEDE) HYMANS (BELGIQUE) LERROUX (ESPAGNE)
VENIZELOS (GRECE) BRANCO (PORTUGAL) MOTTA (SUISSE)
KAROLYI (HONGRIE) LATTIK (ESTHONIE) ERICH (FINLAND)
MARINKOVIC (YOUGOSLAVIE) TITULESKO (ROUMANIE) BORGBJERG
(DANEMARK)

2 To what extent was the League of Nations a success?

FOCUS POINTS
★ How far did weaknesses in the League's organisation and membership make failure inevitable?
★ How successful were the League's attempts at peacekeeping in the 1920s?
★ How important was the League's humanitarian work?
★ How far did the Depression make the work of the League more difficult in the 1930s?

This picture was used as the menu card for a League of Nations banquet in the 1930s. It shows Briand (who was one of the most influential figures in the League) as Moses leading the statesmen of the world to view the 'Promised Land'. The sunrise is labelled 'The United States of Europe'. Discuss:
1 What impression does this picture give you of the League?
2 Does this picture surprise you? Why or why not?

You saw in Chapter 1 that setting up a League of Nations was one of Woodrow Wilson's key ideas for preventing another war. He saw the League as an organisation that would solve international disputes. He hoped that if the Great Powers had to talk to each other they would no longer need or even want to make secret ALLIANCES as they did before the First World War. He thought the League would protect smaller nations from aggression – if they had concerns then the League would be a place where their case would be heard by the world.

Without spoiling the story, Wilson's original plan for the League never happened! This chapter will explain why. However, a scaled-down version of the League was created. How well did it do?

On the one hand people argue that the League achieved a lot.
■ Its humanitarian agencies helped the sick, the poor and the homeless.
■ Its financial agencies helped to stabilise several economies after the war.
■ The League handled 66 major international disputes between the wars and was successful in half of them.

However, the League was unsuccessful in the larger international disputes that involved the major powers. The League failed to stop the Japanese invasion of Manchuria in 1931 and Italy's invasion of Abyssinia in 1935, which had disastrous consequences for international relations in Europe.

So your key question in this chapter is to judge **to what extent** the League succeeded. This is not a question with a 'Yes' or 'No' answer. To tackle a 'to what extent' question you need to:
■ weigh the League's successes against its failures
■ compare the aims of the League with what it actually achieved
■ assess whether the failures were the fault of the League or other factors, and particularly:
  – how far the League's **organisation** weakened it
  – how far the League was let down by its own **members** and the other Great Powers
  – how far the League's work was hampered by the worldwide ECONOMIC DEPRESSION that made the 1930s a dark and dangerous time.

This chapter takes you step by step through those questions so you can reach your own view on this key question: '**To what extent** was the League of Nations a success?'

How far did weaknesses in the League's organisation and membership make failure inevitable?

The birth of the League

SOURCE 1

The front page of the *Daily Express*, 27 December 1918. President Wilson was given a warm reception throughout Europe after the First World War.

Source Analysis

1. Study Source 1. Explain why it is useful as evidence about the state of international relations in December 1918.
2. Some commentators at the time said that they found Wilson to be pompous and arrogant. Is there any evidence to support this in Sources 2 and 3?

SOURCE 2

Merely to win the war was not enough. It must be won in such a way as to ensure the future peace of the world.

President Woodrow Wilson, 1918.

Think!

Which of the three kinds of League proposed by the Allies do you think would be the best at keeping peace:
- a world parliament
- a simple organisation for emergencies only
- a strong organisation with its own army?

SOURCE 3

[If the European powers] had dared to discuss their problems for a single fortnight in 1914 the First World War would never have happened. If they had been forced to discuss them for a whole year, war would have been inconceivable.

President Wilson speaking in 1918.

After the First World War everyone wanted to avoid repeating the mass slaughter of the war that had just ended. They also agreed that a LEAGUE OF NATIONS – an organisation that could solve international problems without resorting to war – would help achieve this. However, there was disagreement about what kind of organisation it should be.

- President Wilson wanted the League of Nations to be like a **world parliament** where representatives of all nations could meet together regularly to decide on any matters that affected them all.
- Many British leaders thought the best League would be a **simple organisation** that would only meet in emergencies. An organisation like this already existed – the CONFERENCE OF AMBASSADORS.
- France proposed **a strong League with its own army**.

It was President Wilson who won. He insisted that discussions about a League should be a major part of the peace treaties and by February 1919 he had drawn up a very ambitious plan for the League.

All the major nations would join the League. They would disarm. If they had a dispute with another country, they would take it to the League. They promised to accept the decision made by the League. They also promised to protect one another if they were invaded. If any member did break the COVENANT (see page 30) and go to war, other members promised to stop trading with it and to send troops if necessary to force it to stop fighting. Wilson's hope was that citizens of all countries would be so much against another conflict that this would prevent their leaders from going to war.

The plan was prepared in a great hurry and critics suggested there was some woolly thinking. Some people were angered by Wilson's arrogant style. He acted as if only he knew the solutions to Europe's problems. Others were worried by his idealism. Under threat of war, would the public really behave in the way he suggested? Would countries really do what the League said? Wilson glossed over what the League would do if they didn't.

Even so, most people in Europe were prepared to give Wilson's plans a try. They hoped that no country would dare invade another if they knew that the USA and other powerful nations of the world would stop trading with them or send their armies to stop them. In 1919 hopes were high that the League, with the United States in the driving seat, could be a powerful peacemaker.

SOURCE 4A

OVERWEIGHTED.

President Wilson. "HERE'S YOUR OLIVE BRANCH. NOW GET BUSY."
Dove of Peace. "OF COURSE I WANT TO PLEASE EVERYBODY; BUT ISN'T THIS A BIT THICK?"

SOURCE 4B

READY TO START.

Two British cartoons from 1919/1920.

Source Analysis

Work in pairs. One of you work with Source 4A and the other work with Source 4B.
1 What is the message of your cartoon? Make sure that you explain what details in the cartoon help to get this message across.
2 Is your cartoon optimistic or pessimistic about the League of Nations? Give reasons.
3 Compare your ideas with your partner's, then write a paragraph comparing the two cartoons.

FOCUS TASK 2.1

Was the League of Nations destined to fail from the start?

Your prediction

You may already have formed an opinion on the League of Nations – but if you haven't, even better! Make your prediction as to how successful you think the League will be **in the 1920s**. For example, how successful do you think it will be in settling the problems left over from the First World War?

To record your prediction, make your own larger copy of this diagram, but with one difference. Redraw the segments to show how successful *you* think it is going to be.

Keep your diagram somewhere you can refer to it again as you will be asked to check back a number of times to reconsider your prediction.

- 50% Successes
- 50% Failures

Think!
Study Figure 5. Write a ten-word slogan summarising each reason for opposing the USA's membership of the League.

A body blow to the League

Back in the USA Woodrow Wilson had problems. Before the USA could even join the League, let alone take a leading role, he needed the approval of his Congress (the American 'Parliament'). And in the USA the idea of a League was not at all popular, as you can see from Figure 5.

FIGURE 5

The League was supposed to enforce the TREATY OF VERSAILLES yet some Americans, particularly the millions who had German ancestors, hated the Treaty itself.

If the League imposed SANCTIONS (e.g. stopping trade with a country that was behaving aggressively) it might be American trade and business that suffered most!

Some feared that joining the League meant sending US soldiers to settle every little conflict around the world. No one wanted that after the casualties of the First World War.

Some feared that the League would be dominated by Britain or France – and would be called to help defend their empires! Many in the US were anti-empires.

Reasons for opposition to the League in the USA.

SOURCE 6

An American cartoon reprinted in the British newspaper the *Star*, June 1919. The original caption said:
'JOHN BULL: "Your bridge, Jonathan. We shan't quarrel about this." [Some of President Wilson's political opponents in the U.S.A. are trying to criticise his League of Nations, by representing that it is a British scheme to exploit the U.S.A.]'

Source Analysis
1 What is the message of the cartoon in Source 6?
2 Explain how the bridge in the cartoon might have been seen by
   a) supporters
   b) opponents of the League.

Together, the critics of Wilson's plans (see Figure 5) put up powerful opposition to the League. They were joined by Wilson's many other political opponents. Wilson's Democratic Party had run the USA for eight troubled years. Its opponents saw the League as an ideal opportunity to defeat him. Wilson toured the USA to put his arguments to the people, but when Congress voted in 1919 he was defeated. So, when the League opened for business in January 1920, the American chair was empty.

SOURCE 7

THE GAP IN THE BRIDGE.

A British cartoon from December 1919. The figure in the white top hat represents the USA.

Source Analysis

Source 7 is one of the most famous cartoons about the League of Nations. On your own copy of the cartoon add annotations to explain the key features. Then write your own summary of the message of the cartoonist.

Think!

Look back to your prediction from Focus Task 2.1 on page 27. Do you want to change your prediction in light of the fact that the USA has not joined the League?

Revision Tip

Be sure you can remember:
- at least two reasons why some Americans were opposed to the USA joining the League (see Figure 5)
- what isolationism means and how it affected the USA's decision.

Wilson defeated

In 1920 Wilson became seriously ill after a stroke. Despite that, he continued to press for the USA to join the League. He took the proposal back to Congress again in March 1920, but they defeated it by 49 votes to 35.

Still the DEMOCRATS did not give up. They were convinced that if the USA did not get involved in international affairs, another world war might follow. In the 1920 election Wilson could not run for president – he was too ill – but his successor made membership of the League a major part of the Democrat campaign.

The REPUBLICAN candidate, Warren Harding, on the other hand, campaigned for America to be ISOLATIONIST (i.e. not to get involved in international alliances but follow its own policies and self-interest). His slogan was to 'return to NORMALCY', by which he meant life as it was before the war, with the USA isolating itself from European affairs. Harding and the Republicans won a landslide victory.

The USA never joined the League. This was a personal rebuff for Wilson and the Democrats, but it was also a body blow to the League.

Factfile

The League of Nations
- The League's home was in Geneva in Switzerland.
- Despite it being the brainchild of the US president, the USA was never a member of the League.
- The most influential part of the League was the COUNCIL – a small group representing the most powerful members. But it was a vast organisation with lots of different parts to fulfil different functions (see chart on pages 32–33).
- The League did not have its own army. But it could call on the armies of its members if necessary.
- One of the jobs of the League was to uphold and enforce the Treaty of Versailles. This included running some of the territories (MANDATES) that had belonged to the defeated countries.
- Forty-two countries joined the League at the start. By the 1930s it had 59 members.

Think!

The League had four main aims:
- discourage aggression
- encourage CO-OPERATION
- encourage DISARMAMENT
- improve living conditions.

As you work through the chapter note down examples that you think could be used as
- evidence of success
- evidence of failure
in each of the aims.

You could record your evidence in a table.

Revision Tip

Make sure you can remember:
- the four aims of the League (the initial letters may help you as they spell out AC/DC)
- one example of the League succeeding or failing in this aim in the 1920s.

The aims of the League

A Covenant set out the aims of the League of Nations. These were:
- to discourage aggression from any nation
- to encourage countries to co-operate, especially in business and trade
- to encourage nations to disarm
- to improve the living and working conditions of people in all parts of the world.

Article 10 = collective security

The Covenant set out 26 Articles or rules, which all members of the League agreed to follow. Probably the most important Article was ARTICLE 10. It said:

> 'The members of the League undertake to preserve against external aggression the territory and existing independence of all members of the League. In case of threat of danger the Council [of the League] shall advise upon the means by which this obligation shall be fulfilled.'

Article 10 really meant COLLECTIVE SECURITY. By acting together (collectively), the members of the League could prevent war by defending the lands and interests of all nations, large or small.

SOURCE 8

The five giants represent the five continents of the Earth. The giants are standing firm together.

At the giants' feet, leaders of all the nations are working, reading and talking together. The League's members came from all five continents. The League believed that strength came from unity.

The famous Spanish artist José Maria Sert was asked to decorate the walls and ceilings of the Assembly Chamber in the League's Headquarters in Geneva, Switzerland. His murals were designed to show the aims and values of the League.

Membership of the League

In the absence of the USA, Britain and France were the most powerful countries in the League. Italy and Japan were also permanent members of the Council. The League had 42 members when it was founded in January 1920. Germany was not allowed to join until it could prove it was a peaceful nation. It was allowed to join in 1926. The USSR was prevented from joining until 1934 as many member states, including Britain and France, did not trust communist states. Throughout the 1920s and 1930s it was Britain and France who usually guided policy. Any action by the League needed their support.

However, both countries were poorly placed to take on this role. Both had been weakened by the First World War. Neither country was quite the major power it had once been. Neither of them had the resources to fill the gap left by the USA. Indeed, some British politicians said that if they had foreseen the American decision, they would not have voted to join the League either. They felt that the Americans were the only nation with the resources or influence to make the League work. In particular, they felt that TRADE SANCTIONS would only work if the Americans applied them.

For the leaders of Britain and France the League posed a real problem. They had to make it work, yet from the start they doubted how effective it could be.

Both countries had other priorities.
- **British** politicians, for example, were more interested in rebuilding British trade and looking after the British empire than in being an international police force.
- **France's** main concern was still Germany. It was worried that without an army of its own the League was too weak to protect France from its powerful neighbour. It did not think Britain was likely to send an army to help it. This made France quite prepared to bypass the League if necessary in order to strengthen its position against Germany.

SOURCE 9

The League of Nations is not set up to deal with a world in chaos, or with any part of the world which is in chaos. The League of Nations may give assistance but it is not, and cannot be, a complete instrument for bringing order out of chaos.

Arthur Balfour, chief British representative at the League of Nations, speaking in 1920.

FIGURE 10

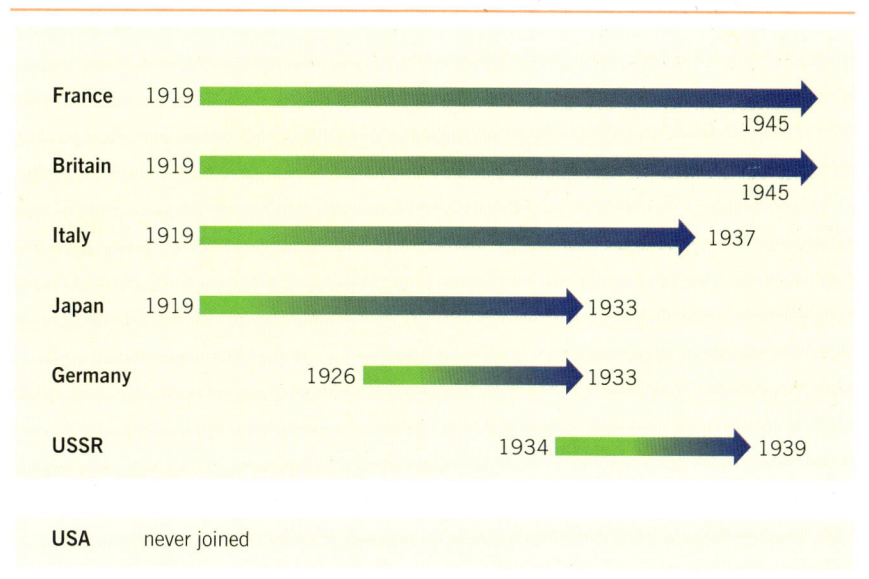

Country	From	To
France	1919	1945
Britain	1919	1945
Italy	1919	1937
Japan	1919	1933
Germany	1926	1933
USSR	1934	1939
USA	never joined	

Membership of the League of Nations. This chart shows only the most powerful nations. More than 50 other countries were also members.

Think!
1. List the strengths and weaknesses of Britain and France as leaders of the League of Nations.
2. France proposed that the League should have an army of its own. Why do you think most people opposed this?
3. Think back to Wilson's ideas for the League. What problems would be caused by the fact that:
   a) the USA
   b) Germany
   were not members of the League?

Think!

1 Study the diagram. Which part of the League would deal with the following problems:
   a) an outbreak of a new infectious disease
   b) a border dispute between two countries
   c) accidents caused by dangerous machinery in factories
   d) complaints from people in Palestine that the British were not running the mandated territory properly?

Organisation of the League

The Covenant laid out the League's structure and the rules for each of the bodies within it – see the diagram below.

The Council
- The Council was a **smaller group** than the Assembly, which met more often, usually about **five times a year** or more often in case of emergency. It included:
  - **permanent members**. In 1920 these were Britain, France, Italy and Japan.
  - **temporary members**. They were elected by the Assembly for three-year periods.
- Each of the permanent members of the Council had a **veto**. This meant that one permanent member could stop the Council acting even if all other members agreed.
- The main aim of the Council was to **resolve disputes by talking**. However, if this did not work, the Council could use a range of powers:
  - MORAL CONDEMNATION: they could decide which country was 'the aggressor', and tell it to stop what it was doing.
  - **Economic and financial sanctions**: members of the League could refuse to trade with the aggressor.
  - **Military force**: the armed forces of member countries could be used against an aggressor.

The Assembly
- This was the League's **'Parliament'**.
- **Every country** in the League sent a representative to the ASSEMBLY.
- The Assembly could **recommend action** to the Council.
- It could also vote on **admitting new members** to the League.
- The Assembly only met **once a year**.
- Decisions made by the Assembly had to be UNANIMOUS – they had to be agreed by all members of the Assembly.

The Secretariat
- The SECRETARIAT was a sort of **civil service** serving all the other bodies within the League.
- It kept **records** of League meetings and prepared **reports**.
- The Secretariat had a key role in **bringing together experts** from across the world on key issues such as health, disarmament and economic matters.

The Permanent Court of International Justice
- The Court was based at the Hague in the Netherlands and was made up of **judges** from the member countries.
- This was meant to play a key role in the League's work by **settling disputes** between countries peacefully.
- If it was asked, the Court would give a decision on a **border dispute** between countries.
- However, the Court had no way of making sure that countries followed its **rulings**.

The International Labour Organization (ILO)
- The ILO **brought together** employers, governments and workers' representatives.
- Its aim was to **improve the conditions** of working people throughout the world.
- It collected statistics and information about working conditions and how to improve them and it tried to **persuade** member countries to adopt its suggestions.

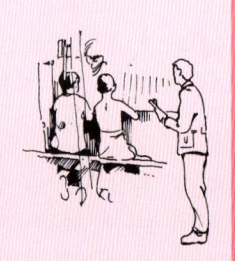

The League of Nations Agencies and Commissions

As well as dealing with disputes between its members, the League also attempted to tackle other major problems. This was done through agencies, COMMISSIONS or committees. The panels below set out the aims of some of these agencies. See Figure 11 on page 34 for a description of some of the actions they took.

The Mandates Commissions

The First World War had led to many **former colonies** of Germany and her allies ending up as League of Nations mandates ruled by Britain and France on behalf of the League. The Mandates Commission was made up of teams of expert advisers whose job was to report to the League on how people in the mandates were being treated. Their aim was to make sure that Britain and France acted in the interests of the people of that territory, not its own interests.

The Refugees Committee

At the end of the First World War there were hundreds of thousands of **refugees who had fled from the areas of conflict**. Some were trying to get back to their homes; others had no homes to go to. The most pressing problems were in former Russian territories: the Balkans, Greece, Armenia and Turkey. It was a huge task.

The Slavery Commission

This Commission worked to **abolish slavery around the world**. It was a particular issue in East Africa but slavery was also a major concern in many other parts of the world. There were also many workers who were not technically slaves but were treated like slaves. The Commission tried to help them too.

The Health Committee

The Health Committee attempted to deal with the problem of **dangerous diseases** and to educate people about **health and sanitation**. The First World War had brought about rapid developments in medicine and ideas about public health and disease prevention. The Health Committee brought experts together and worked with charities and many other independent agencies to collect statistics about health issues, to spread the new ideas and to develop programmes to fight disease.

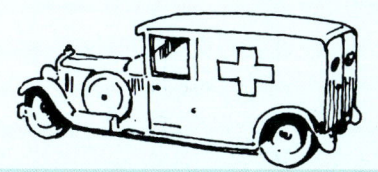

FOCUS TASK 2.2
Were there weaknesses in the League's organisation?

Here is a conversation which might have taken place between two diplomats in 1920.

> Peace at last! The League of Nations will keep large and small nations secure.

> I'm not sure. It might look impressive but I think there are weaknesses in the League.

1. Work in pairs. Choose one statement each and write out the reasons each diplomat might give for his opinion. In your answer make sure you refer to:
   - the membership of the League
   - what the main bodies within the League can do
   - how each body will make decisions
   - how the League will enforce its decisions.
2. Go back to your diagram from page 27 and see if you want to change your predictions about how successful the League will be.

Revision Tip

This is quite a complex chart. Your main aim is to be sure you know the difference between the League's Council and its Assembly.

How successful were the League's attempts at peacekeeping in the 1920s?

The treaties signed at the PARIS PEACE CONFERENCE had created new states and changed the borders of others. Inevitably this led to disputes and it was the job of the League to sort out border disputes. From the start there was so much to do that some disputes were handled by the Conference of Ambassadors. Strictly this was not a body of the League of Nations. But it was made up of leading politicians from the main members of the League – Britain, France and Italy – so it was very closely linked to the League. As you can see from Figure 11 the 1920s was a busy time. This map only shows a small selection of the disputes which involved the League in this period.

> **Think!**
> Four of the problems in Figure 11 are highlighted in **bold text**. As you read about each one, score the League's success on a scale of −5 (a total failure) to +5 (a great success). Make sure you can give a reason for your score.

FIGURE 11

Map of Europe showing disputes in the 1920s:

- **Aaland Islands dispute. Finland & Sweden, 1921**: Finland and Sweden threatened war over the Aaland Islands but Sweden accepted the League's ruling that the islands should belong to Finland.
- Prisoners of war repatriated from Siberia, 1920–22
- **Vilna: Polish–Lithuanian dispute, 1920–29**: In 1920 Poland took control of the Lithuanian capital Vilna. Lithuania appealed to the League for help. The League protested to Poland but the Poles did not pull out. France and Britain were not prepared to act.
- Rights of German settlers in Poland protected, 1923
- Saar territory administered by the League
- Bulgarian refugee settlement, 1926
- Corfu crisis, 1923. See page 35.
- **Prevention of war between Greece & Bulgaria, 1925**. See page 36.

Key:
- Border dispute
- Refugee problem or protection of ethnic minorities
- Other

Some problems dealt with by the League of Nations or the Conference of Ambassadors in the 1920s.

SOURCE 12

The League had been designed to deal with just such a dangerous problem as this. It had acted promptly and fairly and it had condemned the violence of the Italians. But it had lost the initiative. The result was that a great power had once again got away with using force against a small power.

Historians Gibbons and Morican referring to the Corfu crisis in *The League of Nations and the UNO*, 1970.

SOURCE 13

The settlement of the dispute between Italy and Greece, though not strictly a League victory, upheld the principles on which it was based.

From J. and G. Stokes, *Europe and the Modern World*, 1973.

Source Analysis

1. Sources 12 and 13 are referring to the same event. How do their interpretations differ?
2. Could they both be right? Explain your answer.

Think!

'The main problem in the Corfu crisis was not the League's organisation but the attitude of its own members.' Explain whether you agree.

Vilna: Polish–Lithuanian dispute, 1920–29

Poland and Lithuania became independent states after the breakup of the Russian Empire at the end of the war. There had already been some conflict between the two states and the Soviet Union between 1918 and 1920. But on 7 October 1920, Vilna, with its largely Polish-speaking population, became the new seat of the Lithuanian government after negotiations with the League and the withdrawal of Soviet troops. However, two days later, Vilna was annexed by a Polish army and Lithuania appealed to the League of Nations. The League ordered the Polish army to withdraw from the region and wait for a plebiscite. Poland refused and the League was powerless to stop the conflict. France and Britain were not prepared to escalate the situation.

Aaland Islands dispute, 1921

The Aaland Islands, located in the Baltic Sea between Finland and Sweden, was a Finnish territory but whose population was largely Swedish. Many islanders wanted independence from Finland which almost led to conflict between the two countries. The League investigated the dispute and awarded the Aaland Islands to Finland but with protections for Swedish Islanders, including the removal of Finnish troops. Both countries accepted the League's decision.

Corfu, 1923

One of the boundaries that had to be sorted out after the war was the border between Greece and Albania. The Conference of Ambassadors was given this job and it appointed an Italian general called Tellini to supervise it. On 27 August, while surveying the Greek side of the frontier area, Tellini and his team were ambushed and killed. The Italian leader Mussolini was furious and blamed the Greek Government for the murder. On 31 August Mussolini bombarded and then occupied the Greek island of Corfu. Fifteen people were killed.

Greece appealed to the League for help. Fortunately, the Council was already in session, so the League acted swiftly. Articles 12 and 15 of the League of Nations were designed for exactly this situation. They said that when League members were in dispute and there was a danger of war, members could take their dispute to the Council and get a judgement. By 7 September it had prepared its judgement. It condemned Mussolini's actions. It also suggested that Greece pay compensation, but that this would be held by the League to be paid to Italy if, and when, Tellini's killers were found.

Mussolini refused to let the matter rest. He insisted that this dispute had to be settled by the Conference of Ambassadors because, he said, the Council of the League was not competent to deal with the issue. He even threatened to leave the League if this did not happen.

Mussolini would probably not have got his way if the British and French had stood together. Records from the meetings show that the British did not accept the Italian case and were prepared to send warships to force Mussolini out of Corfu. However, the French completely disagreed and backed the Italians, probably because their forces were tied up in the RUHR at this time (see page 16) and could not tackle a dispute with Italy as well. The British were not prepared to act without the French and now argued that Mussolini's actions did not constitute an act of war.

In the end Mussolini got his way and the Conference of Ambassadors made the final ruling on the dispute. The League's ruling was changed. Instead of condemning Mussolini the Conference ordered that the Greeks apologise and pay compensation directly to Italy. On 27 September, Mussolini withdrew from Corfu, boasting of his triumph.

There was much anger in the League over the Ambassadors' actions and League lawyers challenged the decision. However, the ruling was never changed. As historian Zara Steiner says, 'the dispute showed that the weakest of the great powers could get its way when Britain and France agreed to sacrifice justice for co-operation'.

The Geneva Protocol

The Corfu incident demonstrated how the League of Nations could be undermined by its own members. Britain and France drew up the Geneva Protocol in 1924, which said that if two members were in dispute they would have to ask the League to sort out the disagreement and they would have to accept the Council's decision. They hoped this would strengthen the League. But before the plan could be put into effect there was a general election in Britain. The new Conservative government refused to sign the Protocol, worried that Britain would be forced to agree to something that was not in its own interests. So the Protocol, intended to strengthen the League, in fact weakened it.

Bulgaria, 1925

Two years after Corfu, the League was tested yet again. In October 1925, Greek troops invaded Bulgaria after an incident on the border in which some Greek soldiers were killed. Bulgaria appealed for help. It also sent instructions to its army (see Source 14).

The secretary-general of the League acted quickly and decisively, calling a meeting of the League Council in Paris. The League demanded both sides stand their forces down and Greek forces withdraw from Bulgaria. Britain and France solidly backed the League's judgement (and it is worth remembering they were negotiating the Locarno Treaties at the same time – see the Factfile on page 38). The League sent observers to assess the situation and judged in favour of the Bulgarians. Greece had to pay £45,000 in compensation and was threatened with sanctions if it did not follow the ruling.

The Greeks obeyed, although they did complain that there seemed to be one rule for the large states (such as Italy) and another for the smaller ones (such as themselves). Nevertheless the incident was seen as a major success for the League and many observers seemed to forget the shame of the Corfu incident as optimism about the effectiveness of the League soared. Few pointed out that it was not so much the effectiveness of the machinery of the League in this dispute but the fact that the great powers were united in their decision.

SOURCE 14

Make only slight resistance. Protect the refugees. Prevent the spread of panic. Do not expose the troops to unnecessary losses in view of the fact that the incident has been laid before the Council of the League of Nations, which is expected to stop the invasion.

A telegram from the Bulgarian Ministry of War in Sofia to its army commanders, 22 October 1925.

Source Analysis

1. Read Source 14. Why do you think Bulgaria was so optimistic about the League?

Source Analysis

1 Look at Source 15. What impression of the League does this cartoon give you?

SOURCE 15

BALKANDUM AND BALKANDEE.
"JUST THEN CAME DOWN A MONSTROUS DOVE
WHOSE FORCE WAS PURELY MORAL,
WHICH TURNED THE HEROES' HEARTS TO LOVE
AND MADE THEM DROP THEIR QUARREL."—LEWIS CARROLL (adapted).

A cartoon about the Bulgarian crisis in *Punch*, 11 November 1925. The characters are based on Tweedledum and Tweedledee, who were always quarrelling, from the children's book *Alice's Adventures in Wonderland*.

Revision Tip
Border disputes

Make sure you can:
- describe one success in the 1920s and explain why it was a success
- describe one failure in the 1920s and explain why it was a failure

and as a bonus:
- describe and explain one **partial** success or failure.

Success or failure?

The League's most important aims were to try to prevent future wars and to encourage cooperation and compromise between nations. As you can see over the last few pages, the League cannot be considered a complete failure. Even without the USA, Germany or the USSR as members, the League did manage to intervene in border disputes and help different countries avoid conflict by accepting its judgements.

However, it is important to remember that the League was often frustrated by the actions of its own leading members. The League found it very challenging to get more powerful countries, such as Italy, to accept its decisions, especially when these countries were leading members of the League's Council. It was also increasingly clear to many that without Britain and France being willing to act and enforce decisions, the League became less effective and even failed to resolve disputes satisfactorily. Britain and France were prepared to use the League to solve disputes as long as it did not interfere with their national interests and priorities.

You will now look at the League's record on disarmament and the climate of economic recovery and internationalism that developed in the 1920s.

Disarmament

In the 1920s, the League largely failed to bring about disarmament. At the Washington Conference in 1921 the USA, Japan, Britain and France agreed to limit the size of their navies, but that was as far as disarmament ever got.

The failure of disarmament was particularly damaging to the League's reputation in Germany. Germany had disarmed. It had been forced to. But no other countries had disarmed to the same extent. They were not prepared to give up their own armies and they were certainly not prepared to be the first to disarm.

Even so, in the late 1920s, the League's failure over disarmament did not seem too serious because of a series of international agreements that seemed to promise a more peaceful world (see Factfile).

SOURCE 16

> **Source Analysis**
> 1. What is Source 16 commenting on?
> 2. Is the cartoonist praising or criticising someone or something in Source 16? Explain your answer.

A LEAGUE TRIUMPH.
WITH MR. PUNCH'S CONGRATULATIONS TO THE BRITISH COMMISSIONAIRE.

A *Punch* cartoon from 1925. The woman on the billboard represents Germany. 'A League Triumph. With Mr Punch's congratulations to the British Commissionaire.'

SOURCE 17

There was a tendency for nations to conduct much of their diplomacy outside the League of Nations and to put their trust in paper treaties. After the USA assisted Europe financially there seemed to be more goodwill which statesmen tried to capture in pacts and treaties. Many of them, however, were of little value. They represented no more than the hopes of decent men.

Written by historian Jack Watson in 1984.

Factfile

International agreements of the 1920s

- **1921 Washington Conference:** USA, Britain, France and Japan agreed to limit the size of their navies.
- **1922 Rapallo Treaty:** the USSR and Germany re-established DIPLOMATIC RELATIONS.
- **1924 The Dawes Plan:** to avert a terrible economic crisis in Germany, the USA lent money to Germany to help it to pay its REPARATIONS bill (see this page).
- **1925 Locarno treaties:** Germany accepted its western borders as set out in the Treaty of Versailles. This was greeted with great enthusiasm, especially in France. It paved the way for Germany to join the League of Nations.
- **1928 Kellogg–Briand Pact:** 65 nations agreed not to use force to settle disputes. This is also known as the Pact of Paris.
- **1929 Young Plan:** reduced Germany's reparations payments.

FIGURE **18**

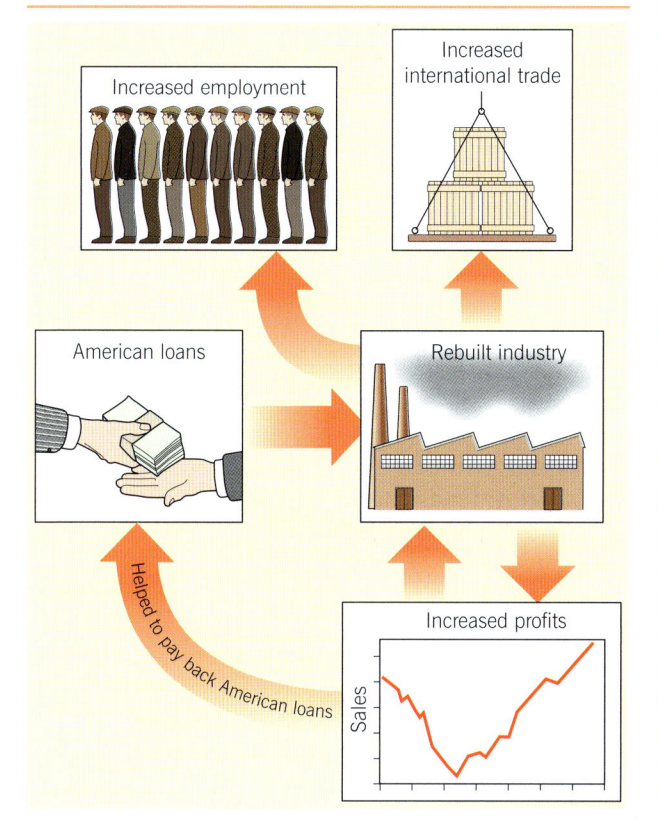

How the Dawes Plan helped recovery in Europe.

Economic recovery

Another reason for optimism in 1928 was that, after the difficult years of the early 1920s, the economies of the European countries were once again recovering. The DAWES PLAN of 1924 had helped to sort out Germany's economic chaos and had also helped to get the economies of Britain and France moving again (see Figure 19).

Increased trade between countries helped to reduce political tension. That is why one of the aims of the League had been to encourage trading links between the countries. When countries trade with one another, they are much less likely to go to war with each other.

Internationalism

Although Wilson's version of the League never happened, the League still achieved a lot in the 1920s. Perhaps most important of all, the League became one of the ways in which the world sorted out international disputes (even if it was not the only way). Historian Zara Steiner has said that 'the League was very effective in handling the "small change" of international diplomacy'. Her implication, of course, is that the League could not deal with 'big' issues, but it was not tested in this way in the 1920s.

Some historians believe that the biggest achievement of the League was the way it helped develop an 'internationalist mind-set' among leaders – it encouraged them to think in terms of collaborating rather than competing. One way it did this was simply by existing! Great and small powers felt that it was worth sending their ministers to League meetings throughout the 1920s and 1930s. This meant they would often talk together when they might not have done so otherwise. Even when powerful countries acted on their own (for example, over Corfu) it was often after their ministers had discussed their plans at League meetings!

FOCUS TASK 2.3

Did the League's weaknesses in membership and organisation affect its attempts at peacekeeping in the 1920s?

Can you find evidence to support or challenge each of the following criticisms of the League's organisation:
- that it would be slow to act
- that members would act in their own interests, not the League's
- that without the USA it would be powerless?

Use a table like this to record your answers:

Criticism	Evidence for	Evidence against

Focus on the Vilna and Aaland Islands disputes and the Corfu and Bulgarian crises first. These will be most useful for your exam. Then look for evidence from the other crises.

Keep your table safe. You will add to it in a later task on page 51.

Once you have completed your table, look at the balance of evidence. Does this suggest to you that the League could have succeeded, or not?

SOURCE 19

One of the League of Nations' projects.

Source Analysis

How useful is this photograph for finding out about the League of Nations?

Think!
1. Study Source 16. What aspects of the League's work do you think it shows?
2. Why do you think the founders of the League wanted it to tackle social problems?
3. The work of the League's commissions affected hundreds of millions of people, yet historians write very little about this side of its work. Why do you think this is?

Revision Tip

The commissions

Make sure you can remember two specific examples of work done by the League's commissions or committees. Choose the ones that you think affected the most people.

How important was the League's humanitarian work?

The League of Nations had set itself a wider task than simply waiting for disputes to arise and hoping to solve them. Through its commissions or committees (see page 33), the League fought poverty, disease and injustice all over the world.

Refugees

It is estimated that in the first few years after the war, about 400,000 prisoners were returned to their homes by the League's agencies. When war led to a refugee crisis in Turkey in 1922, hundreds of thousands of people had to be housed in refugee camps. The League acted quickly to stamp out cholera, smallpox and dysentery in the camps. However, the Refugees Committee was constantly short of funds and its work became more difficult in the 1930s as the international situation became tenser and the authority of the League declined.

Working conditions

The International Labour Organization succeeded in banning poisonous white lead from paint and in limiting the hours that small children were allowed to work. It also campaigned strongly for employers to improve working conditions. It introduced a resolution for a maximum 48-hour week, and an eight-hour day, but a majority of members refused to adopt it because they thought it would cost their industries too much. The ILO was hampered by lack of funds and lack of power. It could not do much more than 'name and shame' countries or organisations that broke its regulations.

Health

As well as collecting statistical information and spreading good practice, it sponsored research into infectious diseases at institutes in Singapore, London and Denmark. These institutes helped develop vaccines and medicines to fight deadly diseases such as leprosy and malaria. The Health Committee is generally regarded as one of the most successful of the League's organisations and its work was continued after 1945 in the form of the World Health Organization.

Slavery and forced labour

It helped free 200,000 slaves in British-owned Sierra Leone. It organised raids against slave owners and traders in Burma. It challenged the use of forced labour to build the Tanganyika railway in Africa, where the death rate among the African workers was a staggering 50 per cent. League pressure brought this down to 4 per cent, which it said was 'a much more acceptable figure'.

Other action

Even in the areas where it could not remove social injustice the League kept careful records of what was going on and provided information on problems such as drug trafficking, prostitution and slavery. The League blacklisted four large German, Dutch, French and Swiss companies which were involved in the illegal drug trade. The League also made recommendations on practical problems such as marking shipping lanes and produced an international highway code for road users.

FOCUS TASK 2.4

How important was the League's humanitarian work?

Use the information on page 40 and refer back to the information on the diagram on page 33.
1. Draw a table like the one below to assess the importance of the humanitarian work of the League of Nations.
2. Add evidence of success and failure in the relevant columns before assessing the overall importance in the last column.
3. Then write a paragraph explaining your overall judgement of the importance of the humanitarian work of the League of Nations.

	Area of humanitarian work				
	Refugees	Working conditions	Health	Slavery	Overall
Evidence of success					
Evidence of failure					
Importance					

When assessing importance consider the following:
- The extent to which the agency or commission achieved its aims.
- The impact the agency or commission had with trying to improve people's living and working conditions.
- The value the League placed on these agencies and their work compared to its other aims, such as disarmament and enforcing the Treaty of Versailles.

FOCUS TASK 2.5

How successful was the League in the 1920s?

It is now time to draw some conclusions to this key question.

Stage 1: Evaluate the League's successes and failures
1. Create four cards like the ones on the right – one for each of the League's aims.
2. On the back of each card summarise your evidence of success or failure in each aim. You will have plenty of detail to use from the table you started in the Think! task on page 30.
3. Based on the evidence on your cards, put the aim you think was achieved to the greatest extent at the top, and that which was achieved to the least extent at the bottom.
4. Write some paragraphs to explain your order and support your paragraphs with evidence from your cards.
5. **Extension:** Suggest one change the League could make to be more effective in one of its objectives. Explain how the change would help. You might find your work on Focus Task 2.3 on page 39 useful for this.

- Discourage aggression
- Encourage co-operation
- Encourage disarmament
- Improve living conditions

Stage 2: Reach an overall judgement
6. Look back to your predictions for the League for the 1920s (page 27). Has the League performed better or worse than you predicted? Redraw your pie chart to show the balance of success and failure in the 1920s.
7. Which of the following statements do you **most** agree with?
    - 'The League of Nations was a great force for peace in the 1920s.'
    - 'Events of the 1920s showed just how weak the League really was.'
    - 'The League's successes in the 1920s were small-scale. Its failures had a higher profile.'

    Explain why you have chosen your statement, and why you rejected the others.

How far did the Depression make the work of the League more difficult in the 1930s?

Most historians agree that in the 1930s the League of Nations was a failure. Figure 1 sums up the three main challenges the League faced in the 1930s and how the League dealt with them. It makes quite depressing reading! However, not all historians agree on how far these failures were the fault of the League and how far other factors beyond the League's control were more important. The biggest of these 'other factors' was the economic depression of the 1930s so let's start with that.

FIGURE 1

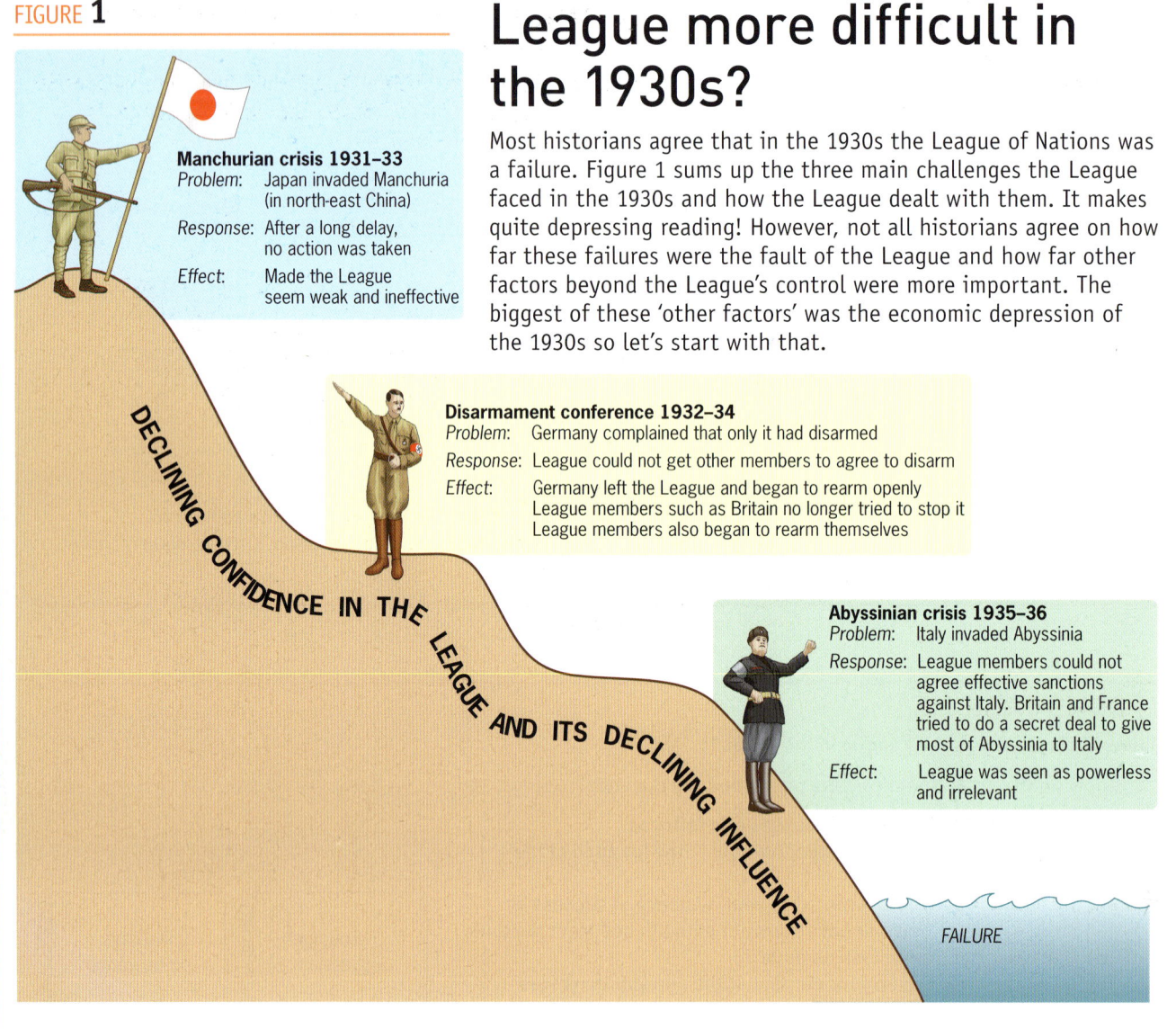

Manchurian crisis 1931–33
- *Problem*: Japan invaded Manchuria (in north-east China)
- *Response*: After a long delay, no action was taken
- *Effect*: Made the League seem weak and ineffective

Disarmament conference 1932–34
- *Problem*: Germany complained that only it had disarmed
- *Response*: League could not get other members to agree to disarm
- *Effect*: Germany left the League and began to rearm openly. League members such as Britain no longer tried to stop it. League members also began to rearm themselves

Abyssinian crisis 1935–36
- *Problem*: Italy invaded Abyssinia
- *Response*: League members could not agree effective sanctions against Italy. Britain and France tried to do a secret deal to give most of Abyssinia to Italy
- *Effect*: League was seen as powerless and irrelevant

DECLINING CONFIDENCE IN THE LEAGUE AND ITS DECLINING INFLUENCE

FAILURE

The challenges faced by the League in the 1930s.

The economic depression

In the late 1920s international trade prospered. The USA, the world's richest nation, was a market for other countries to export to. It also helped economic recovery with loans to many countries, particularly Germany.

In 1929 disaster struck. The WALL STREET CRASH in the USA started a long depression that quickly caused economic problems throughout the rest of the world (see Figure 2).

In the 1930s, as a result of the Depression, much of the goodwill of the late 1920s evaporated.
- As US loans dried up, businesses in many countries went bankrupt, leading to unemployment.

Revision Tip
- The key idea to grasp from Figure 2 is that the Depression created economic problems which led to political problems later on.
- The two most important examples are Germany and Japan so make sure you can describe how the Depression affected them.

- Some countries tried to protect their own industries by putting TARIFFS on imports. But this just meant their trading partners did the same thing and trade got even worse.
- Many countries (including Germany, Japan, Italy and Britain) started to rearm (build up their armed forces) as a way of trying to get industries working and giving jobs to the unemployed. But these new armies caused alarm and tension.

The internationalist spirit of the 1920s was replaced by a more nationalist 'beggar my neighbour' approach in the 1930s (protecting a country's interest at the expense of other countries).

FIGURE 2

The USA
One way that the League of Nations could stop one country invading another was to use economic sanctions. But the Depression made the USA unwilling to help in this because economic sanctions would make its own economy even worse.

Top priority – sort out US economy.
Low priority – help sort out international disputes.

Japan
The Depression threatened to bankrupt Japan. Its main export was silk to the USA, but the USA was buying less silk. So Japan had less money to buy food and raw materials. Its leaders were all army generals. They decided to continue to expand their empire by taking over weaker countries that had the raw materials Japan needed. They started by invading Manchuria (part of China) in 1931.

Plans for Japanese empire

Britain
Britain was one of the leaders of the League of Nations. But, like the USA, it was unwilling to help sort out international disputes while its economy was bad. For example, when Japan invaded Manchuria it did nothing – it did not support economic sanctions against Japan and did not send troops to protect Manchuria.

Top priority – sort out British economy.
Low priority – help sort out international disputes.

Germany
The Depression hit Germany badly. There was unemployment, poverty and chaos. Germany's weak leaders seemed unable to do anything. Many Germans began supporting the Nazi Party and Hitler was appointed chancellor in 1933. He was not good news for international peace. He openly planned to invade Germany's neighbours and to win back land that Germany had lost in the Treaty of Versailles.

He'll make Germany great again.

Italy
In Italy economic problems encouraged Mussolini to try to build an overseas empire to distract people's attention from the difficulties the government faced.

The impact of the Depression on different countries.

FOCUS TASK 2.6
How far did the Depression make the work of the League more difficult in the 1930s?

Study these statements:
a) 'I have not worked since last year.' *anywhere affected*
b) 'I will support anyone who can get the country back to work.' *Germany*
c) 'If we had our own empire we would have the resources we need. Economic depression would not damage us so much.' *Japan + Italy?*
d) 'Reparations have caused this mess.' *Germany*
e) 'The bank has closed. We've lost everything!'
f) 'We need tough leaders who will not be pushed around by the League of Nations or the USA.' *Germany*
g) 'We should tax all foreign goods. That will protect the jobs of our workers.'
1 Suggest in which of the following countries (USA, Britain, France, Germany, Japan or Italy) someone might have said each of the above statements during the Depression. Some might apply to more than one country.
2 Suggest why each viewpoint would worry the League of Nations or make its work harder.

How did the Manchurian crisis weaken the League?

FIGURE 3

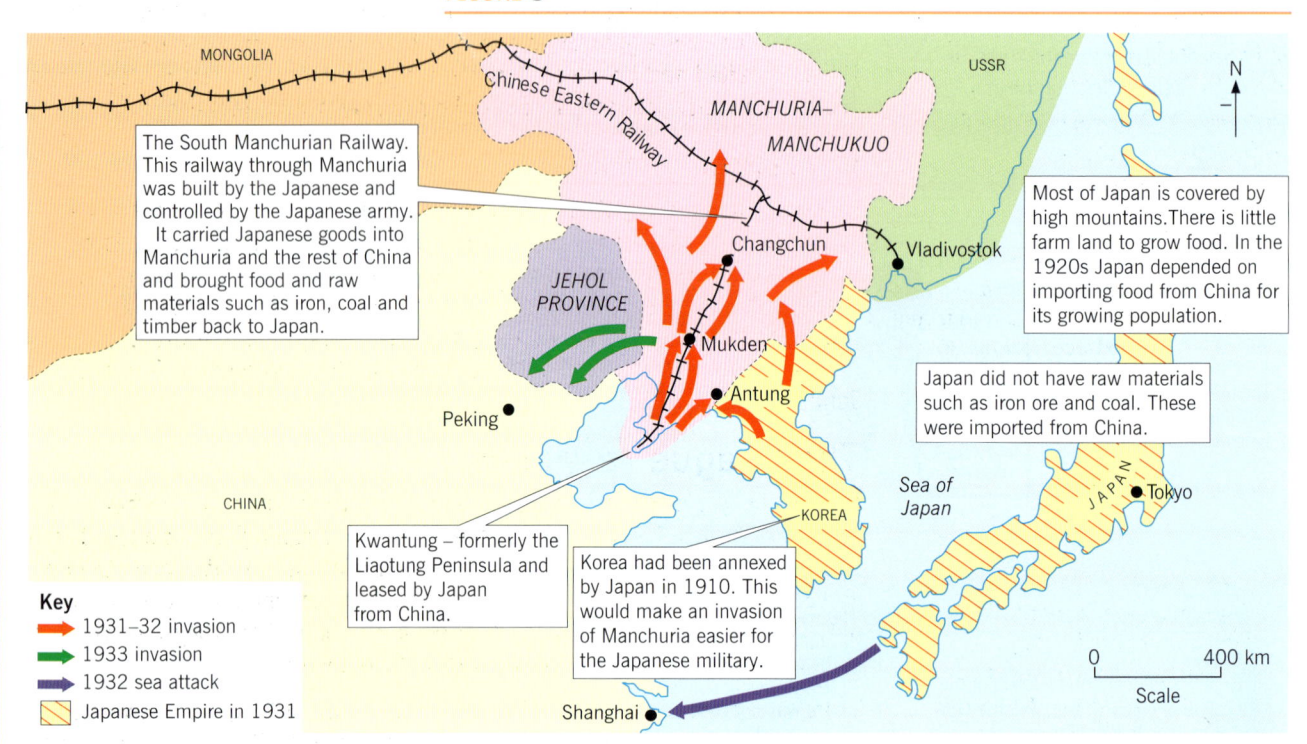

The railways and natural resources of Manchuria.

Map labels:
- The South Manchurian Railway. This railway through Manchuria was built by the Japanese and controlled by the Japanese army. It carried Japanese goods into Manchuria and the rest of China and brought food and raw materials such as iron, coal and timber back to Japan.
- Most of Japan is covered by high mountains. There is little farm land to grow food. In the 1920s Japan depended on importing food from China for its growing population.
- Japan did not have raw materials such as iron ore and coal. These were imported from China.
- Kwantung – formerly the Liaotung Peninsula and leased by Japan from China.
- Korea had been annexed by Japan in 1910. This would make an invasion of Manchuria easier for the Japanese military.

Key
- 1931–32 invasion
- 1933 invasion
- 1932 sea attack
- Japanese Empire in 1931

> **Revision Tip**
>
> Make sure you can explain:
> - what the League decided should happen in Manchuria
> - why it was unable to force Japan to obey.
>
> The first major test for the League came when the Japanese invaded Manchuria in 1931.

Background

Since 1900 Japan's economy and population had been growing rapidly. By the 1920s Japan was a major power with a powerful military, strong industries and a growing empire (see Figure 3). But the Depression hit Japan badly as China and the USA put up tariffs (trade barriers) against Japanese goods. Army leaders in Japan were in no doubt about the solution to Japan's problems – Japan would not face these problems if it expanded its empire to provide resources and markets for Japanese goods.

Invasion 1, 1931

In 1931 an incident in Manchuria gave them an ideal opportunity. The Japanese army controlled the South Manchurian Railway (see Figure 3). When Chinese troops allegedly attacked the railway the Japanese armed forces used this as an excuse to invade and set up a government in Manchukuo (Manchuria), which they controlled. This was known as the Mukden Incident. Japan's civilian government protested but the military were now in charge.

China appeals

China appealed to the League. The Japanese argued that China was in such a state of anarchy that they had to invade in self-defence to keep peace in the area. For the League of Nations this was a serious test. Japan was a leading member of the League. It needed careful handling. What should the League do?

SOURCE 4

I was sad to find everyone [at the League] so dejected. The Assembly was a dead thing. The Council was without confidence in itself. Beneš [the Czechoslovak leader], who is not given to hysterics, said [about the people at the League] 'They are too frightened. I tell them we are not going to have war now; we have five years before us, perhaps six. We must make the most of them.'

The British elder statesman Sir Austen Chamberlain visited the League of Nations late in 1932 in the middle of the Manchurian crisis. This is an adapted extract from his letters.

Source Analysis

1 Source 5 is a comment on this Manchurian crisis. On your own copy of this cartoon add annotations to explain:
   a) the key features
   b) the message
   c) what the cartoonist thinks of the League.
2 Read Source 4. Does Beneš share the same view of the League as the cartoonist in Source 5?

SOURCE 5

A cartoon by David Low, published in a British newspaper in 1933 (see also Source 8 on page 47 for more information about the cartoonist).

The Lytton Report

Britain and France both had colonies in South-East Asia. They did not want to provoke a war with Japan. Many European member states also viewed the incident as a problem far away. Some members even believed that Japanese rule would bring order to the region. Investigation of the Mukden Incident was finally entrusted to Lord Lytton and the Lytton Commission. It took them over a year to present the Lytton Report in September 1932. It was detailed and balanced, but the judgement was very clear. Japan had acted unlawfully. Manchuria should be returned to the Chinese.

Invasion 2, 1933

However, in February 1933, instead of withdrawing from Manchuria the Japanese announced that they intended to invade more of China. They still argued that this was necessary in self-defence. On 24 February 1933 the report from the League's officials was approved by 42 votes to 1 in the Assembly. Only Japan voted against. Smarting at the insult, Japan resigned from the League on 27 March 1933. The next week it invaded Jehol (see Figure 3).

The League responds

The League was powerless. It discussed economic sanctions, but without the USA, Japan's main trading partner, they would be meaningless. Besides, Britain seemed more interested in keeping up a good relationship with Japan than in agreeing to sanctions. The League also discussed banning arms sales to Japan, but the member countries could not even agree about that. They were worried that Japan would retaliate and the war would escalate.

There was no prospect at all of Britain and France risking their navies or armies in a war with Japan. Only the USA and the USSR would have had the resources to remove the Japanese from Manchuria by force and they were not even members of the League.

Consequences

All sorts of excuses were offered for the failure of the League: Japan was so far away; Japan was a special case; Japan did have a point when it said that China was itself in the grip of anarchy. However, the significance of the MANCHURIAN CRISIS was obvious. As many of its critics had predicted, the League was powerless if a strong nation decided to pursue an aggressive policy and invade its neighbours. Japan had committed blatant aggression and got away with it. Back in Europe, both Hitler and Mussolini looked on with interest. Within three years they would both follow Japan's example.

Think!

1 Why did it take so long for the League to make a decision over Manchuria?
2 Did the League fail in this incident because of the way it worked or because of the attitude of its members?

SOURCE 6

To make myself perfectly clear, I would ask: is there anyone within or without Germany who honestly considers the present German regime to be peaceful in its instincts ... Germany is inhibited from disturbing the peace of Europe solely by its consciousness of its present military inferiority.

Professor William Rappard speaking to the League in 1932.

Source Analysis

1. What is the message of Source 7?
2. Why might this cartoon have been published in Germany in July 1933?

SOURCE 7

A German cartoon from July 1933. The parrot represents France. It is calling for more security.

Why did disarmament fail in the 1930s?

The next big failure of the League of Nations was over disarmament. As you saw on page 38, the League had not had success in this area in the 1920s either, but at that stage, when the international climate was better, it had not seemed to matter so much. In the 1930s, however, there was increased pressure for the League to do something about disarmament. The Germans had long been angry that they had been forced to disarm after the First World War while other nations had not done the same. Many countries were actually spending more on armaments than before the First World War.

Disarmament Conference

After the Manchurian crisis, members of the League realised the urgency of the problem. In February 1932 the long-promised Disarmament Conference finally got under way. By July 1932 it had produced resolutions to prohibit bombing of civilian populations, limit the size of artillery, limit the tonnage of tanks, and prohibit chemical warfare. But there was very little in the resolutions to show how these limits would be achieved. For example, the bombing of civilians was to be prohibited, but all attempts to agree to abolish planes capable of bombing were defeated. Even the proposal to ban the manufacture of CHEMICAL WEAPONS was defeated.

German disarmament

It was not a promising start. However, there was a bigger problem facing the Conference – what to do about Germany. The Germans had been in the League for six years. Most people now accepted that they should be treated more equally than under the Treaty of Versailles. The big question was whether everyone else should disarm to the level that Germany had been forced to, or whether the Germans should be allowed to rearm to a level closer to that of the other powers. The experience of the 1920s showed that the first option was a non-starter. But there was great reluctance in the League to allow the second option. The timeline shows how events relating to Germany moved over the next 18 months.

July 1932: Germany proposed all countries disarm to its level. When the Conference failed to agree this principle of 'equality', the Germans walked out.

September 1932: The British sent the Germans a note that went some way to agreeing equality, but the superior tone of the note angered the Germans still further.

December 1932: An agreement was finally reached to treat Germany equally.

January 1933: Germany announced it was coming back to the Conference.

February 1933: Hitler became CHANCELLOR of Germany at the end of January. He immediately started to rearm Germany, although secretly.

May 1933: Hitler promised not to rearm Germany if 'in five years all other nations destroyed their arms'.

June 1933: Britain produced an ambitious disarmament plan, but it failed to achieve support at the Conference.

October 1933: Hitler withdrew from the Disarmament Conference, and soon after took Germany out of the League altogether.

By this stage, all the powers knew that Hitler was secretly rearming Germany already. They also began to rebuild their own armaments. Against that background the Disarmament Conference struggled on for another year but in an atmosphere of increasing futility. It finally ended in 1934.

SOURCE 8

Source Analysis
Look at Source 8. Explain what the cartoonist is saying about:
a) ordinary people
b) political leaders.

David Low's cartoon commenting on the failure of the Disarmament Conference in 1934. Low was one of the most famous cartoonists of the 1930s. He regularly criticised both the actions of dictators around the world and the ineffectiveness of the League of Nations.

Reasons for failure

The Conference failed for a number of reasons. Some say it was all doomed from the start. No one was very serious about disarmament anyway. But there were other factors at work.

It did not help that Britain and France were divided on this issue. By 1933 many British people felt that the Treaty of Versailles was unfair. In fact, to the dismay of the French, the British signed the Anglo-German Naval Agreement with Germany in 1935 that allowed Germany to build up its navy as long as it stayed under 35 per cent of the size of the British navy. Britain did not consult either its allies or the League about this, even though this violated the Treaty of Versailles.

It seemed that each country was looking after itself and ignoring the League.

Revision Tip
Although disarmament was a key aim of the League it never really had much success in this in either the 1920s or the 1930s. The key thing to remember is why this was more serious in the 1930s than in the 1920s. In the 1930s it was serious because Germany used the failure as an excuse for its rapid and risky rearmament programme.

Think!
1. In what ways were each of the following to blame for the failure of the Disarmament Conference:
   a) Germany
   b) Britain
   c) the League itself?
2. Do you think the disarmament failure did less or more damage to the League's reputation than the Manchurian crisis? Give reasons.

How did Mussolini's invasion of Abyssinia damage the League?

FIGURE 9

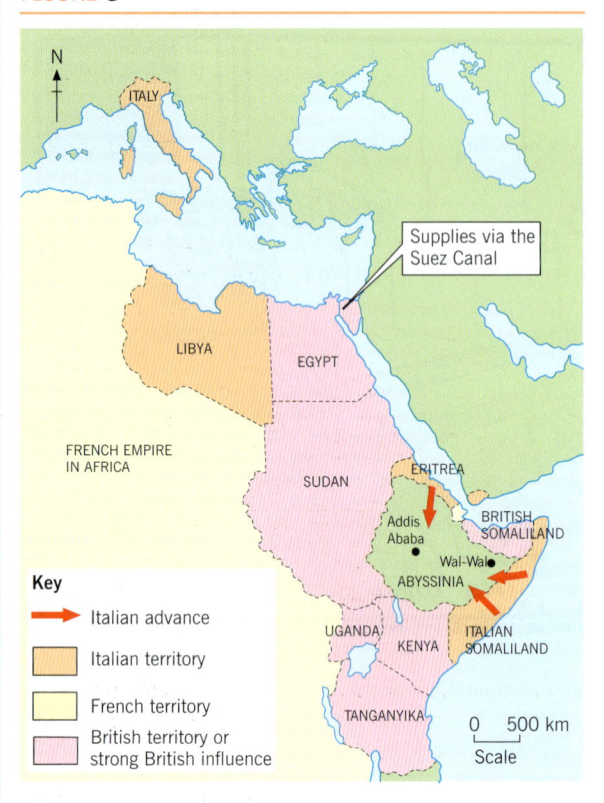

British, French and Italian possessions in eastern Africa.

Think!
To help you analyse these events draw a timeline, from December 1934 to May 1936, down the middle of a piece of paper and use the text to mark the key events on it. On one side put the actions of Mussolini or Hitler, on the other side the actions of Britain, France and the League.

The fatal blow to the League came when the Italian DICTATOR Mussolini invaded Abyssinia in 1935. There were both similarities with and differences from the Japanese invasion of Manchuria.

- **Like Japan**, Italy was a leading member of the League. Like Japan, Italy wanted to expand its empire by invading another country.
- However, **unlike Manchuria**, this dispute was on the League's doorstep. Italy was a European power. It even had a border with France. Abyssinia bordered on the Anglo-Egyptian territory of Sudan and the British colonies of Uganda, Kenya and British Somaliland. Unlike events in Manchuria, the League could not claim that this problem was in an inaccessible part of the world.

Some argued that Manchuria had been a special case. Would the League do any better in this ABYSSINIAN CRISIS?

Background

The origins of this crisis lay back in the previous century. In 1896 Italian troops had tried to invade Abyssinia but had been defeated by a poorly equipped army of tribesmen in the Battle of Adowa. Mussolini wanted revenge for this humiliating defeat. He also had his eye on the fertile land and mineral wealth of Abyssinia. However, most importantly, he wanted glory and conquest. His style of leadership needed military victories and he had often talked of restoring the glory of the Roman Empire.

In December 1934 there was a dispute between Italian and Abyssinian soldiers at the Wal-Wal oasis – 80 km inside Abyssinia. Mussolini took this as his cue and claimed this was actually Italian territory. He demanded an apology and began preparing the Italian army for an invasion of Abyssinia. The Abyssinian emperor Haile Selassie appealed to the League for help.

Phase 1: the League plays for time

From January 1935 to October 1935, Mussolini was supposedly negotiating with the League to settle the dispute. However, at the same time he was shipping his vast army to Africa and whipping up war fever among the Italian people.

To start with, the British and the French failed to take the situation seriously. They played for time. They were desperate to keep good relations with Mussolini, who seemed to be their strongest ally against Hitler. They signed an agreement with him early in 1935 known as the Stresa Pact, which was a formal statement against German REARMAMENT and a commitment to stand united against Germany. At the meeting to discuss this, they did not even raise the question of Abyssinia. Some historians suggest that Mussolini believed that Britain and France had promised to turn a blind eye to his exploits in Abyssinia in return for his joining them in the Stresa Pact.

However, as the year wore on, there was a public outcry against Italy's behaviour. A ballot was taken by the League of Nations Union in Britain in 1934–35. It showed that a majority of British people supported the use of

Source Analysis

1 Study Source 10. At what point in the crisis do you think this might have been published? Use the details in the source and the text to help you decide.
2 Here are three possible reasons why this cartoon was drawn:
   - To inform people in Britain about British and French policy
   - To criticise British and French policy
   - To change British and French policy

   Which do you think is the best explanation?

MILITARY FORCE to defend Abyssinia if necessary. Facing an autumn election at home, British politicians now began to 'get tough'. At an assembly of the League, the British foreign minister, Hoare, made a grand speech about the value of collective security, to the delight of the League's members and all the smaller nations. There was much talking and negotiating. However, the League never actually did anything to discourage Mussolini.

On 4 September, after eight months' deliberation, a committee reported to the League that neither side could be held responsible for the Wal-Wal incident. The League put forward a plan that would give Mussolini some of Abyssinia. Mussolini rejected it.

Phase 2: sanctions or not?

In October 1935 Mussolini's army was ready. He launched a full-scale invasion of Abyssinia. Despite brave resistance, the Abyssinians were no match for the modern Italian army equipped with tanks, aeroplanes and poison gas.

This was a clear-cut case of a large, powerful state attacking a smaller one. The League was designed for just such disputes and, unlike in the Manchurian crisis, it was ideally placed to act. There was no doubting the seriousness of the issue either.

The Covenant (see page 30) made it clear that sanctions must be introduced against the aggressor. A committee was immediately set up to agree what sanctions to impose. Sanctions would only work if they were imposed quickly and decisively. Each week a decision was delayed would allow Mussolini to build up his stockpile of raw materials.

The League banned arms sales to Italy; banned loans to Italy; banned imports from Italy. It also banned the export to Italy of rubber, tin and metals. However, the League delayed a decision for two months over whether to ban oil exports to Italy. It feared the Americans would not support the sanctions. It also feared that its members' economic interests would be further damaged. In Britain, the Cabinet was informed that 30,000 British coal miners were about to lose their jobs because of the ban on coal exports to Italy.

More important still, the Suez Canal, which was owned by Britain and France, was not closed to Mussolini's supply ships. The canal was the Italians' main supply route to Abyssinia and closing it could have ended the Abyssinian campaign very quickly. Both Britain and France were afraid that closing the canal could have resulted in war with Italy. This failure was fatal for Abyssinia.

SOURCE 10

THE AWFUL WARNING.

FRANCE AND ENGLAND (together ?). "WE DON'T WANT YOU TO FIGHT, BUT, BY JINGO, IF YOU DO, WE SHALL PROBABLY ISSUE A JOINT MEMORANDUM SUGGESTING A MILD DISAPPROVAL OF YOU."

A cartoon from *Punch*, 1935, commenting on the Abyssinian crisis. *Punch* was usually very patriotic towards Britain. It seldom criticised British politicians over foreign policy.

Think!
1. How did:
   a) the USA
   b) Britain
   undermine the League's attempts to impose sanctions on Italy?
2. Explain in your own words:
   a) why the Hoare–Laval deal caused such outrage
   b) how it affected attitudes to the League
   c) how the USA undermined the League.

Source Analysis
1. Look at Source 11. What event is the cartoonist referring to when the warrior says 'the matter has been settled elsewhere'?
2. Compare Sources 11 and 12. How far do they agree about the implications of the Abyssinian crisis?

The Hoare–Laval Pact

Equally damaging to the League was the secret dealing between the British and the French that was going on behind the scenes. In December 1935, while sanctions discussions were still taking place, the British and French foreign ministers, Hoare and Laval, were hatching a plan. This aimed to give Mussolini two-thirds of Abyssinia in return for his calling off his invasion! Laval even proposed to put the plan to Mussolini before they showed it to either the League of Nations or Haile Selassie. Laval told the British that if they did not agree to the plan, then the French would no longer support sanctions against Italy.

However, details of the plan were leaked to the French press. It proved quite disastrous for the League. Haile Selassie demanded an immediate League debate about it. In both Britain and France it was seen as a blatant act of treachery against the League. Hoare and Laval were both sacked. But the real damage was to the sanctions discussions. They lost all momentum.

No oil sanctions

The question about whether to ban oil sales was further delayed. In February 1936 the committee concluded that if they did stop oil sales to Italy, the Italians' supplies would be exhausted in two months, even if the Americans kept on selling oil to them. But by then it was all too late. Mussolini had already taken over large parts of Abyssinia. And the Americans were even more disgusted with the ditherings of the French and the British than they had been before and so blocked a move to support the League's sanctions. American oil producers actually stepped up their exports to Italy.

The outcomes

On 7 March 1936 the fatal blow was delivered. Hitler, timing his move to perfection, marched his troops into the RHINELAND, an act prohibited by the Treaty of Versailles (see page 12). If there had been any hope of getting the French to support sanctions against Italy, it was now dead. The French were desperate to gain the support of Italy and were now prepared to pay the price of giving Abyssinia to Mussolini.

Italy continued to defy the League's orders and by May 1936 had taken the capital of Abyssinia, Addis Ababa. On 2 May, Haile Selassie was forced into exile. On 9 May, Mussolini formally annexed the entire country.

The League watched helplessly. Collective security had been shown up as an empty promise. The League of Nations had failed. If the British and French had hoped that their handling of the Abyssinian crisis would help strengthen their position against Hitler, they were soon proved very wrong. In November 1936 Mussolini and Hitler signed an agreement of their own called the Rome–Berlin Axis.

SOURCE 11

A German cartoon from the front cover of the pro-Nazi magazine *Simplicissimus*, 1936. The warrior is delivering a message to the League of Nations (the 'Völkerbund'): 'I am sorry to disturb your sleep but I just wanted to tell you that you should no longer bother yourselves about this Abyssinian business. The matter has been settled elsewhere.'

SOURCE 12

Could the League survive the failure of sanctions to rescue Abyssinia? Could it ever impose sanctions again? Probably there had never been such a clear-cut case for sanctions. If the League had failed in this case there could probably be no confidence that it could succeed again in the future.

Anthony Eden, British foreign minister, expressing his feelings about the crisis to the British Cabinet in May 1936.

SOURCE 13

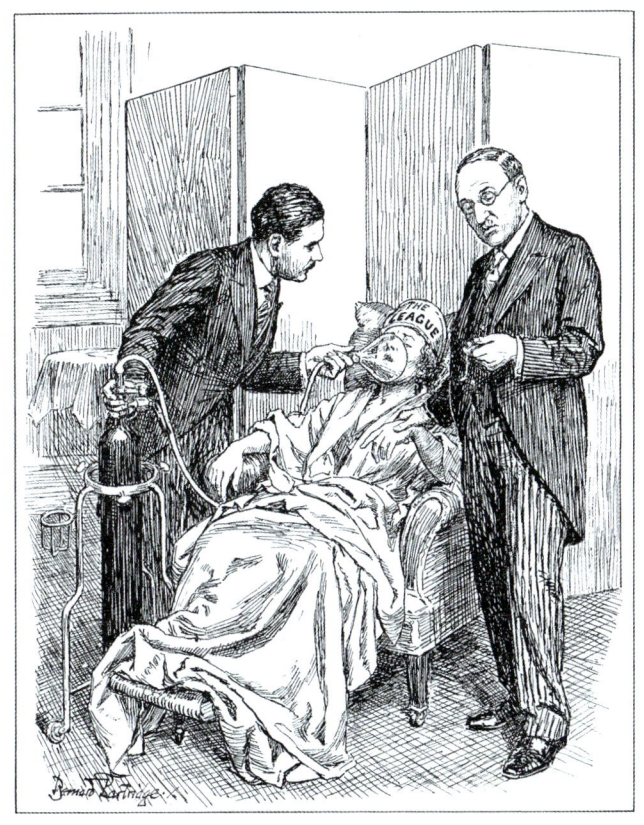

A cartoon from *Punch*, 1938. The doctors represent Britain and France.

Think!
Write a caption for the cartoon in Source 13, showing people's feelings about the League after the Abyssinian crisis. The real caption is on page vi.

FOCUS TASK 2.7
Did the League's weaknesses in membership and organisation affect its attempts at peacekeeping in the 1930s?
1. When the League was set up, its critics said there were weaknesses in its organisation that would make it ineffective. On page 39 you drew up a table to analyse the effect of these weaknesses in the 1920s. Now do a similar analysis for the 1930s.

   What evidence is there in the Manchurian crisis, the disarmament talks and the Abyssinian crisis of the following criticisms of the League:
   - that it would be slow to act
   - that members would act in their own interests
   - that without the USA it would be powerless?
2. 'The way the League was set up meant it was bound to fail.' Explain how far you agree with this statement. Support your answer with evidence from the tables you have compiled for this Focus Task and Focus Task 2.3 on page 39.

A disaster for the League and for the world

Historians often disagree about how to interpret important events. However, one of the most striking things about the events of 1935 and 1936 is that most historians seem to agree about the Abyssinian crisis: it was a disaster for the League of Nations and had serious consequences for world peace.

SOURCE 14

The implications of the conquest of Abyssinia were not confined to East Africa. Although victory cemented Mussolini's personal prestige at home, Italy gained little or nothing from it in material terms. The damage done, meanwhile, to the prestige of Britain, France and the League of Nations was irreversible. The only winner in the whole sorry episode was Adolf Hitler.

Written by historian T.A. Morris in 1995.

SOURCE 15

After seeing what happened first in Manchuria and then in Abyssinia, most people drew the conclusion that it was no longer much use placing their hopes in the League…

Written by historian James Joll in 1976.

SOURCE 16

The real death of the League was in 1935. One day it was a powerful body imposing sanctions, the next day it was an empty sham, everyone scuttling from it as quickly as possible. Hitler watched.

Written by historian A.J.P. Taylor in 1966.

SOURCE 17

Yes, we know that World War began in Manchuria fifteen years ago. We know that four years later we could easily have stopped Mussolini if we had taken the sanctions against Mussolini that were obviously required, if we had closed the Suez Canal to the aggressor and stopped his oil.

British statesman Philip Noel Baker speaking at the very last session of the League in April 1946.

FOCUS TASK 2.8

Why did the League of Nations fail in the 1930s?

Here is a diagram summarising reasons for the failure of the League of Nations in the 1930s. Complete your own copy of the diagram to explain how each weakness affected the League's actions in Manchuria and Abyssinia. We have filled in some points for you. There is one weakness that you will not be able to write about – you will find out about it in Chapter 3.

Failure of the League

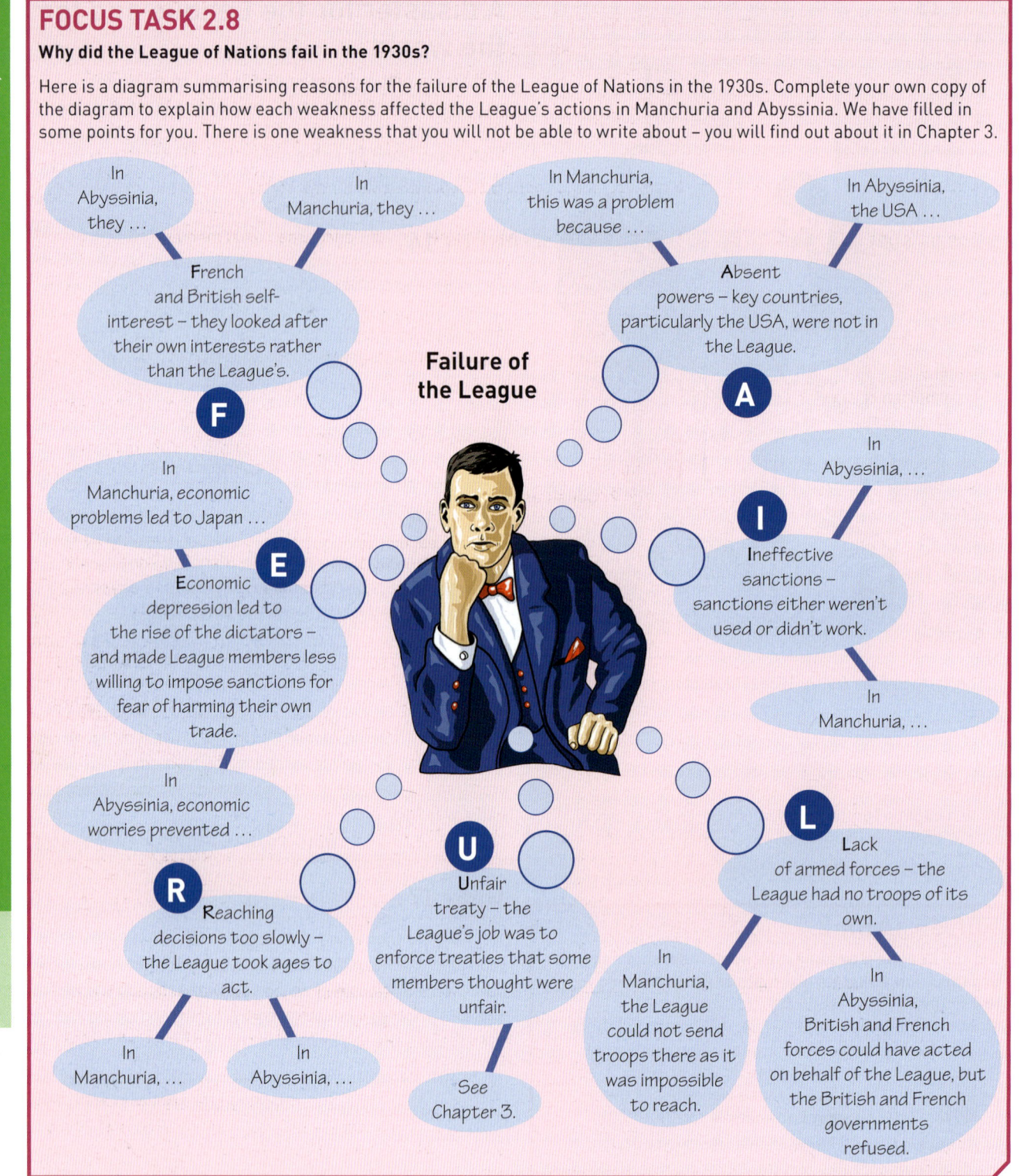

- **F** — French and British self-interest – they looked after their own interests rather than the League's.
  - In Abyssinia, they …
  - In Manchuria, they …

- **A** — Absent powers – key countries, particularly the USA, were not in the League.
  - In Manchuria, this was a problem because …
  - In Abyssinia, the USA …

- **I** — Ineffective sanctions – sanctions either weren't used or didn't work.
  - In Abyssinia, …
  - In Manchuria, …

- **L** — Lack of armed forces – the League had no troops of its own.
  - In Manchuria, the League could not send troops there as it was impossible to reach.
  - In Abyssinia, British and French forces could have acted on behalf of the League, but the British and French governments refused.

- **U** — Unfair treaty – the League's job was to enforce treaties that some members thought were unfair.
  - See Chapter 3.

- **R** — Reaching decisions too slowly – the League took ages to act.
  - In Manchuria, …
  - In Abyssinia, …

- **E** — Economic depression led to the rise of the dictators – and made League members less willing to impose sanctions for fear of harming their own trade.
  - In Manchuria, economic problems led to Japan …
  - In Abyssinia, economic worries prevented …

Revision Tip

The memory aid FAILURE should help you remember these key points for an exam.

PART 1 THE INTER-WAR YEARS, 1919–39

Keywords

Make sure you know these terms, people or events and are able to use them or describe them confidently.
- Abyssinian crisis
- Article 10
- Assembly
- Collective security
- Commissions
- Conference of Ambassadors
- Council
- Covenant
- Disarmament
- Economic depression
- Isolationism
- Manchurian crisis
- Military force
- Moral condemnation
- Normalcy
- Secretariat
- Tariffs
- Trade sanctions
- Unanimous
- Wall Street Crash

FOCUS TASK 2.9

To what extent was the League of Nations a success?

The last few pages have been all about failure. But remember there were successes too. To help you reach a balanced judgement on this key question, use these steps to review your work over the whole chapter.

Stage 1: Evaluate the League's successes and failures in the 1930s

On page 41 you created four cards to summarise the League's successes and failures in the 1920s. Now do the same for the 1930s.

1. Create four cards – one for each of the League's aims.
   - discourage aggression
   - encourage disarmament
   - encourage co-operation
   - improve living conditions.

   On the back of each card summarise evidence of success or failure in each aim in the 1930s. You may not be able to do them all.
2. Based on the evidence on your 1930s cards, put the aim you think was achieved to the greatest extent in the 1930s at the top, and that which was achieved to the least extent at the bottom.
3. Write some paragraphs to explain your order and support your paragraphs with evidence from your cards.
4. If your order is different from the order you had for the 1920s, write a further paragraph explaining how and why this has changed.

Stage 2: Consider reasons for success or failure

5. For each aim decide:
   a) how far you think the League should get credit for its successes or how far other factors (e.g. the economy; the Great Powers) deserve more credit.
   b) how far you think the League should get blamed for its failures; were they more the result of the League's actions or other factors?

Stage 3: Reach a judgement

6. Now it's judgement time. Taking all the work you have done; considering the four aims and its relative success and failure in each one; and taking into account both the 1920s and the 1930s, how does the League score out of 100?
7. Write a short paragraph explaining your mark out of 100.

PRACTICE QUESTIONS

1. (a) Describe the main powers available to the League to sort out international disputes. **[4]**
   (b) Why did the League of Nations fail to impose meaningful sanctions against Italy during the Abyssinian crisis? **[6]**
   (c) 'The League of Nations had failed before the Abyssinian crisis even started.' How far do you agree with this statement? Explain your answer. **[10]**

See pages 148–54 for advice on the different types of questions.

Chapter Summary

To what extent was the League of Nations a success?

1. The League of Nations was set up to solve problems between countries before they led to war.
2. Its methods were mainly diplomacy (talking), trade sanctions, or if necessary using the armies of their members.
3. It was the big idea of President Wilson, but his own country, the USA, never joined and instead returned to its isolationist policy.
4. The leading members were Britain and France, but they had their own interests and bypassed the League when it suited them.
5. The League's structure made it slow to take decisions, which made it less effective in settling international disputes, but it did have some successes in the 1920s.
6. The League's agencies (committees and commissions) were set up to solve social problems such as post-war refugee crises, health problems and slavery/forced labour. It had many successes throughout the 1920s and 1930s.
7. The League was supposed to encourage disarmament but failed to get any countries to disarm.
8. In the 1930s the League's work was made much harder by the economic depression, which made countries less willing to co-operate and helped turn previously democratic countries such as Germany into DICTATORSHIPS.
9. In 1931–32 the League condemned the Japanese invasion of Manchuria and China but was helpless to do anything to stop it.
10. In 1936–37 the League tried to prevent Italy invading Abyssinia but it could not agree what to do and never even enforced trade sanctions.
11. From 1936 the League was seen as irrelevant to international affairs although its agencies continued its humanitarian work.

DAILY SKETCH

CELEBRATE in the best of spirits
SEAGERS GIN
100% PURE 100% PERFECT

PEACE SOUVENIR ISSUE
WIRELESS: P. 19

No. 9,177　　SATURDAY, OCTOBER 1, 1938　　ONE PENNY

PREMIER SAYS 'PEACE FOR OUR TIME'—P. 3

Give Thanks In Church To-morrow

TO-MORROW is Peace Sunday.

Hardly more than a few hours ago it seemed as if it would have been the first Sunday of the most senseless and savage war in history.

The "Daily Sketch" suggests that the Nation should attend church to-morrow and give thanks.

THE fathers and mothers who might have lost their sons, the young people who would have paid the cost of war with their lives, the children who have been spared the horror of modern warfare —let them all attend Divine Service and kneel in humility and thankfulness.

To-morrow should not be allowed to pass without a sincere and reverent recognition of its significance.

MR. CHAMBERLAIN shows the paper that represents his great triumph for European peace to the thousands who gave him such a thunderous welcome at Heston yesterday. It is the historic Anglo-German Pact signed by himself and the Fuehrer, Herr Hitler.

'Determined To Ensure Peace'

WHEN Mr. Chamberlain arrived at Heston last night he said:

"This morning I had another talk with the German Chancellor, Herr Hitler. Here is a paper which bears his name as well as mine. I would like to read it to you:

"'We, the German Fuehrer and Chancellor and the British Prime Minister, have had a further meeting to-day and are agreed in recognising that the question of Anglo-German relations is of the first importance for the two countries and for Europe.

"'We regard the agreement signed last night and the Anglo-German Naval Agreement as symbolic of the desire of our two peoples never to war with one another again.

"'We are resolved that the method of consultation shall be the method adopted to deal with any other questions that may concern our two countries and we are determined to continue our efforts to remove possible sources of difference and thus to contribute to the assurance of peace in Europe.'"

3

How far was Hitler's foreign policy to blame for the outbreak of war in Europe in 1939?

FOCUS POINTS

★ What were the long-term consequences of the Treaty of Versailles?
★ What were the consequences of the failures of the League of Nations in the 1930s?
★ Was the policy of Appeasement justified?
★ How important was the Nazi–Soviet Pact?
★ Why did Britain and France declare war on Germany in September 1939?

The image on the opposite page represents the most famous moment of Appeasement – the policy followed by Britain and France towards Hitler through the 1930s. The British prime minister has returned from a meeting with Hitler having agreed to give him parts of Czechoslovakia, in return for which Hitler promised peace.

If you know the story already then you will know that this agreement proved totally empty – 'not worth the paper it was written on' as they say! Hitler did not keep his word, and probably never meant to.

But just forget HINDSIGHT for a moment and try to join with the people of Britain welcoming back a leader who seemed to be doing his best to preserve a crumbling peace.

You can see from the newspaper there is a genuine desire to believe in the possibility of peace. Chamberlain had not given up on the possibility of peace, nor had the British people. They did not think that war was inevitable – even in 1938. They did all they could to avoid it.

In this chapter your task is to work out why, despite all the efforts of international leaders, and all the horrors of war, international peace finally collapsed in 1939.

Here are some of the factors you will consider. They are all relevant and they are all connected. Your task will be to examine each one, then see the connections and weigh the importance of these different factors.

Opposite is the front page of the *Daily Sketch*, 1 October 1938. Read it carefully and select one or two phrases which suggest or prove that:

- the British people thought Chamberlain was a hero
- the newspaper approves of Chamberlain
- people in Britain genuinely feared a war was imminent in 1938
- Hitler was respected
- Hitler could be trusted
- this agreement would bring lasting peace.

1. The impact of the Treaty of Versailles on Germany

2. The failures of the League of Nations

3. The worldwide economic depression

4. The policy of Appeasement

5. The Nazi–Soviet Pact

6. Hitler's actions and particularly his foreign policy

'Hitler's war'?

Between 1918 and 1933 Adolf Hitler rose from being an obscure and demoralised member of the defeated German army to become the all-powerful Führer, DICTATOR of Germany, with almost unlimited power and an overwhelming ambition to make Germany great once again. His is an astonishing story which you can read about in detail in Chapter 9. Here you will be concentrating on just one intriguing and controversial question: how far was Hitler's foreign policy to blame for the outbreak of war?

Hitler's plans

Hitler was never secretive about his plans for Germany. As early as 1925 he had laid out in his book MEIN KAMPF what he would do if the Nazis ever achieved power in Germany.

Abolish the Treaty of Versailles!

Like many Germans, Hitler believed that the TREATY OF VERSAILLES was unjust.

He hated the Treaty and called the German leaders who had signed it 'The NOVEMBER CRIMINALS'. The Treaty was a constant reminder to Germans of their defeat in the First World War and their humiliation by the Allies. Hitler promised that if he became leader of Germany he would reverse it (see Source 1).

By the time he came to power in Germany, some of the terms had already been changed. For example, Germany had stopped making REPARATIONS payments altogether. However, most points were still in place. The table on page 57 shows the terms of the Treaty that most angered Hitler.

Expand German territory!

The Treaty of Versailles had taken away territory from Germany. Hitler wanted to get that territory back. He wanted Germany to unite with Austria. He wanted German minorities in other countries such as Czechoslovakia to rejoin Germany. But he also wanted to carve out an empire in eastern Europe to give extra LEBENSRAUM or 'living space' for Germans (see Source 2).

Defeat communism!

A German empire carved out of the SOVIET UNION would also help Hitler in one of his other objectives – the defeat of COMMUNISM or BOLSHEVISM. Hitler was anticommunist. He believed that Bolsheviks had helped to bring about the defeat of Germany in the First World War. He also believed that the Bolsheviks wanted to take over Germany (see Source 3).

SOURCE 1

We demand equality of rights for the German people in its dealings with other nations, and abolition of the Peace Treaties of Versailles and St Germain.

From the National Socialist Program, 1920

SOURCE 2

We turn our eyes towards the lands of the east ... When we speak of new territory in Europe today, we must principally think of Russia and the border states subject to her. Destiny itself seems to wish to point out the way for us here.

Colonisation of the eastern frontiers is of extreme importance. It will be the duty of Germany's foreign policy to provide large spaces for the nourishment and settlement of the growing population of Germany.

From Hitler's *Mein Kampf*.

SOURCE 3

We must not forget that the Bolsheviks are blood-stained. That they overran a great state [Russia], and in a fury of massacre wiped out millions of their most intelligent fellow-countrymen ... Germany is the next great objective of Bolshevism. All our strength is needed to raise up our nation once more and rescue it from the embrace of the international python ... The first essential is the expulsion of the Marxist poison from the body of our nation.

From Hitler's *Mein Kampf*.

ACTIVITY

It is 1933. Write a briefing paper for the British Government on Hitler's plans for Germany. Use Sources 1–3 to help you. Conclude with your own assessment on whether the Government should be worried about Hitler and his plans. In your conclusion, remember these facts about the British Government:

- Britain is a leading member of the League of Nations and is supposed to uphold the Treaty of Versailles, by force if necessary.
- The British Government does not trust the communists and thinks that a strong Germany could help to stop the communist threat.

Hitler's actions

This timeline shows how, between 1933 and 1939, Hitler turned his plans into actions.

DATE	ACTION
1933	Took Germany out of the League of Nations; began rearming Germany
1934	Tried to take over Austria but was prevented by Mussolini
1935	Held massive REARMAMENT rally in Germany; reintroduced CONSCRIPTION in Germany
1936	Sent German troops into the RHINELAND; made an anticommunist ALLIANCE with Japan
1937	Tried out Germany's new weapons in the SPANISH CIVIL WAR; made an anticommunist alliance with Italy
1938	Took over Austria; took over the SUDETENLAND area of Czechoslovakia
1939	Invaded the rest of Czechoslovakia; invaded Poland; war

War

SOURCE 4

Any account of the origins and course of the Second World War must give Hitler the leading part. Without him a major war in the early 1940s between all the world's great powers was unthinkable.

British historian Professor Richard Overy, writing in 1996.

Revision Tip
The details in your version of the table below will be a very useful revision aid. So add pictures and highlights to help you learn the information.

Other factors

When you see events leading up to the war laid out this way, it makes it seem as if Hitler planned it all step by step. In fact, this view of events was widely accepted by historians until the 1960s. In the 1960s, however, the British historian A.J.P. Taylor came up with a new interpretation. His view was that Hitler was a gambler rather than a planner. Hitler simply took the logical next step to see what he could get away with. He was bold. He kept his nerve. As other countries gave in to him and allowed him to get away with each gamble, so he became bolder and risked more. In Taylor's interpretation it is Britain, the Allies and the League of Nations who are to blame for letting Hitler get away with it – by not standing up to him. In this interpretation it is other factors that are as much to blame as Hitler himself:
- the worldwide ECONOMIC DEPRESSION
- the weaknesses of the post-war treaties
- the actions of the leading powers – Britain, France, the USA and the USSR.

As you examine Hitler's actions in more detail, you will see that both interpretations are possible. You can make up your own mind which you agree with.

Think!
Hitler and the Treaty of Versailles
1 Draw up a table like this one to show some of the terms of the Treaty of Versailles that affected Germany.
2 As you work through this chapter, fill out the other columns of this 'Versailles chart'.

Terms of the Treaty of Versailles	What Hitler did and when	The reasons he gave for his action	The response from Britain and France
Germany's armed forces to be severely limited			
The Rhineland to be a demilitarised zone			
Germany forbidden to unite with Austria			
The Sudetenland taken into the new state of Czechoslovakia			
The Polish Corridor given to Poland			

3 *How far was Hitler's foreign policy to blame for the outbreak of war in Europe in 1939?*

SOURCE 5

I am convinced that Hitler does not want war … what the Germans are after is a strong army which will enable them to deal with Russia.

British politician Lord Lothian, January 1935.

FIGURE 6

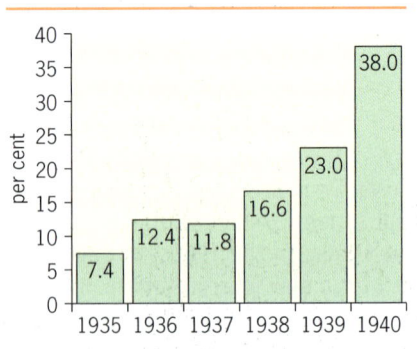

The proportion of German spending that went into armaments, 1935–40.

Year	Per cent
1935	7.4
1936	12.4
1937	11.8
1938	16.6
1939	23.0
1940	38.0

Source Analysis

How far do Figures 6 and 7 prove Source 5 to be wrong?

Think!

1. Fill out the first row of your 'Versailles chart' on page 57 to summarise what Hitler did about rearmament.
2. What factors allowed Hitler to get away with rearming Germany? Look for:
   a) the impact of the Depression
   b) the Treaty of Versailles
   c) the League of Nations
   d) the actions of Britain and France.

Rearmament

Hitler came to power in Germany in 1933. One of his first steps was to increase Germany's armed forces. Thousands of unemployed workers were drafted into the army. This helped him to reduce unemployment, which was one of the biggest problems he faced in Germany. But it also helped him to deliver on his promise to make Germany strong again and to challenge the terms of the Treaty of Versailles.

Hitler knew that German people supported rearmament. But he also knew it would cause alarm in other countries. He handled it cleverly. Rearmament began in secret at first. He made a great public display of his desire not to rearm Germany – that he was only doing it because other countries refused to disarm (see page 46). He then followed Japan's example and withdrew from the League of Nations.

In 1935 Hitler openly staged a massive military rally celebrating the German armed forces and he even reintroduced conscription to the army. He was breaking the terms of the Treaty of Versailles, but he guessed correctly that he would get away with rearmament. Many other countries were using rearmament as a way to fight unemployment. The collapse of the League of Nations Disarmament Conference in 1934 (see pages 48–49) had shown that other nations were not prepared to disarm.

Rearmament was a very popular move in Germany. It boosted Nazi support. Hitler also knew that Britain had some sympathy with Germany on this issue. Britain believed that the limits put on Germany's armed forces by the Treaty of Versailles were too tight. The permitted forces were not enough to defend Germany from attack. Britain also thought that a strong Germany would be a good buffer against communism.

Britain had already helped to dismantle the Treaty by signing the Anglo-German Naval Agreement with Hitler in 1935, allowing Germany to increase its navy to up to 35 per cent of the size of the British navy. The French were angry with Britain about this, but there was little they could do. Through the rest of the 1930s Hitler ploughed more and more spending into armaments (see Figures 6 and 7).

FIGURE 7

	Warships	Aircraft	Soldiers
1932	(30)	(36)	(100,000)
1939	(95)	(8,250)	(950,000)

German armed forces in 1932 and 1939.

The Saar plebiscite

The SAAR region of Germany had been run by the League of Nations since 1919 (see page 34).

In 1935 the League of Nations held the promised plebiscite for people to vote on whether their region should return to German rule. Hitler was initially wary as many of his opponents had fled to the Saar. The League, however, was determined that the vote should take place and Hitler bowed to this pressure. So it seemed that the League was being firm and decisive with Hitler. The vote was an overwhelming success for Hitler. His PROPAGANDA minister Joseph Goebbels mounted a massive campaign to persuade the people of the Saar to vote for the Reich. Around 90 per cent of the population voted to return to German rule. This was entirely legal and within the terms of the Treaty. It was also a real morale booster for Hitler. After the vote Hitler declared that he had 'no further territorial demands to make of France'.

SOURCE 8

A photograph showing German forces moving back into the Saar after the plebiscite in 1935.

Source Analysis

1 Describe the scene shown in Source 8 as though you were reporting it on the radio.
2 Who or what do you think might be represented by the figure being hanged?
3 Do you find this source convincing evidence that the Saar wanted to rejoin Germany?

SOURCE 9

A British cartoon published in January 1935, soon after the Saar plebiscite. The figure in bed is the League of Nations. The caption was 'Sitting up and taking nourishment'. The writing on the wall reads, 'Name: League of Nations; Trouble: Anaemia; Condition: Dying'.

FIGURE 10

Remilitarisation of the Rhineland

In March 1936, Hitler took his first really big risk by moving troops into the Rhineland area of Germany. The Rhineland was the large area either side of the River Rhine that formed Germany's western border with France and Belgium.

The demilitarisation of the Rhineland was one of the terms of the Treaty of Versailles. It was designed to protect France from invasion from Germany. It had also been accepted by Germany in the Locarno Treaties of 1925. Hitler was taking a huge gamble with REMILITARISATION. If he had been forced to withdraw, he would have faced humiliation and would have lost the support of the German army (many of the generals were unsure about him, anyway). Hitler knew the risks, but he had chosen the time and place well.

- **France** and the USSR had just signed a treaty to protect each other against attack from Germany (see Source 11). Hitler used the agreement to claim that Germany was under threat. He argued that in the face of such a threat he should be allowed to place troops on his own frontier.
- Hitler knew that many people in **Britain** felt that he had a right to station his troops in the Rhineland and he was fairly confident that Britain would not intervene. His gamble was over France. Would France let him get away with it?

Key
- January 1935: Saar returned to Germany after a plebiscite
- March 1936: German forces re-enter the Rhineland

The Rhineland.

SOURCE 11

An American cartoon entitled 'Ring-Around-the-Nazi!' published in March 1936 showing the encirclement of Germany by France and the USSR.

SOURCE 12

German troops marching through the city of Cologne in March 1936. This style of marching with high steps was known as goose-stepping.

Think!
Fill out row 2 of your 'Versailles chart' on page 57 to summarise what happened in the Rhineland.

SOURCE 13

At that time we had no army worth mentioning ... If the French had taken any action we would have been easily defeated; our resistance would have been over in a few days. And the Air Force we had then was ridiculous – a few Junkers 52s from Lufthansa and not even enough bombs for them...

Hitler looks back on his gamble over the Rhineland some years after the event.

SOURCE 14

Hitler has got away with it. France is not marching. No wonder the faces of Göring and Blomberg [Nazi leaders] were all smiles.

Oh, the stupidity (or is it the paralysis?) of the French. I learnt today that the German troops had orders to beat a hasty retreat if the French army opposed them in any way.

Written by William Shirer in 1936. He was an American journalist in Germany during the 1930s. He was a critic of the Nazi regime and had to flee from Germany in 1940.

Source Analysis

1. Does Source 11 prove that Hitler was correct when he argued that Germany was under threat? Explain your answer.
2. What do Sources 13 and 14 disagree about? Why might they disagree about it?
3. Why has the cartoonist in Source 15 shown Germany as a goose?
4. Look at the equipment being carried by the goose. What does this tell you about how the cartoonist saw the new Germany?
5. Would you regard reoccupation of the Rhineland as a success for Hitler or as a failure for the French and British? Explain your answer by referring to the sources.

Hitler ordered 20,000 troops into the Rhineland and his generals had orders to retreat if there was any resistance from the French. Despite the rearmament programme, Germany's army was no match for the French army. It lacked essential equipment and air support. In the end, however, Hitler's luck held.

The attention of the League of Nations was on the Abyssinian crisis which was happening at exactly the same time (see pages 51–52). The League condemned Hitler's action but had no power to do anything else. Even the French, who were most directly threatened by the move, were divided over what to do. They were about to hold an election and none of the French leaders was prepared to take responsibility for plunging France into a war. Of course, they did not know how weak the German army was. In the end, France refused to act without British support and so Hitler's big gamble paid off. Maybe next time he would risk more!

SOURCE 15

THE GOOSE-STEP

"GOOSEY GOOSEY GANDER,
WHITHER DOST THOU WANDER?"
"ONLY THROUGH THE RHINELAND—
PRAY EXCUSE MY BLUNDER!"

A British cartoon about the reoccupation of the Rhineland, 1936. *Pax Germanica* is Latin and means 'Peace, German style'.

Source Analysis

1 What can we learn from Source 16 about:
- what happened at Guernica
- the views of French people on Guernica
- the views of the magazine which published the photograph and caption?

2 Use your thinking in Question 1 to write an answer to the question: How useful is Source 16 to a historian studying the Spanish Civil War?

SOURCE 16

Le peuple basque assassiné par les avions allemands
GUERNICA MARTYRE – 26 Avril 1937

A postcard published in France to mark the bombing of Guernica in 1937. The text reads 'The Basque people murdered by German planes. Guernica martyred 26 April 1937'.

FOCUS TASK 3.1

What were the consequences of the failures of the League of Nations in the 1930s?

In Chapter 2 you studied the failures of the League of Nations in the 1930s. You are now in a position to evaluate the impact of those failures on Hitler's actions.

1 Look back over pages 58–62. Look for evidence that the weakness of the League of Nations in the 1930s allowed Hitler to achieve what he did.
2 Write a paragraph describing the effect of each of the following on Hitler's actions:
- the Manchurian crisis
- the failure of DISARMAMENT
- the Abyssinian crisis.

The Spanish Civil War

In 1936 a CIVIL WAR broke out in Spain between supporters of the Republican Government (Republicans) and RIGHT-WING rebels (Nationalists) under General Franco. The war quickly gained an international dimension.

STALIN'S USSR supported the Republican Government (in the form of weapons, aircraft and pilots). Thousands of volunteers from around 50 countries joined International Brigades to support the Republicans. Hitler and Mussolini then declared their support for General Franco as a man who shared their world view.

Britain and France refused to intervene directly, although France did provide some weapons for the Republicans. Germany and Italy also agreed not to intervene but then blatantly did so. Mussolini sent thousands of Italian troops (officially they were 'volunteers'). Germany sent aircraft and pilots who took part in most of the major campaigns of the war including bombing raids on civilian populations (see Source 16). Hitler viewed the Spanish Civil War as a good opportunity to try out his new Luftwaffe (air force) and develop the **Blitzkrieg** tactics the German military would use in future conflicts.

The conflict had important consequences for peace. It strengthened the bonds between Mussolini and Hitler. It encouraged Hitler to believe that Britain and France would not intervene against him if he took further actions against the Treaty of Versailles. Although Britain did not intervene, Hitler's actions alarmed Chamberlain and he ordered massive increases in spending on Britain's armed forces, especially the Royal Air Force. At the same time, the USSR became increasingly suspicious of Britain and France because of their reluctance to get involved in opposing fascism.

Militarism and the Axis

Meanwhile, in the east Japan was under the control of hardline nationalist commanders such as General Tojo. They also had the support of business leaders in Japan. They wanted to extend Japan's empire across Asia so it could compete with other world powers, particularly the USA. In 1937 the Japanese took their next big step with the invasion of China. Some historians regard this as the first campaign of the Second World War.

Hitler and Mussolini saw that they had much in common with the military DICTATORSHIP in Japan. In 1936, Germany and Japan signed an ANTI-COMINTERN PACT, to oppose communism. Comintern was the USSR's organisation for spreading communism to other countries. In 1937, Italy also signed it. This was called the Rome–Berlin Axis alliance.

There was very little Britain or France could do about the Axis, but it was another worrying development, especially as Britain did not have the resources to fight Japan in the Far East and Germany in Europe.

Anschluss with Austria, 1938

With the successes of 1936 and 1937 to boost him, Hitler turned his attention to his homeland of Austria. Hitler believed that the two states belonged together as one German nation. Many in Austria supported the idea of union with Germany. Hitler had tried to take over Austria in 1934, but on that occasion Mussolini had stopped him. But in 1938 the situation was different. Hitler and Mussolini were now allies.

There was a strong Nazi Party in Austria. Hitler encouraged them to stir up trouble for the Government and hold demonstrations demanding union with Germany. Hitler then told the Austrian Chancellor Schuschnigg that only ANSCHLUSS (political union) could sort out these problems. Schuschnigg appealed to Britain and France but it failed to provide any support so Schuschnigg felt he had no option but to call a plebiscite (a referendum) to see what the Austrian people wanted. Hitler was not prepared to risk this – he might lose! He simply sent his troops into Austria in March 1938, supposedly to guarantee a trouble-free plebiscite. Under the watchful eye of the Nazi troops, 99.75 per cent voted for *Anschluss*.

Anschluss was completed without any military confrontation with France and Britain. Chamberlain felt that Austrians and Germans had a right to be united and that the Treaty of Versailles was wrong to separate them.

Once again, Hitler's risky but decisive action had reaped a rich reward – Austria's soldiers, weapons and its rich deposits of gold and iron ore were added to Germany's increasingly strong army and industry. Hitler was breaking yet another condition of the Treaty of Versailles, but it seemed clear to him that Britain and France were not prepared to go to war to defend it. However, Britain and France were not naïve either. Chamberlain increased Britain's rearmament spending further still and made plans for compulsory military service and the preparation of air-raid defences.

Think!
Complete row 3 of your 'Versailles chart' on page 57, summarising what Hitler did about Austria.

Source Analysis
Work in pairs. Take either Source 17 or Source 18.
1 For your source work out:
   a) which character in the cartoon represents Mussolini and which Hitler
   b) what your cartoon suggests about the relationship between Hitler and Mussolini
   c) what is the cartoonist's opinion of the *Anschluss*. Find details in the source to support your view.
2 Compare your answers with your partner's and discuss any points of agreement or disagreement.
3 Write your own paragraph in answer to this question: How far do Sources 17 and 18 agree about the *Anschluss*?

SOURCE 17

GOOD HUNTING
Mussolini. "All right, Adolf—I never heard a shot"

A British cartoon commenting on the *Anschluss*.

SOURCE 18

A Soviet cartoon commenting on the *Anschluss* showing Hitler catching Austria.

Appeasement: for and against!

If Britain and France were not prepared to defend the Treaty of Versailles, would they let Hitler have more of his demands? The short answer is yes, and Britain's policy at this time is known as APPEASEMENT. Neville Chamberlain is the man most associated with this policy (see Profile on page 67) although he did not become prime minister until 1937. Many other British people (probably the majority), including many politicians, were also in favour of this policy. However, there were some at the time who were very critical. Here are the main arguments for and against.

Trusting Hitler
After each new move he made Hitler said this was all he wanted. Yet he often went back on those promises. Appeasement was based on the mistaken idea that Hitler was trustworthy.

Fear of communism
Hitler was not the only concern of Britain and its allies. He was not even their main worry. They were more concerned about the spread of communism and particularly the dangers to world peace posed by Stalin, the new leader in the USSR. Many saw Hitler as the buffer to the threat of spreading communism.

Memories of the Great War
Both British and French leaders, and much of their population, vividly remembered the horrific experiences of the First World War. They wished to avoid another war at almost any cost.

German arms
Germany was rearming publicly and quickly year by year. Hitler claimed he was trying to catch up with other countries, but others could see that Germany was better armed than Britain or France.

British arms
The British Government believed that the armed forces were not ready for war against Hitler. Britain only began rearming in 1935 and INTELLIGENCE suggested the British were some way behind the Germans.

The USA
American support had been vital to Britain's success in the First World War. Britain could not be sure it could face up to Germany without the guarantee of American help. But since 1919 the USA had followed a policy of ISOLATIONISM. American leaders were determined not to be dragged into another European war.

The British empire
For Britain to fight a war against Germany it needed to be sure it had the support of the countries in its empire or Commonwealth. It was not a guaranteed certainty that they would all support a war. There was also the prospect of Japan threatening British interests in Asia, particularly Singapore and even India.

The Treaty of Versailles
Many felt that the Treaty of Versailles was unfair to Germany. Some of Hitler's demands were not unreasonable. They assumed that once these wrongs were put right then Germany would become a peaceful nation again.

Make a stand!
Hitler the gambler took increasing risks. He tried something out to see if there would be any come-back. At some point therefore Britain and France needed to stand up to Hitler to prevent a later bigger and more dangerous move.

The Soviet Union
Hitler made no secret of his plans to expand eastwards. He had openly talked of taking land in Russia. Appeasement sent the message to Stalin and the USSR that Britain and France would not stand in Hitler's way if he invaded Russia.

Hitler's allies
Hitler had already observed how his allies, particularly the right-wing dictatorships in Japan and Italy, had got away with acts of aggression.

Economic problems
Britain and France had large debts (many still left over from fighting the First World War) and huge unemployment as a result of the Depression. They could not afford a war.

FOCUS TASK 3.2

Why did Britain and France follow a policy of Appeasement?

The cards on page 64 show various arguments that were advanced for or against Appeasement. Study the cards, then:
1. Sort them into arguments for and arguments against Appeasement. If there are any you are not sure about leave them aside as you can come back to them.
2. On each card write a 'for' or 'against'.
3. Sort the cards into those that:
   a) would have been obvious to British and French leaders at the time
   b) would only be clear with hindsight.
4. Make notes under the following headings to summarise why Britain followed a policy of Appeasement:
   a) military reasons
   b) economic reasons
   c) fear
   d) public opinion.
5. Use your notes to write a short paragraph to explain in your own words why the British Government followed a policy of Appeasement.

ACTIVITY

Most people in Britain supported the policy of Appeasement. Write a letter to the London *Evening Standard* justifying Appeasement and pointing out why the cartoonist in Source 19 is wrong. Your letter should be written in either 1936 or 1938 and it will need to be different according to which date you pick. You can use some of the arguments from Focus Task 3.2 above in your letter.

Cartoonist David Low

One of the most famous critics was David Low, cartoonist with the popular newspaper the London *Evening Standard*. You have seen many of Low's cartoons in this book already. Low was a fierce critic of Hitler, but also criticised the policy of Appeasement. Source 19 shows one of his cartoons on the issue, but if you visit the British Cartoon Archive website you will be able to see all of Low's cartoons.

SOURCE 19

A cartoon by David Low from the London *Evening Standard*, 1936. This was a popular newspaper with a large readership in Britain.

Source Analysis

Fill out a table like this to analyse Source 19. Fill out a second column to analyse Source 27 on page 68 in the same way.

	Source 19
Date published	
Critical or supportive?	
Of what/whom?	
How can we tell?	
Why was the cartoon published at this time?	

Revision Tip

Make sure you can explain:
- what Appeasement was
- two examples of Appeasement in action.

Be sure you can describe:
- one reason why Chamberlain followed the policy of Appeasement
- one reason why people criticised the policy.

The Sudetenland, 1938

After the Austrian *Anschluss*, Hitler was beginning to feel that he could not put a foot wrong. But his growing confidence was putting the peace of Europe in increasing danger.

FIGURE 20

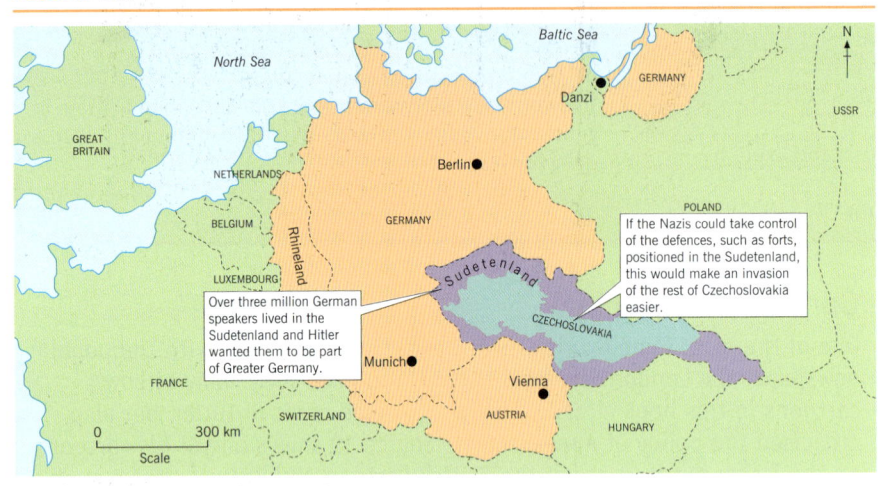

Over three million German speakers lived in the Sudetenland and Hitler wanted them to be part of Greater Germany.

If the Nazis could take control of the defences, such as forts, positioned in the Sudetenland, this would make an invasion of the rest of Czechoslovakia easier.

Central Europe after the *Anschluss*.

Czech fears

Unlike the leaders of Britain and France, Edvard Beneš, the leader of Czechoslovakia, was horrified by the *Anschluss*. He realised that Czechoslovakia would be the next country on Hitler's list for take-over. It seemed that Britain and France were not prepared to stand up to Hitler. Beneš sought guarantees from the British and French that they would honour their commitment to defend Czechoslovakia if Hitler invaded. The French were bound by a treaty and reluctantly said they would. The British felt bound to support the French. However, Chamberlain asked Hitler whether he had designs on Czechoslovakia and was reassured by Hitler's promise (Source 21).

Hitler's threats

Despite what he said to Chamberlain, Hitler did have designs on Czechoslovakia. This new state, created by the Treaty of Versailles, included a large number of Germans – former subjects of Austria–Hungary's empire – in the Sudetenland area. Konrad Henlein, the leader of the Nazis in the Sudetenland, demanded that the area should be part of Germany. In May 1938, Hitler made it clear that he intended to fight Czechoslovakia if necessary. Historians disagree as to whether Hitler really meant what he said. There is considerable evidence that the German army was not at all ready for war. Even so, the news put Europe on full war alert.

SOURCE 21

I give you my word of honour that Czechoslovakia has nothing to fear from the Reich.

Hitler speaking to Chamberlain in 1938.

ACTIVITY

Write a series of newspaper headlines for different stages of the Sudetenland crisis, for example:
- March 1938
- May 1938
- early September 1938
- 30 September 1938.

Include headlines for:
- a Czech newspaper
- a British newspaper
- a German newspaper.

Preparations for war

Unlike Austria, Czechoslovakia would be no walk-over for Hitler. Britain, France and the USSR had all promised to support Czechoslovakia if it came to war. The Czechs themselves had a modern army. The Czechoslovak leader, Beneš, was prepared to fight. He knew that without the Sudetenland and its forts, railways and industries, Czechoslovakia would be defenceless.

All through the summer the tension rose in Europe. If there was a war, people expected that it would bring heavy bombing of civilians as had happened in the Spanish Civil War, and in cities around Britain councils began digging air-raid shelters. Magazines carried advertisements for air-raid protection and gas masks.

SOURCE 22

How horrible, fantastic, incredible it is that we should be digging trenches and trying on gas masks here because of a quarrel in a far-away country between people of whom we know nothing. I am myself a man of peace to the depths of my soul.

From a radio broadcast by Neville Chamberlain, September 1938.

Profile

Neville Chamberlain

- Born 1869.
- He was the son of the famous RADICAL politician Joseph Chamberlain.
- He was a successful businessman in the Midlands before entering politics.
- During the First World War he served in the Cabinet as director general of National Service. During this time he saw the full horrors of war.
- After the war he was health minister and then CHANCELLOR. He was noted for his careful work and his attention to detail. However, he was not good at listening to advice.
- He was part of the government throughout the 1920s and supported the policy of Appeasement towards Hitler. He became prime minister in 1937, although he had little experience of foreign affairs.
- He believed that Germany had real grievances – this was the basis for his policy of Appeasement.
- He became a national hero after the Munich Conference of 1938 averted war.
- In 1940 Chamberlain resigned as prime minister and Winston Churchill took over.

SOURCE 23

Digging air-raid defences in London, September 1938.

Crisis talks

In September the problem reached crisis point. In a last-ditch effort to avert war, Chamberlain flew to meet Hitler on 15 September. The meeting appeared to go well. Hitler moderated his demands, saying he was only interested in parts of the Sudetenland – and then only if a plebiscite showed that the Sudeten Germans wanted to join Germany. Chamberlain thought this was reasonable. He felt it was yet another of the terms of the Treaty of Versailles that needed to be addressed. Chamberlain seemed convinced that, if Hitler got what he wanted, he would at last be satisfied.

On 19 September the French and the British put to the Czechs their plans to give Hitler the parts of the Sudetenland that he wanted. However, three days later at a second meeting, Hitler increased his demands. He said he 'regretted' that the previously arranged terms were not enough. He wanted all the Sudetenland.

SOURCE 24

The Sudetenland is the last problem that must be solved and it will be solved. It is the last territorial claim which I have to make in Europe.

The aims of our foreign policy are not unlimited … They are grounded on the determination to save the German people alone … Ten million Germans found themselves beyond the frontiers of the Reich … Germans who wished to return to the Reich as their homeland.

Hitler speaking in Berlin, September 1938.

To justify his demands, he claimed that the Czech Government was mistreating the Germans in the Sudetenland and that he intended to 'rescue' them by 1 October. Chamberlain told Hitler that his demands were unreasonable. The British navy was MOBILISED. War seemed imminent.

The Munich Agreement

With Mussolini's help, a final meeting was held in Munich on 29 September. While Europe held its breath, the leaders of Britain, Germany, France and Italy decided on the fate of Czechoslovakia.

On 29 September they decided to give Hitler what he wanted. They announced that Czechoslovakia was to lose the Sudetenland. They did not consult the Czechs, nor did they consult the USSR. This is known as the MUNICH AGREEMENT. The following morning Chamberlain and Hitler published a joint declaration, which Chamberlain said would bring 'peace for our time'.

SOURCE 25

People of Britain, your children are safe. Your husbands and your sons will not march to war. Peace is a victory for all mankind. If we must have a victor, let us choose Chamberlain, for the Prime Minister's conquests are mighty and enduring – millions of happy homes and hearts relieved of their burden.

The *Daily Express* comments on the Munich Agreement, 30 September 1938.

SOURCE 26

By repeatedly surrendering to force, Chamberlain has encouraged aggression … our central contention, therefore, is that Mr Chamberlain's policy has throughout been based on a fatal misunderstanding of the psychology of dictatorship.

The *Yorkshire Post*, December 1938.

SOURCE 27

We have suffered a total defeat … I think you will find that in a period of time Czechoslovakia will be engulfed in the Nazi regime. We have passed an awful milestone in our history. This is only the beginning of the reckoning.

Winston Churchill speaking in October 1938. He felt that Britain should resist the demands of Hitler. However, he was an isolated figure in the 1930s.

Source Analysis

1. Study Sources 25–28. Sort them into the categories:
   a) those that support the Munich Agreement
   b) those that criticise the Munich Agreement.
2. List the reasons why each source supports or criticises the agreement.
3. Imagine you are a teacher setting a test.
   - Which of Sources 25–28 would work well for an 'Is it surprising?' question?
   - Which of Sources 25–28 would work well for a 'How useful is this source?' question?
   Explain your answers.

Consequences of the Munich Agreement

Hitler had gambled that the British would not risk war. The prize of the Sudetenland had been given to him without a shot being fired. On 1 October German troops marched into the Sudetenland. At the same time, Hungary and Poland helped themselves to Czech territory where Hungarians and Poles were living.

The Czechs had been betrayed. Beneš resigned and the country descended into chaos. But the rest of Europe breathed a sigh of relief. Chamberlain received a hero's welcome back in Britain, when he returned with the 'piece of paper' – the Agreement – signed by Hitler (see photo in the Profile, page 67).

SOURCE 27

A GREAT MEDIATOR

John Bull. "I've known many Prime Ministers in my time, Sir, but never one who worked so hard for security in the face of such terrible odds."

A British cartoon published in 1938 at the time of the Munich Agreement. John Bull represents Britain.

Triumph or sell-out?

What do you think of the Munich Agreement? Was it a good move or a poor one? Most people in Britain were relieved that it had averted war, but many were soon openly questioning the whole policy of Appeasement. Opinion polls in September 1938 show that the British people did not think Appeasement would stop Hitler. It simply delayed a war, rather than preventing it. And while he hoped for peace Chamberlain continued to increase arms spending in preparation for war.

Think!

Complete row 4 of your 'Versailles chart' on page 57.

Czechoslovakia, 1939: the end of Appeasement

Although the British people welcomed the Munich Agreement, they did not trust Hitler. In an opinion poll in October 1938, 93 per cent said they did not believe him when he said he had no more territorial ambitions in Europe. In March 1939 they were proved right. On 15 March, German troops took over the rest of the country.

FIGURE 29

Key

- October 1938 Teschen taken by Poland
- November 1938 to March 1939 Slovak border areas and Ruthenia taken by Hungary
- October 1938 Sudetenland region given to Germany in the Munich Agreement
- March 1939 Remainder of Czechoslovakia taken under German control
- German border in 1939

Hitler needed the rest of Czechoslovakia for his future plans to invade Poland. He could now invade from two fronts as well as more easily defend Germany in the case of invasion from the east, as Czechoslovakia stabbed into the side of Germany.

The take-over of Czechoslovakia by 1939.

SOURCE 30

German troops entering Prague, the capital of Czechoslovakia, in March 1939.

There was no resistance from the Czechs. Nor did Britain and France do anything about the situation. However, it was now clear that Hitler could not be trusted. For Chamberlain it was a step too far. Unlike the Sudeten Germans, the Czechs were not separated from their homeland by the Treaty of Versailles. This was an invasion. If Hitler continued unchecked, his next target was likely to be Poland and his annexation of Czechoslovakia would allow him to invade Poland from two fronts.

Britain and France told Hitler that if he invaded Poland they would declare war on Germany. The policy of Appeasement was ended. However, after years of Appeasement, Hitler did not actually believe that Britain and France would risk war by resisting him.

> **Think!**
> 1. Choose five words to describe the attitude of the crowd in Source 30.
> 2. Why do you think that there was no resistance from the Czechs?
> 3. Why do you think Britain and France did nothing in response to the invasion?

The Nazi–Soviet Pact, 1939

Look at your 'Versailles chart' from page 57. You should have only one item left. As Hitler was gradually retaking land lost at Versailles, you can see from Figure 29 that logically his next target was the strip of former German land in Poland known as the POLISH CORRIDOR. He had convinced himself that Britain and France would not risk war over this, but he was less sure about Stalin and the USSR. Let's see why.

Stalin's fears

Stalin had been very worried about the German threat to the Soviet Union ever since Hitler came to power in 1933. Even so, Stalin could not reach any kind of lasting agreement with Britain and France in the 1930s. In 1934 he had made the USSR a member of the League of Nations, hoping the League would guarantee his security against the threat from Germany. However, all he saw at the League was its lack of action over Abyssinia and the Spanish Civil War. Politicians in Britain and France had not resisted German rearmament in the 1930s. Indeed, some in Britain seemed even to welcome a stronger Germany as a force to fight communism, which they saw as a bigger threat to British interests than Hitler.

Stalin's fears and suspicions grew in the mid-1930s.
- He signed a treaty with France in 1935 that said that France would help the USSR if Germany invaded the Soviet Union. But Stalin was not sure he could trust the French to stick to it, particularly when they failed even to stop Hitler moving his troops into the Rhineland, which was right on their own border.
- The Munich Agreement in 1938 increased Stalin's concerns. He was not consulted about it. Stalin concluded from the agreement that France and Britain were powerless to stop Hitler or, even worse, that they were happy for Hitler to take over eastern Europe and then the USSR.

Stalin's negotiations

Despite his misgivings, Stalin was still prepared to talk with Britain and France about an alliance against Hitler. The three countries met in March 1939, but Chamberlain was suspicious of the USSR and was reluctant to commit Britain. From Stalin's point of view, France and Britain then made things worse by giving Poland a guarantee that they would defend it if it was invaded. Chamberlain meant the guarantee as a warning to Hitler. Stalin saw it as support for one of the USSR's potential enemies.

Negotiations between Britain, France and the USSR continued through the spring and summer of 1939. However, Stalin also received visits from the Nazi foreign minister Ribbentrop. They discussed a very different deal, a NAZI–SOVIET PACT.

Stalin's decision

In August, Stalin made his decision. On 23 August 1939, Hitler and Stalin, the two arch enemies, signed the Nazi-Soviet Pact and announced the terms to the world. They agreed not to attack one another. Privately, they also agreed to divide Poland between them.

Source Analysis

What is the message of the cartoonist?

SOURCE 31

A Soviet cartoon from 1939. CCCP is Russian for USSR. The French and the British are directing Hitler away from western Europe and towards the USSR.

Source Analysis

1 What do Sources 31 and 32 agree about?
2 Which source do you most trust to tell you about the reasons Stalin signed the Pact?

SOURCE 32

It will be asked how it was possible that the Soviet government signed a non-aggression pact with so deceitful a nation, with such criminals as Hitler and Ribbentrop ... We secured peace for our country for eighteen months, which enabled us to make military preparations.

Stalin, in a speech in 1941.

Why did Stalin sign the Pact?

It was clear what Hitler gained from the Pact. He regarded it as his greatest achievement. It gave him half of Poland and ensured he would not face a war on two fronts if he invaded Poland. He had promised the Russians they could have the rest of Poland as well as the Baltic states, but he never intended to allow Stalin to keep these territories.

It is also clear what Stalin gained from it. It gave him some territory that had once been part of Russia, but that was not the main point. The real benefit was time! Stalin did not expect Hitler to keep his word. He knew he was Hitler's number one target. But he did not trust Britain and France either. He did not think they were strong enough or reliable enough as allies against Hitler. He expected to have to fight Hitler alone at some point. So what he most needed was time to build up his forces to protect the USSR from the attack he knew would come.

Consequences

The Pact cleared the way for Hitler to invade Poland. On 1 September 1939 the Germany army invaded Poland from the west, where they met little resistance. Britain and France demanded he withdraw from Poland or they would declare war. After the experience of the past three years Hitler was certain Britain and France would not actually do anything about this. If he was planning ahead at all, then in his mind the next move would surely be an attack against his temporary ally, the USSR. However, Hitler was in for a surprise. Britain and France kept their pledge. On 3 September they declared war on Germany.

FOCUS TASK 3.3

How important was the Nazi–Soviet Pact?

These statements suggest different reasons why the Nazi–Soviet Pact is important.

A. It showed that 'internationalism' had been completely abandoned.	B. It freed Hitler from the problem of a two-front war, which helped him to conquer Poland and most of Western Europe in 1939–40.	C. It exposed Britain and France's hope that Nazi Germany and the USSR would fight each other rather than them.
D. It showed that Britain feared Stalin's USSR as much as Hitler's Germany.	E. It gave Stalin time to build up forces for future war with Germany.	F. It gave Hitler the confidence to defy Britain and France and attack Poland.

1 In groups decide which statements fit best under each of these headings

The Nazi–Soviet Pact was important because...	
... it demonstrated important aspects of international relations at this time.	... it had direct military and political consequences.

2 Now take one comment from each column and explain:
   a) how the Nazi–Soviet Pact led to this consequence
   b) whether this would have happened anyway, even without the Nazi–Soviet Pact.

FOCUS TASK 3.4

Hitler and the Treaty of Versailles

1 You have been filling out your Versailles chart. Now fill out the final row summarising what Hitler did about Poland.
2 'Germany's bitterness about the Treaty of Versailles was the cause of Hitler's aggressive foreign policy.' How far do you agree with this statement? Explain your answer carefully.

FOCUS TASK 3.5

Was the policy of Appeasement justified?

- The right policy at the right time.
- The wrong policy, but only with hindsight.
- A betrayal of the people of Czechoslovakia.
- A risky policy that purchased valuable time.
- A bad policy but there was no realistic alternative.

1. a) Create five teams with one person acting as a spokesperson and the others working as researchers.
   b) Each team will be arguing for one of the viewpoints above. Use pages 72–3 to collect evidence to support your viewpoint. Then the spokesperson can write a small speech to read to the rest of the class, arguing their case.
   c) Take a vote at the end to see which viewpoint won the argument.
2. Choose one viewpoint that you most agree with and write some well-argued paragraphs to explain your choice:
   a) what the viewpoint means – in your own words
   b) what evidence there is to support it
   c) what evidence there is against it and why you have rejected that evidence
   d) your conclusion as to why this is a good verdict.

Think!

1. What is Source 33 trying to say about the policy of Appeasement?
2. Make a list of the reasons why Appeasement has generally been seen in negative terms.
3. Churchill once remarked to President Roosevelt, 'History will judge us kindly because I shall write the history'. Read Source 34. How should this affect our viewpoints on Appeasement?

Was Appeasement justified?

Chamberlain was not a coward or a weakling. When he had no choice but to declare war in 1939 he did. Most people and most politicians at the time supported Appeasement.

Yet when Hitler broke his promises and the policy did not stop war, the supporters of Appeasement quickly turned against the policy, some claiming that they had been opposed all along. Appeasers were portrayed as naïve, foolish or weak – Source 33 is one of hundreds of examples which parody the policy and the people who pursued it. Historians since then and popular opinion too have judged Chamberlain very harshly. Chamberlain's 'peace for our time' speech is presented as self-deception and a betrayal. Chamberlain and his Cabinet are seen as 'second-rate politicians' who were out of their depth as events unfolded before them. On the other hand, the opponents of Appeasement such as Winston Churchill are portrayed as REALISTS who were far-sighted and brave.

SOURCE 33

'Remember... One More Lollypop, and Then You All Go Home!'

A cartoon by the American artist Dr Seuss published on 13 August 1941 (before the USA entered the Second World War).

SOURCE 34

The Gathering Storm has been one of the most influential books of our time. It is no exaggeration to claim that it has strongly influenced the behaviour of Western politicians from Harry S. Truman to George W. Bush.

... It is a good tale, told by a master story-teller, who did, after all, win the Nobel prize for literature; but would a prize for fiction have been more appropriate?

Professor John Charmley of the University of East Anglia writing about Churchill's account of the 1930s called *The Gathering Storm*.

SOURCE 35

So how did my pre-emptive strategy stand up to a computer stress test? Not as well as I had hoped, I have to confess. The Calm & the Storm made it clear that lining up an anti-German coalition in 1938 might have been harder than I'd assumed. To my horror, the French turned down the alliance I proposed to them. It also turned out that, when I did go to war with Germany, my own position was pretty weak. The nadir [low point] was a successful German invasion of England, a scenario my book rules out as militarily too risky.

Professor Niall Ferguson in an article for the *New York Magazine*, 16 October 2006.

FIGURE 36

In the 1930s, aircraft were generally seen as the most important weapon.

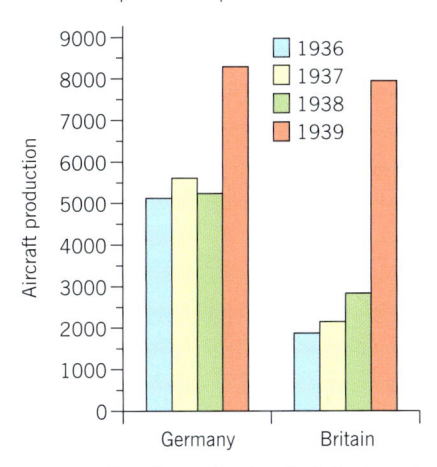

Aircraft production in Britain and Germany, 1936–39.

Until relatively recently the debate has been very one-sided. Yet this debate matters because the failure of Appeasement to stop Hitler has had a profound influence on British and American foreign policy ever since. It is now seen as the 'right thing' to stand up to dictators. But are we learning the right lessons from the story of Appeasement? Before we leap so quickly to judgement on this issue, let's run this argument through three different checks.

Check 1: If Chamberlain had stood up to Hitler in 1938 what would have happened?

The historian Professor Niall Ferguson has set out some 'counter-factual' scenarios – suggesting what might have happened if particular policies were followed. In particular, he has argued that confronting Hitler in 1938 instead of appeasing him 'would have paid handsome dividends. Even if it had come to war over Czechoslovakia, Germany would not have won. Germany's defences were not yet ready for a two-front war'.

Professor Ferguson then had the chance to test his scenario by playing a computer game! *The Calm & the Storm* is a powerful simulation which allows users to make decisions and then computes the possible impact of those decisions. You can read his conclusions in Source 35.

Check 2: Did Appeasement buy time for Chamberlain to rearm Britain?

One of the strongest arguments for Appeasement was that in 1938 Britain simply was not equipped to fight a war with Germany. So did Appeasement allow Britain to catch up?

In the 1960s British historian A.J.P. Taylor argued that Chamberlain had an exaggerated view of Germany's strength. Taylor believed that German forces were only 45 per cent of what British intelligence reports said they were.

But Taylor was writing in 1965 – not much help to Chamberlain in the 1930s. The Government had talked about rearmament since 1935 but Britain only really started rearming when Chamberlain became prime minister in 1937. Chamberlain certainly thought that Britain's armed forces were not ready for war in 1938. His own military advisers and his intelligence services told him this. As you can see from Figure 36 aircraft production increased massively in 1939.

Check 3: Did Chamberlain have any realistic alternatives?

In the 2000s some historians began to accept that Chamberlain made mistakes and that he probably underestimated Hitler and overrated his own abilities. At the same time, they also questioned whether there were any realistic alternatives to the policies that Chamberlain followed which would have stopped Hitler, mainly because Hitler was determined to have a war. British historian Andrew Stedman (Source 37) is a good example.

SOURCE 37

It was easy to criticise Chamberlain from the side-lines. It was more difficult to suggest a constructive, coherent alternative. So what were the other options open to Chamberlain?

1. *Isolation and absolute pacifism*
2. *Economic and Colonial Appeasement*
3. *League of Nations*
4. *Alliances*
5. *Armaments and Defence*
6. *War*

All of these options were considered by Chamberlain. Some were rejected and some were actually tried. In his ultimate failure Chamberlain's achievements deserve to be recognised. It is difficult to believe that the Nazis could have been deterred. War was the Hitler regime's main aim. In failing to achieve peace Chamberlain did at least make clear where the blame lay. History should give him credit for this.

An extract from *Alternatives to Appeasement* by British historian Andrew Stedman, 2011.

FOCUS TASK 3.6

How far was Hitler's foreign policy to blame for the outbreak of war in Europe in 1939?

You have covered a lot of material in the last two chapters. In this task you are going to make sure that you have the important events and developments clear in your mind.

1. Work in groups of six. Each take a blank sheet of paper and write a heading like the ones on the right. On your sheet summarise the ways in which this factor helped to bring about the war.
2. Now come back together as a group and write your own summary of how and why the war broke out. You can use this structure, but set yourself a word limit of 75 words per paragraph, less if you can.

1 The Treaty of Versailles

2 The failures of the League of Nations

3 The worldwide economic Depression

4 The policy of Appeasement

5 The Nazi–Soviet Pact

6 Hitler's actions and particularly his foreign policy

Paragraph 1:
(This is the place to explain how resentment against the Versailles Treaty brought Hitler to power in the first place and guided his actions in the 1930s.)

There were important long-term factors which help to explain why war broke out in 1939. One factor was the Versailles Treaty. It was important because …

Paragraph 2:
(Here you should explain how the failure of the League encouraged Hitler and made him think he could achieve his aims.)

The failure of the League of Nations in the 1930s also contributed towards the outbreak of war. This was because …

Paragraph 3:
(Here you should explain how the Depression was an underlying cause of the failure of the League, Japan's aggression and Hitler's rise to power.)

Economic factors also played an important role. The worldwide economic Depression …

Paragraph 4:
(Here you should briefly describe what Appeasement was, and how instead of stopping Hitler it encouraged him. You could also point out the links between Appeasement and the Depression.)

Another factor which helps to explain the outbreak of war was the policy of Appeasement. Appeasement …

Paragraph 5:
(Here you should explain how the Nazi–Soviet Pact led to the invasion of Poland and how that in turn led to war. You could also point out that these short-term factors probably could not have happened if there had not been a policy of Appeasement.)

There were also key short-term factors which actually sparked off the war. One of these was …

Paragraph 6:
(Here you should comment on Hitler's overall responsibility. How far do you agree that Hitler wanted war, planned for it, and if so does that mean he caused the war?)

Some people describe the Second World War as Hitler's war. I think this is a GOOD/POOR description because…

Paragraph 7:
(Here you should indicate which factor(s) you think were most important.)

All of these factors played important roles. However, [INSERT YOUR CHOICE OF FACTOR(S)] was / were particularly important because …

CHAPTER REVIEW FOCUS TASK

Reaching a judgement

Almost there! In the last task you wrote a clear explanation of the various reasons why peace collapsed by 1939. However, you need to go further. You also need to be able to compare the importance of these reasons (or factors) and see the links between them. For example, if you were asked this question:

'The Nazi–Soviet Pact of 1939 was more important than the policy of Appeasement in causing the Second World War.' How far do you agree with this statement?

what would you say? Most students find it hard to explain what they think and end up **giving information about each factor** (describing events) rather than **making a judgement and supporting it**. This review task helps you to overcome this problem.

Stage 1: Understand and evaluate each factor

There are six major factors. The cards analyse why each one might be seen as:

- a **critical** factor (i.e. the war probably would not have happened without it) or just
- one of several **important** factors (i.e. the war could still possibly have happened without it).
    a) Read the cards carefully to make sure you understand the arguments.
    b) For each of the 'killer sources' 1–7 (on pages 76–77) decide whether this supports the argument that this factor was critical or just one of several important factors.

Factor 1: The Treaty of Versailles
- **Critical?** Versailles and the other treaties created a situation in Europe which made war inevitable. It was only a matter of time before Germany tried to seek revenge, overturn the Treaty and start another war. Many commentators felt at the time that it was only a question of when war might come not whether it would.
- **Important?** The treaties contributed to the tensions of the time but they did not create them. Politicians in the 1930s could have defended the treaties or changed them. It was political choices in the 1930s which caused war not the treaties.

Factor 2: The failure of the League of Nations
- **Critical?** The League of Nations' job was to make sure that disputes were sorted out legally. In the 1920s it created a spirit of co-operation. But, in Manchuria 1931 and Abyssinia 1935–36 the League completely failed to stand up to aggression by Japan and Italy. This encouraged Hitler's aggression from 1936 onwards since he believed no one would try to stop him.
- **Important?** The League never really fulfilled the role of peacekeeper – even in the 1920s it gave in to Italy over Corfu. The failure of the League in the 1930s was important because it encouraged Hitler, but even if the League had been stronger Hitler would still have tried to overturn the Treaty of Versailles and to destroy communism.

Factor 3: The worldwide economic Depression
- **Critical?** The Depression critically weakened the League of Nations. It destroyed the spirit of international CO-OPERATION which had built up in the 1920s, and set countries against each other. Without the Depression leading to these problems there could not have been a war.
- **Important?** The Depression was certainly important – it made Japan and Italy invade Manchuria and Abyssinia. It brought Hitler to power in Germany and started German rearmament. However, it is linked to all the other factors – it did not cause the war in itself. Even with the Depression Hitler could have been stopped if Britain and France had had the will to resist him. The Depression did not make war inevitable.

Factor 4: The policy of Appeasement
- **Critical?** Appeasement was critical because it made Hitler think he could get away with anything. Britain and France could have stopped Hitler in 1936 when he marched troops into the Rhineland but their nerve failed. From this point on Hitler felt he could not lose and took gamble after gamble. As a result of Appeasement he did not even believe Britain would fight him when he invaded Poland in 1939.
- **Important?** The policy of Appeasement only came about because, without the USA, the League of Nations, and its leading members Britain and France, were not strong enough to keep peace. The Depression so weakened Britain and France that they did not have the money to oppose Hitler. The policy of Appeasement would not have been followed without these other factors.

Factor 5: The Nazi–Soviet Pact
- **Critical?** Although Hitler thought that Britain and France would not fight him he was not sure about the Soviet Union. So the Soviet Union was the only country that stood in the way of his plans. Without the Nazi–Soviet Pact, Hitler would not have taken the gamble to invade Poland and war would never have begun.
- **Important?** The Pact allowed Hitler to invade Poland, but war was already inevitable before that – due to Hitler's actions and his hatred of communism. Hitler had made clear his plans to take land from the USSR. Plus it was the policy of Appeasement that drove Stalin to sign the Pact because he thought he could not rely on the support of Britain or France to oppose Hitler.

Factor 6: Hitler's actions
- **Critical?** There could have been no war without Hitler. It was Hitler's vision of *Lebensraum*, his hatred of communism and his determination to reverse the Versailles settlement which led to war. He consciously built up Germany's army and weapons with the intention of taking it to war. At each stage of the road to war from 1936 to 1939 it was Hitler's beliefs, actions or decisions that caused the problem.
- **Important?** Hitler was the gambler. He only did what he could get away with. So without the weakness of the League of Nations, or the reluctance of Britain, France or the Soviet Union to stand up to him; without the flawed Treaty of Versailles; without the economic problems of the 1930s, Hitler would not have got anywhere. He would have been forced to follow a more peaceful foreign policy and there would have been no war.

Stage 2: Investigate connections between factors

From Stage 1 it should be clear to you that these factors are connected to each other. Let's investigate these connections.

a) Make six simple cards with just the factor heading.

b) Display your cards on a large sheet of paper and draw lines connecting them together. Some links are already mentioned on the cards on page 75 but you may be able to think of many more.

c) Write an explanation along each link. For example, between 'the policy of Appeasement' and 'The Nazi–Soviet Pact' you might write:

'The policy of Appeasement helped cause the Nazi–Soviet Pact. It alarmed Stalin so that he felt he had to make his own deal with Hitler thinking that France and Britain would just give him whatever he wanted.'

d) Take a photo of your finished chart.

Stage 3: Rank the factors

Which of these factors is most important? In Stage 2 you will already have started to draw your own conclusions about this. It will be really helpful when you come to answering questions about relative importance if you have already decided what you think! Remember there is no right answer to which is most important, but whatever your view you must be able to support it with key points and with evidence. So:

a) Take your cards and put them in a rank order of importance.

b) To justify your order, in the space between each card you need to be able to complete this sentence: 'X was more important than Y because...'

Stage 4: Compare two factors

Back to the question we started with:

'The Nazi–Soviet Pact of 1939 was more important than the policy of Appeasement in causing the Second World War.' How far do you agree with this statement?

With all the thinking that you have done you should have already made up your mind on what you think, but to help you structure and support your argument you could complete a chart like this. NB If you can include the killer source in your written answer, all the better.

	Reasons more important	Reasons less important
Policy of Appeasement		
Nazi–Soviet Pact		

Killer sources and quotations

SOURCE 1

When war came in 1939, it was a result of twenty years of decisions taken or not taken, not of arrangements made in 1919.

Historian Margaret Macmillan writing in 2001.

SOURCE 2

The failure of the World Disarmament Conference not only crushed the hopes of many supporters of the League of Nations and the disarmament movements but also strengthened the ranks of those who opted for appeasement or some form of pacifism. Pressures for collective action gave way to policies of self-defence, neutrality and isolation. Against such a background, the balance of power shifted steadily away from the status quo nations in the direction of those who favoured its destruction. The reconstruction of the 1920s was not inevitably doomed to collapse by the start of the 1930s. Rather, the demise of the Weimar Republic and the triumph of Hitler proved the motor force of destructive systemic change.

Historian Zara Steiner writing in 2011.

SOURCE 3

If new accounts by historians show that statesmen were able to use the League to ease tensions and win time in the 1920s, no such case appears possible for the 1930s. Indeed, the League's processes may have played a role in that deterioration. Diplomacy requires leaders who can speak for their states; it requires secrecy; and it requires the ability to make credible threats. The Covenant's security arrangements met none of those criteria.

Historian Susan Pedersen writing in 2007.

SOURCE 4

We turn our eyes towards the lands of the east ... When we speak of new territory in Europe today, we must principally think of Russia and the border states subject to her. Destiny itself seems to wish to point out the way for us here. Colonisation of the eastern frontiers is of extreme importance. It will be the duty of Germany's foreign policy to provide large spaces for the nourishment and settlement of the growing population of Germany.

Adolf Hitler, *Mein Kampf*, 1925.

SOURCE 5

The vindictiveness of British and French peace terms helped to pave the way for Nazism in Germany and a renewal of hostilities. World War 2 resulted from the very silly and humiliating punitive peace imposed on Germany after World War 1.

Historian George Kennan writing in 1984.

SOURCE 6

By repeatedly surrendering to force, Chamberlain has encouraged aggression ... our central contention, therefore, is that Mr Chamberlain's policy has throughout been based on a fatal misunderstanding of the psychology of dictatorship.

The Yorkshire Post, December 1938.

SOURCE 7

The effects of the depression encouraged not only the emergence of authoritarian and interventionist governments but led to the shattering of the global financial system. Most European states followed 'beggar-thy-neighbour' tactics [protecting a country's economy at the expense of other countries]. Germany, Hungary, and most of the East European states embarked on defensive economic policies – often at cost to their neighbours.

Historian Zara Steiner writing in 2011.

PRACTICE QUESTIONS

1. (a) What was the policy of Appeasement? **[4]**
   (b) Why was the Munich Agreement of 1938 important to Hitler? **[6]**
   (c) 'Appeasement was a wise policy that delayed war until Britain was ready.' How far do you agree with this statement? Explain your answer. **[10]**

See pages 148–54 for advice on the different types of questions.

Keywords

Make sure you know these terms, people or events and are able to use them or describe them confidently.
- *Anschluss*
- Anti-Comintern Pact
- Appeasement
- *Blitzkrieg*
- Bolshevism
- Communism
- Conscription
- *Lebensraum*
- *Mein Kampf*
- Mobilised
- Munich Agreement
- Nazi–Soviet Pact
- November Criminals
- Polish Corridor
- Radical
- Rearmament
- Remilitarisation
- Spanish Civil War
- Sudetenland

Chapter Summary

How far was Hitler's foreign policy to blame for the outbreak of war in Europe in 1939?

1. The late 1920s had been a time of hope for international relations with a series of agreements that seemed to make the world a more peaceful place with countries co-operating and trading with each other.
2. The Great Depression of the 1930s led to political turmoil in many countries and the rise of the dictators such as Hitler in Germany. Hitler formed alliances with other right-wing regimes in Italy and Japan.
3. Germany was still unhappy about its treatment under the Treaty of Versailles and Hitler set out to challenge the terms of the Treaty of Versailles, first of all by rearming Germany (secretly from 1933, then publicly from 1935).
4. He also challenged the Treaty, for example by sending troops into the DEMILITARISED ZONE of the Rhineland in 1936.
5. The League of Nations and Britain and France did not try to stop Hitler doing these things. This policy was called Appeasement – giving Hitler what he wanted in the hope he would not ask for more.
6. The most famous act of Appeasement was over the Sudetenland – an area of Czechoslovakia that Hitler wanted to take over.
7. In the Munich Agreement (October 1938) Britain and France let Hitler have the Sudetenland as long as he did not try to take over the rest of Czechoslovakia. When Hitler invaded the rest of Czechoslovakia in early 1939 it marked the end of the policy of Appeasement and they told Hitler that any further expansion would lead to war.
8. Although Hitler was very anticommunist and saw Stalin and the USSR as his enemy, he signed a Pact with Stalin in 1939 to not attack each other but to divide Poland between them.
9. When Hitler invaded Poland in September 1939 Britain declared war.
10. Hitler's foreign policy played a major role in causing the Second World War but historians argue that there were other very important factors that contributed as well, particularly the economic Depression, the failures of the League of Nations and the unfairness of the Treaty of Versailles.

PART 2

The Cold War, 1945–75

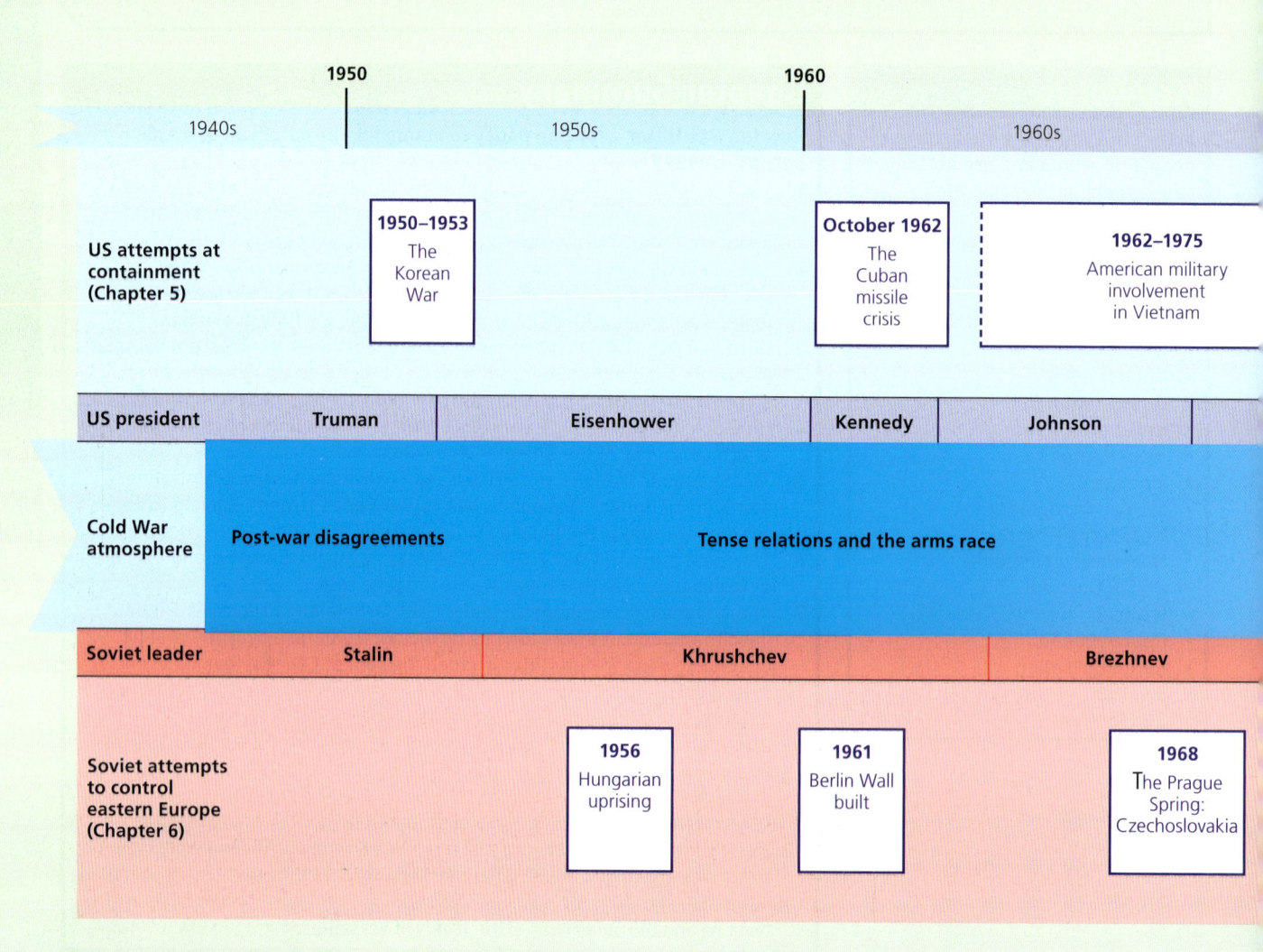

A photo of the Big Three – Churchill, Roosevelt and Stalin – at the Yalta Conference in February 1945.

	1940s	1950	1950s	1960	1960s
US attempts at containment (Chapter 5)		**1950–1953** The Korean War		**October 1962** The Cuban missile crisis	**1962–1975** American military involvement in Vietnam
US president	Truman		Eisenhower	Kennedy	Johnson
Cold War atmosphere	Post-war disagreements		Tense relations and the arms race		
Soviet leader	Stalin		Khrushchev		Brezhnev
Soviet attempts to control eastern Europe (Chapter 6)			**1956** Hungarian uprising	**1961** Berlin Wall built	**1968** The Prague Spring: Czechoslovakia

Focus

The Second World War led to a decisive change in the balance of power around the world. The countries that had dominated European affairs from 1919 to 1939 such as France, Britain and Germany were now much poorer or less powerful. World history was much more affected by what the leaders of the new 'superpowers' (the USA and the USSR) believed and did. So the big story of Part 2 is how the superpowers became enemies, how they clashed (directly or indirectly) during the Cold War and how they tried to influence the affairs of other countries.

- In **Chapter 4** you will examine the short-term causes of the Cold War. Why did the USA and the USSR, who had fought together as allies against Hitler, fall out and enter a 40-year period of tension and distrust?
- One of the USA's obsessions in this Cold War period was to hold back the spread of communism. **Chapter 5** examines why it so feared the spread of communism, how it tried to contain it and helps you to judge how successful it was.
- While the USA was trying to contain communism, the Soviet Union was trying to shore it up in its eastern European neighbours. This was no easy task. It faced frequent protests and problems. In **Chapter 6** you will consider how it did this, how far it succeeded and why in the end it all came crashing down with the demolition of the BERLIN WALL and the collapse of the Soviet Union itself.

The events in these chapters overlap. The timeline below gives you an overview of the main events you will be studying. It would be helpful if you made your own copy and added your own notes to it as you study.

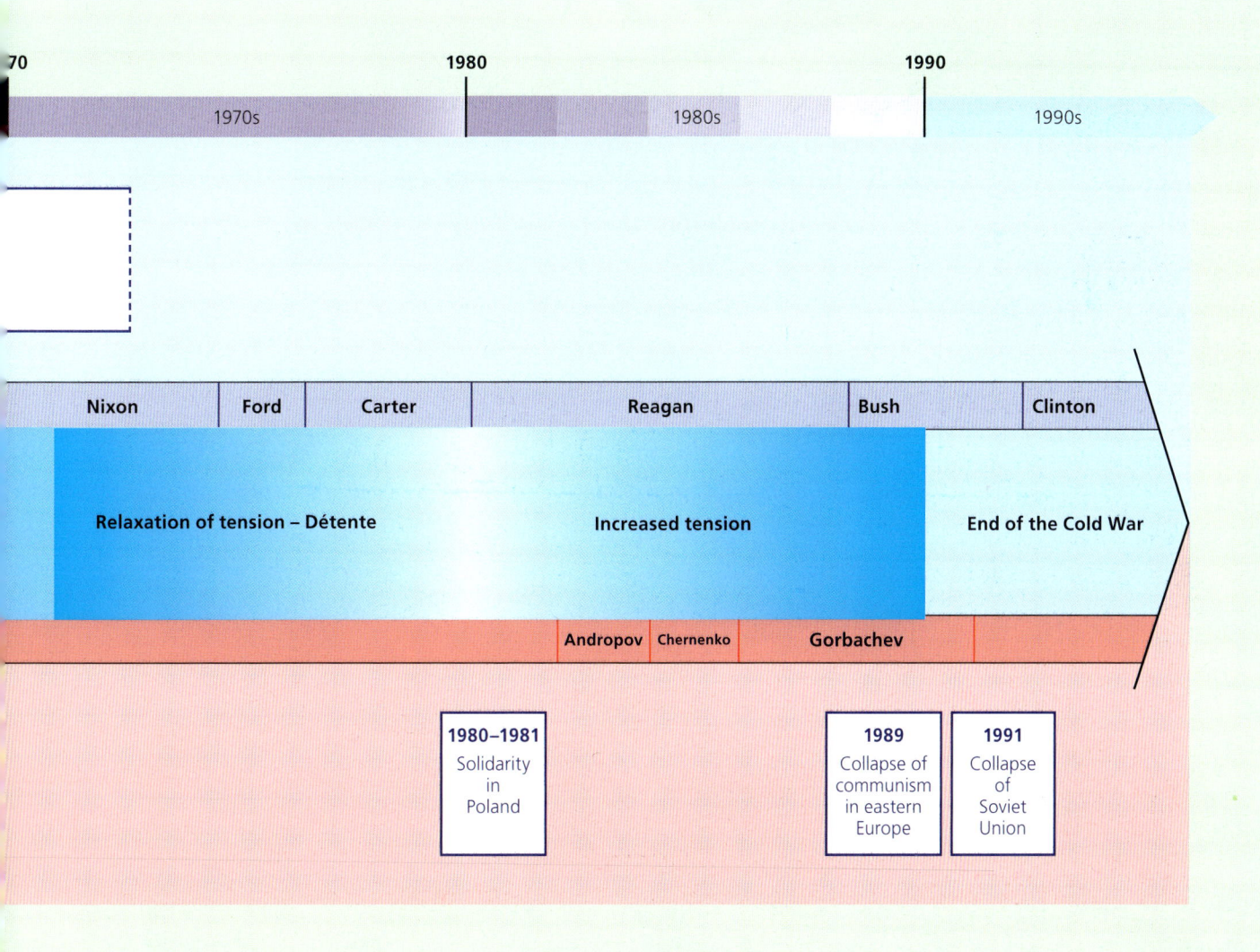

EAST MEETS WEST

4 Who was to blame for the Cold War?

FOCUS POINTS
★ Why did the US–Soviet alliance begin to break down in 1945?
★ How had the USSR gained control of eastern Europe by 1948?
★ How did the United States react to Soviet expansionism?
★ What were the consequences of the Berlin Blockade?
★ Who was the more to blame for starting the Cold War: the United States or the USSR?

In May 1945 American troops entered Berlin from the west, as Russian troops moved in from the east. They met and celebrated victory together. Yet three years later these former allies were arguing over Berlin and war between them seemed a real possibility.

What had gone wrong?

In this chapter you will consider:
- how the wartime ALLIANCE between the USA and the USSR broke down
- how the SOVIET UNION gained control over eastern Europe and how the USA responded
- the consequences of the BERLIN BLOCKADE in 1948.

The key question you will be returning to at the end is who is most to blame for this increasing tension (which became known as the 'COLD WAR').
- Was it the USSR and STALIN with his insistence on taking over and controlling eastern Europe?
- Or was it the USA and President Truman with the TRUMAN DOCTRINE and MARSHALL AID?
- Or should they share the blame? In the post-war chaos in Europe they both saw it as their role to extend their influence, to proclaim the benefits of their own political system and denounce the other side.
- Or was the Cold War inevitable – beyond the control of either country? Is 'blame' the wrong word to use?

Here are some of the factors that you will study in this chapter. At the end you will be asked to become an expert in one of them so you could help yourself by making notes about each one as you read the chapter.

The situation before the Second World War	The personal relationships between various leaders	The conflicting beliefs of the superpowers	The war damage suffered by the USSR
Stalin's take-over of eastern Europe	Marshall Aid for Europe	The Berlin Blockade	

> It is not just cartoons that can have messages. Photos can too. This photo shows American and Soviet soldiers shaking hands in April 1945. It was a staged photograph. The US commander General Bradley knew the Soviet and US troops would meet on 25 April and ordered the poster to be erected. US Army photographers set up the scene.
> 1 What is the message of the photo?
> 2 How far do you trust it to show relations between the USA and the USSR in 1945?

Why did the US–Soviet alliance begin to break down in 1945?

> **ACTIVITY**
>
> Create your own version of the central blue row of the timeline on pages 78–79. You will be adding events and comments to it throughout the chapter to help you in your final Focus Task.
>
> Use the information on these two pages to mark any events or developments that might affect relationships between the USA and the Soviet Union.

Allies against Hitler

The USA, USSR and Britain fought together as allies during the Second World War. However, it was a strategic wartime alliance not a bond of brotherhood. The USSR had been a communist country for more than 30 years. The majority of politicians and business leaders in Britain and the USA hated and feared communist ideas (see the Factfile on page 83). In the past they had helped the enemies of the communists. This made the USSR wary of Britain and the USA. So in many ways the surprising thing is that these old rivals managed a war-time alliance at all. But they did and by 1945 they had defeated Germany.

SOURCE 1

A British cartoon from 1941, with the caption 'Love conquers all'. The figure in the centre of the bench is Stalin and he is being charmed by US President Roosevelt (on the left) and British leader Winston Churchill. The small figure is Hitler. Hitler is shown as Cupid, whose arrows cause people to fall in love.

> **Source Analysis**
>
> Cartoons often criticise particular people or their actions. Sometimes they praise. Sometimes they simply comment on a situation. Would you say Source 1 is criticising, praising or commenting? Explain what features of the cartoon helped you to decide.

SOURCE 2

For Americans, private property was sacred and formed the basis for the rule of law, while for the Soviets private property was the source of all evil and inequality, preventing the development of all humanity to a bright and fair future. While in the West people were taught that if you work harder you better yourself, in the East people were taught that if they work harder, society gets richer and they would share in that. Both systems advocated freedom and democracy, but their understanding of these terms was totally different. Both sides believed that government should be for the benefit of the majority of the population. For the USA, this was ensured by free choice through the ballot box. For Communists, there was no need for free choice because the Communist party understood the hopes and needs of the people even better than the people themselves.

Historian Eleanor Hore of the University of Essex, UK.

Rivals with differing world views

To understand how the alliance broke down we need to understand the beliefs of the two sides.

There was a clash of ideologies between communist and CAPITALIST beliefs as the Factfile (page 83) explains, but this was tied up with strong national pride and a sense of identity as well (see Source 2).

- Most Americans believed passionately that their way of life was best and they were justifiably proud of the leading role the USA took in defeating NAZISM.
- At the same time most Soviet people were equally proud of their country's critical role in defeating Germany (which came at a devastating cost). They too believed their way of life was superior.

Factfile

A clash of ideologies

The USA	The USSR
The USA was capitalist. Business and property were privately owned.	The USSR was communist. All industry was owned and run by the state.
It was a DEMOCRACY. Its government was chosen in free democratic elections.	It was a one-party DICTATORSHIP. Elections were held, but all candidates belonged to the Communist Party.
It was the world's wealthiest country. But as in most capitalist countries, there were extremes – some people were very wealthy while others were very poor.	It was an economic superpower because its industry had grown rapidly in the 1920s and 1930s, but the general standard of living in the USSR was much lower than in the USA. Even so, unemployment was rare and extreme poverty was rarer than in the USA.
For Americans, being free of control by the government was more important than everyone being equal.	For communists, the rights of individuals were seen as less important than the good of society as a whole. So individuals' lives were tightly controlled.
Most Americans firmly believed that other countries should be run in the American way.	Most Soviet people believed that other countries should be run in the communist way.
People in the USA were alarmed by communist theory, which talked of spreading revolution.	COMMUNISM taught that the role of a communist state was to encourage communist revolutions worldwide. In practice, the USSR's leaders tended to take practical decisions rather than be led by this ideology.
Americans generally saw their policies as 'doing the right thing' rather than serving the interests of the USA.	Many in the USSR saw the USA's actions as selfishly building its economic empire and political influence.

ACTIVITY

You need to know the information in the Factfile. Make your own copies of the diagrams on the right and then use the Factfile to make notes around them summarising the two systems.

Superpowers

The USA and the USSR had emerged from the war as the two world 'SUPERPOWERS'. After the Second World War former world-leading powers like Britain and France were effectively relegated to a second division. US leaders felt there was a responsibility attached to being a superpower. In the 1930s, the USA had followed a policy of isolation – keeping out of European and world affairs. The Americans might have disapproved of Soviet communism, but they tried not to get involved. However, by the 1940s the US attitude had changed. Roosevelt had set the Americans firmly against a policy of isolation and this effectively meant opposing communism. There would be no more appeasement of DICTATORS. From now on, every communist action would meet an American reaction.

The Yalta Conference, February 1945

In February 1945 it was clear that Germany was losing the European war, so the Allied leaders met at Yalta in the Ukraine to plan what would happen to Europe after Germany's defeat. The YALTA CONFERENCE went well. Despite their differences, the BIG THREE – Stalin, Roosevelt and Churchill – agreed on some important matters. These are summarised in the tables below.

It seemed that, although they could not all agree, they were still able to negotiate and do business with one another.

> **Revision Tip**
> Make sure you can remember at least two examples of agreement at Yalta and one (the main!) disagreement.

> **ACTIVITY**
> The photo on page 78 of this book shows the Big Three at the Yalta Conference. In 1945 radio was the main medium for news. Imagine you were describing the scene in this photo for a radio audience. Describe for the listeners:
> - the obvious points (such as people you can see)
> - the less obvious points (such as the mood of the scene)
> - the agreements and disagreements the Big Three had come to.

Agreements at Yalta	
✔ **Japan** Stalin agreed to enter the war against Japan once Germany had surrendered.	✔ **Germany** They agreed that Germany would be divided into four zones: American, French, British and Soviet.
✔ **Elections** They agreed that as countries were liberated from occupation by the German army, they would be allowed to hold free elections to choose the government they wanted.	✔ **United Nations** The Big Three all agreed to join the new UNITED NATIONS organisation, which would aim to keep peace after the war.
✔ **War criminals** As Allied soldiers advanced through Germany, they were revealing the horrors of the Nazi CONCENTRATION CAMPS. The Big Three agreed to hunt down and punish war criminals who were responsible for the genocide.	✔ **Eastern Europe** The Soviet Union had suffered terribly in the war. An estimated 20 million Soviet people had died. Stalin was therefore concerned about the future security of the USSR and specifically the risk of another invasion from Europe. The Big Three agreed that eastern Europe should be seen as a 'SOVIET SPHERE OF INFLUENCE'.

SOURCE 3

We argued freely and frankly across the table. But at the end, on every point, unanimous agreement was reached … We know, of course, that it was Hitler's hope and the German war lords' hope that we would not agree – that some slight crack might appear in the solid wall of allied unity … But Hitler has failed. Never before have the major allies been more closely united – not only in their war aims but also in their peace aims.

Extract from President Roosevelt's report to the US Congress on the Yalta Conference.

Disagreements at Yalta
✗ **Poland**   The only real disagreement was about Poland.   • Stalin wanted the border of the USSR to move westwards into Poland. Stalin argued that Poland, in turn, could move its border westwards into German territory.   • Churchill did not approve of Stalin's plans for Poland, but he also knew that there was not very much he could do about it because Stalin's RED ARMY was in total control of both Poland and eastern Germany.   • Roosevelt was also unhappy about Stalin's plan, but Churchill persuaded Roosevelt to accept it, as long as the USSR agreed not to interfere in Greece where the British were attempting to prevent the communists taking over. Stalin accepted this.

SOURCE 4

I want to drink to our alliance, that it should not lose its … intimacy, its free expression of views … I know of no such close alliance of three Great Powers as this … May it be strong and stable, may we be as frank as possible.

Stalin, proposing a toast at a dinner at the Yalta Conference, 1945.

Source Analysis

Behind the scenes at Yalta

The war against Hitler had united Roosevelt, Stalin and Churchill and at the Yalta Conference they appeared to get on well. But what was going on behind the scenes? Sources 5–9 will help you decide.

SOURCE 5

In the hallway [at Yalta] we stopped before a map of the world on which the Soviet Union was coloured in red. Stalin waved his hand over the Soviet Union and exclaimed, 'They [Roosevelt and Churchill] will never accept the idea that so great a space should be red, never, never!'

Milovan Djilas writing about Yalta in 1948.

SOURCE 6

I have always worked for friendship with Russia but, like you, I feel deep anxiety because of their misinterpretation of the Yalta decisions, their attitude towards Poland, their overwhelming influence in the Balkans excepting Greece, the difficulties they make about Vienna, the combination of Russian power and the territories under their control or occupied, coupled with the Communist technique in so many other countries, and above all their power to maintain very large Armies in the field for a long time. What will be the position in a year or two?

Extract from a telegram sent by Prime Minister Churchill to President Truman in May 1945.

SOURCE 7

Perhaps you think that just because we are the allies of the English we have forgotten who they are and who Churchill is. There's nothing they like better than to trick their allies. During the First World War they constantly tricked the Russians and the French. And Churchill? Churchill is the kind of man who will pick your pocket of a kopeck! [A kopeck is a low value Soviet coin.] And Roosevelt? Roosevelt is not like that. He dips in his hand only for bigger coins. But Churchill? He will do it for a kopeck.

Stalin speaking to a fellow communist, Milovan Djilas, in 1945. Djilas was a supporter of Stalin.

SOURCE 8

The Soviet Union has become a danger to the free world. A new front must be created against her onward sweep. This front should be as far east as possible. A settlement must be reached on all major issues between West and East in Europe before the armies of democracy melt.

Churchill writing to Roosevelt shortly after the Yalta Conference. Churchill ordered his army leader Montgomery to keep German arms intact in case they had to be used against the Russians.

SOURCE 9

Once, Churchill asked Stalin to send him the music of the new Soviet Russian anthem so that it could be broadcast before the summary of the news from the Soviet German front. Stalin sent the words [as well] and expressed the hope that Churchill would set about learning the new tune and whistling it to members of the Conservative Party. While Stalin behaved with relative discretion with Roosevelt, he continually teased Churchill throughout the war.

Written by Soviet historian Sergei Kudryashov after the war.

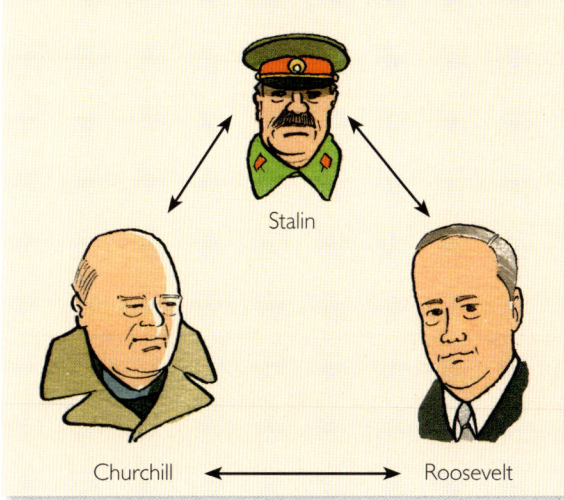

1. Draw a simple diagram like this and use Sources 5–9 to summarise what each of the leaders thought of the other.
2. How do Sources 5–9 affect your impression of the Yalta Conference?
3. How far do you trust these sources to tell you what the leaders actually thought of each other?

The Potsdam Conference, July 1945

In May 1945, three months after the Yalta Conference, Allied troops reached Berlin. Hitler committed suicide. Germany surrendered. The war in Europe was won.

A second conference of the Allied leaders was arranged for July 1945 in the Berlin suburb of Potsdam. However, in the five months since Yalta a number of changes had taken place which would greatly affect relationships between the leaders.

Changes since Yalta

1 Stalin's armies were occupying most of eastern Europe

Soviet troops had liberated country after country in eastern Europe, but instead of withdrawing his troops Stalin had left them there. Refugees were fleeing out of these countries fearing a communist take-over. Stalin had set up a communist government in Poland, ignoring the wishes of the majority of Poles. He insisted that his control of eastern Europe was a defensive measure against possible future attacks.

2 America had a new president

On 12 April 1945, President Roosevelt died. He was replaced by his vice-president, Harry Truman. Truman was a very different man from Roosevelt. He was much more anticommunist than Roosevelt and was very suspicious of Stalin. Truman and his advisers saw Soviet actions in eastern Europe as preparations for a Soviet take-over of the rest of Europe.

3 The Allies had tested an atomic bomb

On 16 July 1945 the Americans successfully tested an ATOMIC BOMB at a desert site in the USA. At the start of the POTSDAM CONFERENCE, Truman informed Stalin about it.

Think!
1. At Yalta, Churchill and Roosevelt had agreed with Stalin that eastern Europe would be a Soviet 'sphere of influence'. Do you think Source 10 is what they had in mind?
2. Explain how each of the three changes since Yalta described in the text might affect relationships at Potsdam.
3. What is your overall impression of Source 11:
   a) a reasonable assessment of Stalin based on the facts
   b) an overreaction to Stalin based on fear and prejudice against the USSR?
   Use extracts from the source to support your view.

SOURCE 10

This war is not as in the past; whoever occupies a territory also imposes on it his own social system. Everyone imposes his own system as far as his army has power to do so. It cannot be otherwise.

Stalin speaking soon after the end of the Second World War about the take-over of eastern Europe.

SOURCE 11

Unless Russia is faced with an iron fist and strong language another war is in the making. Only one language do they understand — 'how many [army] divisions have you got?' ... I'm tired of babying the Soviets.

President Truman, writing to his Secretary of State in January 1946.

Stalin v. Truman

The Potsdam Conference finally got under way on 17 July 1945. Not surprisingly, it did not go as smoothly as Yalta.

To change the situation further still, in July there was an election in Britain. Winston Churchill was defeated, so half way through the conference he was replaced by a new prime minister, Clement Attlee. In the absence of Churchill, the conference was dominated by rivalry and suspicion between Stalin and Truman. A number of issues arose on which neither side seemed able to appreciate the other's point of view (see table on page 87).

SOURCE 12

An official publicity photograph of the leaders of the Big Three at the Potsdam Conference. The new British prime minister Clement Atlee is on the left, new US president Harry Truman is in the centre and Stalin is on the right.

Think!
Compare Source 12 with the photo of the Yalta Conference on page 78 (which you analysed in the Activity on page 84).
1. How is this picture similar or different?
2. How accurately do you think this picture represents relations at the Potsdam Conference?

Disagreements at Potsdam

✗ Germany	✗ Reparations	✗ Eastern Europe
Stalin wanted to incapacitate Germany completely to protect the USSR against future threats. Truman did not want to repeat the mistake of the TREATY OF VERSAILLES.	Twenty million Russians had died in the war and the Soviet Union had been devastated. Stalin wanted compensation from Germany. Truman, however, was once again determined not to repeat the mistakes at the end of the First World War and resisted this demand.	At Yalta, Stalin had won agreement from the Allies that he could set up pro-Soviet governments in eastern Europe. He said, 'If the Slav [the majority of east European] people are united, no one will dare move a finger against them'. Truman became very unhappy about Russian intentions and soon adopted a 'get tough' attitude towards Stalin.

FOCUS TASK 4.1
Why did the US–Soviet alliance begin to break down in 1945?

Under the following headings, make notes to summarise why the Allies began to fall out in 1945:
- Personalities
- Actions by the United States
- Actions by the USSR
- Misunderstandings

Revision Tip
Your notes from the Focus Task will be useful for revision. Make sure you can remember one example of each reason for the falling out.

4 Who was to blame for the Cold War?

Source Analysis

1. How do Sources 13 and 14 differ in their interpretation of Stalin's actions?
2. Explain why they see things so differently.
3. How do Sources 15 and 16 differ in their interpretation of Churchill?
4. Explain why there are differences.

How did the USSR gain control of eastern Europe by 1948?

The 'iron curtain'

The Potsdam Conference ended without complete agreement on any of the disagreements on the previous page. Over the next nine months, Stalin achieved the domination of eastern Europe that he was seeking. By 1946 Poland, Hungary, Romania, Bulgaria and Albania all had communist governments which owed their loyalty to Stalin. Churchill described the border between Soviet-controlled countries and the West as an 'IRON CURTAIN' (see Source 13). The name stuck.

SOURCE 13

A shadow has fallen upon the scenes so lately lighted by the Allied victory. From Stettin on the Baltic to Trieste on the Adriatic, an iron curtain has descended. Behind that line lie all the states of central and eastern Europe. The Communist parties have been raised to power far beyond their numbers and are seeking everywhere to obtain totalitarian control. This is certainly not the liberated Europe we fought to build. Nor is it one which allows permanent peace.

Winston Churchill speaking in the USA, in the presence of President Truman, March 1946. Letters and telegrams between Truman and Churchill suggest that Truman was aware of what Churchill planned to say and approved.

SOURCE 14

The following circumstances should not be forgotten. The Germans made their invasion of the USSR through Finland, Poland and Romania. The Germans were able to make their invasion through these countries because, at the time, governments hostile to the Soviet Union existed in these countries. What can there be surprising about the fact that the Soviet Union, anxious for its future safety, is trying to see to it that governments loyal in their attitude to the Soviet Union should exist in these countries?

Stalin, replying to Churchill's speech (Source 13).

SOURCE 15

A British cartoon commenting on Churchill's 'iron curtain' speech, in the *Daily Mail*, 6 March 1946.

SOURCE 16

A Soviet cartoon. Churchill is shown with two flags, the first proclaiming that 'Anglo-Saxons must rule the world' and the other threatening an 'iron curtain'. Notice who is formed by his shadow!

Source Analysis

What is the message of the cartoonist?

Think!

Some historians say that Churchill is as much to blame for the post-war distrust between the Soviet Union and the West as Roosevelt, Truman or Stalin. What evidence is there on pages 84–88 to support or challenge this view?

FOCUS TASK 4.2

How had the USSR gained control of eastern Europe by 1948?

'The only important factor in the communist take-over of eastern Europe was armed force.' How far do you agree with this statement?
1. List events which support it.
2. List other methods the communists used.
3. Decide how far you agree with the statement on a scale of 1–5. Explain your score carefully.

Stalin strengthens his grip

Figure 17 shows how Stalin extended Soviet power across eastern Europe. With communist governments established throughout eastern Europe, Stalin gradually tightened his control in each country. The SECRET POLICE imprisoned anyone who opposed communist rule.

Cominform

In October 1947, Stalin set up the Communist Information Bureau, or COMINFORM, to co-ordinate the work of the communist parties of eastern Europe. Cominform regularly brought the leaders of each communist party to Moscow to be briefed by Stalin and his ministers. This also allowed Stalin to keep a close eye on them. He spotted independent-minded leaders and replaced them with people who were completely loyal to him. The only communist leader who escaped this close control was Tito in Yugoslavia. He resented being controlled by Cominform and was expelled for his hostility in 1948.

Revision Tip

Make sure you can remember two examples of methods that the USSR and the communist parties used to take power in eastern Europe.

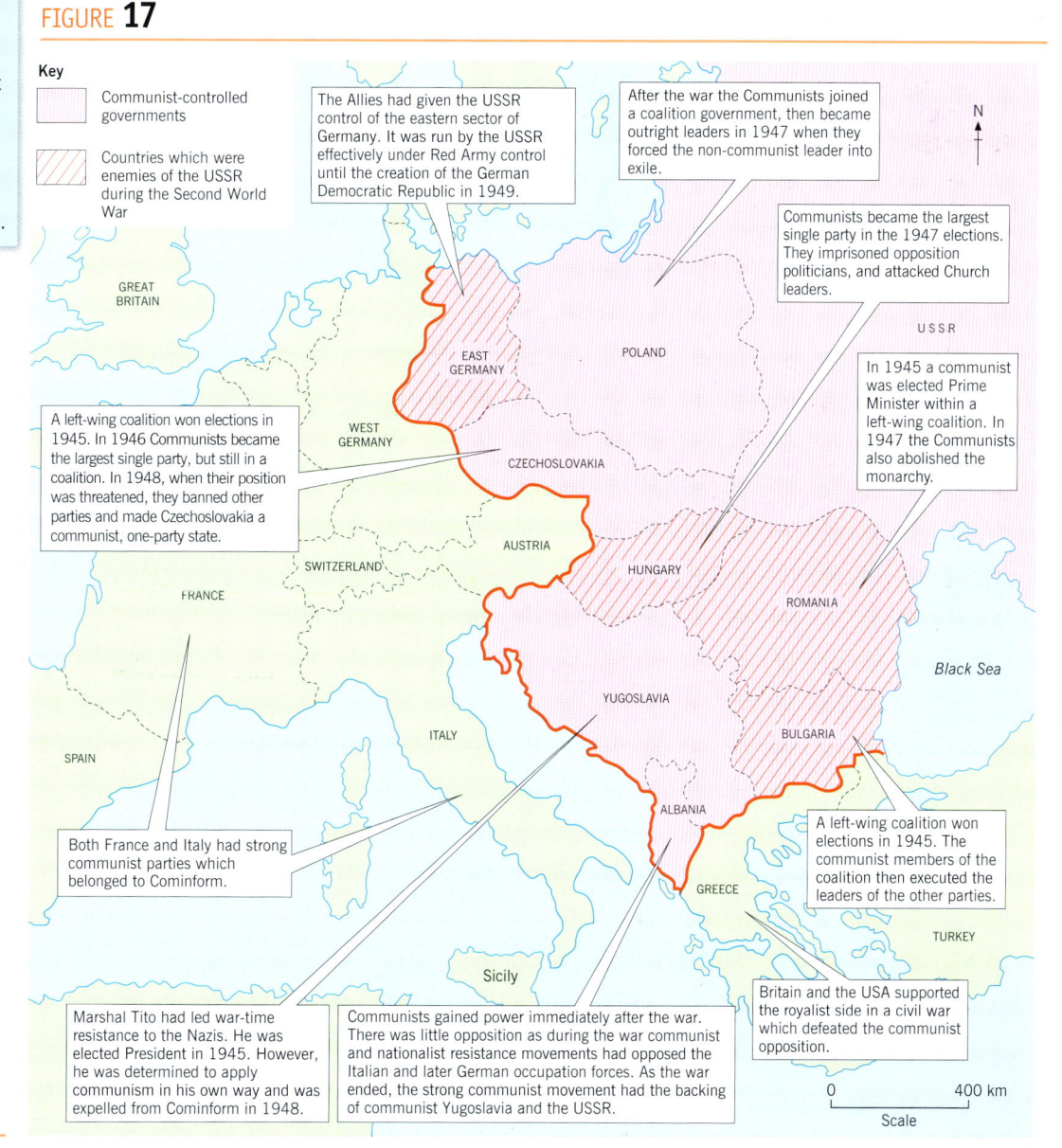

FIGURE 17

Key:
- Communist-controlled governments
- Countries which were enemies of the USSR during the Second World War

East Germany: The Allies had given the USSR control of the eastern sector of Germany. It was run by the USSR effectively under Red Army control until the creation of the German Democratic Republic in 1949.

Poland: After the war the Communists joined a coalition government, then became outright leaders in 1947 when they forced the non-communist leader into exile.

Hungary: Communists became the largest single party in the 1947 elections. They imprisoned opposition politicians, and attacked Church leaders.

Romania: In 1945 a communist was elected Prime Minister within a left-wing coalition. In 1947 the Communists also abolished the monarchy.

Czechoslovakia: A left-wing coalition won elections in 1945. In 1946 Communists became the largest single party, but still in a coalition. In 1948, when their position was threatened, they banned other parties and made Czechoslovakia a communist, one-party state.

Bulgaria: A left-wing coalition won elections in 1945. The communist members of the coalition then executed the leaders of the other parties.

France and Italy: Both France and Italy had strong communist parties which belonged to Cominform.

Yugoslavia: Marshal Tito had led war-time resistance to the Nazis. He was elected President in 1945. However, he was determined to apply communism in his own way and was expelled from Cominform in 1948.

Albania: Communists gained power immediately after the war. There was little opposition as during the war communist and nationalist resistance movements had opposed the Italian and later German occupation forces. As the war ended, the strong communist movement had the backing of communist Yugoslavia and the USSR.

Greece: Britain and the USA supported the royalist side in a civil war which defeated the communist opposition.

The communists in eastern Europe, 1945–48.

> **Source Analysis**
>
> 1 Do Sources 18 and 19 have the same message?
> 2 Source 18 is a British source. Does it seem likely that similar documents were being produced by the American Government? Give reasons.

How did the USA react to Soviet expansion?

The WESTERN POWERS were alarmed by Stalin's take-over of eastern Europe. Roosevelt, Churchill and their successors had accepted that Soviet security needed friendly governments in eastern Europe. They had agreed that eastern Europe would be a Soviet 'sphere of influence' and that Stalin would heavily influence this region. However, they had not expected such complete communist domination. They felt it should have been possible to have governments in eastern Europe that were both democratic and friendly to the USSR. Stalin saw his policy in eastern Europe as making himself secure, but Truman could only see the spread of communism.

SOURCE 18

After all the efforts that have been made and the appeasement that we followed to try and get a real friendly settlement, not only is the Soviet government not prepared to co-operate with any non-Communist government in eastern Europe, but it is actively preparing to extend its hold over the remaining part of continental Europe and, subsequently, over the Middle East and no doubt the Far East as well. In other words, physical control of Europe and Asia and eventual control of the whole world is what Stalin is aiming at – no less a thing than that. The immensity of the aim should not betray us into thinking that it cannot be achieved.

Extract from a report by the British Foreign Secretary to the British Cabinet in March 1948. The title of the report was 'The Threat to Civilisation'.

SOURCE 19

An American cartoon commenting on Stalin's take-over of eastern Europe. The bear represents the USSR.

As you can see from Figure 17 on page 89, by 1948 Greece and Czechoslovakia were the only eastern European countries not controlled by communist governments. It seemed to the Americans that not only Greece and Czechoslovakia but even Italy and France were vulnerable to communist take-over. Events in two of these countries were to have a decisive effect on America's policy towards Europe.

Greece, 1947

When the Germans retreated from Greece in 1944, there were two rival groups – the monarchists and the communists – who wanted to rule the country. Both had been involved in resistance against the Nazis. The communists wanted Greece to be a SOVIET REPUBLIC. The monarchists wanted the return of the king of Greece. Churchill sent British troops to Greece in 1945 supposedly to help restore order and supervise free elections. In fact, the British supported the monarchists and the king was returned to power.

In 1946, the USSR protested to the United Nations that British troops were a threat to peace in Greece. The United Nations took no action and so the communists tried to take control of Greece by force. A CIVIL WAR quickly developed. The British could not afford the cost of such a war and announced on 24 February 1947 that they were withdrawing their troops. Truman stepped in. Paid for by the Americans, some British troops stayed in Greece. They tried to prop up the king's government. By 1950 the royalists were in control of Greece, although they were a very weak government, always in crisis.

SOURCE 20

I believe that it must be the policy of the United States to support free peoples who are resisting attempted subjugation by armed minorities or by outside pressures ... The free peoples of the world look to us for support in maintaining those freedoms.

If we falter in our leadership, we may endanger the peace of the world.

President Truman speaking on 12 March 1947, explaining his decision to help Greece.

The Truman Doctrine

American intervention in Greece marked a new era in the USA's attitude to world politics, which became known as 'the Truman Doctrine' (see Source 20).

Under the Truman Doctrine, the USA was prepared to send money, equipment and advice to any country which was, in the American view, threatened by a communist take-over. Truman accepted that eastern Europe was now communist. His aim was to stop communism from spreading any further. This policy became known as CONTAINMENT.

The Marshall Plan

Truman believed that communism succeeded when people faced poverty and hardship. He sent the Secretary of State and former US Army general George Marshall to assess the economic state of Europe. What he found was a ruined economy (see Figure 21). The countries of Europe owed $11.5 billion to the USA. There were extreme shortages of all goods. Most countries were still rationing bread. There was such a coal shortage in the hard winter of 1947 that in Britain all electricity was turned off for a period each day. Churchill had described Europe as 'a rubble heap, a breeding ground of hate'.

FIGURE 21

Problems in post-war Europe: Homeless people; Refugees; Shortage of food and clothing; Cost of rebuilding damaged homes; Damage caused by war to infrastructure (roads, bridges, etc.); Debts from cost of war effort; Shortage of fuel.

Marshall suggested that about $17 billion would be needed to rebuild Europe's prosperity. 'Our policy', he said, 'is directed against hunger, poverty, desperation and chaos.'

In December 1947, Truman put his plan to Congress. For a short time, the American Congress refused to grant this money. Many Americans were becoming concerned by Truman's involvement in foreign affairs. Besides, $17 billion was a lot of money!

Czechoslovakia, 1948

Americans' attitude changed when the communists took over the government of Czechoslovakia. Czechoslovakia had been ruled by a coalition government which, although it included communists, had been trying to pursue policies independent of Moscow. The communists came down hard in March 1948. Anti-Soviet leaders were purged. One pro-American minister, Jan Masaryk, was found dead below his open window. The communists said he had jumped. The Americans suspected he'd been pushed. Immediately, Congress accepted the MARSHALL PLAN and made $17 billion available over a period of four years.

Think!

Explain in just 120 characters how events in
a) Greece
b) Czechoslovakia

affected American policy in Europe.

Think!

1. Draw a diagram to summarise the aims of Marshall Aid. Put political aims on one side and economic aims on the other. Draw arrows and labels to show how the two are connected.
2. Which of the problems in post-war Europe shown in Figure 21 do you think would be the most urgent for Marshall Aid to tackle? Explain your choice.

Marshall Aid

On the one hand, Marshall Aid was an extremely generous act by the American people. On the other hand, it was also motivated by American self-interest.

- The USA wanted to create new markets for American goods. The Americans remembered the disastrous effects of the DEPRESSION of the 1930s and Truman wanted to do all he could to prevent another worldwide slump.
- Many in the US Government argued that Aid should only be given to states which embraced democracy and free markets – in other words, a government and economy the USA would approve of. They wanted an 'Open Door' to these countries as the policy was called, with no trade TARIFFS or other restrictions to stop US companies.

Stalin viewed Marshall Aid with suspicion. After expressing some initial interest, he refused to have anything more to do with it. He also forbade any of the eastern European states to apply for Marshall Aid. Stalin's view was that the anticommunist aims behind Marshall Aid would weaken his hold on eastern Europe. He also felt that the USA was trying to dominate as many states as possible by making them dependent on dollars.

SOURCE 22

An American cartoon, 1949.

SOURCE 23

A Soviet cartoon commenting on Marshall Aid. Marshall's rope spells out the words 'Marshall Plan' and the lifebelt magnet is labelled 'Aid to Europe'.

Source Analysis

1. Do Sources 22 and 23 support or criticise Marshall Aid?
2. Do you think the sources give a fair impression of Marshall Aid? Explain your answer.

FOCUS TASK 4.3

How did the USA react to Soviet expansionism?

1. Work in pairs to write two accounts of US policy in Europe. One of you should write from the point of view of the Americans; the other should write from the point of view of the Soviets. The sources and text on pages 90–92 will help you.

   You should include reference to:
   a) US actions in the Greek Civil War in 1947
   b) the Truman Doctrine
   c) Soviet action in Czechoslovakia in 1948
   d) the Marshall Plan and Marshall Aid.

   As you consider each event, try to use it to make one side look reasonable or the other side unreasonable – or both!

2. Was the distrust between the USA and the USSR a problem of action (what each side is actually doing) or interpretation (how things are seen)?

Revision Tip

Stalin and Truman saw Marshall Aid differently. Try to sum up each view in a sentence.

The Berlin Blockade: causes and consequences

By 1948 the distrust between the USA and the USSR was alarming. The two sides actually increased their stocks of weapons. A propaganda war developed. Each side took every opportunity to denounce the policies or the plans of the other. Truman and Stalin were anxious to show each other and their own people that they would not be pushed around. Despite all the threatening talk, the two sides had never actually fired on one another. But in 1948 it looked like they might. The clash came over Germany.

FIGURE 24

The four zones of Germany in 1948.

The problem of Germany

After the war, Germany was divided into four zones (see Figure 24). At first the US plan, known as the Morgenthau Plan, was to remove all German industry and make it an agricultural country so it could never again wage a modern war. However, as Truman grew more concerned about the USSR, he decided that a strong Germany might be a useful ally. It was also clear that if German industries were not allowed to recover then millions of Germans would simply starve. In 1946, Britain, France and the USA combined their zones. This region became known as West Germany in 1949.

SOURCE 25

A Soviet cartoon from 1947. It shows (from left to right) the USA, Britain and France. The three sticks tied together are labelled 'American zone', 'British zone' and 'French zone'. The building is labelled 'Yalta and Potsdam Agreements'.

Source Analysis

Explain what Source 25 is saying about the actions of the USA, Britain and France in Germany in 1947.

Stalin blockades Berlin

Stalin felt he had to show Western leaders that he would fight back if they encroached on the Soviet 'sphere of influence'. Although Berlin was also divided into four zones, the city itself lay deep in the Soviet zone and was linked to the western areas by roads, railways and canals. In June 1948, Stalin blocked these supply lines, stopping the Western Powers reaching their zones of Berlin. If the USA tried to ram the roadblocks or railway blocks, it could be seen as an act of war. Stalin expected Truman to announce a humiliating withdrawal from Berlin, which would give the Soviets control of Berlin and a propaganda victory.

The Berlin airlift

The Americans believed that the situation in West Berlin was an important test case. If they gave in to Stalin on this issue and withdrew, the western zones of Germany might be next to fall to the communist USSR. Truman ordered that aircraft should fly supplies into Berlin. This was known as the BERLIN AIRLIFT. As the first planes took off from their bases in West Germany, everyone feared that the Soviets might shoot them down – an undeniable act of war. People waited anxiously as the planes flew over Soviet territory, but no shots were fired. For the next ten months, West Berlin received all the supplies it needed in this way – everything from food and clothing to building materials and oil. Stalin eventually lifted the BLOCKADE in May 1949.

Source Analysis

Explain why Source 26 is a useful source to historians investigating US policy on Berlin.

SOURCE 26

We refused to be forced out of the city of Berlin. We demonstrated to the people of Europe that we would act and act resolutely, when their freedom was threatened. Politically it brought the people of Western Europe closer to us. The Berlin blockade was a move to test our ability and our will to resist.

President Truman, speaking in 1949.

Consequences of the Berlin Blockade

The end of the Berlin Blockade did not end Cold War tensions. But it had several important consequences for Cold War relationships.

- **A powerful symbol:** Berlin became a powerful symbol of Cold War rivalry. From the US point of view, it was an oasis of democratic freedom in the middle of communist repression; from the Soviet point of view, it was a cancer growing in the workers' paradise of East Germany.
- **Cold War flashpoint:** Berlin was also a Cold War flashpoint. It was one of the few places where US and Soviet troops faced each other directly (and on a daily basis), and it would be vulnerable if the Soviets chose to act. Later in the Cold War, Berlin would become even more significant.
- **Cold War patterns of thinking and acting:** Despite the mistrust shown by the superpowers, the crisis in Berlin suggested that there would not be a direct war between them. There would be other types of conflict. Each side would never trust the other and would never accept that the other had a valid case or was acting responsibly or morally and would use propaganda to criticise the other side. They would fight 'proxy wars' – helping any state, group or individual opposed to the other side, no matter what that state, group or individual was like. There were also more formal alliances (see below).

SOURCE 27

Article 3: To achieve the aims of this Treaty, the Parties will keep up their individual and collective capacity to resist armed attack.

Article 5: The Parties agree that an armed attack against one or more of them in Europe or North America shall be considered an attack against them all.

Extracts from the NATO Charter.

Source Analysis
What evidence is there in Source 27 and Figure 28 to indicate that NATO was a purely defensive alliance?

Factfile

The Warsaw Pact and NATO membership in 1955

Warsaw Pact: Soviet Union; Albania; Bulgaria; Czechoslovakia; East Germany; Hungary; Poland; Romania

NATO: USA; Belgium; Canada; Denmark; France; West Germany; Greece; Iceland; Italy; Luxembourg; Netherlands; Norway; Portugal; Turkey; UK

Revision Tip
For the topic of the Berlin Blockade, aim to be able to explain (with examples):
- how the Allies started to rebuild Germany
- one reason this alarmed Stalin
- two important consequences of the blockade.

NATO and the Warsaw Pact

During the blockade, war between the USSR and the USA seemed a real possibility. At the height of the crisis, the Western Powers met in Washington DC and signed an agreement to work together. The new organisation, formed in April 1949, was known as NATO (North Atlantic Treaty Organization). Source 27 shows the main terms of the NATO charter. Although the USSR was critical of NATO, Stalin took no further action. However, when West Germany was allowed to join NATO in 1955, the new Soviet leader, Khrushchev, created a defensive alliance called the Warsaw Pact. This pact included the USSR and the main communist states in eastern Europe. Its members promised to defend each other if any one of them was attacked.

FIGURE 28

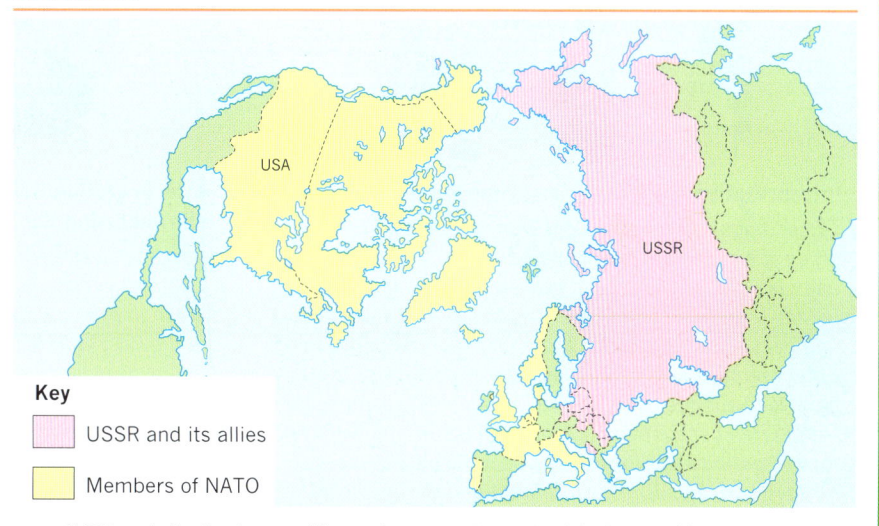

Key
- USSR and its allies
- Members of NATO

NATO and the Soviet satellites of eastern Europe. With the establishment of NATO, Europe was once again home to two hostile armed camps, just as it had been in 1914.

FOCUS TASK 4.4
What were the consequences of the Berlin Blockade?
Here are some consequences of the Berlin Blockade.
- The Soviet Union and the West both claimed a victory.
- The Western Allies set up a military alliance called NATO.
- Many Westerners left Berlin for good.
- The airlift showed the West's commitment to Berlin.
- The airlift kept Berlin working.
- Berlin became a symbol of Cold War tension.
- It ended the four-power administration of Germany and Berlin and split Germany into two blocs. Germany remained a divided country for 40 years.
- There was no fighting – the dispute ended peacefully.
- It heightened fear of the Soviet Union in the West.
- The airlift improved relations between Germans and the Allies (who had so recently been at war).

Write each consequence on a card. Then:
a) divide the cards into short-term and long-term consequences
b) choose two which you think are the most significant consequences and explain your choice.

FOCUS TASK 4.5

Who was more to blame for starting the Cold War: the United States or the USSR?

This is a highly controversial question which is still being debated today (as you can see from Interpretations A and B)!

Interpretation A: US historian Lynne Viola, writing in 2002.

The orthodox view of the Cold War greatly simplified the study of history for American audiences. There were enemies (them) and us and our friends. There were truth tellers (American historians) and there were liars (Soviet falsifiers). Best of all, there were no sources because no American historian could use a Soviet archive so it was very hard to challenge the view with evidence. As a consequence – and often because many American historians were either former politicians or wanted to become politicians – a great American success story unfolded as Americans and democracy were made to look very good indeed by their actions towards an unreasonable enemy.

Interpretation B: British historian Joseph Smith, summarising the Soviet view, 2001.

Soviet writers agreed on the importance of the Truman Doctrine in contributing to the conflict between East and West. In their opinion, American imperialism was the cause of the Cold War. After the Truman Doctrine was enunciated, Soviet news agencies criticised it as part of a calculated strategy to expand the capitalist system throughout Europe. The Marshall Plan was similarly condemned as an American plot to encircle the Soviet Union with hostile capitalist states. In addition, the United States was accused of endangering Soviet security by creating NATO and proceeding to remilitarise West Germany.

Work in small groups. Five people per group would be ideal.

You are going to investigate who was to blame for the Cold War. The possible verdicts you might reach are:

A The USA was most to blame.
B The USSR was most to blame.
C Both sides were equally to blame.
D No one was to blame. The Cold War was inevitable.

This is our suggested way of working.

1 Start by discussing the verdicts together. Is one more popular than another in your group? You will probably find it helpful to consider Interpretations A and B as well.
2 **a)** Each member of the group should research how one of the following factors helped to lead to the Cold War:
   – the situation before the end of the Second World War (pages 82–83)
   – the personal relationships between the various leaders (pages 85–87)
   – the conflicting beliefs of the superpowers (pages 82–83)
   – the war damage suffered by the USSR (pages 84 and 87)
   – Stalin's take-over of eastern Europe (pages 88–89)
   – Marshall Aid for Europe (pages 91–92)
   – the Berlin Blockade (pages 93–95).

   You can start with the page numbers given. You can introduce your own research from other books or the internet if you wish.
   b) Present your evidence to your group and explain which, if any, of the verdicts A–D your evidence most supports.
3 As a group, discuss which of the verdicts now seems most sensible.
4 Write a balanced essay on who was to blame, explaining why each verdict is a possibility but reaching your own conclusion about which is best. The verdicts A–D give you a possible structure for your essay. Write a paragraph on each verdict, selecting relevant evidence for your group discussion. A final paragraph can explain your overall conclusion.

Revision Tip

It is useful to think about big questions like 'who was most to blame...' but it is also useful to think about the role of specific factors so turn your research for question 2 of Focus Task 4.5 into revision cards and share them with your fellow students.

Keywords

Make sure you know these terms, people or events and are able to use them or describe them confidently.

- Atomic bomb
- Alliance
- Appeasement
- Berlin airlift
- Berlin Blockade
- Capitalism
- Cominform
- Communism
- Democracy
- Dictatorship
- Iron curtain
- Isolationism
- Marshall Aid
- Marshall Plan
- NATO
- Potsdam Conference
- Soviet sphere of influence
- Soviet Union
- Superpower
- Truman Doctrine
- West/The Western Powers
- Yalta Conference

Chapter Summary

Who was to blame for the Cold War?

1. The USSR was a communist country with a ONE-PARTY STATE; the USA was a capitalist democracy. They had very different ideas about how a country should be run and had been enemies throughout the 1930s. However, because they had a shared enemy (Hitler) they were allies during the Second World War.
2. When it was clear that Germany was going to be defeated their leaders met together at Yalta (in the USSR) to plan what would happen after the war. The US and Soviet leaders, Roosevelt and Stalin, appeared to get on well, although behind the scenes there were tensions and disagreements.
3. They agreed that after the war Germany (and its capital Berlin) would be divided into four sectors run by Britain, the USA, France and the USSR, and that eastern Europe would be a Soviet 'sphere of influence'.
4. After the war ended the countries met again at Potsdam in Germany but by this time much had changed: Roosevelt had been replaced as president by Truman; Stalin's troops were occupying most of eastern Europe; and the Americans had dropped an atomic bomb.
5. Relations between the USA and USSR quickly deteriorated and a Cold War started (a Cold War is the threat of war and deep mistrust but no outright fighting).
6. All the countries of eastern Europe elected or had forced on them a communist government that was allied to the USSR. The division between communist east and capitalist west became known as the iron curtain.
7. The USA wanted to stop communism spreading – the Truman Doctrine said that America would help any country that was resisting outside pressure (by which Truman meant communism). This marked a decisive end to US isolationism.
8. The USA offered financial help (Marshall Aid) to countries in western Europe to rebuild.
9. The USSR saw Marshall Aid and the Truman Doctrine as a threat to the USSR, which might lead to an attack on the USSR itself.
10. Berlin became the first focus of Cold War tension when it was blockaded by Stalin to prevent supplies getting into the US/British/French sectors. The Western allies responded with the Berlin airlift.

PRACTICE QUESTIONS

1. (a) What agreements were made at the Yalta Conference? **[4]**
   (b) Why was the Truman Doctrine important? **[6]**
   (c) 'The USA was more responsible than the USSR in causing the Cold War in the late 1940s.' How far do you agree with this statement? Explain your answer **[10]**

See pages 148–54 for advice on the different types of questions.

IS THIS TOMORROW

5 How effectively did the United States contain the spread of communism?

FOCUS POINTS

This key question will be explored through case studies of the following:
- ★ The United States and events in Korea, 1950–53
- ★ The United States and events in Cuba, 1959–62
- ★ American involvement in Vietnam, 1955–75

Although the USA was the world's most powerful nation, in 1950 it seemed to President Truman that events were not going America's way, particularly with regard to COMMUNISM.

- As you have seen in Chapter 4 most of eastern Europe had fallen under the influence of the communist USSR 1945–48.
- China became communist in 1949. The Americans had always regarded China as their strongest ally in the Far East. Between 1946 and 1949 they gave billions of dollars of aid to the Nationalist Government in China, largely to prevent a communist take-over. That had failed. Suddenly a massive new communist state had appeared on the map.
- Also in 1949 the Soviet leader STALIN announced that the USSR had developed its own ATOMIC BOMB. The USA was no longer the world's only nuclear power.
- Furthermore, American spies reported to President Truman that Stalin was using his network (Cominform) to help communists win power in Malaya, Indonesia, Burma, the Philippines and Korea. The USA had visions of the communists overrunning all of Asia, with country after country being toppled like a row of dominoes.

There was already strong anticommunist feeling in the USA. These developments made it stronger. There was no doubt in the minds of American leaders (indeed most American people) that this spread should be resisted. If they could have done, they would have liked to turn back the communist advances but that was unrealistic. So from 1947 onwards the USA followed the policy of CONTAINMENT – holding back communism so it did not spread any further. But as the 1950s dawned this looked like a serious challenge.

In this chapter you will investigate:
- the different methods the USA used to try to contain the spread of communism
- how successful these methods were during the Korean War, the Cuban Missile Crisis and the Vietnam War – using the case studies to make up your own mind.

← This is the cover of a comic book published in the USA in 1947.
1. What impression does this comic cover give you of:
   a) the USA?
   b) communism?
2. What is the message of this picture?

Think!

The situation in Korea has sometimes been compared to the situation in Germany in 1945 (which you studied in Chapter 4). Explain:
a) how these situations were similar
b) how they were different.

Case study 1: The Korean War

Origins

Outbreak of the Korean War

Korea had been ruled by Japan until 1945. At the end of the Second World War the northern half was liberated by Soviet troops and the southern half by Americans. When the war ended:

- **the North** remained communist-controlled, with a communist leader who had been trained in the USSR, and with a Soviet-style one-party system
- **the South** was anticommunist. It was not very democratic, but the fact that it was anticommunist was enough to win it the support of the USA.

There was bitter hostility between the North's communist leader, Kim Il Sung, and Syngman Rhee, president of South Korea. REUNIFICATION did not seem likely. In 1950 this hostility spilled over into open warfare. North Korean troops overwhelmed the South's forces. By September 1950 all except a small corner of south-east Korea was under communist control (see Figure 5, map 1).

The US response

As you have already seen in Chapter 4, US President Truman was determined to contain communism – to stop it spreading further. In his view, Korea was a glaring example of how communism would spread if the USA did nothing (see Source 1). Containment was the aim, but there were different ways to achieve this aim. Truman's attitude was that the USA would do anything (short of all-out war) to stop the spread of communism.

President Truman immediately sent advisers, supplies and warships to the seas around Korea. However, he was aware that if he was going to take military action it would look better to the rest of the world if he had the support of other countries, especially if he had the support of the UNITED NATIONS. In fact, the ideal situation would be a UN intervention in the Korean War rather than an American one.

United Nations Resolution 84

Truman put enormous pressure on the UN Security Council to condemn the actions of the North Koreans and to call on them to withdraw their troops. The USA was the biggest single contributor to the UN BUDGET and was therefore in a powerful position to influence its decisions. However, this did not mean the USA always got its own way and it would probably have failed this time except for some unusual circumstances.

In the Cold War atmosphere of 1950, each SUPERPOWER always denounced and opposed the other. Normally, in a dispute such as this, the SOVIET UNION would have used its right of veto to block the call for action by the UN. However, the USSR was BOYCOTTING the UN at this time over another issue (whether communist China should be allowed to join the UN). So when the resolution was passed, the USSR was not even at the meeting so could not use its veto. So Truman was able to claim that this was a UN-sponsored operation, even if Soviet newspapers and other media claimed that the decision was not valid.

Under the resolution (see Source 2) the UN committed itself to using its members' armies to drive North Korean troops out of South Korea. Eighteen states provided troops or support of some kind. These were mostly allies of the USA and included Britain. However, by far the largest part of the UN force was American. The commander, General MacArthur, was also American.

SOURCE 1

Korea is a symbol to the watching world. If we allow Korea to fall within the Soviet orbit, the world will feel we have lost another round in our match with the Soviet Union, and our prestige and the hopes of those who place their faith in us will suffer accordingly.

The US State Department, 1950.

SOURCE 2

The UN will render such assistance to the republic of Korea as may be necessary to restore international peace and security to the area.

Resolution 84 passed by the United Nations in 1950.

SOURCE 3

If the UN is ever going to do anything, this is the time, and if the UN cannot bring the crisis in Korea to an end then we might as well just wash up the United Nations and forget it.

American Senator Tom Connally speaking in 1950. He was a Republican and strongly anticommunist.

Development

September 1950 – the UN force advances

United Nations forces stormed ashore at Inchon in September 1950 (see Figure 5, map 2). At the same time, other UN forces and South Korean troops advanced from Pusan. The North Koreans were driven back beyond their original border (the 38th parallel) within weeks.

SOURCE 4

Source Analysis

Source 4 makes a comparison with earlier events you may have studied in this book – see Chapter 2. Use that knowledge to write a 100-word explanation of the message of this cartoon for someone who does not know anything about the League of Nations.

A cartoon by David Low, 1950.

FIGURE 5

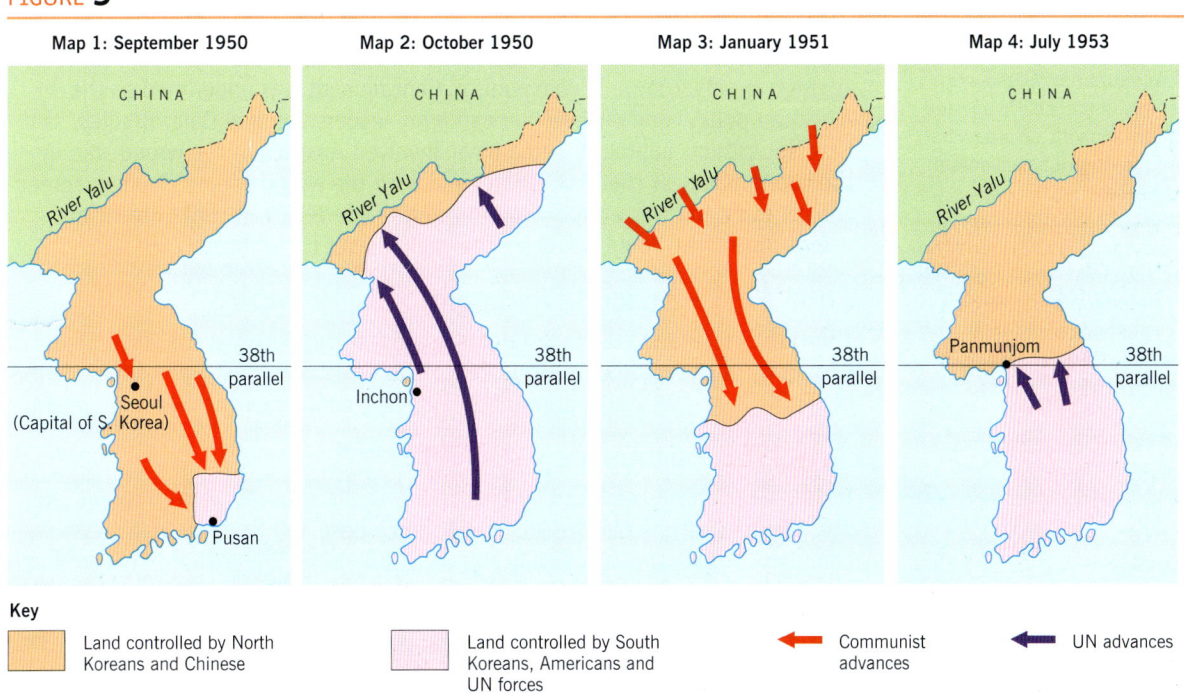

Map 1: September 1950
Map 2: October 1950
Map 3: January 1951
Map 4: July 1953

Key
- Land controlled by North Koreans and Chinese
- Land controlled by South Koreans, Americans and UN forces
- Communist advances
- UN advances

The 38th parallel was the border between North and South Korea from 1945 to June 1950.

The Korean War, 1950–53.

How effectively did the United States contain the spread of communism?

SOURCE 6

Had they [the Chinese] intervened in the first or second months it would have been decisive, [but] we are no longer fearful of their intervention. Now that we have bases for our Air Force in Korea, there would be the greatest slaughter.

General MacArthur speaking in October 1950.

Profile

General Douglas MacArthur (1880–1964)

- Born 1880. His father was a successful army leader.
- Trained at West Point, the top American military academy.
- Fought in the First World War. Became the youngest commander in the American army in France. Received 13 medals for bravery.
- During the Second World War he was the commander of the war against the Japanese. He devised the 'island-hopping' strategy that allowed the Americans to defeat the Japanese.
- In 1945 he personally accepted the Japanese surrender, and from 1945 to 1951 he virtually controlled Japan, helping the shattered country get back on its feet.
- He was aged 70 when he was given command of the UN forces in Korea.
- He tried unsuccessfully to run for US president in 1952.

SOURCE 7

Even the reports to the UN were censored by [American] state and defence departments. I had no connection with the United Nations whatsoever.

From General MacArthur's memoirs.

October 1950 – the UN force presses on

MacArthur had quickly achieved the original UN aim of removing North Korean troops from South Korea. But the Americans did not stop. Despite warnings from China's leader, Mao Tse-tung, that if they pressed on China would join the war, the UN approved a plan to advance into North Korea.

By October, US forces had reached the Yalu River and the border with China (see Figure 5, map 2). The nature of the war had now changed. It was clear that MacArthur and Truman were after a bigger prize, one which went beyond containment. As the UN forces advanced and secured their positions (see Source 6), Truman and MacArthur saw an opportunity to remove communism from Korea entirely. Even Mao's warnings were not going to put them off.

November 1950 – the UN force retreats

MacArthur underestimated the power of the Chinese. Late in October 1950, 200,000 Chinese troops (calling themselves 'People's Volunteers') joined the North Koreans. They launched a blistering attack. They had soldiers who were strongly committed to communism and had been taught by their leader to hate the Americans. They had modern tanks and planes supplied by the Soviet Union. The United Nations forces were pushed back into South Korea.

Conditions were some of the worst the American forces had known, with treacherous cold and blinding snowstorms in the winter of 1950–51. The Chinese forces were more familiar with fighting in the jagged mountains, forested ravines and treacherous swamps – as the landscape was similar to many areas of China.

April 1951 – MacArthur is sacked

At this point, Truman and MacArthur fell out. MacArthur wanted to carry on the war. He was ready to invade China and even use nuclear weapons if necessary. Truman, on the other hand, felt that saving South Korea was good enough. Communism had been contained. The risks of starting a war that might bring in the USSR were too great, and so an attack on China was ruled out.

However, in March 1951 MacArthur blatantly ignored the UN instruction and openly threatened an attack on China. In April Truman removed MacArthur from his position as commander and brought him back home. He rejected MacArthur's aggressive policy towards communism. Containment was underlined as the American policy. One of the American army leaders, General Omar Bradley, said that MacArthur's approach would have 'involved America in the wrong war, in the wrong place, at the wrong time, and with the wrong enemy'. Truman agreed with Bradley and was effectively returning to the policy of containment and accepting that he could not drive the communists out of North Korea.

June 1951 – peace talks begin

The fighting finally reached stalemate around the 38th parallel (see Figure 5, map 4) in the middle of 1951. Peace talks between North and South Korea began in June 1951, although bitter fighting continued for two more years.

July 1953 – armistice

In 1952 Truman was replaced by President Eisenhower, who wanted to end the war. Stalin's death in March 1953 made the Chinese and North Koreans less confident. An ARMISTICE was finally signed in July 1953. The border between North and South Korea was much the same as it had been before war started in 1950.

> **Think!**
> Use the text on pages 100–02 to write some extra bullet points for the Profile describing:
> a) MacArthur's personality and beliefs
> b) his actions in Korea.

Consequences of the Korean War

The casualties on all sides were enormous – but particularly among civilians (see Figure 8 and Source 9).

FIGURE 8

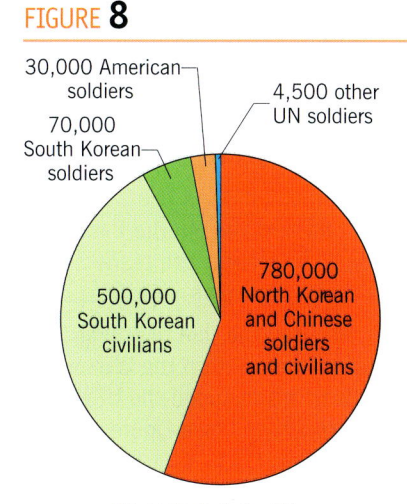

- 30,000 American soldiers
- 4,500 other UN soldiers
- 70,000 South Korean soldiers
- 500,000 South Korean civilians
- 780,000 North Korean and Chinese soldiers and civilians

Total killed: 1.4 million

Civilian and military deaths in the Korean War. American military deaths per year of conflict were actually higher than the Vietnam War.

SOURCE 9

Civilian casualty in the early stages of the Korean War as South Koreans fled from the advancing North Koreans.

A success for containment?

In one sense the Korean War was a success for the USA. The cost and the casualties were high but it showed that the USA had the will and the means to contain communism. South Korea remained out of communist hands.

On the other hand it showed the limits of the policy. The USA had to accept that North Korea remained communist. It also highlighted tensions among American leaders. Hardline anticommunist politicians and military leaders wanted to go beyond containment – to push back communism. They thought that Truman had shown weakness in not going for outright victory. More moderate politicians and commanders argued that this would not be worth the risk.

These tensions would affect US policy over the coming decades, and North Korea would continue to trouble the USA long after the Cold War ended. With support from China, North Korea developed into a hardline communist DICTATORSHIP and eventually became a nuclear power, threatening the USA's allies Japan and South Korea.

FOCUS TASK 5.1

Was the Korean War a success for containment?

Draw up your own copy of this table. You will use it to compare the three case studies. At this stage, just focus on the Korean War. You are going to revisit this task at the end of the Cuban Missile Crisis and the Vietnam War as well. We have started it off for you. Your completed chart will be a useful revision tool.

Case study	Why were the Americans worried?	What methods did the Americans use to contain communism?	What problems did they face?	What was the outcome?	Success or failure (out of 10) with reasons supported by evidence
Korea	Communist North Korea invaded capitalist South Korea				

SOURCE 10

We shall never have a secure peace and a happy world so long as Soviet Communism dominates one-third of all the world's people and is in the process of trying to extend its rule to many others. Therefore we must have in mind the liberation of these captive peoples. Now liberation does not mean war. Liberation can be achieved by processes short of war.

J.F. Dulles, US Secretary of State, speaking on his appointment in 1952.

Methods of containment

There was no doubt at all in the minds of American leaders that communism had to be resisted. The question was how to do it. The Korean War showed the Americans that they could not just send their soldiers to fight a war whenever they saw a problem (see Source 10). It was too expensive and it did not really work very well. Instead American policy focused on two other methods of containment: building ALLIANCES and developing ever more powerful weapons.

Alliances with anticommunist countries

The USA created a network of anticommunist alliances around the world: SEATO in South East Asia and CENTO in Central Asia and the Middle East. The USA gave money, advice and arms to these allies. In return, the leaders of these countries suppressed communist influence in their own countries.

The USSR saw these alliances as aggressive. They accused the USA of trying to encircle the communist world. In 1955 the Soviet Union set up the Warsaw Treaty Organisation, better known as the WARSAW PACT. This included the USSR and all the communist east European countries except Yugoslavia (see Figure 11).

FIGURE 11

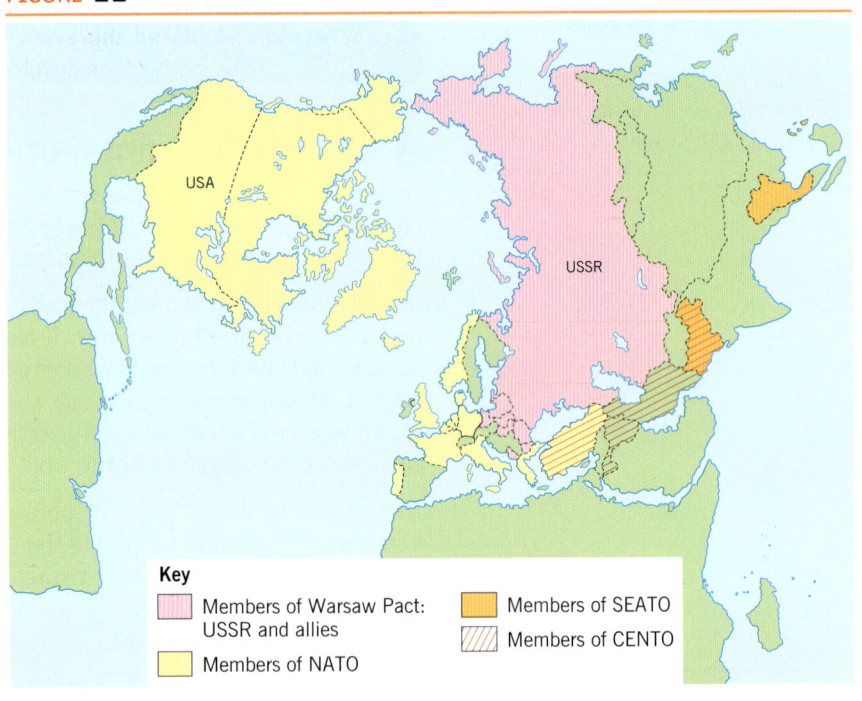

Key
- Members of Warsaw Pact: USSR and allies
- Members of NATO
- Members of SEATO
- Members of CENTO

Membership of the organisations allied to the USA and USSR in 1955.

Building more powerful nuclear weapons

The Americans had developed their first atomic bomb in 1945. They did not share the secret of their bomb with the USSR, even while they were still allies. When the USA dropped the first bombs on Hiroshima and Nagasaki in August 1945, 70,000 people were killed instantly. The awesome power of the explosions and the incredible destruction caused by the bombs made Japan surrender within a week. It was clear to the USA that atomic bombs were the weapons of the future. Just threatening to use such weapons could help contain communism.

The same was clear to the USSR! The result was an ARMS RACE to build ever more powerful weapons and to place them where they could best threaten your enemy. This was to prove a key factor in our next case study: the Cuban Missile Crisis.

Revision Tip

Make sure you can remember:
- one example of the USA creating an alliance to contain communism
- one example of it using the threat of nuclear weapons to try to contain communism.

Case study 2: The Cuban Missile Crisis

For many historians – and people at the time – the Cuban Missile Crisis was the most serious incident in the Cold War. To understand why, we need to look closely at Cold War tensions at the time and particularly the nuclear 'arms race'.

Origins of the Cuban Missile Crisis

The arms race and nuclear deterrence

Through the 1960s the USA and the USSR were locked in a nuclear arms race. Each side developed ever bigger, more deadly and more flexible weapons. They both spent vast amounts of money on new weapons.

They spied on one another to steal technological secrets. The USSR tended to use spies. The USA favoured hi-tech spying such as the U2 plane – a plane which flew so high it could not be shot down but took incredibly detailed photos of the ground.

Each side perfected nuclear bombs that could be launched from submarines or planes. The USA placed short-range nuclear weapons in Turkey (one of their CENTO allies). Both sides developed ICBMs, which could travel from continent to continent in half an hour.

By the early 1960s both sides had enough nuclear weapons to destroy the other side. The USA had more than the USSR, but the advantage did not really matter because both sides had enough to destroy each other many times over. On each side the theory was that such weapons made them more secure. The 'NUCLEAR DETERRENT' meant the enemy would not dare attack first, because it knew that, if it did, the other would strike back before its bombs had even landed and it too would be destroyed. This policy also became known as MAD (Mutually Assured Destruction). Surely no side would dare strike first when it knew the attack would destroy itself too.

The Cuban Revolution

Cuba is a large island just 160 km from Florida in the southern USA. It had long been an American ally. Americans owned most of the businesses on the island and they had a huge naval base there (see Figure 18 on page 108). The Americans also provided the Cuban ruler, General Batista, with economic and military support. Batista was a DICTATOR. His rule was corrupt and unpopular. The Americans supported Batista primarily because he was just as opposed to communism as they were.

Source Analysis

How far do Sources 12 and 13 agree about Cuba's relationship with the USA before the revolution?

SOURCE 12

We considered it part of the United States practically, just a wonderful little country over there that was of no danger to anybody, as a matter of fact it was a rather important economic asset to the United States.

American TV reporter Walter Cronkite.

SOURCE 13

I believe there is no country in the world ... whose economic colonisation, humiliation and exploitation were worse than in Cuba, partly as a consequence of US policy during the Batista regime. I believe that, without being aware of it, we conceived and created the Castro movement, starting from scratch.

President Kennedy speaking in 1963.

Enter Fidel Castro

There was plenty of opposition to Batista in Cuba itself. In 1959, after a three-year campaign, Fidel Castro overthrew Batista. Castro was charming, clever and also ruthless. He quickly killed, arrested or exiled many political opponents. Castro was also a clever propagandist. He was very charismatic and he had a vision for a better Cuba, which won over the majority of Cubans.

The USA was taken by surprise at first and decided to recognise Castro as the new leader of Cuba. However, within a short period of time relations between the two countries grew worse. There were two important reasons:

- There were thousands of Cuban exiles in the USA who had fled from Castro's rule. They formed powerful pressure groups demanding action against Castro.
- Castro took over some American-owned businesses in Cuba, particularly agricultural businesses. He took their land and distributed it to his supporters among Cuba's PEASANT farmer population.

The USA responds

As early as June 1960, US President Eisenhower authorised the US Central Intelligence Agency (CIA) to investigate ways of overthrowing Castro. The CIA provided support and funds to Cuban exiles. It also investigated ways to disrupt the Cuban economy, such as damaging sugar plantations. American companies working in Cuba refused to co-operate with any Cuban businesses that used oil or other materials which had been imported from the USSR. The American media also broadcast a relentless stream of criticism of Castro and his regime (see Source 15 for example).

Castro responded to US hostility with a mixed approach. He assured Americans living in Cuba that they were safe and he allowed the USA to keep its naval base. He said he simply wanted to run Cuba without interference. However, by the summer of 1960 he had allied Cuba with the Soviet Union. Soviet leader Khrushchev signed a trade agreement giving Cuba $100 million in economic aid. Castro also began receiving arms from the Soviet Union and American spies knew this.

> **Source Analysis**
>
> 1 Apart from the caption in Russian, how else can you tell that the cartoon in Source 14 is a Soviet cartoon?
> 2 What is the cartoonist's view of the situation?

SOURCE 14

A 1960 Soviet cartoon. The notice held by the US Secretary of State says to Castro in Cuba: 'I forbid you to make friends with the Soviet Union.'

Factfile

Bay of Pigs invasion

- Cuban exiles were funded and trained by the CIA and supported by US air power.
- The plan was originally devised by President Eisenhower's Government but Kennedy approved it when he became president. Training began in April 1960. The invasion took place on 17 April 1961.
- Cuban security services knew that the invasion was coming.
- The invasion was a complete failure. US INTELLIGENCE, which stated that Cuban people would rebel against Castro, proved to be wrong.

Kennedy ordered extensive investigations into the disaster. Key failings were identified:

- lack of secrecy so that USA could not deny its involvement
- poor links between various US departments
- failure to organise resistance inside Cuba
- insufficient Spanish-speaking staff.

'The Bay of Pigs' invasion

In January 1961 the USA's new president, John F Kennedy, broke off DIPLOMATIC RELATIONS with Cuba. Castro thought that the USA was preparing to invade his country. He was right. Kennedy was no longer prepared to tolerate a Soviet satellite in the USA's 'sphere of influence'. However, the Americans did not want to invade directly. Instead President Kennedy put into action a plan that had been devised under Eisenhower. He supplied arms, equipment and transport for 1400 anti-Castro exiles to invade Cuba intending to overthrow Castro.

In April 1961 the exiles landed at the BAY OF PIGS (see Factfile). The invasion failed disastrously. They were met by 20,000 Cuban troops, armed with tanks and modern weapons. Castro captured or killed them all within days.

The impact of the invasion

The half-hearted invasion suggested to Cuba and the Soviet Union that, despite its opposition to communism in Cuba, the USA was unwilling to get directly involved in Cuba. The Soviet leader Khrushchev was scornful of Kennedy's pathetic attempt to oust communism from Cuba.

Historians too argue that the Bay of Pigs fiasco further strengthened Castro's position in Cuba. It suggested to the USSR that Kennedy was weak (see Source 16). It also made Castro and Khrushchev very suspicious of US policy.

SOURCE 15

By October 1962 the historic friendship between Cuba and the USA was gone. Behind this change was the story of the betrayal of the Cuban people. It began with Fidel Castro triumphantly entering Havana in 1959. Castro promised democracy and freedom and for a time it appeared to most Cubans that they were liberated. But it soon became apparent that Castro had sold out to Premier Khrushchev of the Communists.

Commentary from an American TV programme made in 1962.

SOURCE 16

I think he [Khrushchev] did it [was so aggressive in the meeting] because of the Bay of Pigs. He thought that anyone who was so young and inexperienced as to get into that mess could be beaten; and anyone who got into it and didn't see it through had no guts. So he just beat the hell out of me.

If he thinks I'm inexperienced and have no guts, until we remove those ideas we won't get anywhere with him.

Kennedy speaking after a meeting with Khrushchev in 1961.

Source Analysis
How reliable is this source?

FOCUS TASK 5.2

How did the USA react to the Cuban revolution?

1. The President has asked his advisers how he should deal with Cuba. Here are some suggestions they might have made:

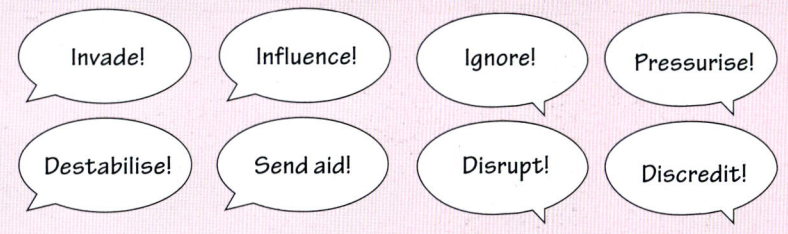

   Invade!   Influence!   Ignore!   Pressurise!

   Destabilise!   Send aid!   Disrupt!   Discredit!

   Record examples you can find of the USA doing any of these things. If you find examples of American actions that are not covered by these words record them too.

2. Place these actions on a 'containment continuum' like this:

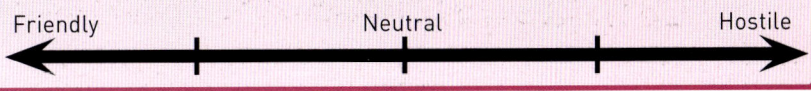

   Friendly —————— Neutral —————— Hostile

Revision Tip

From these two pages you should make sure you remember:

- one reason why the USA disliked Castro's Government
- how the USA initially tried to contain communism on Cuba.

5 How effectively did the United States contain the spread of communism?

The October crisis

Khrushchev arms Castro

After the Bay of Pigs fiasco, Soviet arms flooded into Cuba. In May 1962 the Soviet Union announced publicly for the first time that it was supplying Cuba with arms. By July 1962 Cuba had the best-equipped army in Latin America. By September it had thousands of Soviet missiles, plus patrol boats, tanks, radar vans, missile erectors, jet bombers, jet fighters and 5000 Soviet technicians to help maintain the weapons.

The Americans watched all this with great alarm. They seemed ready to tolerate conventional arms being supplied to Cuba, but the big question was whether the Soviet Union would dare to put nuclear missiles on Cuba. In September Kennedy's own Intelligence Department said that it did not believe the USSR would send nuclear weapons to Cuba. The USSR had not taken this step with any of its SATELLITE STATES before and the US Intelligence Department believed that the USSR would consider it too risky to do it in Cuba. On 11 September, Kennedy warned the USSR that he would prevent 'by whatever means might be necessary' Cuba becoming an offensive military base – by which, everyone knew, he meant a base for nuclear missiles. The same day the USSR assured the USA that it had no need to put nuclear missiles on Cuba and no intention of doing so.

The US discovers nuclear sites

On Sunday, 14 October 1962, an American spy plane flew over Cuba. It took amazingly detailed photographs of missile sites in Cuba. Despite the USSR's reassurances that they did not intend to provide nuclear missiles to Cuba, to the military experts two things were obvious: these *were* nuclear missile sites, and they *were* being built by the USSR.

More photo reconnaissance followed over the next two days. This confirmed that some sites were nearly finished but others were still being built. Some were already supplied with missiles, others were awaiting them. The experts said that the most developed of the sites could be ready to launch missiles in just seven days. American spy planes also reported that twenty Soviet ships were currently on the way to Cuba carrying missiles.

SOURCE 17

[Estimates were that the] missiles had an atomic warhead [power] of about half the current missile capacity of the entire Soviet Union. The photographs indicated that missiles were directed at certain American cities. The estimate was that within a few minutes of their being fired 80 million Americans would be dead.

President Kennedy's brother, Robert Kennedy, describing events on Thursday 18 October in the book he wrote about the crisis, *13 Days*.

FIGURE 18

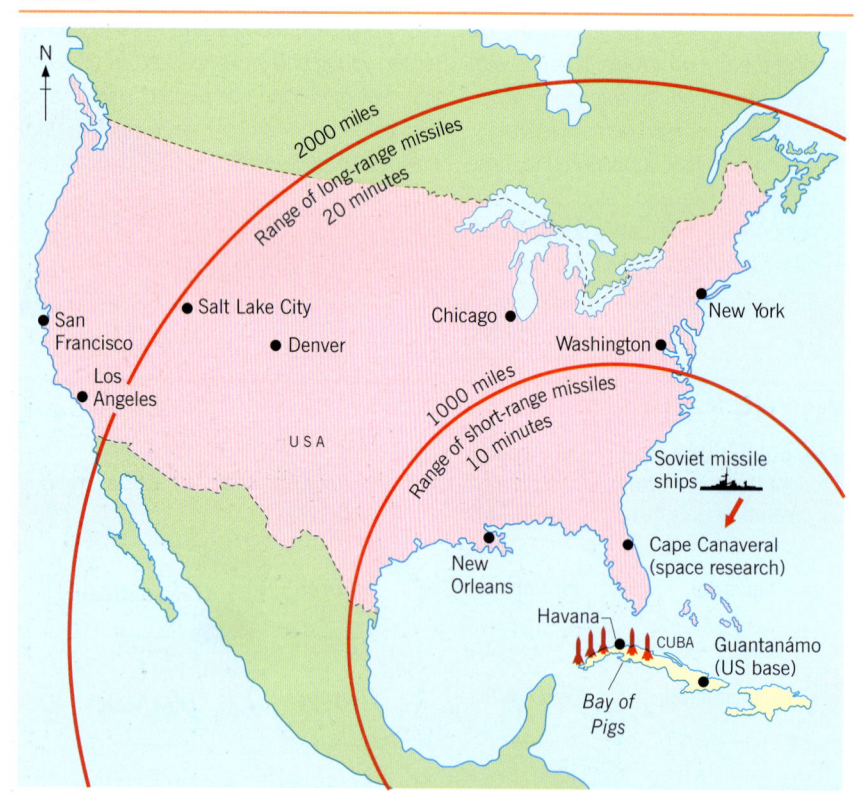

Map showing the location of Cuba and the range of the Cuban missiles.

ACTIVITY

How should President Kennedy deal with the Cuban crisis?

On Tuesday 16 October, President Kennedy was informed of the discovery. He formed a special team of advisers called Ex Comm. They came up with several choices.

Work in groups. You are advisers to the President. You have to reduce Ex Comm's five options to just two for the President to choose between. When you have made your decision explain why you have rejected the three you have.

Option 1 Do nothing?

For: The Americans still had a vastly greater nuclear power than the Soviet Union. The USA could still destroy the Soviet Union, so – the argument went – the USSR would never use these missiles. The biggest danger to world peace would be to overreact to this discovery.

Against: The USSR had lied about Cuban missiles. Kennedy had already issued his solemn warning to the USSR. To do nothing would be another sign of weakness.

Option 2 Surgical air attack?

An immediate selected air attack to destroy the nuclear bases themselves.

For: It would destroy the missiles before they were ready to use.

Against:
1. Destruction of all sites could not be guaranteed. Even one left undamaged could launch a counter-attack against the USA.
2. The attack would inevitably kill Soviet soldiers. The Soviet Union might retaliate at once.
3. To attack without advance warning was seen as immoral.

Option 3 Invasion?

All-out invasion of Cuba by air and sea.

For: An invasion would not only get rid of the missiles but Castro as well. The American forces were already trained and available to do it.

Against: It would almost certainly guarantee an equivalent Soviet response, either to protect Cuba, or within the SOVIET SPHERE OF INFLUENCE – for example, a take-over of Berlin.

Option 4 Diplomatic pressures?

To get the United Nations or other body to intervene and negotiate.

For: It would avoid conflict.

Against: If the USA was forced to back down, it would be a sign of weakness.

Option 5 Blockade?

A ban on the Soviet Union bringing in any further military supplies to Cuba, enforced by the US navy who would stop and search Soviet ships. And a call for the Soviet Union to withdraw what was already there.

For: It would show that the USA was serious, but it would not be a direct act of war. It would put the burden on Khrushchev to decide what to do next. The USA had a strong navy and could still take the other options if this one did not work.

Against: It would not solve the main problem – the missiles were already on Cuba. They could be used within one week. The Soviet Union might retaliate by blockading Berlin as it had done in 1948.

Tue 16 October ....

What happened next?

President Kennedy was informed of the missile build-up. Ex Comm formed.

Sat 20 October ....
Kennedy decided on a BLOCKADE of Cuba.

Mon 22 October ....
Kennedy announced the blockade and called on the Soviet Union to withdraw its missiles. He addressed the American people:

SOURCE 19

Source Analysis

1 What words and phrases in Source 19 reveal how serious Kennedy believed the situation was in October 1962?
2 Kennedy was renowned as a skilled communicator. How did he convince his audience that he was in the right?

Good Evening, My Fellow Citizens:

Within the past week, unmistakable evidence has established the fact that a series of offensive missile sites is now in preparation on Cuba.

... Acting, therefore, in the defence of our own security and of the entire Western Hemisphere, and under the authority entrusted to me by the Constitution, I have directed that the following initial steps be taken immediately:

First: a strict quarantine on all offensive military equipment under shipment to Cuba ... Second: continued and increased close SURVEILLANCE of Cuba ... Third: we will regard any nuclear missile launched from Cuba against any nation in the Western Hemisphere as an attack on the United States, requiring a full retaliatory response upon the Soviet Union.

Extract from President Kennedy's TV broadcast to the American people on 22 October 1962.

Tue 23 October ....
Kennedy received a letter from Khrushchev saying that Soviet ships would not observe the blockade. Khrushchev did not admit the presence of nuclear missiles on Cuba.

Wed 24 October ....
The blockade began. The first missile-carrying ships, accompanied by a Soviet submarine, approached the 500-mile (800-km) blockade zone. Then suddenly, at 10.32 a.m., the twenty Soviet ships which were closest to the zone stopped or turned around.

SOURCE 20

Source Analysis

1 Source 20 is a British cartoon. Pretend you did not know this. Explain why it is unlikely to be an American or Soviet cartoon.
2 What is its attitude to the two sides in the crisis?

"INTOLERABLE HAVING YOUR ROCKETS ON MY DOORSTEP!"

A cartoon by Vicky (Victor Weisz) from the *London Evening Standard*, 24 October 1962.

Thu 25 October	**Despite the Soviet ships turning around,** intensive aerial photography revealed that work on the missile bases in Cuba was proceeding rapidly.
Fri 26 October	**Kennedy received a long personal letter from Khrushchev.** The letter claimed that the missiles on Cuba were purely defensive, but went on: 'If assurances were given that the USA would not participate in an attack on Cuba and the blockade was lifted, then the question of the removal or the destruction of the missile sites would be an entirely different question.' This was the first time Khrushchev had admitted the presence of the missiles.
Sat 27 October a.m.	**Khrushchev sent a second letter** – revising his proposals – saying that the condition for removing the missiles from Cuba was that the USA withdraw its missiles from Turkey. **An American U-2 plane was shot down** over Cuba. The pilot was killed. The President was advised to launch an immediate reprisal attack on Cuba.
Sat 27 October p.m.	**Kennedy decided to delay** an attack. He also decided to ignore the second Khrushchev letter, but accepted the terms suggested by Khrushchev on 26 October. He said that if the Soviet Union did not withdraw, an attack would follow.

SOURCE 21

It was a beautiful autumn evening, the height of the crisis, and I went up to the open air to smell it, because I thought it was the last Saturday I would ever see.

Robert McNamara talking about the evening of 27 October 1962. McNamara was one of Kennedy's closest advisers during the Cuban Crisis.

Sun 28 October	**Khrushchev replied to Kennedy:** 'In order to eliminate as rapidly as possible the conflict which endangers the cause of peace ... the Soviet Government has given a new order to dismantle the arms which you described as offensive and to crate and return them to the Soviet Union.'

SOURCE 22

A cartoon from the British newspaper, the *Daily Mail*.

Source Analysis

1. Does Source 22 give the impression that either Khrushchev or Kennedy has the upper hand?
2. Explain whether you think the events of the crisis on these pages support that view.

Think!

Kennedy described Wednesday 24 October and Saturday 27 October as the darkest days of the crisis. Use the information on these pages to explain why.

5 *How effectively did the United States contain the spread of communism?*

Why did the Soviet Union place nuclear missiles on Cuba?

It was an incredibly risky strategy. The USSR had supplied many of its allies with CONVENTIONAL WEAPONS but this was the first time that any Soviet leader had placed nuclear weapons outside Soviet territory. Why did Khrushchev take such an unusual step? He must have known that it would cause a crisis. What's more, the Soviets and Cubans made no attempt at all to camouflage the sites, and even allowed the missiles to travel on open deck. This has caused much debate as to what Khrushchev was really doing. Historians have suggested various possible explanations.

To bargain with the USA
If Khrushchev had missiles on Cuba, he could agree to remove them in return for some American concessions.

To test the USA
In the strained atmosphere of Cold War politics the missiles were designed to see how strong the Americans really were – whether they would back off or face up.

To trap the USA
Khrushchev wanted the Americans to find them and be drawn into a nuclear war. He did not even try to hide them.

To close the missile gap
Khrushchev was so concerned about the MISSILE GAP between the USSR and the USA that he would seize any opportunity he could to close it. With missiles on Cuba it was less likely that the USA would ever launch a 'first strike' against the USSR.

To defend Cuba
Cuba was the only communist state in the Western Hemisphere, and it had willingly become communist rather than having become communist as a result of invasion by the USSR. In addition, Cuba was in 'Uncle Sam's backyard'. As Castro himself put it: 'The imperialist cannot forgive that we have made a socialist revolution under the nose of the United States.' Just by existing, Castro's Cuba was excellent PROPAGANDA for the USSR.

To strengthen his own position in the USSR
The superiority of the USA in nuclear missiles undermined Khrushchev's credibility inside the USSR. His critics pointed out that he was the one who had urged the USSR to rely on nuclear missiles. Now, could he show that the USSR really was a nuclear power?

Think!
1. Which of the explanations above do Sources 23 and 24 support?
2. Talking in private Khrushchev called the missiles 'a hedgehog in Uncle Sam's pants'. Which of the explanations does this statement support?
3. Which explanation do you think Khrushchev's actions on 26 and 27 October support (see page 111)?
4. Choose the explanation(s) that you think best fits what you have found out about the crisis. Explain your choice.

SOURCE 23

From the territory of the Soviet Union, the medium-range missiles couldn't possibly reach the territory of the USA, but deployed on Cuba they would become strategic nuclear weapons. That meant in practical terms we had a chance to narrow the differences between our forces.

General Anatoly Gribkov, commander, Soviet forces, Cuba.

SOURCE 24

In addition to protecting Cuba, our missiles would have equalized what the West likes to call the 'balance of power'. The Americans had surrounded our country with military bases and threatened us with nuclear weapons, and now they would learn just what it feels like to have enemy missiles pointing at you …

Khrushchev writing in his memoirs in 1971.

Outcomes of the Cuban Missile Crisis...

...for Kennedy and the USA

- Kennedy came out of the crisis with a greatly improved reputation in his own country and throughout the West. He had stood up to Khrushchev and made him back down.
- Kennedy had also resisted the hardliners in his own Government. They had wanted the USA to invade Cuba – to turn back communism. However, the crisis highlighted the weakness of their case. Such intervention was not worth the high risk.
- On the other hand, he did secretly agree to remove the missiles from Turkey. This was awkward for him as the decision to remove them should have been a decision for NATO. His NATO allies were unhappy that Kennedy had traded them during the crisis but accepted this was better than a nuclear war.
- Kennedy also had to accept that Castro's Cuba would remain a communist state in America's backyard.

...for Khrushchev and the USSR

- In public Khrushchev was able to highlight his role as a responsible peacemaker, willing to make the first move towards compromise.
- There was no question that keeping Cuba safe from American attack was a major achievement for the USSR. Cuba was a valuable ally and proved a useful base from which to support communists in South America.
- Khrushchev did also get the USA to withdraw its nuclear missiles from Turkey. However, Khrushchev promised to keep this secret so he was unable to use it for propaganda purposes.
- The USA was criticised by some of its own allies. Newspaper articles in Britain, for example, commented that the USA was unreasonable to have missiles in Turkey and yet object to Soviet missiles in Cuba.
- On the other hand, Khrushchev had been forced to back down and remove the missiles. Soviet military leaders were particularly upset at the terms of the withdrawal. They were forced to put missiles on the decks of their ships so the Americans could count them. They felt this was a humiliation.
- The USSR still lagged behind the USA in the arms race. The USSR developed its stockpile of ICBMs at a huge financial cost, but it never caught up with the USA.
- In 1964 Khrushchev himself was forced from power by his enemies inside the USSR. Many commentators believe that the Cuban Missile Crisis contributed to this.

...for the Cold War

- The crisis helped thaw Cold War relations between the USA and the USSR. Both leaders had seen how their brinkmanship had nearly ended in nuclear war. They were now more prepared to take steps to reduce the risk of nuclear war. For example:
  - A permanent 'hot line' phone link was set up direct from the White House to the Kremlin.
  - In 1963, they signed a Nuclear Test Ban Treaty. It did not stop the development of weapons, but it limited tests and was an important step forward.
- Although it was clear the USSR could not match US technology or numbers of weapons, it was also clear this was not necessary. The Soviet nuclear arsenal was enough of a threat to make the USA respect the USSR. It is significant that for the rest of the Cold War the superpowers avoided direct confrontation and fought through their allies where possible.

...for Castro's Cuba

- Castro was very upset by Khrushchev's deal with America but he had to accept it. He needed the support of the USSR.
- Cuba stayed communist and highly armed. The nuclear missiles were removed but Cuba remained an important base for communist operations in South America and for a CIVIL WAR in Angola in the 1970s.
- Castro kept control of the American companies and economic resources he nationalised during his revolution.

Think!
1. Use the information on this page to fill out a table of positive and negative outcomes for the USA and the USSR.
2. Who do you think gained the most from the Cuban Missile Crisis?

FOCUS TASK 5.3
Was the Cuban Missile Crisis a success for containment?

Look back at your table from page 103. Complete a second row for the Cuban Missile Crisis.

Revision Tip
Make sure you can remember from this case study:
- one reason that the Cuban Crisis might be seen as a success for containment
- one reason it might be seen as a failure.

Case study 3: The Vietnam War

Although Americans were relieved at the outcome of the Cuban Crisis it did not reduce their fear of communism. Very soon they found themselves locked in a costly war in Vietnam, which put a massive question mark over the very policy of containment.

Origins of the Vietnam War

Vietnam had a long history of fighting outsiders.

Fighting the Japanese

Before the Second World War, Vietnam (or INDOCHINA as it was called then) had been ruled by France. During the war the region was conquered by the Japanese. They treated the Vietnamese people savagely. As a result, a strong anti-Japanese resistance movement (the Viet Minh) emerged under the leadership of communist Ho Chi Minh.

Ho inspired the Vietnamese people to fight the Japanese. When the Second World War ended, the Viet Minh entered the northern city of Hanoi in 1945 and declared Vietnam independent.

Fighting the French

The French had other ideas. In 1945 they came back wanting to rule Vietnam again, but Ho was not prepared to let this happen. Another nine years of war followed between the Viet Minh, who controlled the north of the country, and the French, who controlled much of the south.

From 1949 Ho was supported by China, which had become a communist state in 1949. As we have seen in the Cold War, the USA responded by helping those who opposed the communists. It poured $500 million a year into the French war effort. Despite this the French were unable to hold on to the country and pulled out of Vietnam in 1954.

A peace conference was held in Geneva and the country was divided into North and South Vietnam until elections could be held to decide its future (see Source 25).

The USA responds

Under the terms of the ceasefire, elections were to be held within two years to reunite the country. You will remember how the USA criticised Stalin for not holding free elections in Soviet-controlled eastern Europe after the war (see pages 89–92). In Vietnam in 1954 the USA applied a different rule. It prevented the elections from taking place.

Why did the Americans do this? Their policy was a strange combination of determination and ignorance. President Eisenhower and his Secretary of State JF Dulles were convinced that China and the USSR were planning to spread communism throughout Asia. The idea was often referred to as the DOMINO THEORY. If Vietnam fell to communism, then Laos, Cambodia, Thailand, Burma and possibly even India might also fall – just like a row of dominoes. The Americans were determined to resist the spread of communism in Vietnam, which they saw as the first domino in the row. However, their methods and policies showed their ignorance of the Vietnamese people and the region.

SOURCE 25

It was generally agreed that had an election been held, Ho Chi Minh would have been elected Premier ... at the time of the fighting, possibly 80 per cent of the population would have voted for the communist Ho Chi Minh as their leader.

President Eisenhower writing after the Vietnam War.

SOURCE 26

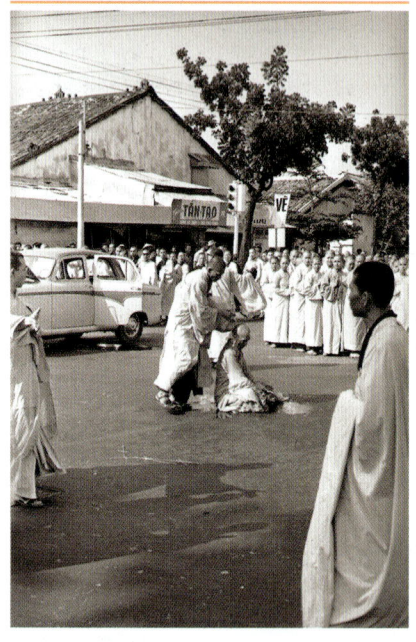

Quang Duc, a 73-year-old Buddhist priest, is about to be set on fire in protest against the attacks on Buddhist shrines by the government of South Vietnam in 1963.

> **Think!**
> 1 Many neutral observers in Vietnam were critical of US policy towards Diem's regime. Explain why.
> 2 Explain how US politicians would have defended their policies.

Financial support for Diem's regime

In 1955 the Americans helped Ngo Dinh Diem to set up the Republic of South Vietnam. They supported him because he was bitterly anticommunist. However, Diem's regime was very unpopular with the Vietnamese people.

- He belonged to the LANDLORD class, which treated the Vietnamese PEASANTS with contempt.
- He was a Christian and showed little respect for the Buddhist religion of most Vietnamese peasants (see Source 26).
- Diem's regime was also extremely corrupt.

The Americans were concerned and frustrated by his actions, but as Dulles said, 'We knew of no one better.' The USA supported Diem's regime with around $1.6 billion in the 1950s. Diem was overthrown by his own army leaders in November 1963, but the governments that followed were equally corrupt. Even so, they also received massive US support.

The emergence of the Viet Cong

The actions of these anticommunist governments increased support among the ordinary peasants for the communist-led National Front for the Liberation of South Vietnam, which was set up in December 1960. This movement was usually called the VIET CONG. It included South Vietnamese opponents of the Government, but also large numbers of communist North Vietnamese taking their orders from Ho Chi Minh. Peasants who did not support the Viet Cong faced intimidation and violence from them.

The Viet Cong started a guerrilla war against the South Vietnamese Government. Using the HO CHI MINH TRAIL (see Figure 27), the Viet Cong sent reinforcements and ferried supplies to guerrilla fighters. These fighters attacked South Vietnamese Government forces, officials and buildings. They also attacked American air force and supply bases.

In response the South Vietnamese Government launched their 'strategic hamlet' programme, which involved moving peasant villages from Viet Cong-controlled areas to areas controlled by the South Vietnamese Government. The Americans helped by supplying building materials, money, food and equipment for the villagers to build improved farms and houses. In practice this policy backfired as the peasants resented it – and corrupt officials pocketed money meant to buy supplies for the villagers.

US involvement escalates

By 1962 President Kennedy was sending military personnel (he always called them 'advisers') to help the South Vietnamese army fight the Viet Cong. However, Kennedy said he was determined that the USA would not 'blunder into war, unclear about aims or how to get out again'. He was a keen historian himself and had studied the USA's past successes and failures. He was well aware from the Korean War ten years earlier what could and could not be achieved by military intervention.

However, President Kennedy was assassinated in 1963. His successor, Lyndon Johnson, was more prepared than Kennedy to commit the USA to a full-scale conflict in Vietnam to prevent the spread of communism.

The Tonkin Gulf Resolution

In August 1964, North Vietnamese patrol boats opened fire on US ships in the Gulf of Tonkin. In a furious reaction, the US Congress passed the Tonkin Gulf Resolution, which gave the President power to 'take all necessary measures to prevent further aggression and achieve peace and security'.

FIGURE 27

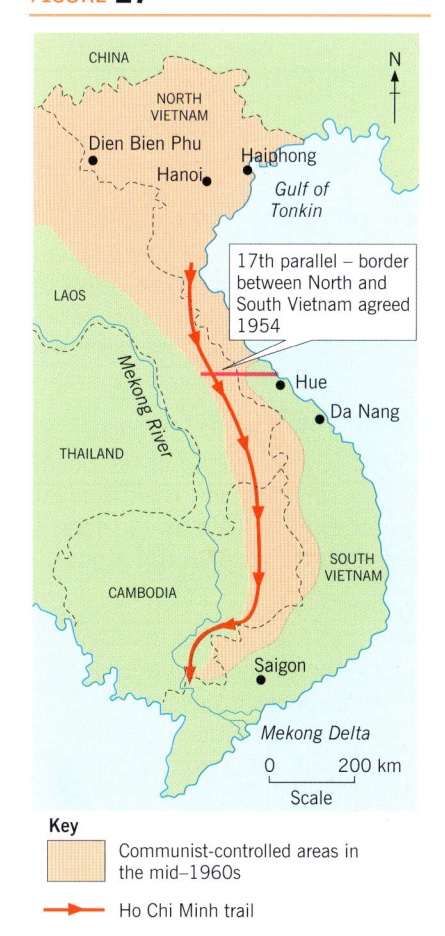

Vietnam in the mid-1960s showing the Ho Chi Minh Trail.

Source Analysis
Compare Source 28 with Source 1 on page 100. How similar are the arguments used in 1964 about Vietnam to those used in 1950 about Korea?

It effectively meant that Johnson could take the USA into a full-scale war if he felt it was necessary, and very soon he did.

- **In February 1965 the US started** OPERATION ROLLING THUNDER – a gigantic bombing campaign against North Vietnamese cities, factories, army bases and the Ho Chi Minh Trail, which continued for three years.
- **On 8 March 1965**, 3500 US marines, combat troops rather than advisers, came ashore at Da Nang.

The USA was now officially at war in Vietnam.

SOURCE 28

First is the simple fact that South Vietnam, a member of the free world family, is striving to preserve its independence from Communist attack. Second, South East Asia has great significance in the forward defence of the USA. For Hanoi, the immediate object is limited: conquest of the south and national unification. For Peking, however, Hanoi's victory would only be a first step towards eventual Chinese dominance of the two Vietnams and South East Asia and towards exploitation of the new strategy in other parts of the world.

Robert McNamara, US Defence Secretary, explaining in 1964 why he supported the policy of sending US troops to Vietnam.

FIGURE 29

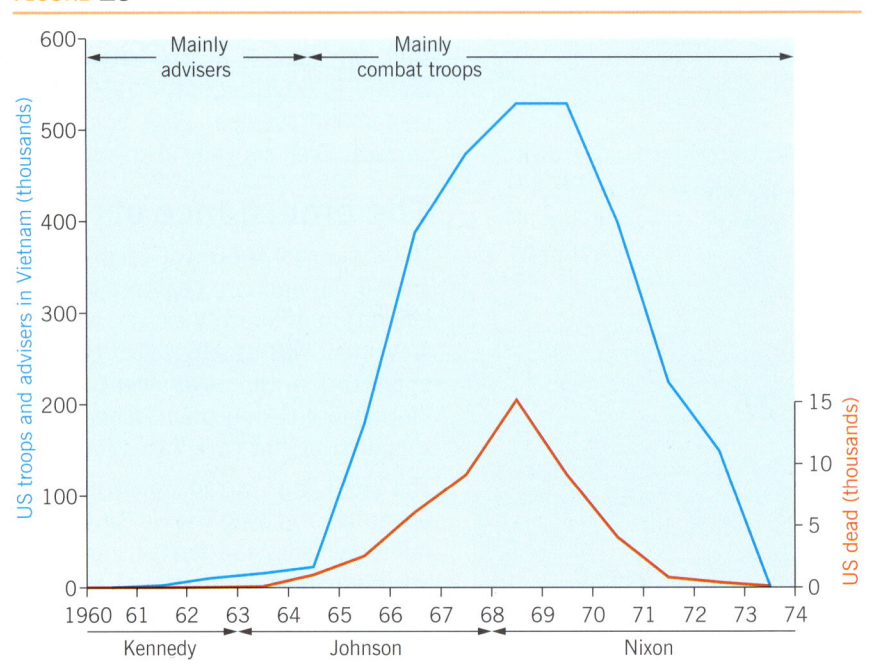

Graph showing escalating US involvement in Vietnam, 1960–74. The blue line shows US personnel. The red line shows US deaths. US troops were not the only foreign soldiers fighting in Vietnam. About 46,000 Australian and New Zealand troops fought too.

Why did the US send troops to Vietnam?

The answer to this question may seem obvious! It was because of the policy of containment and the 'domino theory'. That is certainly how the President and his advisers explained it (see Source 28 for example). However, there is a more controversial view held by some historians that powerful groups within the USA wanted a war.

In 1961 President Eisenhower himself warned that America had developed a powerful 'military–industrial complex'. The Government gave huge budgets to the military commanders. These budgets were spent on weapons made by some of America's biggest companies. Thus, both the armed forces and business actually gained from conflict. Eisenhower did not accuse business and military leaders of anything, but in his last speech as president he warned the American people not to let these groups become too influential. Some historians believe that this was a factor in American involvement in Vietnam, but it is hotly disputed by others.

FOCUS TASK 5.4
Why did the USA get increasingly involved in Vietnam?

1. Draw a timeline of the period 1945–65.
2. Mark on it increasing American involvement using the following headings:
   - No direct American involvement
   - Financial support
   - Political involvement
   - Military involvement
3. Write annotations to show the date on which each of these phases started and what events triggered the increasing involvement.
4. Choose two events that you think were critical in increasing the USA's involvement in the war in Vietnam. Explain your choice.

Revision Tip
Make sure you can recall:
- two reasons why communism was becoming stronger in Vietnam
- two measures taken by the USA to resist the spread of communism.

Tactics and strategy in the Vietnam War

With HINDSIGHT it is easy to see that the American decision to get fully involved in the war was a huge gamble. But political leaders did not have the benefit of hindsight. They made their decision on the basis of what they knew and believed at the time. They knew their technology and firepower was superior to the Viet Cong and they believed that would allow them to win the war.

However, they were soon proved wrong. As time wore on it became clear that the USA needed more than money and technology to win this kind of war. On the next two pages you will find out why by comparing Viet Cong and US tactics. Focus Task 5.5 will direct your reading.

FOCUS TASK 5.5

Why couldn't the Americans win?

Stage 1: Understand the tactics

1 Work in pairs. Take either the Viet Cong or the Americans. Use page 118 or 119 to find out about your side's tactics. Create a diagram by drawing two concentric circles (one inside the other) on a large piece of paper.
- In the inner circle record the tactics.
- In the outer circle the reason for using those tactics.
- Draw lines to show how the tactics and reasons are connected.

Compare your diagram with your partner's.

Stage 2: Thinking it through

2 Make your own table like this, then using your research from stage 1 record in columns 2 and 4 how far each side had these qualities. You can add further rows if you think of other important qualities.

Qualities	The US army	▲ or ▲	Viet Cong
Well-trained soldiers			
The right technology			
Reliable supplies and equipment			
Effective tactics			
Support from the Vietnamese population			
Motivated and committed soldiers			
Intelligence			

3 Next, in each row of column 3, draw some scales to show which way the balance falls for this quality. Did the USA or the Viet Cong have the advantage?

4 Now think about the overall picture – how the strengths and weaknesses work together.
   a) Were the armies finely balanced? Or was the balance strongly weighted to one side or the other?
   b) Which quality was most important in determining who won the war? Was one so important that being ahead in that area meant that other advantages or disadvantages did not matter?

Stage 3: Explaining your conclusions

5 Now write up your answer. You could use this structure:
   a) Describe how the failure of the US army was a combination of its own weaknesses and Viet Cong strengths.
   b) Give balanced examples of US successes and failures.
   c) Give balanced examples of Viet Cong successes and failures.
   d) Choose one American weakness and one Viet Cong strength that you think were absolutely vital in preventing the USA from beating the Viet Cong and explain the significance of the points you have chosen.

Revision Tip

Find five reasons why the USA could not defeat the Viet Cong. Make sure you can recall:
- two or three strengths of the Viet Cong (with examples)
- two or three weaknesses of the USA (with examples).

Viet Cong tactics and troops

In early 1965 the Viet Cong had about 170,000 soldiers. They were heavily outnumbered and outgunned. They were no match for the US and South Vietnamese forces in open warfare. In November 1965 in the La Dreng Valley, US forces killed 2000 Viet Cong for the loss of 300 troops. However, this did not daunt Ho Chi Minh.

Guerilla warfare

Ho used GUERRILLA WARFARE. Guerrilla is a Spanish word which literally means 'little war'. Guerrilla warfare meant avoiding big battles and using hit-and-run raids. Guerrillas did not wear uniform. They were hard to tell apart from the peasants in the villages. They had no known base camp or headquarters. They worked in small groups. They attacked then disappeared into the jungle, into the villages or into tunnels (see Figure 31).

Guerrilla attacks aimed to wear down enemy soldiers and wreck their morale. US soldiers lived in constant fear of ambushes or booby traps such as pits filled with sharpened bamboo stakes – 11 per cent of US casualties were caused by booby traps. Another 51 per cent were from ambushes or hand-to-hand combat. The Viet Cong favoured close-quarter fighting because it knew that the Americans would not use their air power for fear of hitting their own troops.

Civilians

Ho knew how important it was to keep the population on his side. The Viet Cong fighters were courteous and respectful to the Vietnamese peasants. They helped them in the fields during busy periods. However, they were quite prepared to kill peasants who opposed them or who co-operated with their enemies. They also conducted a campaign of terror against the police, tax collectors, teachers and any other employees of the South Vietnamese Government. Between 1966 and 1971 the Viet Cong killed an estimated 27,000 civilians.

Supplies

The Viet Cong depended on supplies from North Vietnam that came along the Ho Chi Minh Trail. US and South Vietnamese planes bombed this constantly, but 40,000 Vietnamese worked to keep it open whatever the cost.

Commitment

The total of Viet Cong and North Vietnamese dead in the war has been estimated at 1 million – far higher than US losses. However, this was a price that Ho Chi Minh was prepared to pay. Whatever the casualties, there were replacement troops available. The greatest strength of the Viet Cong fighters was that they simply refused to give in.

> **Think!**
> 1. One Viet Cong leader said: 'The people are the water. Our armies are the fish.' What do you think he meant?
> 2. Find evidence on pages 118–22 to support the view that:
>   - the Viet Cong had the support of the people
>   - the US and South Vietnam forces did not.

SOURCE 30

I remember sitting at this wretched little outpost one day with a couple of my sergeants. We'd been manning this thing for three weeks and running patrols off it. We were grungy and sore with jungle rot and we'd suffered about nine or ten casualties on a recent patrol. This one sergeant of mine said, 'You know, Lieutenant, I don't see how we're ever going to win this.' And I said, 'Well, Sarge, I'm not supposed to say this to you as your officer – but I don't either.' So there was this sense that we just couldn't see what could be done to defeat these people.

Philip Caputo, a lieutenant in the Marine Corps in Vietnam in 1965–66, speaking in 1997.

FIGURE 31

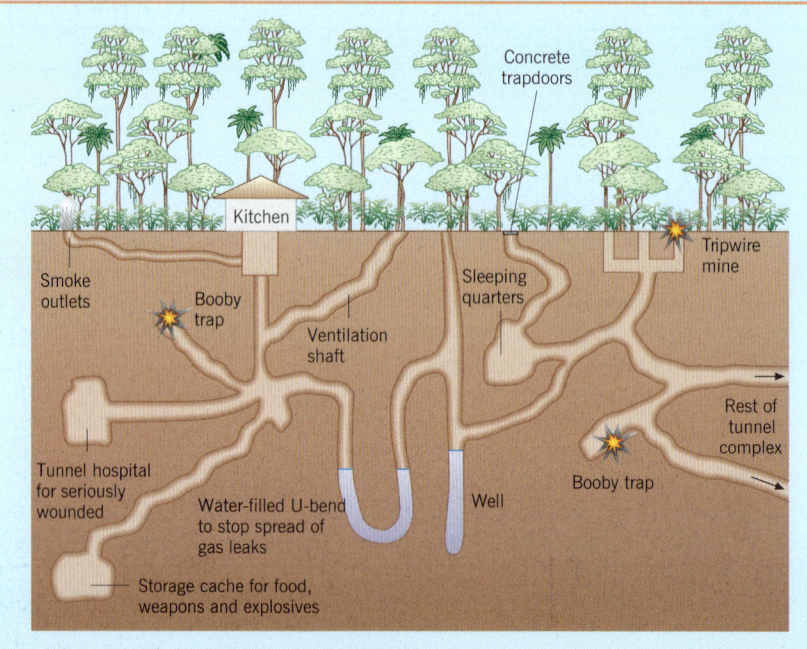

A Viet Cong tunnel complex. To avoid the worst effects of American air power, the Viet Cong built a vast network of underground tunnels, probably around 240 km of them.

US tactics and troops

Bombing

The main US tactic was bombing. For seven years from 1965–72 the USA bombed military, industrial and civilian targets in North Vietnam; they bombed the Ho Chi Minh Trail; they bombed Vietnam's neighbours Laos and Cambodia (who were sympathetic to the Viet Cong).

To some extent bombing worked. It damaged North Vietnam's war effort and it disrupted supply routes. From 1970 to 1972, intense bombing of North Vietnam forced it to negotiate for peace. However, air power could not defeat the communists. Even after major air raids on North Vietnam in 1972, the communists were still able to launch a major assault on the South. Even more important, civilian casualties helped turn the Vietnamese people against the Americans.

Search and destroy

To combat guerrilla warfare the US commander General Westmoreland developed a policy OF SEARCH AND DESTROY. He set up heavily defended US bases in South Vietnam near to the coasts. From here helicopters full of troops would descend on a village and search out and destroy any Viet Cong forces they found. Soldiers had to send back reports of body counts.

Search-and-destroy missions did kill Viet Cong soldiers, but there were problems.
- The raids were often based on inadequate information.
- Inexperienced US troops often walked into traps.
- Innocent villages were mistaken for Viet Cong strongholds. For every Viet Cong weapon captured by search and destroy, there was a body count of six. Many of these were innocent civilians.
- Search-and-destroy tactics made the US and South Vietnamese forces very unpopular with the peasants. It pushed them towards supporting the Viet Cong.

SOURCE 32

You would go out, you would secure a piece of terrain during the daylight hours, [but at night] you'd surrender that – and I mean literally surrender … you'd give it up, because … the helicopters would come in and pick you up at night and fly you back to the security of your base camp.

Lieutenant Colonel George Forrest, US Army.

Chemical weapons

The USA also used CHEMICAL WEAPONS to combat the Viet Cong.
- AGENT ORANGE was a highly toxic 'weedkiller' sprayed from planes to destroy the jungle where the Viet Cong hid. The Americans used 82 million litres of Agent Orange to spray thousands of square kilometres of jungle.
- NAPALM was another widely used chemical weapon. It destroyed jungles where guerrillas might hide. It also burned through skin to the bone.
- Many civilians and soldiers were also killed or harmed by these chemical weapons.

Conscription and morale

In the early stages of the war most US troops were professional soldiers. Morale was good and they performed well. However, as the war intensified the US needed more soldiers so they introduced the DRAFT (CONSCRIPTION). As soon as young men left school or college they could be called up into the US army. So from 1967:
- Many soldiers were young men who had never been in the army before. The average age of US troops was only 19.
- The conscripts knew little about Vietnam – and some cared little about DEMOCRACY or communism. They just wanted to get home alive. In contrast the Viet Cong were fighting for their own country, and a cause many of them believed in.
- Morale among the US conscripts was often very low. To tackle this problem the generals introduced a policy of giving troops just a one-year term of service. This backfired because as soon as the soldiers gained experience they were sent home.

SOURCE 33

Napalm bombs exploding in a village in the Mekong Delta, that was believed to be a Viet Cong position, March 1965.

SOURCE 34

In the end anybody who was still in that country was the enemy. The same village you'd gone in to give them medical treatment … you could go through that village later and get shot at by a sniper. Go back in and you would not find anybody. Nobody knew anything. We were trying to work with these people, they were basically doing a number on us. You didn't trust them anymore. You didn't trust anybody.

Fred Widmer, an American soldier, speaking in 1969.

The Tet Offensive

Despite these problems the official American view of the war from 1965 to 1967 was that it was going reasonably well. The US and South Vietnamese forces were killing large numbers of Viet Cong. Although they were struggling against guerrilla tactics they were confident that the enemy was being worn down. The press reports reflected this positive view.

This confidence was shattered early in 1968. During the New Year holiday, Viet Cong fighters attacked over 100 cities and other military targets. One Viet Cong commando unit tried to capture the US embassy in Saigon. US forces had to fight to regain control room by room. Around 4500 Viet Cong fighters tied down a much larger US and South Vietnamese force in Saigon for two days.

A turning point

In many ways the Tet Offensive was a disaster for the communists. They had hoped that the people of South Vietnam would rise up and join them. They didn't. The Viet Cong lost around 10,000 experienced fighters and were badly weakened by it.

However, the Tet Offensive proved to be a turning point in the war because it raised hard questions in the USA about the war.

- There were nearly 500,000 troops in Vietnam and the USA was spending $20 billion a year on the war. So why had the communists been able to launch a major offensive that took US forces completely by surprise?
- US and South Vietnamese forces quickly retook the towns captured in the offensive, but in the process they used enormous amounts of artillery and air power. Many civilians were killed. The ancient city of Hue was destroyed. Was this right?

Media reaction

Until this point media coverage of the war was generally positive, although some journalists were beginning to ask difficult questions in 1967. During the Tet Offensive the gloves came off. CBS journalist Walter Cronkite (see Source 35) asked 'What the hell is going on? I thought we were winning this war'. Don Oberdorfer of *The Washington Post* later wrote (in 1971) that as a result of the Tet Offensive 'the American people and most of their leaders reached the conclusion that the Vietnam War would require greater effort over a far longer period of time than it was worth'.

SOURCE 35

CBS News journalist Walter Cronkite reporting in Vietnam in February 1968. He was regarded as the most trusted man in America.

SOURCE 36

The Tet Offensive was the decisive battle of the Vietnam War because of its profound impact on American attitudes about involvement in Southeast Asia. In the aftermath of Tet, many Americans became disillusioned … To the American public and even to members of the administration, the offensive demonstrated that US intervention … had produced a negligible effect on the will and capability of the Viet Cong and North Vietnamese.

Extract from *The Tet Offensive: Intelligence Failure in War* by James Wirtz.

SOURCE 37

One does not use napalm on villages and hamlets sheltering civilians if one is attempting to persuade these people of the rightness of one's cause. One does not defoliate [destroy the vegetation of] the country and deform its people with chemicals if one is attempting to persuade them of the foe's evil nature.

Richard Hamer, an American journalist, comments on US policy failure in Vietnam, 1970.

Source Analysis

1 Who or what is the cartoonist criticising in Source 38?
2 Which do you think is more effective as a criticism of the Vietnam War – Source 37, 38 or 39? Give reasons based on the source and your knowledge of the USA at this time.

SOURCE 38

"There's Money Enough To Support Both Of You — Now, Doesn't That Make You Feel Better?"

An American cartoon from 1967.

The peace movement in the USA

For a war on such a scale the Government had to have the support of the American people. With deaths and injuries to so many young Americans, PUBLIC OPINION had been turning against the war even before the Tet Offensive. After it the trickle of antiwar feeling became a flood:

- **Cost:** The war was draining money that could be used to better purposes at home (see Sources 38 and 39). Yet despite all that spending the USA did not seem to be any closer to winning the war.
- **Inequality:** The draft exposed racial inequality in the USA: 30 per cent of African Americans were drafted compared to only 19 per cent of white Americans; 22 per cent of US casualties were black Americans, even though this group made up only 11 per cent of the total US force. World champion boxer Muhammad Ali refused to join the army on the grounds of his Muslim faith. He was stripped of his world title and his passport was removed. Ali was a follower of the RADICAL Black Power group called Nation of Islam. They argued: How could they fight for a country which discriminated against them at home? As Muhammed Ali pointed out, 'I ain't go no quarrel with them Viet Cong!'
- **Purpose:** Most damaging of all, an increasing number of Americans felt deeply uncomfortable about what was going on in Vietnam.

'What are we fighting for?'

The Vietnam War was a media war. Thousands of television, radio and newspaper reporters, and a vast army of photographers sent back to the USA and Europe reports and pictures of the fighting. The newspapers showed crying children burned by American napalm bombs (see Source 33). Television showed prisoners being tortured or executed, or women and children watching with horror as their house was set on fire. To see such casual violence beamed into the living rooms of the USA was deeply shocking to the average American. Was this why 900,000 young Americans had been drafted? Instead of Vietnam being a symbol of a US crusade against communism, Vietnam had become a symbol of defeat, confusion and moral corruption. The most powerful illustration of this was the My Lai massacre (see page 122).

Protest

The antiwar protests, led by students and civil rights campaigners, reached their height during 1968–70.

- In the first half of 1968, there were over 100 demonstrations against the Vietnam War involving 40,000 students. Frequently, the protest would involve burning the American flag – a criminal offence in the USA and a powerful symbol of the students' rejection of American values. Students taunted the American President Lyndon B Johnson with the chant 'Hey, Hey LBJ; how many kids did you kill today?'
- In November 1969, almost 700,000 antiwar protesters demonstrated in Washington DC. It was the largest political protest in American history.

SOURCE 39

The promises of the Great Society have been shot down on the battlefields of Vietnam ... The war has put us in the position of protecting a corrupt government. We are spending $500,000 to kill every Viet Cong soldier while we spend only $53 for every person considered to be in poverty in the USA.

Civil rights leader Martin Luther King speaking in the USA in April 1968. The Great Society was President Johnson's plan for reforms to help the poorest in the USA.

SOURCE 40

Most of the soldiers had never been away from home before they went into service. They thought they were going to do something courageous on behalf of their country, something which they thought was in the American ideal.

But it didn't mean slaughtering whole villages of women and children. One of my friends, when he told me about it, said: 'You know it was a Nazi kind of thing.' We didn't go there to be Nazis. At least none of the people I knew went there to be Nazis.

Written by Ronald Ridenhour, a US soldier in Vietnam. He was not at My Lai, but interviewed many witnesses and started a campaign to pressure the US authorities to investigate properly.

Think!
1. Why do you think it took twelve months for anyone to do anything about the massacre?
2. Why was the massacre so shocking to the American public?

Source Analysis
Source 41 was written by someone who worked for the US army. Does that make it a trustworthy source?

The My Lai massacre

In March 1968, a unit of young American soldiers called Charlie Company started a search-and-destroy mission. They had been told that in My Lai there was a Viet Cong headquarters, and 200 Viet Cong guerrillas. They had been ordered to destroy all houses, dwellings and livestock. They had been told that all the villagers would have left for market because it was a Saturday. Most of them were under the impression that they had been ordered to kill everyone they found in the village.

Early in the morning of 16 March, Charlie Company arrived in My Lai. In the next four hours, between 300 and 400 civilians were killed. They were mostly women, children and old men. Some were killed as they worked in their fields; others in their homes. Many were mown down by machine-gun fire as they were herded into an irrigation ditch. No Viet Cong were found. Only three weapons were recovered.

'Something dark and bloody'

At the time, the army treated the operation as a success. The commanding officer's report said that twenty non-combatants had been killed by accident in the attack, but the rest of the dead were recorded as being Viet Cong.

However, twelve months later, a letter arrived in the offices of 30 leading politicians and government officials in Washington. It was written by Ronald Ridenhour, an American soldier who had served in Vietnam and who personally knew many of the soldiers who took part in the massacre. He had evidence, he said, of 'something rather dark and bloody' that had occurred in My Lai – or Pinkville as the American soldiers called it. He recounted in detail the stories he had been told about what had taken place and asked Congress to investigate.

Investigation

Soon after, *Life* magazine, one of the most influential magazines in the USA, published photographs of the massacre at My Lai that had been taken by an official army photographer. This triggered an investigation that ended in the trial for mass murder of Lieutenant William Calley. He was an officer in Charlie Company. He had personally shot many of the people in the irrigation ditch at My Lai. In September 1969 he was formally charged with murdering 109 people. Ten other members of the company and the commanding officers were also charged.

Aftermath

The revelations were deeply shocking to the American people. The charges were also too much for the army. They placed responsibility on Calley. They denied that Calley was acting under orders. His senior officers were acquitted. After a long court case surrounded by massive media attention and publicity, Calley was found guilty of the murder of 22 civilians. In August 1971 he was sentenced to twenty years' hard labour. In November 1974 he was released.

SOURCE 41

I think I was in a kind of daze from seeing all these shootings and not seeing any returning fire. The Americans were rounding up the people and shooting them, not taking any prisoners ... I was part of it, everyone who was there was part of it and that includes the General and the Colonel flying above in their helicopters ... I did not pay any attention to who did it. By that time I knew what the score was. It was an atrocity ... I notice this one small boy had been shot in the foot ... he was walking toward the group of bodies looking for his mother ... then suddenly I heard a crack and ... I saw this child flip on top of the pile of bodies. The GI just stood and walked away. No remorse. Nothing.

Ron Haeberle, the US army official photographer. His black and white pictures for the army and his colour photographs taken with his own private camera had a dramatic public impact.

The withdrawal from Vietnam

After the Tet Offensive President Johnson concluded that the war could not be won militarily. He reduced the bombing campaign against North Vietnam and instructed his officials to begin negotiating for peace with the communists.

Johnson also announced that he would not be seeking re-election as president. It was an admission of failure. In the election campaign both candidates campaigned to end US involvement in Vietnam. The antiwar feeling was so strong that if they had supported continuing the war they would have had no chance of being elected anyway. It was no longer a question of 'could the USA win the war?' but 'how can the USA get out of Vietnam without it looking like a defeat?'

A new president

In November 1968 Richard Nixon was elected president. From 1969 to 1973 he and his National Security Adviser Henry Kissinger worked to end US involvement in Vietnam. This was not easy because the bigger question of how to contain world communism – the one that had got the USA into Vietnam in the first place – had not gone away. They did not want to appear simply to hand Vietnam to the communists. They used a range of strategies.

Improved relations with USSR and China

In 1969 the USSR and China fell out. It seemed possible that there would even be a war between these two powerful communist countries. As a result, both the USSR and China tried to improve relations with the USA.

'Vietnamisation' of the war effort

In Vietnam Nixon began handing responsibility for the war to South Vietnamese forces and withdrawing US troops (a process they called VIETNAMISATION). Between April 1969 and the end of 1971 almost 400,000 US troops left Vietnam.

Peace negotiations with North Vietnam

From early 1969, Kissinger had regular meetings with the chief Vietnamese peace negotiator, Le Duc Tho.

Increased bombing

At the same time Nixon increased bombing campaigns against North Vietnam to show he was not weak. US and South Vietnamese troops also invaded Viet Cong bases in Cambodia, causing outrage across the world, and even in the USA.

'Peace with honour'

In Paris in January 1973 all parties signed a peace agreement. Nixon described it as 'peace with honour'. Others disagreed (see Source 42), but the door was now open for Nixon to pull out all US troops. By 29 March 1973 the last American forces had left Vietnam.

It is not clear whether Nixon really believed he had secured a lasting peace settlement. But within two years, without the support of the USA, South Vietnam had fallen to the communists. One of the bleakest symbols of American failure in Vietnam was the televised news images of desperate Vietnamese men, women and children trying to clamber aboard American helicopters taking off from the US embassy. All around them communist forces swarmed through Saigon. After 30 years of constant conflict, the struggle for control of Vietnam had finally been settled and the communists had won.

Source Analysis

1 Describe the attitude of Source 42 to the agreement of January 1973.
2 Are you surprised by this source?

SOURCE 42

FOR WHOM THE BELL TOLLS

… the nation began at last to extricate itself from a quicksandy war that had plagued four Presidents and driven one from office, that had sundered the country more deeply than any event since the Civil War, that in the end came to be seen by a great majority of Americans as having been a tragic mistake.

… but its more grievous toll was paid at home – a wound to the spirit so sore that news of peace stirred only the relief that comes with an end to pain. A war that produced no famous victories, no national heroes and no strong patriotic songs, produced no memorable armistice day celebrations either. America was too exhausted by the war and too chary of peace to celebrate.

Reaction to the agreement of January 1973 in the influential American news magazine *Newsweek*, 5 February 1973.

How did the Vietnam War affect the policy of containment?

The American policy of containment was in tatters.
- It had failed **militarily**. The war had shown that even the USA's vast military strength could not stem the spread of communism.
- It had also failed **strategically**. Not only did the USA fail to stop South Vietnam going communist, but the heavy bombing of Vietnam's neighbours, Laos and Cambodia, actually helped the communist forces in those countries to win support. By 1975 both Laos and Cambodia had communist governments. Instead of slowing down the domino effect in the region, American policies actually speeded it up.
- It was also a **propaganda disaster**. The Americans had always presented their campaign against communism as a moral crusade. But atrocities committed by American soldiers and the use of chemical weapons damaged the USA's reputation. In terms of a crusade for 'democracy' the Americans were seen to be propping up a government that did not have the support of its own people.

Theses failures greatly affected the USA's future policies towards communist states. After the war, the Americans tried to improve their relations with China. They ended their block on China's membership of the UN. The President made visits to China. The USA also entered into a period of greater understanding with the Soviet Union. In fact, during the 1970s both the Soviet Union and China got on better with the USA than they did with each other.

The Americans also became very suspicious of involving their troops in any other conflict that they could not easily and overwhelmingly win. This was an attitude that continued to affect American foreign policy into the twenty-first century.

Revision Tip
You can use the cards from Focus Task 5.6 below for your revision. Take a photo of your completed layout showing and annotating the connections. This will be a good essay plan if you have to write on this topic for an assignment. Make sure you can remember one piece of evidence to go with each point.

FOCUS TASK 5.6
Why did the US policy of containment fail in Vietnam?

Despite all the money it spent and the effort they put in, the USA failed to contain the spread of communism to South Vietnam. You are now going to consider the reasons for this.

1. Make cards like these. On each card write an explanation or paste a source which shows the importance of the reason, i.e. how it damaged the policy of containment. Add other cards if you think there are reasons you should consider.
2. Lay your cards out on a large sheet of paper and add lines to show connections between the reasons. Write an explanation of the connection.

| US military tactics in Vietnam | The unpopularity of the South Vietnamese regime | The experience of the Viet Cong and the inexperience of the American soldiers | Opposition in the USA | Other countries' support for the Viet Cong |

Revision Tip
All these case studies (Korea, Cuba, Vietnam) are important because they each show different aspects of containment in action. Make sure you are equally confident about each one and can explain in your own words whether it was a success or failure for containment.

FOCUS TASK 5.7
How effectively did the United States contain the spread of communism?
1. Look back at your chart from page 103. Complete it for the Vietnam War.
2. You have now looked at three very different case studies of the USA's attempts to contain communism. Using the work you have done for Focus Tasks 5.1, 5.3 and 5.6 on pages 103, 113 and this page, explain:
   - how far the policy of containment succeeded
   - the main reasons for its success or failure.

Keywords

Make sure you know these terms, people or events and are able to use them or describe them confidently.

- Agent Orange
- Armistice
- Arms race
- Atomic bomb/H bomb
- Bay of Pigs
- Blockade
- Capitalism
- CENTO
- CIA
- Cold War
- Cominform
- Communism
- Containment
- Conventional weapons
- Democracy
- Dictator
- Diplomatic relations
- Domino theory
- Draft
- Guerrilla warfare
- Ho Chi Minh Trail
- ICBM
- Indochina
- Intelligence (as in CIA)
- Landlord/peasant
- MAD
- Missile gap
- Napalm
- Nuclear deterrent
- Operation Rolling Thunder
- Satellite state
- Search and destroy
- SEATO
- Surveillance
- Tet Offensive
- United Nations
- US sphere of influence
- Viet Cong
- Viet Minh
- Vietnamisation
- Warsaw Pact

Chapter Summary

Containment
1. The USA was anticommunist and wanted to limit the spread of communism around the world – this policy was called containment.

Korea
2. When a communist government tried to take over in Korea in 1950 the USA sent troops to help prevent Korea falling to the communists.
3. The result was a stalemate and in 1953 Korea was divided into a communist north (friendly towards China) and a capitalist south (friendly towards the USA).

Cuba
4. Cuba turned communist in 1959. Cuba is a large island very close to the USA.
5. In the 1960s there was a nuclear arms race between the USA and USSR with ever more dangerous nuclear weapons being developed and tested by both sides.
6. The Soviet leader Khrushchev sent nuclear weapons to Cuba. The USA and much of the world were worried that this might lead to the first nuclear war with dreadful consequences.
7. The US President Kennedy ordered a blockade of Cuba to prevent the weapons arriving and the crisis was averted. Better relations between the two leaders followed.

Vietnam
8. The next area of worry was South-east Asia where communism was very strong. The USA believed in the domino theory – if one country turned communist then the neighbouring countries would follow so they wanted to stop any country turning communist.
9. In 1954 following a civil war Vietnam was divided into a communist north and a capitalist south but the north, with the help of communist China, tried to take over the south too.
10. The USA decided to help the south to resist the threat of the communist north by first sending money and advisers then combat troops.
11. They got more and more involved, to the point where hundreds of thousands of US troops were fighting in Vietnam (the USA introduced conscription to provide enough soldiers), and thousands were being killed each year.
12. Despite all this investment the USA was not winning this war. The war lost support at home and the USA decided to withdraw from Vietnam and leave South Vietnam to its fate. It finally fell to the communists in 1975.

PRACTICE QUESTIONS

1. (a) Describe the Bay of Pigs incident of 1961. **[4]**
   (b) Why did Khrushchev put nuclear missiles on Cuba in 1962? **[6]**
   (c) 'The Cuban Missile Crisis was a victory for the USA.' How far do you agree with this statement? Explain your answer. **[10]**

See pages 148–54 for advice on the different types of questions.

Before

After

6 How secure was the USSR's control over eastern Europe, 1948–c.1989?

FOCUS POINTS

★ Why was there opposition to Soviet control in Hungary in 1956 and Czechoslovakia in 1968, and how did the USSR react to this opposition?
★ How similar were events in Hungary in 1956 and in Czechoslovakia in 1968?
★ Why was the Berlin Wall built in 1961?
★ What was the significance of Solidarity in Poland for the decline of Soviet influence in eastern Europe?
★ How far was Gorbachev personally responsible for the collapse of Soviet control over eastern Europe?

In Chapter 4 you saw how the SOVIET UNION took control of eastern Europe. You are now going to return to that story and see how far the Soviet Union was able to maintain that control.

You will investigate:
- how the Soviet Union took control in eastern Europe and how it tried to maintain control
- why and how some people challenged Soviet control and what happened to them when they did
- how, finally, changes in the Soviet Union led to the collapse of all the communist regimes in eastern Europe and indeed the collapse of the Soviet Union itself.

The key question you will consider is 'how secure' was this control.

The Soviet Union almost certainly did not feel it was secure. It kept up constant pressure on the governments and people of eastern Europe. It was really only the threat of sending in the RED ARMY that propped up some of the communist regimes in the region long after their people had lost faith in their government. In the end it was Mikhail Gorbachev's unwillingness to prop them up any longer with Soviet troops that signalled the end of Soviet domination.

So which of these graphs do you think is likely to be the best representation of Soviet control through this period? This is your 'hypothesis'. You will decide later if you were right.

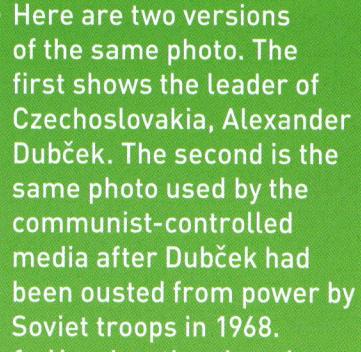

> Here are two versions of the same photo. The first shows the leader of Czechoslovakia, Alexander Dubček. The second is the same photo used by the communist-controlled media after Dubček had been ousted from power by Soviet troops in 1968.
> 1 How has the photo been changed?
> 2 Why might the photo have been changed?
> 3 What does this tell you about communist control of Czechoslovakia in 1968?

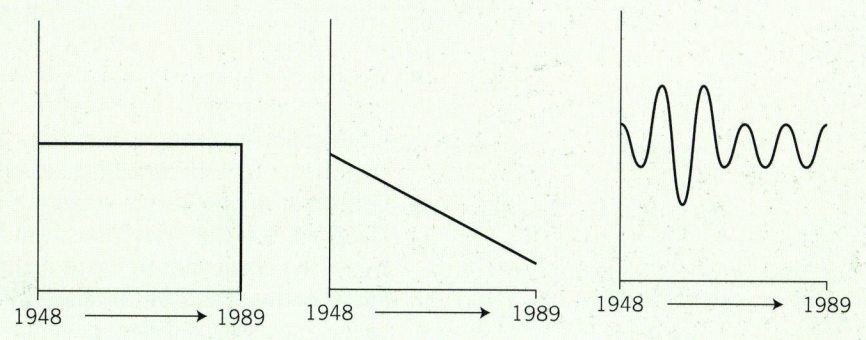

How did the Soviet Union control eastern Europe?

As you saw in Chapter 4, after the Second World War the communists quickly gained control of eastern Europe with the help of the Soviet Union and the Red Army (see Figure 17 on page 89).

Soviet leader STALIN was determined that eastern Europe would be a SOVIET SPHERE OF INFLUENCE. This meant that eastern Europe would be dominated politically and economically by the USSR. The eastern European countries were controlled by their communist governments, but Stalin kept tight control of them, particularly through the Cominform (see Factfile). For Stalin, eastern Europe would serve as a buffer against a future attack on the USSR. He also wanted the resources of eastern Europe to help rebuild the USSR's industries and economy after the terrible damage caused by the war against Germany. He used COMECON to ensure this.

Factfile

Cominform
- Cominform stands for the Communist Information Bureau.
- Stalin set up the Cominform in 1947 as an organisation to co-ordinate the various communist governments in eastern Europe.
- The office was originally based in Belgrade in Yugoslavia but moved to Bucharest in Romania in 1948 after Yugoslavia was expelled by Stalin because it would not do what the Soviet Union told it to do.
- Cominform ran meetings and sent out instructions to communist governments about what the Soviet Union wanted them to do.

Comecon
- Comecon stands for the Council for Mutual Economic Assistance.
- It was set up in 1949 to co-ordinate the industries and trade of the eastern European countries.
- The idea was that members of Comecon traded mostly with one another rather than trading with the West.
- Comecon favoured the USSR far more than any of its other members. It provided the USSR with a market to sell its goods. It also guaranteed it a cheap supply of raw materials. For example, Poland was forced to sell its coal to the USSR at one-tenth of the price that it could have got selling it on the open market.
- It set up a bank for socialist countries in 1964.

Revision Tip
Make sure you can explain in your own words:
- the role of Cominform and Comecon
- the role of the Red Army in keeping control of eastern Europe.

The impact on ordinary people

For some people of eastern Europe the communists initially brought hope. The Soviet Union had achieved amazing industrial growth before the Second World War. Maybe, by following Soviet methods, they could do the same. However, the reality of Soviet control of eastern Europe was very different from what people had hoped for.

- **Freedom** Countries that had a long tradition of free speech and democratic government suddenly lost the right to criticise the government. Newspapers were censored. Non-communists were put in prison for criticising the government. People were forbidden to travel to countries in western Europe. Protests, such as those in East Germany in 1953, were crushed by security forces.
- **Wealth** Between 1945 and 1955 eastern European economies did recover, but soon wages in eastern Europe fell behind the wages in other countries. People in eastern Europe were short of coal to heat their houses. Clothing and shoes were very expensive.
- **Consumer goods** People could not get consumer goods like radios, electric kettles or televisions, which were becoming common in the West. The economies of Eastern Europe were geared towards helping the Soviet Union. Factories produced items such as machinery or electric cables, not what ordinary people wanted.

Stalin to Khrushchev: a new era?

When Stalin died in 1953 many people in eastern Europe hoped for a more relaxed form of rule. After some power struggles in the USSR the new leader who emerged in 1955 was Nikita Khrushchev. He appeared to be very different from Stalin. He talked of peaceful CO-EXISTENCE with the West. He talked of improving the lives of ordinary citizens. He closed down Cominform and released thousands of political prisoners. In an astonishing speech in 1956 he openly denounced Stalin for his harsh rule.

This new approach from the Soviet leader encouraged some critics of communist rule. In the summer of 1956 large demonstrations broke out in Poland. Protestors demanded reforms and the appointment of the Polish war-time resistance leader Wladyslaw Gomulka as the new Polish leader. There were violent clashes between protesters and Polish police. Gomulka was not the loyal ally Khrushchev would have wanted, but he compromised and accepted Gomulka as the new Polish leader. At the same time he moved Soviet tanks and troops to the Polish border just to make it clear that he would only compromise so far.

The world watched with interest. Who was the real Khrushchev – the compromiser with new ideas or the Soviet leader who moved tanks to the Polish border? In October 1956 the answer would become clear as Khrushchev faced a crisis in Hungary. You will investigate his response in the Case Study on pages 130–31.

SOURCE 1

A 1959 Soviet cartoon. The writing on the snowman's hat reads 'Cold War'. Khrushchev is drilling through the Cold War using what the caption calls 'miners' methods'. The cartoon uses very strong visual images like Khrushchev's modern style of clothing to emphasise his new ideas. And of course he is breaking up the Cold War!

Revision Tip

Make sure you know two ways in which Khrushchev appeared to be different from Stalin in 1955.

ACTIVITY

Look at Source 1.
1. Make a list of the features of the cartoon that show Khrushchev as a new type of leader.
2. Design another cartoon that shows him relaxing the Soviet grip on eastern Europe. Think about:
   - how you would show Khrushchev
   - how you would represent the states of eastern Europe (as maps? as people?)
   - how you would represent Soviet control (as a rope? getting looser? tighter?).

You could either draw the cartoon or write instructions for an artist to do so.

Case study 1: Hungary, 1956

From 1949 to 1956 Hungary was led by a hardline communist called Mátyás Rákosi. Hungarians hated the restrictions imposed on them. Most Hungarians felt bitter about losing their FREEDOM OF SPEECH. They lived in fear of the SECRET POLICE. They resented the presence of thousands of Soviet troops and officials in their country. Some areas of Hungary even had Russian street signs, Russian schools and shops. Worst of all, Hungarians had to pay for Soviet forces to be in Hungary.

SOURCE 2

Living standards were declining and yet the papers and radio kept saying that we had never had it so good. Why? Why these lies? Everybody knew the state was spending the money on armaments. Why could they not admit that we were worse off because of the war effort and the need to build new factories? … I finally arrived at the realisation that the system was wrong and stupid.

A Hungarian student describes the mood in 1953.

SOURCE 3

… wearing clothes patterned after Western styles, showing interest in jazz, expressing liberalism in the arts – was considered dangerous in the eyes of the people's democracy. To cite a small example … My university colleague, John, showed up at lectures one day several weeks before the revolution in a new suit and a striped shirt and necktie, which he had received from an uncle in the United States through gift-parcel channels. His shoes were smooth suede and would have cost one month's wages in Hungary. After class John was summoned by the party officer. He received a tongue-lashing and was expelled.

Written by László Beke, a student who helped lead the Hungarian uprising in 1956, in *A Student's Diary: Budapest October 16–November 1, 1956*.

FOCUS TASK 6.1

Why was there opposition to Soviet control in Hungary in 1956?

1. Use the text and Sources 2 and 3 to list reasons why some Hungarians were opposed to communist control – for example, they resented the presence of Soviet troops.
2. List the changes proposed by Nagy's Government.
3. Which of these proposed changes do you think would be most threatening to the USSR? Give reasons.

What happened?

- **Opposition:** In June 1956 a group within the Communist Party in Hungary opposed Rákosi. He appealed to Khrushchev for help. He wanted to arrest 400 leading opponents. Moscow would not back him. Khrushchev ordered Rákosi to be retired 'for health reasons'.
- **Protest:** The new leader, Ernö Gerö, was no more acceptable to the Hungarian people. Discontent came to a head with a huge student demonstration on 23 October, when the giant statue of Stalin in Budapest was pulled down.
- **Reform:** The USSR allowed a new government to be formed under the well-respected Imre Nagy. In October Soviet troops and tanks that had been stationed in Hungary since the Second World War began to withdraw. Hungarians created thousands of local councils to replace Soviet power. Several thousand Hungarian soldiers defected from the army to the rebel cause, taking their weapons with them.
- **Plans:** Nagy's Government began to make plans. It would hold free elections, create impartial courts and restore farmland to private ownership. It wanted the total withdrawal of the Soviet army from Hungary. It also planned to leave the WARSAW PACT and declare Hungary neutral in the Cold War struggle between East and West. There was widespread optimism that the new American President Eisenhower, who had been the wartime supreme commander of all Allied Forces in western Europe, would support the new independent Hungary with armed troops if necessary.

How did the Soviet Union respond?

Khrushchev at first seemed ready to accept some of the reforms. However, he could not accept Hungary leaving the Warsaw Pact. In November 1956 thousands of Soviet troops and tanks moved into Budapest. The Hungarians did not give in. Two weeks of bitter fighting followed. Some estimates put the number of Hungarians killed at 30,000. However, the latest research suggests about 3000 Hungarians and up to 1000 Russians were killed. Another 200,000 Hungarians fled across the border into Austria to escape the communist forces.

The WESTERN POWERS protested to the USSR but sent no help; they were too preoccupied with a crisis of their own (the Suez crisis in the Middle East).

Revision Tip

Test yourself to see if you can remember:
- two important reasons that the Hungarians rebelled against Soviet control in 1956
- two changes brought about by Nagy
- how Khrushchev reacted at first, then changed his mind, then changed it again.

SOURCE 4

In Hungary thousands of people have obtained arms by disarming soldiers and militia men ... Soldiers have been making friends with the embittered and dissatisfied masses ... The authorities are paralysed, unable to stop the bloody events.

From a report in a Yugoslav newspaper. Yugoslavia, although communist, did not approve of Soviet policies.

Source Analysis

1 How do Sources 4 and 5 differ in the impression they give of the Hungarian uprising?
2 Why do you think they differ?
3 Does the photo in Source 7 give the same impression as either Source 4 or Source 5?
4 Work in pairs. Study Sources 4–7 and choose one source. Try to convince your partner that your source is the most useful source for studying events in Hungary in 1956.

Think!

1 Look back at Figure 17 in Chapter 4 (page 89). Why do you think Hungary's membership of the Warsaw Pact was so important to the Soviet Union?
2 Why do you think the Hungarians received no support from the West?
3 Explain which of these statements you most agree with:

> The speed at which the Red Army crushed resistance in Hungary shows how completely the Soviet Union controlled Hungary.

> The severity of the Red Army in dealing with Hungary in 1956 shows how fragile the Soviet hold on Hungary really was.

SOURCE 5

We have almost no weapons, no heavy guns of any kind. People are running up to the tanks, throwing in hand grenades and closing the drivers' windows. The Hungarian people are not afraid of death. It is only a pity that we cannot last longer. Now the firing is starting again. The tanks are coming nearer and nearer. You can't let people attack tanks with their bare hands. What is the United Nations doing?

A telex message sent by the Hungarian rebels fighting the communists. Quoted in George Mikes, *The Hungarian Revolution*, 1957.

SOURCE 6

October 27, 1956. On my way home I saw a little girl propped up against the doorway of a building with a machine gun clutched in her hands. When I tried to move her, I saw she was dead. She couldn't have been more than eleven or twelve years old. There was a neatly folded note in her pocket she had evidently meant to pass on through someone to her parents. In childish scrawl it read: 'Dear Mama, Brother is dead. He asked me to take care of his gun. I am all right, and I'm going with friends now. I kiss you. Kati.'

Written by László Beke, a Hungarian student.

SOURCE 7

A photograph of Erika Szeles, a fifteen-year-old rebel, taken by a news photographer from Denmark in 1956. Erika helped the rebels as a nurse and then took up a weapon and fought. She was killed by Soviet troops in a fire fight in November 1956. The photograph appeared on the front cover of several newspapers and magazines in western Europe and the USA.

Outcomes

Khrushchev put János Kádár in place as leader. Kádár took several months to crush all resistance. Around 35,000 anticommunist activists were arrested and 300 were executed. Kádár cautiously introduced some of the reforms demanded by the Hungarian people. However, he did not waver on the central issue – membership of the Warsaw Pact.

Case study 2: Czechoslovakia and the Prague Spring, 1968

Twelve years after the brutal suppression of the Hungarians, Czechoslovakia posed a similar challenge to Soviet domination of eastern Europe. Khrushchev had by now been ousted from power in the USSR. A new leader, Leonid Brezhnev, had replaced him.

What happened?

In the 1960s a new mood developed in Czechoslovakia.

- **New leader:** In 1967 the old Stalinist leader was replaced by Alexander Dubček. He proposed a policy of 'socialism with a human face': less CENSORSHIP, more freedom of speech and a reduction in the activities of the secret police. Dubček was a committed communist, but he believed that COMMUNISM did not have to be as restrictive as it had been before he came to power. He had learned the lessons of the Hungarian uprising and reassured Brezhnev that Czechoslovakia had no plans to pull out of the Warsaw Pact or Comecon.
- **New ideas:** As censorship eased, opponents were able to criticise the failings of communist rule, expose corruption and ask awkward questions about events in the country's recent past. This period became known as 'the PRAGUE SPRING' because of all the new ideas that seemed to be appearing everywhere. By the summer even more RADICAL ideas were emerging. There was even talk of allowing another political party, the Social Democratic Party, to be set up as a rival to the Communist Party.

SOURCE 8

In Czechoslovakia the people who were trusted [by the Communist government] were the obedient ones, those who did not cause any trouble, who didn't ask questions. It was the mediocre man who came off best.

In twenty years not one human problem has been solved in our country, from primary needs like flats, schools, to the more subtle needs such as fulfilling oneself ... the need for people to trust one another ... development of education.

I feel that our Republic has lost its good reputation.

From a speech given by Ludvik Vaculik, a leading figure in the reform movement, in March 1968.

SOURCE 9

The Director told them they would produce 400 locomotives a year. They are making seventy.

And go look at the scrapyard, at all the work that has been thrown out. They built a railway and then took it down again. Who's responsible for all this? The Communist Party set up the system.

We were robbed of our output, our wages ... How can I believe that in five years' time it won't be worse?

Ludvik Vaculik quotes from an interview he had with the workers in a locomotive factory run by the communists.

SOURCE 10

All the different kinds of state in which the Communist Party has taken power have gone through rigged trials ... There must be a fault other than just the wrong people were chosen. There must be a fault in the theory [of communism] itself.

Written by Luboš Dubrovsky, a Czech writer, in May 1968.

How did the Soviet Union respond?

The Soviet Union was very suspicious of the changes taking place in Czechoslovakia. So were the other communist leaders in eastern Europe. They worried that the new ideas might spread. Brezhnev came under pressure from the East German and Polish leaders to clamp down on reform in Czechoslovakia.

Through the summer the USSR tried various tactics to slow Dubček down.
- To intimidate the Czechs, Soviet, Polish and East German troops performed public training exercises right on the Czech border.
- It thought about imposing economic SANCTIONS – for example, cancelling wheat exports to Czechoslovakia – but didn't because it thought that the Czechs would ask for help from the West.
- In July the USSR held a summit conference with the Czechs. Dubček agreed not to allow a new Social Democratic Party. However, he insisted on keeping most of his reforms. The tension seemed to ease.

Then on 20 August 1968, to the stunned amazement of the Czechs and the outside world, Soviet tanks moved into Czechoslovakia. There was little violent resistance. Dubček was removed from power. Dubček's experiment in SOCIALISM with a human face had not failed; it had simply proved unacceptable to the other communist countries.

FOCUS TASK 6.2

Why was there opposition to Soviet control in Czechoslovakia in 1968?

1. Use the text and Sources 8–10 to find evidence for opposition to Soviet control in Czechoslovakia using the following headings:
   a) Social problems (e.g. living and working conditions, education)
   b) Economic problems (e.g. production, wages)
   c) Communist control.
2. Draw a diagram to summarise Dubček's reforms.
3. Which reforms do you think would have threatened Soviet control the most? Explain your answer.

SOURCE 11

Yesterday troops from the Soviet Union, Poland, East Germany, Hungary and Bulgaria crossed the frontier of Czechoslovakia … The Czechoslovak Communist Party Central Committee regard this act as contrary to the basic principles of good relations between socialist states.

A Prague radio report, 21 August 1968.

SOURCE 12

The party and government leaders of the Czechoslovak Socialist Republic have asked the Soviet Union and other allies to give the Czechoslovak people urgent assistance, including assistance with armed forces. This request was brought about … by the threat from counter revolutionary forces …working with foreign forces hostile to socialism.

A Soviet news agency report, 21 August 1968.

SOURCE 13

Czechs demonstrating against the occupation in Prague, August 1968.

SOURCE 14

A street cartoon in Prague.

Source Analysis

1. Explain how and why Sources 11 and 12 differ in their interpretation of the Soviet intervention.
2. What is the message of Source 14?

SOURCE 15

When internal and external forces hostile to socialism attempt to turn the development of any socialist country in the direction of the capitalist system, when a threat arises to the cause of socialism in that country, a threat to the socialist commonwealth as a whole – it becomes not only a problem for the people of that country but also a general problem, the concern of all socialist countries.

The Brezhnev Doctrine.

Outcomes

Unlike Nagy in Hungary, Dubček was not executed. But he was gradually downgraded. First he was sent to be ambassador to Turkey, then expelled from the Communist Party altogether. Photographs showing him as leader were 'censored' (see page 126).

It was clear that reforming ideas were regarded as a threat to communist rule by all of the communist leaders. We now know from a release of documents from the Soviet archives that the suppression of Czechoslovakia was driven just as much by other eastern European leaders (particularly Walter Ulbricht of East Germany) as it was by Brezhnev. These leaders feared that their own people would demand the same freedom that Dubček had allowed in Czechoslovakia.

The Brezhnev Doctrine

The Czechoslovak episode also gave rise to the BREZHNEV DOCTRINE. The essentials of communism were defined as:
- a one-party system
- to remain a member of the Warsaw Pact.

FOCUS TASK 6.3

How similar were the uprisings of 1956 and 1968?

One question which historians often consider is how similar the uprisings of 1956 in Hungary and 1968 in Czechoslovakia actually were. The table below gives you a number of ways to compare the two events. Work through pages 130–31 and pages 132–33, make your own copy then complete the table.

Issue	Hungary, 1956	Czechoslovakia, 1968	How similar? Give reasons
Aims of rebels			
Attitude towards communism			
Attitude towards democracy			
Attitude towards the USSR			
Attitude towards the West			
Why the USSR intervened			
How the USSR intervened			
Response of the rebels			
Casualties			
Eventual outcome			

Here are a few points to help you get the table started, but you will have to decide where they fit and add your own as well.
- Abolish secret police
- Around 200,000 fled the country
- Because of the threat to leave the Warsaw Pact
- Dubček downgraded
- Fear that other states would demand the same freedoms
- Less censorship
- Pitched battles in the streets
- Wanted a more human form of communism
- Wanted free elections with more than one party
- Withdraw Soviet troops

Revision Tip

You don't need to learn this whole table but be sure you can explain:
- two ways in which the Hungarian and Czech uprisings were similar
- two ways in which they were different.

FOCUS TASK 6.4

How secure was Soviet control of Hungary and Czechoslovakia?

Here are various events from the two invasions. For each event decide where it should go on this line. Does it suggest that Soviet control was weak, strong or somewhere in between?

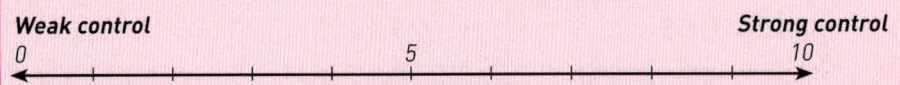

Weak control 0 — 5 — **Strong control** 10

There may be some events that you think could be used to support either view. Whatever you decide you must include notes to explain your decision.

Hungary
- Imre Nagy forms new government
- Khruschev sends in troops
- Nagy imprisoned and executed
- Nagy's plans
- Opposition to Rákosi
- Rákosi not supported by Moscow
- Rákosi removed
- Rebellion
- Soviet tanks move in and then withdraw
- Two weeks of fierce street fighting

Czechoslovakia
- Censorship eased in Czechoslovakia
- Czech communist leaders were heavily criticised for corrupt and incompetent rule
- Plans to set up Social Democratic Party
- USSR argued with Dubček to slow down the pace of reform
- Troops carried out training exercises on the border of Czechoslovakia
- The USSR considered sanctions against Czechoslovakia but feared they would not work
- Tanks moved into Prague on 20 August 1968
- There was little violent resistance in Czechoslovakia
- Dubček was removed
- The Brezhnev Doctrine

Case study 3: The Berlin Wall

SOURCE 16

A 1959 Soviet cartoon – the caption was: 'The socialist stallion far outclasses the capitalist donkey.'

Source Analysis
1 Look at Source 16. What is the aim of this cartoon?
2 How might someone living in a communist country react to it?

SOURCE 17

West Berlin ... has many roles. It is more than a showcase of liberty, an island of freedom in a Communist sea. It is more than a link with the free world, a beacon of hope behind the iron curtain, an escape hatch for refugees. Above all, it has become the resting place of Western courage and will ... We cannot and will not permit the Communists to drive us out of Berlin.

President Kennedy speaking in 1960, before he became president.

You have already seen how Berlin was a battleground of the Cold War (see Source 17). In 1961 it also became the focus of the Soviet Union's latest attempt to maintain control of its east European satellites.

The problem

The crushing of the Hungarian uprising (see pages 130–31) had confirmed for many people in eastern Europe that it was impossible to fight the communists. For many, it seemed that the only way of escaping the repression was to leave altogether. Some wished to leave eastern Europe for political reasons – they hated the communists – while many more wished to leave for economic reasons. As standards of living in eastern Europe fell further and further behind the West, the attraction of going to live in a CAPITALIST state was very great.

The contrast was particularly great in the divided city of Berlin. Living standards were tolerable in the East, but just a few hundred metres away in West Berlin, East Germans could see some of the prize exhibits of capitalist West Germany – shops full of goods, great freedom, great wealth and great variety. This had been done deliberately by the WESTERN POWERS. They had poured massive investment into Berlin. East Germans could also watch West German television.

In the 1950s East Germans were still able to travel freely into West Berlin. From there they could travel on into West Germany. It was very tempting to leave East Germany, with its harsh communist regime and its hardline leader, Walter Ulbricht. By the late 1950s thousands were leaving and never coming back (see Figure 18).

FIGURE 18

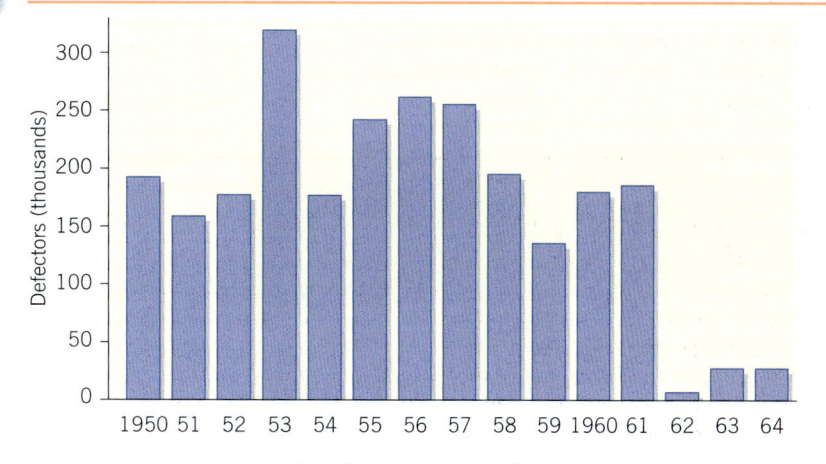

Number of people crossing from East to West Germany, 1950–64.

Those who were defecting were very often highly skilled workers or well-qualified managers. The communist government could not afford to lose these high-quality people. More importantly, from Khrushchev's point of view, the sight of thousands of Germans fleeing communist rule for a better life under capitalism undermined communism generally.

The solution

In 1961 the USA had a new president, the young and inexperienced John F Kennedy. Khrushchev thought he could bully Kennedy and chose to pick a fight over Berlin. He insisted that Kennedy withdraw US troops from the city. He was certain that Kennedy would back down. Kennedy refused. However, all eyes were now on Berlin. What would happen next?

At two o'clock in the morning on Sunday 13 August 1961, East German soldiers erected a barbed-wire barrier along the entire frontier between East and West Berlin, ending all free movement from East to West. It was quickly replaced by a concrete wall. All the crossing points from East to West Berlin were sealed, except for one. This became known as CHECKPOINT CHARLIE.

Families were divided. Berliners were unable to go to work; chaos and confusion followed. Border guards kept a constant look-out for anyone trying to cross the wall. They had orders to shoot people trying to defect. Hundreds were killed over the next three decades.

SOURCE 19

A

B

A section of the Berlin Wall.

SOURCE 20

People escape from East Berlin during a Sunday walk.

SOURCE 21

The Western powers in Berlin use it as a centre of subversive activity against the GDR [the initial letters of the German name for East Germany]. In no other part of the world are so many espionage centres to be found. These centres smuggle their agents into the GDR for all kinds of subversion: recruiting spies; sabotage; provoking disturbances.

The government presents all working people of the GDR with a proposal that will securely block subversive activity so that reliable safeguards and effective control will be established around West Berlin, including its border with democratic Berlin.

A Soviet explanation for the building of the wall, 1961.

Outcomes

For a while, the wall created a major crisis. Access to East Berlin had been guaranteed to the Allies since 1945. In October 1961 US diplomats and troops crossed regularly into East Berlin to find out how the Soviets would react.

On 27 October Soviet tanks pulled up to Checkpoint Charlie and refused to allow any further access to the East. All day, US and Soviet tanks, fully armed, faced each other in a tense stand-off. Then, after eighteen hours, one by one, five metres at a time, the tanks pulled back. Another crisis, another retreat.

The international reaction was relief. Khrushchev ordered Ulbricht to avoid any actions that would increase tension. Kennedy said, 'It's not a very nice solution, but a wall is a hell of a lot better than a war.' So the wall stayed, and over the following years became the symbol of division – the division of Germany, the division of Europe, the division of communist East and democratic West. The communists presented the wall as a protective shell around East Berlin. The West presented it as a prison wall.

SOURCE 22

There are some who say, in Europe and elsewhere, we can work with the Communists. Let them come to Berlin.

President Kennedy speaking in 1963 after the building of the Berlin Wall.

SOURCE 23

A Soviet cartoon from the 1960s. The sign reads: 'The border of the GDR (East Germany) is closed to all enemies.' Notice the shape of the dog's tail.

> **Revision Tip**
> You need to be able to give:
> - two reasons that the Soviet Union built the Berlin Wall
> - a full explanation of each reason.

FOCUS TASK 6.5

Why was the Berlin Wall built in 1961?

Stage 1

Work in pairs. Make a poster or notice to be stuck on the Berlin Wall explaining the purpose of the wall. One of you make a poster for the East German side and the other make a poster for the West German side. You can use pictures and quotations from the sources in this chapter or use your own research.

Make sure you explain in your poster the reasons why the wall was built and what the results of building the wall will be.

Stage 2

Do you think the building of the Berlin Wall shows that communist control of East Germany was weak or that it was strong?

In pairs, one of you will argue communist control was weak and the other that is was strong. Choose evidence from pages 135–37 to write a short speech supporting your viewpoint.

When you have heard all of the speeches, take a class vote.

Case study 4: Solidarity in Poland, 1980–81

SOURCE 24

- More pay
- End to censorship
- Same welfare benefits as police and party workers
- Broadcasting of Catholic church services
- Election of factory managers

Some of Solidarity's 21 demands.

Profile

Lech Walesa

- Pronounced Lek Fowensa.
- Born 1943. His father was a farmer.
- He went to work in the shipyards at Gdansk.
- In 1976 he was sacked from the shipyard for making 'malicious' statements about the organisation and working climate.
- In 1978 he helped organise a union at another factory. He was dismissed.
- In 1979 he worked for Eltromontage. He was said to be the best automotive electrician. He was sacked.
- With others, he set up Solidarity in August 1980 and became its leader.
- He was a committed Catholic.
- In 1989 he became the leader of Poland's first non-communist government since the Second World War.

Throughout the years of communist control of Poland there were regular protests. However, they were generally more about living standards and prices than attempts to overthrow communist government. During the first half of the 1970s Polish industry performed well so the country was relatively calm. But in the late 1970s the Polish economy hit a crisis and 1979 was the worst year for Polish industry since communism had been introduced. This is what happened next.

July 1980	The Government announced increases in the price of meat.
August 1980	Workers at the Gdansk shipyard, led by Lech Walesa, put forward 21 demands to the Government, including free TRADE UNIONS and the right to strike (see Source 24). They also started a free trade union called SOLIDARITY. Poland had trade unions but they were ineffective in challenging government policies.
30 August 1980	The Government agreed to all 21 of Solidarity's demands.
September 1980	Solidarity's membership grew to 3.5 million.
October 1980	Solidarity's membership was 7 million. Solidarity was officially recognised by the Government.
January 1981	Membership of Solidarity reached its peak at 9.4 million – more than a third of all the workers in Poland.

Reasons for Solidarity's success

You might be surprised that the Government gave in to Solidarity in 1980. There are many different reasons for this.

- The union was strongest in those industries that were most important to the Government – shipbuilding and heavy industry. A GENERAL STRIKE in these industries would have devastated Poland's economy.
- In the early stages the union was not seen by its members as an alternative to the Communist Party. More than 1 million members (30 per cent) of the Communist Party joined Solidarity.
- Lech Walesa was very careful in his negotiations with the Government and worked to avoid provoking a dispute that might bring in the Soviet Union.
- The union was immensely popular. Almost half of all workers belonged. Lech Walesa was a kind of folk hero.
- Solidarity had the support of the Catholic Church, which was still very strong in Poland.
- The Government was playing for time. It hoped Solidarity would break into rival factions. Meanwhile the Government drew up plans for MARTIAL LAW (rule by the army).
- The Soviet Union also had half an eye on the West. Solidarity had gained support in the West in a way that neither the Hungarian nor the Czech rising had. Walesa was well known in the Western media and people in the West bought Solidarity badges to show their support. The scale of the movement ensured that the Soviet Union treated the Polish crisis cautiously.

Revision Tip

Make sure you know:
- two demands made by Solidarity in 1980
- one reason why Solidarity was crushed in 1981
- one reason why you think the rise and fall of Solidarity is a significant event in history.

SOURCE 25

Inequality and injustice are everywhere. There are hospitals that are so poorly supplied that they do not even have cotton, and our relatives die in the corridors; but other hospitals are equipped with private rooms and full medical care for each room. We pay fines for traffic violations, but some people commit highway manslaughter while drunk and are let off ... In some places there are better shops and superior vacation houses, with huge fenced-in grounds that ordinary people cannot enter.

Extract from 'Experience and the Future', a report drawn up in 1981 by Polish writers and thinkers who were not members of the Communist Party. They are describing the inequality in Poland between Communist Party members and ordinary people.

Think!
Between August 1980 and December 1981, Solidarity went through some rapid changes. Choose two moments in this period that you think were particularly important in the rise and fall of Solidarity and explain why they were important.

FIGURE 26

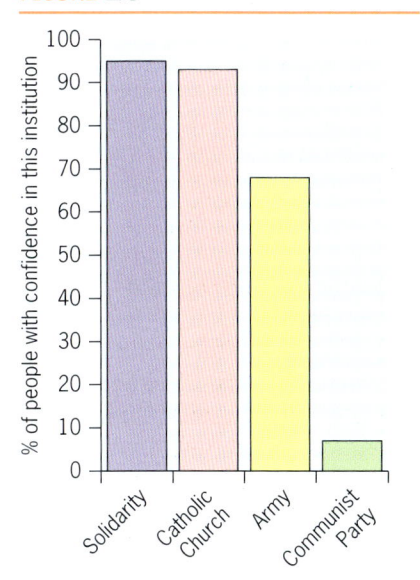

The results of an opinion poll in Poland, November 1981. The people polled were asked whether they had confidence in key institutions in Poland. It is known that 11 per cent of those polled were Communist Party members.

Martial law

In February 1981 the situation changed. The civilian prime minister 'resigned' and the leader of the army, General Jaruzelski, took over. From the moment he took office, people in Poland, and observers outside Poland, expected the Soviet Union to 'send in the tanks' at any time, especially when the Solidarity Congress produced an 'open letter' saying that they were campaigning not only for their own rights but for the rights of workers throughout the COMMUNIST BLOC. It proclaimed that the Poles were fighting 'For Your Freedom and For Ours'.

Jaruzelski and Walesa negotiated to form a government of national understanding but when that broke down in December, after nine months of tense relationships, the communist Government acted. Brezhnev ordered the Red Army to carry out 'training manoeuvres' on the Polish border. Jaruzelski introduced martial law. He put Walesa and almost 10,000 other Solidarity leaders in prison. He suspended Solidarity.

Reasons for the crushing of Solidarity

Military DICTATORS are not required to give reasons for their actions. But if they were, what might Jaruzelski have to say?

- Solidarity was acting as a political party. The Government declared that it had secret tapes of a Solidarity meeting setting up a new provisional government – without the Communist Party.
- Poland was sinking into chaos. Almost all Poles felt the impact of food shortages. Rationing had been introduced in April 1981. Wages had increased by less than INFLATION. Unemployment was rising.
- Solidarity itself was also tumbling into chaos. There were many different factions. Some felt that the only way to make progress was to push the communists harder until they cracked under the pressure. Strikes were continuing long after the Solidarity leadership had ordered them to stop.

The Soviet Union had seen enough. It thought the situation in Poland had gone too far. If Poland's leaders would not restore communist control in Poland, then it would. This was something the Polish leaders wanted to avoid.

The significance of Solidarity

In the story of Soviet control of eastern Europe, Solidarity was significant for a number of reasons:

- It highlighted the failure of communism to provide good living standards and this undermined communism's claim to be a system which benefited ordinary people.
- It highlighted inefficiency and corruption (see Source 25 for example).
- It showed that there were organisations which were capable of resisting a communist government.
- It showed that communist governments could be threatened by 'PEOPLE POWER'.

It also highlighted the nature of Soviet control. The only thing that kept the communists in power was force or the threat of force backed by the USSR. When Jaruzelski finally decided to use force, Solidarity was easily crushed. The lesson was clear. If MILITARY FORCE was not used, then communist control seemed very shaky indeed. If Soviet policy were to change, communist control would not survive. What do you expect to happen next?

FOCUS TASK 6.6
What was the significance of Solidarity for the decline of Soviet influence in eastern Europe?

'Solidarity died as quickly as it started, having achieved nothing.'

How far do you agree with this statement? Support your answer with evidence from page 138 and this page.

Profile

Mikhail Gorbachev

- Born 1931. One grandfather was a KULAK – a landowning peasant – who had been sent to a prison camp by Stalin because he resisted Stalin's policy of COLLECTIVISATION. The other grandfather was a loyal Communist Party member.
- His elder brother was killed in the Second World War.
- Studied law at Moscow University in the 1950s. Became a persuasive speaker.
- Worked as a local Communist Party official in his home area. By 1978 he was a member of the Central Committee of the party and in charge of agriculture.
- In 1980 he joined the POLITBURO.
- He was a close friend of Andropov, who became Soviet leader in 1983. He shared many of Andropov's ideas about reforming the USSR. When Andropov was leader, he was effectively second in command.
- In 1985 he became leader of the USSR.
- In October 1990 he was awarded the NOBEL PEACE PRIZE.

Enter Mikhail Gorbachev

Gorbachev became leader of the Soviet Union in 1985. He was an unusual mix of IDEALIST, optimist and REALIST.

- The realist in him could see that the USSR was in a terrible state. Its economy was very weak. It was spending far too much money on the ARMS RACE. It was locked into an unwinnable war in Afghanistan.
- The idealist in Gorbachev believed that communist rule should make life better for the people of the USSR and other communist states. As a loyal communist and a proud Russian, he was offended by the fact that goods made in Soviet factories were shoddy, living standards were higher in the West and that many Soviet citizens had no loyalty to the Government.
- The optimist in Gorbachev believed that a reformed communist system of government could give people pride and belief in their country. He definitely did not intend to dismantle communism in the USSR and eastern Europe, but he did want to reform it radically.

Gorbachev's policies in eastern Europe

Gorbachev also had a very different attitude to eastern Europe from Brezhnev. In March he called the leaders of the Warsaw Pact countries together. This meeting should have been a turning point in the history of eastern Europe. He had two messages.

'We won't intervene'

SOURCE 27

The time is ripe for abandoning views on foreign policy which are influenced by an imperial standpoint. Neither the Soviet Union nor the USA is able to force its will on others. It is possible to suppress, compel, bribe, break or blast, but only for a certain period. From the point of view of long-term big time politics, no one will be able to subordinate others. That is why only one thing – relations of equality – remains. All of us must realise this …

Gorbachev speaking in 1987.

Gorbachev made it very clear to the countries of eastern Europe that they were responsible for their own fates. However, most of the Warsaw Pact leaders were old-style, hardline communists. To them, Gorbachev's ideas were too radical and they simply did not believe he meant what he said.

'You have to reform'

Gorbachev also made it clear that they needed to reform their own countries. He did not think communism was doomed. In fact, he felt the opposite was true. Gorbachev believed the communist system could provide better healthcare, education and transport. The task in the USSR and eastern Europe was to renew communism so as to match capitalism in other areas of public life. However, they did not believe him on this count either.

In the next few year these leaders would realise they had made a serious error of judgement.

Revision Tip

Identify two problems in the USSR that led to Gorbachev's new policy towards eastern Europe.

Think!

Why do you think the Warsaw Pact leaders did not believe Gorbachev when he told them the Soviet Union would no longer interfere in the internal affairs of other communist countries?

SOURCE 28

Polish, Hungarian and Romanian dogs get to talking. 'What's life like in your country?' the Polish dog asks the Hungarian dog.

'Well, we have meat to eat but we can't bark. What are things like where you are from?' says the Hungarian dog to the Polish dog.

'With us, there's no meat, but at least we can bark,' says the Polish dog.

'What's meat? What's barking?' asks the Romanian dog.

Example of anticommunist jokes collected by researchers in eastern Europe in the 1980s.

SOURCE 29

A

The Soviet Union would remain a one party state even if the Communists allowed an opposition party to exist. Everyone would join the opposition party.

B

When American college students are asked what they want to do after graduation, they reply: 'I don't know, I haven't decided'. Russian students answer the same question by saying: 'I don't know, they haven't told me'.

Anticommunist jokes told by US President Reagan to Mikhail Gorbachev at their SUMMIT MEETINGS in the late 1980s.

Source Analysis

1. Why do you think President Reagan was so fond of jokes like those in Source 29A and B?
2. Do you think it is strange that Gorbachev was upset by these jokes? Explain your answer.
3. Can jokes really be useful historical sources? Explain your answer.
4. If you think jokes are useful sources, do you think the joke in Source 28 is more or less useful than the jokes in Source 29? Explain your answer.

Gorbachev's reforms

He had to be cautious, because he faced great opposition from hardliners in his own Government, but gradually he declared his policies. The two key ideas were GLASNOST (openness) and PERESTROIKA (restructuring).

- *Glasnost*: He called for open debate on government policy and honesty in facing up to problems. It was not a detailed set of policies but it did mean radical change.
- In 1987 his *perestroika* programme allowed market forces to be introduced into the Soviet economy. For the first time in 60 years it was no longer illegal to buy and sell for profit.

He then went on to:
- **Reduce defence spending**: The nuclear arms race was an enormous drain on the Soviet economy at a time when it was in trouble anyway. After almost 50 years on a constant war footing, the Red Army began to shrink.
- **Improve international relations**: Gorbachev brought a new attitude to the USSR's relations with the wider world. He withdrew Soviet troops from Afghanistan, which had become such a costly yet unwinnable war. In speech after speech, he talked about international trust and CO-OPERATION as the way forward for the USSR, rather than confrontation.

Gorbachev and President Reagan

Ronald Reagan became US president in January 1981. He was president until 1988. He had only one policy towards the USSR – get tough. He criticised its control over eastern Europe and increased US military spending. In a way, Reagan's toughness helped Gorbachev.

- It was clear by the late 1980s that the USSR could not compete with American military spending. This helped Gorbachev to push through his military spending cuts.
- Reagan got on quite well with Gorbachev himself. As SUPERPOWER relations improved, the USSR felt less threatened by the USA. This meant there was less need for the USSR to control eastern Europe.

Implications for eastern Europe: 'Listen to your people'

As Gorbachev introduced his reforms in the USSR the demand rose for similar reforms in eastern European states as well. Most people in these states were sick of the poor economic conditions and the harsh restrictions that communism imposed. Gorbachev's policies gave people some hope for reform.

In July 1988 Gorbachev made a speech to the leaders of the Warsaw Pact countries. He planned to withdraw large numbers of troops, tanks and aircraft from eastern Europe. Hungary was particularly eager to get rid of Soviet troops and, when pressed, Gorbachev seemed to accept this. In March 1989 he made clear again that the Red Army would not intervene to prop up communist regimes in eastern Europe. What followed was staggering.

The collapse of communism in eastern Europe

1 — May 1989
Hungarians begin dismantling the barbed-wire fence between Hungary and non-communist Austria.

2 — June
In Poland, free elections are held for the first time since the Second World War. Solidarity wins almost all the seats it contests. Eastern Europe gets its first non-communist leader, President Lech Walesa.

3 — September
Thousands of East Germans on holiday in Hungary and Czechoslovakia refuse to go home. They escape through Austria into West Germany.

4 — October
There are enormous demonstrations in East German cities when Gorbachev visits the country. He tells the East German leader Erich Honecker to reform. Honecker orders troops to fire on demonstrators but they refuse.

Gorbachev makes it clear that Soviet tanks will not move in to 'restore order'.

5 — November
East Germans march in their thousands to the checkpoints at the Berlin Wall. The guards throw down their weapons and join the crowds. The Berlin Wall is dismantled.

6 — November
There are huge demonstrations in Czechoslovakia. The Czech government opens its borders with the West, and allows the formation of other parties.

7 — December
In Romania there is a short but very bloody revolution that ends with the execution of the communist dictator Nicolae Ceausescu.

8 — The Communist Party in Hungary renames itself the Socialist Party and declares that free elections will be held in 1990.

9 — In Bulgaria, there are huge demonstrations against the communist government.

10 — March 1990
Latvia leads the Baltic republics in declaring independence from the USSR.

Key
- Territory taken over by USSR at end of Second World War
- Soviet-dominated communist governments
- Other communist governments

People power

The western media came up with a phrase to explain the events on page 142 – people power. Communist control was toppled because ordinary people were not prepared to accept it any longer. They took control of events. It was not political leaders guiding the future of eastern Europe in 1989 but ordinary people.

Source Analysis

Study Source 30. We are going to study the story **in** the source.
1. What is the man in the foreground doing?
2. Would this have been possible at an earlier date? Why?
3. Who are the men watching from above? Why is it significant that they are just watching?
4. How would you summarise this scene: joyful? sad? powerful? other words?

Now let's think about the story **of** the source:

5. What is significant about the fact that the photographer was even able to take this picture?
6. The photographer was probably a freelance photographer who hoped to sell this picture to as many different newspapers as he could. Do you think he would have been successful? Why?
7. Which countries would have been most likely to publish this photograph? Why?

SOURCE 30

A demonstrator pounds away at the Berlin Wall as East German border guards look on from above, 4 November 1989. The wall was dismantled five days later.

SOURCE 31

For most west Europeans now alive, the world has always ended at the East German border and the Wall; beyond lay darkness ... The opening of the frontiers declares that the world has no edge any more. Europe is becoming once more round and whole.

The Independent, November 1989.

Revision Tip
Remember two examples of 'people power' weakening communist control of eastern Europe in 1989–90.

Reunification of Germany

With the Berlin Wall down, West German CHANCELLOR Helmut Kohl proposed a speedy REUNIFICATION of Germany. Germans in both countries embraced the idea enthusiastically.

Despite his idealism, Gorbachev was less enthusiastic. He expected that a new united Germany would be friendlier to the West than to the East. But after many months of hard negotiations, not all of them friendly, Gorbachev accepted German reunification and even accepted that the new Germany could become a member of NATO. This was no small thing for Gorbachev to accept. Like all Russians, he lived with the memory that it was German aggression in the Second World War that had cost the lives of 20 million Soviet citizens.

On 3 October 1990, Germany became a united country once again.

The collapse of the USSR

Even more dramatic events were to follow in the Soviet Union itself.

1990

MARCH
- Gorbachev visited the Baltic state of **Lithuania** – part of the Soviet Union. Its leaders put their views to him. They were very clear. They wanted independence. They did not want to be part of the USSR. Gorbachev was for once uncompromising. He would not allow this. But in March they did it anyway.
- Almost as soon as he returned to Moscow from Lithuania, Gorbachev received a similar demand from the Muslim Soviet Republic of **Azerbaijan**. What should Gorbachev do now? He sent troops to Azerbaijan to end rioting there. He sent troops to Lithuania. But as the summer approached, the crisis situation got worse.

MAY
- The **Russian Republic**, the largest within the USSR, elected Boris Yeltsin as its president. Yeltsin made it clear that he saw no future in a Soviet Union. He said that the many REPUBLICS that made up the USSR should become independent states.

JULY
- **Ukraine** declared its independence. Other republics followed.
- By the end of 1990 nobody was quite sure what the USSR meant any longer. Meanwhile, Gorbachev was an international superstar. In October 1990 Gorbachev received the **Nobel Peace Prize** for his contribution to ending the Cold War.

1991

APRIL
- The Republic of **Georgia** declared its independence.

AUGUST
- The USSR was disintegrating. Reformers within the USSR itself demanded an end to the Communist Party's domination of government. Gorbachev was struggling to hold it together, but members of the communist elite had had enough.
- Hardline Communist Party members and leading military officers attempted a COUP to take over the USSR. The plotters included Gorbachev's prime minister, Pavlov, and the head of the armed forces, Dimitry Yazov. They held Gorbachev prisoner in his holiday home in the Crimea. They sent tanks and troops onto the streets of Moscow. This was the old Soviet way to keep control. Would it work this time?
- Huge crowds gathered in Moscow. They strongly opposed this military coup. The Russian president, Boris Yeltsin, emerged as the leader of the popular opposition. Faced by this resistance, the conspirators lost faith in themselves and the coup collapsed.
- This last-ditch attempt by the Communist Party to save the USSR had failed. A few days later, Gorbachev returned to Moscow.

DECEMBER
- Gorbachev might have survived the coup, but it had not strengthened his position as Soviet leader. He had to admit that the USSR was finished and he with it. In a televised speech on 25 December 1991, Gorbachev announced his own resignation and the end of the Soviet Union (see Source 32).

> **Think!**
> Think of a suitable headline for each of the six 'episodes' in the collapse of the USSR (shown as yellow bands in the table above).

The end of the Cold War

Think!
Read Source 32 carefully. Three statements are in bold.

Do you agree or disagree with each statement? For each statement, write a short paragraph to:
a) explain what it means, and
b) express your own view on it.

SOURCE 32

A sense of failure and regret came through his [Gorbachev's] Christmas Day abdication speech – especially in his sorrow over his people 'ceasing to be citizens of a great power'. Certainly, if man-in-the-street interviews can be believed, **the former Soviet peoples consider him a failure**.

History will be kinder. The Nobel Prize he received for ending the Cold War was well deserved. Every man, woman and child in this country should be eternally grateful.

His statue should stand in the centre of every east European capital; for it was Gorbachev who allowed them their independence. The same is true for the newly independent countries further east and in Central Asia. No Russian has done more to free his people from bondage since Alexander II who freed the serfs.

From a report on Gorbachev's abdication speech, 25 December 1991, in the US newspaper the *Boston Globe*.

SOURCE 33

He had no grand plan and no predetermined policies; but if Gorbachev had not been Party General Secretary, the decisions of the late 1980s would have been different. The USSR's long-lasting order would have endured for many more years, and almost certainly the eventual collapse of the order would have been much bloodier than it was to be in 1991. The irony was that Gorbachev, in trying to prevent the descent of the system into general crisis, proved instrumental in bringing forward that crisis and destroying the USSR.

Extract from *History of Modern Russia* by historian Robert Service, published 2003. In this extract he is commenting on the meeting in March 1985.

SOURCE 34

Mikhail Gorbachev giving a speech in Ottawa, Canada, 30 May 1990.

SOURCE 35

Doonesbury — BY GARRY TRUDEAU

Panel 1: AN EPIPHANY. LOOK AT THE FACTS, SIR. THE SOVIETS ARE IN THE THROES OF PERESTROIKA, THE CHINESE ARE RESTRUCTURING THEIR ECONOMY...

Panel 2: FROM POLAND TO VIETNAM, DISCREDITED COMMUNIST ECONOMIC AND POLITICAL MODELS ARE BEING CHALLENGED, WHILE CAPITALIST VALUES ARE EMBRACED! / WHAT ARE YOU SAYING HERE, HOWARD?

Panel 3: I'M SAYING THE COLD WAR IS OVER, SIR! IT'S OVER, AND WE WON! / WE WON?

Panel 4: WITHIN HOURS, TIMES SQUARE ERUPTED. U.S.A.! WE'RE NUMBER ONE! VICTORY! COLD WAR OVER!

A cartoon by Doonesbury which appeared in the *Guardian* on 13 June 1988.

FOCUS TASK 6.7

How far was Gorbachev personally responsible for the collapse of Soviet control over eastern Europe?

You are making a documentary film called 'The Collapse of the Red Empire' to explain the how and why of the collapse of Soviet control of eastern Europe. The film will be 60 minutes long.

1. Decide what proportion of this time should concentrate on:
   a) people power
   b) problems in the USSR
   c) actions by Western leaders such as Reagan
   d) actions of political leaders in eastern Europe
   e) Mikhail Gorbachev.
2. Choose one of these aspects and summarise the important points, stories, pictures or sources that your film should cover under that heading.

Keywords

Make sure you know these terms, people or events and are able to use them or describe them confidently.

- Berlin Wall
- Brezhnev Doctrine
- Censorship
- Checkpoint Charlie
- Co-existence
- Comecon
- Cominform
- Communism
- Communist bloc
- De-Stalinisation
- Freedom of speech
- *Glasnost*
- Iron curtain
- Martial law
- NATO
- Nobel Peace Prize
- One-party state
- People power
- *Perestroika*
- Politburo
- Prague Spring
- Red Army
- Reunification
- Secret police
- Socialism
- Solidarity
- Soviet republics
- Summit meeting
- Superpower
- Trade union
- Warsaw Pact

FOCUS TASK 6.8

How secure was Soviet control over eastern Europe, 1948–c.1989?

You now know a lot about Soviet control of eastern Europe:
- how and why communists seized control of each country in the 1940s (Chapter 4)
- how the Soviet Union successfully crushed opposition and threats to control from the 1950s to the 1980s
- how the communist regimes of eastern Europe and the USSR collapsed so suddenly in 1989-90.

Here are the three graphs from page 127. Which do you think best represents the story of Soviet control of eastern Europe?

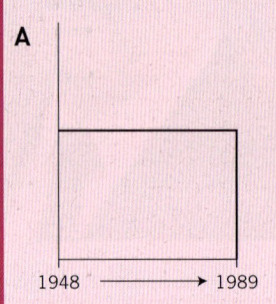

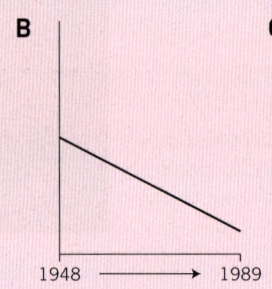

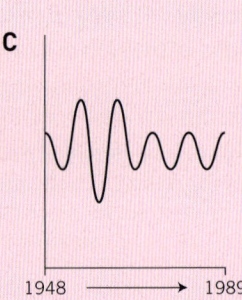

A 1948 → 1989

B 1948 → 1989

C 1948 → 1989

If you pick Graph A, you think Soviet control stayed steady for years, then collapsed in 1989.

If you pick Graph B, you think Soviet control gradually decreased over time.

If you pick Graph C, you think Soviet control fluctuated in response to various crises.

If you think none of them is right, draw your own instead. Explain your graph using evidence from this chapter. You could refer back to your work for Focus Tasks 6.3, 6.4 and 6.6 on pages 134 and 139.

Chapter Summary

How secure was the USSR's control over eastern Europe, 1948–c.1989?

1. After the Second World War, communist governments were elected or forced on most countries of eastern Europe.
2. They were not directly ruled by the USSR but their communist governments did what the USSR wanted and when they did not the USSR sent troops and tanks (the Red Army) to force them to follow the USSR's wishes.
3. Life in these countries was tightly controlled with censorship, a secret police and all industry directed to meeting the needs of the Soviet Union rather than making goods for ordinary people.
4. The countries formed a military alliance called the Warsaw Pact – the members would defend each other if any member was attacked.
5. In Hungary in 1956 the communist Government was very unpopular and the people resented the lack of freedom. There were demonstrations and protests. A new leader was chosen (with Soviet approval) who promised greater freedom but when he also decided to leave the Warsaw Pact the USSR changed its mind and sent the Red Army to crush the rising.
6. In 1961 an increasing number of people in communist East Germany were leaving by crossing into capitalist West Germany. The USSR responded by building the Berlin Wall – and stopping all movement from East to West Berlin. It stayed in place for 28 years and became a symbol of Cold War tension.
7. In Czechoslovakia in 1968 after mass protests the communist Government tried to introduce more freedom for its people. Again, the Soviet Union sent the Red Army to crush the protests.
8. In 1980 a trade union in Poland called Solidarity led a protest movement against communist control that was tolerated to start with until the army took over in Poland and Solidarity was crushed.
9. In 1985 Gorbachev became leader of the USSR. He believed the USSR needed to change and he introduced two key ideas: *glasnost* (openness) and *perestroika* (restructuring).
10. He also told the communist governments of eastern Europe that the USSR was no longer going to intervene to prop them up. They were on their own. In 1988 he began to withdraw Soviet troops from eastern Europe.
11. The impact of this was not immediately clear but by 1989 people in eastern Europe began to test what this meant in practice. First of all Hungarians began to dismantle the barbed-wire fence between Hungary and the West. Over the rest of the summer of 1989 people acted similarly throughout eastern Europe, culminating with the dismantling of the Berlin Wall (while troops looked on) in November.
12. Gorbachev was awarded the Nobel Peace Prize for helping to end the Cold War between the USA and the USSR but he was not popular in the USSR. The USSR fragmented and he resigned as leader on Christmas Day 1991.

PRACTICE QUESTIONS

Structured questions

1. (a) What were *glasnost* and *perestroika*? **[4]**
   (b) Why did Mikhail Gorbachev change Soviet policy towards eastern Europe? **[6]**
   (c) 'Gorbachev almost singlehandedly ended communist control of eastern Europe.' How far do you agree with this statement? Explain your answer. **[10]**

Document questions

1. Study Source 16 on page 135. What is the cartoonist's message? Explain your answer using details of the source and your own knowledge. **[7]**
2. Study Source 17 and Figure 18 on page 135. Does Figure 18 prove Kennedy was right in Source 17? Explain your answer using details of the sources and your own knowledge. **[8]**
3. Study Sources 20 and 21 on page 136. How far do these two sources disagree? Explain your answer using details of the sources and your own knowledge. **[8]**
4. Study Source 23 on page 137. Why was this source published at this time? Explain your answer using details of the source and your knowledge. **[7]**
5. Study Sources 16–23 on pages 135–37. How far do these sources provide convincing evidence that the Berlin Wall was built to contain the West? Use the sources to explain your answer. **[9]**

See pages 148–67 for advice on the different types of questions.

Focus on: Structured Questions

The Core Content you have studied in Section A will be examined in both Paper 1 Structured Questions and Paper 2 Document Questions. The main difference between the two papers is that the Document Questions paper is a source-based paper while the Structured Questions paper is made up of structured essay questions.

The information in this section is based on the Cambridge International syllabus. You should always refer to the appropriate syllabus document for the year of examination to confirm the details and for more information. The syllabus document is available on the Cambridge International website at www.cambridgeinternational.org.

Structure

Section A of the Structured Questions paper examines the Core Content and consists of structured essay questions.

Structured essay questions usually have a similar structure and require you to describe, explain and reach a supported judgement.

Description means giving an account from your own knowledge.

Explanation means using your own knowledge to explain why or how something happened.

A supported judgement means your own opinion about something based on relevant contextual knowledge. It is important to be balanced – i.e. to examine different points of view before reaching a judgement.

The tasks in this book will have developed the skills and knowledge for you to do all these things.

Section A questions usually have a similar structure:
- You are given a **simple statement** – however, you are *not* asked questions on this; it is simply intended to focus your thinking.

Then there are three sub-questions testing different skills:
a) A **knowledge** or **description** question. This will often begin 'describe' or 'what'.
b) An **explanation** question. This will begin with 'why'.
c) A **judgement** question. One common type of question gives you a statement to agree or disagree with. You need to make a judgement and back up your judgement with evidence and argument.

For example:

> a) What were Germany's main territorial losses under the Treaty of Versailles? [4]
> b) Why did Clemenceau and Lloyd George disagree about how to treat Germany at the Paris Peace Conference? [6]
> c) 'The Treaty of Versailles was a fair settlement.' How far do you agree with this statement? Explain your answer. [10]

Think before you write

It is a common mistake for students to launch straight into writing as soon as they see the question, but our advice is that you spend some time thinking before you do so.

1 Choose your question carefully

Read *all* questions carefully before you decide which to answer. You should have revised enough to give you a choice of questions, but don't immediately opt for your favourite topic. Sometimes your less favoured topic might have a question which is easier to answer or which suits you better.

2 Read the questions carefully

This might sound obvious but there is a skill to it.
- Look for **command words** such as 'describe' or 'explain' which let you know what type of skills you have to use.
- Identify **the topic** and the sub-topic. Questions will often focus on an event, individual or historical issue.
- Look for **dates**. If dates are given they will be important.

3 Plan your answer

If you think through your answer first, then writing it is easy. If you skip the thinking and just start writing, the risks are:
- Your writing will be muddled.
- You will write in an illogical order.
- Your points won't lead to your conclusion.
- Even more likely, you will keep thinking of something more to say and will run out of time.

4 Plan your time

Running out of time is *not* unlucky, it is a mistake! The marks for each sub-question guide you as to how long to spend.

Worked examples: The Inter-war Years, 1919–39

These first examples are based on the content of Chapters 1 to 3.

How to approach description-style questions

Description questions may not use the word 'describe' but that is what you need to do. For example:

> What were Germany's main territorial losses under the Treaty of Versailles? **[4]**

The questions, example answers and comments that appear on pages 148–54 were written by the author. In an examination, the way marks would be awarded to answers like these may be different.

✓ This will be straightforward if you have revised thoroughly. You simply have to display accurate knowledge. However, bear in mind you still have to select facts which are relevant to the question. Selection is a vital skill for a historian. Questions like this have a strict content focus. Don't waste time giving information that is not relevant.

> Under the Treaty of Versailles Germany lost 10 per cent of its land and all of its overseas colonies, so many Germans ended up living in other countries. Some German land was given to its European neighbours. Alsace-Lorraine was given to France and West Prussia was given to Poland to ensure that Poland had a sea port.

Here is an example we have written of a good answer. It uses plenty of relevant knowledge to thoroughly describe the main territorial losses under the Treaty of Versailles.

How to approach explanation-style questions

Here is an example of an explanation question.

> Why did Clemenceau and Lloyd George disagree about how to treat Germany at the Paris Peace Conference? **[6]**

✓ **Read the question carefully** to see what you have to explain. The focus is on:
- Clemenceau and Lloyd George (not on Wilson)
- how to treat Germany.

You need to **select**, from your knowledge of the Peace Conference, examples of *how* and *why* these two people (Clemenceau and Lloyd George) disagreed about this specific thing (how to treat Germany). You probably know a lot more about the Peace Conference than this but once again it is vital to remain focused and not give unnecessary information.

Use a paragraph structure to help you fully develop your answer. Many teachers use Point, Evidence, Explain (PEE) to help students. You might have another technique.

✗ **A common error** which students make is to describe the disagreements rather than giving reasons for them.

> This answer gets straight to the point and gives valid reasons about why the leaders disagreed about how to treat Germany. There is no wasting time on irrelevant or background information.

> The opening sentence of each paragraph clearly states a reason for disagreement. The rest of each paragraph explains clearly why Clemenceau held this view and why Lloyd George held a different view.

Lloyd George and Clemenceau disagreed over what to do about Germany because Clemenceau saw Germany as a bigger threat than Lloyd George did. During the war France suffered massive damage to its industries, towns and agriculture. Over two-thirds of French troops were killed or injured in the war. Germany's population was still much greater than France's (75 million compared to 40 million) and Germany had invaded France in 1870 and 1914. Lloyd George did not see Germany as a threat in the same way. In fact he wanted to rebuild Germany so that British industries could start trading with Germany.

Lloyd George and Clemenceau also disagreed about what measures would work. Clemenceau thought the best way to get future peace was to cripple Germany by breaking it up into separate states, reducing its army and forcing it to pay huge fines. Lloyd George believed this would not work. It would simply make Germany want revenge in the future. So although he favoured fines and some limits on German arms he did not think Germany should be treated as harshly as Clemenceau did.

How to approach judgement-style questions

An important skill at this stage of your studies is to be able to think like a historian and make a judgement. Can you:
- weigh up different factors – whether you think one factor is more important than others
- decide how far you agree or disagree with a particular opinion?

Here is an example of a judgement question.

> 'The Treaty of Versailles was a fair settlement.' How far do you agree with this statement? Explain your answer. **[10]**

✓ You need to plan your answer to this question before you start writing so that you remain focused on the topic throughout your answer. So make sure you:
- Step 1: understand the statement.
- Step 2: list key points which support and oppose the statement.
- Step 3: decide on your argument (the view that you are best able to support with evidence).

You are then ready to write your answer.

There are many different ways to structure your answer. Many teachers advise students to:
- explain reasons to agree with the statement
- explain reasons to disagree
- finally, to express your judgement as to how far you agree.

There is not a right or wrong judgement to reach as long as you can explain yourself and support it with valid knowledge. Make sure you can write balanced answers that use your wider knowledge of the topic, as it is rare in History that there is ever a single cause for any event.

✗ **A common error** is to only give your own view without considering another or giving it little or no explanation.

> **The first three paragraphs give reasons why historians or people at the time would argue the Treaty was fair. These could be all put in a single paragraph but it can help organise your thinking to put a point per paragraph.**

There are many arguments to support the view that the Treaty of Versailles was a fair settlement. To begin with, it was strongly believed that Germany had started the war and was therefore responsible for it. It was certainly true that Germany invaded neutral Belgium in 1914, which broke international treaties.

Another argument was that most of the fighting on the western front took place in Belgium and France. France lost around 1.6 million troops and civilians as well as suffering huge damage to industry, towns and agriculture. There was no fighting on German soil and so there was a strong case that Germany should pay compensation.

A third argument was that the Treaty was not as harsh as its critics claimed. Germany certainly lost territory in the Versailles settlement – 10 per cent of its land, all colonies, 12.5 per cent of its population. However, it could have been a lot harsher. Clemenceau wanted Germany to be broken up into small states. And when we look at the Treaty of Brest-Litovsk, which Germany forced Russia to sign in 1918, we can see that Germany was much harsher in its terms with Russia than the Allies were with Germany at Versailles.

> **This paragraph gives reasons why historians or people at the time might argue the Treaty was unfair.**

Of course, there were terms that were seen as unfair. Germans regarded the Treaty as a diktat because they were not consulted about it. They also believed that the Allies operated double standards. For example, the German army was limited to 100,000 men but France and Britain and most other countries did not reduce their armed forces to the same levels. Another term that could be seen as unfair was the fact that many Germans were left outside Germany as a result of the Treaty.

> **The conclusion states a clear judgement, supported with evidence.**

Overall, I agree with the statement. Obviously no treaty will be seen as fair by all sides but the Treaty of Versailles was as fair as it possibly could have been, and was a lot fairer on Germany than it might have been. The arguments against the Treaty were mainly complaints from the German point of view at the time, as many Germans believed the peace treaty would be based on Wilson's 14 Points and were not happy about the reparation payments or War Guilt Clause imposed by other countries such as France.

Worked examples: The Cold War, 1945–c.1989

These examples are based on the content of Chapters 4–6.

How to approach description-style questions

Description questions may not use the word 'describe' but that is what you need to do. For example:

> What agreements were made at the Yalta Conference? [4]

✓ This will be straightforward if you have revised thoroughly. You simply have to display accurate knowledge. However bear in mind you still have to select facts which are relevant to the question. Selection is a vital skill for a historian. Questions like this have a strict content focus so don't waste time giving information that is not relevant.

✗ **A common error** is writing too much for a four-mark question – this will waste time.

> They agreed to divide Germany into four occupation zones run by Britain, France, the USA and the Soviet Union, and they agreed to allow free elections to take place in eastern Europe. They also all agreed to join a new United Nations Organisation to try to keep world peace after the war. Finally, Stalin agreed to help the Allies in the war against Japan when Germany was defeated.

> Here is an example we have written of a good answer. It uses plenty of relevant knowledge to thoroughly describe many of the agreements made at the Yalta Conference.

How to approach explanation-style questions

Here is an example of an explanation question.

> Why was the Truman Doctrine important? [6]

✓ **Read the question carefully** to see what you have to explain.

The focus for this question is on:
- the Truman Doctrine
- why it was important.

You need to **select**, from your knowledge of the Truman Doctrine, examples of *how* and *why* it was important. It is vital to remain focused and not give unnecessary information.

Use a paragraph structure to help you fully develop your answer. Many teachers use Point, Evidence, Explain (PEE) to help students. You might have another technique.

✗ **A common error** is to describe the policy rather than giving reasons why it was important.

> The Truman Doctrine was important because it marked an increase in tension between the USA and USSR and could even be seen as the start of the Cold War. The US President Harry Truman was angry and concerned at the way that Stalin had established communist regimes in many eastern European states in the period 1946-47. Although the Soviet leader Stalin saw this as a defensive policy against possible future invasions, Truman regarded it as Stalin trying to build an empire. His response was the Truman Doctrine, designed to stop any further spread of communism.
>
> Under the Truman Doctrine the USA said it would send money, equipment and advice to any country which was, in American eyes, threatened by a communist take-over. He did not offer troops. Most of the communist take-overs had been carried out by communist sympathisers inside each country who had been helped by Stalin. Truman therefore chose to help opponents of communism in a similar sort of way. This way he could oppose the spread of communism without triggering a war.

Annotations:
- This is a good clear opening.
- This is quite an interesting point but it is not really answering the question.
- This section explains what Truman's concerns were and why he responded to those concerns with the Truman Doctrine.

How to approach judgement-style questions

An important skill at this stage of your studies is to be able to think like a historian and make a judgement. Can you:
- weigh up different factors – whether you think one factor is more important than others
- decide how far you agree or disagree with a particular opinion?

Here is an example of a judgement question.

> 'The USA was more responsible than the USSR in causing the Cold War in the late 1940s.' How far do you agree with this statement? Explain your answer. [10]

✓ You need to plan your answer before you start writing so you remain focused on the topic in the question. Make sure you:
- Step 1: understand the statement.
- Step 2: list key points which support and oppose the statement.
- Step 3: decide on your argument (the view that you are best able to support with evidence).

You are then ready to write your answer.

There are many different ways to structure your answer. Many teachers advise students to:
- explain reasons to agree with the statement
- explain reasons to disagree
- finally to express your judgement as to how far you agree.

There is not a right or wrong judgement to reach as long as you can explain yourself and support your judgement with valid knowledge. Make sure you can write balanced answers that use your wider knowledge of the topic as it is rare in History that there is ever a single cause for any event.

✗ **A common error** is to only give your own view without considering another or giving it little or no explanation.

Comments (left margin)

- Good start – very clear what is being said here.
- Again, very clear what point is being made – and this is then followed up with supporting facts.
- Once again it is very clear what point is being made and it is followed up well with supporting evidence.
- This is still a strong balancing point although it is not quite as crystal clear as the two paragraphs before. The reader has to wait to find out what point is being made.
- This is a sensible conclusion. If you really wanted to go the extra mile you could possibly refer to the work of a historian you have read to fully develop a paragraph like this.

Essay

In some respects the statement is correct. The USA could be accused of causing the Cold War in some ways. One reason for this was the attitude of US President Truman towards Stalin and the USSR. His predecessor Roosevelt had had relatively good relations with Stalin. Truman was much more anti-communist and aggressive towards the USSR. He was very critical of Stalin's actions in eastern Europe. He tried to intimidate Stalin at the Potsdam Conference by telling Stalin the USA had developed an atomic bomb. He also encouraged former British Prime Minister Winston Churchill to give the 'iron curtain' speech in 1947, which was a major cause of tension.

There were other ways in which the USA could be seen as responsible for the Cold War. One of these was the USA's Marshall Aid programme. This programme channelled billions of dollars of economic aid into the countries which had been affected by the war, mostly countries in western Europe. However, it was only available to countries that agreed to have democratic governments like the USA and capitalist economies, like the USA. The Soviets saw this as 'dollar imperialism' – trying to create an empire of states which were dependent on US dollars.

On the other hand it could be argued that the USSR was more responsible for the Cold War. At the end of the Second World War Soviet troops drove German forces out of eastern Europe. However, after Germany surrendered in 1945 the Soviet forces stayed in most eastern European states. At the same time Stalin encouraged and supported communist supporters within states like Poland, Hungary and Czechoslovakia to take control of these countries and set up communist governments which supported the USSR. This caused a great deal of tension with the USA and Britain who saw this as the USSR building an empire and planning to take over the rest of Europe as well.

Overall, I believe that the statement is incorrect and that neither the USA nor USSR were more to blame for the Cold War. The real difficulty was that each side was unable to understand the viewpoint of the other side because of their differing ideologies. As a result they tended to misunderstand and misinterpret each other's actions and this is what caused the worst of the tension.

Focus on: Document Questions

> The information in this section is based on the Cambridge International syllabus. You should always refer to the appropriate syllabus document for the year of examination to confirm the details and for more information. The syllabus document is available on the Cambridge International website at www.cambridgeinternational.org.

Paper 2 Document Questions will also be based on your study of the Core Content in Chapters 1 to 6. The difference between the Structured Questions paper and the Document Questions paper is that Document Questions are source-based investigations. They test your ability to use your knowledge and skill to evaluate a range of sources and use them to answer an historical question. This question will be drawn from the Core Content. You will have been told in advance what general area this investigation will be based on. For example: 'How effectively did the USA contain the spread of communism?'

Features

- This paper includes a range of **sources**. Typically you will find some pictures and a range of different types of written sources.
- Sources are not designed to catch you out, but usually some sources **agree** with each other, some **disagree** and some do a bit of both!
- This paper includes **five questions** – you have to answer them all.
- These questions typically take you **step-by-step** through the sources: using, evaluating and comparing them towards a final question that gets you using all the sources to answer the big question.
- The skill you need to answer source-based questions is to **think like an historian**. This means doing more than extracting basic information from a source. It means considering the following:
  — **Purpose**: why the source was produced.
  — **Audience**: the audience for the source.
  — **Methods**: the methods used in the source to convince its audience.
  — **Attitudes**: what the source reveals about the person/people who made it, for example their attitudes, values, concerns. The makers may be angry, afraid, unhappy, outraged ... and much more.
  — **Tone**: sources may deny, criticise, mock, praise, accuse, threaten or warn, and this will allow you to make inferences about the author of the source.
- As well as the content of the sources, you will also need to use your **background knowledge** to evaluate the sources (e.g. your knowledge of events might confirm what is being said in a source, or your knowledge of a particular group might help you to evaluate a source produced by that group).

Advice

- **Read through all the sources** before you start writing anything.
- Read through **all the questions** as well. Note the marks for each so you know how much time to spend.
- Always **support your answers with details from the sources**. For written sources use actual words or phrases from the source to support your answer. For visual sources describe relevant features from the source and explain how they support your answer.
- **Use your background knowledge** whenever it's helpful, but **don't include background knowledge just for its own sake** if it's got nothing to do with the source or the question.
- When you use your own knowledge avoid saying 'my knowledge tells me...'. Just **state what you know**.
- **Avoid speculation** – so avoid using words like 'might' and 'could' (such as 'The author might be a supporter so he could be biased...').
- **Avoid phrases such** as 'we don't know what else...' or 'she could have forgotten...'. This type of phrase could apply to any source so does not display any skill or knowledge.
- Sources might support or challenge each other. When you explain how Source X supports or challenges Source Y, **be specific** – use details from the sources to support your explanation.
- **Don't include your own personal views which are not historical** (such as, 'I think it was awful the way the USA used chemical weapons in Vietnam...').

Question types

- This page gives examples of question types. You could encounter any type of question about any type of source so this is not comprehensive! These are only a small selection of possible question types.
- It is also important to remember that your answers to the different types of question will vary depending on the actual source – there is no 'one size fits all' formula.
- On pages 157–59 and 162–65 are some worked examples with our comments. On pages 160–61 and 166–67 are sets of practice questions we have put together.

'What is the message?'

The source could be a cartoon, or a poster or part of a speech – something where the creator is trying to make a particular point.

Think about the following:
- What is the cartoonist/speaker/artist for or against? These sources are not made simply to inform. They might criticise, disapprove or maybe mock.
- How do you know? What details in the source tell you the maker's view?
- Why then? Why was the message relevant at that point in time?
- Note: For message questions, you do not need to comment on reliability.

Comparison: 'How far do Sources X and Y agree about...?'

Look for:
- similarities and/or differences in the **content** of the sources
- similarities and/or differences at a more subtle level, for example in the **attitudes** shown, or the **purpose**. For example, two text sources may agree about events or details (e.g. that the USSR did place missiles in Cuba) but differ in attitude (e.g. one might be critical of the USSR whereas the other is supportive).

'How useful is Source X for...?'

All sources are useful for something so think in terms of 'How is this source useful...?' Even a biased source is useful for telling you about the attitudes of the person or organisation who created them.

For example, an American poster accusing communists of crimes is not reliable evidence about communists but it is very useful in showing how far Americans were worried about communism.

Purpose: 'Why was Source X published at this time?'

Work out the message of the source and then think about why this message was relevant at the time or what the maker of the source wanted to achieve by getting that message across.

For example did they want to change people's attitudes or behaviour (e.g. getting them to join a movement or contribute funds to a particular cause).

Is Source X surprising

These questions test your knowledge and understanding of the period in which the source was created.

Look for whether the **events** and **attitudes** in the source are surprising given what you know about the context of the time.

For example, you might be surprised to hear a speech by President Richard Nixon building friendly relations with communist China in the 1970s although the USA was traditionally very anticommunist. Or you might not be surprised because you know he was trying to end the Vietnam War and this involved improved relations with China.

'How reliable is Source X about...?'

A source is never reliable or unreliable in itself. It all depends on what you are using it for.

Think about the following:
- **The author**. The caption may tell you something about the author or you may know something from your contextual knowledge. Explain whether the author can be trusted to tell the truth about particular people, issues or events.
- **The tone.** If the source uses emotive language or a biased tone this will affect how far you trust the source's view of particular people, issues or events.
- **Knowledge**. Does the source fit with or contradict your own knowledge about particular people, issues or events?
- **Cross-referencing**. Sometimes you will be asked to compare sources, but even if you are not you can use other sources in the paper to support or contradict the source and to comment on their reliability.

Conclusion: 'How far do Sources A–G support this statement?'

This is worth most marks. It builds on the previous questions and asks you to use as many sources as possible in your answer.

Make sure you:
- Address both sides of the argument: how the sources support and how they don't support the statement.
- Work through source by source, explaining whether and how they support or challenge the statement.
- Start a new paragraph for each source.
- When you make use of a source in your answer, don't just refer to it by letter. Use relevant detail from the source to show how it supports or challenges the statement.

Worked examples based on the Inter-war years 1919–39 content

The questions, example answers and comments that appear on pages 157–67 were written by the authors. In an examination, the way marks would be awarded to questions like these may be different.

SOURCE A

The Sudetenland is the last problem that must be solved and it will be solved. It is the last territorial claim which I have to make in Europe.

The aims of our foreign policy are not unlimited … They are grounded on the determination to save the German people alone … Ten million Germans found themselves beyond the frontiers of the Reich … Germans who wished to return to the Reich as their homeland.

Hitler speaking in Berlin, September 1938.

> Recognises that biased and untrustworthy sources are useful! In this case, we may not be able to **trust** what Hitler is saying, but it is still **useful** in revealing how Hitler manipulated the situation.

1 Study Source A. How useful is this source to an historian? Explain your answer using details of the source and your knowledge. **[7]**

> The source is definitely useful because it tells us how Hitler was publicly portraying the issue of the Sudetenland to the German people and the rest of the world. He says that it is the 'last territorial claim' Germany has in Europe. Even though this turned out not to be true, it is still useful to show us the methods Hitler used to get what he wanted. He was using the language of peace because he was trying to take the Sudetenland without having to fight for it. He worried that Britain and France would fight alongside Czechoslovakia to stop him and hoped that promising to leave Czechoslovakia alone would prevent this. The source also gives us an insight into why some people in Britain supported Appeasement and helps explain why the Munich Agreement was generally popular in Britain after it was signed.

SOURCE B

A British cartoon published in the *News of the World*, shortly after the Munich Agreement.

2 Study Source B. What is the message of the cartoonist? Explain your answer using details of the source and your knowledge. **[7]**

> Good idea to start your answer in this way. It gets you straight to the point. This answer has carefully and correctly identified that the source is supportive of the Munich Agreement.

> The message that the cartoonist was trying to put across is that Chamberlain has done a good job by signing the Munich Agreement, avoiding a crisis and averting taking the world to war, and moving it towards peace.

> You can see this because he's shown as tough and strong with his sleeves rolled up, successfully rolling the globe across the sheer drop to war below.

> The cartoonist clearly thinks that giving Hitler the Sudetenland in 1938 was the right decision.

> The answer has not simply described the cartoon but has actually **used** the details to **support** the point made above.

> Understands the **context** in which this cartoon was drawn, and gets this across, without too much unnecessary detail.

SOURCE C

People of Britain, your children are safe. Your husbands and your sons will not march to war. Peace is a victory for all mankind. If we must have a victor, let us choose Chamberlain, for the Prime Minister's conquests are mighty and enduring – millions of happy homes and hearts relieved of their burden.

The *Daily Express* comments on the Munich Agreement, 30 September 1938.

SOURCE D

We have suffered a total defeat ... I think you will find that in a period of time Czechoslovakia will be engulfed in the Nazi regime. We have passed an awful milestone in our history. This is only the beginning of the reckoning.

Winston Churchill speaking in October 1938. He felt that Britain should resist the demands of Hitler. However, he was an isolated figure in the 1930s.

3 Study Sources C and D. How far does Source D prove Source C wrong? Explain your answer using details of the sources and your knowledge. **[8]**

> In some ways Source D does prove Source C wrong. The newspaper says that the Munich Agreement will bring peace – 'your husbands and sons will not march to war'. This is contradicted by Churchill when he says 'This is only the beginning of the reckoning'. The overall impression given by Source C is that people are relieved by the Munich Agreement, whereas Churchill seems to prove this wrong by being very critical of it.
>
> However, Source D cannot prove Source C wrong about people's reactions to the Munich Agreement. Lots of people in Britain were relieved that it had averted war, or at least delayed it in the short term. This can be seen by looking at Source B, where the cartoonist seems to support Chamberlain's actions, showing how he has dealt well with a tricky situation.

Uses the content of the sources to show how they disagree. This is a useful starting point – it is saying that Source D says Source C is wrong about people's attitudes to the Munich Agreement. It is important to explain 'wrong about what?'.

Improves the answer because it looks at the issue of 'proof' in a different way. By **cross-referencing** Source C with another source on the paper, it can be shown that while Churchill may be right about the Munich Agreement in general, he cannot prove Source C wrong about people's **reactions to it**.

SOURCE E

By repeatedly surrendering to force, Chamberlain has encouraged aggression ... our central contention, therefore, is that Mr Chamberlain's policy has throughout been based on a fatal misunderstanding of the psychology of dictatorship.

Extract from an article in a British newspaper, the *Yorkshire Post*, published in December 1938.

4 Study Sources E and F. Does Source E make Source F surprising? Explain your answer using details of the sources and your knowledge. **[8]**

SOURCE F

A GREAT MEDIATOR

John Bull. "I've known many Prime Ministers in my time, Sir, but never one who worked so hard for security in the face of such terrible odds."

A British cartoon published in 1938 at the time of the Munich Agreement. John Bull represents Britain.

Source E does make Source F surprising because the message in Source E suggests that Chamberlain's policy of appeasing Germany has been a failure and has 'encouraged aggression', whereas in Source F the cartoonist portrays Chamberlain as 'a great mediator' who has saved Britain from war against Germany. Many politicians in Britain as well as much of the public still remembered the horrors and casualties caused by the Great War and were desperate to avoid a conflict with Germany, even if it meant that Hitler was appeased and given the Sudetenland in the Munich Agreement. This makes Source F less surprising. However, Source F is still surprising as politicians such as Churchill and some newspapers believed that Appeasement was a mistake and would encourage Hitler to take over even more territory in the future.

> A thorough response which clearly compares and contrasts the two sources and uses good source details to support the explanations of why Source F is surprising. The answer also uses some good contextual knowledge to give balance to the argument over surprise, though some more precise knowledge or examples would have helped develop the explanation further.

5 Study Sources A–F. How far do these sources provide convincing evidence that the crisis in Czechoslovakia was a failure for Appeasement? Use the sources to explain your answer. **[9]**

> A well-balanced answer that uses all of the sources to address the question. Each source is analysed individually and well-selected details from each of the sources are used to support the arguments. There is some attempt to use contextual knowledge to evaluate the reliability of Source A but this is not necessary for this question. It is important to make sure each source is referenced by its source letter or by relevant quotations or descriptions of source content.

Source A was written by Hitler and suggests that after the Sudetenland has been given to Germany, he will make no more territorial claims in Europe. Hitler says that it is 'the last problem that must be solved' which suggests that Appeasement was not a failure but instead would avoid war against Germany in the future. However, the source is not completely trustworthy because Hitler clearly had ambitions to expand eastwards and retake the Polish Corridor which was land lost in the Treaty of Versailles and he eventually planned to invade the East to create Lebensraum for the German Reich.

Source B also suggests that the Munich Agreement was a success for Appeasement. Chamberlain is seen in the cartoon carefully manoeuvring the world away from war suggesting that the Munich Conference helped achieve future peace in Europe.

Source C is a newspaper article which expresses the idea that Chamberlain's actions at the Munich Conference were a great success and have avoided war. The Daily Express reads 'People of Britain, your children are safe.' Many families still remembered the horrors of the Great War and many newspapers voiced their relief when the Munich Agreement was signed.

Source D, however, was a speech by Churchill who was a vocal opponent of Appeasement and Chamberlain. Churchill says that 'Czechoslovakia will be engulfed in the Nazi regime' which suggests that the Munich Conference was a failure for Appeasement and would lead to further German expansion in the near future.

Source E, which is an article in the Yorkshire Post, implies that Chamberlain is a failure and the Munich Agreement has actually 'encouraged aggression' by giving in to Hitler's demands over the Sudetenland.

Source F views the Munich Conference and Chamberlain's actions as a success rather than a failure. In the cartoon, Chamberlain is being congratulated by John Bull who represents the British public. This indicates to the reader that the cartoonist believes Chamberlain has helped maintain peace and security in Europe and thus avoided war with Germany thanks to his diplomatic actions.

Practice: How successful was the League of Nations in the 1920s?

SOURCE A

The League was created, first and foremost, as a security organisation. But in this respect it fell badly short of its original aims. There was no way to guarantee that members would carry out their obligations to enforce sanctions or undertake military force where it might be needed. But it was not without its achievements. For most countries attendance at League meetings in the 1920s was seen as essential, because the foreign ministers of the major powers were almost always present. The small and middle sized states found the League was a vital platform for them to talk about their interests and concerns. Even those outside the League, including the United States, found it useful to attend League-sponsored Conferences and similar events. Without exaggerating its importance the League developed useful ways of handling inter-state disputes. For the most part the League handled the 'small change' of international diplomacy. It was not a substitute for great power diplomacy as Wilson had hoped, but it was an additional resource which contributed to the handling of international politics.

An American historian writing in 2005.

SOURCE B

Despite its poor historical reputation, the League of Nations should not be dismissed as a complete failure. Of sixty-six international disputes it had to deal with (four of which had led to open hostilities), it successfully resolved thirty-five important disputes and quite legitimately passed back twenty to the traditional channels of diplomacy where major powers negotiated settlements outside the League. It failed to resolve eleven conflicts. Like its successor the United Nations, it was capable of being effective.

A British historian writing in 2009.

SOURCE C

BALKANDUM AND BALKANDEE.
"JUST THEN CAME DOWN A MONSTROUS DOVE
WHOSE FORCE WAS PURELY MORAL,
WHICH TURNED THE HEROES' HEARTS TO LOVE
AND MADE THEM DROP THEIR QUARREL."—LEWIS CARROLL (adapted).

A British cartoon about the conflict between Greece and Bulgaria, published in December 1925.

SOURCE D

The League Council felt that our role under the League Covenant was to do everything we could to promote a settlement, and since the two parties had willingly agreed to accept the decision of the Conference of Ambassadors our job from this point was to do everything we could to help the Ambassadors make decisions which were in line with the opinions expressed in the Assembly in Geneva. In this I believe we acted rightly and properly.

British Government minister Lord Robert Cecil writing in October 1923 about the Corfu crisis. Cecil was the British minister responsible for League of Nations matters.

SOURCE E

In response to the successive menaces of Mussolini we muzzled the League, we imposed the fine on Greece without evidence of her guilt and without reference to the International Court of Justice, and we disbanded the Commission of Enquiry. A settlement was thus achieved. At the time I felt that British public opinion will wonder how it came about that we entered into the dispute upon a firm moral basis and that in the end we forced Greece to accept a settlement that was unjust. Corfu was evacuated by the Italians, but the League of Nations had suffered a defeat from which its prestige has never recovered.

British Government official Sir Harold Nicolson writing in 1929, soon after he resigned from the British diplomatic service after criticising one of his ministers.

SOURCE F

Greek forces have invaded our sovereign territory. Make only slight resistance. Protect the refugees. Prevent the spread of panic. Do not expose the troops to unnecessary losses in view of the fact that the incident has been laid before the Council of the League of Nations, which is expected to stop the invasion.

A telegram from the Bulgarian Ministry of War in Sofia to its army commanders, 22 October 1925.

SOURCE G

A cartoon published in the USA in 1919. The title of the cartoon was 'The League of Nations Bridge' and the character on the right (John Bull, representing Britain) is saying: 'Your bridge, Jonathan. We shan't quarrel about this.'

---

1. Study Sources A and B.
   How far do Sources A and B agree about the League of Nations? Explain your answer using details from the sources. **[8]**
2. Study Source C.
   What is the message of the cartoonist? Explain your answer using details from the source and your own knowledge. **[7]**
3. Study Sources D and E.
   Why do these sources give such different accounts of the League's actions over Corfu? Explain your answer using details from the sources and your own knowledge. **[8]**
4. Study Source F.
   Are you surprised by Source F? Explain your answer using details from the source and your own knowledge. **[8]**
5. Study Sources A–G.
   'The League of Nations was very successful in the 1920s.' How far do these sources support this statement? Use the sources to explain your answer. **[9]**

Worked examples based on the Cold War 1945–c.1989 content

(a) Study Sources A and B. How far do these sources disagree over reasons why some people opposed the war in Vietnam? Explain your answer using details of the sources and your knowledge. **[8]**

SOURCE A

The Tet Offensive was the decisive battle of the Vietnam War because of its profound impact on American attitudes about involvement in Southeast Asia. In the aftermath of Tet, many Americans became disillusioned … To the American public and even to members of the administration, the offensive demonstrated that US intervention … had produced a negligible effect on the will and capability of the Viet Cong and North Vietnamese.

Extract from *The Tet Offensive: Intelligence Failure in War* by James Wirtz.

SOURCE B

One does not use napalm on villages and hamlets sheltering civilians if one is attempting to persuade these people of the rightness of one's cause. One does not defoliate [destroy the vegetation of] the country and deform its people with chemicals if one is attempting to persuade them of the foe's evil nature.

Richard Hamer, an American journalist comments on US policy failure in Vietnam, 1970.

A very focused start to the response. This part starts by explaining the opinions implied in Source A and uses some good contextual knowledge to support the explanation.

> Sources A and B disagree over the main reasons why some people were opposed to US involvement in the Vietnam War. Source A suggests many Americans became 'disillusioned' after the Tet Offensive in 1968 when the Viet Cong launched a surprise offensive in over one hundred cities and against key US and South Vietnamese military targets. Many in the USA saw the surprise attack as evidence that American money and lives were being wasted in the conflict in Vietnam as the Viet Cong were clearly undefeated and supported by many in South Vietnam.
>
> Contrastingly, Source B opposes the war in Vietnam because of the inhumanity associated with the chemical warfare tactics used by US forces against the Vietnamese population. The author comments on the use of 'napalm on villages' and the use of chemicals which 'deform its people'. The USA used napalm bombs to attack settlements they believed to be Viet Cong strongholds and used Agent Orange, a strong chemical to to clear vegetations and jungle cover to stop supplies from the North down the Ho Chi Minh Trail. Both weapons caused horrific injuries to civilians and soldiers alike, and Agent Orange was known to lead to birth defects.

This part makes the vital contrast between the two sources by explaining the different opinion portrayed in Source B and is supported by some in-depth contextual knowledge.

SOURCE C

We were not in My Lai to kill human beings. We were there to kill ideology that is carried by – I don't know – pawns. Blobs. Pieces of flesh. And I wasn't in My Lai to destroy intelligent men. I was there to destroy an intangible idea ... To destroy Communism.

From Lieutenant Calley's account of the event, *Body Count*, published in 1971.

SOURCE D

This was a time for us to get even. A time for us to settle the score. A time for revenge – when we can get revenge for our fallen comrades. The order we were given was to kill and destroy everything that was in the village. It was to kill the pigs, drop them in the wells; pollute the water supply ... burn the village, burn the hootches as we went through it. It was clearly explained that there were to be no prisoners. The order that was given was to kill everyone in the village. Someone asked if this meant the women and children. And the order was: everyone in the village, because those people that were in the village – the women, the kids, the old men – were VC ... or they were sympathetic to the Viet Cong.

The testimony of US Army Sergeant Hodge to the official US Army investigation into My Lai in 1970.

(b) Study Sources C and D. Why do they differ in their accounts of what happened at My Lai in 1968? Explain your answer using details of the sources and your knowledge. **[8]**

> Even though this response has not yet tackled the question of **why** the sources differ, it is a good approach because we can see the sources are being **compared to each other**, and not dealt with in isolation.

> In Source C, Lieutenant Calley gives the impression that the massacre at My Lai was not really a massacre or a revenge operation: 'We were not in My Lai to kill human beings.' But in Source D, Sergeant Hodge says it was revenge - the operation was 'a time for us to get even'.
>
> I think the sources say different things because at the time they were produced, Calley and other officers in Charlie Company had been charged with murder for what happened at My Lai. So Hodge is trying to put the blame for what happened on his senior officers, placing all the responsibility on them, whilst Calley is trying to justify his actions. He's trying to appeal to people's fear of communism.

> This part now successfully tackles the question of **why** the sources differ and uses the **context and purpose** of the sources to fully explain this.

SOURCE E

"There's Money Enough To Support Both Of You — Now, Doesn't That Make You Feel Better?"

An American cartoon from 1967.

(c) Study Source E. What is the message of the cartoonist? Explain your answer using details of the source and your knowledge. **[7]**

> The cartoonist is criticising President Lyndon Johnson for lying to the American people when he says there is enough money to fight the Vietnam War and help poorer areas of the USA (shown by the ragged woman labelled US Urban Needs). The cartoonist clearly thinks that the Vietnam War is getting all the money and poor Americans are being ignored.
>
> This was published in 1967 and by this time a lot of the US media were starting to question American involvement.

This answer correctly identifies that this cartoonist is **critical** of America's sustained involvement.

SOURCE F

The American military was not defeated in Vietnam –

The American military did not lose a battle of any consequence. From a military standpoint, it was almost an unprecedented performance. This included Tet 68, which was a major military defeat for the VC and NVA.

The United States did not lose the war in Vietnam, the South Vietnamese did –

The fall of Saigon happened 30 April 1975, two years AFTER the American military left Vietnam. The last American troops departed in their entirety 29 March 1973. How could we lose a war we had already stopped fighting? We fought to an agreed stalemate.

The Fall of Saigon –

The 140,000 evacuees in April 1975 during the fall of Saigon consisted almost entirely of civilians and Vietnamese military, NOT American military running for their lives.

There were almost twice as many casualties in Southeast Asia (primarily Cambodia) the first two years after the fall of Saigon in 1975 than there were during the ten years the US was involved in Vietnam.

An extract from a website, www.slideshare.net, 'Vietnam War Statistics', by an American ex-serviceman.

(d) Study Source F. How reliable is this source about the Vietnam War? Explain your answer using details of the source and your knowledge. **[7]**

> I don't think Source F is very reliable at all about the Vietnam War. I think the source's whole purpose seems to be to convince people that America shouldn't be embarrassed about its actions in Vietnam and that it could have won the war had it chosen to stay because the author is very selective in the evidence put forward, such as the fact that Saigon did not technically fall to North Vietnam until after the Americans left. He neglects evidence such as the fact America spent $110 billion on the war and had been there over ten years without securing victory.

This is a very good response which tackles the question of reliability in different ways. First, the answer uses **contextual knowledge** to challenge details in the source, and second, the answer examines the purpose of the source and uses that to question its reliability.

(e) Study Sources A–F. How far do these sources provide convincing evidence that there was support for US involvement in Vietnam? Use the sources to explain your answer. **[9]**

> Source A does not support the statement there was support for US involvement in Vietnam. The author of 'The Tet Offensive', James Wirtz, clearly views the attack by the Viet Cong as a turning point in the war in Vietnam which led to more Americans opposing direct US involvement when he says it '…had produced a negligible effect on the will and capability of the Viet Cong and North Vietnamese'. This means that he is questioning the impact the US military are having in the Vietnam War and believes this will begin to turn the US public against it.
>
> Source B also suggests that many Americans were critical of US involvement in Vietnam. The source implies that US military tactics, particularly its use of chemical weapons such as 'napalm' and 'chemicals' which were used against the Vietnamese population were turning many in South Vietnam against the Americans and likely in favour of the communists.
>
> Source C could suggest that some Americans, especially those in the military, supported US involvement as they believed that the war's aim was to 'destroy Communism'. Many in the USA feared that if the Communists were successful in taking over South Vietnam it would have a domino effect and would spread to neighbouring countries like Laos and Cambodia. This is why the US government followed a policy of containment.
>
> Source D suggests that lower ranking soldiers also supported the war as they could get 'revenge for … fallen comrades'. This implies that many soldiers had been deeply affected by the horrors they encountered when fighting the guerrilla tactics used by the Viet Cong. However, the source could also be used as evidence to show why some Americans might oppose the war as it was not only affecting the mental health of the US soldiers, most of whom were very young, but was also leading to the deaths of innocent Vietnamese civilians as in the My Lai Massacre of 1968: 'the order was: everyone in the village, because those people … were VC'.
>
> Source E is an American cartoon which is criticising President Johnson. The message of the cartoonist suggests that Johnson is wasting public money on the Vietnam War and neglecting social problems at home such as urban poverty. Some in the US media were beginning to disapprove of the US government for wasting money on the Vietnam War.
>
> Source F was written by an ex-serviceman of the Vietnam War. He clearly supported US involvement in the conflict believing that the USA were victorious against the Viet Cong and did not 'lose a battle of any consequence'. He points the blame on the fall of Saigon on the south Vietnamese army and believed that the war was a stalemate.

> This answer uses all of the available sources which is important for this question. There are plenty of references directly to the sources, including some relevant quotations and descriptions of detail which support the arguments and explanations. Most importantly, the answer is balanced and examines both sides of the argument convincingly.

Practice: What caused the Cold War?

SOURCE A

We (Roosevelt, Churchill and Stalin) argued freely and frankly across the table. But at the end on every point unanimous agreement was reached … We know, of course, that it was Hitler's hope and the German war lords' hope that we would not agree – that some slight crack might appear in the solid wall of allied unity … But Hitler has failed. Never before have the major allies been more closely united – not only in their war aims but also in their peace aims.

Extract from President Roosevelt's report to the US Congress on the Yalta Conference, April 1945.

SOURCE B

I have always worked for friendship with Russia but, like you, I feel deep anxiety because of their misinterpretation of the Yalta decisions, their attitude towards Poland, their overwhelming influence in the Balkans excepting Greece, the difficulties they make about Vienna, the combination of Russian power and the territories under their control or occupied, coupled with the Communist technique in so many other countries, and above all their power to maintain very large Armies in the field for a long time. What will be the position in a year or two?

Extract from a telegram sent by Prime Minister Churchill to President Roosevelt in May 1945.

SOURCE D

A Soviet cartoon published in 1946.

SOURCE C

OPERATION UNTHINKABLE
REPORT BY THE JOINT PLANNING STAFF

We have examined Operation Unthinkable. As instructed, we have taken the following assumptions on which to base our examination:

Great Britain and the United States have full assistance from the Polish armed forces and can count upon the use of German manpower and what remains of German industrial capacity …

Owing to the special need for secrecy, the normal staffs in Service Ministries have not been consulted.

OBJECT

The overall or political object is to impose upon Russia the will of the United States and British Empire. The only way we can achieve our object with certainty and lasting results is by victory in a total war.

Extract from a top secret document called Operation Unthinkable. It was presented by the Army Chiefs to Churchill in May 1945 but the research and planning had begun in February 1945.

SOURCE E

A shadow has fallen upon the scenes so lately lighted by the Allied victory. From Stettin on the Baltic to Trieste on the Adriatic, an iron curtain has descended. Behind that line lie all the states of central and eastern Europe. The Communist parties have been raised to power far beyond their numbers and are seeking everywhere to obtain totalitarian control. This is certainly not the liberated Europe we fought to build. Nor is it one which allows permanent peace.

A speech by Winston Churchill on 5 March, 1946. It was given in the USA and was broadcast widely. At the time Churchill was no longer British prime minister.

SOURCE F

The following circumstances should not be forgotten. The Germans made their invasion of the USSR through Finland, Poland and Romania. The Germans were able to make their invasion through these countries because, at the time, governments hostile to the Soviet Union existed in these countries. What can there be surprising about the fact that the Soviet Union, anxious for its future safety, is trying to see to it that governments loyal in their attitude to the Soviet Union should exist in these countries?

A speech by Soviet leader Stalin given on 15 March, 1946. It was broadcast in the USSR and reported in Britain and the USA.

SOURCE G

A publicity photograph of the Big Three taken at the Yalta Conference in 1945.

1. Study Sources A and B.
   How far do Sources A and B agree? Explain your answer using details from the sources. **[8]**
2. Study Source C.
   Are you surprised by Source C? Explain your answer using details from the source and your own knowledge. **[7]**
3. Study Source D.
   What is the cartoonist's message? Explain your answer using details from the sources and your own knowledge. **[8]**
4. Study Sources E and F.
   How far do you think Source E influenced Source F? Explain your answer using details from the sources and your own knowledge. **[8]**
5. Study Sources A–G.
   'The Cold War began because Churchill had such a poor relationship with Stalin.' How far do these sources support this statement? Use the sources to explain your answer. **[9]**

Advice for Cambridge O Level History students

> The Cambridge O Level History syllabus was harmonised with Cambridge IGCSE History in 2020 so this advice is particularly for teachers and students who are used to the O Level assessment and reiterates the skills that will be needed. The content between Cambridge IGCSE and O Level is identical.

Paper 1 Structured Questions

- Both the Cambridge IGCSE and O Level syllabuses use the same format for Structured Questions and it will require students to answer questions on their chosen Core Content and chosen Depth Study options.
- Questions will require students to use their own knowledge to describe, explain and make judgements.
- Students will need to have developed good time management skills to answer each of the different types of question and it is vital that all of the exam-style questions are practised in lessons.
- The ability to write extended answers is also important for success. Students will need to give balanced explanations and use their own knowledge to reach supported judgements in order to produce the best answers.

Paper 2 Document Questions

- Both the Cambridge IGCSE and O Level syllabuses use the same format for Document Questions and it will require students to use a range of sources on a prescribed topic from their chosen Core Content option. The Cambridge International website tells you the prescribed topic in each examination session.
- Students will need to be able to interpret, compare, evaluate and make judgements about the sources using their own knowledge to support their answers.
- Time management will, once again, be key to success, so it is important that students get to work with and annotate different types of sources such as pictures, written sources, photographs and cartoons and think about why the author made the source or the significance of the time period it was made (or both!).

One difference

- The only difference between the assessment of the two syllabuses is that the O Level syllabus DOES NOT include Coursework or Alternative to Coursework. Students take only two papers Paper 1 Structured Questions and Paper 2 Document Questions.

SECTION 2
Depth Studies

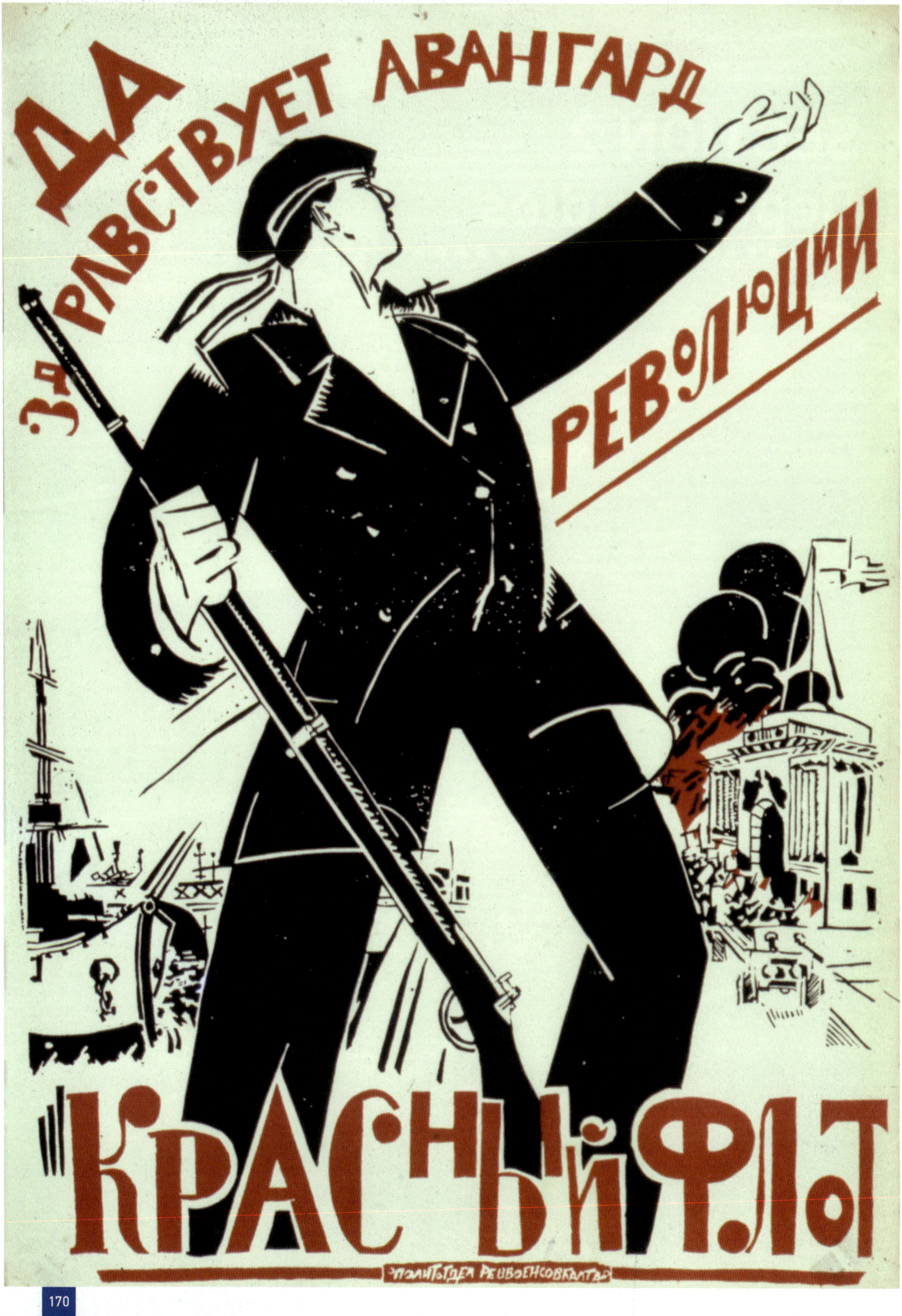
ДА ЗДРАВСТВУЕТ АВАНГАРД
РЕВОЛЮЦИИ
КРАСНЫЙ ФЛОТ

7 Russia, 1905–41

KEY QUESTIONS
7A Why did the Tsarist regime collapse in 1917?
7B How did the Bolsheviks gain power, and how did they consolidate their rule?
7C How did Stalin gain and hold on to power? What was the impact of Stalin's economic policies?

In 1905 Russia was a vast but backward agricultural country. Its industry was underdeveloped, its people mainly poor and uneducated. It was ruled by a TSAR who had complete power. In March 1917 the Tsar was overthrown and in November of the same year the Bolsheviks took over the running of Russia. Over the next 30 years the country was transformed by STALIN into a modern industrial state which became a world SUPERPOWER.

In **7A** you will investigate why the Tsar's regime survived one revolution in 1905 but then collapsed in 1917. What changed?

In **7B** you will explore how the Bolsheviks (Communists) under LENIN seized power in 1917 and, against all the odds, held on to power.

In **7C** you will look at how Stalin became the new leader of Russia (by this time the USSR) after Lenin, how he changed the SOVIET UNION, and the consequences of his rule for his people.

Timeline
This timeline shows the period you will be covering in this chapter. Some of the key dates are filled in already. To help you gain a complete picture of the period, make your own much larger version of the timeline and add other details to it as you work through the chapter.

Here is a poster from 1920 showing a sailor from the Kronstadt naval base near St Petersburg. It was produced by the Communists. The text says 'Long live the vanguard of the Revolution: the Red Fleet'.

On pages 187–200 you will be looking at the period from which this poster comes. Try to answer the following questions (you will have to guess intelligently) and then keep your answers and check whether you were right.
1 How would you describe the poster's view of the sailor – for example, cowardly, weak, brave?
2 Does this mean the sailors support the Communists or the other way around?
3 Do you get the impression that Russia is a peaceful place at this time?
4 Would you expect the relationship between the Communists and the sailors to change in the next few months?

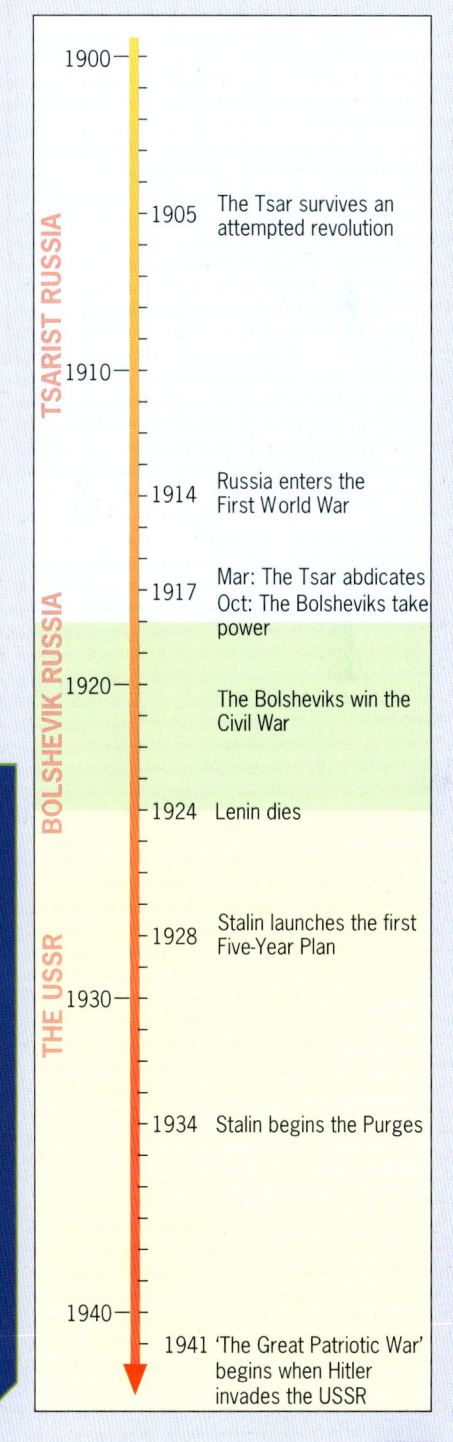

TSARIST RUSSIA
- 1900
- 1905 The Tsar survives an attempted revolution
- 1910
- 1914 Russia enters the First World War
- 1917 Mar: The Tsar abdicates / Oct: The Bolsheviks take power

BOLSHEVIK RUSSIA
- 1920 The Bolsheviks win the Civil War
- 1924 Lenin dies

THE USSR
- 1928 Stalin launches the first Five-Year Plan
- 1930
- 1934 Stalin begins the Purges
- 1940
- 1941 'The Great Patriotic War' begins when Hitler invades the USSR

7A Why did the Tsarist regime collapse in 1917?

FOCUS

When Nicholas II was crowned tsar of Russia in 1894, the crowds flocked in their thousands to St Petersburg to cheer the new tsar, whom they called 'the Little Father of Russia'.

Twenty-three years later, he had been removed from power and he and his family were prisoners. Perhaps the Tsar might have asked himself how this had happened, but commentators had predicted collapse long before 1917. In fact some people think the surprise is that the Tsar had actually survived so long. How could one man rule such a vast and troubled empire? So your focus in 8.1 is why, having survived for 23 troubled years, did the Tsar's regime finally collapse **in 1917**?

Focus Points

- How well did the Tsarist regime deal with the difficulties of ruling Russia up to 1914?
- How did the Tsar survive the 1905 Revolution?
- How far was the Tsar weakened by the First World War?
- Why was the revolution of March 1917 successful?

The Russian empire

As you can see from Figure 1 Russia was a vast empire, more than 3000 miles wide and very varied with arctic waste to the north and hot desert to the south.

FIGURE 1

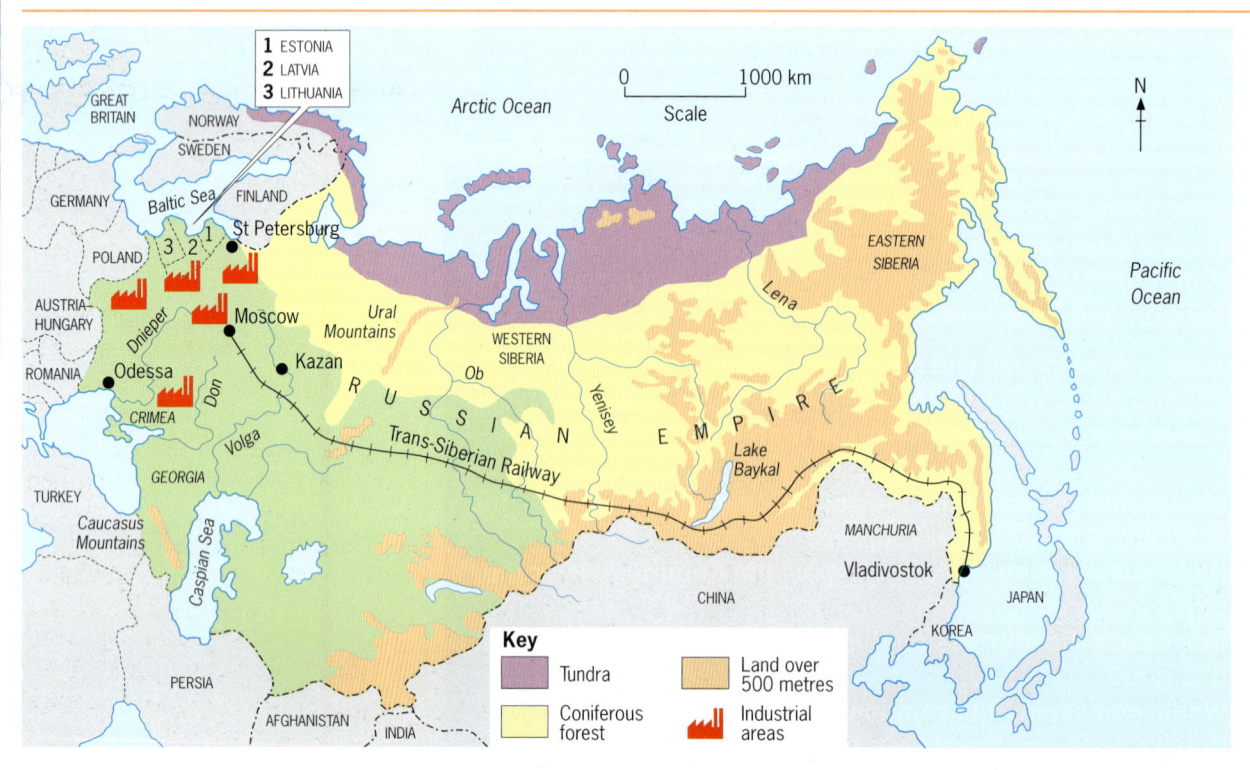

The Russian empire in 1900.

SOURCE 2

Let all know that I, devoting all my strength to the welfare of the people, will uphold the principle of autocracy as firmly and as unflinchingly as my late unforgettable father.

Part of Tsar Nicholas II's coronation speech in 1894.

Think!
1. Draw up your own chart to summarise the tsarist system of government.
2. Describe and explain at least two ways in which Nicholas II made Russia's government weak.

Profile

Tsar Nicholas II

- Born 1868.
- Crowned as tsar in 1896.
- Married to Alexandra of Hesse (a granddaughter of Queen Victoria).
- Both the Tsar and his wife were totally committed to the idea of the tsar as autocrat – absolute ruler of Russia.
- Nicholas regularly rejected requests for reform.
- He was interested in the Far East. This got him into a disastrous war with Japan in 1905.
- He was not very effective as a ruler, unable to concentrate on the business of being tsar.
- He was a kind, loving family man but did not really understand the changes Russia was going through.
- By 1917 he had lost control of Russia and abdicated.
- In 1918 he and his family were shot by Bolsheviks during the Russian CIVIL WAR.

The Tsar and his Government

Autocracy

This huge and diverse empire was ruled by one man, the tsar, who had absolute power. By the early twentieth century most European countries had given their people at least some say in how they were run, but Tsar Nicholas was still committed to the idea of AUTOCRACY.

He would not listen to any calls for political reform or greater DEMOCRACY in Russia. Most Russian nobles supported him in this view. He also had the support of the army commanders, the Church and the bureaucracy that ran the government.

Control and repression

Through the army, Church and bureaucracy the Tsar exercised oppressive control over the Russian people. Newspapers were censored and political parties banned. The police had a special force with 10,000 officers whose job was to concentrate on dealing with political opponents of the regime. The Tsar's SECRET POLICE force, the OKHRANA, was very effective, sending thousands to prison or exile in Siberia. Backing them up was the army, particularly the terrifying COSSACK regiments, which could be relied on to put down any disturbances. A loyal army was crucial to the Tsar's regime.

In the countryside each peasant belonged to a *mir* or village commune which controlled their daily lives. Each area had a 'land captain' – a local noble who dealt with crimes and disputes. Larger regions had governors – aristocrats appointed by the Tsar. They had powers to arrest people, put down trouble, censor newspapers and so on. Some of them were tyrants running their regions like little police states.

There were some elected officials in towns and district councils called ZEMSTVA, but these were dominated by the nobles and professional classes (such as doctors, lawyers). The *zemstva* did some good work in areas such as health and education and gave people useful experience in running local government. Some people wanted a national *zemstvo* through which elected representatives could help run the country but the Tsar and his regime would not accept this.

Chaos and incompetence

There is a different story to tell though. There had been some great tsars in the past but most historians and even some of the Tsar's supporters at the time agreed that Tsar Nicholas was not actually a very good ruler.

He worked hard but he avoided making big decisions and wasted time by getting involved in the tiniest details of government. He personally answered letters from peasants and appointed provincial midwives. He even wrote out the instructions for the royal car to be brought round! He did not delegate day-to-day tasks. In a country as vast as Russia this was a major problem.

Nicholas also felt threatened by able and talented ministers. He refused to chair the Council of Ministers because he disliked confrontation. He encouraged rivalry between ministers which caused chaos, because different government departments refused to co-operate with each other. He also appointed family members and friends from the court to important positions even though many were incompetent or even corrupt, making huge fortunes from bribes.

Revision Tip
- Make sure you can describe at least two ways in which the Tsar's Government crushed opponents.
- You should be able to explain the *zemstvo*.
- Make sure you can explain at least one weakness of the government system.

The Russian people

The nationalities

Many people in the Russian empire were not actually Russians. Only 40 per cent of the Tsar's subjects spoke Russian as their first language. These other groups were called NATIONALITIES because they really belonged to a different nation. Some nationalities, for example the COSSACKS, were loyal to the Tsar. Others, for example the Poles and Finns, hated Russian rule. Jewish people were seen as a separate group and often suffered racial prejudice and even attacks called pogroms which were encouraged by the government.

Peasants and the countryside

Around 80 per cent of Russia's population were peasants who lived in communes. Before 1861, peasants were known as serfs, who were bound to the landlord class. When they were freed from this near slavery in 1861, some peasants were able to buy more land to farm and become prosperous. These wealthier peasants were called KULAKS, but only accounted for about four per cent of the peasant class by the early 1900s. Most of the peasants remained very poor and lived and worked in terrible conditions. The peasants had no access to education to help them improve their farming methods and life was strictly controlled. They were also heavily taxed by the government. Many peasant families also owed Redemption Taxes – a kind of loan the peasants were made to pay the government for the freedom they gained from their landlords. Life expectancy was only 40 years in some areas.

The land issue

One big issue was that the landlord classes and the kulaks had most of the good farmland. Many peasants barely grew enough food to feed their families, especially as the population was rising. This was known as the peasant 'land issue'. Dissatisfaction led to increasing riots and land seizures in the countryside in the early 1900s. Farming methods were also outdated and many peasants still had little access to modern farming methods, machinery or fertilisers. This often led to years when harvests were poor and sometimes even famine. The famines of 1901–02 and 1906–08 saw starvation and disease in many provinces of the Russian empire. This affected the peasants far more than the upper classes, which increased the divide between the rich and poor. Despite this most peasants remained loyal to the Tsar, mainly because of the teachings of the Church. However, some peasants began to support RADICAL political parties calling for revolution. These parties wanted to seize the land from the aristocrats and the Church and share it out amongst the peasants.

Industrial workers and the cities

From the later nineteenth century, the tsars had been keen to see Russia become an industrial power. The senior minister Sergei Witte introduced policies that led to the rapid growth of industry. Oil and coal production trebled; iron production quadrupled. Some peasants left the countryside to work in these newly developing industries. However, their living

FIGURE 3

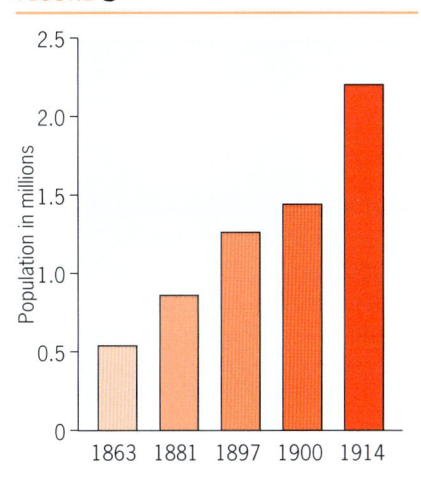

Graph showing the growth of St Petersburg.

(Population in millions: 1863 ≈ 0.5; 1881 ≈ 0.85; 1897 ≈ 1.25; 1900 ≈ 1.45; 1914 ≈ 2.2)

conditions hardly improved. Workers, who made up about four per cent of the population by 1900, were jammed into slum housing in the cities. They had to share kitchens and toilets between multiple families, especially in St Petersburg and Moscow. Within a short distance of the Tsar's glittering palaces workers suffered from illnesses, alcoholism and appalling working conditions. The average working day was 11.5 hours long and pay was very low. With food shortages and rising bread prices, it was hard to feed a family. Some workers and their families even had to sleep in the factories where they worked and were exposed to the poisonous fumes. Most workers had no access to insurance if they were injured and couldn't work. TRADE UNIONS and striking were illegal until 1905 so there was no way for workers to protest for better pay and conditions. This led to increased protests and even strikes in many industrial areas which had to be crushed by the Cossacks and the army. Many workers began supporting radical political parties that opposed the Tsar.

SOURCE 4

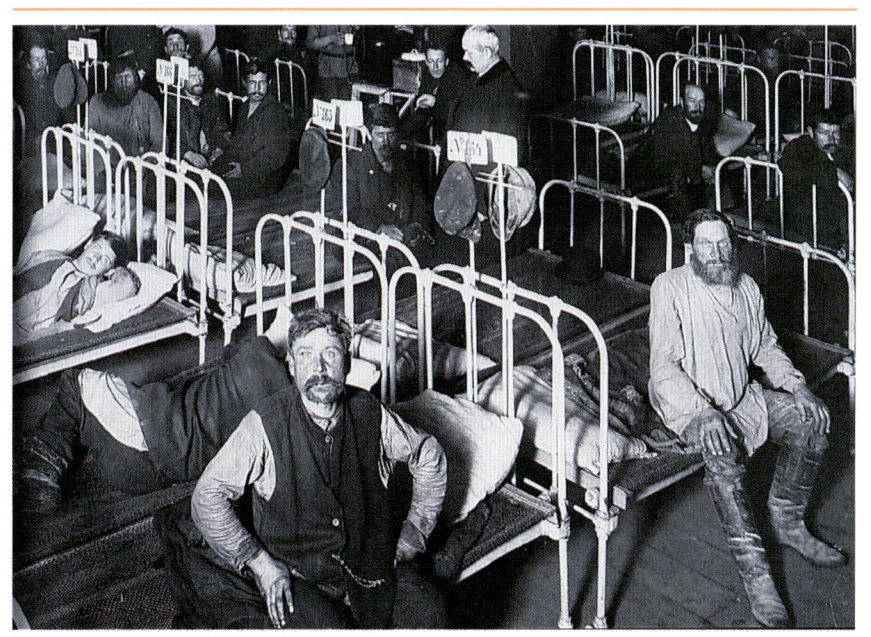

Workers' living conditions: a dormitory in Moscow. Urban workers made up about 4 per cent of the population in 1900.

The capitalists

As a result of INDUSTRIALISATION, a new class began to emerge in Russia – the CAPITALISTS. They were landowners, industrialists, bankers, traders and businessmen. Until this time, Russia had had only a small middle class which included people such as shopkeepers, lawyers and university lecturers. The capitalists increased the size of Russia's middle class, particularly in the towns. Their main concerns were the management of the economy which led some to demand a greater say in how the government was run. The capitalists were also concerned about controlling their workforce. Clashes between workers and capitalists were to play an important role in Russia's history in the years up to 1917.

Political opposition to the Tsar

The tsarist government faced opposition from three particular political groups.

Liberals

From the later 1800s many middle-class men and some women had received a university education. The universities became hotbeds of student radicalism. This meant that by the early 1900s many middle-class people wanted greater democracy in Russia. They demanded political reform, particularly a DUMA, an assembly similar to the British Parliament. They pointed out that Britain still had a king but also a powerful parliament. These people were called liberals.

Radicals

Two other groups were more deeply opposed to the Tsar. They believed that violent revolution was the answer to the people's troubles.

- **The SOCIALIST REVOLUTIONARIES (SRs)** were a radical movement. Their main aim was to carve up the huge estates of the nobility and hand them over to the peasants. They believed in violent struggle. They were responsible for the assassination of two government officials, as well as the murder of a large number of Okhrana (police) agents and spies. They had support in the towns and the countryside.
- **The Social Democratic Party** was a smaller but more disciplined party which followed the ideas of Karl Marx (see Factfile). In 1903 the party split itself into Bolsheviks and MENSHEVIKS. The **Bolsheviks** (led by Lenin) believed it was the job of the party to create a revolution whereas the **Mensheviks** believed Russia was not ready for revolution.

Both of these organisations were illegal and many of their members had been executed or sent in exile to Siberia. Many of the leading Social Democrat leaders were forced to live abroad (including Vladimir Ilyich Lenin who will figure significantly in this story later on).

In the Tsar's autocratic system there was no way for these opposition groups to voice their discontent. It all added up to a very volatile situation. Only the formidable forces of the state were keeping the lid on the tensions. In 1905 the lid was about to blow.

Revision Tip
- Make sure you know the difference between the SRs and the Social Democrats.
- It is also important to make sure you don't get Bolsheviks and Mensheviks mixed up!

Think!
Look back at Source 4. Do you think these men would be more likely to be influenced by the Church and its message of loyalty to the Tsar or the revolutionary views of the Social Democratic Party? Explain your answer.

Factfile

Marxist theory
- Karl Marx was a German writer and political thinker. He believed that history was dominated by class struggle and revolution.
- Marx believed that the middle classes would take control from the monarchy and aristocracy.
- There would then be a revolution in which the workers (the proletariat) would overthrow the middle classes.
- For a short while the Communist Party would rule but eventually there would be no need for any government as all would live in a peaceful communist society.

SOURCE 5

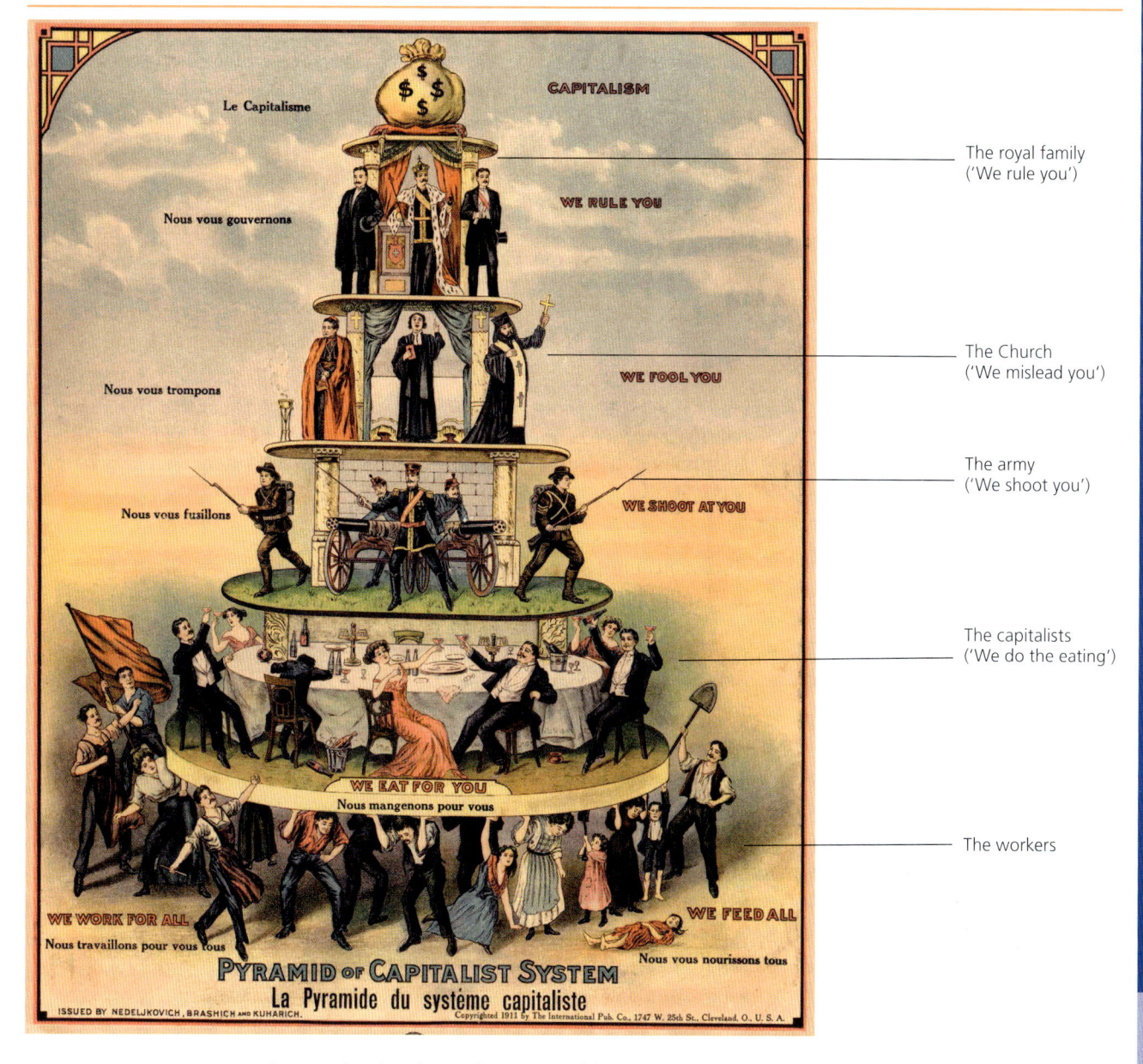

Pyramid of Capitalist System
La Pyramide du système capitaliste

ISSUED BY NEDELJKOVICH, BRASHICH AND KUHARICH. Copyrighted 1911 by The International Pub. Co., 1747 W. 25th St., Cleveland, O., U.S.A.

- CAPITALISM / Le Capitalisme
- WE RULE YOU / Nous vous gouvernons — The royal family ('We rule you')
- WE FOOL YOU / Nous vous trompons — The Church ('We mislead you')
- WE SHOOT AT YOU / Nous vous fusillons — The army ('We shoot you')
- WE EAT FOR YOU / Nous mangeons pour vous — The capitalists ('We do the eating')
- WE WORK FOR ALL / Nous travaillons pour vous tous — WE FEED ALL / Nous vous nourrissons tous — The workers

Cartoon showing the tsarist system. This was published in Switzerland by exiled opponents of the Tsar.

ACTIVITY

You are a minister of the Tsar in 1903. Write a report for him, informing him truthfully of the situation in Russia.

Your report should mention:
- inefficient and corrupt government
- the condition of the peasants
- conditions for the workers
- opposition groups.

Source Analysis

Source 5 was drawn by opponents of the Tsar's regime in exile. Discuss how far you think it is an accurate view of Russian society. Think about:
- ways in which its claims are supported by the information and sources in the text
- ways in which its claims are not supported by the information and sources in the text
- aspects of life in Russia that are not covered by the drawing.

SOURCE 6

A third of Russia lives under emergency legislation. The numbers of the regular police and of the secret police are continually growing. The prisons are overcrowded with convicts and political prisoners. At no time have religious persecutions [of Jews] been so cruel as they are today. In all cities and industrial centres soldiers are employed and equipped with live ammunition to be sent out against the people. Autocracy is an outdated form of government that may suit the needs of a central African tribe but not those of the Russian people who are increasingly aware of the culture of the rest of the world.

Part of a letter from the landowner and writer Leo Tolstoy to the Tsar in 1902. The letter was an open letter – it was published openly as well as being sent to the Tsar.

SOURCE 7

Lord, we workers, our children, our wives and our old, helpless parents have come, Lord, to seek truth, justice and protection from you.

We are impoverished and oppressed, unbearable work is imposed on us, we are despised and not recognised as human beings. We are treated as slaves, who must bear their fate and be silent. We have suffered terrible things, but we are pressed ever deeper into the abyss of poverty, ignorance and lack of rights.

We ask but little: to reduce the working day to eight hours and to provide a minimum wage of a rouble a day.

Officials have taken the country into a shameful war. We working men have no say in how the taxes we pay are spent.

Do not refuse to help your people. Destroy the wall between yourself and your people.

From the Petition to the Tsar presented by Father Gapon, 1905.

The 1905 revolution

You have already seen there was a lot of discontent in Russia. It would hardly be a surprise if this erupted in revolution at some stage. In 1905 it did. What finally turned the discontent into revolution?

Economic problems

In the late nineteenth century Russian industry and cities had grown rapidly. This caused stresses and strains as people flooded into towns and cities, often living and working in appalling conditions. After 1900 this growth stopped. Russia was hit by ECONOMIC DEPRESSION – wages fell, factories and mines closed and people were thrown out of work. This led to strikes and unrest. When the police set up 'approved' trade unions to try to control the workers, this only led to more strikes.

The problems deepened with a poor harvest in 1901 which led to hunger and peasant revolt. The only answer the Government could come up with to this growing discontent was further repression (see Source 6).

War with Japan

The Tsar hoped that the Russo–Japanese War, 1904–05, would help to unite his subjects behind him. This might have happened if it had been successful, but the Russia experienced a series of disastrous defeats on land and at sea. Russian casualties have been estimated at around 50,000 dead. The Russian surrender of Port Arthur to the Japanese in January 1905, and the sinking of the Russian Baltic Fleet at the Battle of Tsushima in May 1905, caused a huge loss in morale for the military and at home.

Many Russians had believed that Japan had an inferior military to Russia, but the war had proved the opposite. Although many Russians did not care about Japan or the Tsar's lands thousands of miles away, some were angered by the incompetence of the Tsar and his commanders in losing to the Japanese. As 1904 ended and winter began to bite, the discontent reached new heights.

Bloody Sunday

These tensions all came together on Sunday, 22 January 1905. A crowd of 200,000 protesters, led by the priest Father Gapon, came to the Winter Palace to give a petition to the Tsar (see Source 7). Many of the marchers carried pictures of the Tsar to show their respect for him.

The Tsar was not in the tWinter Palace. He had left St Petersburg when the first signs of trouble appeared. The protesters were met by a regiment of soldiers and mounted Cossacks. Without warning, the soldiers opened fire and the Cossacks charged. It was a decisive day. The Tsar finally lost the respect of the ordinary people of Russia. Bloody Sunday sparked a wave of strikes and disturbances which quickly spread to other cities.

> ### Source Analysis
> 1 Read Source 7. Make two lists:
>   a) the petitioners' complaints
>   b) their demands.
> 2 Are these demands revolutionary demands? Explain your answer.
> 3 Choose two words to sum up the attitude of the petitioners to the Tsar in Source 7.
> 4 a) Describe in detail what you can see in Source 8.
>   b) What do you think the artist is trying to show?
>   c) How might this event change the attitude of the petitioners (see your answer to question 3)?

Think!

Source 8 was published in France, where many opponents of the Tsar lived in exile. How might they have made use of this image and others like it?

SOURCE 9

Saturday 21 January

A clear frosty day. Went for a long walk. Since yesterday all the factories and workshops in St Petersburg have been on strike. Troops have been brought in to strengthen the garrison. The workers have conducted themselves calmly hitherto. At the head of the workers is some socialist priest: Gapon.

Sunday 22 January

A painful day. There have been serious disorders in St Petersburg because workmen wanted to come up to the Winter Palace. Troops had to open fire in several places in the city; there were many killed and wounded. God, how painful and sad! Mama arrived from town, straight to church. I lunched with all the others. Went for a walk with Misha. Mama stayed overnight.

Extracts from the Tsar's diary over the weekend of Bloody Sunday.

SOURCE 8

A painting of Bloody Sunday by the Russian artist Ivan Vladimirov, painted soon after the event. Vladimirov was a Realist painter. Realists tended to use a very vivid and lifelike style of painting and many of them used this style to highlight what they saw as social or political problems.

FOCUS TASK 7.1

Why was the Tsar facing revolution in 1905?

THE TSAR SURVIVES

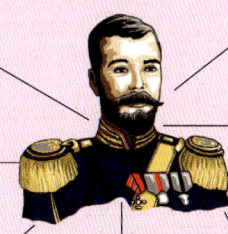

Discontented peasants were treated harshly, suffered poor health and envied the land of the landlords.

Discontented nationalities were treated as second-class citizens in Russia and suffered discrimination.

Discontented workers suffered appalling living and working conditions.

War with Japan increased discontent amongst several different classes.

Discontented middle classes were unhappy with the Tsar's inefficient government and wanted some say in the running of the country.

Political opposition groups wanted to topple the Tsar and stirred up and organised peasants and workers.

Economic problems throughout the early 1900s depression, and bad harvests, led to food shortages.

Bloody Sunday – the vicious massacre of innocent demonstrators.

The diagram show a range of factors which contributed to the outbreak of revolution in 1905. Historians often organise such causes into categories:

Long-term or structural factors	Short-term or trigger factors
Underlying factors which make a revolution possible or likely. They are the logs on a fire before a spark sets it alight. They can build up for a long time.	Factors which spark off the revolution but without the structural factors they could not cause a revolution. Factors like these help to explain why the revolution happened in 1905 rather than an earlier date or a later date.

1. Study the factors in the diagram above. On your own copy of the diagram colour code the factors you think are structural factors and the factors you think are trigger factors.
2. Add brief notes to your diagram to explain how each of the factors was either a structural or trigger factor.
3. The X Factor. Think about this question:

'Without X the 1905 Revolution would never have happened'. How far do you agree?

Look through the factors again and decide which factor you think would be best candidate to be the X Factor. When you have decided, write a paragraph explaining your decision.

Revision Tip

Make sure you can remember your X factor from Q. 3 and two others to compare with it. This will be useful for the Paper 1 Structured Questions, 10-mark and Paper 4 Alternative to Coursework part b) questions.

How did the Tsar survive the 1905 Revolution?

Tsarism in danger

Bloody Sunday sparked a wave of strikes which started in St Petersburg and then spread to other cities and even to other provinces in the empire, such as Poland and Finland. Barricades appeared in the streets accompanied by riots and violence. By the end of 1905, over half of Russian workers were on strike. The Tsar's uncle was assassinated and it seemed the Tsar might well lose control of Russia. All sorts of groups joined the workers demanding change. These included:

- the liberals and middle classes who wanted civil rights and a say in government
- students who wanted freedom in the universities
- the nationalities demanding independence.

However, they did not combine to form a united opposition and lacked political leadership.

In June 1905 the sailors on Battleship Potemkin mutinied. They killed seven of their officers and took charge of the ship. This was dangerous for the Tsar who needed the armed forces to remain loyal. In the countryside, PEASANTS attacked LANDLORDS and seized land. Workers' councils (or SOVIETS) were formed, becoming particularly strong in St Petersburg and Moscow. Revolutionaries like TROTSKY returned from exile to join in. Lenin, who was in exile in London, ordered the Bolsheviks to encourage the workers to take radical action against the government (Source 10). In September a GENERAL STRIKE began which brought Russian industry to a standstill. The revolution reached its peak in December 1905. Thousands of workers in Moscow joined an armed rebellion in protest against poor living and working conditions. This was known as the Moscow uprising. The Bolsheviks and Socialist Revolutionaries set up a committee to organise the rebellion, stockpiled weapons and erected barricades. An army had to be sent from St Petersburg to crush the uprising as the Moscow garrison could not be trusted not to mutiny and join the rebellion. Things looked very bleak for the Tsar and his regime.

SOURCE 11

The oath which We took as Tsar compels Us to use all Our strength, intelligence and power to put a speedy end to this unrest which is so dangerous for the State. The relevant authorities have been ordered to take measures to deal with direct outbreaks of disorder and to protect people who only want to go about their daily business in peace.

However, in view of the need to speedily implement earlier measures to pacify the country, we have ordered the government to take the following measures in fulfilment of our unbending will:

1. *Fundamental civil freedoms will be granted to the population, including freedom of conscience, speech, assembly and association.*
2. *Participation in the Duma will be granted to those classes of the population which are at present deprived of voting powers, insofar as is possible in the short period before the calling of the Duma, and this will lead to the development of a universal franchise.*
3. *It is established as an unshakeable rule that no law can come into force without its approval by the State Duma and representatives of the people will be given the opportunity to take real part in the supervision of the legality of government bodies.*

We call on all true sons of Russia to remember the homeland, to help put a stop to this unprecedented unrest and, together with this, to devote all their strength to the restoration of peace to their native land.

Nicholas II
Tsar of all the Russias

Extracts from the Tsar's October Manifesto.

SOURCE 10

Events of the greatest historical importance are developing in Russia. The proletariat has risen against tsarism. The slogan of the heroic St. Petersburg proletariat, "Death or freedom!" is reverberating throughout Russia. The revolution is spreading. The government is beginning to lose its head. From the policy of bloody repression it is attempting to change to economic concessions to save itself by throwing a sop to the workers or promising the nine-hour day. But the lesson of Bloody Sunday cannot be forgotten. The demand of the insurgent St. Petersburg workers must become the demand of all the striking workers. Immediate overthrow of the government — this was the slogan with which even the St. Petersburg workers who had believed in the tsar answered the massacre of January 9th. Their leader, the priest Georgi Gapon, declared after that bloody day: "We no longer have a tsar. A river of blood divides the tsar from the people. Long live the fight for freedom!"

'Long live the revolutionary proletariat!' say we.

Bolshevik leader Vladimir Lenin (see page 193) commenting on events in Russia in 1905.

Source Analysis

1. Read Source 10. Do you think it is more useful as evidence about the revolution or about Lenin? Explain your answer.
2. Read Source 11. Do you think the October Manifesto was a clever move?
3. Do you get the impression the Tsar believed in the October Manifesto?
4. Do you think 'Nightmare' is a good title for Source 12?

The October Manifesto

Things were so bad at the end of September that the Tsar was persuaded, unwillingly, to issue the October Manifesto (see Source 11). This offered the people an elected parliament called the Duma, the right to free speech and the right to form political parties. This divided the Tsar's opponents. The liberals were delighted, feeling this had achieved their main aim, and the middle classes, desperate to end the violence and disorder, now supported moves to end the revolution.

The army restores tsarist rule

The Tsar made peace with Japan and brought his troops back to help put down the trouble. To ensure their loyalty he promised them better pay and conditions. Now the Government moved to restore order.

- In December 1905 the leaders of the St Petersburg and Moscow soviets were arrested. This led to fighting in Moscow and other cities but the workers were no match for the army and their resistance was crushed.
- In the countryside it took much of 1906 to bring peasant unrest under control. The Tsar promised financial help in setting up a peasants' bank to help them buy land but it was force that won the day. Troops were sent out in huge numbers to crush the peasants and the nationalities. Thousands were executed or imprisoned. Beatings and rape were used to terrify peasants into submission.

It was clear that no revolution would succeed if the army stayed loyal to the Tsar.

SOURCE 12

An illustration from the anti-tsarist Russian magazine *Leshii*, published in 1906. The title was 'Nightmare: the aftermath of a Cossack punishment expedition'.

Revision Tip
- Make sure you can list two examples of the weaknesses/mistakes of the revolutionaries.
- Also make sure you can explain two measures taken by the Tsar which helped him survive.

FOCUS TASK 7.2
How did the Tsar survive the 1905 revolution?

Copy and complete the diagram. Describe how each of the factors helped the Tsar survive and bring Russia back under control. We have started one branch for you.

THE TSAR SURVIVES

- The October manifesto
- Dealing with workers' leaders
- The role of the army
- Use of brutal force
- Lack of united opposition

All the different groups – workers, peasants, liberals etc. – had different aims and never united together to bring down the Tsar's Government.

FIGURE 13

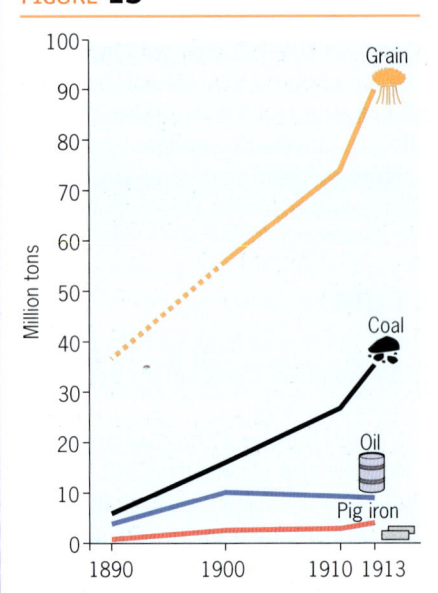

Agricultural and industrial production, 1890–1913.

(Chart showing Grain, Coal, Oil and Pig iron production in million tons from 1890 to 1913. Grain rises from about 55 to over 90; Coal rises from about 6 to 36; Oil rises to about 10 then declines slightly; Pig iron remains low.)

SOURCE 15

Year	Strikes	Strikers
1905	13,995	2,863,173
1906	6,114	1,108,406
1907	3,573	740,074
1908	892	176,101
1909	340	64,166
1910	222	46,623
1911	466	105,110
1912	2,032	725,491
1913	2,404	887,096
1914	3,534	1,337,458

These figures were compiled by the Tsar's Ministry of Trade and Industry.

SOURCE 16

Let those in power make no mistake about the mood of the people ... never were the Russian people ... so profoundly revolutionised by the actions of the government, for day by day, faith in the government is steadily waning.

Guchkov, a Russian conservative in the Duma, 1913. By 1913, even staunch supporters of the Tsar were beginning to want change.

The troubled years, 1905–14

The Tsar survived the 1905 revolution, but some serious questions remained. Nicholas needed to reform Russia and satisfy at least some of the discontented groups that had joined the revolution in 1905. The Duma deputies who gathered for its first meeting in 1906 were hopeful that they could help to steer Russia on a new course. They were soon disappointed (see Source 14). The Tsar continued to rule without taking any serious notice of them. The first and second Dumas were very critical of the Tsar. They lasted less than a year before Nicholas sent them home. In 1907 Tsar Nicholas changed the voting rules so that his opponents were not elected to the Duma. This third Duma lasted until 1912, mainly because it was much less critical of the Tsar than the previous two. But by 1912 even this 'loyal' Duma was becoming critical of the Tsar's ministers and policies.

SOURCE 14

The two hostile sides stood confronting each other. The court side of the hall resounded with orchestrated cheers as the Tsar approached the throne. But the Duma deputies remained completely silent. It was a natural expression of our feelings towards the monarch, who in the twelve years of his reign had managed to destroy all the prestige of his predecessors. The feeling was mutual: not once did the Tsar glance towards the Duma side of the hall. Sitting on the throne he delivered a short, perfunctory speech in which he promised to uphold the principles of autocracy.

From the memoirs of Duma deputy Obolensky, published in 1925. He is describing the first session of the Duma in April 1906.

Stolypin's reforms

In 1906 the Tsar appointed a tough new prime minister – Peter STOLYPIN. Stolypin used a 'carrot and stick' approach to Russia's problems.

- **The stick:** He came down hard on strikers, protesters and revolutionaries. Over 20,000 were exiled and over 1000 hanged (the noose came to be known as 'Stolypin's necktie'). This brutal suppression effectively killed off opposition to the regime in the countryside until after 1914.
- **The carrot:** Stolypin also tried to win over the peasants with the 'carrot' they had always wanted – land. He introduced a series of agricultural reforms which allowed the kulaks to opt out of the *mir* communes and buy up land to create larger, more efficient farms. The Peasants' Land Bank lent over 600 million roubles to the kulaks between 1906 and 1907, which helped boost agricultural production (see Figure 13). However, 90 per cent of land in the fertile west was still run by inefficient communes in 1916. Farm sizes remained small. Most poorer peasants did not benefit from the reforms and continued to live in poor conditions and to remain discontented.

Stolypin also tried to boost Russia's industries. There was impressive economic growth between 1908 and 1911. But Russia was still far behind modern industrial powers such as Britain, Germany and the USA.

Stolypin was assassinated in 1911, but the Tsar was about to sack him anyway. He worried that Stolypin was trying to change Russia too much. Nicholas had already blocked some of Stolypin's plans for basic education for the people and regulations to protect factory workers. The Tsar was influenced by the landlords and members of the court. They saw Stolypin's reforms as a threat to the traditional Russian society in which everyone knew their place.

Think!
1. Make two lists:
   a) Stolypin's achievements
   b) Stolypin's failings.
2. If you were a senior adviser to the Tsar, which of Sources 13–16 would worry you most? Explain your answer.

SOURCE 17

Russian cartoon published in 1916. The caption reads: 'The Russian Tsars at home'.

Source Analysis
Look at Source 17. How does the cartoonist suggest that Rasputin is an evil influence on the Tsar and Tsarina?

Rising discontent
Relations between the Tsar and his people became steadily worse. The year 1913 saw huge celebrations for the 300th anniversary of the Romanovs' rule in Russia. The celebrations were meant to bring the country together, but enthusiasm was limited.

Discontent grew, especially among the growing industrial working class in the cities. The industrial growth had not really helped them. The profits were going to the capitalists, or they were being paid back to banks in France which had loaned the money to pay for much of Russia's industrial growth. Very little of this new wealth found its way back to the urban workers. Their wages stayed low while the cost of food and housing was rising. Living and working conditions had not really improved – they were still appalling. Strikes were on the rise (see Source 15), including the highly publicised Lena gold field strike where troops opened fire on striking miners.

The army and police dealt with these problems and for the Tsar's opponents it must have seemed as if the Tsar's Government were firmly in control. However, some of the Tsar's supporters were less sure (see Source 16). Industrialists were concerned by the way the Tsar chose to appoint loyal but unimaginative and sometimes incompetent ministers.

Rasputin
Some of the Tsar's supporters were particularly alarmed about the influence of a strange and dangerous figure – Gregory Yefimovich, generally known as Rasputin. The Tsar's son Alexis was very ill with a blood disease called haemophilia. Through hypnosis, it appeared that Rasputin could control the disease. He was greeted as a miracle worker by the Tsarina (the Tsar's wife). Before long, Rasputin was also giving her and the Tsar advice on how to run the country. People in Russia were very suspicious of Rasputin. He was said to be a drinker and a womaniser. His name means 'disreputable'. The Tsar's opponents seized on Rasputin as a sign of the Tsar's weakness and unfitness to rule Russia. The fact that the Tsar either didn't notice their concern or, worse still, didn't care showed just how out of touch he was.

FOCUS TASK 7.3
How well did the Tsarist regime deal with the difficulties of ruling Russia up to 1914?

Here are some issues facing the Tsar's Government. Give the Government a score between 1 and 5 to say how well it was doing on each issue. Write a comment to explain your reasons for each score.
- Providing strong leadership and running the country effectively
- Growing modern industry to make Russia powerful
- Making the workers more contented to reduce strikes and unrest
- Making agriculture more productive and efficient
- Improving the lives of the peasants
- Responding to the demands of people for a say in government
- Dealing with opposition within Russia
- Defending the country from its enemies

Revision Tip
A common question about this period is how stable Russia was before 1914. Was it so stable that it could have survived if there had been no war? To prepare for this kind of question make sure you can explain:
- two ways in which Russia could be seen as stable before 1914
- two ways in which Russia was unstable in the period.

FOCUS TASK 7.4

How far was the Tsar weakened by the First World War?

The First World War had a massive impact on Russia. Your task is to use the material on pages 184–85 to present an overview of how the war affected four different groups of people in Russian society. The groups are:

- the army
- the workers
- the middle classes
- the aristocracy.

As you read through pages 184–85 make notes about the impact of war on each group and how far that weakened the Tsar's ability to rule Russia effectively.

SOURCE 18

The army had neither wagons nor horses nor first aid supplies ... We visited the Warsaw station where there were about 17,000 men wounded in battle. At the station we found a terrible scene: on the platform in dirt, filth and cold, on the ground, even without straw, wounded men, who filled the air with heart-rending cries, dolefully asked: 'For God's sake order them to dress our wounds. For five days we have not been attended to.'

From a report by Michael Rodzianko, president of the Duma.

FIGURE 19

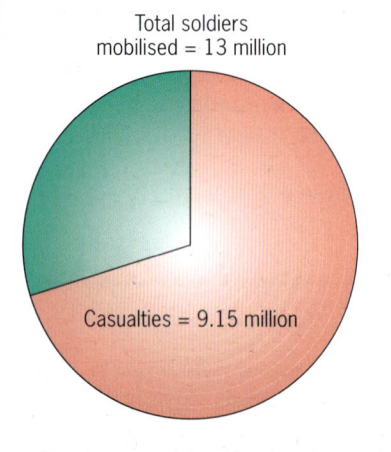

Total soldiers mobilised = 13 million

Casualties = 9.15 million

Russian casualties (dead and wounded) in the First World War.

War and revolution

In August 1914 Russia entered the First World War. Tensions in the country seemed to disappear. The Tsar seemed genuinely popular with his people and there was an instant display of patriotism. The good feeling, however, was very short-lived. Before long the Tsar began to lose the support of key sectors of Russian society.

The army

The Russian army was a huge army of conscripts. At first, the soldiers were enthusiastic. They felt that they were fighting to defend their country against the Germans rather than showing any loyalty to the Tsar. Russian soldiers fought bravely, but they stood little chance against the German army. They were badly led and treated appallingly by their aristocrat officers. They were also short of rifles, ammunition, artillery and shells. Many did not even have boots.

The Tsar took personal command of the armed forces in September 1915. This made little difference to the war, since Nicholas was not a particularly able commander. However, it did mean that people held Nicholas personally responsible for the defeats and the blunders. The defeats and huge losses continued throughout 1916. It is not surprising that by 1917 there was deep discontent in the army.

Peasants and workers

It did not take long for the strain of war to alienate the peasants and the workers. The huge casualty figures left many widows and orphans needing state war pensions which they did not always receive.

Despite the losses, food production remained high until 1916. By then, the Government could not always be relied on to pay for the food produced. The Government planned to take food by force but abandoned the idea because it feared it might spark a widespread revolt.

By 1916 there was much discontent in the cities. War contracts created an extra 3.5 million industrial jobs between 1914 and 1916. The workers got little in the way of extra wages. They also had to cope with even worse overcrowding than before the war. There were fuel and food shortages. The rail network could not cope with the needs of the army, industry and the populations of the cities. The prices of almost everything got higher and higher. As 1916 turned into 1917, many working men and women stood and shivered in bread queues and cursed the Tsar.

The middle classes

The middle classes did not suffer in the same way as the peasants and workers, but they too were unhappy with the Tsar by the end of 1916. Many middle-class activists in the *zemstva* were appalled by reports such as Source 18. They set up their own medical organisations along the lines of the modern Red Cross, or joined war committees to send other supplies to the troops. These organisations were generally far more effective than the government agencies. By 1916 many industrialists were complaining that they could not fulfil their war contracts because of a shortage of raw materials (especially metals) and fuel. In 1915 an ALLIANCE of Duma politicians, the Progressive Bloc, had urged the Tsar to work with them in a more representative style of government that would unite the people. The Tsar dismissed the Duma a month later.

FIGURE 20

The average worker's wage in 1917 was 5 roubles a day. This would buy you:

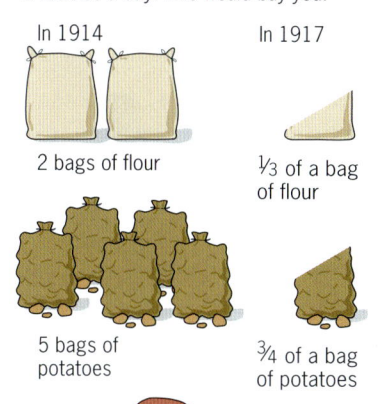

In 1914: 2 bags of flour
In 1917: 1/3 of a bag of flour

In 1914: 5 bags of potatoes
In 1917: 3/4 of a bag of potatoes

In 1914: 5 kilograms of meat
In 1917: 0.8 kilograms of meat

Prices in Russia, 1914–17.

Revision Tip

The war was a critical factor in causing revolution in 1917. Make sure you can list one example of how the war alienated each of the key groups: army, peasants and workers, middle classes, aristocracy.

FIGURE 22

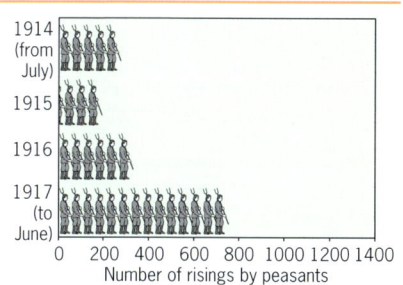

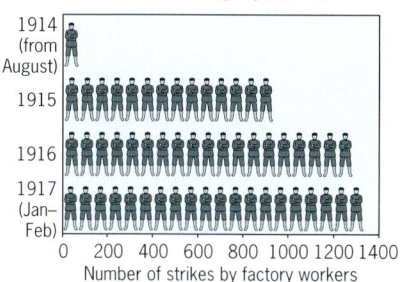

Number of risings by peasants (1914 from July, 1915, 1916, 1917 to June), scale 0–1400.

Number of strikes by factory workers (1914 from August, 1915, 1916, 1917 Jan–Feb), scale 0–1400.

Peasant risings and strikes, 1914–17.

Revision Tip

Make sure you can explain why the mutiny of the army was the key factor.

The aristocracy

The situation was so bad by late 1916 that the Council of the United Nobility was calling for the Tsar to step down. The junior officers in the army (mostly from the aristocrat class) had suffered devastating losses in the war. The CONSCRIPTION of 13 million peasants meant landlords had no workers for their estates. Most of all, many of the leading aristocrats were appalled by the influence of Rasputin over the government of Russia (see Source 17). When the Tsar left Petrograd (the new Russian version of the Germanic name St Petersburg) to take charge of the army, he left his wife in control of the country. The fact that she was German started rumours flying in the capital. There were also rumours of an affair between her and Rasputin. Ministers were dismissed and then replaced. The concerns were so serious that a group of leading aristocrats murdered Rasputin in December 1916.

SOURCE 21

I asked for an audience and was received by him [the Tsar] on March 8th. 'I must tell Your Majesty that this cannot continue much longer. No one opens your eyes to the true role which this man is playing. His presence in Your Majesty's court undermines confidence in the Supreme Power and may have an evil effect on the fate of the dynasty and turn the hearts of the people from their Emperor' ... My report did some good. On March 11th an order was issued sending Rasputin to Tobolsk; but a few days later, at the demand of the Empress, this order was cancelled.

M. Rodzianko, president of the Duma, March 1916.

The March 1917 revolution

As 1917 dawned, few people had great hopes for the survival of the Tsar's regime. In January strikes broke out all over Russia. In February the strikes spread. They were supported and even joined by members of the army. The Tsar's best troops lay dead on the battlefields. These soldiers were recent conscripts and had more in common with the strikers than their officers. On 7 March workers at the Putilov steelworks in Petrograd went on strike. They joined with thousands of women – it was International Women's Day – and other discontented workers demanding that the Government provide bread. From 7 to 10 March the number of striking workers rose to 250,000. Industry came to a standstill. The Duma set up a Provisional Committee to take over the government. The Tsar ordered them to disband. They refused. On 12 March the Tsar ordered his army to put down the revolt by force. They refused. This was the decisive moment. Some soldiers even shot their own officers and joined the demonstrators. They marched to the Duma demanding that they take over the government. Reluctantly, the Duma leaders accepted – they had always wanted reform rather than revolution, but now there seemed no choice.

On the same day, revolutionaries set up the Petrograd Soviet again, and began taking control of food supplies to the city. They set up soldiers' committees, undermining the authority of the officers. Soviets were also set up in many other towns and cities across Russia, but these others tended to look to the Petrograd Soviet for leadership and guidance. It was not clear who was in charge of Russia, but it was obvious that the Tsar was not! On 15 March he issued a statement that he was abdicating. There was an initial plan for his brother Michael to take over, but Michael refused: Russia had finished with tsars.

FOCUS TASK 7.5

How important was the war in the collapse of the Tsarist regime?

Historians have furiously debated this question since the revolution took place. There are two main views:

> **View 1**
> The Tsar's regime was basically stable up to 1914, even if it had some important problems to deal with. It was making steady progress towards becoming a modern state, but this progress was destroyed by the coming of war. Don't forget that this war was so severe that it also brought Germany, Austria-Hungary and Turkey to their knees as well.

> **View 2**
> The regime in Russia was cursed with a weak tsar, a backward economy and a class of aristocrats who were not prepared to share their power and privileges with the millions of ordinary Russians. Revolution was only a matter of time. The war did not cause it, although it may have speeded up the process.

Divide the class into two groups.

One group has to find evidence and arguments to support View 1, the other to support View 2.

You could compare notes in a class discussion or organise a formal debate.

FOCUS TASK 7.6

Why was the March 1917 revolution successful?

The Tsar faced a major revolution in 1905 but he survived. Why was 1917 different? Why was he not able to survive in 1917?

The military failures of the war (Questioned deaths, competence of Tsar and Government)

Duma formed provisional government (Alternatives to Tsar's Government)

The workers (Strikes, unrest)

Mutiny of the army

Shortages at home (Food, fuel, rising prices)

Tsarina and Rasputin (Damaged reputations)

Tsar's supporters (Aristocrats, middle classes, army officers had lost faith in Tsar as leader)

Stage 1
1. Copy the headings in this diagram. They show seven reasons why the Tsar was forced to abdicate in March 1917.
2. For each of the factors, write one or two sentences explaining how it contributed to the fall of the Tsar. We have provided some hints to get you started.
3. Draw lines between any of the factors that seem to be connected. Label your line explaining what the link is.

Stage 2
4. In pairs or small groups, discuss the following points:
   a) Which factors were present in 1905?
   b) Were these same factors more or less serious than in 1905?
   c) Which factors were not present in 1905?
   d) Were the new factors decisive in making the March 1917 revolution successful?

Key Question Summary

Why did the Tsarist regime collapse in 1917?
1. The Tsar was a weak, indecisive leader whose Government did not run the country well.
2. The regime had lost the support and loyalty of the people.
   a) The workers were deeply resentful because their living and working conditions had improved little despite the wealth produced by rapidly developing industry.
   b) The peasants would only be satisfied when they owned the land. Some improvements had been made by the land reforms but most peasants were still very poor.
3. The middle classes wanted a say in government. The Tsar refused to respond to this demand and would not work with the Duma, even during the war.
4. The Russian army had done badly in the war, losing many lives, and the Tsar was held responsible for this.
5. The Tsarina and Rasputin had damaged the reputation of the royal family and made a terrible mess of running the country when the Tsar went to the warfront. Even top aristocrats and army generals thought the Tsar was unfit to run Russia.
6. The war had caused extreme shortages in St Petersburg leaving an angry strike-prone, discontented population which exploded in March 1917.
7. The crucial factor was when the soldiers mutinied and went over to the side of the people. The Tsar's rule had depended on the army. Without it he was powerless.

7B How did the Bolsheviks gain power, and how did they consolidate their rule?

FOCUS

If you had asked Russians in Petrograd in March 1917 what they thought of the Bolsheviks, most would probably have said, 'Who are the Bolsheviks?' Yet this small party quite dramatically seized control of Russia just six months later in November 1917.

Once in power most people thought the Bolsheviks would survive only a few weeks. They had a formidable set of enemies lined up against them. In the first few days they could not even get into the central bank to get money to run the government. Yet, against all the odds, they did survive.

So your focus on pages 187–200 is all about how they did it. It all begins with the problems facing the PROVISIONAL GOVERNMENT of Russia in March 1917.

Focus Points
- How effectively did the Provisional Government rule Russia in 1917?
- Why were the Bolsheviks able to seize power in November 1917?
- Why did the Bolsheviks win the Civil War?
- How far was the New Economic Policy a success?

Revision Tip
Make sure you can clearly explain what is meant by dual power.

Dual power: The Provisional Government and the Petrograd Soviet

After the abdication of the Tsar the Duma's Provisional Committee (usually called the Provisional Government) took charge. The Provisional Government was made up of many different political parties. When it was first established the key posts in the Government went to men from a range of parties in the hope of persuading the people that the different groups in Russia were being fairly represented.

However, the Provisional Government faced the problem that not all Russians accepted it as the new government of the country. Many Russians, especially the industrial workers and many in the army and navy, regarded the Petrograd Soviet as the body which truly represented them. Historians refer to the situation in Russia as 'dual power', where there were two possible bodies who could claim to run the government.

Many Russians played it safe, partly to see which of these bodies might be better for them and partly to make sure that if one did triumph they would not be on the losing side. Even some of the politicians in the Provisional Government also belonged to the Petrograd Soviet, such as Justice Minister Alexander KERENSKY. It was a confused and confusing time, with many different parties claiming to represent the people and striving to represent their followers (see Factfile).

Factfile

Major political parties in Russia 1917
- **Kadets**: Full name was the Constitutional Democratic Party. They were mostly middle-class liberals. They wanted Russia to become a parliamentary democracy with full rights for all citizens including minority groups and Jewish people. They also supported laws for improved living and working conditions. Their main support came from minorities and middle-class professionals, particularly university professors and lawyers.
- **Progressive Party**: Moderate middle-class liberals with beliefs fairly similar to the Kadets.
- **Octobrists**: Mainly middle-class party, which was originally founded in 1905. Supported modernising developments in Russia such as better education and industrialisation. Also supported the idea of a constitutional monarchy which was clearly impossible after the Tsar abdicated.
- **Socialist Revolutionary Party**: A democratic party which was more radical and revolutionary than the middle-class parties. They had the largest amount of popular support with a great deal of support from peasants and many industrial workers. Demanded that landlords' estates be divided up between the peasants and improved pay and conditions for workers. Committed to a democratic CONSTITUTION.
- **Mensheviks**: As you have already seen, the Mensheviks were one wing of the old Social Democratic Party. They were socialists and they believed that ultimately the workers should have complete control of the country and all of its assets – land, industry, roads, railways, housing. Many Mensheviks took part in the 1905 revolution. Unlike the Bolsheviks they were prepared to work with other groups to achieve their ultimate aim of a socialist state. There was one Menshevik minister in the Provisional Government.
- **Bolsheviks**: The Bolsheviks were led by Lenin. They were socialists like the Mensheviks but they believed that the workers could only take power by a violent revolution which would overthrow the existing rulers.

The Provisional Government, March to October 1917

The success of the Provisional Government would depend on how well it handled three key issues:
- To stay in the war or make peace.
- To distribute land to the peasants or ask thems to wait until elections had been held.
- How to feed the starving workers in the cities.

Most ordinary Russians were hoping for instant and radical action. However, the Provisional Government was dominated by middle-class liberals, particularly the Kadets. The Provisional Government promised Russia's allies that it would continue the war. It also urged the peasants to be restrained and wait for elections before taking any land. The plan was to hold free elections to take place to elect a new Constituent Assembly that would carry out such a major change. It was a very cautious message for a people who had just gone through a revolution.

SOURCE 1

The Provisional Government should do nothing now which would break our ties with the allies. The worst thing that could happen to us would be separate peace. It would be ruinous for the Russian revolution, ruinous for international democracy …

As to the land question, we regard it as our duty at the present to prepare the ground for a just solution of the problem by the Constituent Assembly.

A Provisional Government minister explains why Russia should stay in the war, 1917.

Think!
Read Source 1. How popular do you think the Provisional Government's policies on the war and land would be with the peasants and the soldiers?

The Petrograd Soviet

The newly formed Petrograd Soviet held the real power in Petrograd. It had the support of key workers like the railwaymen, and, crucially, the soldiers. In March 1917 the Petrograd Soviet issued Soviet Order Number One. This instructed all units in the army and navy to elect representatives to the Soviet and to elect committees to oversee the unit and control the weapons, rather than the officers. It could control what went on in the city and in reality it had the resources to undermine anything the Provisional Government decided to do (see Source 2). Its members were generally more radical than the Provisional Government. However, it was dominated by the Socialist Revolutionaries who supported the idea of a new Constituent Assembly (not least because they expected to win elections to the new Assembly). The Soviet had a small number of Bolshevik members but they were outnumbered by Mensheviks and Socialist Revolutionaries who took a more cautious approach. The Soviet decided to work with the Provisional Government in the spring and summer of 1917. But this was not an open-ended promise of support and the situation was always likely to change.

SOURCE 2

The Provisional Government possesses no real power and its orders are executed only in so far as this is permitted by the Soviet of Workers' and Soldiers' Deputies, which holds in its hands the most important elements of actual power, such as troops, railroads, postal and telegraph service.

A letter from Guchkov, minister for war in the Provisional Government, to General Alekseyev, 22 March 1917.

Lenin and the rise of the Bolsheviks

Despite this CO-OPERATION one man was determined to push the revolution further. He was Lenin, leader of the Bolsheviks (see page 193). When he heard of the March revolution he immediately returned to Russia from exile in Europe. The Germans even provided him with a special train, hoping that he might cause more chaos in Russia!

When Lenin arrived at Petrograd station, he set out the Bolshevik programme in his April Theses. In ten key points he set out the main points of the Bolshevik position. He condemned Russia's involvement in the war. He urged the people to support the Bolsheviks in a second revolution. He condemned the Provisional Government. He called for land to be given to the peasants and for the banks to be taken into state control. Lenin's slogans 'Peace, Land and Bread' and 'All power to the soviets' contrasted sharply with the cautious message of the Provisional Government. Support for the Bolsheviks increased quickly (see Source 3 and Figure 4), particularly in the soviets and in the army. By October party membership was around 500,000 and the Bolsheviks had a majority in the Petrograd Soviet and the Moscow Soviet and in the All–Russia Congress of Soviets (a sort of parliament where representatives of the different Soviets met).

Source Analysis
Study Source 3, Figure 4 and Source 5. Is it possible to say whether one is more useful as evidence about Russia in 1917? Use the sources/figure and your own knowledge to explain your answer.

SOURCE 3

A painting (made some time afterwards) of Lenin arriving at Petrograd railway station returning from exile, 1917. It was made by the artist Mikhail Sokolov, an opponent of the tsarist regime.

FIGURE 4

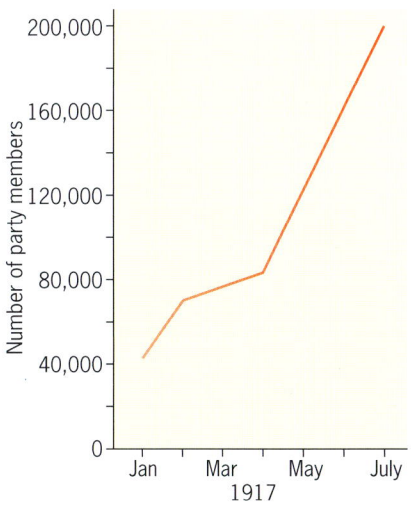

Growth of Bolshevik support, 1917.

Revision Tip
List:
- two weaknesses of the Provisional Government
- two strengths of the Provisional Government
- two strengths of the Bolsheviks.

SOURCE 5

The Bolshevik speaker would ask the crowd 'Do you need more land?'

'Do you have as much land as the landlords do?'

'But will the Kerensky government give you land? No, never. It protects the interests of the landlords. Only our party, the Bolsheviks, will immediately give you land…'

Several times I tried to take the floor and explain that the Bolsheviks make promises which they can never fulfil. I used figures from farming statistics to prove my point; but I saw that the crowded square was unsuitable for this kind of discussion.

A Menshevik writer, summer 1917.

SOURCE 6

A sudden and disastrous change has occurred in the attitude of the troops … Authority and obedience no longer exist … for hundreds of miles one can see deserters, armed and unarmed, in good health and in high spirits, certain they will not be punished.

A Russian officer reporting back to the Provisional Government, 1917.

The Provisional Government collapses

In the second half of 1917, the Provisional Government's authority steadily collapsed.

- The war effort was failing. Soldiers had been deserting in thousands from the army. Kerensky became minister for war and rallied the army for a great offensive in June. It was a disaster. The army began to fall apart in the face of a German counter-attack (see Source 6). The deserters decided to come home.
- Desertions were made worse because another element of the Provisional Government's policy had failed. The peasants ignored the orders of the Government to wait. They were simply taking control of the countryside. The soldiers, who were mostly peasants, did not want to miss their turn when the land was shared out.

July 1917: Kerensky defeats the Bolsheviks

The Provisional Government's problems got worse in the summer. In July (the 'July Days'), Bolshevik-led protests against the war turned into a rebellion. However, when Kerensky produced evidence that Lenin had been helped by the Germans, support for the rebellion fell. Lenin, in disguise, fled to Finland. Kerensky used troops to crush the rebellion and took over the government. Kerensky was appointed Prime Minister of the Provisional Government after the July Days had been crushed. He quickly set out to restore order. Kerensky appointed General Kornilov as the new commander of the Russian Army.

However, Kerensky was in a very difficult situation. In the cities, strikes, lawlessness and violence were rife. The upper and middle classes expected him to restore order. Kerensky seemed unable to do anything about this or the deteriorating economic situation. There was little reason for the ordinary people of Russia to be grateful to the Provisional Government (see Sources 8 and 9).

SOURCE 7

Troops loyal to the Provisional Government fire on Bolshevik demonstrators during the July Days.

SOURCE 8

Cabs and horse-drawn carriages began to disappear. Street-car service was erratic. The railway stations filled with tramps and deserting soldiers, often drunk, sometimes threatening. The police force had vanished in the first days of the Revolution. Now 'revolutionary order' was over. Hold-ups and robberies became the order of the day. Politically, signs of chaos were everywhere.

H.E. Salisbury, *Russia in Revolution*.

SOURCE 9

Week by week food became scarcer … one had to queue for long hours in the chill rain … Think of the poorly clad people standing on the streets of Petrograd for whole days in the Russian winter! I have listened in the bread-lines, hearing the bitter discontent which from time to time burst through the miraculous good nature of the Russian crowd.

John Reed, an American writer who lived in Petrograd in 1917.

Source Analysis

How far do you think Source 9 is a reliable source about the situation in Russia under the Provisional Government? Use the source, your knowledge and the other sources in this section to explain your answer.

Revision Tip

Add to your list from the previous Revision Tip on page 189:
- two more strengths of the Bolsheviks in late 1917
- two more weaknesses of the Provisional Government.

September 1917: Kerensky relies on the Bolsheviks

General Kornilov and other army leaders were now fed up with the chaos. They decided to restore order by crushing the Petrograd Soviet and the Provisional Government as well as remove the threat of the Bolsheviks. Kerensky knew that his garrison was no match for Kornilov's approaching army. He turned to the Soviets for help, many of whom were Bolsheviks. He even released many of the Bolshevik leaders who had been arrested after the July Days, including Leon Trotsky. The Bolsheviks organised themselves into units called the Red Guards and were given weapons and ammunition by Kerensky to defend Petrograd. When Kornilov's army approached Petrograd, many of his soldiers began to desert as they did not want to fight members of the Soviet. Kornilov's attempted coup had failed and Petrograd was saved. This is sometimes called the Kornilov Affair.

But it was hardly a victory for Kerensky. In fact, by October Kerensky's Government was doomed.
- It had tried to carry on the war and failed. It had therefore lost the army's support.
- It had tried to stop the peasants from taking over the land and so lost their support too.
- Without peasant support it had failed to bring food into the towns and food prices had spiralled upwards. This had lost the Government any support it had from the urban workers.

In contrast, the Bolsheviks were promising what the people wanted most (bread, peace, land). It was the Bolsheviks who had removed the threat of Kornilov. By the end of September 1917, the Bolsheviks had control of the Petrograd Soviet and Leon Trotsky was its chairman. They also controlled the soviets in Moscow and other major cities.

What do you think happened next?

FOCUS TASK 7.7

How effectively did the Provisional Government rule Russia in 1917?

Step 1
1. Here is a list of some decisions that faced the Provisional Government when it took over in March 1917:
   a) what to do about the war
   b) what to do about land
   c) what to do about food.

   For each one, say how the Government dealt with it, and what the result of the action was.
2. Based on your answers to question 1, how effective do you think the Provisional Government was? Give it a mark out of ten.

Step 2
3. Read through pages 187–91 again. Think about how effectively the Provisional Government dealt with their opponents:
   - Petrograd Soviet
   - Bolsheviks
   - Kornilov's attempted COUP.
4. Based on your answers to question 3, would you revise the score you gave the Government in question 2?

Step 3
5. Now reach an overview score. Out of ten, how effective was the Provisional Government? Write a paragraph to explain your score.

FOCUS TASK 7.8

Why were the Bolsheviks able to seize power in November 1917?

1. Using the material on pages 192–93 and your answers to Think! sum up how these two factors contributed to Bolshevik success:
   a) Bolshevik organisation
   b) Bolshevik leadership.
2. Now read Source 15 (on page 193). Below are some of these 'other mighty factors at work'. Write some notes under each heading to explain how each one helped the Bolsheviks. The first has been done for you with hints for the others:
   - Collapse of the Tsar's regime - *This had left a power vacuum. It was difficult to set up a new democratic regime which everybody would support.*
   - War (people war-weary, disruption)
   - Army disintegrating (officers and soldiers in St Petersburg)
   - Peasants (had already begun to seize land)
   - Desperate economic situation (desperate people)

SOURCE 10

The Provisional Government has been overthrown. The cause for which the people have fought has been made safe: the immediate proposal of a democratic peace, the end of land owners' rights, workers' control over production, the creation of a Soviet government. Long live the revolution of workers, soldiers and peasants.

Proclamation of the Petrograd Soviet, 8 November 1917.

Revision Tip

You need to be able to explain at least three factors that brought the Bolsheviks to power. Ideally, make these factors the three you think are most important.

The November Revolution

By the end of October 1917, Lenin was convinced that the time was right for the Bolsheviks to seize power. They had the support of many workers and control of the Soviet. Lenin convinced the other Bolsheviks to act swiftly. It was not easy – some, such as Kamenev, felt that Russia was not ready – but neither he nor any other Bolshevik could match Lenin in an argument. Trotsky organised the Military-Revolutionary Committee to oversee the planned seizure of power from the Provisional Government using the Red Guards to seize strategic locations in Petrograd. On 6 November at 9 am, the Committee issued a statement denouncing the Provisional Government and the seizure of power began.

The Bolsheviks seize power

- During the night of 6 November, the Red Guards led by Leon Trotsky took control of post offices, bridges and the State Bank.
- On 7 November, Kerensky awoke to find the Bolsheviks were in control of most of Petrograd. Through the day, with almost no opposition, the Red Guards continued to take over railway stations and other important targets. A small pro-Bolshevik fleet then sailed into Petrograd harbour to assist the Red Guards. The sailors at the Kronstadt naval base proclaimed their support for the Bolshevik Revolution.
- On the evening of 7 November, the cruiser Aurora fired a blank signal shot that was the signal for the Red Guards to storm Winter Palace (again, without much opposition) and arrest the ministers of the Provisional Government.
- Kerensky managed to escape and tried to rally loyal troops. When this failed, he fled into exile.
- On 8 November an announcement was made to the Russian people (see Source 10).

Why did the Bolsheviks succeed?

Despite what they claimed, the Bolsheviks did not have the support of the majority of the Russian people. So how were they able to carry out their take-over in November 1917?

- The unpopularity of the Provisional Government was a critical factor – there were no massive demonstrations demanding the return of Kerensky!
- A second factor was that the Bolsheviks were a disciplined party dedicated to revolution, even though not all the Bolshevik leaders believed this was the right way to change Russia.
- The Bolsheviks had some 800,000 members, and their supporters were also in the right places, including substantial numbers of soldiers and sailors. (The Bolsheviks were still the only party demanding that Russia should pull out of the war.)
- The major industrial centres, and the Petrograd and Moscow Soviets especially, were also pro-Bolshevik.
- The Bolsheviks also had some outstanding personalities in their ranks, particularly Trotsky and their leader Lenin.
- The Bolsheviks had used their newspaper, Pravda, to spread the Bolshevik message to the Russian people and had mounted an effective propaganda campaign against the Provisional Government and its failures.

Think!

Work in pairs, taking either Lenin or Trotsky.
1. Using Sources 11–16 add extra bullet points to the profiles of Lenin or Trotsky on page 193 covering:
   - why he appealed to people
   - his personal qualities
   - his strengths as a leader.
2. Finally, write a short (150–200 word) explanation of the contribution of your individual to the Bolsheviks' success in 1917.

Profile

Vladimir Ilyich Lenin

- Born 1870 into a respectable Russian family.
- Thrown out of Kazan University for his political ideas.
- Exiled to Siberia 1897–1900.
- 1900–03 lived in various countries writing the revolutionary newspaper *Iskra* ('The Spark').
- Leader of the Bolsheviks from 1903.
- Lived in exile, 1905–17.
- Led the Bolsheviks to power in November 1917.

Profile

Leon Trotsky

- Born 1879 into a respectable and prosperous Jewish family.
- Exceptionally bright at school and university.
- Politically active – arrested in 1900 and deported to Siberia.
- Escaped to London in 1902. Met Lenin.
- Joined the Social Democratic Party, but was Menshevik not Bolshevik.
- Imprisoned for his role in the 1905 revolution but escaped.
- Edited *Pravda*, the newspaper of the Social Democratic Party.
- Returned to Russia in 1917. Played a key role in the Bolshevik Revolution.
- Became Commissar for War and led the Bolsheviks to victory in the Civil War 1918-20.

SOURCE 11

Lenin … was the overall planner of the revolution: he also dealt with internal divisions within the party and provided tight control, and a degree of discipline and unity which the other parties lacked.

S.J. Lee, *The European Dictatorships*, 1987.

SOURCE 12

This extraordinary figure [Lenin] was first and foremost a professional revolutionary. He had no other occupation. A man of iron will and inflexible ambition, he was absolutely ruthless and used human beings as mere material for his purpose … his ordinary appearance disposed the crowd in his favour. 'He is not one of the gentlefolk, he is one of us', they would say.

The Times, writing about Lenin after his death, 1924.

SOURCE 13

The struggle was headed by Lenin who guided the Party's Central Committee, the editorial board of *Pravda*, and who kept in touch with the Party organisations in the provinces … He frequently addressed mass rallies and meetings. Lenin's appearance on the platform inevitably triggered off the cheers of the audience. Lenin's brilliant speeches inspired the workers and soldiers to a determined struggle.

Soviet historian Y. Kukushkin, *History of the USSR*, 1981.

SOURCE 14

Now that the great revolution has come, one feels that however intelligent Lenin may be he begins to fade beside the genius of Trotsky.

Mikhail Uritsky, 1917. Uritsky was a Bolshevik activist and went on to play an important role in Bolshevik governments after 1917.

SOURCE 15

*The [November] Revolution has often and widely been held to have been mainly Lenin's revolution. But was it? Certainly Lenin had a heavier impact on the course [of events] than anyone else. The point is, however, that great historical changes are brought about not only by individuals. There were **other mighty factors at work** as well in Russia in 1917 … Lenin simply could not have done or even co-ordinated everything.*

Historian Robert Service, writing in 1990.

SOURCE 16

Under the influence of his [Trotsky's] tremendous activity and blinding success, certain people close to Trotsky were even inclined to see in him the real leader of the Russian revolution … It is true that during that period, after the thunderous success of his arrival in Russia and before the July days, Lenin did keep rather in the background, not speaking often, not writing much, but largely engaged in directing organisational work in the Bolshevik camp, whilst Trotsky thundered forth at meetings in Petrograd. Trotsky's most obvious gifts were his talents as an orator and as a writer. I regard Trotsky as probably the greatest orator of our age. In my time I have heard all the greatest parliamentarians and popular tribunes of socialism and very many famous orators of the bourgeois world and I would find it difficult to name any of them whom I could put in the same class as Trotsky.

From *Revolutionary Silhouettes* by Anatoly Lunacharsky, published in 1918. The book was a series of portraits of leading revolutionaries. The author was a Bolshevik activist and knew Lenin and Trotsky well.

FIGURE 17

The Treaty of Brest-Litovsk, 1918.

Lenin in power

Lenin and the Bolsheviks had promised the people bread, peace and land. Lenin knew that if he failed to deliver, the Bolsheviks would suffer the same fate as the Provisional Government.

Lenin immediately set up the Council of People's Commissars (the Sovnarkom). It issued its first decree on 8 November, announcing that Russia was asking for peace with Germany. There followed an enormous number of decrees from the new government that aimed to strengthen the Bolsheviks' hold on power (see Factfile). The peasants were given the nobles' lands. The factories and industries were put into the hands of the workers. The Bolsheviks were given power to deal ruthlessly with their opponents – and they did (see page 195).

The Bolshevik dictatorship

Lenin had also promised free elections to the new Constituent Assembly. Elections were held in late 1917. As Lenin had feared, the Bolsheviks did not gain a majority. Their rivals, the peasant-based Socialist Revolutionaries, were the biggest party when the Assembly opened on 18 January 1918. They gained 370 seats to the Bolsheviks' 175 and 162 seats for the other parties.

Lenin solved this problem in his typically direct style. He sent the Red Guards to close down the Assembly. After brief protests (again put down by the Red Guards) the Assembly was forgotten. Lenin instead used the All-Russia Congress of Soviets to pass his laws as it did contain a Bolshevik majority.

Russia's democratic experiment therefore lasted less than 24 hours, but this did not trouble Lenin's conscience. He believed he was establishing a DICTATORSHIP of the proletariat, which in time would give way to true COMMUNISM.

Making peace

The next promise that Lenin had to make good was for peace. He put Trotsky in charge of negotiating a peace treaty. He told Trotsky to try to spin out the peace negotiations as long as possible. He hoped that very soon a socialist revolution would break out in Germany as it had in Russia. By February 1918, however, there was no revolution and the Germans began to advance again. Lenin had to accept their terms in the TREATY OF BREST-LITOVSK in March 1918.

The Treaty was a severe blow to Russia. You can see how much land was lost in Figure 17, but this was not the whole story. Russia's losses included 34 per cent of its population, 32 per cent of its agricultural land, 54 per cent of its industry, 26 per cent of its railways and 89 per cent of its coalmines. A final blow was the imposition of a fine of 300 million gold roubles. It was another example of Lenin's single-minded leadership. If this much had to be sacrificed to safeguard his revolution, then so be it. Many Russians, including revolutionaries, were opposed to the signing of the Treaty.

Factfile

Bolshevik decrees, 1917

8 November
- Land belonging to Tsar, Church and nobles handed over to peasants.
- Russia asked for peace with Germany.

12 November
- Working day limited to eight hours; 48-hour week; rules made about overtime and holidays.

14 November
- Workers to be insured against illness or accident.

1 December
- All non-Bolshevik newspapers banned.

11 December
- The opposition Constitutional Democratic Party (Kadets) banned; its leaders arrested.

20 December
- Cheka (secret police) set up to deal with 'spies and counter-revolutionaries'.

27 December
- Factories put under control of workers' committees.
- Banks put under Bolshevik government control.

31 December
- Marriages could take place without a priest if desired.
- Divorce made easier.

Think!
Study the Factfile. Which of the Bolshevik decrees would you say aimed to:
a) keep the peasants happy
b) keep the workers happy
c) increase Bolshevik control
d) improve personal freedom in Russia?

Revision Tip
- List two factors which would have generated support for the Bolsheviks.
- List two factors which would have created opposition to them.

Factfile

The Whites

'Whites' was a very broad term and was applied to any anti-Bolshevik group(s). Whites were made up of:
- Socialist Revolutionaries
- Mensheviks
- supporters of the Tsar
- landlords and capitalists who had lost land or money in the revolution
- the Czech Legion (former prisoners of war).

The Whites were also supported for part of the Civil War by foreign troops from the USA, Japan, France and Britain. They were sent by their governments to try to force Russia to rejoin the war against Germany.

Opposition and Civil War

Lenin's activities in 1917–18 were bound to make him enemies. He survived an attempted assassination in August 1918 (he was hit three times). In December he set up a secret police force called the Cheka to crush his opponents.

By the end of 1918 an unlikely collection of anti-Bolshevik elements had united against the Bolsheviks. They became known as the Whites (in contrast to the Bolshevik Reds) and consisted of enemies of the Bolsheviks from inside and outside Russia (see Factfile). By spring 1918 three separate White armies were marching on Bolshevik-controlled western Russia. Generals Yudenich and Denikin marched towards Petrograd and Moscow, while Admiral Kolchak marched on Moscow from central southern Russia.

FIGURE 18

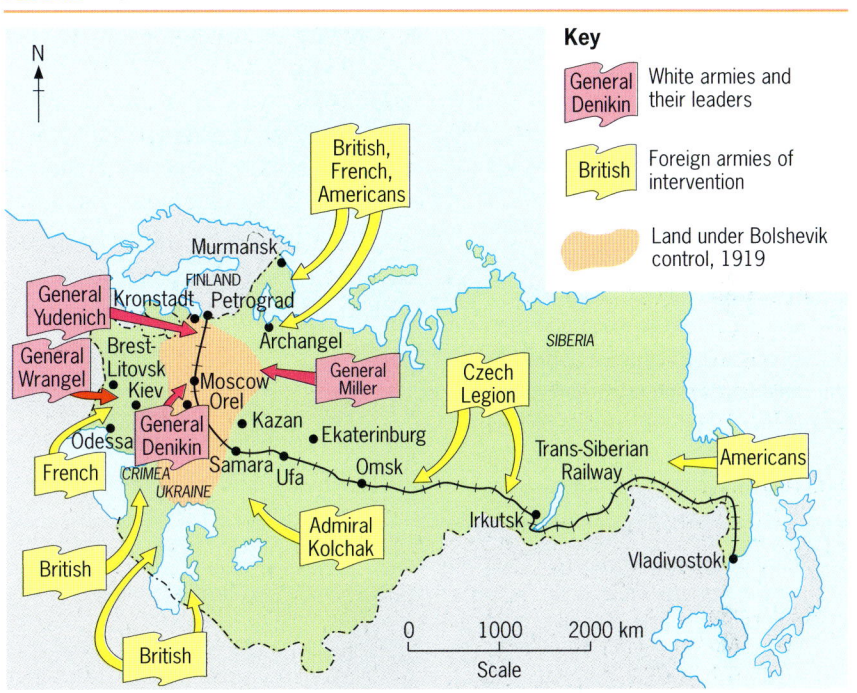

The main developments of the Civil War.

FIGURE 19

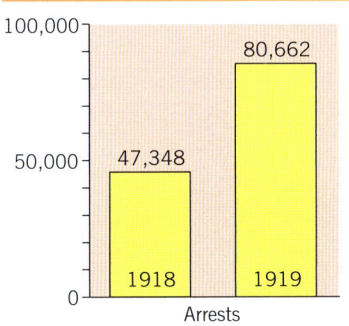

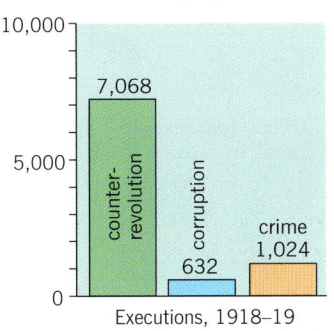

Arrests:
- 1918: 47,348
- 1919: 80,662

Executions, 1918–19:
- counter-revolution: 7,068
- corruption: 632
- crime: 1,024

The Red Terror.

Revision Tip

Make sure you can explain two ways in which the Bolshevik Red Terror helped them fight the Civil War.

The reaction of the Bolsheviks was ruthless and determined. In an amazingly short time, Leon Trotsky created a new RED ARMY of over 300,000 men. They were led by former tsarist officers. Trotsky made sure of their loyalty by holding their families hostage and by appointing political commissars to watch over them. The Cheka terrorised the populations of Bolshevik territories so that nobody co-operated. This period was known as the Red Terror – see Figure 19. In July 1918, White forces were approaching Ekaterinburg where the Tsar was being held. The Bolshevik commander ordered the execution of the Tsar and his family. Lenin could not risk the Tsar being rescued and returned as leader of the Whites. The fighting was savage with both sides committing terrible acts of cruelty.

Through harsh discipline and brilliant leadership, Trotsky's Red Army began to turn back the White forces. Kolchak's forces were destroyed towards the end of 1919 and at the same time the foreign 'armies of intervention' withdrew. The Whites were not really a strong alliance, and their armies were unable to work together. Trotsky defeated them one by one. The last major White army was defeated in the Crimea in November 1920.

> **Source Analysis**
>
> 1 Use Sources 20 and 21 to describe how the Civil War affected ordinary people.
> 2 Do you think Source 21 was painted by opponents or supporters of the Bolsheviks?
> 3 Look at Source 25. Who is controlling the White forces?
> 4 Who do you think Source 23 is talking to?

Why did the Bolsheviks win the Civil War?

The Red Army was no match for the armies that were still fighting on the Western Front in 1918. However, compared to the Whites, the Red Army was united and disciplined. It was also brilliantly led by Trotsky, who even traveled around Bolshevik-held Russia in his armoured train giving inspirational speeches to the Red Army units.

The Bolsheviks also kept control over their heartlands in western Russia.

- They made sure that the towns and armies were fed, by forcing peasants to hand over food and by rationing supplies (see Source 22). Lenin ordered special grain requisitioning squads to seize grain and foodstuffs. Anyone who opposed them were shot or imprisoned.
- They took over the factories of Moscow and Petrograd so that they were able to supply their armies with equipment and ammunition.
- The Red Terror imposed strict control (see Figure 19 and Source 20).

SOURCE 20

In the villages the peasant will not give grain to the Bolsheviks because he hates them. Armed companies are sent to take grain from the peasant and every day, all over Russia, fights for grain are fought to a finish.

In the Red Army, for any military offence, there is only one punishment, death. If a regiment retreats against orders, machine guns are turned on them. The position of the bourgeoisie [middle class] defies all description. Payments by the banks have been stopped. It is forbidden to sell furniture. All owners and managers of works, offices and shops have been called up for compulsory labour. In Petrograd hundreds of people are dying from hunger. People are arrested daily and kept in prison for months without trial.

> The Red Terror, observed by a British businessman in Russia in 1918.

SOURCE 22

Having surrounded the village [the Whites] fired a couple of volleys in the direction of the village and everyone took cover. Then the mounted soldiers entered the village, met the Bolshevik committee and put the members to death … After the execution the houses of the culprits were burned and the male population under forty-five whipped … Then the population was ordered to deliver without pay the best cattle, pigs, fowl, forage and bread for the soldiers as well as the best horses.

> Diary of Colonel Drozdovsky, from his memoirs written in 1923. He was a White commander during the Civil War.

SOURCE 21

Members of the Red Guard requisition grain from peasants during the Civil War.

SOURCE 23

For the first time in history the working people have got control of their country. The workers of all countries are striving to achieve this objective. We in Russia have succeeded. We have thrown off the rule of the Tsar, of landlords and of capitalists. But we still have tremendous difficulties to overcome. We cannot build a new society in a day. We ask you, are you going to crush us? To help give Russia back to the landlords, the capitalists and the Tsar?

> Red propaganda leaflet, *Why Have You Come to Murmansk?*

The Bolsheviks used propaganda to raise fears about the intentions of the foreign armies in league with the Whites (Source 24, page 197). A propaganda train spread communist ideas across Russia. Propaganda also raised fears about the possible return of the Tsar and landlords (Source 23).

SOURCE 24

The Civil War, 1918–1920, was a time of great chaos and estimates of Cheka executions vary from twelve to fifty thousand. But even the highest figure does not compare to the ferocity of the White Terror ... for instance, in Finland alone, the number of workers executed by the Whites approaches 100,000.

R. Appignanesi, *Lenin for Beginners*, 1977.

Source Analysis

'Most Russians saw the Bolsheviks as the lesser of two evils.'
Explain how Sources 20, 22, 23 and 24 support or challenge this statement.

Revision Tip

- List two weaknesses of the Whites.
- List two strengths of the Bolsheviks.
- Decide for yourself whether White weaknesses or Bolshevik strengths were more important.

Finally, the Reds had important territorial advantages. Their enemies were spread around the edge of Russia while they controlled the centre and also the all-important railway system. This enabled them to move troops and supplies quickly and effectively by rail, while their enemies used less efficient methods.

SOURCE 25

Bolshevik propaganda cartoon, 1919. The dogs represent the White generals Denikin, Kolchak and Yudenich.

FOCUS TASK 7.9

Why did the Bolsheviks win the Civil War?

1. Draw a table and use the text to make notes about how each of these factors helped the Bolsheviks win.
   - Unity
   - Leadership
   - Communications, e.g. railways
   - Geography
   - Support of the workers
   - Support of the peasants
   - The Red Army
   - Foreign intervention
   - Propaganda

2. Now write some paragraphs to show how some of these factors were connected. Two examples are shown below.

Linking Geography and Communications:

In such a vast country communications were a key to success. The Bolsheviks held the central industrial area which included all the main railway lines out of Moscow and Petrograd. This meant that they could get soldiers and military supplies to the different fronts much more easily that the Whites who found it very difficult to communicate with each other and move troops around the edges of the centre.

Linking Foreign intervention and Propaganda:

The foreign intervention was a gift to the Reds. They could use it in their propaganda to show that the Red Army was fighting foreign invaders.

The Whites, in contrast with the Bolsheviks, were not united.
- They were made up of many different groups, all with different aims.
- They were also widely spread so they were unable to co-ordinate their campaigns against the Reds. Trotsky was able to defeat them one by one.
- They had limited support from the Russian population. Russian peasants did not especially like the Bolsheviks, but they preferred them to the Whites. If the Whites won, the peasants knew the landlords would return. Both sides were guilty of atrocities, but the Whites in general caused more suffering to the peasants than the Reds.

Economic policy

War Communism

WAR COMMUNISM was the name given to the harsh economic measures the Bolsheviks adopted during the Civil War in order to survive. It had two main aims. The first aim was to put communist theories into practice by redistributing (sharing out) wealth among the Russian people. The second aim was to help with the Civil War by keeping the towns and the Red Army supplied with food and weapons.

- All large factories were taken over by the Government.
- Production was planned and organised by the new government agency called Vesenkha (Supreme Economic Council).
- Discipline for workers was strict and strikers could be shot.
- Peasants had to hand over surplus food to the Government. If they didn't, they could be shot.
- Food was rationed.
- Free enterprise became illegal – all production and trade was state-controlled.

SOURCE 26

Starving children photographed during the Russian famine of 1921.

War Communism achieved its aim of winning the war, but in doing so it caused terrible hardship. By 1921, industrial output had fallen to just one-fifth of 1913 levels. The currency collapsed which resulted in bartering – 90 per cent of wages were paid with goods rather than money. Peasants refused to co-operate in producing more food because the Government simply took it away. This led to food shortages which, along with the bad weather in 1920 and 1921, caused a terrible famine. Some estimates suggest that 7 million Russian people died in this famine. There were even reports of cannibalism.

Kronstadt Rising

As you saw on page 192 the sailors from the Kronstadt naval base were strong supporters of the Bolsheviks during the revolution and the Civil War. However, they were concerned at the impact that Bolshevik policies were having on ordinary Russians. Sailors from two of the battleships at Kronstadt passed a resolution calling on the Bolsheviks to change their policies. They made fifteen demands, including new elections, FREEDOM OF SPEECH, equal rations and the scrapping of the militia units which were taking peasants' grain.

This was a potentially serious threat to Lenin and the Bolsheviks. Lenin issued a statement claiming the rebellion was a plot by the White force. He demanded the rebels surrender. They refused, so in early March Trotsky's forces stormed the Kronstadt base. There was heavy fighting and although there are no reliable figures about casualties the death toll was probably in the thousands. Thousands more of the rebels were executed or imprisoned in labour camps. Nevertheless, the rebellion had affected Lenin. Because the Kronstadt sailors had been among the strongest supporters of Lenin and Bolshevism in 1917–20, Lenin began to think that he had to make concessions.

> **Source Analysis**
>
> Why do you think the photograph in Source 26 was taken and published in 1921? Use the source and your knowledge to explain your answer.

> **Think!**
>
> Why do you think Lenin was more worried about the revolt of the sailors than about starvation among the peasants?

SOURCE 27

Our poverty and ruin are so great that we cannot at one stroke restore large-scale socialist production . . . we must try to satisfy the demands of the peasants who are dissatisfied, discontented and cannot be otherwise . . . there must be a certain amount of freedom to trade, freedom for the small private owner. We are now retreating, but we are doing this so as to then run and leap forward more vigorously.

Lenin, introducing the NEP at the Party Congress, 1921.

The New Economic Policy

In March 1921, at the Party Congress, Lenin announced some startling new policies which he called the NEW ECONOMIC POLICY (NEP). The NEP effectively brought back capitalism for some sections of Russian society. Peasants were allowed to sell surplus grain for profit and would pay tax on what they produced rather than giving some of it up to the Government.

FIGURE 28

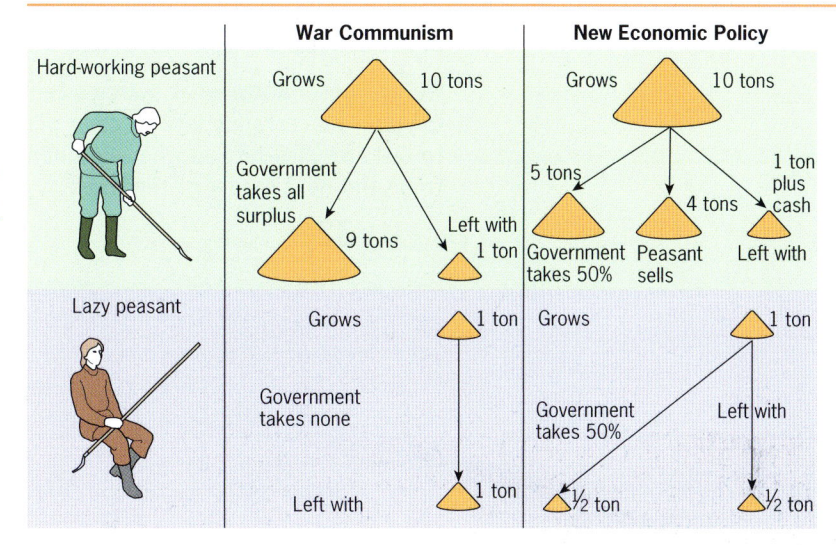

How the NEP differed from War Communism.

In the towns, small factories were handed back into private ownership and private trading of small goods was allowed. The NEPMEN were the beneficiaries.

Lenin made it clear that the NEP was temporary and that the vital heavy industries (coal, oil, iron and steel) would remain in state hands. Nevertheless, many Bolsheviks were horrified when the NEP was announced, seeing it as a betrayal of communism. As always, Lenin won the argument and the NEP went into operation from 1921 onwards. By 1925 there seemed to be strong evidence that it was working, as food production in particular rose steeply. However, increases in production did not necessarily improve the situation of industrial workers.

SOURCE 29

Poor, starving old Russia, Russia of primitive lighting and the meal of a crust of black bread, is going to be covered by a network of electric power stations. The NEP will transform the Russian economy and rebuild a broken nation. The future is endless and beautiful.

Bukharin, speaking in 1922. He was a leading Bolshevik and a strong supporter of the NEP.

Source Analysis

Does the evidence of Figure 30 prove that the NEP was a success? Explain your answer with reference to Sources 27 and 29.

Revision Tip
- Make sure you can explain the aims of War Communism.
- List two effects of War Communism.
- List two key features of the NEP.

FIGURE 30

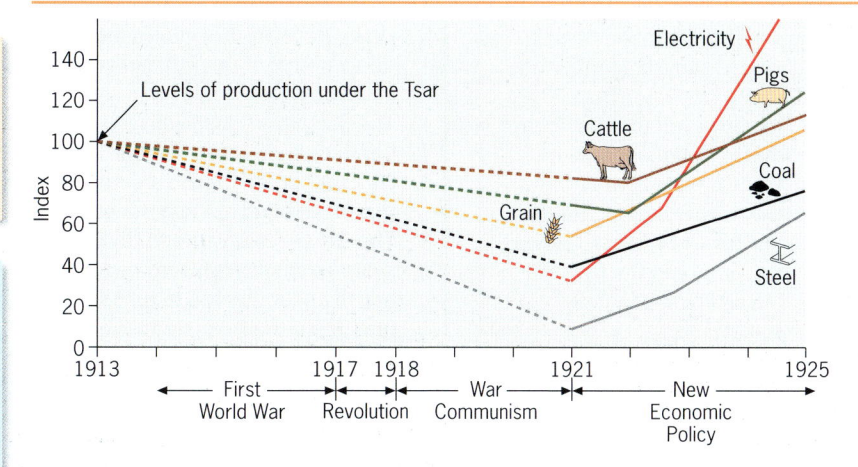

Production under the New Economic Policy, 1921–25.

SOURCE 31

Lenin did more than any other political leader to change the face of the twentieth-century world. The creation of Soviet Russia and its survival were due to him. He was a very great man and even, despite his faults, a very good man.

The British historian A.J.P. Taylor writing in the 1960s.

The death of Lenin and the creation of the USSR

Lenin did not live to see the recovery of the Russian economy. He suffered several strokes in 1922 and 1923 which left him paralysed and which led to his death in January 1924. He was a remarkable man by any standards. He led Russia through revolution and civil war and even in 1923 he supervised the drawing up of a new Constitution that turned the Russian Empire into the Union of Soviet Socialist Republics. Source 31 gives the opinion of a British historian.

We will never know what policies Lenin would have pursued if he had lived longer – he certainly left no clear plans about how long he wanted the NEP to last. He also left another big unanswered question behind him: who was to be the next leader of the USSR?

SOURCE 32

In the late 1980s and 1990s, Soviet archives were opened up as the Communist regime came to an end. These revealed a much harder, more ruthless Lenin than the 'softer' image he had enjoyed amongst left-wing historians and groups. For instance, a memorandum, first published in 1990, reveals his ordering the extermination of the clergy in a place called Shuya …

Lenin believed that revolutionaries had to be hard to carry out their role, which would inevitably involve spilling the blood of their opponents. Although hard and tough on others, it seems that Lenin was not personally brave. He left the fighting to others.

An extract from *Communist Russia under Lenin and Stalin*. This was an A-level History textbook published in 2002.

Source Analysis

From all you have found out about Lenin, do you agree with Source 32? (Don't forget to look at Source 31.)

FOCUS TASK 8.10

How did the Bolsheviks consolidate their rule?

1 Draw a timeline from 1917 to 1924, and mark on it the events of that period mentioned in the text.
2 Mark on the timeline:
   a) one moment at which you think Bolshevik rule was most threatened
   b) one moment at which you think it was most secure.
3 Write an explanation of how the Bolsheviks made their rule more secure. Mention the following:
   ■ the power of the Red Army
   ■ treatment of opposition
   ■ War Communism
   ■ the New Economic Policy
   ■ the Treaty of Brest-Litovsk
   ■ the victory in the Civil War
   ■ the promise of a new society
   ■ propaganda.
4 Is any one of these factors more important than any of the others? Explain your answer.

Key Question Summary

How did the Bolsheviks gain power and how did they hold on to power?

1 After the Tsar's abdication, a Provisional Government was set up to run Russia until elections could be held to choose a new government.
2 The Petrograd Soviet had the real power in the capital because it controlled the army and the workers in the factories.
3 The Provisional Government was weak and failed to deal with the problems of the war and the land to the satisfaction of the people. The economic situation continued to deteriorate throughout 1917.
4 Lenin returned to Russia and announced, in the April Theses, that his party, the Bolsheviks, would end the war, give the land to the peasants and ensure that the people got food. This brought them popular support although an attempt by some Bolsheviks to stage a rising in the July Days was a failure.
5 However, after Kornilov's attempted coup, they had enough support to take control of the Petrograd Soviet. On Lenin's urging, they seized power in October 1917.
6 The Bolsheviks dealt with any internal opposition ruthlessly by using the Cheka.
7 Lenin ended the war by the Treaty of Brest-Litovsk.
8 He crushed the newly elected Constituent Assembly because the Bolsheviks did not win the elections.
9 The Bolsheviks won the Civil War and kept the economy going through a system called War Communism. War Communism worked but it was very harsh and it started to turn former supporters against the Communists (including the Kronstadt sailors).
10 Lenin introduced a compromise – the New Economic Policy – which allowed the economy to recover and bring the people respite and some prosperity. By 1924 the Bolsheviks were firmly in power and had CONSOLIDATED their position.

7C Stalin's Russia

FOCUS

Most people thought Trotsky was the person most likely to succeed Lenin. Yet not only did Stalin become the new leader of the USSR, but over the next 40 years he changed it radically. He created a modern industrial state that became a superpower but he also created a TOTALITARIAN state where opposition was not tolerated and where the government imprisoned or murdered millions of its own citizens.

How did Stalin gain and hold on to power?

Focus Points

- Why did Stalin, and not Trotsky, emerge as Lenin's successor?
- Why did Stalin launch the Purges?
- What methods did Stalin use to control the Soviet Union?
- How complete was Stalin's control over the Soviet Union by 1941?

What was the impact of Stalin's economic policies?

Focus Points

- Why did Stalin introduce the Five-Year Plans?
- Why did Stalin introduce collectivisation?
- How successful were Stalin's economic changes?
- How were the Soviet people affected by these changes?

In this section you will look at two overlapping themes: how Stalin modernised the USSR and how he controlled it.

Source Analysis

1. Study Source 1. What achievements is Stalin pointing out?
2. Which figure can you see top left? Why do you think he has been placed in this position?
3. Why do you think this poster was produced at the end of the 1930s?

SOURCE 1

An official poster from the mid to late 1930s showing Stalin pointing out the achievements of the USSR and its people.

Factfile

Stalin's steps to power

- **1923** Lenin calls for Stalin to be replaced. Trotsky calls him 'the party's most eminent mediocrity'.
- **1924** Lenin's death. Stalin attends funeral as chief mourner. Trotsky does not turn up (tricked by Stalin).
- **1924** Stalin, Kamenev and Zinoviev form the triumvirate that dominates the Politburo, the policy-making committee of the Communist Party. Working together, these three cut off their opponents (Trotsky and Bukharin) because between them they control the important posts in the party.
- **1925** Trotsky sacked as War Commissar. Stalin introduces his idea of Socialism in One Country.
- **1926** Stalin turns against Kamenev and Zinoviev and allies himself with Bukharin.
- **1927** Kamenev, Zinoviev and Trotsky all expelled from the Communist Party.
- **1928** Trotsky exiled to Siberia. Stalin begins attacking Bukharin.
- **1929** Trotsky expelled from USSR and Bukharin expelled from the Communist Party.

SOURCE 3

Trotsky refrained from attacking Stalin because he felt secure. No contemporary, and he least of all, saw in the Stalin of 1923 the menacing and towering figure he was to become. It seemed to Trotsky almost a joke that Stalin, the wilful and sly but shabby and inarticulate man in the background, should be his rival.

Historian I. Deutscher in *The Prophet Unarmed, Trotsky 1921–1929*, published in 1959.

Stalin or Trotsky?

When Lenin died in 1924 there were several leading Communists who were possible candidates to take his place. Among the contenders were Kamenev and Zinoviev, leading Bolsheviks who had played important parts in the Bolshevik Revolution of 1917, and Bukharin, a more moderate member of the party who favoured the NEP and wanted to introduce communism gradually to the USSR. However, the real struggle to succeed Lenin was between two bitter rivals, Joseph Stalin and Leon Trotsky. The power struggle went on for some time and it was not until 1929 that Stalin made himself completely secure as the supreme leader of the USSR. Stalin achieved this through a combination of political scheming, the mistakes of his opponents and the clever way in which he built up his power base in the Communist Party.

Lenin's Testament

Source 2 shows Lenin's opinions of Trotsky and Stalin. As Lenin lay dying in late 1923 Trotsky seemed most likely to win. He was a brilliant speaker and writer, as well as the party's best political thinker, after Lenin. He was also the man who had organised the Bolshevik Revolution and was the hero of the Civil War as leader of the Red Army (see page 196).

SOURCE 2

Comrade Stalin, having become Secretary General, has unlimited authority in his hands and I am not sure whether he will always be capable of using that authority with sufficient caution.

Comrade Trotsky, on the other hand, is distinguished not only by his outstanding ability. He is personally probably the most capable man in the present Central Committee, but he has displayed excessive self-assurance and preoccupation with the purely administrative side of the work.

Lenin's Testament. This is often used as evidence that Stalin was an outsider. However, the document contained many remarks critical of other leading Communists as well. It was never published in Russia, although, if it had been, it would certainly have damaged Stalin.

Trotsky's mistakes

So how did Trotsky lose this contest? Much of the blame lies with Trotsky himself. He was brilliant, but also arrogant and high-handed. He often offended other senior party members. More importantly, he failed to take the opposition seriously. He made little effort to build up any support in the ranks of the party. And he seriously underestimated Stalin, as did the other contenders. No one saw Stalin as a threat. They were all more concerned with each other. Stalin kept in the shadows, not taking a clear position and seeming to be the friend and ally of different groups. This allowed him to become steadily more powerful without the others realising it.

Trotsky also frightened many people in the USSR. They were worried he might become a DICTATOR, especially because he had a great deal of support in the army. Trotsky argued that the future security of the USSR lay in trying to spread permanent revolution across the globe until the whole world was communist. Many people were worried that Trotsky would involve the USSR in new conflicts and that his radical policies might split the party.

Luck

As it often does in history, chance also played a part. Trotsky was unfortunate in falling ill late in 1923 with a malaria-like infection – just when Lenin was dying, and Trotsky needed to be at his most active.

SOURCE 4

Lenin and Stalin. Stalin made the most of any opportunity to appear close to Lenin. This photograph is a suspected fake.

Profile

Joseph Stalin

- Born 1879 in Georgia. His father was a shoemaker and an alcoholic.
- Original name was Iosif Dzhugashvili but changed his name to Stalin (man of steel).
- Twice exiled to Siberia by the tsarist secret police, he escaped each time.
- Made his name in violent bank raids to raise party funds.
- He was slow and steady, but very hardworking.
- He also held grudges and generally made his enemies suffer.
- Became a leading communist after playing an important role in defending the Bolshevik city of Tsaritsyn (later Stalingrad) during the Civil War.
- Had become undisputed party leader by 1929.

Think!

In groups, look at the following statements and decide on a scale of 1–5 how far you agree with them.
- Stalin was a dull and unimaginative politician.
- Stalin appeared to be a dull and unimaginative politician.
- Trotsky lost the contest because of his mistakes.
- Stalin trusted to luck rather than careful planning.
- Stalin was ruthless and devious.

Try to find evidence on these two pages to back up your judgements.

Stalin's cunning

We have already seen that Stalin was a clever politician and he planned his bid for power carefully. He made great efforts to associate himself with Lenin wherever possible and got off to an excellent start at Lenin's funeral. He played a trick on Trotsky. Stalin cabled Trotsky to tell him that Lenin's funeral was to be on 26 January, when it was in fact going to be on the 27th. Trotsky was away in the south of Russia and would not have had time to get back for the 26th, although he could have got back for the 27th. As a result, Trotsky did not appear at the funeral whereas Stalin appeared as chief mourner and Lenin's closest comrade and follower.

He was also extremely clever in using his power within the Communist Party. He took on many boring but important jobs including the post of General Secretary. He used these positions to put his own supporters into important posts and remove people likely to support his opponents from the Party. He was also very good at political manoeuvring. First of all he allied himself with Zinoviev and Kamanev to push out Trotsky. Then he allied himself with Bukharin in the debate about the NEP (see page 199) to defeat Zinoviev and Kamanev and later get them, along with Trotsky, expelled from the Party. All the time he was building his own power base, bringing in his supporters to the Party Congress and Central Committee to make sure he was chosen as leader. Finally, he turned on Bukharin and his supporters, removing them from powerful positions. By 1929 he was the unchallenged leader.

Stalin's policies also met with greater favour than Trotsky's. Stalin proposed that in future the party should try to establish 'Socialism in One Country' rather than try to spread revolution worldwide. The idea that they could achieve SOCIALISM on their own appealed to the Russian sense of NATIONALISM. Finally, Stalin appeared to be a straightforward Georgian peasant – much more a man of the people than his intellectual rivals. To a Soviet people weary of years of war and revolution, Stalin seemed to be the man who understood their feelings.

FOCUS TASK 7.11

Why did Stalin and not Trotsky emerge as Lenin's successor?

Use pages 202–03 and your own research to complete the following:

1. In groups of four, two will promote Trotsky as the new leader and two will promote Stalin.
2. One person will need to design and draw a propaganda poster to promote their leader and the other will need to write a short speech explaining why their leader is the better choice for the Soviet Union.
3. Listen to the speeches and study the posters and then write notes under the following headings to explain why Stalin rather than Trotsky emerged as the new leader of Russia.

Write notes under the following headings to explain why Stalin rather than Trotsky emerged as the new leader of Russia.
- Trotsky's strengths and weaknesses in the leadership contest
- Why other contenders underestimated Stalin
- How Stalin outmanoeuvred other contenders
- Why Stalin's policies were attractive to Party members

Then combine your notes to write your own account in answer to the question: 'Why did Stalin and not Trotsky emerge as Lenin's successor?'

Revision Tip

- List two mistakes made by Trotsky.
- List two strengths or clever actions of Stalin.

Modernising the USSR: 1 – Industrialisation

SOURCE 5

Throughout history Russia has been beaten again and again because she was backward … All have beaten her because of her military, industrial and agricultural backwardness. She was beaten because people have been able to get away with it. If you are backward and weak, then you are in the wrong and may be beaten and enslaved. But if you are powerful, people must beware of you.

It is sometimes asked whether it is not possible to slow down industrialisation a bit. No, comrades, it is not possible … To slacken would mean falling behind. And those who fall behind get beaten … That is why Lenin said during the October Revolution: 'Either perish, or overtake and outstrip the advanced capitalist countries.' We are 50 to 100 years behind the advanced countries. Either we make good the difference in ten years or they crush us.

Stalin speaking in 1931.

Think!
Look at the different reasons Stalin had for wanting to modernise the USSR. Which do you think he would have placed as his top priority?

Why did Stalin want to modernise Soviet industry?

Security
It might seem clear from Source 5 why Stalin wanted to give the USSR a modern industrial economy. Security was certainly a key factor. The First World War had shown that a country could only fight a modern war if it had the industries to produce the weapons and other equipment which were needed – it was impossible to equip an army with rifles and uniforms without the factories to make them. And those factories needed iron, steel, textiles and other resources to turn into rifles and uniforms. And without coal and electricity to power them there would not be any factories anyway. It is also worth noting that Stalin planned for many of the new industrial projects to be further east in the USSR, potentially safer from invasion.

Power and control
But this was not the only reason. As you have already seen, Stalin was a cunning political operator who made alliances with different groups in order to dispose of his rivals. By 1928 he had allied himself to Bukharin and his supporters, who believed in the NEP. In order to undermine Bukharin he switched his position and became a supporter of greater state planning and control and the construction of large projects like railways and hydro-electric dams. Once he removed Bukharin and other opponents the industrialisation programme also became a powerful means of controlling the country. Many political prisoners were sent to work in appalling conditions in labour camps' building projects like the White Sea to Baltic Canal. The fate of these prisoners often discouraged others. Similarly, anyone who complained or criticised Stalin's programme could be accused of undermining the country's progress.

Socialism in One Country
This was closely connected to his policy of 'Socialism in One Country'. This policy had a lot of support in the Communist Party and in the USSR generally. Stalin saw an opportunity to harness nationalist pride to develop the economy. When Stalin took power, much of Russia's industrial equipment had to be imported. Stalin wanted to make the USSR self-sufficient so that it could make everything it needed for itself. He wanted the USSR to compete on equal terms with the economies of the West. He hoped to see a time when the West would be importing goods from the USSR not the other way around. He also wanted to improve standards of living in Russia with better housing, mass education and health care so that people would value communist rule.

Ideology
Marxist theory viewed the workers as crucial in creating a communist society, but by 1928 only about one in five Russians were industrial workers. Stalin wanted to modernise industry rapidly to build a power base of working-class support. He also wanted to remove the NEPmen who were viewed as a capitalist class of traders.

Reasons Stalin wanted to modernise Soviet industry

Personal reputation
Finally, Stalin probably saw modernising industry as a means of establishing his own personal reputation. Lenin had made big changes to the USSR. Stalin wanted to prove himself as a great leader by bringing about even greater changes. He would be able to point to dams, factories, railways and electricity pylons and take the credit for these achievements, helped by a formidable propaganda machine of films, posters, painting and music.

FIGURE 6

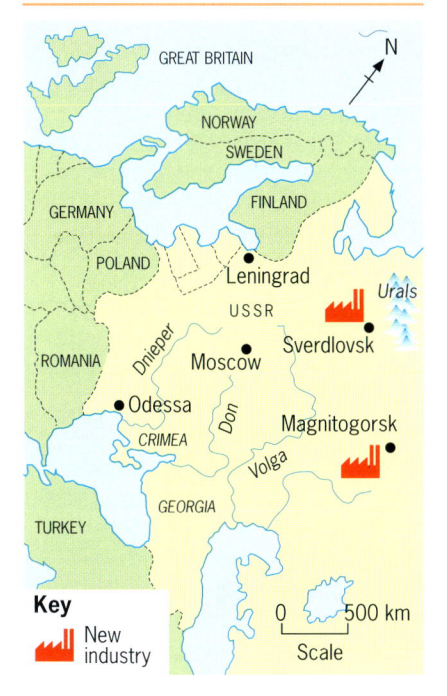

Locations of the new industrial centres.

The Five-Year Plans

Stalin ended Lenin's NEP and set about achieving modernisation through a series of FIVE-YEAR PLANS. These plans were drawn up by GOSPLAN, the state planning organisation that Lenin had set up in 1921. It set ambitious targets for production in the vital heavy industries (coal, iron, oil, electricity). The plans were very complex but they were set out in such a way that by 1929 every worker knew what he or she had to achieve.

| GOSPLAN set overall targets for an industry. | ▶ | Each region was told its targets. | ▶ | The region set targets for each mine, factory, etc. | ▶ | The manager of each mine, factory, etc. set targets for each foreman. | ▶ | The foremen set targets for each shift and even for individual workers. |

The first Five-Year Plan (1982–32) focused on the major industries and although most targets were not met, the achievements were still staggering. The USSR increased production and created a foundation on which to build the next Five-Year Plans. The USSR was rich in natural resources, but many of them were in remote places such as Siberia. So whole cities were built from nothing and workers taken out to the new industrial centres. Foreign observers marvelled as huge new steel mills appeared at Magnitogorsk in the Urals and Sverdlovsk in central Siberia. New dams and hydro-electric power fed industry's energy requirements. Russian 'experts' flooded into the Muslim REPUBLICS of central Asia such as Uzbekistan and Kazakhstan, creating industry from scratch in previously undeveloped areas.

The second Five-Year Plan (1933–37) built on the achievements of the first. Heavy industry was still a priority, but other areas were also developed. Mining for lead, tin, zinc and other minerals intensified as Stalin further exploited Siberia's rich mineral resources. Transport and communications were also boosted, and new railways and canals were built. The most spectacular showpiece project was the Moscow underground railway.

Stalin also wanted industrialisation to help improve Russia's agriculture. The production of tractors and other farm machinery increased dramatically. In **the third Five-Year Plan**, which was begun in 1938, some factories were to switch to the production of consumer goods. However, this plan was disrupted by the Second World War.

FOCUS TASK 7.12
Why did Stalin introduce the Five-Year Plans?

Study the reasons set out on page 204 as well as Source 5. Now draw your own version of this diagram with much larger bubbles. 
- In the speech bubbles summarise the reasons for his plans Stalin would have set out to a public audience.
- In the thought bubbles summarise the other reasons which you think Stalin might have kept to himself.

Revision Tip
You need to be able to explain at least two reasons why Stalin introduced the Five-Year Plans. Make sure you can explain rather than just describe what he did.

The impact of industrialisation on Russian people

Targets, hard work and propaganda
Any programme as extreme as Stalin's Five-Year Plans was bound to carry a cost. In the USSR this cost was paid by the workers. Many foreign experts and engineers were called in by Stalin to supervise the work and in their letters and reports they marvel at the toughness of the Russian people.

The workers were constantly bombarded with propaganda, posters, slogans and radio broadcasts. They all had strict targets to meet and were fined if they did not meet them.

The most famous worker was Alexei Stakhanov. In 1935, with two helpers and an easy coal seam to work on, he managed to cut an amazing 102 tons of coal in one shift. This was fourteen times the average for a shift. Stakhanov became a 'Hero of Socialist Labour' and the propaganda machine encouraged all Soviet workers to be STAKHANOVITES.

Slave labour
On the great engineering projects, such as dams and canals, many of the workers were prisoners who had been sentenced to hard labour for being political opponents, or suspected opponents, of Stalin, or for being kulaks (rich peasants) or Jewish people. Many other prisoners were simply unfortunate workers who had had accidents or made mistakes in their work but had been found guilty of 'sabotage'.

On these major projects conditions were appalling and there were many deaths and accidents. It is estimated that 100,000 workers died in the construction of the Belomor Canal.

Wages and living conditions
In the towns and cities, most housing was provided by the state, but overcrowding was a problem. Most families lived in flats and were crowded into two rooms, which were used for living, sleeping and eating. What's more, wages actually fell between 1928 and 1937. In 1932 a husband and wife who both worked earned only as much as one man or woman had in 1928.

At the same time, the concentration on heavy industry meant that there were few consumer goods (such as clothes or radios) that ordinary people wanted to buy.

Women workers
The first Five-Year Plan revealed a shortage of workers, so from 1930 the Government concentrated on drafting more women into industry. It set up thousands of new crèches and day-care centres so that mothers could work. By 1937 women were 40 per cent of industrial workers (compared to 28 per cent in 1927), 21 per cent of building workers and 72 per cent of health workers. Four out of five new workers recruited between 1932 and 1937 were women.

The impact of industrialisation on Russian people

Control
To escape punishments and harsh conditions, or to try to get better wages and bonuses, workers moved jobs frequently (in some industries three times a year). This did not help industry or society to stabilise. To try to prevent this, internal passports were introduced to prevent the movement of workers inside the USSR.

Training
By the late 1930s many Soviet workers had improved their conditions by acquiring well-paid skilled jobs and earning bonuses for meeting targets. Unemployment was almost non-existent. In 1940 the USSR had more doctors per head of population than Britain. Education became free and compulsory for all and Stalin invested huge sums in training schemes based in colleges and in the workplace.

Repression
Stalin was also quite prepared to destroy the way of life of the Soviet people to help industrialisation. For example, in the republics of central Asia the influence of Islam was thought to hold back industrialisation, so between 1928 and 1932 it was repressed. Many Muslim leaders were imprisoned or deported, mosques were closed and pilgrimages to Mecca were forbidden.

Punishments and blame
On the other hand, life was very harsh under Stalin. Factory discipline was strict and punishments were severe. Lateness or absences were punished by sacking, and that often meant losing your flat or house as well. In the headlong rush to fulfil targets, many of the products were of poor quality. Some factories over-produced in massive amounts while others had to shut down for short periods because they could not get parts and raw materials. However, things did improve under the second and third Five-Year Plans.

Blaming the workers was a good way of excusing mistakes made by management, although many workers were unskilled ex-peasants and did sometimes cause damage to machinery and equipment.

SOURCE 7

We got so dirty and we were such young things, small, slender, fragile. But we had our orders to build the metro and we wanted to do it more than anything else. We wore our miners' overalls with such style. My feet were size four and the boots were elevens. But there was such enthusiasm.

Tatyana Fyodorova, interviewed as an old lady in 1990, remembers building the Moscow Metro.

SOURCE 8

Half a billion cubic feet of excavation work ... 25,000 tons of structural steel ... without sufficient labour, without necessary quantities of the most rudimentary materials. Brigades of young enthusiasts arrived in the summer of 1930 and did the groundwork of railroad and dam ... Later groups of peasants came ... Many were completely unfamiliar with industrial tools and processes...

J. Scott, *Behind the Urals*, 1943.

Think!
Draw a diagram of a see-saw. List the benefits of industrialisation on one side and the downsides on the other. Finally, decide which way the see-saw will tip for the Russian people.

Achievements of the Five-Year Plans

There is much that could be and was criticised in the Five-Year Plans. For example:

- There was much inefficiency, duplication of effort and waste.
- There was also an immense human cost. One feature of the plans was spectacular building projects, such as the Dnieprostroi Dam, which were used as a showcase of Soviet achievement. The Moscow Metro was particularly impressive with vast stations and stunning architectural design. But many thousands of workers were killed in making them.

However, the fact remains that by 1937 the USSR was a modern, industrial state and it was this that saved it from defeat when Hitler invaded in 1941. Figure 9 shows how production increased.

FIGURE 9

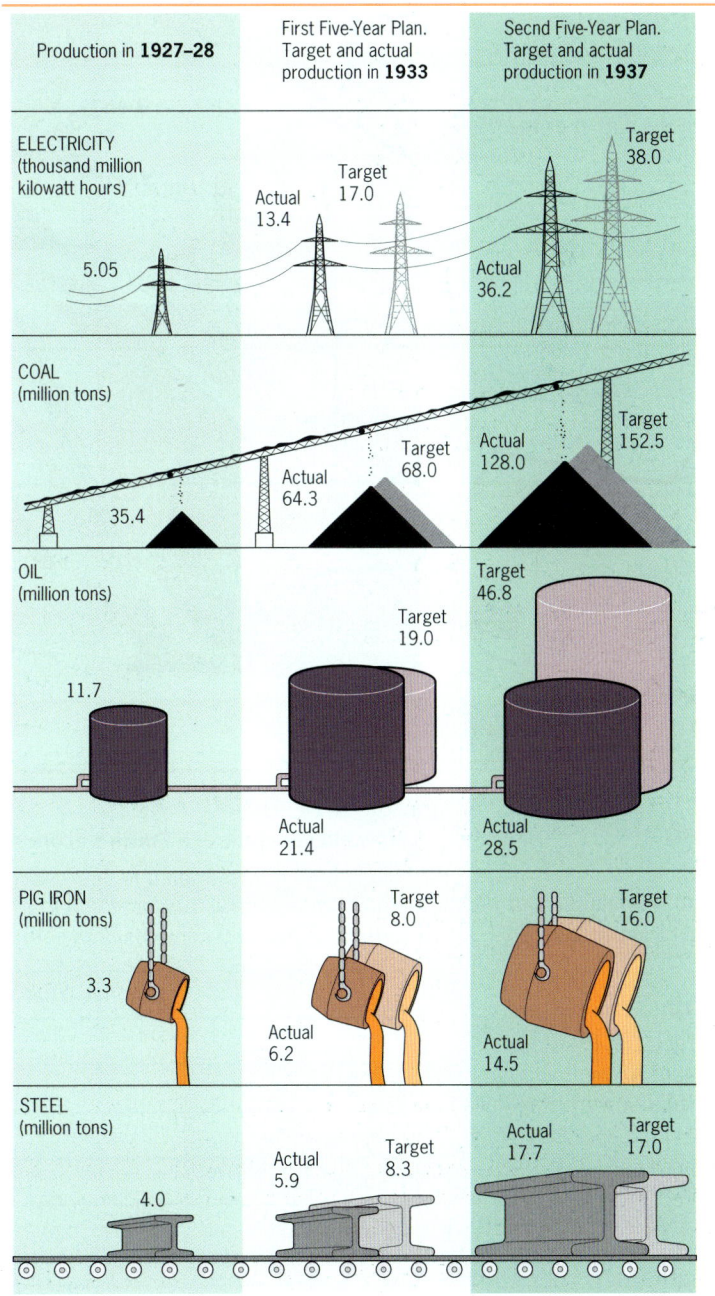

	Production in 1927–28	First Five-Year Plan. Target and actual production in 1933	Second Five-Year Plan. Target and actual production in 1937
ELECTRICITY (thousand million kilowatt hours)	5.05	Actual 13.4; Target 17.0	Target 38.0; Actual 36.2
COAL (million tons)	35.4	Actual 64.3; Target 68.0	Actual 128.0; Target 152.5
OIL (million tons)	11.7	Target 19.0; Actual 21.4	Target 46.8; Actual 28.5
PIG IRON (million tons)	3.3	Target 8.0; Actual 6.2	Target 16.0; Actual 14.5
STEEL (million tons)	4.0	Actual 5.9; Target 8.3	Actual 17.7; Target 17.0

The achievements of the Five-Year Plans.

Source Analysis

1 What is the message of Source 11?
2 How could Stalin use Figures 10 and 12 to support the claims of Source 11?

FIGURE 10

	1913	1928	1940
Gas (billion m³)	0.02	0.3	3.4
Fertilisers (million tons)	0.07	0.1	3.2
Plastics (million tons)	–	–	10.9
Tractors (thousand)	–	1.3	31.6

The growth in the output of the USSR, 1913–40.

FIGURE 12

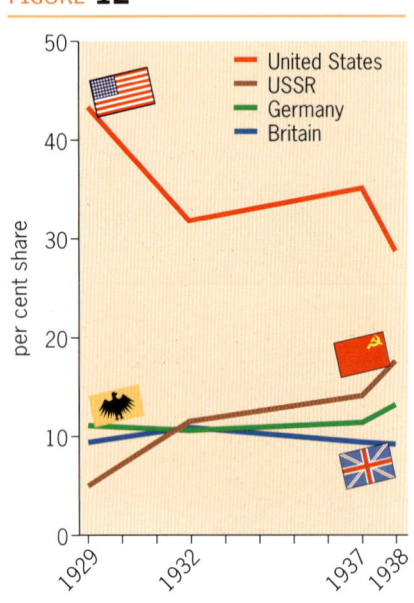

Graph showing share of world manufacturing output, 1929–38.

Revision Tip

- Make sure you can list at least two successes of the Five-Year Plans and explain why they were successes.
- Make sure you can list at least two failures of the Five-Year Plans and explain why they were failures.

Behind the propaganda

The Five-Year Plans were used very effectively for propaganda purposes (see Source 11). Stalin had wanted the Soviet Union to be a beacon of socialism and his publicity machine used the successes of industrialisation to further that objective. But the sources need careful evaluation.

SOURCE 11

Soviet propaganda poster, 1933. In the top half, the hand is holding the first Five-Year Plan. The capitalist is saying (in 1928), 'Fantasy, Lies, Utopia.' The bottom half shows 1933.

FOCUS TASK 7.13

How successful were Stalin's economic changes? 1: The Five-Year Plans

Use all the information and sources in this section to assess the Five-Year Plans for industry. Copy and complete a table like the one below. Fill out column 2. You will come back to column 3 on page 211.

	The Five-Year Plans	Collectivisation
Policy		
Aims		
Key features		
Successes		
Failures		

Modernising the USSR: 2 – Collectivisation

Why did Stalin want to modernise Soviet agriculture?

Feeding the workers

For the enormous changes of the Five-Year Plans to be successful, Stalin needed to modernise the USSR's agriculture as well. Agriculture was the biggest single resource the USSR had. The vast majority of Russians worked in agriculture and he wanted to make the fullest use of this resource.

Stalin's industrialisation programme had created a huge army of workers, many living in newly built towns, who were working in industry and not producing food. They needed to be fed and yet as early as 1928 the country was already 2 million tons short of the grain it needed to feed its workers. The USSR was actually importing food. This was bad from an economic point of view. It was also humiliating from a political view that a country with such huge agricultural resources could not feed its own people.

Food exports

Stalin also wanted to try to raise money for his industrialisation programme by selling exports of surplus food abroad. He could only do this if he could fully exploit the USSR's agricultural resources and massively increase food production. If he could do this he could develop industry further and improve living standards for workers.

Reasons Stalin wanted to modernise Soviet agriculture

Building his reputation

Stalin probably thought that modernising agriculture would also enhance his reputation in the same way that the Five-Year Plans for industry would. The full propaganda machine of the USSR was MOBILISED. It praised the modernisation of agriculture and celebrated the arrival of new techniques and machinery, especially tractors. It also relentlessly attacked those who opposed him.

Ending the NEP

The NEP had proved popular with the peasants, especially the more prosperous peasants known as kulaks. Kulaks usually owned more and better land than the average peasant which meant they could grow more food and sell the surplus food for profit. Small merchants also benefited from the NEP. They bought the surplus food from the peasants and kulaks and sold it in the towns and cities for a profit. These merchants were often called NEPmen. Stalin had built a lot of support within the Communist Party with his ideas about Socialism in One Country. He had also undermined Bukharin by opposing the NEP. It was unacceptable to Stalin to have the countryside operating the old NEP.

Stalin also knew that the kulaks and NEPmen would never support him. He thought that by removing them he could replace them with peasants who would gain from his new agricultural policies and would therefore be more loyal to him. The struggle between Stalin and the kulaks and other peasants who opposed him would turn out to be bitter and incredibly destructive.

FOCUS TASK 7.14

Why did Stalin introduce collectivisation?

On page 204 you saw that Stalin wanted to modernise industry for the following reasons:
- security
- power and control
- ideology
- Socialism in One Country
- personal reputation.

1. How many of these apply to his reasons for modernising agriculture? Explain your answers with examples.
2. Are there any extra reasons or factors in addition to the list above which explain why Stalin wanted to modernise agriculture?

SOURCE 13

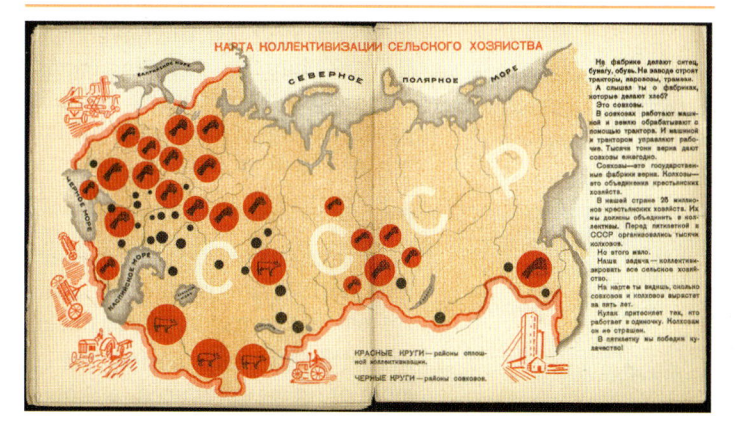

A map of the USSR from a Soviet children's book. It was explaining how agriculture was being reorganised in the USSR.

Revision Tip

Make sure you can explain at least two aims of collectivisation.

The impact of collectivisation on Russian people

The plan

It would not be easy to modernise the USSR's agriculture. Stalin's method was collectivisation – forcing the farmers to combine their lands and cattle and farm them together (collectively) – see Factfile.

Most peasants were still working on small plots of land using age-old methods. Making the peasants work on larger farms meant that:
- It would be easier to make efficient use of tractors, fertilisers and other modern methods of farming. This would produce more food.
- Mechanised farming would require fewer workers and release large numbers of peasants to work in growing industries.
- It would be easier to collect grain and taxes from larger farms.
- It would also be a more socialist way of farming as farmers would co-operate rather than selling their own food for a profit.

Resistance

There was one big problem with collectivisation. The peasants did not want to hand over their animals and tools and be ordered around by farm managers. All they wanted was to farm their own piece of land without interference from the Government. This applied particularly to kulaks – richer peasants who owned larger farms and employed agricultural labourers.

The Government sent out activists, backed up by the secret police, to 'persuade' them. A massive propaganda campaign was organised to inform peasants of the advantages of joining a collective farm. Some did join, but many resisted bitterly. They preferred to slaughter and eat their animals rather than allow them to be taken. They burnt crops and even their houses. In some areas there was armed resistance.

Dekulakisation

The Government blamed the kulaks for all the trouble and Stalin announced that 'We must liquidate the kulaks as a class'. In practice, anybody who resisted became a kulak. In 1931 alone, the secret police deported over 1.5 million peasants to GULAGS. Others were executed by firing squads and some fled to the cities to find work. This campaign was known as 'dekulakisation'.

Famine

This process in 1930–32 caused huge disruption in the countryside and there were severe food shortages. This, combined with a poor harvest in 1932, led to a famine on an unimaginable scale, particularly in Ukraine, in the years 1932–33. The Government would not acknowledge the famine and still sent out requisitioning gangs to collect grain for the workers and to export to other countries. Millions starved, perhaps as many as 13 million people. It was a man-made human tragedy of immense proportions. The way of life of millions of peasants had been destroyed.

Impact

Despite the famine, Stalin did not ease off. By 1934 there were no kulaks left. By 1941 almost all agricultural land was organised under the collective system. Stalin had achieved his aim of collectivisation.

After this traumatic period, the countryside did settle down and gradually more grain was produced, although the numbers of animals did not reach pre-collectivisation levels until 1940. Stalin had achieved his aim: he had established control of the grain supply and collectivised the peasants. Moreover, he had a ready supply of labour for the factories.

Factfile

Collectivisation
- Peasants were to put their lands together to form large joint farms ('KOLKHOZ') but could keep small plots for personal use.
- Animals and tools were to be shared.
- Motor tractors were provided by government.
- Ninety per cent of produce would be sold to the state and the profits shared.
- The remaining 10 per cent of produce was to feed the 'kolkhoz'.

Revision Tip
- Make sure you can list at least two successes of collectivisation and explain why they were successes.
- Make sure you can list at least two failures of collectivisation and explain why they were failures.

SOURCE 14

In order to turn a peasant society into an industrialised country, countless material and human sacrifices were necessary. The people had to accept this, but it would not be achieved by enthusiasm alone ... If a few million people had to perish in the process, history would forgive Comrade Stalin ... The great aim demanded great energy that could be drawn from a backward people only by great harshness.

Anatoli Rybakov, *Children of the Arbat*, 1988.

Source Analysis
Read Source 15. Why do you think the only reports of the famine came from Western journalists?

SOURCE 15

'How are things with you?' I asked one old man. He looked around anxiously to see that no soldiers were about. 'We have nothing, absolutely nothing. They have taken everything away.' It was true. The famine is an organised one. Some of the food that has been taken away from them is being exported to foreign countries. It is literally true that whole villages have been exiled. I saw myself a group of some twenty peasants being marched off under escort. This is so common a sight that it no longer arouses even curiosity.

The *Manchester Guardian*, 1933.

SOURCE 16

Stalin, ignoring the great cost in human life and misery, claimed that collectivisation was a success; for, after the great famines caused at the time … no more famines came to haunt the Russian people. The collective farms, despite their inefficiencies, did grow more food than the tiny, privately owned holdings had done. For example, 30 to 40 million tons of grain were produced every year. Collectivisation also meant the introduction of machines into the countryside. Now 2 million previously backward peasants learned how to drive a tractor. New methods of farming were taught by agricultural experts. The countryside was transformed.

Historian E. Roberts, *Stalin, Man of Steel*, published in 1986.

Revision Tip
Remember:
- one way industrialisation made life better and one way it made it worse
- one way collectivisation made life better and one way it made life worse.

FOCUS TASK 7.15
How successful were Stalin's economic policies? 2: Collectivisation
1. You started a chart on page 208. Now complete column 3 to assess the policy of collectivisation.
2. Which policy do you think was more effective: the Five-Year Plans or collectivisation? Support your answer with evidence from pages 205–11.

FOCUS TASK 7.16
How were Soviet people affected by Stalin's economic policies?
1. Use pages 204–11 and your own research to weigh up the overall effects of Stalin's economic policies on the Soviet people.
2. Work in groups of four. Each person in the group should represent one of the following:
    - An industrial worker
    - A peasant (rich and poor)
    - A Russian woman
    - A Communist Party official
3. Write a short speech giving evidence of how Stalin's economic policies have affected you. Remember to consider the positive and negative impacts.
4. Once you have listened to all of the speeches, compile the evidence in a table like this:

Evidence that Stalin's economic policies made life better	Evidence that Stalin's economic policies made life worse

Try to find at least two pieces of evidence on each side and make sure you can explain why it could be used as evidence for each argument.

Key Question Summary
What was the impact of Stalin's economic policies?
1. From 1928, Stalin embarked on a radical programme of change to modernise the USSR.
2. He initiated Five-Year Plans for industry in which production targets were set for every industry right down to individual factories.
3. The first two Five-Year Plans concentrated mainly on heavy industry – iron, coal and steel – and to a lesser extent on mining, chemicals and transport.
4. A feature of the plans was gigantic spectacular projects like the Moscow Metro.
5. The plans were very successful. Production from heavy industries rose dramatically, huge new industrial plants were built, new cities appeared and a modern industrial state was created. However, the quality of goods was often poor and there were inefficiencies.
6. Stalin needed to make farming more modern to produce the food he needed for the workers. He used collectivisation to do this.
7. Many peasants resisted and were shot, sent to labour camps or exiled. Millions fled to the new cities to become workers.
8. As a result of this disruption, food production fell and there was a famine in parts of the USSR, especially Ukraine, in 1932–33.
9. However, Stalin had got what he wanted from collectivisation: food for the workers, food to export abroad, more industrial workers and control of the peasants and the food supply.
10. The Russian people paid a high cost for Stalin's economic policies.

SOURCE 17

A tribute to Comrade Stalin was called for. Of course, everyone stood up ... for three minutes, four minutes, the 'stormy applause, rising to an ovation' continued ... Who would dare to be the first to stop? After all, NKVD men were standing in the hall waiting to see who quit first! After 11 minutes the director [of the factory] ... sat down ... To a man, everyone else stopped dead and sat down. They had been saved!

... That, however, was how they discovered who the independent people were. And that was how they eliminated them. The same night the factory director was arrested.

Alexander Solzhenitsyn, *Gulag Archipelago*, published in 1973. Solzhenitsyn lost his Soviet citizenship as a result of this book.

SOURCE 18

Stalin shown holding a young child, Gelya Markizova, in 1936. Stalin had both of her parents killed. This did not stop him using this image on propaganda leaflets to show him as a kind, fatherly figure.

Source Analysis

Choose either Source 19 or 21.
1 Summarise the message of the cartoon in your own words.
2 Do you think either of these cartoons could have been published in the USSR?

How did Stalin control the Soviet Union?

Terror

Using terror to control Russians was a feature of the Tsar's regime and the communist state under Lenin, but Stalin took it to a new level. He was determined to crush any opposition from inside or outside the Communist Party. He used his secret police, the NKVD, and gulags to terrorise his people into obedience.

The Purges

By 1934, some leading communists wanted to slow the pace of industrialisation to make life more bearable for ordinary Russians. When Sergei Kirov suggested this at a Party conference, he was widely supported. There was talk of him replacing Stalin as leader.

Soon after, Kirov was mysteriously murdered (probably on Stalin's orders) then Stalin used this as an excuse to 'purge' the Communist Party of his opponents (supposedly to unmask spies and conspirators). He arranged a series of SHOW TRIALS where leading Bolsheviks confessed to their crimes, probably because of torture or threats to their families. In the first big trial in 1936 Kamenev and Zinoviev were tried along with fourteen others. Bukharin was tried in 1938. Stalin removed all of the 'Old Bolsheviks' (party leaders who were part of the 1917 Revolution). Out of these six Politburo members, only Stalin remained. Four of them were executed and Trotsky, who was in exile in Mexico, was assassinated by a Soviet agent in 1940. However, these PURGES were not restricted to leading Party members. Around 500,000 Communist Party members were arrested and either executed or sent to labour camps. Those left learned to carry out Stalin's orders to the letter.

The Purges went beyond the Communist Party. Anybody suspected of disloyalty to Stalin was arrested. Many people were denounced by neighbours trying to prove they were loyal. University lecturers and teachers, miners and engineers, factory managers and ordinary workers disappeared.

Stalin also purged the army, removing 25,000 officers, including its supreme commander, Marshal Tukhachevsky, who had disagreed with Stalin. Finally he purged the NKVD itself by executing its chiefs, Yagoda and Yezhov.

By 1937 an estimated 18 million people had been transported to labour camps. Ten million died. Stalin seriously weakened the USSR by removing so many able individuals. He had also succeeded in destroying any sense of independent thinking. Everyone who was spared knew that their lives depended on thinking exactly as Stalin did.

SOURCE 19

Russian exiles in France made this mock travel poster in the late 1930s. The text says: 'Visit the USSR's pyramids!'

A new Constitution

In 1936 Stalin created a new Constitution for the USSR. It gave freedom of speech and free elections to the Russian people. This was, of course, a cosmetic measure. Only Communist Party candidates were allowed to stand in elections, and only approved newspapers and magazines could be published.

Propaganda

Despite all this, if you had visited the Soviet Union in the 1930s, you would probably have found that most Soviet citizens admired, or even loved, Stalin. They saw him as a great leader driving them forward to a great future.

This is partly because of the Soviet propaganda machine. Stalin understood the power of ideas and the media. Newspapers were censored or run by government agencies. The radio was under state control. The state used propaganda extensively in posters, information leaflets and public events.

They created a 'cult of personality'. There were photographs and statues everywhere (most homes had their own portrait of Stalin on the wall). Processions in praise of Stalin were held regularly in towns and cities. Streets were named after Lenin and Stalin and even the capital city, Petrograd, was renamed Leningrad. He was presented as a super-human being, almost godlike.

Stalin enjoyed the worship he received. Moreover, he wanted to make himself an important historical figure. He had history books rewritten to show himself and Lenin as the only real heroes of the Revolution. Others, like Trotsky, were removed from the story.

SOURCE 20

One of Stalin's opponents deleted from a photograph, 1935. Techniques of doctoring pictures became far more sophisticated in the 1930s. This allowed Stalin to create the impression that his enemies had never existed.

SOURCE 21

A cartoon published by Russian exiles in Paris in 1936. The title of the cartoon is 'The Stalinist Constitution' and the text at the bottom reads 'New seating arrangements in the Supreme Soviet'.

SOURCE 22

These men lifted their villainous hands against Comrade Stalin. By lifting their hands against Comrade Stalin, they lifted them against all of us, against the working class ... against the teaching of Marx, Engels, Lenin ... Stalin is our hope, Stalin is the beacon which guides all progressive mankind. Stalin is our banner. Stalin is our will. Stalin is our victory.

From a speech made by Communist leader Nikita Khrushchev in 1937, at the height of the Purges. (Khrushchev later became leader of the USSR and in 1956 announced a 'DE-STALINISATION' programme.

Revision Tip

You should have a view on whether terror or propaganda was more important in securing Stalin's rule. You need to:
- know at least two events which show how the terror regime worked
- be able to describe at least two examples of propaganda
- practise explaining which you think was more important – it does not matter which you decide as long as you can explain your reasoning.

FOCUS TASK 7.17

Why did Stalin launch the Purges?

Some say that Stalin launched the Purges because he was power-mad and paranoid. Do you agree with this? Here are other possible reasons. Using the evidence on this page, which of these seem most believable? Which can you discount altogether?
- To ensure his economic policies succeeded
- To remove potential rivals in the Communist Party
- To ensure the army stayed loyal
- To remove independent thinkers
- To boost his reputation as the supreme ruler of Russia.

Society and culture under Stalin

FOCUS TASK 7.18

How were Soviet people affected by Stalin's rule?

Work with a partner to produce a presentation to answer this question. You will find useful information on pages 206, 210 and 214–16 but you could do further research in the library or online.

You will need to look at as many as possible of the following aspects of life in the USSR:
- industrialisation
- the growth of towns and cities
- collectivisation
- control and terror
- religion
- music and arts
- education
- social attitudes.

For each aspect:

Slide 1 should summarise the policy. Follow 'the rule of five' for presentations – maximum five bullet points, maximum five words per bullet. For example:

Industrialisation – summary
- Aim: to modernise USSR
- Be able to challenge West
- Five Year Plans
- Key industries developed
- Significant achievements

Slide 2 should explain how groups, individuals, organisations or nationalities gained from the policy. If the answer is none, say so!

Industrialisation – winners
- No unemployment
- Training
- Work for women
- State provided accommodation

Slide 3 should be a 'loser' slide. Again, if there are no losers, say so.

Religion

Religion came under sustained attack. Many churches were closed, priests deported and church buildings pulled down. Priests were not allowed to vote. By 1939 only one in forty churches still held regular services in the USSR. Despite this, in the 1937 census, around 60 per cent of Russians said that they were Christians. Muslims were banned from practising Islamic law and women encouraged to abandon the veil. In 1917 there were 26,000 mosques in Russia but by 1939 there were only 1300.

Music and arts

Music and arts were carefully monitored by the NKVD. Poets and playwrights praised Stalin either directly or indirectly. Composers such as Shostakovich wrote music praising him and lived in dread of Stalin's disapproval. Artists and writers were forced to adopt a style Socialist Realism. This meant that paintings and novels had to glorify ordinary workers, inspire people with socialism, and help build the future. Paintings showed happy collective farm workers in the fields or workers striving in the factories. It was a similar situation with literature (see Source 23).

SOURCE 23

Whoever said that Soviet literature contains only real images is profoundly mistaken. The themes are dictated by the Party. The Party deals harshly with anybody who tries to depict the real state of affairs in their literature.

Is it not a fact that all of you now reading these lines saw people dying in the streets in 1932? People, swollen with hunger and foaming at the mouth, lying in their death throes in the streets. Is it not a fact that whole villages full of people perished in 1932? Does our literature show any of these horrors, which make your hair stand on end? No. Where will you find such appalling things depicted in Soviet literature? You call it realism?

A protest note pinned on the walls of a college by students in November 1935.

Think!
1 Why did Stalin try to reduce the influence of religion?
2 How effective were his policies?
3 What does the story of Shostakovich tell historians about life for musicians under Stalin? Use the internet to look up other artists or writers such as Maxim Gorky.

SOURCE 24

I, a Young Pioneer of the Soviet Union, in the presence of my comrades, solemnly promise to love my Soviet motherland passionately, and to live, learn and struggle as the great Lenin bade us and the Communist Party teaches us.

The promise made by each member of the Young Pioneers.

SOURCE 25

Interviews with Soviet citizens who fled the USSR in the Second World War showed that support for welfare policies, support for strong government and patriotic pride were all robust – and this was from a sample of persons who had shown their hatred of Stalin by leaving the country.

An extract from *A History of Modern Russia* by Robert Conquest, published in 2003. Conquest is a well-known historian in this field.

Education and youth organisations

By the early 1930s Stalin set about reforming the Soviet education system. The discipline of teachers and parents was emphasised. Strict programmes of work were set out for key subjects like mathematics, physics and chemistry. History textbooks presented Stalin's view of history. There were compulsory lessons in socialist values and how a Soviet citizen should behave. Children under fifteen joined the Pioneers where they were indoctrinated with communist views, encouraged to be loyal to the state and to behave like a good citizens.

Women in Stalin's USSR

Women were given the same educational and employment opportunities as men. By 1935 some 42 per cent of all industrial workers were women. The Second Five-Year Plan in particular would have failed without the huge influx of women workers. Some women were enrolled into technical training programs and management positions; although the vast majority of women remained in relatively low-paid industrial jobs or traditional roles.

The Communists challenged traditional views about women and the family. Communists thought that women should be free and not tied down to men by marriage. They envisaged that children would be looked after in crèches and kindergartens. Divorce was made very easy and there was abortion on demand. However, the reality did not live up to the dream. Many men abandoned their wives as soon as they became pregnant. In 1927 two-thirds of marriages in Moscow ended in divorce. The promised state kindergartens never appeared and thousands of women were left to manage as best they could with jobs and children.

The Great Retreat

By the mid-1930s the regime attempted to re-impose traditional family values and discipline, often called 'the Great Retreat'.
- Abortion was made illegal except to protect the health of the mother.
- Divorce was made more difficult. Divorcing couples had to go to court and pay a fee.
- Divorced fathers had to pay maintenance for their children.
- Mothers received cash payments of 2000 roubles per year for each child up to age five.
- A new law in 1935 allowed the NKVD to deal harshly with youth crime.
- Parents could be fined if their children caused trouble.

It is very hard to judge the impact of these measures although they tended to have a much greater impact on women than men as they restricted many of the new opportunities which had opened up. Overall, however, interviews with survivors from the period suggest that most people supported the Great Retreat policies.

Equality

One of the main aims of communism was to make people more equal and life fairer for all members of society. Critics of communism have usually pointed out that it made life equally bad for everyone in society. There is some evidence to support this.
- The buying power of a worker's wage fell by over 50 per cent during the first Five-Year Plan.
- The average worker in 1930s Moscow ate only 20 per cent of the meat and fish he ate in 1900.
- Housing was hard to find and expensive.
- It was difficult to get clothing, shoes and boots. Queuing to buy goods became part of life.

> **Revision Tip**
>
> A major area of debate is whether the Soviet people gained or lost more under Stalin. Find two examples of gains and losses in this period and make sure you can explain why you chose them.

On the other hand, there were some positives. Health care improved enormously. Education improved and public libraries became available. Literacy was a high priority. Sports facilities were good in most towns and cities.

However, despite its ideology communism created a new social hierarchy.
- If you were ambitious, you could join the new 'class' of skilled workers or become a foreman, supervisor or technician.
- Above them was an army of managers. Managers could get items like clothing and luxuries in the official Party shops.
- At the very top was a new ruling class – the *nomenclatura*. This was the group loyal to Stalin who took all the top jobs in the Communist Party and government. They and their families enjoyed many privileges such as better housing, food, clothes and schools for their children.

These groups did well out of the new industrial society. Their support was vital in helping Stalin control Soviet society.

The nationalities

Russia and the USSR were not the same thing. Russia was the dominant republic in a large collection of republics (the USSR), which included many different languages, religions and national identities.

Stalin regarded the nationalities with suspicion. In 1932 a new regulation required Soviet citizens to carry identity booklets which specified their nationality. Many nationalities found that their homelands were dramatically changed by many Russian migrant workers who were sent to develop new industrial projects.

In some areas whole populations were deported from their homes because Stalin did not trust them. Between 1935 and 1938 Stalin deported members of at least nine different ethnic groups. For example, when Japan began to expand in the Far East Stalin deported 142,000 Koreans from his easternmost borders. Other groups were persecuted because of long-standing prejudices. For example, Jewish people still suffered discrimination and the Finnish population in the region around Leningrad fell by one-third during the 1930s.

SOURCE 26

Pages from a children's textbook published in the Soviet Republic of Uzbekistan in central Asia, near to Afghanistan. Under Stalin children of the nationalities were taught about the benefits of communism in their own language because it was thought to be more effective. Here the people are benefitting from the introduction of tractors and it is interesting to note that the tractor driver is a woman.

How complete was Stalin's control over the Soviet Union by 1941?

By 1941 Stalin was the supreme unchallenged leader of Soviet Russia, but how far was he in complete control?

On the one hand…
In the Purges, which had mainly ended in 1938, Stalin had:
- removed all the old Bolsheviks capable of forming an alternative government and replacing him as leader
- removed the main officers in the army likely to cause him any trouble
- cowed intellectuals in education, sciences and the arts, making them unlikely to voice criticisms of his policies
- terrified the population at large who did not know where accusations of disloyalty might come from and feared being picked up by the secret police
- got rid of many of the unruly and disruptive elements in society by sending them to the Gulag where they might prove more useful as slave labour.

The vast organisation of the secret police, the NKVD, stood behind Stalin and behind the NKVD lay the terror of the Gulag CONCENTRATION CAMPS.

Stalin's position was cemented by the cult of the personality, which led many Russians to regard him as an almost superhuman leader whom they revered and even loved. Those who did not go along with the hype were very reluctant to voice their views in public. Stalin had complete control of the media and propaganda, which repeated the message that Stalin was great and the only person who could lead Russia to a bright future.

But on the other hand…
Soviet Russia was a still a difficult country to rule.
- Stalin found it difficult to control regions away from Moscow. People, including Communist officials, ran their own areas to suit themselves and would not always carry out instructions from the centre.
- There was a lot of bribery and corruption, especially as everybody had to reach unrealistic production targets in industry. Nobody, even Communist Party officials, wanted to be accused of not fulfilling targets, so they fiddled the figures, produced sub-standard goods or simply did not tell the centre what was going on.
- Even those higher up cheated and manipulated the system so they could escape any blame. The whole central planning system was rough and unwieldy despite the fact that it achieved its broad aims.

Soviet Russia in the 1930s was never very stable. Millions of people moved around as industrialisation created vast new centres and peasants were thrown off the land. People came and went seeking jobs and accommodation or trying to escape the authorities. Thousands changed jobs regularly so they could not be tracked down and subjected to the harsh labour laws, or to get better wages, especially if they were skilled workers. In all this fluid mix there were embittered, rebellious and criminal elements as well as young people who would not conform to Soviet laws, rules and regulations. Some historians think the Purges were in part an attempt to control this moving mass and weed out the troublemakers. But Stalin could never really bring this 'quicksand society' under control.

In the countryside, Stalin had subdued the peasants through collectivisation but most were still aggrieved by the loss of their land and independence. They adapted to the Stalinist system but resisted where they could. They made life difficult for farm managers, were insubordinate, neglected their jobs, were apathetic and generally did not work hard. Agriculture never performed as well as it should have done.

We know that Stalin tried to control things personally as far as he could. He sent out a constant stream of notes and letters giving very specific instructions about what should be done, even down to particular industrial plants. In letters to his henchmen Stalin talks frequently about fulfilling targets 'with unrelenting firmness and ruthlessness'. These could be used as evidence of Stalin's control but the frustration expressed in the letters can also be seen as evidence that Stalin was not able to get them to do what he wanted (see Source 27 for example).

SOURCE 27

There are abominations in the supply of metal for the Stalingrad Tractor Plant and the Moscow and Gorky auto plants. It is disgraceful that the windbags at the People's Commissariat of Heavy Industry have still not gotten around to straightening out the supply system. Let the Central Committee place under its continuous supervision, without delay, the plants that are supplying them and make up for this disruption.

Stalin writing in 1932 to his deputy, Kaganovich.

FOCUS TASK 8.19

Stage 1: What methods did Stalin use to control the USSR?
Draw up and complete a table to make notes and record examples for the methods of control listed. You can add more/different methods if you wish.
- Terror
- Purges
- Force
- Propaganda
- The cult of personality
- Education and youth groups
- Mass media and the arts
- Improved living conditions

Stage 2: How complete was Stalin's control over the Soviet Union by 1941?
Now use your notes from Stage 1 to write an answer to this question:
'By 1941 Stalin had complete control of the Soviet Union because he had crushed all opposition.' How far do you agree with this statement? Explain your answer.
You should structure this in three sections or paragraphs:
1. The argument that Stalin was in control. Here you should include:
   - examples of the methods he used
   - evidence that these methods actually worked (e.g. source extracts).
2. The argument that Stalin was not in control or that his control was not as great as it appeared. Here you should include:
   - examples of resistance to Stalin and his methods
   - an explanation of how serious this resistance was.
3. Your overall judgement as to how complete his control really was (e.g. that his control was not complete but the resistance was limited).

Keywords

Make sure you know these terms, people or events and are able to use them or describe them confidently.
- Autocracy
- Bolshevik
- Capitalist
- Civil War
- Collectivisation
- Communist
- Cossack
- Duma
- Five-Year Plan
- Gulag
- Industrialisation
- Kerensky
- Kolkhoz
- Kulak
- Lenin
- Marxist
- Mensheviks
- Nationalities
- NEPmen
- New Economic Policy
- NKVD
- Okhrana
- Peasants
- Propaganda
- Provisional Government
- Purges
- Show trials
- Social Democratic Party
- Socialist Revolutionaries
- Soviet Union
- Soviets
- Stakhanovite
- Stalin
- Stolypin
- Trotsky
- Tsar
- Tsarina
- USSR
- War Communism
- *Zemstva*

Key Question Summary

How did Stalin gain and hold on to power?

1. Stalin emerged as the new leader of Russia through a mixture of political cunning, ruthlessness and the mistakes of the other contenders.
2. He gained control of the Party machine and could appoint his supporters to key positions. He outmanoeuvred his opponents by playing them off against each other.
3. Stalin's policy of 'Socialism in one country' was popular and appealed to Russian nationalism.
4. Stalin used terror to control the USSR, backed by an effective secret police force and the Gulag labour camps.
5. From 1936 he used the Purges to make sure he remained leader. He set up show trials to get rid of the old Bolsheviks who might form an alternative government and to frighten others.
6. He purged the Communist Party to make sure it would carry out his orders without question.
7. He purged the army to get rid of any officers who might be disloyal to him.
8. He undertook a general purge of the population to instil fear so that they would do as they were told. He got rid of leading members of the intelligentsia in education and the arts. He also got rid of troublesome individuals on the fringes of society who did not fit into the Stalinist system.
9. A cult of the personality promoted Stalin as a godlike leader who could guide the USSR to a great future.
10. Stalin tried to control what people thought through the mass media, education, the arts and culture in general. He tried to suppress religion but was not successful.

PRACTICE QUESTIONS

Structured questions

1. (a) What were the Five-Year Plans? **[4]**
   (b) Why was Stalin so committed to modernising industry in the USSR? **[6]**
   (c) 'The Five-Year Plans brought glory to Stalin but misery to his people.' How far do you agree with this statement? Explain your answer. **[10]**

Alternative to Coursework questions

1. a) Write an account of tactics used by the Reds in the Russian Civil War. **[15]**
   b) Discuss the importance of Trotsky to the outcome of the Russian Civil War. **[25]**

See pages 338–55 for advice on the different types of questions.

DIE NSDAP SICHERT DIE VOLKSGEMEINSCHAFT

VOLKSGENOSSEN
BRAUCHT IHR RAT UND HILFE
SO WENDET EUCH AN DIE
ORTSGRUPPE

8 Germany, 1918–45

KEY QUESTIONS
8A Was the Weimar Republic doomed from the start?
8B Why was Hitler able to dominate Germany by 1934?
8C How effectively did the Nazis control Germany, 1933–45?
8D What was it like to live in Nazi Germany?

Germany emerged from the First World War in a state of chaos. The new WEIMAR Government struggled from crisis to crisis. Out of this confusion Adolf Hitler and the Nazis emerged as the most powerful group in Germany and led the nation into a period of DICTATORSHIP ending in an international war and the deaths of tens of millions of people.

How could this happen in a modern, democratic European state?

In **8A** you will investigate how the Weimar Republic was created out of post-war chaos and how its leaders tried to solve the problems left over from the war.

In **8B** you will focus on the same period but view it through a different lens and examine the reasons for the birth and growth of the Nazi Party. You will see how its early failures turned into a runaway success after the ECONOMIC DEPRESSION hit Germany in the early 1930s.

The Nazis had a very specific vision of what Germany should be like and they did not tolerate opposition. In **8C** you will examine how they imposed their will on the German people through a combination of terror and PROPAGANDA.

In **8D** you will see how specific groups of people were affected by Nazi rule – young people, women, workers and farmers – and how the lives of Germans began to change again as a result of the Second World War.

Timeline
This timeline shows the period you will be covering in this chapter. Some of the key dates are filled in already. To help you get a complete picture of the period make your own much larger version and add other details to it as you work through the chapter.

THE WEIMAR REPUBLIC
- 1918 The end of the First World War
- 1920
- 1923 Stresemann becomes Chancellor of Germany
- 1929 The Wall Street Crash is followed by a worldwide depression
- 1930

THE THIRD REICH
- 1933 Hitler becomes Chancellor of Germany
- 1939 The Second World War begins
- 1940
- 1941 The USA joins the war
- 1945 Germany is defeated by the Allies. Hitler kills himself

This Nazi poster from the 1930s encouraged people to turn to Nazi-led community groups for help and advice.
1. Using this source, describe the Nazis' ideal family.
2. What are the Nazis offering this ideal family and how is it represented in the poster?
3. Does this poster give the impression that people were afraid of the Nazis?
4. What message is the poster trying to convey to Germans?

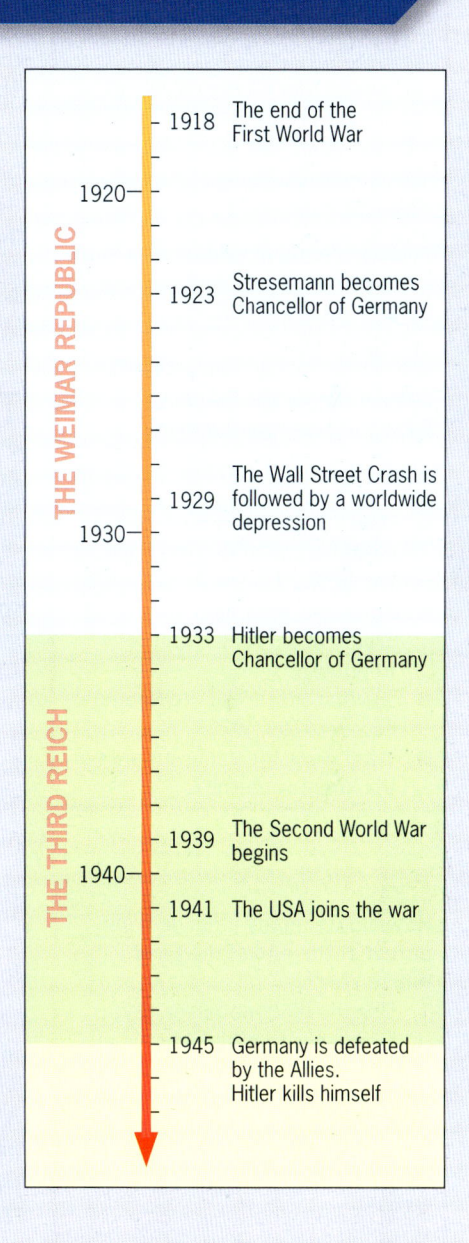

FOCUS

The democratic Weimar Government was set up in 1919, but it collapsed in 1933 and was replaced by a Nazi dictatorship. Was this inevitable? Many have argued it was because of:

- a weak CONSTITUTION
- huge post-war problems
- being forced to sign the TREATY OF VERSAILLES.

However, others would disagree because there were significant political economic and cultural achievements, especially from 1924–29.

There is plenty of evidence on both sides of the debate. As you study these events you can reach your own conclusions on these issues and arrive at your own judgement about whether the Weimar Republic was doomed to fail.

Focus Points

- How did Germany emerge from defeat at the end of the First World War?
- What was the impact of the Treaty of Versailles on the Republic?
- To what extent did the Republic recover after 1923?
- What were the achievements of the Weimar period?

FOCUS TASK 8.1

How did Germany emerge from defeat at the end of the First World War?

1. Use the information on these two pages to make a list of all the challenges facing Ebert when he took over in Germany in 1918. You could organise the list into sections:
   - Political challenges
   - Social challenges
   - Economic challenges.
2. Imagine you are advising Ebert. Explain what you think are the three most serious challenges that need tackling urgently.
3. Take a class vote and see if you can all agree on which are the most serious challenges.

8A Was the Weimar Republic doomed from the start?

The impact of the First World War

In 1914 the Germans were a proud people. Their KAISER – virtually a DICTATOR – was celebrated for his achievements. Their army was probably the finest in the world. A journey through the streets of Berlin in 1914 would have revealed prospering businesses and a well-educated and well-fed workforce. There was great optimism about the power and strength of Germany.

Four years later a similar journey would have revealed a very different picture. Although little fighting had taken place in Germany itself, the war had still destroyed much of the old Germany. The proud German army was defeated. The German people were surviving on turnips and bread, and even the flour for the bread was mixed with sawdust to make it go further. A flu epidemic was sweeping the country, killing thousands of people already weakened by lack of food.

The end of the old Germany

By the autumn of 1918 Germany had clearly lost the war. Germany was in a state of chaos, as you can see from the diagram on page XXX. The Allies offered Germany peace, but under strict conditions. One condition was that Germany should become more democratic and that the Kaiser should abdicate. When the Kaiser refused, sailors in northern Germany mutinied and took over the town of Kiel. This triggered other revolts. The Kaiser's old enemies, the Socialists, led uprisings of workers and soldiers in other German ports. Soon, other German cities followed. In Bavaria an independent Socialist Republic was declared. On 9 November 1918 the Kaiser abdicated his throne and left Germany for the Netherlands. This is often referred to as the German Revolution of 1918.

On 10 November, the Socialist leader Friedrich Ebert became the new Chancellor of Germany. With the cooperation of the German army EBERT signed an ARMISTICE with the Allies on 11 November. He and his government were often referred to by right-wing opponents as the 'November Criminals' for signing the ceasefire.

The war was over and Ebert announced a new government would be set up in Germany – a REPUBLIC. Ebert introduced many reforms including the 8-hour working day and improved benefits for the sick, elderly and unemployed. A new Constitution was drawn up and the first elections for the new parliament took place in January 1919. In February 1919 Ebert was elected the first President of the new German Republic. However, the Republic faced many problems, as you can see in the diagram on the next page.

Revision Tip

Make sure you can:
- describe one social, one economic and one political impact of the war on Germany.
- explain how at least two of these factors made it difficult for the new German Government.

Impact of the war on Germany by 1918

ECONOMIC IMPACT
Germany was virtually bankrupt

- National income was about one-third of what it had been in 1913. 
- There were acute shortages of food. By 1918 Germany was producing only 50 per cent of the milk and 60 per cent of the butter and meat it had produced before the war. Fuel was short and people were cold. Nearly 300,000 people died from starvation and hypothermia in 1918.
- War left 600,000 widows and 2 million children without fathers – by 1925 the state was spending about one-third of its BUDGET in war pensions.  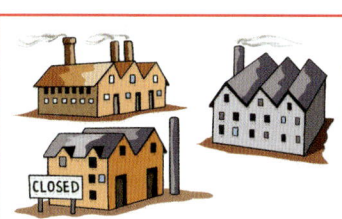
- Industrial production was about two-thirds of what it had been in 1913.

POLITICAL IMPACT
Germany had a revolution and became an unstable democratic republic. Groups with extremist political views tried to gain power.

- Stresses of war led to a revolution in October–November 1918. There was fighting between RIGHT-WING groups and LEFT-WING groups.
- Many ex-soldiers and civilians despised the new democratic leaders and came to believe that the heroic leader Field Marshal Hindenburg had been betrayed by weak politicians – this was known as the 'stab in the back' myth.

SOCIAL IMPACT
The war had deepened divisions in German society

- There were huge gaps between the living standards of the rich and the poor. 
- One and a half million demobilised soldiers returned to society, many disillusioned.
- Many German workers were bitter at the restrictions placed on their earnings during the war while the factory owners made vast fortunes from the war. 
- Many Germans were angry about losing the war. There was a wave of unrest, especially in cities like Berlin. Law and order was breaking down in a country where people were used to order and discipline.

A new Germany: The Weimar Republic

In January 1919 free elections took place for the first time in Germany's history. Ebert's party won the largest share of the vote and he became the president of the Weimar Republic. It was called this because, to start with, the new Government met in the small town of Weimar rather than in the German capital, Berlin. Even in February 1919, Berlin was thought to be too violent and unstable.

The success of the new Government would depend on two key factors:

- **Factor 1: The Constitution:** Would the new Constitution provide a practical, workable solution to the challenge of ruling Germany? It was designed to be as democratic as possible and to represent the many different groups which made up German society. The Factfile on the next page explains how the Constitution worked.
- **Factor 2: The German people:** Would the German people accept an almost instant change from the traditional, autocratic German system of government to this new democratic system?

The prospects for this did not look good. The reaction of politicians and many ordinary Germans was unenthusiastic. Ebert faced opposition from both right and left.

- **On the right wing**, nearly all the Kaiser's former advisers remained in their positions in the army, judiciary, civil service and industry. They restricted what the new Government could do. Many still hoped for a return to rule by the Kaiser. A powerful myth developed that men such as Ebert had 'stabbed Germany in the back' and caused the defeat in the war.
- **On the left wing** there were many communists who believed that at this stage what Germany actually needed was a communist revolution, just like Russia's in 1917.

The government ministers assembled in the town of Weimar after the first elections in January 1919 to draw up a new constitution.

The Constitution

- Ebert signed the Weimar Constitution into law in August 1919. It was a FEDERAL Republic with a President as head of state instead of the Kaiser. It divided Germany into states which had their own governments.
- There was UNIVERSAL SUFFRAGE – all adults over the age of 20 could vote and all German citizens had equal rights (freedom of religion, the right to own private property, for example).
- The REICHSTAG (Parliament) was elected every four years by proportional representation – if a party won 20 per cent of the votes they gained 20 per cent of the seats.
- The President was the head of state and was elected every seven years. Day-to-day government was the responsibility of the CHANCELLOR who was both appointed by, and could be dismissed by, the President.
- In a crisis, the Constitution gave the President emergency powers (Article 48) to pass decrees which did not need the approval of the Reichstag. Ebert used Article 48 136 times while in office. Article 48 sometimes saved the new Weimar Republic from uprisings as it allowed the President to act swiftly and mobilise the army. Some criticised it for making the President too powerful during crises.
- The Chancellor needed the support of half of the Reichstag to pass new laws.
- In the January 1919 elections there were eighteen different parties that won seats in the Reichstag. Ebert's Social Democratic Party won

38 per cent of the seats and was the largest party, but as you can see, it did not win a majority. This led to COALITIONS being formed with smaller parties which often led to slow decision-making and ineffective government. There was a total of seven different coalitions with different Chancellors between 1919 and 1923!

FOCUS TASK 8.2

What were the strengths and weaknesses of the Weimar Constitution?

1. Make a list of what you think seem to be the **strengths** of the Weimar Constitution.
2. Here are some concerns expressed at the time about the **weaknesses** of the Constitution. For each one explain how the Constitution might allow such things to happen.
   - The Constitution is too democratic – even small and extreme parties could get seats in the Reichstag.
   - If the Chancellor cannot get the support of the Reichstag he will be unable to pass any laws or other measures, or it will take an enormous amount of time to get measures through.
   - If the various parties in the Reichstag refuse to work together there could be a stalemate.
   - The president might abuse his powers under Article 48.

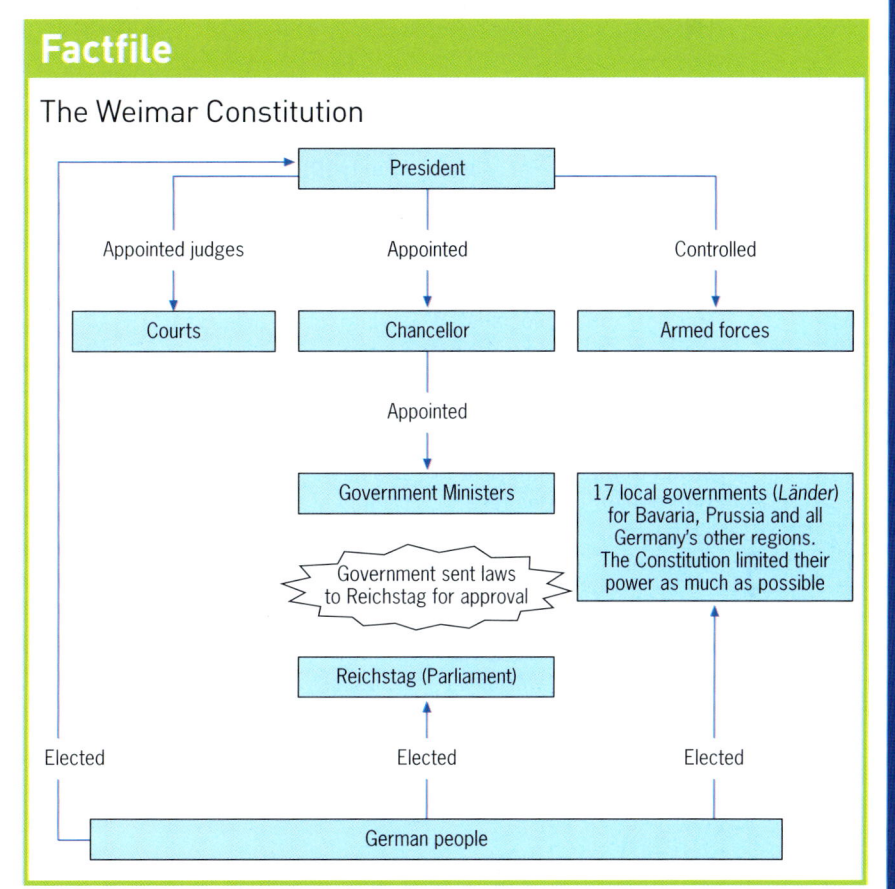

Factfile

The Weimar Constitution

- **President** (elected by German people)
  - Appointed judges → **Courts**
  - Appointed → **Chancellor** → Appointed → **Government Ministers**
  - Controlled → **Armed forces**
- Government sent laws to Reichstag for approval
- **Reichstag (Parliament)** – Elected by German people
- 17 local governments (*Länder*) for Bavaria, Prussia and all Germany's other regions. The Constitution limited their power as much as possible – Elected by German people

The main political parties in Germany, 1919–33

Left-wing parties generally wanted greater equality in society. Socialists or social democrats wanted to achieve this by distributing the wealth more fairly by increasing taxes on the rich and business or by nationalising industries and banks. Liberals wanted to create greater equality by introducing reforms and protecting people's rights and democratic freedoms. Centre-left parties like the socialists and liberals supported the Weimar democracy.

Far-left parties like the communists wanted a workers' revolution like in Russia in 1917. They wanted to seize control of the government by revolution, confiscate property and land from the ruling classes and create a state-controlled economy. Communists opposed the Weimar democracy.

Right-wing parties generally wanted to conserve the traditional class system and allow private enterprise to flourish (capitalism). Conservative parties wanted to achieve this through support for the German army, the established churches and by protecting the privileges of the ruling elites such as landlords and industrialists.

Far-right parties were anti-Weimar nationalists. They wanted a strong government and a powerful army and were very anti-communist. Some nationalists, like the Nazis, also had racist and anti-Semitic policies.

The political spectrum

Far-left ← Centre → Far-right

	Communist Party of Germany (KPD)	Social Democratic Party of Germany (SPD)	German Democratic Party (DDP)	German People's Party (DVP)	Centre Party	German National People's Party (DNVP)	National Socialist German Workers' Party (NSDAP) or Nazi Party
Political position	Far-left revolutionary; Marxist; anti-Weimar	Left-wing moderate; socialist; pro-Weimar	Centre-left liberal; pro-Weimar	Centre-right liberal; pro-Weimar	Right-wing conservative and pro-Weimar	Far-right conservative-nationalist; anti-Weimar	Far-right extreme nationalist; anti-Weimar
Main policies	Workers' revolution to set up Soviet-style communist system in Germany	Democratic socialist policies to improve welfare system for workers and unemployed	Liberal policies to protect equality of rights and improve welfare system	Liberal policies to protect rights but more pro-business	Conservative policies – pro-business and pro-Catholic	Nationalist policies to restore monarchy and oppose the Weimar Republic and the Treaty of Versailles	Racist and anti-Semitic policies; oppose Weimar Republic and abolish Treaty of Versailles; reclaim lost German territory
Support base	Workers; some ex-soldiers and sailors	Industrial workers	Middle classes	Wealthy, educated middle class; industrialists	Catholics; some wealthy middle class	Industrialists; ex-soldiers, especially officer class; landowners	Mainly lower middle class and peasant farmers; members included workers, unemployed, ex-soldiers
Significance	The Communist Party saw an increase in support during economic problems after the crises of 1923; distrusted the Social Democratic Party of Ebert after he made a deal with the *Freikorps* and army to crush the Spartacist Uprising in 1919	The Social Democratic Party was the single most popular party in the early 1920s, though it never received a majority of the votes, forcing Ebert to agree to coalitions; anti-communist	Declined in popularity in the early 1920s and seen as increasingly out of touch with the problems of ordinary Germans	Led by Gustav Stresemann who would serve as Chancellor (1923) and foreign minister (1923–29); popular in the early and mid-1920s but this decreased in the late 1920s	Third largest party for much of the Weimar period and formed part of many coalitions; some in the party supported monarchy, others the Republic; increasingly right-wing by the late 1920s	The main nationalist party before 1930 when it lost votes to the Nazis; supported Hindenburg's election as President in 1925; made a temporary alliance with the Nazis in 1931 – the Harzburg Front – which supported Hitler	A fringe party for most of the 1920s but rapidly increased its popularity after the 1929 Wall Street Crash and Depression of the 1930s; largest party in the Reichstag by 1932 and Hitler appointed Chancellor in 1933

Factfile

German federal election results

January 1919

Political party	Percentage of votes won
Social Democratic Party	38%
Centre Party	20%
German Democratic Party	19%
German National People's Party	10%
Independent Social Democratic Party	8%
Other	5%

June 1920

Political party	Percentage of votes won
Social Democratic Party	22%
Independent Social Democratic Party	18%
German National People's Party	15%
German People's Party	14%
Centre Party	14%
German Democratic Party	8%
German Communist Party	2%
Other	7%

May 1924

Political party	Percentage of votes won
Social Democratic Party	21%
German National People's Party	19%
Centre Party	13%
German Communist Party	13%
German People's Party	9%
Nazi Party	7%
German Democratic Party	6%
Other	12%

December 1924

Political party	Percentage of votes won
Social Democratic Party	26%
German National People's Party	20%
Centre Party	14%
German People's Party	10%
German Communist Party	9%
German Democratic Party	6%
Nazi Party	4%

The Republic in danger, 1919–24

From the start, Ebert's Government faced violent opposition from both left-wing and right-wing opponents.

The threat from the Left

One left-wing group was known as the SPARTACISTS. They were communists led by Karl Liebknecht and Rosa Luxemburg. Their party was much like Lenin's Bolsheviks, which had just taken power in Russia. They wanted a Germany ruled by workers' councils or soviets.

In January 1919 the Spartacists launched their bid for power. Joined by rebel soldiers and sailors, they set up soviets in many towns. Not all soldiers were on the side of the Spartacists, however. Some anticommunist ex-soldiers had formed themselves into vigilante groups called FREIKORPS. Ebert made an agreement with the commanders of the army and the *Freikorps* to put down the rebellion. Bitter street fighting and heavy casualties followed. Eventually the *Freikorps* won and Liebknecht and Luxemburg were murdered.

The Spartacist rising was soon followed by another rebellion in Bavaria in the south of Germany. Ebert used the same tactics as he had used against the Spartacists. The *Freikorps* moved in to crush the revolt in May 1919. Around 600 communists were killed.

In 1920 there was more communist agitation in the RUHR industrial area. Again police, army and *Freikorps* clashed with communists. There were 2000 casualties.

Ebert's ruthless measures against the communists created lasting bitterness between them and his Socialist Party. However, it gained approval from many in Germany. Ebert was terrified that Germany might go the same way as Russia (at that time rocked by bloody civil war). Many Germans shared his fears. Even so, despite these defeats, the communists remained a powerful antigovernment force in Germany throughout the 1920s.

The threat from the Right

At the same time, Ebert's Government faced violent opposition from the Right. His right-wing opponents were largely people who had grown up in the successful days of the Kaiser's Germany. They resented the new Germany and above all they deeply resented the humiliating Treaty of Versailles, which they blamed Ebert for agreeing to (see page 229).

In March 1920 Dr Wolfgang Kapp led 5000 *Freikorps* into Berlin in a rebellion known as the KAPP PUTSCH ('PUTSCH' means rebellion). The army refused to fire on the *Freikorps* and it looked as if Ebert's Government was doomed. However, it was saved by the German people, especially the industrial workers of Berlin. They declared a GENERAL STRIKE which brought the capital to a halt with no transport, power or water. After a few days Kapp realised he could not succeed and fled the country. He was hunted down and died while awaiting trial. It seemed that Weimar had support and power after all.

Even so, the rest of the rebels went unpunished by the courts and judges. Ebert's Government struggled to deal with the political violence in Germany. Political assassinations were frequent. In the summer of 1922 Ebert's Jewish foreign minister Walther Rathenau was murdered by extremists. Then in November 1923 Adolf Hitler led an attempted rebellion in Munich, known as the MUNICH PUTSCH (see page 236). Both Hitler and the murderers of Rathenau received short prison sentences. It seemed that Weimar's right-wing opponents had friends in high places.

Revision Tip

Make sure you can describe:
- at least one strength and one weakness of the Weimar Constitution, and why it was a strength or weakness
- at least one example of left-wing and one example of right-wing revolts and how each was defeated.

Think!

1. Draw up a table like the one below to compare the various threats from Left and Right described on this page.

	Left wing	Right wing
Name of group		
Leadership		
Demands/aims		
Supported by		
Methods		
How defeated		
Consequences		

2. What differences can you see between how Ebert's Government treated left-wing and right-wing extremists? How can you explain this?

SOURCE 1

Versailles was a scandal and a disgrace and … the dictate signified an act of highway robbery against our people.

Extract from Hitler's biography *Mein Kampf*, 1925.

FOCUS TASK 8.3

What was the impact of the Treaty of Versailles on the Republic?

1 **Research:** Using all the information and sources on pages 229–31 and pages 14–17 in Chapter 1, find out the impact of the Treaty on:
   a) German territory
   b) the armed forces
   c) German attitudes and national pride
   d) the economy
   e) political stability.
2 **Reach a judgement:** Which of these do you think was most damaging to the Weimar Republic in:
   ■ the short term (in 1920)
   ■ the long term (by 1923)?

Support your answer with evidence from your research.

The Treaty of Versailles

The biggest crisis for the new republic came in May 1919 when the terms of the Treaty of Versailles were announced. You can read more about this in Chapter 1. Most people in Germany were appalled, but the right-wing opponents of Ebert's Government were particularly angry. They blamed Ebert's Government for betraying Germany.

Germany lost:
- 10 per cent of its land
- all of its overseas colonies
- 12.5 per cent of its population
- 16 per cent of its coal and 48 per cent of its iron industry.

In addition:
- Its army was reduced to 100,000; it was not allowed to have an air force; its navy was reduced.
- Germany had to accept blame for starting the war and was forced to pay REPARATIONS.

Most Germans were appalled. Supporters of the Weimar Government felt betrayed by the Allies. The Kaiser was gone – why should they be punished for his war and aggression? Opponents of the regime turned their fury on Ebert.

Ebert himself was very reluctant to sign the Treaty, but he had no choice. Germany could not go back to war. However, in the minds of many Germans, Ebert and his Weimar Republic were forever to blame for the Treaty. The injustice of the Treaty became a rallying point for all Ebert's opponents. They believed that the German army had been 'stabbed in the back' by the Socialist and Liberal politicians who agreed an armistice in November 1918. They believed that Germany had not been beaten on the battlefield, but that it had been betrayed by its civilian politicians who didn't dare continue the war. The Treaty was still a source of bitterness in Germany when Hitler came to power in 1933.

> **Revision Tip**
> Make sure you can describe at least two ways (one political, one economic) the Treaty affected Germany.

SOURCE 2

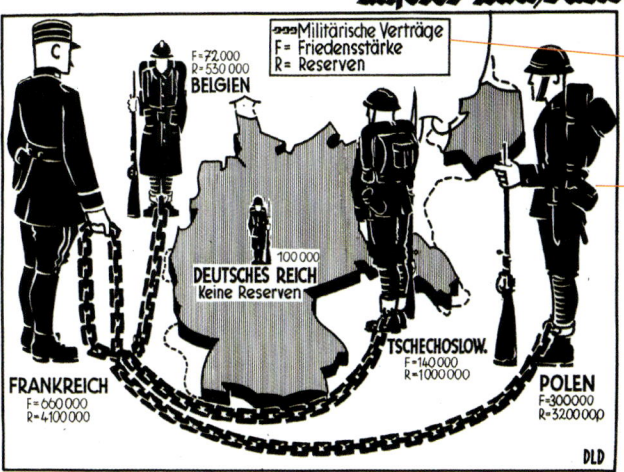

Nazi cartoon commenting on the military terms of the Versailles treaty.

- The text reads: 'The Mammoth Military superiority of our neighbours'.
- The chains = military treaties; F = peacetime strength; R = reserve soldiers.
- The German Reich (centre) is surrounded by France, Belgium, Czechoslovakia and Poland (from left to right).

> **Source Analysis**
> Study Source 2 carefully.
> 1 What point is the cartoonist making about the relationship between France and Germany?
> 2 What point is the cartoonist making about the relationship between France and the other countries?

SOURCE 3

There was widespread hunger, squalor and poverty and – what really affected us – there was humiliation. The French ruled with an iron hand. If they disliked you walking on the pavement, for instance, they'd come along with their riding crops and you'd have to walk in the road.

The memories of Jutta Rudiger, a German woman living in the Ruhr during the French occupation.

Source Analysis

Work in pairs. One study Source 4 and the other Source 5. Explain the message of your source to your partner.
- Remember to make a valid inference (for example, the cartoonist is saying...).
- Then remember to support the inference with a detail from the source (for example this is shown in the cartoon by...).

Economic disaster

The Treaty of Versailles destabilised Germany politically, but Germans also blamed it for another problem – economic chaos. See if you agree that the Treaty of Versailles was responsible for economic problems in Germany.

Reparations

The Treaty of Versailles forced Germany to pay reparations to the Allies. The reparations bill was announced in April 1921. It was set at £6600 million, to be paid in annual instalments of 2 per cent of Germany's annual output. The Germans protested that this was an intolerable strain on the economy, which they were struggling to rebuild after the war, but their protests were ignored.

The occupation of the Ruhr

The first instalment of £50 million was paid in 1921, but in 1922 nothing was paid. Ebert did his best to play for time and to negotiate concessions from the Allies, but the French in particular ran out of patience. They too had war debts to pay to the USA. So in January 1923 French and Belgian troops entered the Ruhr (quite legally under the Treaty of Versailles) and began to take what was owed to them in the form of raw materials and goods.

The results of the occupation of the Ruhr were disastrous for Germany. The Government ordered the workers to go on strike. That way, there would be nothing for the French to take away. The French reacted harshly, killing over 100 workers and expelling over 100,000 protesters from the region. More importantly, the halt in industrial production in Germany's most important region caused the collapse of the German currency.

SOURCE 4

A TRANSPARENT DODGE.
Germany. "HELP! HELP! I DROWN! THROW ME THE LIFE-BELT!"
Mr. Lloyd George. ⎱ "TRY STANDING UP ON YOUR FEET."
M. Briand . . . ⎰

A British cartoon from 1921. The two watchers are the leaders of France and Britain.

SOURCE 5

A 1923 German poster discouraging people from buying French and Belgian goods, as long as Germany is under occupation. The poster reads, 'Hands off French and Belgian goods as long as Germany is raped!' Bochun and Essen are two industrial towns in the Ruhr.

SOURCE 6

A photograph taken in 1923 showing a woman using worthless banknotes to start her fire.

SOURCE 7

	1918	0.63 marks
	1922	163 marks
January	1923	250 marks
July	1923	3465 marks
September	1923	1,512,000 marks
November	1923	201,000,000,000 marks

The rising cost of a loaf of bread in Berlin.

Revision Tip

Hyperinflation

Make sure you can describe:
- two causes and two effects of hyperinflation
- two actions Stresemann took to tackle the crisis
- one reason why Germans blamed the Treaty of Versailles for hyperinflation.

Weimar Republic 1919–23

You also need to be able to:
- describe at least two other challenges facing the Weimar Republic 1919–23
- explain why each one was a challenge
- take a view on which of your two challenges was most threatening.

Hyperinflation

Because it had no goods to trade and because it needed to pay the striking workers in the Ruhr, the Government simply printed money. For the Government this seemed an attractive solution. It paid off its debts in worthless marks, including war loans of over £2200 million. The great industrialists were able to pay off all their debts as well.

This set off a chain reaction. With so much money in circulation, but not enough goods to buy with it, prices and wages rocketed, but people soon realised that this money was worthless. Workers needed wheelbarrows to carry home their wages. Wages began to be paid daily instead of weekly. The price of goods could rise between joining the back of a queue in a shop and reaching the front!

Poor people suffered, but in some ways those who lost most were middle-class Germans. A prosperous middle-class family would find that their savings, which might have bought a house in 1921, by 1923 would not even buy a loaf of bread. Pensioners found that their monthly pension would not even buy one cup of coffee. The Government had lost the support of the middle classes.

It was clear to all, both inside and outside Germany, that the situation needed urgent action. In August 1923 a new government under Gustav Stresemann took over.
- He called off the passive resistance in the Ruhr.
- He called in the worthless marks and burned them, replacing them with a new currency called the Rentenmark.
- He negotiated to receive American loans under the DAWES PLAN.
- He even renegotiated the reparations payments.

The economic crisis was solved very quickly. Some historians suggest that this is evidence that Germany's problems were not as severe as its politicians at the time had made out.

It was also increasingly clear, however, that the hyperinflation had done great political damage to the Weimar Government. Their right-wing opponents had yet another problem to blame them for, and many linked it to the hated Treaty of Versailles which the Government had signed. They blamed reparations and the Weimar politicians who had agreed to pay them. Many Germans never forgave them.

SOURCE 8

One afternoon I rang Aunt Louise's bell. The door was opened merely a crack. From the dark came a broken voice: 'I've used 60 billion marks' worth of gas. My milk bill is 1 million. But all I have left is 2000 marks. I don't understand any more.'

E. Dobert's memoir, *Convert to Freedom*, published in 1941. Dobert was a working-class German who converted to Nazism.

FOCUS TASK 8.4

What was the most serious challenge for the Weimar Republic in the period 1919–23?

The diagram on the right shows the challenges which faced the Weimar Republic,1919–23. At the moment they are shown as equally serious. Redraw the diagram so that the most serious challenge is largest, the next most serious is next largest, and so on. Add notes to each sector explaining why it was a serious challenge.

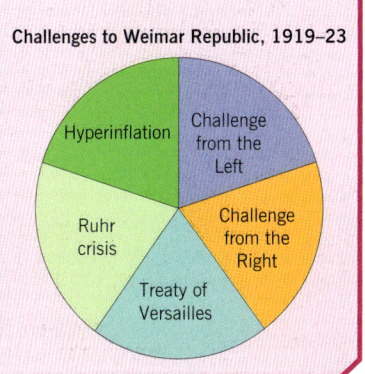

Challenges to Weimar Republic, 1919–23
- Hyperinflation
- Challenge from the Left
- Challenge from the Right
- Treaty of Versailles
- Ruhr crisis

FIGURE 9

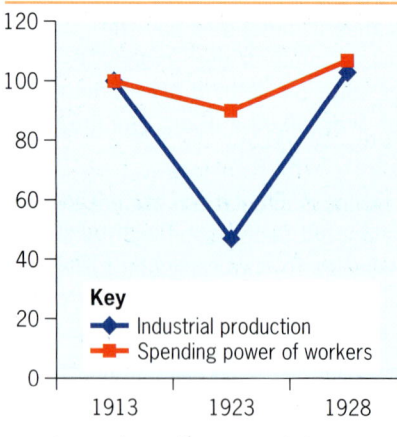

Comparison of aspects of the German economy in 1913, 1923 and 1928.

Key:
- Industrial production
- Spending power of workers

The Weimar Republic under Stresemann, 1923–29

Although Chancellor for only a few months, Gustav Stresemann was a leading member of every government from 1923 to 1929. He was a more skilful politician than Ebert, and, as a right-winger, he had wider support. He was also helped by the fact that through the 1920s the rest of Europe was gradually coming out of its post-war depression.

Achievement 1: The economy

Slowly but surely, Stresemann rebuilt Germany's prosperity. Under the Dawes Plan (see pages 38 and 39), reparations payments were spread over a longer period, and 800 million marks in loans from the USA poured into German industry. Some of the money went into German businesses to help them replace old equipment with the latest technology. Some went into public works like swimming pools, sports stadia and apartment blocks. As well as providing facilities, these projects created jobs.

By 1927 German industry seemed to have recovered very well. In 1928 Germany finally achieved the same levels of production as before the war and regained its place as the world's second greatest industrial power (behind the USA). Wages for industrial workers rose and for many Germans there was a higher standard of living.

Reparations were being paid and exports were on the increase. The Government was even able to increase welfare benefits and wages for state employees.

Achievement 2: Politics

Even politics became more stable. There were no more attempted revolutions after 1923. One politician who had been a leading opponent of Ebert in 1923 said that 'the Republic is beginning to settle and the German people are becoming reconciled to the way things are'. Figure 10 shows that the parties that supported Weimar DEMOCRACY did well in these years. By 1928 the moderate parties had 136 more seats in the Reichstag than the RADICAL parties. Hitler's Nazis gained less than 3 per cent of the vote in the 1928 election. Just as importantly, some of the parties who had co-operated in the 'revolution' of 1918 began to co-operate again.

Think!
1. List the factors that helped Germany's economy to recover, for example reduced reparations.
2. In what ways did economic recovery affect the lives of ordinary Germans?

FIGURE 10

Support for the main political parties in Germany, 1919–28.

Key:
- Left wing opposed to the Republic
- Left wing supporting the Republic
- Right wing opposed to the Republic

Revision Tip
- Make sure you can describe how the Dawes Plan worked.
- Describe one way in which German politics was more settled in this period.
- Practise explaining to someone else why the Nazis were unsuccessful in this period.

SOURCE 11

A photograph of a Berlin nightclub in 1920.

FOCUS TASK 8.5
Weimar culture

The Weimar period saw many cultural developments, especially in Berlin.

Carry out some research online to find at least three sources from the Weimar period and copy and paste them into a document. Then write a short description of each of the sources. You should include one source from each of the following categories:
- Cinema
- Architecture
- Art

SOURCE 12

What we have today is a coalition of ministers, not a coalition of parties. There are no government parties, only opposition parties. This state of things is a greater danger to the democratic system than ministers and parliamentarians realise.

Gustav Stolper, a Reichstag member for the DDP in 1929.

Achievement 3: Culture

There was also a cultural revival in Germany. In the Kaiser's time there had been strict CENSORSHIP, but the Weimar Constitution allowed free expression of ideas. Writers and poets flourished, especially in Berlin. Artists in Weimar Germany turned their back on old styles of painting and tried to represent the reality of everyday life, even when that reality was sometimes harsh and shocking. Artists like George Grosz produced powerful paintings such as *Pillars of Society*, which criticised politicians and business, Church and army leaders of the Weimar period. It showed them as callous and mindless. Other paintings highlighted how soldiers had been traumatised by their experiences in the war.

The famous BAUHAUS style of design and architecture developed. Artists such as Walter Gropius, Paul Klee and Wassily Kandinsky taught at the Bauhaus design college in Dessau. The Bauhaus architects and designers rejected traditional styles to create new and exciting buildings and objects. They produced designs for anything from chairs and desk lamps to art galleries and factories. The first Bauhaus exhibition attracted 15,000 visitors.

The 1920s were a golden age for German cinema, producing one of its greatest ever international stars, Marlene Dietrich, and one of its most celebrated directors, Fritz Lang. Berlin was famous for its daring and liberated nightlife. Going to clubs was a major pastime. In 1927 there were 900 dance bands in Berlin alone. Cabaret artists performed songs criticising political leaders that would have been banned in the Kaiser's days. These included songs about sex that would have shocked an earlier generation of Germans.

Achievement 4: Foreign policy

Stresemann's greatest triumphs were in foreign policy. In 1925 he signed the Locarno Treaties, guaranteeing not to try to change Germany's western borders with France and Belgium. As a result, in 1926 Germany was accepted into the League of Nations. Here Stresemann began to work, quietly but steadily, on reversing some of the terms of the Treaty of Versailles, particularly those concerning reparations and Germany's eastern frontiers. By the time he died in 1929, Stresemann had negotiated the YOUNG PLAN, which further lightened the reparations burden on Germany and led to the final removal of British, French and Belgian troops from the RHINELAND.

Problem 1: The economy

The economic BOOM in Weimar Germany was precarious. The US loans could be called in at short notice, which would cause ruin in Germany.

The boom also increased inequality. The main economic winners in Germany were big businesses (such as the steel and chemicals industries) which controlled about half of Germany's industrial production. Other winners were big landowners, particularly if they owned land in towns – the value of land in Berlin rose by 700 per cent in this period. The workers in the big industries gained as well. Most Weimar governments were sympathetic towards the unions, which led to improved pay and conditions. However, even here there were concerns as unemployment began to rise – it was 6 per cent of the working population by 1928.

The main losers were the peasant farmers and sections of the middle classes. The peasant farmers had increased production during the war. In peacetime, they were producing too much. They had loans to pay back but not enough demand for the food they produced. Many small business owners became disillusioned during this period. Small shopkeepers saw their businesses threatened by large department stores (many of which were owned by Jewish people). A university lecturer in 1913 earned ten times as much as a coal miner. In the 1920s he only earned twice as much. These people began to feel that the Weimar Government offered them little.

FOCUS TASK 8.6
To what extent did the Weimar Republic recover after 1923?

Draw a diagram like this then complete it to summarise the strengths (+) and weaknesses (-) of the Weimar Republic in 1929.

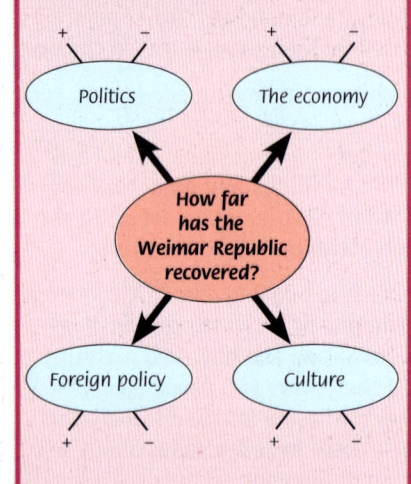

[Diagram: central node "How far has the Weimar Republic recovered?" connecting to four nodes — Politics, The economy, Foreign policy, Culture — each with + and - attached.]

You could give each sector a mark out of ten.

Finally, you need to decide on an overall judgement: in your opinion, how far had the Weimar Republic recovered? In your answer, do remember that, in the view of many historians, it was probably a major achievement for the Weimar Republic just to have survived.

Problem 2: Politics
Despite the relative stability of Weimar politics in this period, both the Nazis and Communists were building up their party organisations. Even during these stable years there were four different Chancellors and it was only the influence of party leaders which held the party coalitions together (see Source 12).

More worrying for the Republic was that around 30 per cent of the vote regularly went to parties opposed to the Republic. Most serious of all, the right-wing organisations which posed the greatest threat to the Republic were quiet rather than destroyed. The right-wing Nationalist Party (DNVP) and the Nazis began to collaborate closely and make themselves appear more respectable. Another event which would turn out to be very significant was that the German people elected a new president in 1925 who was opposed to democracy. Hindenburg even wrote to the (exiled) Kaiser for approval before he took up the post!

Problem 3: Culture
Weimar culture was colourful and exciting to many. However, for others living in Germany's villages and country towns, the culture of the cities represented moral decline, made worse by American immigrants and Jewish artists and musicians. As you have read, the Bauhaus design college was in Dessau. What you were not told is that it was in Dessau because it was forced out of Weimar by hostile town officials.

Organisations such as the Wandervogel movement were a reaction to Weimar culture. The Wandervogel called for a return to simple country values. It wanted to see more help for the countryside and less decadence in the towns. It was a powerful feeling, which the Nazis successfully used in later years.

Problem 4: Foreign policy
There was also the question of international relations. Nationalists attacked Stresemann for joining the League of Nations and for signing the Locarno Pact because it meant Germany accepted the Treaty of Versailles. Communists also attacked Locarno, seeing it as part of a plot against the communist government in the USSR.

Key Question Summary

Was the Weimar Republic doomed from the start?
1. Germany emerged from the First World War in a poor state, short of food and goods and in debt. It was an angry, bitter and divided society – politically (between left- and right-wing views) and socially (rich and poor).
2. The Weimar Republic was created in this turbulent time. Its Constitution was very democratic but it had weaknesses. In particular, its system of proportional representation meant that it was difficult for any political party to get a clear majority and provide strong government.
3. Its leaders signed the armistice to end the war (the 'stab in the back') and the hated Treaty of Versailles. This gave some Germans a poor view of democratic government and the Weimar Republic from the beginning.
4. Challenges from the Left (Spartacists, 1919) and Right (Kapp Putsch, 1920 and Munich Putsch, 1923) created political instability.
5. The Treaty of Versailles harmed Germany economically (reparations, loss of territory and industry) and psychologically (WAR GUILT, national pride).
6. One consequence of the Treaty, the occupation of the Ruhr, led to the hyperinflation of 1923.
7. The economy recovered after 1924 as Germany was put on a sounder financial footing. However, prosperity depended on American loans, and unemployment remained a problem.
8. Germany became more stable politically after 1924 and extremists parties, like the Nazis, did not do well in elections through the 1920s.
9. Given the problems that the Weimar Republic started with it was an achievement just to have survived to 1929. This proved it was not 'doomed from the start'.

Revision Tip
Make sure you can describe:
- one example of cultural achievement and one example of economic achievement in this period
- one group who were winners in the Weimar period and explain why they were winners
- one group who were losers in the Weimar period and explain why they were losers.

Profile

Adolf Hitler – the early years, 1889–1919

- Born in Austria in 1889.
- He got on badly with his father but was fond of his mother.
- At sixteeen he left school and went to Vienna to become a painter. He did not succeed and between 1909 and 1914 he was 'down and out' living on the streets of Vienna.
- During this period he developed his hatred of foreigners and Jewish people.
- In 1914 Hitler joined the German army and served with distinction, winning the Iron Cross.
- Hitler found it very hard to accept the armistice and was completely unable to accept the Treaty of Versailles.
- He despised Weimar democracy and like many Germans looked back to the 'glorious days' of the Kaiser.
- After the war, Hitler stayed working for the army spying on extremist groups. This is how he came across the German Workers' Party. He liked their ideas and joined in 1919.

Factfile

Twenty-Five Point Programme

The most important points were:
- the abolition of the Treaty of Versailles
- union of Germany and Austria
- only 'true' Germans to be allowed to live in Germany. Jewish people in particular were to be excluded
- large industries and businesses to be nationalised
- generous old-age pension
- a strong central government.

8B Why was Hitler able to dominate Germany by 1934?

FOCUS

Stresemann's Government succeeded in stabilising Germany. However, as you have already seen, the extremist opponents of the Weimar Government had not disappeared. Through the 1920s they were organising and regrouping, waiting for their chance to win power.

One of these extremist groups was the Nazi Party. You are now going to look back at what it had been doing since 1919 and examine its changing fortunes through the 1920s and early 1930s.

Your key question examines how the Nazis turned themselves from an obscure fringe party in the 1920s to the most popular party in Germany by 1933. You will see that there are a range of factors including Hitler's skills as a leader and the economic Depression that hit Germany in the 1930s.

You will also examine the ruthless way that once elected as Chancellor Hitler CONSOLIDATED his power by removing all possible opposition.

Focus Points

- What did the Nazi Party stand for in the 1920s?
- Why did the Nazis have little success before 1930?
- Why was Hitler able to become Chancellor by 1933?
- How did Hitler consolidate his power in 1933–34?

Hitler and the Nazis

The Nazis began as the German Workers' Party, led by Anton Drexler. In 1919 Adolf Hitler joined the party. Drexler soon realised that Hitler had great talent and within months he had put him in charge of propaganda and the political ideas of the party. In 1920 the party announced its Twenty-Five Point Programme (see Factfile), and renamed itself the National Socialist German Workers' Party, or Nazis for short.

In 1921 Hitler removed Drexler as leader. Hitler's energy, commitment and above all his power as a speaker were soon attracting attention, as you can see from Source 1.

Hitler had a clear and simple appeal. He stirred nationalist passions in his audiences. He gave them scapegoats to blame for Germany's problems: the Allies, the Versailles Treaty, the 'November Criminals' (the Socialist politicians who signed the Treaty), the Communists and the Jewish people.

His meetings were so successful that his opponents tried to disrupt them. To counter this, he set up the SA, also known as Stormtroopers or Brownshirts, in 1921. These hired thugs protected Hitler's meetings but also disrupted those of other parties.

SOURCE 1

The most active political force in Bavaria at the present time is the National Socialist Party … It has recently acquired a political influence quite disproportionate to its actual numerical strength … Adolf Hitler from the very first has been the dominating force in the movement and the personality of this man has undoubtedly been one of the most important factors contributing to its success … His ability to influence a popular assembly is uncanny.

American intelligence report on political activities in Germany, 1922.

SOURCE 2

Hitler knew how to whip up those crowds jammed closely in a dense cloud of cigarette smoke – not by argument, but by his manner: the roaring and especially the power of his repetitions delivered in a certain infectious rhythm … He would draw up a list of existing evils and imaginary abuses and after listing them, in higher and higher crescendo, he screamed: 'And whose fault is it? It's all … the fault … of the Jews!'

A person who went to Nazi meetings describes the impact of Hitler's speeches.
From *A Part of Myself: Portrait of an Epoch*, by C. Zuckmayer, 1966.

The Munich Putsch, 1923

By 1923 the Nazis were still very much a minority party, but Hitler had given them a high profile. In November 1923 Hitler believed that the moment had come for him to topple the Weimar Government. The Government was preoccupied with the economic crisis. Stresemann had just called off Germany's passive resistance in the Ruhr (see page 16). On 8 November, Hitler hijacked a local government meeting and announced he was taking over the government of Bavaria. He was joined by the old war hero Ludendorff.

Nazi Stormtroopers, many of them under the command of Ernst Röhm (see Profile on page 238), began taking over official buildings. The next day, however, the Weimar Government forces hit back. Police rounded up the Stormtroopers and in a brief exchange of shots sixteen Nazis were killed by the police. The rebellion broke up in chaos. Hitler escaped in a car, while Ludendorff and others stayed to face the armed police. Hitler had gambled and miscalculated and his revolution had failed. But this was not quite the end of the story.

SOURCE 3

A painting of the Munich Putsch made by Arthur Wirth, one of the Nazis who took part in it. Hitler is in the centre and Ludendorff is in the black hat to Hitler's right.

Revision Tip
- Make sure you can describe two aims of the Nazis before 1923.
- Explain one way in which the Munich Putsch was a disaster for the Nazis and one way it was a success.

Source Analysis
1. What impression does Source 3 give of the Putsch and Hitler's role in it?
2. Why would you have concerns about it as a source for finding out what happened?

SOURCE 4

When I resume active work, it will be necessary to pursue a new policy. Instead of working to achieve power by armed conspiracy we shall have to take hold of our noses and enter the Reichstag against the Catholic and Marxist deputies. If out-voting them takes longer than out-shooting them, at least the results will be guaranteed by their own constitution. Any lawful process is slow. Sooner or later we shall have a majority and after that we shall have Germany.

Hitler, writing while in prison in 1923.

Factfile

Hitler's views

In *Mein Kampf* and his later writings, Hitler set out the main Nazi beliefs:
- National Socialism: This stood for loyalty to Germany, racial purity, equality and state control of the economy.
- Racism: The Aryans (white Europeans) were the Master Race. All other races and especially Jewish people were inferior.
- Armed force: Hitler believed that war and struggle were an essential part of the development of a healthy Aryan race.
- Living space ('*Lebensraum*'): Germany needed to expand as its people were hemmed in. This expansion would be mainly at the expense of Russia and Poland.
- The Führer: Debate and democratic discussion produced weakness. Strength lay in total loyalty to the leader (the Führer).

Source Analysis

1 Read Source 5. List the demands made by Goebbels.
2 Would you say this source appeals more to the hearts of German people than to their minds? Support your answer with evidence from the source.

The aftermath of the Munich Putsch

In the short term, the Munich Putsch was a disaster for Hitler. He had miscalculated the mood of the German people and the Nazis had been humiliated. People did not rise up to support him. He and other leading Nazis were arrested and charged with treason.

However, from a longer-term point of view, the Putsch turned out to be less of a disaster. At his trial Hitler gained enormous publicity for himself and his ideas, as his every word was reported in the newspapers.

In fact, Hitler so impressed the judges that he and his accomplices got off very lightly. Ludendorff was freed altogether and Hitler was given only five years in prison, even though the legal guidelines said that high treason should carry a life sentence. In the end, Hitler only served nine months of the sentence and did so in great comfort in Landsberg Castle. This last point was very significant. It was clear that Hitler had some sympathy and support from important figures in the legal system. Because of his links with Ludendorff, Hitler probably gained the attention of important figures in the army. Time would show that Hitler was down, but not out.

The Nazis in the wilderness, 1924–29

Hitler used his time in prison to write a book, *Mein Kampf* (My Struggle), which clarified and presented his ideas about Germany's future (see Factfile and Sources 1–3 on pages 235 and 236).

It was also while in prison that he came to the conclusion that the Nazis would not be able to seize power by force. They would have to work within the democratic system to achieve power but, once in power, they could destroy that system (see Source 4).

As soon as he was released from prison, Hitler set about rebuilding the Nazi Party so that it could take power through democratic means. He saw the Communists building up their strength through youth organisations and recruitment drives. Soon the Nazis were doing the same.

Their candidates stood in the Reichstag elections for the first time in May 1924 and won 32 seats. Encouraged by this, Hitler created a network of local Nazi parties which in turn set up the HITLER YOUTH, the Nazi Students' League and similar organisations.

SOURCE 5

Three million people lack work and sustenance … The illusion of freedom, peace and prosperity that we were promised … is vanishing …

Thus we demand the right of work and a decent living for every working German.

While the soldier was fighting in the trenches to defend his Fatherland, some Jewish profiteer robbed him of hearth and home. The Jew lives in palaces … Therefore we demand homes for German soldiers and workers. If there is not enough money to build them, drive the foreigners out so that Germans can live on German soil.

These days anyone has the right to speak in Germany – the Jew, the Frenchman, the Englishman, the League of Nations. Everyone but the German worker. He has to shut up and work. Every four years he elects a new set of torturers, and everything stays the same. Therefore we demand the annihilation of this system of exploitation!

Extracts from a pamphlet called 'We demand', written in 1927 by Nazi propaganda expert Joseph Goebbels.

Hitler's henchmen

Hitler had many loyal followers who helped organise the Nazis to increase their support and membership. Below are some of the most important of Hitler's henchmen in this period, many of whom were also instrumental later in the period in Hitler's rise to power.

Profile

Ernst Röhm
(Chief of Staff of the SA)

Background
Röhm served as a captain in the German army in the First World War and received the Iron Cross for bravery. In 1919 he joined the Nazi Party and took part in the failed Munich Putsch (see page 236) leading 2,000 men to march on the War Ministry. He left the Nazi Party in 1925 for a role in Bolivia but returned after Hitler asked him to lead the SA during the Depression.

Importance
Röhm was a violent man who despised Jews and communists. He organised the SA into a powerful paramilitary force and won the loyalty of its members. By 1931 the SA numbered over one million. SA members marched, sang songs and held parades, and also attacked communists and Jews on the streets. After the Wall Street Crash, Rohm stirred up trouble to make the government look weak and to make many Germans fear a communist revolution was imminent.

Profile

Joseph Goebbels
(Gauleiter (District leader) of Berlin and Head of Nazi Propaganda in 1928)

Background
Goebbels joined the Nazi Party in 1924 after taking an interest in Hitler during his trial for the Munich Putsch. He supported Hitler when it looked like the Nazi Party might break up into factions in 1926. As Gauleiter in Berlin, he drew large crowds to his speeches and like Hitler, was a charismatic public speaker. He was elected to the Reichstag in 1928 and by 1930 the Nazi Party in Berlin was second in size only to the Party in Munich.

Importance
Goebbels was in charge of Nazi propaganda during the Depression and targeted different groups in Germany to win their votes by propagating the idea of the FÜHRER MYTH. He used posters, rallies and the Nazi newspaper, the *Volkischer Beobachter* (People's Observer), to promise jobs for the unemployed workers, to crush communism to appeal to the middle class and industrialists and to protect the racial purity of the peasant farmers.

Profile

Heinrich Himmler
(Reichsführer-SS)

Background

Himmler had not fought in the war and failed to make a successful career in the military as a young man. In 1923, he joined the Nazi Party and took part in the Munich Putsch as part of Röhm's SA men. In 1925 he joined the newly formed SS (then a part of the SA), which was used as the personal bodyguard for Nazi leaders. He persuaded Hitler to separate the SS from the SA in 1927 and in 1929 was made head of the SS (Reichsführer-SS). He quickly expanded the SS and by 1933 it had over 50,000 members.

Importance

Himmler's SS were fiercely loyal to Hitler who sometimes doubted the loyalty and discipline of the SA. They were well-trained and were meant to represent the Nazi Party elite – members even had to prove their Aryan heritage as far back as 1800! The intelligence service of the SS (the SD) was used to root out opponents and threats to Hitler in the Nazi Party and was led by Himmler's deputy, Reinhard Heydrich.

Profile

Hermann Goering
(Early SA leader and President (Speaker) of the Reichstag from 1932)

Background

Goering was a First World War fighter pilot ace who received the 'Blue Max' medal for his 22 victories in the air. He joined the Nazi Party in 1922 and led the SA during the Munich Putsch where he was shot in the groin. He became addicted to morphine for the rest of his life to cope with the pain. He was a leading party member who was elected to the Reichstag in 1928. In 1932, when the Nazis were the largest party, he was appointed as President of the Reichstag (not to be confused with the President of the Republic).

Importance

Goering was an early supporter of Hitler and was born into an aristocratic family with ties to many wealthy and influential German families, especially in the military. His background served the Nazi Party well when it needed funds to win the elections. Like many Nazis, he promoted the 'stab in the back myth'. His aviation background would serve Hitler well when the Nazis got into power and he needed to build a new air force.

Profile

Rudolf Hess
(Hitler's private secretary; Chairman of the Nazi Party and Deputy Führer in 1933)

Background

After serving in the war, Hess joined the Nazi Party in 1920 and allegedly introduced the idea of *Lebensraum* to Hitler. He joined the SA in 1921 and took part in the *Munich Putsch*. He was imprisoned with Hitler and other Nazis at Landsberg Prison and assisted Hitler in writing Mein Kampf. He helped increase the size of the SA and followed Hitler on his election campaigns around Germany as a close friend.

Importance

Hess was trusted by Hitler and as his private secretary had unbridled access to him at all times. All official orders passed through his office before reaching Hitler and he oversaw the Nazi Party organisation as a whole. He often gave the opening speech at the Nuremberg Rallies before introducing Hitler. Hess was loyal to Hitler and was rewarded with the honour of Deputy Führer when Hitler was appointed Chancellor of Germany in 1933.

A change of strategy

As you can see from Source 5 (on page 237), by 1927 the Nazis were still trying to appeal to German workers. However, most workers supported either the Socialists or the Communists. In the 1928 elections the Nazis gained only twelve Reichstag seats (a quarter of the Communist vote). Although their antisemitic policies gained them some support, they had failed to win over the workers. Although the Nazis argued that workers were exploited, in fact urban industrial workers felt that they were doing rather well in Weimar Germany in the years up to 1929.

Target the farmers

Other groups in society were doing less well, however. The Nazis found that they gained more support from groups such as the peasant farmers in northern Germany and middle-class shopkeepers and small business people in country towns.

Unlike Britain, Germany still had a large rural population that lived and worked on the land – probably about 35 per cent of the entire population. They were not sharing in Weimar Germany's economic prosperity. The Nazis highlighted the importance of the peasants in their plans for Germany, promising to help agriculture if they came to power. They praised the peasants as racially pure Germans (see the image in Source 7 for example). Nazi propaganda also contrasted the supposedly clean and simple life of the peasants with that of the allegedly corrupt, immoral, crime-ridden cities (for which they blamed Jewish people). The fact that the Nazis despised Weimar culture also gained them support among some conservative people in the towns, who saw Weimar's flourishing art, literature and film achievements as immoral.

SOURCE 7

A Nazi election poster from 1928, showing a farmer. The caption says 'Work, freedom and bread! Vote for the National Socialists.'

SOURCE 6

At one of the early congresses I was sitting surrounded by thousands of SA men. As Hitler spoke I was most interested at the shouts and more often the muttered exclamations of the men around me, who were mainly workmen or lower-middle-class types. 'He speaks for me … Ach, Gott, he knows how I feel' … One man in particular struck me as he leant forward with his head in his hands, and with a sort of convulsive sob said: 'Gott sei Dank [God be thanked], he understands.'

E. Amy Buller, *Darkness over Germany*, published in 1943. Buller was an anti-Nazi German teacher.

Strengthen the SA

In 1925 Hitler enlarged the SA. About 55 per cent of the SA came from the ranks of the unemployed. Many were ex-servicemen from the war. He also set up a new group called the SS. The SS were similar to the SA but were fanatically loyal to Hitler personally. Membership of the party rose to over 100,000 by 1928.

Spread the message

Hitler appointed Joseph Goebbels to take charge of Nazi propaganda. Goebbels was highly efficient at spreading the Nazi message. He and Hitler believed that the best way to reach what they called 'the masses' was by appealing to their feelings rather than by rational argument. Goebbels produced posters, leaflets, films and radio broadcasts; he organised ralliessuch as the annual Nuremberg Rally; he set up photo opportunities; and leading party members were even trained how to deliver speeches in public.

But ... no breakthrough

Despite these shifting policies and priorities, there was no electoral breakthrough for the Nazis. Even after all their hard work, in 1928 they were still a fringe minority party who had the support of less than 3 per cent of the population. They were the smallest party with fewer seats than the Communists. The prosperity of the Stresemann years and Stresemann's success in foreign policy made Germans uninterested in extreme politics.

FOCUS TASK 8.7

What did the Nazi Party stand for in the 1920s?

1 Using the information and sources from pages 235–41, draw up a diagram or chart to represent the Nazis' ideas. You can use this for revision so make the headings big and bold. You can use the ones below and/or add others of your own:
- The Treaty of Versailles
- Greater Germany
- The German people
- *Lebensraum*
- Race and Jewish people
- Government/Weimar Republic
- Economic policies
- Social policies.

2 What was the biggest change in Nazi policy after 1923?

FOCUS TASK 8.8

Stage 1: Why did the Nazis have little success before 1930?

Below are some factors which explain the Nazis' lack of success.

At the moment these factors are organised in alphabetical order. Work in groups to rearrange these factors into what you think is their order of importance:
- Disastrous Putsch of 1923
- Disruption of meetings by political enemies
- Lack of support in the police and army
- Most industrial workers supported left-wing parties
- Nazi aims were irrelevant to most Germans
- Successes of Weimar Government (for example in the economy, foreign policy)

Stage 2: What successes did the Nazis have before 1930?

The 1920s was not a good period for the Nazis but it was not a complete failure. Draw a line and mark one end 'Total failure' and the other end 'Great success'. In the middle, write 'Important development'. Now consider where the following events and developments belong on the line:
- The 25 Points
- Hitler's speaking ability
- Munich Putsch
- Hitler's trial after the Munich Putsch
- Changing policies targeting different groups to win support
- Expanding the SA
- Appointing Goebbels in charge of propaganda

Add notes to explain your placing. NB You may show the same event or development twice if its success changed at different times.

Keep this work safe. It will be useful for Focus Task 8.9 on page 244.

The Depression and the rise of the Nazis

In 1929 the American STOCK MARKET crashed and sent the USA into a disastrous ECONOMIC DEPRESSION. In a very short time, countries around the world began to feel the effects of this depression. Germany was particularly badly affected. American bankers and businessmen lost huge amounts of money in the CRASH. To pay off their debts they asked German banks to repay the money they had borrowed. The result was economic collapse in Germany. Businesses went bankrupt, workers were laid off and unemployment rocketed. And Germany still had to pay the hated reparations from the Treaty of Versailles. The Government tried to act but the Weimar Constitution, with its careful balance of power, made firm and decisive action by the Government difficult.

SOURCE 8

The German mining region of Upper Silesia in 1932: unemployed miners and their families moved into shacks in a shanty town because they had no money to pay their rent.

Enter the Nazis!

Hitler's ideas now seemed to have a special relevance:
- Is the Weimar Government indecisive? Then Germany needs a strong leader!
- Are reparations adding to Germany's problems? Then kick out the Treaty of Versailles!
- Is unemployment a problem? Let the unemployed join the army, build Germany's armaments and be used for public works like road building!

The Nazis' Twenty-Five Points (see Factfile on page XXX) were very attractive to those most vulnerable to the Depression: the unemployed, the elderly and the middle classes. Hitler offered them culprits to blame for Germany's troubles – the Allies, the 'November Criminals' and Jewish people. None of these messages was new and they had not won support for the Nazis in the Stresemann years. The difference now was that the democratic parties simply could not get Germany back to work.

In the 1930 elections the Nazis got 107 seats. In November 1932 they got nearly 200. They did not yet have an overall majority, but they were the biggest single party.

Revision Tip
- Can you describe two effects of the Depression on Germans?
- Make sure you can explain two ways in which the Depression helped the Nazis.

Think!
Draw a diagram to show how the Wall Street Crash in New York could lead to miners losing their jobs in Silesia (Source 8). You could refer to Chapter 2 or Chapter 9.

FIGURE 9

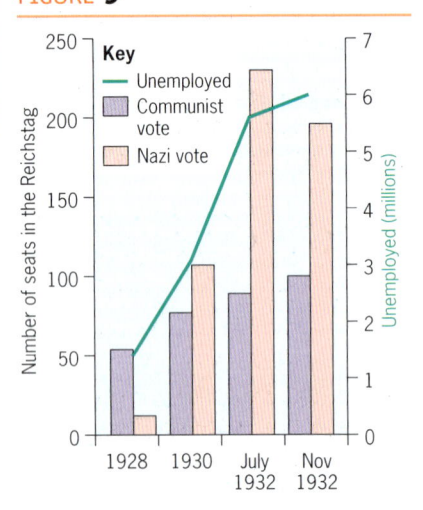

Support for the Nazis and Communists, and unemployment, 1928–32.

SOURCE 10

An English translation of a 1931 Nazi election poster.

SOURCE 11

A Nazi election poster from July 1932. The Nazis proclaim 'We build!' and promise to provide work, freedom and bread. They accuse the opposing parties of planning to use terror, corruption, lies and other strategies as the basis for their government.

Why did the Nazis succeed in elections?

The simple answer is: the Depression. But there were many other important factors that allowed the Nazis to seize this opportunity.

Factor 1: Nazi campaigning

Nazi campaign methods were modern and effective.

The Nazis' greatest campaigning asset was Hitler. He was a powerful speaker. Hitler ran for president in 1932. Despite his defeat, the campaign raised his profile hugely. He was years ahead of his time as a communicator. Using films, radio and records he brought his message to millions. He travelled by plane on a hectic tour of rallies all over Germany. He appeared as a dynamic man of the moment, the leader of a modern party with modern ideas. At the same time, he was able to appear to be a man of the people, someone who knew and understood the people and their problems.

Nazi posters and pamphlets such as Sources 10 and 11 could be found everywhere. Their rallies impressed people with their energy, enthusiasm and sheer size.

The Nazis relied on generalised slogans – 'uniting the people', 'going back to traditional values' – but they were never very clear about what this meant in terms of policies. This made it hard to criticise them. When they were criticised for a specific policy, they were quite likely to drop it. (For example, when industrialists expressed concern about Nazi plans to nationalise industry, they simply dropped the policy.) The Nazis repeated at every opportunity that they believed Jewish people, communists, Weimar politicians and the Treaty of Versailles were the causes of Germany's problems. They expressed contempt for Weimar's democratic system and said that it was unable to solve Germany's economic problems.

They backed up their campaigns with practical action. For example, Nazis organised soup kitchens and provided shelter in hostels for the unemployed.

SOURCE 12

My mother saw a storm trooper parade in the streets of Heidelberg. The sight of discipline in a time of chaos, the impression of energy in an atmosphere of universal hopelessness seems to have won her over.

Albert Speer, writing in 1931. Later, he was to become an important and powerful Nazi leader.

Revision Tip

Note two examples of increasing Nazi support and be ready to explain why.

SOURCE 13

Our opponents accuse us National Socialists, and me in particular, of being intolerant and quarrelsome. They say that we don't want to work with other parties. They say the National Socialists are not German at all, because they refuse to work with other political parties. So is it typically German to have thirty political parties? I have to admit one thing – these gentlemen are quite right. We are intolerant. I have given myself this one goal – to sweep these thirty political parties out of Germany.

Hitler speaking at an election rally, July 1932.

Think!
1 In a sentence explain 'negative cohesion' to someone who has never heard the phrase.
2 Do you think Gordon Craig was right that people supported the Nazis for negative reasons rather than positive reasons?

FOCUS TASK 8.9
How did the Depression help the Nazis?

1 The Depression:
- made Weimar politicians look weak and indecisive
- made Germany less able to pay reparations
- increased unemployment and poverty in Germany
- increased support for communism.

Write these factors onto separate cards and divide into groups. Find examples for each of the factors using pages 242–44. Next, put them in priority order – which factor helped the Nazis gain electoral support the most? Explain your judgement.

2 Decide how far you agree with the following statement. Give it a score out of five (five would mean total agreement).
'Without the economic depression in Germany the Nazis would have remained a minority party.'
Write a short paragraph explaining your score.

Factor 2: 'Negative cohesion'
Cohesion means bringing together. The historian Gordon Craig believed the Nazis benefited from 'NEGATIVE COHESION'. People supported the Nazis not because they shared Nazi views (that would be positive cohesion) but because they shared Nazi fears: 'If you hate what I hate, then I'll support you!'

Factor 3: Disillusionment with democracy
Perhaps the biggest negative was a dissatisfaction with democracy in Weimar Germany. Politicians seemed unable to tackle the problems of the Depression. When the Depression began to bite, Chancellor Brüning actually cut government spending and welfare benefits. He urged Germans to make sacrifices. Brüning called new elections in 1930. This was a disastrous decision as it gave the Nazis the opportunity to exploit the discontent in Germany. Unemployment was heading towards 6 million and the average German's income had fallen by 40 per cent since 1929.

Factor 4: The Communist threat
As the crisis deepened, Communist support was rising too. The Nazis turned this to their advantage. 'Fear of COMMUNISM' was another shared negative.

There were frequent street battles between communist gangs and the police. Large unruly groups of unemployed workers gathered on street corners. In contrast, the SA and SS gave an impression of discipline and order. Many people felt the country needed this kind of order (see Source 12), and many unemployed men signed up with the SA in order to be involved in the Nazi Party.

Business leaders feared the Communists because of their plans to introduce state control of businesses. They were also concerned about the growing strength of Germany's TRADE UNIONS. They felt the Nazis would combat these threats and some began to put money into Nazi campaign funds.

Farmers were also alarmed by the Communists. In the USSR, the communist government had taken over all of the land. Millions of peasants had been killed or imprisoned in the process. In contrast, the Nazis promised to help Germany's desperately struggling small farmers.

Factor 5: Decadence
As for modern decadent Weimar culture – the Nazis could count on all those who felt traditional German values were under threat. The Nazis talked about restoring these old-fashioned values.

Factor 6: Weak opposition
The SOCIAL DEMOCRATIC PARTY made a grave mistake in thinking that German people would not fall for these vague promises and accusations. They also failed to work with other parties, particularly the Communists. But Ebert's crushing of the Communists in 1919–20 left too many bitter memories and the Nazis exploited the divisions among their opponents.

The result
Nazi support rocketed. For example, in Neidenburg in East Prussia Nazi support rose from 2.3 per cent in 1928 to over 25 per cent in 1931, even though the town had no local Nazi Party and Hitler never went there. We know from the work of W.S. Allen that many Germans, especially middle-class Germans, supported Hitler in villages, towns and cities across Germany. In rural communities the Nazis gained many votes from those who shared their views about the decadent cities.

How did Hitler become Chancellor?

July 1932

After the Reichstag elections of July 1932 the Nazis were the largest single party (with 230 seats) but did not have an overall majority. Hitler demanded the post of Chancellor. However, Hindenburg was suspicious of Hitler and refused. He allowed the current Chancellor Franz von Papen to carry on. He then used his emergency powers to pass the measures that von Papen hoped would solve the unemployment problem. However, von Papen was soon in trouble. He had virtually no support in the Reichstag and so called yet another election.

November 1932

In the November 1932 elections the Nazis again came out as the largest party, although their share of the vote fell. Hitler regarded the election as a disaster. He had lost more than 2 million votes along with 38 seats in the Reichstag. The signs were that the Hitler tide had finally turned. The Nazis started to run out of funds. Hitler is said to have threatened suicide.

December 1932

Hindenburg again refused to appoint Hitler as Chancellor. In December 1932 he chose Kurt von Schleicher, one of his own advisers and a bitter rival of von Papen. But within a month, however, von Schleicher too was forced to resign.

By this time it was clear that the Weimar system of government was not working. The system of balances and proportional representation meant that no political group was able to provide strong rule. This had left the 84-year-old President Hindenburg to more or less run the country using his emergency powers, supported by army leaders and rich industrialists. In one sense, Hindenburg had already overthrown the principles of democracy by running Germany with emergency powers. If he was to rescue the democratic system, he needed a Chancellor who actually had support in the Reichstag.

January 1933

Hindenburg appointed Hitler. Through January 1933 Hindenburg and von Papen met secretly with industrialists, army leaders and politicians. On 30 January, to everyone's surprise, they offered Hitler the post of Chancellor. With only a few Nazis in the Cabinet and von Papen as Vice Chancellor, they were confident that they could limit Hitler's influence and resist his extremist demands. The idea was that the policies would be made by the Cabinet, which was filled with conservatives like von Papen. Hitler would be there to get support in the Reichstag for those policies and to control the Communists.

So Hitler ended up as Chancellor through a behind-the-scenes deal by some German aristocrats. Both Hindenburg and von Papen were sure that they could control Hitler. They were very wrong.

Revision Tip
Describe three events (in date order) that brought Hitler to power in 1933.

FOCUS TASK 8.10
Why was Hitler able to become Chancellor by 1933?
Here is a list of factors that helped Hitler come to power.

Hitler's strengths
- Hitler's speaking skills
- Propaganda campaigns
- Their criticisms of the Weimar system of government
- Nazi policies
- Support from big business
- Violent treatment of their opponents

Opponents' weaknesses
- Failure to deal with the Depression
- Failure to co-operate with one another
- Attitudes of Germans to the democratic parties

Other factors
- Weaknesses of the Weimar Republic
- Scheming of Hindenburg and von Papen
- The impact of the Depression
- The Treaty of Versailles
- Memories of the problems of 1923

1. For each factor, write down one example of how it helped Hitler.
2. Give each factor a mark out of 10 for its importance in bringing Hitler to power.
3. Choose what you think are the five most important factors and write a short paragraph on each, explaining why you have chosen it.
4. If you took away any of those factors, would Hitler still have become Chancellor?
5. Were any of those five factors also present in the 1920s?
6. If so, explain why the Nazis were not successful in the 1920s.

Factfile

Reichstag Fire Decree

A Dutch communist called Marinus van der Lubbe was found at the scene of the Reichstag Fire. He was later charged with treason and executed. Hitler blamed the attack on the Communists and claimed a revolution was imminent. He demanded Hindenburg used Article 48 to grant the government emergency powers. With these powers Hitler was able to:

- suspend civil liberties, such as the freedom of expression and freedom of the press and the freedom to organise and assemble
- increase police powers and use the SA as an auxiliary police force
- use the police and the SA to arrest over 4000 communist leaders and shut down the anti-Nazi press.

This effectively removed the communist threat, helped prevent opposition from trade unions and helped the Nazis to increase their share of the vote in the March elections.

Hitler consolidates his position

It is easy to forget, but when Hitler became Chancellor in January 1933 he was in a very precarious position (see Source 14). Few people thought he would hold on to power for long. Even fewer thought that by the summer of 1934 he would be the supreme dictator of Germany. He achieved this through a clever combination of methods – some legal, others dubious. He also managed to defeat or reach agreements with those who could have stopped him.

Step 1: The Reichstag Fire

Once he was Chancellor, Hitler took steps to complete a Nazi take-over of Germany. He called another election for March 1933 to try to get an overall Nazi majority in the Reichstag. He used the same tactics as in previous elections, but now he had the resources of state media and control of the streets. Even so, success was in the balance. Then on 27 February there was a dramatic development: the Reichstag building burnt down. Hitler blamed the Communists and declared that the fire was the beginning of a communist uprising. He demanded special emergency powers to deal with the situation and was given them by President Hindenburg. The Nazis used these powers to arrest Communists, break up meetings and frighten voters.

There have been many theories about what caused the fire, including that it was an accident, the work of a madman, or a Communist plot. Many Germans at the time thought that the Nazis might have started the fire themselves.

SOURCE 14

Source Analysis

This source can be interpreted in different ways.
- Does it show Hitler pressing down and controlling von Papen and Hindenburg or
- Is it saying that without these men holding Hitler up he would be nowhere?

Come to your own decision as to which is the best interpretation and explain your answer.

A British cartoon from early 1933. Hitler, as Chancellor, is being supported by Hindenburg and Von Papen.

THE TEMPORARY TRIANGLE.
Von Hindenburg and Von Papen (together)—
"FOR HE'S A JOLLY GOOD FELLOW,
FOR HE'S A JOLLY GOOD FELLOW."

Think!

1. Some people suggest that the Nazis burnt down the Reichstag themselves. Explain why the Nazis might have wanted to do this.
2. Explain why the Enabling Act was so important to Hitler.
3. In the Night of the Long Knives, why might Hitler have executed people such as von Schleicher who were nothing to do with the SA?
4. Why do you think Hitler chose the support of the army over the support of the SA?

Revision Tip

- Make sure you can describe how the Nazis reacted to the Reichstag Fire.
- Can you explain how the Enabling Act helped Hitler secure his power?

SOURCE 15

The defeat in 1918 did not depress me as greatly as the present state of affairs. It is shocking how day after day naked acts of violence, breaches of the law, barbaric opinions appear quite undisguised as official decree. The Socialist papers are permanently banned. The 'Liberals' tremble. The Berliner Tageblatt was recently banned for two days; that can't happen to the Dresdener Neueste Nachrichten, it is completely devoted to the government ... I can no longer get rid of the feeling of disgust and shame. And no one stirs; everyone trembles, keeps out of sight.

An extract for 17 March 1933 from the diary of Victor Klemperer, a Jewish man who lived in Dresden and recorded his experiences from 1933 to 1941.

Step 2: The Enabling Act

In the election, the Nazis won their largest-ever share of the votes and, with the support of the smaller Nationalist Party, Hitler had an overall majority. Using the SA and SS, he then intimidated the Reichstag into passing the ENABLING ACT which allowed him to make laws without consulting the Reichstag. Only the SPD voted against him. Following the election, the Communists had been banned. The Catholic Centre Party decided to co-operate with the Nazis rather than be treated like the Communists. In return, they retained control of Catholic schools. The Enabling Act made Hitler a virtual dictator. For the next four years if he wanted a new law he could just pass it. There was nothing President Hindenburg or anyone else could do.

Even now, Hitler was not secure. He had seen how the Civil Service, the judiciary, the army and other important groups had undermined the Weimar Republic. He was not yet strong enough to remove his opponents, so he set about a clever policy that mixed force, concessions and compromise (see Factfile below).

Factfile

Nazi consolidation of power

- **30 January 1933** Hitler appointed Chancellor; Goering minister of interior.
- **17 February** Goering ordered local police forces to co-operate with the SA and SS.
- **27 February** Reichstag fire. Arrest of 4000 Communists and other Nazi opponents on the same night.
- **28 February** Emergency Decree issued by Hindenburg:
  – police to arrest suspects and hold them without trial, search houses, ban meetings, close newspapers and radio stations
  – Hitler took over regional governments.
- **5 March** Reichstag elections: government used control of radio and police to intimidate opponents. Nazi election slogan was 'The battle against Marxism'. Won 43.9 per cent of vote.
- **13 March** Goebbels appointed head of Ministry for Propaganda. Took control of all media.
- **24 March** The Enabling Act allowed Hitler to pass decrees without the President's involvement. This made Hitler a legal dictator.
- **7 April** Civil Service administration, court, and education purged of 'alien elements', i.e. Jewish people and other opponents of the Nazis.
- **1 May** Workers granted May Day holiday.
- **2 May** Trade unions banned; all workers to belong to new German Labour Front (DAF).
- **9 June** Employment Law: major programme of public works (e.g. road building) to create jobs.
- **14 July** Law against the Formation of New Parties: Germany became a ONE-PARTY STATE.
- **20 July** CONCORDAT (agreement) with the Roman Catholic Church: government protected religious freedom; Church banned from political activity.
- **January 1934** All state governments taken over.
- **30 June** NIGHT OF THE LONG KNIVES.
- **August** On death of Hindenburg, Hitler became Führer. German armed forces swore oath of loyalty to him.

Revision Tip

- Choose three events from the Factfile and make sure you can describe them accurately.
- Give the Enabling Act and the Night of The Long Knives marks out of ten for their importance. Now prepare two points that justify your marks.

Step 3: The Night of the Long Knives

Within a year any opponents (or potential opponents) of the Nazis had either left Germany or been taken to CONCENTRATION CAMPS run by the SS. Other political parties were banned.

Hitler was still not entirely secure, however. The leading officers in the army were not impressed by him and were particularly suspicious of Hitler's SA and its leader Ernst Röhm. The SA was a badly disciplined force (in comparison with the army that is). What's more, Röhm talked of making the SA into a second German army to begin a 'second revolution'. This would achieve some of the Nazi Party's more socialist aims from their 25-Point Programme. Röhm's nearly four million strong SA was also increasingly causing chaos on the streets with the communists gone.

Hindenburg even threatened to enforce martial law if nothing was done. This would have seen the German army take control of law and order in Germany and with it, Nazi rule. Hitler himself was also suspicious of Röhm and feared that Röhm's control over the SA men made him a potentially dangerous rival.

Hitler had to choose between the army and the SA. He made his choice, after leading Nazis such as Himmler and Goering persuaded him of Röhm's intentions, and acted ruthlessly. On the weekend of 29–30 June squads of SS men broke into the homes of Röhm and other leading figures in the SA and arrested them. Hitler accused Röhm of plotting to overthrow and murder him. Over the weekend Röhm and possibly as many as 400 others were executed. These included the former Chancellor von Schleicher, a fierce critic of Hitler, and others who actually had no connection with Röhm. This purge came to be known as the Night of the Long Knives.

Hindenburg thanked Hitler for his 'determined action which has nipped treason in the bud'. The army said it was well satisfied with the events of the weekend.

The SA was not disbanded. It remained as a Nazi paramilitary organisation, but was very much subordinate to the SS. Many of its members were absorbed by the army and the SS.

SOURCE 16

A Swiss cartoon commenting on the Night of the Long Knives. Röhm was the head of the SA and Heines was his deputy. The caption for the cartoon is: 'And the Führer said: Only death can drive us apart.'

Step 4: The army oath

President Hindenburg died on 2 August 1934, at the age of 86. Hitler used the Enabling Act to pass a law that abolished the position of President and combined its powers with that of the Chancellor. This meant Hitler was now Germany's head of state and head of government. His new title was 'Führer und Reichskanzler' ('Leader and Chancellor of the Reich'). Hindenburg's death had removed the last obstacle to Hitler's absolute control over Germany.

On the day that Hindenburg died, the entire army swore an oath of personal loyalty to Adolf Hitler as Führer of Germany.

The army agreed to stay out of politics and to serve Hitler. In return, Hitler spent vast sums on REARMAMENT, brought back CONSCRIPTION and made plans to make Germany a great military power again.

FOCUS TASK 8.11
How did Hitler consolidate his power in 1933–34?

1 Work in groups of three or four. Draw your own copy of the following graph:

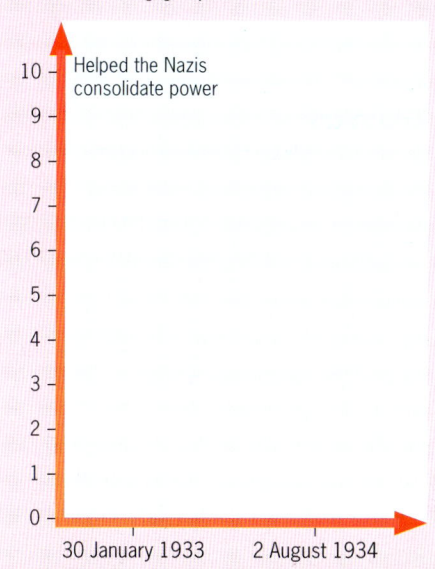

(Graph: y-axis labelled 0 to 10 'Helped the Nazis consolidate power'; x-axis from 30 January 1933 to 2 August 1934)

2 Use the Factfile on page 247 and choose at least eight of the 16 key events. You must include the following four events:
- Reichstag Fire and Emergency Decree
- Enabling Act
- Concordat
- Night of the Long Knives

Decide where you would place each one, as well as four more, on your timeline based on how far they helped the Nazis consolidate power.

3 Add a brief explanation for each event on your timeline justifying your decision.

Key Question Summary

Why was Hitler able to dominate Germany by 1934?

1 The Nazi Party was formed in 1919 and Hitler soon became its leader.
2 Its 25-point programme appealed to ex-soldiers and those on the Right but it did not enjoy wider support.
3 While in prison after the Munich Putsch of 1923, Hitler wrote *Mein Kampf*, setting out his ideas.
4 The Nazi Party reorganised itself in the 1920s but was still a fringe party in the 1928 elections.
5 The Great Depression led to unemployment and economic hardship, circumstances in which the Nazis could flourish.
6 Nazi criticisms of the Weimar Government and the Treaty of Versailles were popular along with their ideas on rebuilding Germany.
7 They used innovative techniques – rallies, slogans, films, radio, posters and pamphlets – to put across their ideas.
8 Hitler was a great asset as a highly effective speaker who appeared to understand the people's problems and express their hopes.
9 Disillusionment with the Weimar Republic pushed Germans towards extremist parties, both the Nazis and the Communists.
10 There was violence and lawlessness and groups like businessmen and farmers, who feared communism, liked the Nazis' anticommunist message.
11 The Nazis became the biggest single party in the 1932 elections.
12 The leaders of the Weimar Republic thought they could use Hitler to their advantage by making him Chancellor. But he used emergency powers and the Enabling Act to establish himself as dictator.

8C How effectively did the Nazis control Germany, 1933–45?

> ### FOCUS
> There was supposed to be no room for opposition of any kind in Nazi Germany. The aim was to create a TOTALITARIAN state. In a totalitarian state there can be no rival parties, no political debate. Ordinary citizens must divert their whole energy into serving the state and doing what its leaders want.
>
> In this section you will examine how the Nazis combined the strategies of terror and propaganda to control Germany.
>
> ### Focus Points
> - How much opposition was there to the Nazi regime?
> - How effectively did the Nazis deal with their political opponents?
> - How did the Nazis use culture and the mass media to control the people?
> - Why did the Nazis persecute many groups in German society?
> - Was Nazi Germany a totalitarian state?

The Nazi seizure of power

Nazi aims

Achieving political power was only the beginning of Nazi ambition. Hitler wanted power in order to reshape Germany. The Nazis wanted to build:

- **A strong Germany.** Hitler blamed Germany's problems on weak leadership. He wanted strong leadership as in the days of the Kaiser. He wanted strong Germans, ready for war who were able to restore Germany's military pride.
- **A racially pure Germany.** Hitler believed in Aryan supremacy and blamed Jewish people for many of Germany's problems. He wanted to remove Jewish people and other non-Aryans from any positions of leadership.
- **A People's Community** (or *Volk*). The Nazis wanted people to give their hearts and minds to Hitler. In the VOLK people would see their contribution to Germany as more important than their own fulfilment.

They intended to eliminate anything that stood in the way of achieving these aims. They started immediately Hitler took power in January 1933. The speed and ruthlessness of this take-over took many Germans by surprise. Political opposition was decapitated – its leaders imprisoned or intimidated into silence.

Case study: The Nazi seizure of power in Northeim

The historian W.S. Allen wrote a groundbreaking book in the 1960s. He interviewed hundreds of people in the small town of Northeim in northern Germany about their experience of living under Nazi rule. He compiled an incredibly thorough account of how the Nazis took control in this one town. This process is summarised in the diagram on the opposite page.

The steps that took place in Northeim were replicated in thousands of other small towns and communities around Germany.

How the Nazis seized power in the town of Northeim	
	**1. They took over the council by bullying and intimidation.** They had a majority of 15:5 on the council. Before the first council meeting the police arrested one opposition councillor. At the meeting they stationed SA officers all around the room and refused to let opposition councillors speak. Opposition councillors walked out in protest and were spat on by the SA officers as they left. The council never met again. That was the end of democracy in Northeim.
	**2. They set up a search of all houses in Northeim** supposedly looking for illegal guns and ammunition. They ransacked homes and arrested 22 people. Seven were taken to the local concentration camp. The deeper impact of this was that ordinary Northeimers got the message that the violence the Nazis used against political opponents would also be applied to any person who stepped out of line.
	**3. They ordered *Gleichschaltung* (co-ordination) of all organisations.** They argued that because the Nazis were a majority in national government that all local bodies should also have a Nazi majority. The four sports clubs in Northeim were combined into one Nazi-run sports club. Even the singing groups and choirs were combined as the Nazi-led 'Mixed choral singing club of 1933'. The aim was that whenever ordinary people got together to do anything they would be watched by a loyal Nazi.
	**4. They organised boycotts of Jewish businesses.** A newspaper campaign told Northeimers not to shop at Jewish-run businesses. SA men were stationed outside to turn people away.
	**5. They ended unemployment.** This had been a key reason the Nazis had been elected. In June 1933 there were 500 registered unemployed in Northeim; within three months there were none. Most were put to work repairing roads and clearing the woods around the town. However, socialists were dismissed from jobs which were then given to Nazis. Unemployed socialists were offered physically demanding work in the local quarry but only if they agreed to give up politics.
	**6. They produced relentless propaganda.** In the first three months of Nazi power they organised a torrent of propaganda events including the ceremonial burning of the Weimar flag; a book burning to destroy unacceptable books; and a torchlight parade, joined by 3000 people, through the streets to the park where the local Nazi leader Ernst Girmann gave a speech saying, 'The individual is nothing! The Volk is everything! Once we unite internally, we shall defeat the enemy!'
	**7. Northeimers rushed to join the Nazi party.** Northeimers could quickly see that to get anywhere in Nazi Germany you had to join the party. By May membership had rocketed to 1200 people in a town of 10,000. Many of these were not Nazi fanatics. They joined to keep safe or to keep their jobs.

FOCUS TASK 8.12

How did the Nazis control Germany?

Summarise these two pages in a table with the following headings:
- Organisation
- Methods
- Controlled by
- Duties
- How it helped Hitler make his position secure.

Crushing opposition: The Nazi police state

The Nazis had a range of powerful ways to terrorise the German people. The main organisations and methods are summarised below. However you will quickly see as you read about each one that their roles overlap. If it seems confusing, it was! Modern research suggests that Nazi Germany was in many ways chaotic and disorganised. Nazi officials competed with each other to get Hitler's approval. The result was often a jumble of different organisations competing with each other and getting in each other's way.

However, even if it was confusing exactly who did what to whom there is no doubting the overall impression they generated – that the Nazi terror machine was everywhere. It very effectively scared most opposition into submission.

The Gestapo

- The GESTAPO was the secret state police. It was commanded by Reinhard Heydrich.
- Gestapo agents had sweeping powers. They could arrest citizens and send them to concentration camps without trial or even explanation.
- They were believed to have a network of 'informers' listening in on people's conversations.
- It seems that the Gestapo was the organisation most feared by ordinary citizens. However, recent research has shown that Germans believed the Gestapo was much more powerful than it actually was. As a result, ordinary Germans informed on each other because they thought the Gestapo would find out anyway.

SOURCE 1

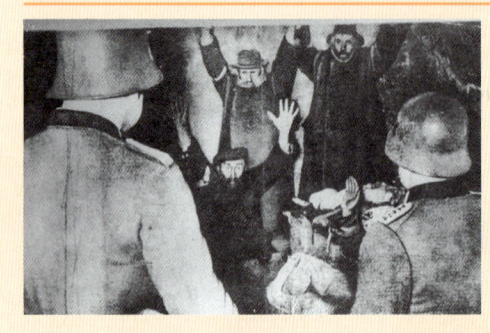

Gestapo officers making an arrest. It was probably staged as propaganda to increase the fear of the Gestapo.

The SS

- After virtually destroying the SA in 1934, the SS grew into a huge organisation with many different responsibilities. It had 1 million staff by 1944. It was led by Heinrich Himmler (see page 239).
- SS men were Aryans, very highly trained and totally loyal to Hitler.
- Under Himmler, the SS had the main responsibility for crushing opposition and carrying out Nazi racial policies.
- There were three particularly important sub-divisions:
  - **The SD** was the SS's own internal security service. The SD would investigate potential disloyalty within the armed forces or politically sensitive cases (e.g. a crime committed by a senior Nazi).
  - **The Death's Head units** were responsible for the concentration camps and the transportation and murder of Jewish people.
  - **The Waffen-SS** – armoured regiments that fought alongside the regular army.
- As its power grew, the SS set up its own courts. Around 200,000 Germans were sent to concentration camps by these courts.

SOURCE 2

SS guards after taking over the Berlin broadcasting station in 1933.

FIGURE 3

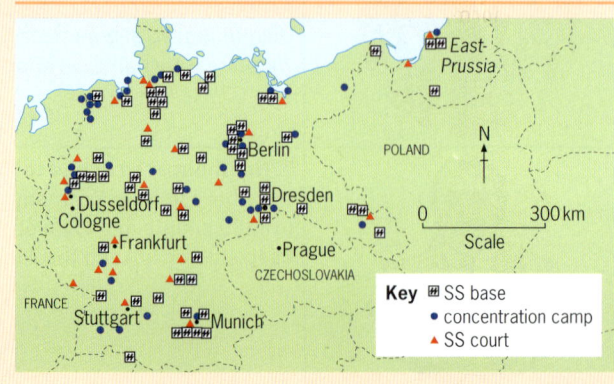

Map showing the locations and types of SS activities 1933–37.

Source Analysis

1 Study Sources 1–5. Does it seem strange that these activities were photographed by the Nazis?
2 Can you think why these pictures were published and why the Nazis did not try to hide what was happening?

Revision Tip

- Make sure you can describe at least two methods of control used by the Nazis.
- Choose one method and make sure you can explain how it was effective.

Concentration camps

- Concentration camps were the Nazis' ultimate sanction against their own people.
- The first camps were set up as soon as Hitler took power in 1933. They were makeshift prisons in disused factories and warehouses. Purpose-built camps were soon built, usually in isolated rural areas.
- Jewish people, socialists, communists, trade unionists, churchmen and anyone else brave enough to criticise the Nazis ended up in these camps. Historians estimate that around 1.3 million Germans spent at least some time in a concentration camp between 1933 and 1939.
- These camps were run by SS Death's Head units.
- Prisoners were forced to do hard labour. Food was limited and prisoners suffered harsh discipline, beatings and random executions.
- The aim was to 'correct' opponents of the regime. However, by the late 1930s, deaths in the camps were increasingly common and very few people came out alive.

SOURCE 4

Political prisoners at the Oranienburg concentration camp near Berlin.

The police and the courts

- Top jobs in local **police** forces were given to high-ranking Nazis reporting to Himmler.
- As a result, the police added political 'snooping' to their normal law-and-order role. They were, of course, under strict instructions to ignore crimes committed by Nazi agents.
- Similarly, the Nazis controlled **magistrates, judges and the courts**. They appointed all the judges and sacked those they disapproved of.
- This led to self-imposed control – magistrates knew what they were expected to do and did it. They knew they would not last long if they did not. This meant that opponents of Nazism rarely received a fair trial.

SOURCE 5

German judges swearing their loyalty to the Nazi regime at the criminal courts in Berlin.

Propaganda in Nazi Germany

One reason why opposition to Hitler was so limited was the work of Dr Joseph Goebbels, minister for enlightenment and propaganda. Goebbels passionately believed in Hitler as the saviour of Germany. His mission was to make sure that others believed this too. Throughout the twelve years of Nazi rule Goebbels constantly kept his finger on the pulse of PUBLIC OPINION and decided what the German public should and should not hear. He aimed to use every resource available to him to make people loyal to Hitler and the Nazis.

The Nuremberg rallies

Goebbels organised huge rallies, marches, torch-lit processions and meetings. Probably the best example was the NUREMBERG RALLY which took place in summer each year. There were bands, marches, flying displays and Hitler's brilliant speeches. The rallies brought some colour and excitement into people's lives. They gave them a sense of belonging to a great movement. The rallies also showed the German people the power of the state and convinced them that 'every other German' fully supported the Nazis. Goebbels also recognised that one of the Nazis' main attractions was that they created order out of chaos and so the whole rally was organised to emphasise order.

> **Source Analysis**
>
> Look at Source 6. How does the rally:
> a) make it clear who the leader is
> b) give people a sense of belonging
> c) provide colour and excitement
> d) show the power of the state
> e) show the Nazis' ability to create order out of chaos?

SOURCE 6

A Hitler speaks to the assembled Germans.

B A parade through the streets.

C German youth marching with spades.

The annual rally at Nuremberg. The whole town was taken over and the rally dominated radio broadcasts and newsreels.

Control of media and culture

Less spectacular than the rallies but possibly more important was Goebbels' control of media and culture. The diagram below summarises how he used them to spread Nazi messages. This was in stark contrast with the freedom of expression allowed in Weimar Germany.

Goebbels was supported in this work by the terror state. For example, when he wanted to close down an anti-Nazi newspaper, silence an anti-Nazi writer, or catch someone listening to a foreign radio station, the SS and the Gestapo were there to do that work for him.

Books
- No books could be published without Goebbels' permission. Not surprisingly the bestseller in Nazi Germany was Hitler's book, *Mein Kampf*.
- In 1933 Goebbels organised a high-profile 'book-burning'. Nazi students publicly burned books that included ideas unacceptable to the Nazis.

Art
- Artists suffered the same kinds of restriction as writers. Only Nazi-approved painters could show their works.
- These usually had to be paintings or sculptures of heroic-looking Aryans, military figures or images of the ideal Aryan family.

Newspapers
- Within months of the Nazi take-over, Jewish editors and journalists found themselves out of work and anti-Nazi newspapers were closed down.
- Those that remained were not allowed to print anti-Nazi articles. German newspapers became dull reading and Germans bought fewer newspapers as a result – circulation fell by about 10 per cent.

Cinema
- All films – factual or fictional, thrillers or comedies – had to carry a pro-Nazi message.
- The newsreels before each feature film told of the greatness of Hitler and the achievements of Nazi Germany. There is evidence that Germans avoided these by arriving late!
- Goebbels censored all foreign films coming into Germany.

Music
- He banned JAZZ music, which had been popular in Germany as elsewhere around Europe. He banned it because it was 'Black' music and black people were considered an inferior race.

Radio
- Goebbels also loved new technology and quickly saw the potential of radio broadcasting for spreading the Nazi message.
- He made cheap radios available so all Germans could buy one (see Source 8 on page 256) and he controlled all the radio stations. Listening to broadcasts from the BBC was punishable by death.
- Just in case people did not have a radio Goebbels placed loudspeakers in the streets and public bars.
- Hitler's speeches and those of other Nazi leaders were repeated on the radio over and over again until the ideas expressed in them – German expansion into eastern Europe, the inferiority of Jewish people – came to be accepted as normal by the German people.

Posters
- If people missed the radio broadcasts they would see the posters. Goebbels plastered Germany with posters proclaiming the successes of Hitler and the Nazis and attacking their opponents.

Source Analysis

What can you infer from Sources 7 and 8 about the effectiveness of Nazi propaganda?

Think!

In groups, discuss which of the following statements you most agree with.
- **A** Goebbels' work was more important to Nazi success than that of Himmler (head of the SS).
- **B** Himmler's work was more important to Nazi success than Goebbels'.
- **C** The techniques of repression and propaganda go hand in hand – neither would work without the other.

Revision Tip

- Make sure you can describe at least two things the Nazis banned and one thing the Nazis promoted.
- Be ready to explain why Goebbels thought the use of modern technology was important.

SOURCE 7

There are cinema evenings to be caught up with, very enjoyable ones – if only there were not each time the bitterness of the Third Reich's triumphalism. The renewal of German art … enthusiastic welcome for the Führer in X or Y … Goebbels' speech on culture … the biggest lecture theatre in the world, the biggest autobahn in the world, etc. etc. – the biggest lie in the world, the biggest disgrace in the world. It can't be helped.

From the diary of Victor Klemperer for 8 August 1937.

SOURCE 8

Poster advertising cheap Nazi-produced radios. The text reads 'All Germany hears the Führer on the People's Radio.' The radios had only a short range and were unable to pick up foreign stations.

FOCUS TASK 8.13

How did the Nazis use culture and the mass media to control the people?

Use your own wider research to find out about one of the following examples of Goebbels' use of culture or mass media:
- a book banned by the Nazis or an artwork banned by the Nazis
- *The Triumph of the Will*: a propaganda film made by the Nazis
- Heinrich Hoffman's photographs of Hitler
- *Der Sturmer*.

There are many other examples you can choose.

For your chosen example, research and then write a short explanation of how this was used by the Nazis. It could be one or more of:
- marginalising groups the Nazis disliked
- persuading Germans to believe in Nazi ideology
- building national pride
- strengthening the cult of personality around Hitler.

Think!
1. In what ways was the Berlin Olympics a propaganda success for Goebbels?
2. In what ways was it a failure?
3. Why do you think Nazi propaganda was more successful within Germany than outside it?
4. You have already come across many examples of Nazi propaganda. Choose one example which you think is the cleverest piece of propaganda. Explain your choice.

Revision Tip
- Try to remember two ways the Nazis exploited the 1936 Olympics.
- Explain one way in which the Olympics were a propaganda success for the Nazis and one way they were a failure.

Case study: The 1936 Olympics

One of Goebbels' greatest challenges came with the 1936 Olympic Games in Berlin. Other Nazis were opposed to holding the Games in Berlin, but Goebbels convinced Hitler that this was a great propaganda opportunity both within Germany and internationally.

Goebbels and Hitler also thought that the Olympics could be a showcase for their doctrine that the Aryan race was superior to all other races. However, there was international pressure for nations such as the USA to BOYCOTT the Games in protest against the Nazis' repressive regime and anti-Jewish politics. In response, the Nazis included one token Jewish person in their team!

Goebbels built a brand new stadium to hold 100,000 people. It was lit by the most modern electric lighting. He brought in television cameras for the first time. The most sophisticated German photo-electronic timing device was installed. The stadium had the largest stopclock ever built. With guests and competitors from 49 countries coming into the heart of Nazi Germany, it was going to take all Goebbels' talents to show that Germany was a modern, civilised and successful nation. No expense was spared. When the Games opened, the visitors were duly amazed at the scale of the stadium, the wonderful facilities and the efficiency of the organisation. However, they were also struck, and in some cases appalled, by the almost fanatical devotion of the people to Hitler and by the overt presence of army and SS soldiers who were patrolling or standing guard everywhere.

To the delight of Hitler and Goebbels, Germany came top of the medal table, way ahead of all other countries. However, to their great dismay, a black athlete, Jesse Owens, became the star of the Games. He won four gold medals and broke eleven world records in the process. The ten black members of the American team won thirteen medals between them. So much for Aryan superiority!

To the majority of German people, who had grown used to the Nazi propaganda machine, the Games appeared to present all the qualities they valued in the Nazis – a grand vision, efficiency, power, strength and achievement. However, to many foreign visitors who were not used to such blatant propaganda it backfired on the Nazi regime.

SOURCE 9

The stadium built for the 1936 Olympics.

Factfile

Religion in Germany in the 1930s

Most Germans were Christian in the 1930s. Approximately one-third of Christians were Catholic and two-thirds were Protestant.

When the Nazis took control after 1933, the Protestant Church split into two distinct groups:
- The German Christians under Müller were prepared to swear loyalty to Hitler and promote Nazi racial ideas.
- The Confessing Church, which included Niemöller and Bonhoeffer, resisted the German Christian movement and opposed the Nazification of religion.

The German Faith Movement, which emerged as an alternative religion, tried to tempt Germans away from Christianity and towards an older, pagan form of worship. This emphasised worship of the sun, loyalty to Hitler and the peasant farmer 'blood and soil' philosophy. It only managed to attract about 200,000 followers or 0.3 per cent of the total population.

SOURCE 10

Most postwar accounts have concentrated on the few German clerics who did behave bravely ... But these were few. Most German church leaders were shamefully silent. As late as January 1945, the Catholic bishop of Würzburg was urging his flock to fight on for the Fatherland, saying that 'salvation lies in sacrifice'.

British historian and journalist Charles Wheeler, writing in 1996.

Revision Tip

Make sure you can describe:
- one example of collaboration between the Nazis and the Churches
- at least one example of conflict between the Nazis and the Churches.

The Nazis and the Churches

The relationship between the Churches and the Nazis was complicated. In the early stages of the Nazi regime, there was some CO-OPERATION between the Nazis and the Churches. Hitler signed a Concordat with the Catholic Church in 1933. This meant that Hitler agreed to leave the Catholic Church alone and allowed it to keep control of its schools. In return, the Church agreed to stay out of politics.

Hitler tried to get all of the Protestant Churches to come together in one official Reich Church. The Reich Church was headed by the Protestant Bishop Ludwig Müller (see Source 11). However, many Germans still felt that their true loyalties lay with their original Churches in their local areas rather than with this state-approved Church.

Hitler even encouraged an alternative religion to the Churches, the pagan German Faith Movement.

Many churchgoers either supported the Nazis or did little to oppose them. However, there were some very important exceptions. The Catholic Bishop Galen criticised the Nazis throughout the 1930s. In 1941 he led a popular protest against the Nazi policies of killing mentally ill and physically disabled people, forcing the Nazis temporarily to stop. He had such strong support among his followers that the Nazis decided it was too risky to try to silence him because they did not want trouble while Germany was at war.

Protestant ministers also resisted the Nazis. Pastor Martin Niemöller was one of the most high-profile critics of the regime in the 1930s. Along with Dietrich Bonhoeffer, he formed an alternative Protestant Church to the official Reich Church. These church leaders suffered a similar fate to Hitler's political opponents. Niemöller spent the years 1938–45 in a concentration camp for resisting the Nazis. Dietrich Bonhoeffer preached against the Nazis until the Gestapo stopped him in 1937.

SOURCE 11

An official photograph of the National Synod (the ruling body) of the German Evangelical Church (the largest of Germany's Protestant churches) in 1933. The man in the centre is Bishop Ludwig Müller, a close ally of Hitler. Hitler forced the Church to accept him as its leader in 1933.

FOCUS TASK 8.14

Why did the Nazis persecute many groups in German society?

You have seen how the Nazis persecuted people who opposed them politically, e.g. the Communists, socialists and trade unionists. But why did they persecute so many other groups?

1 Work in teams of five, each representing one of the minority groups below. Each team will use the information on pages 259–61 and their own research to investigate:
   a) why the Nazis targeted their group
   b) what actions the Nazis took against them.
   - Group 1: Gay and lesbian people
   - Group 2: People with physical or mental health disorders
   - Group 3: Roma
   - Group 4: Asocials
   - Group 5: Jewish people
2 Complete a table to summarise this information. You will need to ask the other teams about their research to complete the table.

Revision Tip

Make sure you can describe how the Nazis persecuted Jewish people and one other group. It is important to be able to explain Nazi theories on race and how these led to persecution.

Factfile

Nazi race theory

The Nazis believed that the Germans were members of the Aryan race who were the *herrenvolk*, or master race, destined to rule. This included mainly white, northern Europeans. Germans who could prove their Aryan heritage received an 'Aryan Certificate'.

According to Nazi racial ideas, below the Aryans there were lesser races such as Slav, African and Asian. And at the bottom of the Nazi hierarchy came the *Untermenschen* ('sub-human') races. This group included Jews and Roma, who were viewed by the Nazis as parasitic and a danger to the healthy Aryan race. The *Mischling* were Germans of mixed race ancestry. This included people with at least one Jewish grandparent. These ideas formed the basis of the 1935 Nuremberg Laws.

The persecution of minorities

Through their twelve years in power the Nazis persecuted any group that they thought challenged Nazi ideals. Gay and lesbian people were seen as a threat to Nazi ideas about family life; people with mental health disorders were a threat to Nazi ideas about Germans being a perfect master race; Roma and Jewish people were thought to be inferior people.

Methods of persecution varied.

- Organisations for gay and lesbian people were shut down. Homosexuality was already a crime and there was a lot of antigay prejudice even before 1933 so the Nazis exploited this prejudice. Books by gay authors were banned. Around 100,000 gay people were arrested with around 50,000 sent to prison. Figures are unclear but between 5000 and 10,000 of these ended up in concentration camps. They were forced to wear a pink triangle to mark them out.
- A so-called 'euthanasia programme' was begun in 1939 against people with mental health disorders: at least 5000 babies and children were killed between 1939 and 1945 either by injection or by starvation. Between 1939 and 1941, 72,000 patients with mental health conditions were gassed before a public outcry in Germany itself ended the extermination.
- The attempted extermination of the Roma, on the other hand, did not cause an outcry. Five out of six Roma living in Germany in 1939 were killed by the Nazis.
- Similarly, there was little or no complaint about the treatment of so-called 'asocials' – alcoholics, the homeless, prostitutes, habitual criminals and beggars – who were rounded up off the streets and sent to concentration camps.

Jewish people

The most vicious persecution was the Nazi treatment of the Jewish population in which ANTISEMITISM culminated in the dreadful slaughter of the 'FINAL SOLUTION'.

Hitler's antisemitism

Antisemitism means hatred of Jewish people. Throughout Europe, Jewish people had experienced discrimination for hundreds of years. They were often treated unjustly in courts or forced to live in ghettos. One reason for this persecution was religious, in that Jewish people were blamed for the death of Jesus Christ. Another reason was that the Nazis promoted the idea that Jewish people tended to be better off, owning more stores and successful businesses.

Hitler hated Jewish people. In his years of poverty in Vienna, he became obsessed by the fact that they ran many of the most successful businesses, particularly the large department stores. This offended his idea of the superiority of Aryans. Hitler also blamed Jewish businessmen and bankers for Germany's defeat in the First World War. He thought they had forced the surrender of the German army.

SOURCE 12

To read the pages [of Hitler's Mein Kampf] is to enter a world of the insane, a world peopled by hideous and distorted shadows. The Jew is no longer a human being, he has become a mythical figure, a grimacing leering devil invested with infernal powers, the incarnation of evil.

A. Bullock, *Hitler: A Study in Tyranny*, published in 1990.

Factfile

Nazi eugenics

Nazi eugenics refers to the attempts the Nazis made to biologically 'improve' the Aryan race. The Nazis believed that to ensure a thriving future Aryan master race, Aryans should only marry Aryans and raise Aryan children. This eugenics programme meant those deemed non-Aryan in Germany were barred from marrying Aryans. Many non-Aryans were also sterilised, including many of the 20,000 black people living in the Rhineland.

The Nazis also believed that people with hereditary mental and physical conditions, such as Down's syndrome, should not be allowed to have children. They argued that people with these conditions wasted public money. Many were sterilised and in 1939 the 'Aktion T-4' euthanasia programme saw a total of 200,000 people deemed 'unfit for life'.

All this in the name of 'racial hygiene'.

SOURCE 14

I hate the treatment of the Jews. I think it is a bad side of the movement and I will have nothing to do with it. I did not join the party to do that sort of thing. I joined the party because I thought and still think that Hitler did the greatest Christian work for twenty-five years. I saw seven million men rotting in the streets, often I was there too, and no one ... seemed to care ... Then Hitler came and he took all those men off the streets and gave them health and security and work.

H. Schmidt, Labour Corps leader, in an interview in 1938.

SOURCE 15

I feel the urge to present to you a true report of the recent riots, plundering and destruction of Jewish property. Despite what the official Nazi account says, the German people have nothing whatever to do with these riots and burnings. The police supplied SS men with axes, house-breaking tools and ladders. A list of the addresses of all Jewish shops and flats was provided and the mob worked under the leadership of the SS men. The police had strict orders to remain neutral.

Anonymous letter from a German civil servant to the British consul, 1938.

Early measures against Jewish people

As soon as Hitler took power in 1933 he began to mobilise the full powers of the state against Jewish people.

- They were immediately **banned** from the Civil Service and a variety of public services such as broadcasting and teaching.
- At the same time, SA and later SS troopers organised **boycotts** of Jewish shops and businesses (see Source 13), which were marked with a star of David.
- Goebbels' **propaganda** experts bombarded German children and families with anti-Jewish messages.
- In daily life Jewish people faced **discrimination**. They might be refused jobs or refused service in shops. In schools, Jewish children were humiliated and then segregated.

SOURCE 13

SA and SS men enforcing the boycott of Jewish shops, April 1933. The sign tells Germans not to buy from Jewish people.

The Nuremberg Laws

In September 1935 at the annual Nuremberg Rally, Hitler announced two new anti-Semitic laws. Collectively they are known as the Nuremberg Laws.

- The 'Law for the Protection of German Blood and German Honour' made it illegal for Jews to marry or have sex with Aryans.
- The 'Reich Citizenship Law' classified Germans into different racial groups:
  - Aryans of pure German blood
  - *Mischling* or mixed race
  - Non-Aryans, including Jews.

Only Aryans were given full German citizenship. A further decree later in the year added Roma and black Germans to the list of non-Aryans.

Kristallnacht

In November 1938 a young Jewish man killed a German diplomat in Paris. The Nazis used this as an excuse to launch a violent revenge on Jewish people. Plain-clothes SS troopers were issued with pickaxes and hammers

Source Analysis

1 Read Sources 14–17. How useful is each source to a historian looking at the German reaction to *Kristallnacht*?
2 Taken together, do they provide a clear picture of how Germans felt about *Kristallnacht*?

SOURCE 16

Until Kristallnacht, many Germans believed Hitler was not engaged in mass murder. [The treatment of the Jews] seemed to be a minor form of harassment of a disliked minority. But after Kristallnacht no German could any longer be under any illusion. I believe it was the day that we lost our innocence. But it would be fair to point out that I myself never met even the most fanatic Nazi who wanted the extermination [mass murder] of the Jews. Certainly we wanted the Jews out of Germany, but we did not want them to be killed.

Alfons Heck, member of the Hitler Youth in 1938, interviewed for a television programme in 1989.

Revision Tip

It is important that you can describe how persecution of Jewish people increased in the 1930s. Make sure you can:
- describe the 1933 boycott, the Nuremberg Laws and *Kristallnacht*
- explain how each was more severe than the one before it.

Think!

Could Germans have protested effectively about *Kristallnacht*? Explain your answer with reference to pages 260–62.

---

and the addresses of Jewish businesses. They ran riot, smashing up Jewish shops and workplaces. Ninety-one Jewish people were murdered. Hundreds of synagogues were burned. Twenty thousand Jewish peoples were taken to concentration camps. Thousands more left the country. This event became known as KRISTALLNACHT or 'The Night of Broken Glass'. Many Germans watched the events of *Kristallnacht* with alarm and concern. The Nazi-controlled press presented *Kristallnacht* as the spontaneous reaction of ordinary Germans against the Jewish people. Most Germans did not believe this. However, hardly anyone protested. The few who did were brutally murdered. The Jews were even fined one billion marks as a lot of the damaged property was rented by Jews from German owners.

After Kristallnacht, Nazi policies towards Jews got increasingly harsh. Jewish children were banned from German schools. By the end of 1938 all the remaining Jewish businesses were confiscated.

Before war broke out again in September 1939, there were still nearly 200,000 Jews living in Germany (there had been nearly 500,000 in 1933). The Nazis enforced new restrictive laws to make it easier for the authorities to identify Jewish people. They were forced to add new first names to their identification papers ('Israel' for men and 'Sarah' for women). They had a red 'J' stamped on their passports. As the war continued, Nazi policy towards the Jews in Germany and occupied Europe would become more brutal and increasingly radical.

SOURCE 17

[The day after Kristallnacht] the teachers told us: don't worry about what you see, even if you see some nasty things which you may not understand. Hitler wants a better Germany, a clean Germany. Don't worry, everything will work out fine in the end.

Henrik Metelmann, member of the Hitler Youth, in 1938.

SOURCE 18

An anti-Semitic cartoon from the Nazi newspaper *Der Stürmer*, 1935. The Nazis promoted the idea that Jewish people owned many shops and businesses so they could target them for Nazi attacks.

SOURCE 19

Frustration and disappointment with the realities of everyday life under Nazism led ordinary Germans to grumble and complain, but seldom to engage in behaviour that can be appropriately termed 'resistance'. Why? Organised terror played a central role. But the most important mechanism of social integration was Hitler's charismatic leadership. The 'Hitler Myth' secured loyalty to the regime of even those who opposed the Nazi movement itself. Millions of Germans believed the Führer would right all wrongs in Germany if only the abuses could be brought to his attention. Hitler's foreign policy and military successes also convinced ordinary Germans (at least until Stalingrad) that the Führer was a brilliant, infallible statesman and general who was leading Germany to world power.

From *The Hitler Myth* by Ian Kershaw, published in 2001.

FOCUS TASK 8.15

How much opposition was there to the Nazi regime, 1933–39?

As Source 19 makes clear, there was very little opposition to the Nazis between 1933 and 1939. The interesting thing however is to compare these 'peacetime' years with the war years. So this task provides a baseline.

Take these examples from the text and rate them by degree of threat to the Nazi regime. Use a scale of 0–10 (0 means no impact at all on the Nazis; 10 means it would topple the regime).
- Meeting secretly
- Sabotaging factories or railways
- Distributing anti-Nazi leaflets
- Not listening to Nazi radio broadcast
- Not giving the Heil Hitler salute
- Hanging your own flags in church instead of Nazi flags
- Helping Jewish people escape from Germany
- Grumbling about the Nazis
- Telling jokes about Hitler

Opposition to Nazi rule, 1933–39

The Nazis achieved a remarkable level of control over ordinary Germans. Through their mix of ruthless violence and constant propaganda they forced people to do what they wanted. Not all Germans became Nazis, but most kept their fears or opposition to themselves because they felt powerless or unwilling to risk their lives by saying or doing unacceptable things. Even the persecution of minorities, which nowadays seems so horrific, faced little opposition.

However, some Germans did find their own ways to oppose the Nazis.

Political opposition

The Nazis had not killed or imprisoned all the socialists. Some socialists did still meet secretly, but they had lost their leaders and were divided from each other so their activities were small scale. There were no attempts to challenge or topple the Nazi regime until well into the Second World War. However, in the 1930s there was some sabotage of factories, railways and army stores. The Gestapo claimed to have broken up 1000 opposition meetings in 1936 (probably many more took place). They record having seized 1.6 million anti-Nazi leaflets in 1936 alone. You could conclude from this either that the political opposition were still active (that is a lot of leaflets!) or that it was powerless (what good was a leaflet against the barrage of Nazi propaganda?).

Social opposition

Social opposition means people or groups who tried to keep their own identity or refused to accept and conform to Nazi ideals. This was much more common than political opposition. Historians have identified many examples of this, particularly once the novelty of the Nazis had worn off and the nature of their rule was clearer to ordinary Germans.

There was widespread apathy towards parades and propaganda, particularly after 1936. For example:
- local party officials reported that they increasingly had to bully people to attend Nazi rallies
- the Nazis had to use 'radio wardens' to force people to listen to Hitler's speeches.

The Gestapo reported a lot of complaining in bars, trains and other public places. They reported that some people refused to give the Heil Hitler salute, others told jokes about Hitler and the Nazis or refused to contribute to party funds.

Some national Church leaders publicly criticised the Nazis. At the local level some resisted, for example Joseph Fath was reported for hanging his own flags in his church instead of Nazi flags, and Pastor Grueber risked his life protecting Jewish people and helping them to escape the Nazis.

We have little idea of how typical these examples are because Nazi opponents left little evidence – they tried to cover their tracks – so even this information comes via the Nazis' own records, which obviously have to be handled carefully. However, the picture that emerges is that non-co-operation was quite common and private grumbling about the Nazis was probably very widespread. Indeed, one Gestapo report commented disapprovingly that grumbling had become a national pastime. While the Nazis may have silenced opposition they had not won the 'hearts and minds' of the German people. In the next section (9D) you will examine this in more detail.

FOCUS TASK 8.16

Review: How effectively did the Nazis control Germany, 1933–39?

The table below lists various groups in Germany who the Nazis tried to control. Look back over pages 258–62 and gather examples of how they did this. Write that in column 2. In column 3 give the Nazis a score out of 5 for effectiveness (5 would be total control). In column 4 explain your score using evidence.

Group	Examples of methods used to control	Your judgement on effectiveness of control	Evidence to support your judgement
Political opponents			
Churches	Collaborating, e.g. Concordat with Catholic Church	Effective	Made important concessions to Catholic Church; relatively little conflict between Nazis and Catholic Church
Jewish people			

You can add three further rows to this table for young people, women and workers as you study Chapter 8D.

Key Question Summary

How effectively did the Nazis control Germany, 1933–39?

1. The Nazis had a powerful range of organisations to control Germany: the SS, the Gestapo, the police and the courts, and concentration camps.
2. There was little opposition because of the terror they inspired, economic progress and success in foreign affairs, overturning the Treaty of Versailles and making Germany a strong military power.
3. The Nazis built a highly successful propaganda machine and used mass media to control what people knew.
4. They sought to control culture, banning books which contained ideas they did not like. Paintings, plays and films had to put across a pro-Nazi message and show idealised images of the Aryan family.
5. The Nazis persecuted many groups that did not fit with their notions of racial purity, such as disabled people, gay and lesbian people and Roma.
6. They particularly persecuted the Jewish people, depriving them of their jobs, businesses and homes and forcing them into ghettos.

SECTION 2 DEPTH STUDIES

FOCUS

You have seen how Hitler and the Nazis tried to control Germany. You have also seen how they persecuted groups they saw as 'outsiders'. In this section you will examine the effect of Nazi rule on the majority of Germans. Hitler wanted to create a *Volksgemeinschaft* – a NATIONAL COMMUNITY of Germans. This meant young people, women, workers, farmers, businesspeople. But did this vision become a reality? In this section you will examine the experiences of these different groups.

Focus Points

- How did young people react to the Nazi regime?
- How successful were Nazi policies towards women and the family?
- Did most people in Germany benefit from Nazi rule?
- How did the coming of war change life in Nazi Germany?

8D What was it like to live in Nazi Germany?

Young people in Nazi Germany

The Nazis reorganised every aspect of life to win children's loyalty and to shape their ideas.

At school

If you had been a sixteen-year-old Aryan living in Nazi Germany you would probably have been a strong supporter of Adolf Hitler. At school your teacher would probably be an approved teacher who had been on a training course run by the National Socialist Teachers Alliance. At school you would learn about the history of Germany. You would be outraged to find out how the German army was 'stabbed in the back' by the weak politicians who had made peace. You might well remember the hardships of the 1920s for yourself, but at school you would be told how these were caused by Jewish people squeezing profits out of honest Germans. By the time you were a senior pupil, your studies in history would make you confident that loyalty to the Führer was right and good. Your biology lessons would inform you that you are special as a member of the Aryan race that is superior in intelligence and strength to the *Untermenschen* or 'sub-human' Jewish people and Slavs of eastern Europe. In maths you would be set questions like the one in Source 2. You would not be expecting to go to university. Between 1933 and 1938 the number of university places fell from 128,000 to just 58,000.

SOURCE 1

It is my great educative work I am beginning with the young. We older ones are used up ... We are bearing the burden of a humiliating past ... But my magnificent youngsters! Are there finer ones in the world? Look at these young men and boys! What material! With them I can make a new world.

Hitler, speaking in 1939.

SOURCE 2

The Jews are aliens in Germany. In 1933 there were 66,060,000 inhabitants of the German Reich of whom 499,862 were Jews. What is the percentage of aliens in Germany?

A question from a Nazi maths textbook, 1933.

SOURCE 3

All subjects – German language, History, Geography, Chemistry and Mathematics – must concentrate on military subjects, the glorification of military service and of German heroes and leaders and the strength of a rebuilt Germany. Chemistry will develop a knowledge of chemical warfare, explosives, etc, while Mathematics will help the young to understand artillery, calculations, ballistics.

A German newspaper, heavily controlled by the Nazis, approves of the curriculum in 1939.

SOURCE 4

8.00	German (every day)
8.50	Geography, History or Singing (alternate days)
9.40	Race Studies and Ideology (every day)
10.25	Recess, Sports and Special Announcements (every day)
11.00	Domestic Science or Maths (alternate days)
12.10	Eugenics or Health Biology (alternate days)
1.00–6.00	Sport
Evenings	Sex education, Ideology or Domestic Science (one evening each)

The daily timetable for a girls' school in Nazi Germany

Think!

1. Do you think the real aim of the question in Source 2 is to improve mathematical skills?
2. Read Source 4. Eugenics is the study of how to produce perfect offspring by choosing parents with ideal qualities. How would this help the Nazis?

SOURCE 5

It was a great feeling. You felt you belonged to a great nation again. Germany was in safe hands and I was going to help to build a strong Germany. But my father of course felt differently about it. [He warned] 'Now Henrik, don't say to them what I am saying to you.' I always argued with my father as I was very much in favour of the Hitler regime which was against his background as a working man.

Henrik Metelmann describes what it was like being a member of the Hitler Youth in the 1930s.

New schools for future German leaders

The Nazis set up three new types of selective school to recruit future Nazi Party officials and leaders:
- National Political Institutes of Education or 'Napolas' – 35 of these were set up by the SS and the German army to train future officers. About 6,000 children attended these.
- Adolf Hitler Schools – twelve of these were set up and run by the Hitler Youth and the SS to find future SS leaders. Children were indoctrinated with Nazis ideas rather than taught academic subjects.
- The Reichsschule Feldafing was a single school created and funded by the Nazi Party leaders to prepare the very best students for the highest Nazi positions.

In the Hitler Youth

Outside school your indoctrination continued. If you were a boy you would probably have been in the German Young People (*Deutsches Jungvolk*) from the age of ten to fourteen. Girls had similar organisations called the League of German Girls. Then you would have moved on to the Hitler Youth (for boys) or the LEAGUE OF GERMAN MAIDENS (for girls). You would have marched in exciting parades with loud bands. You would probably be physically fit. Your leisure time would also be devoted to Hitler and the Nazis. You would be a strong cross-country runner, and confident at reading maps. After years of summer camps, you would be comfortable camping out of doors and if you were a boy you would know how to clean a rifle and keep it in good condition. If you were a girl you would be taught sewing, cooking and other domestic tasks. You would also be taught about race and how to be a good German mother.

You would be attracted to the Nazi youth movements by the leisure opportunities they offered. There were really no alternatives. All other youth organisations had been absorbed or made illegal. By 1936 the Hitler Youth had around 6 million members. However, if you did not join this would have been looked on with surprise and suspicion. When it was time to apply for an apprenticeship or a job one of the first things an employer will ask will be whether you had been in the Hitler Youth.

SOURCE 6

Hitler looked over the stand, and I know he looked into my eyes, and he said: 'You my boys are the standard bearers, you will inherit what we have created.' From that moment there was not any doubt I was bound to Adolf Hitler until long after our defeat. Afterwards I told my friends how Hitler had looked into my eyes, but they all said: 'No! It was my eyes he was looking into.'

A young German describes his feelings after a Hitler Youth rally.

SOURCE 7

Members of the Hitler Youth in the 1930s. From a very early age children were encouraged to join the Nazi youth organisations. It was not compulsory, but most young people did join.

SOURCE 8

Children have been deliberately taken away from parents who refused to acknowledge their belief in National Socialism ... The refusal of parents to allow their young children to join the youth organisation is regarded as an adequate reason for taking the children away.

A German teacher writing in 1938.

SOURCE 9

Early one morning, a neighbour of ours, a trade-union secretary, was taken away in a car by the SS and police. His wife had great difficulty finding out what had happened to him. My mother was too scared to be seen talking to her and Father became very quiet and alarmed and begged me not to repeat what he had said within our four walls about the whole Nazi set-up ...

I loved it when we went on our frequent marches, feeling important when the police had to stop the traffic to give us right of way and passing pedestrians had to raise their arm in the Nazi salute. Whenever we were led out on a march, it was always into the working-class quarters. We were told that this was to remind the workers, but I sometimes wondered what we wanted to remind them of, after all most of our fathers were workers.

From *Through Hell for Hitler*, the memoirs of Henrik Metelmann, published in 1970. Metelmann came from a working-class family.

Think!
1. Make a list of the main differences between your life and the life of a sixteen-year-old in Nazi Germany.
2. Totalitarian regimes throughout history have used children as a way of influencing parents. Why do you think they do this?
3. Read Source 5. Why do you think Henrik's father asks Henrik not to repeat what he says to him?

At home

As a child in Nazi Germany, you might well feel slightly alienated (estranged) from your parents because they are not as keen on the Nazis as you are. They expect your first loyalty to be to your family, whereas your Hitler Youth leader makes it clear that your first loyalty is to Adolf Hitler. You find it hard to understand why your father grumbles about Nazi regulation of his working practices – surely the Führer (Hitler) is protecting him? Your parents find the idea of Nazi inspectors checking up on the teachers rather strange. For you it is normal.

SOURCE 10

Illustration from a Nazi children's book. The children are being taught to distrust Jewish people

The whole story?

The previous three text panels probably gave you the impression that the Nazis really did control the hearts and minds of young people. However, this might not be the whole story. We know from interviews with Hitler Youth members after the war that while many of them enjoyed the activities they tended to switch off when lectured about Nazi ideas. We have reports from anti-Nazi spies that by 1938 many Hitler Youth members saw the organisation as boring, although we have to take care with evidence like this. We also know that despite all the lectures on health, diseases like diphtheria and scarlet fever increased in the 1930s. However, even when the Nazis made all other youth organisations except the Hitler Youth illegal in 1936, and made membership of the Hitler Youth compulsory in 1939, there were still over a million children who never joined! We also know that juvenile crime rose during the 1930s and 175,000 young people were convicted of crimes in 1939 alone. Juvenile crime increased dramatically once war began, and so did youth resistance. Find out more about this on page 276.

SOURCE 11

We didn't know much about Nazi ideals. Nevertheless, we were politically programmed: to obey orders, to cultivate the soldierly virtue of standing to attention and saying 'Yes, Sir' and to stop thinking when the word Fatherland was uttered and Germany's honour and greatness were mentioned.

A former member of the Hitler Youth looks back after the war.

Revision Tip

- Make sure you can describe:
  - at least one way the Nazis tried to control young people
  - at least two ways the Nazis tried to win over young people.
- Record two points which show that Nazi youth policies succeeded and two points which show they failed.

Source Analysis

What does Source 12 reveal about the Nazis' view of women?

Factfile

The Three Ks

Women in Nazi Germany were expected to contribute towards creating a racially pure community, or *Volksgemeinschaft*. Nazi policy and propaganda (see Source 12) idealised the racially pure Aryan woman and her family. In schools and Hitler Youth organisations girls were taught the three Ks – *Kinder*, *Küche*, *Kirche* (Children, Kitchen, Church).

The National Socialist Women's League, or Nazi Women's League, was set up to promote the three Ks and encourage women to leave the workplace and become mothers. Marriage loans of 1000 marks were offered to newlyweds if the woman left her workplace. Other incentives and restrictions were established by the Nazis:

- women were barred from government professions, such as the army and the civil service
- women were awarded the Mother's Cross for having four, six or eight healthy Aryan children
- women were encouraged not to smoke, drink or wear make-up
- women were expected to be tall, fit and naturally beautiful to ensure fertility.

FOCUS TASK 8.17

How did young people react to the Nazi regime?

1. In pairs, you are going to write two short diary accounts of life as a young person in Nazi Germany. One person needs to write about their experiences from a positive point of view. The other person needs to write about the negative experiences they have had as a young person under Nazi rule.
2. Use pages 264–67 to write three paragraphs to explain why the Nazis were successful in winning young people over. Include the following points:
   - why the Nazis wanted to control young people
   - how they set about doing it
   - what the attractions of the youth movements were.
3. The Nazi regime was not successful in keeping the loyalty of all young people. Add a fourth paragraph to your essay to explain why some young people rejected the Nazi youth movements.

Women in Nazi Germany

SOURCE 12

A painting showing the Nazis' view of an ideal German family.

Young girls and women were expected to be fit and healthy in line with Nazi racial theory. They were expected to marry Aryan men and raise large families for the fatherland. The Nazis used the SA to humiliate German women who married Jewish or non-Aryan men (see Source 13) and in 1935 the Nuremberg Laws made it illegal for Aryans and non-Aryans to marry.

Nazi attitudes to women

Hitler and most Nazis had a very traditional view of the role of the German woman as wife and mother. Many German men and *women* agreed. In the traditional rural areas and small towns, many women felt that the proper role of a woman was to support her husband. There was also resentment towards working women in the early 1930s, since they were seen as keeping men out of jobs. It all created a lot of pressure on women to conform to traditional roles.

There were some prominent women in Nazi Germany. Leni Riefenstahl was a high-profile film producer. Gertrude Scholz-Klink was head of the Nazi Women's Bureau, although she was excluded from any important discussions (such as the one to conscript female labour in 1942). Many working-class girls and women gained the opportunity to travel and meet new people through the Nazi women's organisation. Overall, however, opportunities for women were limited. Married professional women were forced to give up their jobs and discrimination against women applicants for jobs was encouraged.

SOURCE 13

A German woman and her Jewish boyfriend being publicly humiliated by the SA in 1933. The notices say: (woman) 'I'm the biggest pig in town and only get involved with Jews'; (man) 'As a Jewish boy I always take only German girls up to my room'.

Rewards for mothers

The Nazis offered tempting financial incentives for married couples to have at least four children. Mothers got a 'Gold Cross' for having eight children. Posters, radio broadcasts and newsreels all celebrated the ideas of motherhood and homebuilding. The German Maidens' League reinforced these ideas, focusing on a combination of good physical health and housekeeping skills. This was reinforced at school. With all these encouragements the birth rate did increase from fifteen per thousand in 1933 to twenty per thousand in 1939. There was also an increase in pregnancies outside marriage. These girls were looked after in state maternity hostels.

> **Factfile**
>
> **Lebensborn**
>
> This SS-run organisation encouraged unmarried women to bear children for the Führer by getting impregnated by SS men in state-run brothels. The children were then adopted by Aryan families. About 8,000 *Lebensborn* children were born in Germany in this way. During the war, the organisation also started to kidnap children with Aryan features from occupied Europe. It is believed that around 100,000 children from Poland were kidnapped.

> **Revision Tip**
> - You need to be able to describe at least two aspects of Nazi policy towards women.
> - Make sure you can explain why the Nazis wanted women out of the workplace.
> - Find two points you could use as evidence in an essay to argue that Nazi policies on women were successful.

The impact of war

By 1937, industry was beginning to run out of male workers due to conscription and the increasing demands of the rearmament programme. The Nazis therefore did a U-turn on their original policies on women. They abolished the marriage loan. They made it compulsory for many women to undertake a 'duty year' where they would work for a year on farms or in industry. The number of women in work increased, but not by as much as the Nazis needed and far less than had worked in Weimar Germany.

Women were also still expected to have children. It was a very confusing set of policies! When war broke out in 1939, women were even allowed to join the German armed forces as auxiliaries such as nurses, secretaries and even camp guards. By the end of the war, nearly half a million women had served in the armed forces. Almost 4,000 women worked in the Nazi camp system, including the extermination camps.

SOURCE 14

I went to Sauckel [the Nazi minister in charge of labour] with the proposition that we should recruit our labour from the ranks of German women. He replied brusquely that where to obtain which workers was his business. Moreover, he said, as Gauleiter [a regional governor] he was Hitler's subordinate and responsible to the Führer alone ... Sauckel offered to put the question to Goering as Commissioner of the Four-Year Plan ... but I was scarcely allowed to advance my arguments. Sauckel and Goering continually interrupted me. Sauckel laid great weight on the danger that factory work might inflict moral harm on German womanhood; not only might their 'psychic and emotional life' be affected but also their ability to bear children.

Goering totally concurred. But just to be absolutely sure, Sauckel went immediately to Hitler and had him confirm the decision. All my good arguments were therefore blown to the winds.

Albert Speer, *Inside The Third Reich*, 1970. Speer was minister of armaments and war production.

> **FOCUS TASK 8.18**
>
> **How successful were Nazi policies towards women and the family?**
>
> Read these two statements:
>
> *Nazi policy for women was a success.*
>
> *Nazi policy for women was a failure.*
>
> For each statement explain whether you agree or disagree with it and use examples from the text to support your explanation.

Women who resisted Nazi rule

Many women in Nazi Germany silently opposed the regime and its policies towards them and their families, especially after they had enjoyed the same freedoms as men in the Weimar period. It has been estimated that women represented nearly 15 per cent of the various resistance movements that existed in Nazi Germany.

Communist student Liselotte Herrmann opposed the appointment of Hitler as Chancellor and informed foreign governments about Nazi rearmament plans. She was later arrested and executed in 1938 – the first mother to face the death penalty in the Nazi regime.

Twenty women from Dusseldorf passed information to foreign governments about the concentration camps where their family members had been sent.

Libertas Schulze-Boysen and Mildred Harnack-Fish were both members of the Kreisau Circle. They were both arrested and executed.

Maria Terwiel helped spread the sermons of Bishop Galen about the Nazi euthanasia programme and helped any Jews flee abroad.

Workers, farmers and businesses in Nazi Germany

Economic recovery and rearmament

The Nazi election campaigns had promised to solve the unemployment problem in Germany caused by the Depression. In 1933, there were still nearly six million Germans out of work. By 1939 this number was below half a million. Nazi leaders declared it an 'economic miracle' thanks to Hitler's leadership. But is this the whole story?

YES, it was a miracle!

The Nazis tackled the economic problems with energy and commitment. The biggest issue was unemployment. Hitler appointed the economist, **Dr Hjalmar Schacht**, as his economics minister and President of the Reichsbank. Schacht created a 'New Plan' which included:

- Huge **public works projects** rebuilding German cities and extending the motorways, or AUTOBAHNS, and railways, funded by government investment.
- A compulsory National Labour Service (RAD) for young men (18–25) to work on these public works projects for six months.
- Major house-building programmes and grandiose new public building projects, such as the Reich Chancellery in Berlin.
- The reintroduction of **conscription** into the army, in 1935. More jobs became available when Hitler announced that Germany would have a world-class air force (the Luftwaffe). This reduced unemployment and created work in related industries, such as weapons, uniforms and engineering.

In 1936, Hitler demanded a more rapid **rearmament** programme to prepare Germany for war. **Goering** was named head of the **Four Year Plan** and became a virtual economic dictator. His aim was to create a war economy and make Germany self-sufficient (autarky). Goering increased the production of raw materials, such as iron ore, oil and explosives, for rearmament. He persuaded industries to switch from making consumer goods to making synthetic materials like rubber. He tightened controls on prices and wages and used forced labour. He used billions of marks of government money to fund this and handed out lucrative contracts to industrialists who supported the rearmament programme.

The German economy did grow and unemployment fell. Industrial production doubled between 1933 and 1939. The number of Germans out of work halved in the first two years of Nazi rule. Government investment rose from about four billion marks in 1933 to over 20 billion marks by 1938.

NO, there was no miracle!

The Nazis were lucky that the worst effects of the Depression had passed by the time Hitler came to power. World trade was already starting to recover. The unemployment figures look impressive, but the Nazis achieved this at the expense of many in Germany.

- Jews had been forced from many professions and were replaced by Germans.
- Many Jewish businesses had been confiscated and given to Germans to run.
- Conscription rapidly caused unemployment to decrease by making military service compulsory.
- Women were encouraged to leave their jobs for men.

Furthermore, real wages were by 1938 only at the same level as they had been in 1929 before the Depression. Many workers were made to work

---

Think!

As you read through pages 270–73, you will come across a number of individuals, organisations and terms in bold type in the text, **like this**. You could add more of your own if you wish. Draw up a table containing definitions of the words, or explanations of their importance to the Nazi's economic policies. The completed table will help you with your revision. You could organise your table like this:

Key word/term/person	Definition/explanation

longer hours for the same money. People had less access to consumer goods as Hitler moved towards a war economy. Finally, the German economy was near bankruptcy. Total government debt had quadrupled between 1933 and 1939 of which nearly 60 per cent had been spent on rearmament!

The Nazis and the workers

Hitler promised (and delivered) lower unemployment which helped to ensure popularity among **industrial workers**. These workers were important to the Nazis: Hitler needed good workers to create the industries that would help to make Germany great. The Nazis never really won the hearts of the workers but they did provide a range of benefits which kept most workers reasonably happy.

- Schemes such as STRENGTH THROUGH JOY **(KDF)** gave them cheap theatre and cinema tickets, organised courses, trips and sports events.
- Many thousands of workers saved five marks a week in the state scheme to buy the **Volkswagen Beetle**, the 'people's car'. It became a symbol of the prosperous new Germany, even though no workers ever received a car because all car production was halted by the war in 1939.
- Another important scheme was the BEAUTY OF LABOUR movement. This improved working conditions in factories. It introduced features not seen in many workplaces before, such as washing facilities and low-cost canteens.

SOURCE 16

Previously unemployed men assemble for the building of the first autobahn, September 1933.

What was the price of these advances? Workers lost their main political party, the SDP. They lost their trade unions and for many workers this remained a source of bitter resentment. All workers had to join the **DAF (General Labour Front)** run by **Dr Robert Ley**. This organisation kept strict control of workers. They could not strike for better pay and conditions. In some areas, they were prevented from moving to better-paid jobs. Wages remained comparatively low, although prices were also strictly controlled. Even so, by the late 1930s, many workers were grumbling that their standard of living was still lower than it had been before the Depression (see Figure 15).

FIGURE 15

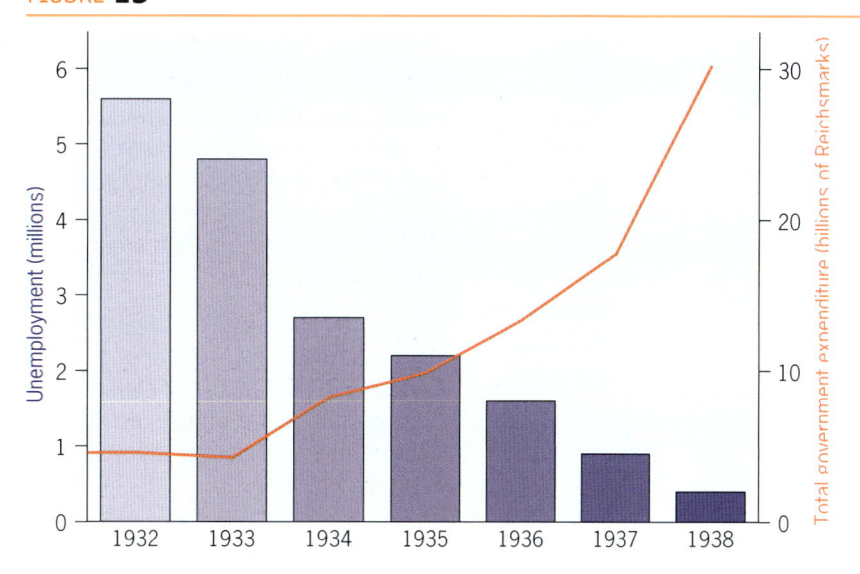

Unemployment and government expenditure in Germany, 1932–38.

The Nazis and the farming communities

The **farmers** had been an important factor in the Nazis' rise to power. Hitler introduced a series of measures to help them. In September 1933 he introduced the **Reich Food Estate** under **Richard Darré**. This set up central boards to buy agricultural produce from the farmers and distribute it to markets across Germany. It gave the peasant farmers a guaranteed market for their goods at guaranteed prices. The second main measure was the **Reich Entailed Farm Law**: banks could not seize their land if they could not pay loans or mortgages. This ensured that peasants' farms stayed in their hands.

The Reich Entailed Farm Law also had a racial aim. Part of the Nazi philosophy was **'Blood and Soil'**, the belief that the peasant farmers were the basis of Germany's master race. They would be the backbone of the new German empire in the east. As a result, their way of life had to be protected. As Source 18 shows, the measures were widely appreciated.

However, some peasants were not thrilled with the regime's measures. More efficient, go-ahead farmers were held back by having to work through the same processes as less efficient farmers. The Reich Entailed Farm Law stated that only the eldest child inherited the farm. As a result, many children of farmers left the land to work for better pay in Germany's industries. **Rural depopulation** ran at about 3 per cent per year in the 1930s – the exact opposite of the Nazis' aims!

FIGURE 17

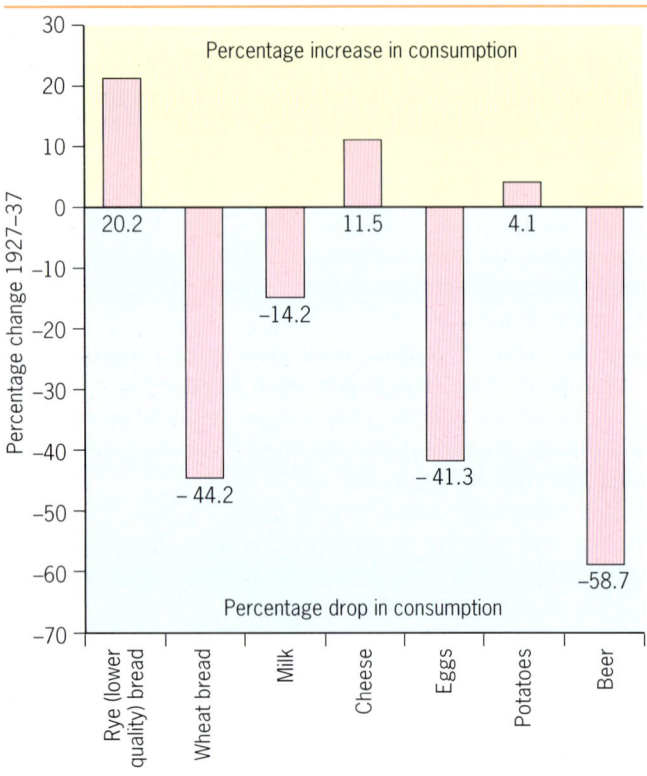

Annual food consumption in working-class families, 1927–37 (% change).

Percentage change 1927–37:
- Rye (lower quality) bread: 20.2
- Wheat bread: −44.2
- Milk: −14.2
- Cheese: 11.5
- Eggs: −41.3
- Potatoes: 4.1
- Beer: −58.7

SOURCE 18

Thousands of people came from all over Germany to the Harvest Festival celebrations ... We all felt the same happiness and joy. Harvest festival was the thank you for us farmers having a future again. I believe no statesman has ever been as well loved as Adolf Hitler was at that time.

Lusse Essig's memories of the 1930s. Lusse was a farm worker who later worked for the Agriculture Ministry.

Big business and the middle classes

The record of the Nazis with the **middle classes** was also mixed. Certainly many middle-class business people were grateful to the Nazis for eliminating the Communist threat to their businesses and properties. They also liked the way in which the Nazis seemed to be bringing order to Germany. For the owners of small businesses it was a mixed picture. If you owned a small engineering firm, you were likely to do well from government orders as rearmament spending grew in the 1930s. However, if you produced consumer goods or ran a small shop, you might well struggle. Despite Hitler's promises, the large department stores which were taking business away from local shops were not closed.

It was **big business** that really benefited from Nazi rule. The big companies no longer had to worry about troublesome trade unions and strikes. Companies such as the chemicals giant IG Farben gained huge government contracts to make explosives, fertilisers and even artificial oil from coal. Other household names today, such as Mercedes and Volkswagen, prospered from Nazi policies.

Revision Tip

Look back at pages 270–73. There is a lot here and it might help you to get right down to basics, so make sure you can describe:
- two ways in which the Nazis helped tackle the problem of unemployment
- two ways the Nazis tried to improve life for workers
- one way the Nazis tried to improve life for farmers
- one reason each why the middle classes and big business might have approved of the Nazis.

FOCUS TASK 8.19

Did most people in Germany benefit from Nazi rule?

Here are some claims that the Nazi propaganda machine made about how life in Germany had been changed for the better during the 1930s:
- 'Germans now have economic security.'
- 'Germans no longer need to feel inferior to other states. They can be proud of their country.'
- 'The Nazi state looks after its workers very well indeed.'
- 'The Nazis have ensured that Germany is racially pure.'
- 'The Nazis are on the side of the farmers and have rescued Germany's farmers from disaster.'
- 'The Nazis have made Germany safe from communism.'

You are now going to decide how truthful these claims actually are.
1 Look back over pages 264–73. Gather evidence that supports or opposes each claim. You could work in groups, taking one claim each.
2 For each claim, decide whether, overall, it is totally untrue; a little bit true; mostly true; or totally true.
3 Discuss:
   a) Which of the groups you have studied do you think benefited most from Nazi rule?
   b) Who did not benefit from Nazi rule, and why not?

'National community': Volksgemeinschaft

We have divided this section by social group, but the Nazis would not want Germans to see their society that way. Hitler wanted all Germans (or more exactly all 'racially pure' Germans) to think of themselves as part of a **national community**, or *Volksgemeinschaft*. Under Nazi rule, workers, farmers and so on would no longer see themselves primarily as workers or farmers; they would see themselves as Germans. Their first loyalty would not be to their own social group but to Germany and the Führer. They would be so proud to belong to a great nation that was racially and culturally superior to other nations that they would put the interests of Germany before their own. Hitler's policies towards each group were designed to help win this kind of loyalty to the Nazi state.

The evidence suggests that the Nazis never quite succeeded in this: Germans in the 1930s certainly did not lose their self-interest, nor did they embrace the national community wholeheartedly. However, the Nazis did not totally fail either! In the 1930s Germans did have a strong sense of national pride and loyalty towards Hitler. For the majority of Germans, the benefits of Nazi rule made them willing – on the surface at least – to accept some central control in the interests of making Germany great again.

FOCUS TASK 8.20

How did the Nazis try to create a national community?

1 On pages 264–73 you have seen how the Nazis tried to win over various groups in German society. Use the table below to record the ways they did this and how far you think they succeeded.

Group	How and why they were important to Nazis	Nazi policies	Evidence the policies succeeded	Evidence of failure or lack of success
Young people				
Women				
Workers				
Farmers				
Businesses				

2 Nazi methods of control have been compared to a 'carrot and stick' approach. You offer carrots (or anything nice to eat!) to get a donkey to work for you but you use the stick to beat them in case they don't. For each of the groups above explain whether you think the stick or the carrot was more important in maintaining Nazi control and persuading each to play their part in the national community.

Factfile

Germany's war economy

- When war broke out it did not bring massive changes to the German economy because Germany had been preparing for it since the mid-1930s.
- In the early stages of the war, Germany was short of raw materials. This was made worse when the British navy blockaded sea routes into Germany.
- As the German forces conquered territories they took raw materials and goods from these territories. For example, Germany took around 20 per cent of Norway's entire production in 1940.
- From 1942 German production was shifted towards armaments to supply the army fighting against Russia.
- Huge corporations like IG Farben produced chemicals, explosives and the infamous gas used in the death camps.
- German factories used forced labour from occupied countries. Most factories had a significant number of prisoners in their workforce and estimates suggest that forced labourers made up around 25 per cent of the workforce.
- By 1944 there had been a vast increase in military production. Production of aircraft and tanks trebled compared to 1942.
- Production was hampered by Allied bombing and some factories were moved underground.
- There is an ongoing debate about the effectiveness of the Nazi war economy. The traditional view is that the economy was mismanaged until 1942 and then improved. However, this account is based on the writings of Albert Speer. Some historians believe he exaggerated his own importance and that the war economy became more efficient after 1942 simply because Germany focused production away from civilian goods and onto military equipment.

The impact of the Second World War on Germany

Through the 1930s, Hitler fulfilled his promises to the German people that he would:
- reverse the Treaty of Versailles
- rebuild Germany's armed forces
- unite Germany and Austria
- extend German territory into eastern Europe.

He fulfilled each of these aims, but started the Second World War in the process.

Germans had no great enthusiasm for war. People still had memories of the First World War. But in war, as in peacetime, the Nazis used all methods available to make the German people support the regime.

Food rationing was introduced soon after war began in September 1939. Clothes rationing followed in November 1939. Even so, from 1939 to 1941 it was not difficult to keep up civilian morale because the war went spectacularly well for Germany. Hitler was in control of much of western and eastern Europe and supplies of luxury goods flowed into Germany from captured territories.

However, in 1941 Hitler took the massive gamble of invading the SOVIET UNION, and for the next three years his troops were engaged in an increasingly expensive war with Russian forces who 'tore the heart out of the German army', as the British war leader, Winston Churchill, put it. As the tide turned against the German armies, civilians found their lives increasingly disrupted. They had to cut back on heating, work longer hours and recycle their rubbish. Goebbels redoubled his censorship efforts. He tried to maintain people's support for the war by involving them in it through asking them to make sacrifices. They donated an estimated 1.5 million fur coats to help to clothe the German army in Russia.

At this stage in the war, the German people began to see and hear less of Hitler. His old speeches were broadcast by Goebbels, but Hitler was increasingly preoccupied with the detail of the war. In 1942 the 'Final Solution' began (see pages 278–79), which was to kill millions of Jewish civilians in German-occupied countries.

From 1942, Albert Speer began to direct Germany's war economy (see Factfile). All effort focused on the armament industries. Postal services were suspended and letter boxes were closed. All places of entertainment were closed, except cinemas – Goebbels needed these to show propaganda films. Women were drafted into the labour force in increasing numbers. Country areas had to take evacuees from the cities and refugees from eastern Europe.

These measures were increasingly carried out by the SS. In fact, the SS became virtually a state within the German state. This SS empire had its own armed forces, armaments industries and labour camps. It developed a business empire that was worth a fortune. However, even the SS could not win the war, or even keep up German morale.

With defeat looming, support for the Nazis weakened. Germans stopped declaring food they had. They stayed away from Nazi rallies. They refused to give the 'Heil Hitler' salute when asked to do so. Himmler even contacted the Allies to ask about possible peace terms.

FOCUS TASK 8.21

How did the coming of war change life in Germany?

1. Draw a timeline from 1939 to 1945 down the middle of a page.
2. On the left, make notes from pages 274–78 on how the war was going for Germany's army.
3. On the right, make notes to show how the war affected Germans at home in Germany.
4. Choose one change from the right-hand column that you think had the greatest impact on ordinary Germans and explain your choice.

The bombing of Dresden

It was the bombing of Germany which had the most dramatic effect on the lives of German civilians. In 1942 the Allies decided on a new policy towards the bombing of Germany. Under Arthur 'Bomber' Harris the British began an all-out assault on both industrial and residential areas of all the major German cities. One of the objectives was to destroy German industry, the other was to lower the morale of civilians and to terrorise them into submission.

The bombing escalated through the next three years, culminating in the bombing of Dresden in February 1945 which killed between 35,000 and 150,000 people in two days. Sources 20–22 tell you more about that bombing.

The end of the war

By 1945 the German people were in a desperate state. Food supplies were dwindling. Already 3.5 million German civilians had died. Refugees were fleeing the advancing Russian armies in the east.

Three months after the massive destruction of Dresden, Germany's war was over. Hitler, Goebbels and other Nazi war leaders committed suicide or were captured. Germany surrendered. It was a shattered country. The Nazi promises lay in tatters and the country was divided up into zones of occupation run by the British, French, US and Soviet forces (see page XX).

SOURCE 19

Goebbels does not always tell you the truth. When he tells you that England is powerless do you believe that? Have you forgotten that our bombers fly over Germany at will? The bombs that fell with these leaflets tell you … The war lasts as long as Hitler's regime.

Translation of a leaflet dropped by the Allies on Berlin.

SOURCE 20

The greatest effect on [civilian] morale will be produced if a new blow of catastrophic force can be struck at a time when the situation already appears desperate.

From a secret report to the British Government, 1944.

Think!
What do Sources 19–22 tell you about:
a) the aims of the bombing
b) the success of the bombing?

Revision Tip
Make sure you can:
- describe three changes which the war caused for Germans
- explain how at least one change affected Germans for the worse.

SOURCE 21

The centre of Dresden after the bombing in February 1945.

FIGURE 22

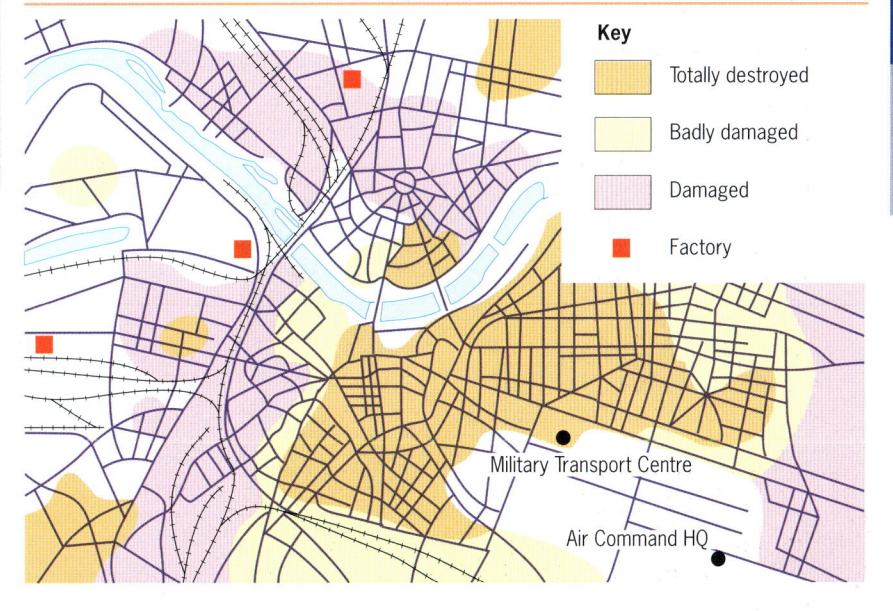

A map showing the destruction of Dresden. Dresden was an industrial city, but the major damage was to civilian areas.

SOURCE 23

The formation of cliques, i.e. groupings of young people outside the Hitler Youth, has been on the increase before and particularly during the war to such a degree that one must speak of a serious risk of political, moral and criminal subversion of our youth.

From a report by the Nazi youth leadership, 1942.

Revision Tip
- The Edelweiss Pirates and Swing movements are important examples of resistance. Make sure you can describe each movement.
- Prepare two points to argue that the Pirates were a more serious threat to the Nazis than the Swing movement.

How did war affect young people?

In 1939 membership of a Nazi youth movement was made compulsory. But by this time many of the experienced leaders had been drafted into the German army. Many of the movements were now run by older teenagers who rigidly enforced Nazi rules. They even forbade other teenagers from meeting informally with their friends.

As the war progressed, the activities of the youth movements focused increasingly on the war effort and military drill. The popularity of the movements decreased and indeed an anti-Hitler Youth movement appeared. The Nazis identified two distinct groups of young people who they were worried about: the Swing movement and the EDELWEISS PIRATES.

The 'Swing' movement

This was made up mainly of middle-class teenagers. They went to parties where they listened to English and American music and sang English songs. They danced American dances such as the 'jitterbug' to banned jazz music. They accepted Jewish people at their clubs. They talked about and enjoyed sex. They were deliberately 'slovenly'. The Nazis issued a handbook helping the authorities to identify these degenerate types.

The Edelweiss Pirates

The Edelweiss Pirates were working-class teenagers. They were not an organised movement, and groups in various cities took different names: 'The Roving Dudes' (Essen); the 'Kittelbach Pirates' (Düsseldorf); the 'Navajos' (Cologne). The Nazis, however, classified all the groups under the single name 'Edelweiss Pirates' and the groups did have a lot in common.

The Pirates were mainly aged between fourteen and seventeen (Germans could leave school at fourteen, but they did not have to sign on for military service until they were seventeen). They sang songs, just like the Hitler Youth, but changed the lyrics to mock Germany, and when they spotted bands of Hitler Youth they taunted and sometimes attacked them.

The Pirates' activities caused serious worries to the Nazi authorities in some cities. In December 1942 the Gestapo broke up 28 groups containing 739 adolescents. The Nazi approach to the Pirates was different from their approach to other minorities. As long as they needed future workers and future soldiers they could not simply exterminate all these teenagers or put them in concentration camps (although Himmler did suggest that). They therefore responded uncertainly – sometimes arresting the Pirates, sometimes ignoring them.

In 1944 in Cologne, Pirate activities escalated. They helped to shelter army deserters and escaped prisoners. They stole armaments and took part in an attack on the Gestapo during which its chief was killed. The Nazi response was to round up the so called 'ringleaders'. Thirteen were publicly hanged in November 1944.

Neither of the groups described above had strong political views. They were not political opponents of the Nazis. But they resented and resisted Nazi control of their lives.

SOURCE 24

An Edelweiss Pirates youth group in an undated photograph.

How did war affect Jewish people and other persecuted groups?

You have already seen how the Nazis persecuted Jewish people and other minority groups in Germany in the 1930s. Once the war began, this persecution reached new depths of brutality. At the same time, it became more carefully organised.

SOURCE 25

A photograph, probably taken by German army photographers, of Jewish people arriving at the Warsaw ghetto in 1940.

Polish ghettos

After invading Poland in 1939, the Nazis set about 'Germanising' western Poland. This meant transporting Poles from their homes and replacing them with German settlers. Around one in five Poles died, either in the fighting or as a result of racial policies in the period 1939–45. Polish Jewish people were rounded up and transported to the big cities. Here they were herded into sealed areas, called ghettos. Able-bodied Jews were used for slave labour but the young, the old and the sick were left to die of hunger and disease.

SOURCE 26

I saw much suffering. The ghetto was very overcrowded. There was a typhoid epidemic. Many buildings, including where I lived with my grandfather, were under quarantine.

During the winter I was very cold; to keep warm I stayed in bed covered by whatever I could find. I was continuously hungry. I was dreaming of the white Kaiser rolls that I had for breakfast before the war in Katowice. In the ghetto, young starving children were begging for food, dead bodies were lying in the streets.

I had relatives who lived across from the notorious Pawiak prison, run by the Gestapo, where executions took place daily. On one visit to their house, crossing a checkpoint manned by police, I was beaten up by a policeman for no reason at all, but simply because I was there.

In the early summer of 1942, my mother decided that for my survival it was necessary for me to be smuggled out of the ghetto. It was just in time, because the transport of Warsaw Jews to the death camp of Treblinka started a few months later.

Ed Herman's memories of the Warsaw ghetto, published on a website in 2013. Herman was nine years old in 1940.

Mass murder

In 1941, Germany invaded the USSR. Within weeks the Nazis found themselves in control of 3 million Soviet Jews (in addition to the Jewish people in all the other countries they had conquered). German forces had orders to round up and shoot Communist Party activists and their Jewish supporters. The executions were carried out by special SS units called *Einsatzgruppen*. By the autumn of 1941, mass shootings were taking place all over occupied eastern Europe. In Germany, all Jewish people were ordered to wear the star of David on their clothing to mark them out.

SOURCE 27

Wedding rings taken from people killed at Buchenwald concentration camp.

The 'Final Solution'

In January 1942, a group of senior Nazis met at Wannsee, a suburb of Berlin, to discuss what they called the 'Final Solution' to the 'Jewish Question'. There, Himmler, head of the SS and Gestapo, was put in charge of the systematic killing of all Jewish people within Germany and German-occupied territory. Slave labour and death camps were built at Auschwitz, Treblinka and Chelmno in Poland, among other places. The old, the sick and young children were killed immediately. The rest were sent to work at the labour camps. Some were used for medical experiments. Six million Jewish people, 500,000 European Roma and countless political prisoners, Jehovah's Witnesses, gay and lesbian people and Russian and Polish prisoners of war were sent to these camps, where they were worked to death, gassed or shot.

SOURCE 28

A child's drawing of prisoners arriving at the Auschwitz death camp.

Think!

1. There are many websites, TV programmes and books about the mass murders during the war. Some of these contain shocking images of dead bodies, gas chambers, cremation ovens and other horrors. We have chosen Sources 27 and 28 instead. Why do you think we did this?
2. The systematic killing of the Jewish people by the Nazis is generally known today as the Holocaust, which means 'sacrifice'. Many people prefer the Jewish term *Sho'ah*, which means 'destruction'. Why do you think this is?

Who resisted?

Many Jewish people escaped from Germany before the killing started. Other Jewish people managed to live under cover in Germany and the occupied territories. Some joined resistance groups. Gad Beck, for example, led the Jewish resistance to the Nazis in Berlin. He was finally captured in April 1945. On the day he was due to be executed, he was rescued by troops from the Jewish regiment of the Soviet army. There were 28 known groups of Jewish fighters, and there may have been more. Many Jewish people fought in the resistance movements in the Nazi-occupied lands. In 1945, the Jewish people in the Warsaw ghetto in Poland rose up against the Nazis and held out against them for four weeks. There were armed uprisings in five concentration camps, and Greek Jews managed to blow up the gas ovens at Auschwitz.

We also know that many Germans and others helped Jewish people by hiding them and smuggling them out of German-held territory. The industrialist Oskar Schindler protected and saved many people by getting them on to his 'list' of workers. The Swedish diplomat Raoul Wallenberg worked with other resisters to provide Jewish people with Swedish and US passports to get them out of the reach of the Nazis in Hungary. He disappeared in mysterious circumstances in 1945. Of course, high-profile individuals such as these were rare. Most of the successful resisters were successful because they kept an extremely low profile and were discovered neither by the Nazis at the time, nor by historians since then.

Revision Tip

- Make sure you can describe the ghettos and the Final Solution.
- Identify three examples that show how Nazi actions against Jewish people and other groups became more violent as the war went on.

Who was responsible?

Was the 'Final Solution' planned from the start?

Historians have long debated how far Hitler had planned this 'Final Solution'. Some historians (intentionalists) believe that the whole process had been carefully planned, for years. Others (structuralists) argue that there was no clear plan and that the policy of mass murder evolved during the war years. Lack of evidence makes it difficult to know for sure. Hitler had made speeches in which he talked of the annihilation of Jewish people, but there are no documents with his signature and no record of him ever giving any orders directly relating to the extermination of Jewish people. The Nazis kept the programme as secret as they could, so there are relatively few documents.

Responsibility

Although historians disagree about whether Hitler planned this, they do generally agree that Hitler was ultimately responsible. However, other individuals and organisations shared responsibility. The genocide would not have been possible without:

- **the Civil Service bureaucracy** who collected, stored and supplied information about Jewish people
- **police forces in Germany and the occupied territories:** many victims of the Nazis were actually seized by the police rather than the Gestapo or SS
- **the SS:** Adolf Eichmann devised a system of transporting Jewish people to collection points and then on to the death camps. He was also in charge of looting the possessions of Jewish people. The SS Death's Head battalions and Einsatzgruppen also carried out many of the killings
- **the Wehrmacht (the German armed forces):** army leaders were fully aware of what was going on
- **industry:** companies such as Volkswagen and Mercedes had their own slave labour camps. The chemical giant IG Farben competed with other companies for the contract to make the Cyclon B gas that was used in the gas chambers
- **the German people:** antisemitism was widespread. They may not have wanted mass murder but they turned a blind eye to it. Many German civilians went further and took part in some aspect of the HOLOCAUST, but ignored the full reality (see Source 29).

SOURCE 29

The extermination of the Jews is the most dreadful chapter in German history, doubly so because the men who did it closed their senses to the reality of what they were doing by taking pride in the technical efficiency of their actions and, at moments when their conscience threatened to break in, telling themselves that they were doing their duty … Others took refuge in the enormity of the operation, which lent it a convenient depersonalisation. When they ordered a hundred Jews to get on a train in Paris or Amsterdam, they considered their job accomplished and carefully closed their minds to the thought that eventually those passengers would arrive in front of the ovens of Treblinka.

US historian Gordon Craig, writing in 1978.

Think!

The war clearly increased persecution of Jewish people and other minorities:
1. War massively increased the numbers of Jewish people and other groups who came under Nazi control.
2. War allowed leading Nazis to pursue their racial policies even more fiercely than they previously had.
3. War made it difficult to resist Nazi racial policies and brought opportunities for individuals and groups who took part in persecution.

Work through pages 277–79 and find examples to use as evidence of each development above.

Did the war increase opposition to the Nazi regime?

You have already read some examples of opposition to Nazi control during the war, such as the Edelweiss Pirates (page 276) and Gad Beck leading Jewish resistance in Berlin (page 278). The war increased opposition in other ways.

Organised resistance groups emerged

One of the best-known resistance groups was the White Rose, run by Hans and Sophie Scholl and friends. The White Rose published and distributed anti-Nazi leaflets. This was a small movement, although its members were certainly brave. The Scholls were executed in February 1943.

Church leaders challenged Nazi policies

The Catholic Bishop Clemens Galen had criticised the Nazis throughout the 1930s. In 1941, he led a popular protest against the Nazi policy of killing people with mental or physical disorders, which forced the Nazis to stop this programme temporarily. Galen had such strong support that the Nazis decided it was too risky to try to silence him – they did not want social unrest while Germany was at war.

Dietrich Bonhoeffer had also preached against the Nazis until the Gestapo stopped him in 1937. He then became involved with members of the army's intelligence services who were secretly opposed to Hitler. He helped Jewish people to escape from Germany. In 1942, he asked Allied commanders what peace terms they would offer Germany if Hitler was overthrown. He was arrested in October 1942 and hanged shortly before the end of the war, in April 1945.

Army leaders plotted against Hitler

The only group that really had much chance of overthrowing the Nazis was the army. Some leaders had challenged Hitler in the 1930s. For example, General von Fritsch and Field-Marshall von Blomberg argued against Hitler's plan to invade Germany's neighbours, fearing a disastrous war. Hitler had them removed – Fritsch because the Nazis 'found out' his wife was a prostitute and von Blomberg was accused of being gay.

As the war progressed the army became increasingly indivisible from the Nazi regime. Even so, there were attempts by senior army officers to assassinate Hitler. We know of five attempts between June 1940 and December 1943, but they all failed.

The July Bomb Plot, 1944

The closest to success came in July 1944. By this stage, many army officers were sure that the war was lost and that Hitler was leading Germany to ruin. One of these was a colonel in the army, Count von Stauffenberg. On 20 July he planted a bomb in Hitler's conference room. The plan was to kill Hitler, close down the radio stations, round up the other leading Nazis and take over Germany. It failed on all counts because the revolt was poorly planned and organised. Hitler survived and the Nazis took a terrible revenge, killing 5000 people.

Low-level resistance increased

The many types of lower-level resistance which we noted on page 262 increased as well. SS and Gestapo reports were increasingly concerned about the discontent and disillusionment caused by bombing raids,

---

FOCUS TASK 8.22

How did war affect opposition to the Nazi regime?

Using these two pages or your own additional research, list examples of opposition to Nazi rule during the war years. For each example:
a) Decide whether you think it was a new type of opposition **caused by war** or whether it already existed and was **made worse by war**. You will need to refer back to your work on page 262.
b) On a scale of 0–10, decide how serious each type of opposition was. A mark of 10 would mean a genuine threat to overthrow Hitler.
c) Now decide which of the factors on page 281 (terror, the 'Hitler myth', etc.) would have been most effective in stopping each type of resistance from succeeding.

shortages and heavy casualties. This was leading to increasing loss of control, for example civilians hiding food from the authorities.

However...

We must be careful not to exaggerate opposition to the regime or the war effort. In fact, support for the war remained remarkably strong almost to the end. When Protestant church minister Wilhelm Kenath criticised the war at the funeral of a young soldier in May 1943 he was reported to the Nazis by several mourners. Among ordinary Germans there was a misplaced faith in Hitler that he would find a way to lead them to victory.

Why was there not more opposition to the Nazis?

When you know the way the story of Nazi Germany developed and the disaster that Hitler proved to be for Germany and its people it is hard to understand why there was not more opposition. Here is a review of the main explanations:

Terror

This has to be top of any list of explanations. The Nazi police state was designed to scare Germans into submission, and it worked. It continued long into the war. Even in the final days of the war, when all seemed lost, the local Gestapo still rounded up and hung some saboteurs who had blown up a railway track to help the enemy.

The 'Hitler myth'

Hitler was a charismatic leader. Nazi propaganda had built him up still further into a godlike figure who controlled Germany's destiny. Even Germans who disliked the Nazis still respected Hitler personally and did not blame him for many of the unpleasant or unfair things which Nazi officials did. This belief in Hitler remained strong and was only shaken towards the end of the Second World War.

Divided opposition

Left-wing groups such as the Communists and the Social Democrats were the natural enemies of Nazism. They were both banned. However, these groups did not trust each other and were not prepared to work together. They were leaderless and divided. They never mounted any co-ordinated resistance.

Approval

Many people were pleased with the Nazis. They had been swept to power in 1933 because of the failings of Weimar democracy. Hitler had delivered on many of his promises. He had restored German pride internationally. He had got the economy moving again. Even those who did not support all Nazi policies were prepared to tolerate them for the sake of the stability and prosperity the Nazis had brought. This continued well into the early years of the war.

Propaganda and censorship

Censorship and propaganda meant that the newspapers and radio only spread news of Nazi achievements. This did not let up in wartime; in fact it increased. After Kristallnacht in 1938, when they could see that many Germans were unhappy with it, the Nazis kept all future measures against Jewish people secret and did not publicise them in the way they had their anti-Jewish policies in the early 1930s.

FOCUS TASK 8.23
Was Nazi Germany a totalitarian state?

A totalitarian state is one where:
- no opposition is allowed
- people are expected to show total loyalty and obedience to the state
- every aspect of life is controlled by the state for its own benefit.

You are going to prepare for a debate on the question: Was Nazi Germany a totalitarian state? Clearly Hitler wanted Germany to be like this, but did the Nazis achieve it?

Stage A: Research

Read through this chapter gathering as much evidence as you can about where Nazi Germany fits on this continuum.

Total control ⟷ No control

Use the text and the sources and your own research. Here are a few references to get you started.

Page 247
Factfile
Summarises the step-by-step Nazi consolidation of power.

Page 276
Source 24
An Edelweiss Pirates youth group in an undated photograph.

Page 257
Source 7
The diary of Victor Klemperer for 8 August 1937 describes his experience of going to the cinema.

Page 260
Source 14
H. Schmidt, Labour Corps leader, in an interview in 1938, describes his attitude to Nazi policy towards Jewish people.

Page 254
Source 6
Photos of the annual Nazi rally at Nuremberg – a celebration of Nazi power and discipline.

Page 269
Source 14
Albert Speer, who was the Nazis' minister of armaments and war, writes in 1970 about how he tried to affect Nazi policy on women workers.

Page 279
Source 29
American historian Gordon Craig writes in 1978 about the attitudes of Nazi officials to their role in the Final Solution.

Page 258
Source 10
British historian and journalist Charles Wheeler, writing in 1996, describes how Church leaders responded to the Nazis.

Be sure to note where you found each extra piece of evidence. If possible, share your evidence with others. Discuss it.

Stage B: Reach your judgement

1 Taking all the evidence, do you think that the Nazis managed to turn Germany into a totalitarian state? Where on the continuum would you put Nazi rule?
2 Would your answer change if you chose particular years: 1936, 1939, 1941, 1945.

Stage C: Write your speech

Aim for just one minute (200–250 words). State your view. Use evidence to support your arguments.

Keywords

Make sure you know these terms, people or events and are able to use them or describe them confidently.

- Antisemitism
- Autobahn
- Bauhaus
- Beauty of Labour
- Chancellor
- Coalition Communist (Bolshevik)
- Concentration camp
- Concordat
- Conscription
- Consolidation
- Constitution
- Dawes Plan
- Democracy
- Diktat
- Edelweiss Pirates
- Enabling Act
- Federal
- Final Solution
- *Freikorps*
- Führer
- Gestapo
- *Gleichschaltung* (co-ordination)
- Hitler Youth
- Holocaust
- Hyperinflation
- Kaiser
- *Kristallnacht*
- League of German Maidens
- *Mein Kampf*
- Munich Putsch
- National Community (*Volksgemeinschaft*)
- Nazism
- Negative cohesion
- Night of the Long Knives
- Nuremberg Laws
- Nuremberg rally
- Propaganda
- Rearmament
- Reichstag
- Reparations
- Republic
- Ruhr
- SA
- Spartacists
- SS
- Strength Through Joy
- Totalitarian
- Treaty of Versailles
- Universal suffrage
- *Volk*
- Weimar

Key Question Summary

What was it like to live in Nazi Germany?

1. Young people were expected to join the Hitler Youth. There were separate organisations for boys and girls.
2. The boys focused on activities that taught them to be soldiers. The girls focused on healthy living and preparing for motherhood.
3. The school curriculum was also used to indoctrinate young people. Teachers were among the keenest supporters of the Nazis.
4. Not all young people liked the Nazis and once the war started opposition to the Hitler Youth among young people increased and groups like the Edelweiss Pirates actively resisted.
5. The Nazis rewarded German women for having children – the more the better. They discouraged women from working and encouraged them to stay at home and look after children.
6. However, later on they also needed women to become workers so they had to change their policies to encourage women to do both.
7. The Nazis promised to end unemployment, which they did, but only by drafting hundreds of thousands of people into the army or putting political opponents to forced labour.
8. The economy recovered in the 1930s but business was geared towards getting ready for war, making weapons or becoming self-sufficient in raw materials.
9. For those who did not fit Nazi ideas life was terrible. The Jewish people suffered in particular, facing restrictions, then persecution or exile, and in the end forced labour and genocide.
10. The war went well for Germany to start with. However, after Germany invaded Russia in 1941 the tide turned. German resources were directed into fighting an unwinnable war against the USSR. The German economy and the Nazi regime collapsed.

PRACTICE QUESTIONS

Structured questions

1. (a) What was the Munich Putsch? **[4]**
   (b) Why did the Nazis launch the Munich Putsch in 1923? **[6]**
   (c) 'The Munich Putsch was a total failure for Adolf Hitler.' How far do you agree with this statement? Explain your answer. **[10]**

Alternative to Coursework questions

1. a) Write an account of the development of the Nazi Party between 1924 and 1930. **[15]**
   b) Discuss the impact the Depression had on Nazi electoral success between 1930 and 1932. **[25]**

See pages 338–55 for advice on the different types of questions.

284

9 The United States, 1919–41

KEY QUESTIONS
9A How far did the US economy boom in the 1920s?
9B How far did US society change in the 1920s?
9C What were the causes and consequences of the Wall Street Crash?
9D How successful was the New Deal?

At the end of the First World War the USA was the richest and most powerful country in the world. The next two decades were a turbulent time: a BOOM then a bust; a time of opportunity for some but a time of trauma for others.

In **9A** you will look at the booming US economy in the 1920s. You will look at the causes of this economic boom and also its consequences. Most important of all, you will investigate which Americans shared in the new prosperity and what happened to those who did not.

In **9B** you will examine the changes that took place in the 1920s, particularly for women, immigrants and African Americans.

In **9C** you will examine the economic disaster that plunged the USA into crisis – the WALL STREET CRASH of 1929 – and how the Crash led to a deep economic DEPRESSION.

In **9D** you will look at the NEW DEAL: the measures President Roosevelt used to help the USA recover. You will examine the range of measures taken, the thinking behind those measures and how people reacted to them. Most of all you will think hard about whether or not the New Deal should be seen as a success or not.

Timeline
This timeline shows the period you will be covering in this chapter. Some of the key dates are filled in already. To help you get a complete picture of the period make your own much larger version and add other details to it as you work through the chapter.

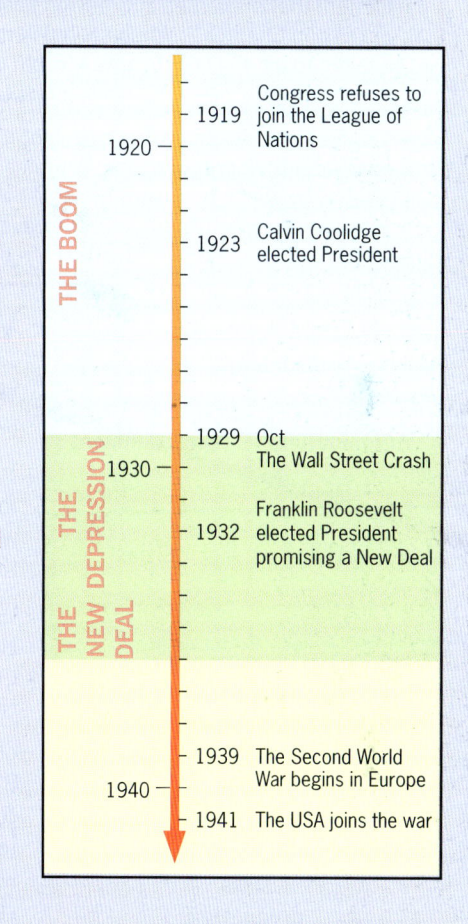

THE BOOM
- 1919 Congress refuses to join the League of Nations
- 1923 Calvin Coolidge elected President

THE NEW DEPRESSION DEAL
- 1929 Oct The Wall Street Crash
- 1932 Franklin Roosevelt elected President promising a New Deal
- 1939 The Second World War begins in Europe
- 1941 The USA joins the war

This photo was taken in California by Dorothea Lange during the Great Depression of the early 1930s. It was taken in a temporary camp for workers who had come to California to find a job. It is called 'Migrant Mother' and is one of the most famous and widely used photographs about this period.
1 What impression does this photo give you of the woman?
2 This was a carefully constructed photo – what does the photographer want you to feel and think and how has she achieved that?

9A How far did the US economy boom in the 1920s?

FOCUS

As you saw in Chapter 1, after the First World War President Wilson determined that from then on the USA should take a lead in world affairs. He proposed an international LEAGUE OF NATIONS that would be like a world parliament that prevented aggression between countries. As you saw in Chapter 2, Wilson failed in this attempt. He even failed to get the USA to agree to join the League at all.

Instead Wilson was defeated and the USA turned its back on Europe, a policy known as 'isolationism'. A new president, Warren Harding, promised a return to 'normalcy' by which he meant life as it had been before the war. Americans turned their energies to what they did best – making money! Over the next ten years the USA, already the richest country in the world, became richer still as its economy boomed.

In 9.1 you will examine the reasons for this boom and also the extent. You will also see that while some people in America benefited greatly from the boom there were significant proportions – possibly even the majority – who did not share in the boom at all.

Focus Points
- On what factors was the economic boom based?
- Why did some industries prosper while others did not?
- Why did agriculture not share in the prosperity?
- Did all Americans benefit from the boom?

Think!
What was the boom?

- Automobiles
- Entertainment
- Advertising
- Cities
- Electricity
- Transport
- Credit
- Mass consumption
- Mass production

1. These cards show nine key features of the 1920s economic boom. Make your own set of cards – large enough to write some information on the back.
2. As you read this chapter write notes on each card to summarise how this was changing in the 1920s and how it contributed to the boom.
3. Working on a larger piece of paper, make notes about how these different features are linked.

NB Keep your cards. They will be useful for Focus Task 9.1 on page 292. They will also be useful for revision.

What was the boom?

The 'boom' is the name given to the dynamic growth of the American economy in the decade after the First World War.

In the 1920s American businesses grew more quickly than ever before. They found faster and cheaper ways of making goods than ever before. As production went up prices came down so ordinary people bought more household goods than ever before: millions of fridges and cars were sold; hundreds of millions of nylon stockings.

Many families bought new houses in the suburbs of America's rapidly growing cities. And with money to spare they spent more on leisure – so the music, radio, cinema industries and even sport were booming.

Company profits were booming and confidence was booming too. Business leaders were prepared to take risks and ordinary people were too. Banks had money to spare so they invested it in the STOCK MARKET or lent it to ordinary Americans to do so. The value of stocks and SHARES went up and up.

The Government built more roads than ever before. More homes were supplied with electricity and phone lines than ever before. There was more building being done in the boom years of the 1920s than ever before. And, as if to symbolise the massive confidence of the time, cities built higher skyscrapers than ever before.

It seemed that everything was going up, up, up!

This may all sound too good to be true – and it was! The whole system came crashing down with a bang in 1929 but that is another story which you will investigate on page XXX. For now you will focus on the boom years and why exactly American industry was so successful in the 1920s.

Revision Tip
Make sure you can describe at least three aspects of the boom.

Think!
Why did it benefit American industry to have raw materials, especially coal, oil and cotton, so easily available within the USA?

Factors behind the economic boom

Industrial strength

The USA was a vast country, rich in natural resources. It had a growing population (123 million by 1923). Most of this population was living in towns and cities. They were working in industry and commerce, usually earning higher wages than in farming. So these new town dwellers became an important market for the USA's new industries. Most US companies had no need to export outside the USA, and most US companies had access to the raw materials they needed in the USA.

FIGURE 1

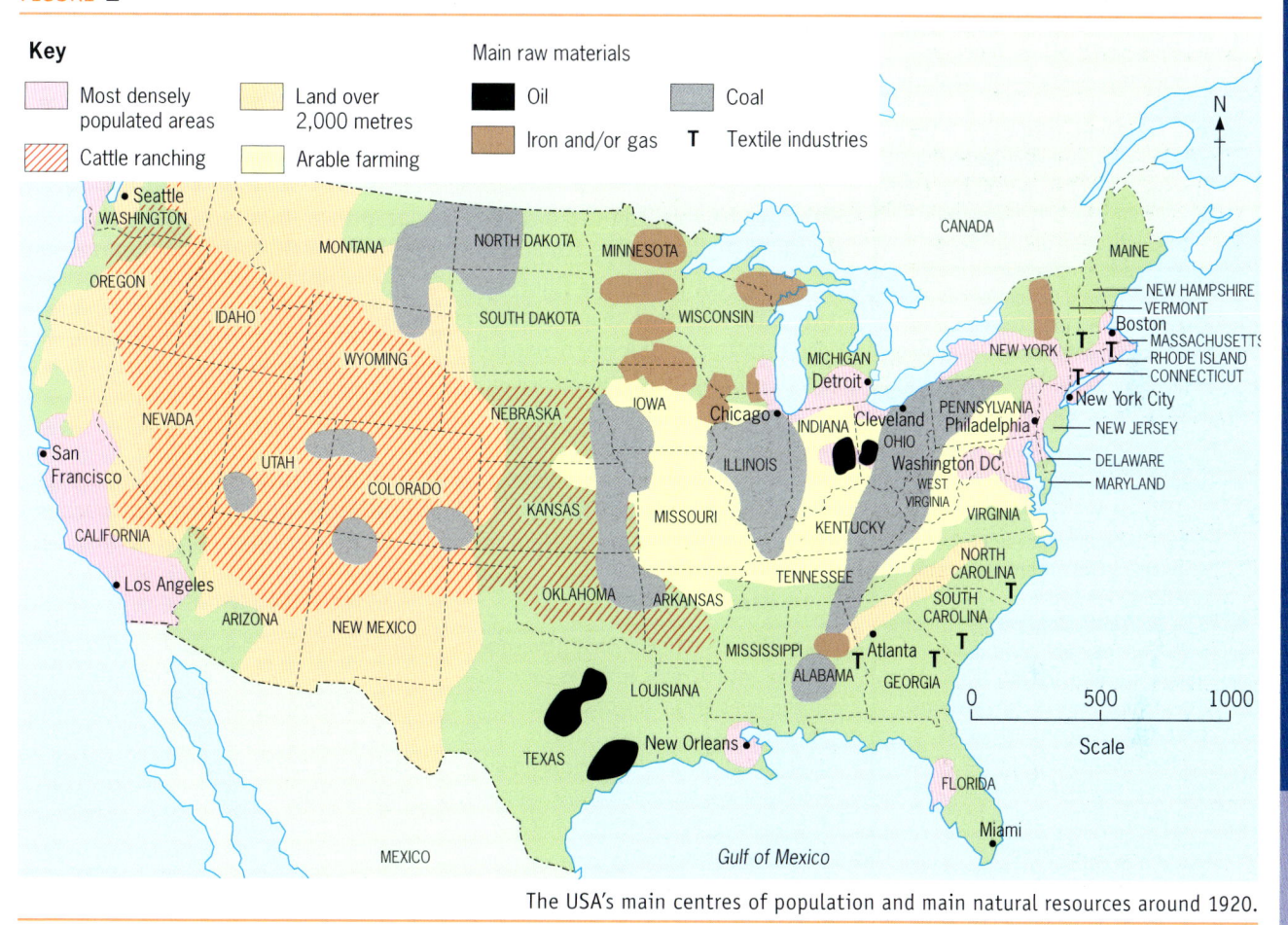

Key
- Most densely populated areas
- Cattle ranching
- Land over 2,000 metres
- Arable farming

Main raw materials
- Oil
- Iron and/or gas
- Coal
- T Textile industries

The USA's main centres of population and main natural resources around 1920.

By the time of the First World War, the USA led the world in most areas of industry. It had massive steel, coal and textile industries. It was the leading oil producer. It was foremost in developing new technology such as motor cars, telephones and electric lighting. In fact, electricity and electrical goods were a key factor in the USA's economic boom. Other new industries such as chemicals were also growing fast. The USA's new film industry already led the world.

The managers of these industries were increasingly skilled and professional, and they were selling more and more of their products not just in the USA but in Europe, Latin America and the Far East.

American agriculture had become the most efficient and productive in the world. In 1914, most Americans would have confidently stated that American agriculture and industry were going from strength to strength.

Revision Tip
On this page and the next four there are quite a few factors explaining the boom. Focus on two per page. Make sure you can explain how the factor contributed to the boom.

Factfile

US system of government

- **The federal system:** The USA's federal system means that all the individual states look after their own internal affairs (such as education). Questions that concern all of the states (such as making treaties with other countries) are dealt with by Federal (National) Government in Washington D.C.
- **The Constitution:** The CONSTITUTION lays out how the government is supposed to operate and what it is allowed to do.
- **The president:** He (or she) is the single most important politician in the USA. The president is elected every four years. However, the Constitution of the USA is designed to stop one individual from becoming too powerful. Congress and the SUPREME COURT both act as 'watchdogs', checking how the president behaves.
- **Congress:** Congress is made up of the Senate and the House of Representatives. The main functions of Congress are to pass laws, which are sometimes proposed by the president, and to agree government taxes and spending.
- **The Supreme Court:** This is made up of judges, who are usually very experienced lawyers. Their main task is to make sure that American governments do not misuse their power or pass unfair laws. They have the power to say that a law is unconstitutional (against the Constitution), which usually means that they feel the law would harm American citizens.
- **Parties:** There are two main political parties, the REPUBLICANS and the DEMOCRATS. In the 1920s and 1930s, the Republicans were stronger in the industrial north of the USA while the Democrats had more support in the south. On the whole, Republicans in the 1920s and 1930s preferred government to stay out of people's lives if possible. The Democrats were more prepared to intervene in everyday life.

The First World War

The Americans tried hard to stay out of the fighting in the First World War. But throughout the war they lent money to the Allies, and sold arms and munitions to Britain and France. They sold massive amounts of foodstuffs as well. This one-way trade gave American industry a real boost. In addition, while the European powers slugged it out in France, the Americans were able to take over Europe's trade around the world. American exports to the areas controlled by European colonial powers increased during the war.

There were other benefits as well. Before the war Germany had one of the world's most successful chemicals industries. The war stopped it in its tracks. By the end of the war the USA had far outstripped Germany in the supply of chemical products. Explosives manufacture during the war also stimulated a range of by-products which became new American industries in their own right. Plastics and other new materials were produced.

Aircraft technology was improved during the First World War. From 1918 these developments were applied to civilian uses. In 1918 there were virtually no civilian airlines. By 1930 the new aircraft companies flew 162,000 flights a year.

Historians have called the growth and change at this time the USA's second industrial revolution. The war actually helped rather than hindered the 'revolution'.

When the USA joined the fighting it was not in the war long enough for it to drain American resources in the way it drained Europe's. There was a downturn in the USA when war industries readjusted to peacetime, but it was only a blip. By 1922 the American economy was growing fast once again.

Republican policies

A third factor behind the boom was the policies of the Republican Party. From 1920 to 1932 all the US presidents were Republican, and Republicans also dominated Congress. Here are some of their beliefs.

1 Laissez-faire

Republicans believed that government should interfere as little as possible in the everyday lives of the people. This attitude is called 'LAISSEZ-FAIRE'. In their view, the job of the president was to leave businesspeople alone to do their job. That was where prosperity came from.

This was closely related to their belief in 'rugged individualism'. They admired the way Americans were strong and got on with solving their own problems.

2 Protective tariffs

The Republicans believed in import TARIFFS which made it expensive to import foreign goods. For example, in 1922 Harding introduce the Fordney–McCumber tariff which made imported food expensive in the USA. These tariffs protected businesses against foreign COMPETITION and allowed American companies to grow even more rapidly.

3 Low taxation

The Republicans kept taxation as low as possible. This brought some benefits to ordinary working people, but it brought even more to the very wealthy. The Republican thinking was that if people kept their own money, they would spend it on American goods and wealthy people would reinvest their money in industries.

4 Powerful trusts

TRUSTS were huge super-corporations, which dominated industry. Woodrow Wilson and the Democrats had fought against trusts because they believed it was unhealthy for men such as Carnegie (steel) and Rockefeller (oil) to have almost complete control of one vital sector of industry. The Republicans allowed the trusts to do what they wanted, believing that the 'captains of industry' knew better than politicians did about what was good for the USA.

Republican presidents and the economic boom of the 1920s

Profile

President Warren Harding
(In office: 1921–23)

Famous quote

'Return to normalcy', which meant he wanted to return to traditional American ideas after the First World War.

Economic policies

Following the post-war depression between 1920 and 1921, Harding passed a number of measures to help the economy. In 1921, Harding's Treasury Secretary, Andrew Mellon, convinced Congress to cut income tax for both higher and lower earners. The effect was the start of economic recovery as wages, profits and productivity increased. Harding removed many government regulations that had been in place during the war. He cut government spending from 6.5 per cent to 3.5 per cent. In 1921 he signed the Federal Highway Act, which saw $160 million of investment in highways. This created many jobs within the road building industry. Most importantly, in 1922 he signed the Fordney–McCumber Tariff Act. This Act protected US industry and made foreign goods more expensive. As a result of his economic successes, Harding is viewed by many economists as laying the foundations of the boom.

Profile

President Calvin Coolidge
(In office: 1923–29)

Famous quote

'After all, the chief business of the American people is business', which meant he promoted consumerism and the creation of personal wealth.

Economic policies

Coolidge continued with the same economic policies as Harding. In 1924 he passed the Revenue Act which cut income tax for a further two million Americans. After two more tax cuts in 1926 and 1928, only the wealthiest two per cent of taxpayers paid income tax!

Coolidge was also a firm believer in laissez-faire policies. In 1926 he vetoed (rejected) a bill to set up a farm board that would buy surplus produce from farmers. Since the end of the war, farmers had been struggling economically. According to Coolidge, agriculture, 'must stand on an independent business basis.' This meant he did not believe it was the government's job to help them. He also believed in modernising agriculture which would later lead to overproduction and economic problems in the 1930s.

Profile

President Herbert Hoover
(In office: 1929–33)

Famous quote

'Put a chicken in every cooking pot, and a car in every garage', which meant the government was committed to every American sharing in the prosperity.

Economic policies

Hoover was committed to his own brand of laissez-faire policies which he dubbed 'rugged individualism'. This meant that every American should look after their own interests without relying on help from the government. His ideas could not have come at a worse time. Economic growth in the USA had been slowing down since 1927. Farmers in particular were hard hit by continually falling prices and low incomes.

When the Depression set in during the early 1930s, Hoover did attempt to use the government to try to help farmers and banks, but never retreated from his core beliefs. He even introduced a further tariff in 1930 called the Smoot–Hawley Tariff. He was labelled the 'do-nothing' president by opponents and lost the election in 1932. You will learn more about this in Chapter 10.

FIGURE 2

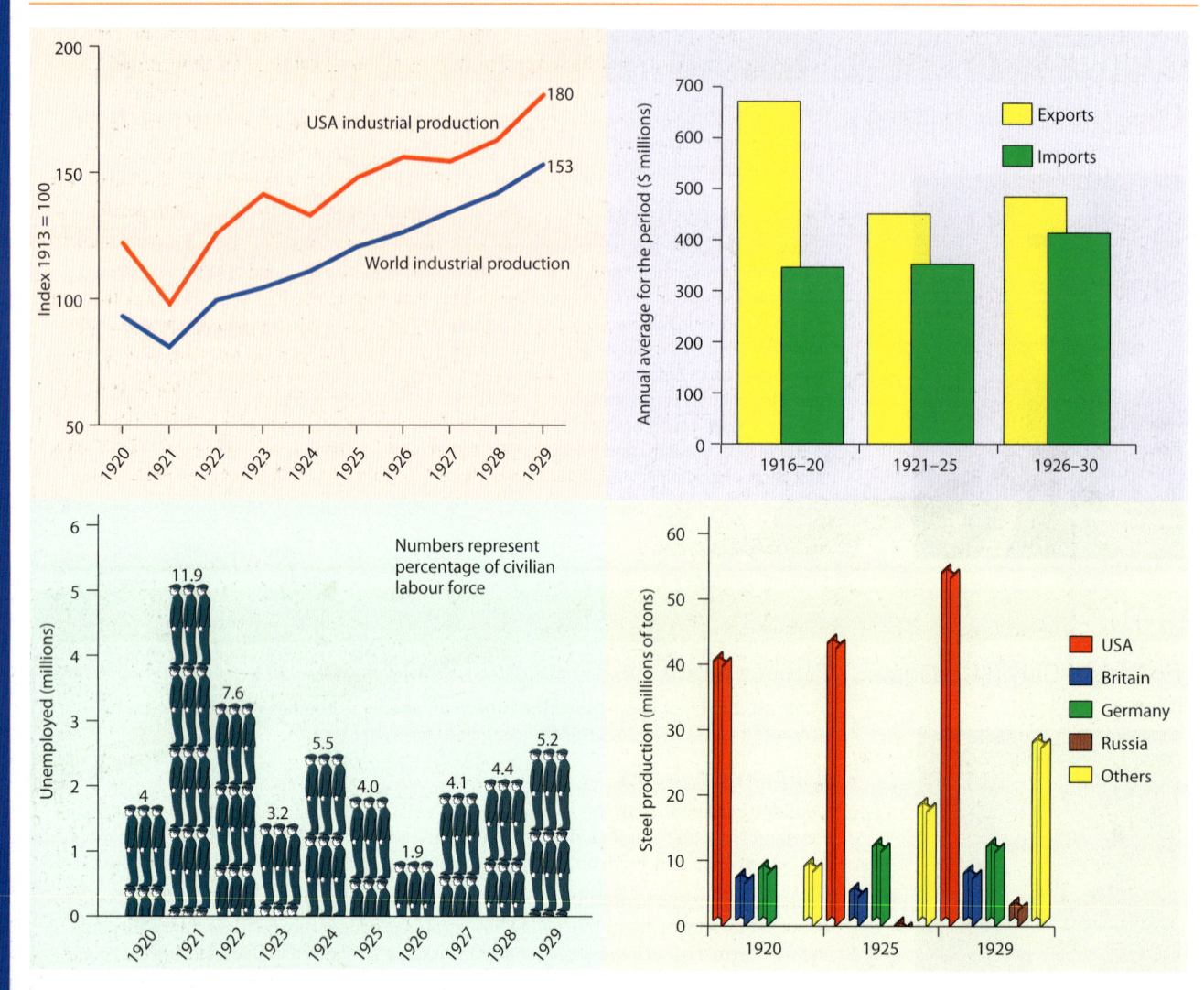

The growth of the US economy in the 1920s.

Think!
1. How could the Republicans use Figure 2 to justify their policies?
2. How could critics of Republican policies use Figure 2 to attack the Republicans?

Revision Tip
Which factors have you chosen from pages 287–92? Practise explaining how they caused the boom rather than just describing them.

New industries, new methods

Through the 1920s new industries and new methods of production were developed in the USA. The country was able to exploit its vast resources of raw materials to produce steel, chemicals, glass and machinery. Electricity was changing America too. Before the First World War industry was still largely powered by coal. By the 1920s electricity had taken over. In 1918 only a few homes were supplied; by 1929 almost all urban homes had it. These new industries in turn became the foundation of an enormous boom in consumer goods. Telephones, radios, vacuum cleaners and washing machines were mass-produced on a vast scale. MASS PRODUCTION methods meant that huge amounts of goods could be produced much more cheaply and so more people could afford them.

Things that used to be luxuries were now made cheaper by new inventions and mass production. For example, silk stockings had once been a luxury item reserved for the rich. In 1900 only 12,000 pairs had been sold. In the 1920s rayon was invented, which was a cheaper substitute for silk. In 1930, 300 million pairs of stockings were sold to a female population of around 100 million.

> **Think!**
> Why were mass production techniques so crucial to production and consumption of goods made by the new industries?

The car

The most important of these new booming industries was the motor-car or automobile industry. The motor car had only been developed in the 1890s. The first cars were built by blacksmiths and other skilled craftsmen. They took a long time to make and were very expensive. In 1900 only 4000 cars were made. Car production was revolutionised by Henry Ford. In 1913 he set up the world's first moving ASSEMBLY LINE, in a giant shed in Detroit. Each worker on the line had one or two small jobs to do as the skeleton of the car moved past him. At the beginning of the line, a skeleton car went in; at the end of the line was a new car. The most famous of these was the Model T. More than 15 million were produced between 1908 and 1925. In 1927 they came off the assembly line at a rate of one every ten seconds. In 1929, 4.8 million cars were made. In 1925 they cost $290. This was only three months' wages for an American factory worker.

SOURCE 3

The new roads gave rise to a new truck industry. In 1919 there were 1 million trucks in the USA. By 1929 there were 3.5 million.

SOURCE 4

Ford's assembly line in 1913.

By the end of the 1920s the motor industry was the USA's biggest industry. As well as employing hundreds of thousands of workers directly, it also kept workers in other industries in employment. Glass, leather, steel and rubber were all required to build the new vehicles. Automobiles used up 75 per cent of US glass production in the 1920s! Petrol was needed to run them. And a massive army of labourers was busily building roads throughout the country for these cars to drive on. In fact, road construction was the biggest single employer in the 1920s.

Owning a car was not just a rich person's privilege, as it was in Europe. There was one car to five people in the USA compared with one to 43 in Britain, and one to 7000 in Russia. The car made it possible for people to buy a house in the suburbs, which further boosted house building. It also stimulated the growth of hundreds of other smaller businesses, ranging from hot-dog stands and advertising billboards to petrol stations and holiday resorts.

> **Think!**
> 1 Study the information and sources on this page and make a list of the ways in which the motor industry changed. Use the following headings:
> - Jobs people did
> - Other industries
> - Where people lived
> - How people lived
> 2 Discuss: Was the car industry more important than other factors in changing America?

FIGURE **5**

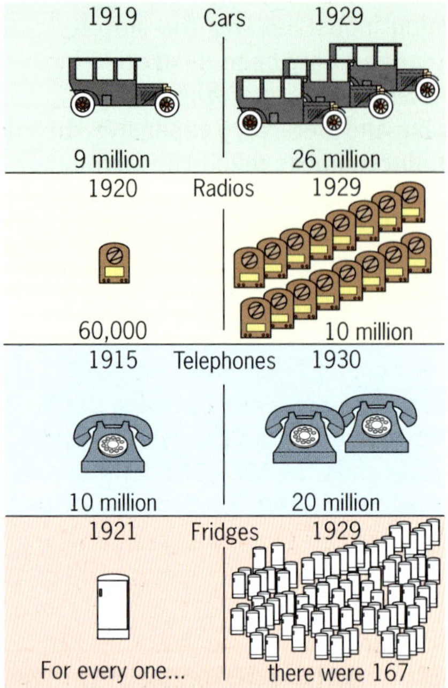
1919
Cars
1929
9 million
26 million
1920
Radios
1929
60,000
10 million
1915
Telephones
1930
10 million
20 million
1921
Fridges
1929
For every one...
there were 167

Sales of consumer goods, 1915–30. Overall, the output of American industry doubled in the 1920s.

Mass consumption

It is no good producing lots of goods if people don't buy them. Mass production requires MASS CONSUMPTION. So, the big industries used sophisticated sales and marketing techniques to get people to buy their goods. New electrical companies such as Hoover became household names. They used the latest, most efficient techniques proposed by the 'Industrial Efficiency Movement'.

- Mass nationwide advertising had been used for the first time in the USA during the war to get Americans to support the war effort. Many of the advertisers who had learned their skills in wartime PROPAGANDA now set up agencies to sell cars, cigarettes, clothing and other consumer items. Poster advertisements on billboards, radio advertisements and travelling salesmen encouraged Americans to spend.
- There was a huge growth in the number of MAIL-ORDER companies. People across America, especially in remote areas, could buy the new consumer goods from catalogues. In 1928 nearly one-third of Americans bought goods from Sears, Roebuck and Company catalogue. This greatly expanded the market for products.
- Even if they did not have the money, people could borrow it easily. Or they could take advantage of the new 'Buy now, pay later' HIRE PURCHASE schemes. Eight out of ten radios and six out of ten cars were bought on CREDIT. Before the war, people expected to save up until they could afford something. Now they could buy on credit.
- A brand-new kind of shop emerged – the chain store – the same shop selling the same products all across the USA, such as Woolworth's and American Stores.

This all worked very well as you can see from Figure 5.

A state of mind

The 1920s saw a change in attitude for many Americans as the economy started to recover. In the post-war depression, thrift – being careful with money and saving – was seen as a good quality. But as the economy of the 1920s picked up, Americans became more confident. They began to spend more on consumer goods and entertainment, and they placed a high value on owning things. This confidence was supported by the Republican policies of laissez-faire and low taxation (see page 288). America became a consumer society.

This confidence was also apparent in the way banks lent money to businesses and consumers, as banks were confident they would see debts paid back with interest. Companies expanded and invested in new machinery and technology, and as consumer demand increased, profits soared. Consumers bought more goods on credit and many borrowed from banks to buy shares in companies. Between 1920 and 1929, stocks in the major companies quadrupled in value. Confidence is vital to any economic boom, and in the 1920s there was a huge amount of confidence in the American stock market.

FOCUS TASK 9.1

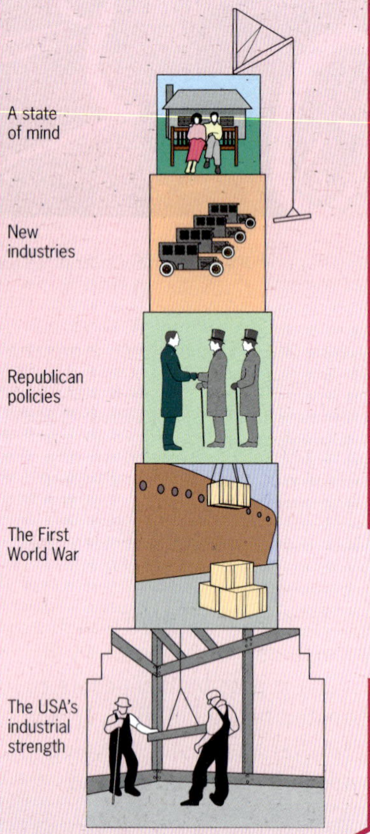
A state of mind
New industries
Republican policies
The First World War
The USA's industrial strength

On what factors was the economic boom based?

The diagram on the left shows you the main factors on which the economic boom in the 1920s was based. Put a copy of the diagram in the centre of a large piece of paper. Write notes to summarise how each factor contributed to the boom using pages 287–92.

Revision Tip

So have you got five or more factors which explain the boom? If so:

- choose two factors you think were connected and practise explaining how they were connected
- decide which one you think is the most important (or if you think the boom cannot be explained that way, say why).

Problems in the farming industry

SOURCE 6

A cartoon showing the situation faced by American farmers in the 1920s.

While many Americans were enjoying the boom, farmers most definitely were not. Total US farm income dropped from $22 billion in 1919 to just $13 billion in 1928. There were a number of reasons why farming had such problems.

- **Declining exports:** After the war, Europe imported far less food from the USA. This was partly because Europe was poor, and it was partly a response to US tariffs which stopped Europe from exporting to the USA (see page 290).
- **New competitors:** Farmers were also struggling against competition from the highly efficient Canadian and Argentinian wheat producers. All of this came at a time when the population of the USA was actually falling and there were fewer mouths to feed.
- **Over-production:** Underlying all these problems was OVER-PRODUCTION. From 1900 to 1920, while farming was doing well, more and more land was being farmed. Improved machinery, especially the combine harvester, and improved fertilisers made US agriculture extremely efficient. The result was that by 1920 it was producing surpluses of wheat which nobody wanted.
- **Falling prices:** Prices plummeted as desperate farmers tried to sell their produce. In 1921 alone, most farm prices fell by 50 per cent. Hundreds of rural banks collapsed in the 1920s and there were five times as many farm bankruptcies as there had been in the 1900s and 1910s.
- **Prohibition:** In 1920 Prohibition was introduced across the USA. The alcohol industry was a major consumer of American wheat and barley. Demand for these resources fell as a result.

Not all farmers were affected by these problems. Rich Americans wanted fresh vegetables and fruit throughout the year. Shipments of lettuce to the cities, for example, rose from 14,000 crates in 1920 to 52,000 in 1928. But for most farmers the 1920s were a time of hardship.

This was a serious issue. About half of all Americans lived in rural areas, mostly working on farms or in businesses that sold goods to farmers. Problems in farming therefore directly affected more than 60 million Americans.

Six million rural Americans, mainly farm labourers, were forced off the land in the 1920s. Many of these were unskilled workers who migrated to the cities, where there was little demand for their labour. African Americans were particularly badly hit. They had always done the least skilled jobs in the rural areas. As they lost their jobs on the farms, three-quarters of a million of them became unemployed.

It is no surprise that farming communities were the fiercest critics of the 'laissez-faire' policies of the Republican Party.

Source Analysis

1. Do you think the cartoonist who drew Source 6 is sympathetic towards the farmer?
2. What is the cartoonist's attitude towards the towns and cities?

Revision Tip

Make sure you know at least two reasons why agriculture was facing problems in the 1920s and that you understand what is meant by the terms 'overproduction' and 'tariffs'.

FOCUS TASK 9.2

Why did agriculture not share in the prosperity?

Write a 200-word caption explaining the message of Source 6. Refer to details in the source but also use the information in the text to explain the details, for example, the reasons why the farmer might be looking enviously (or angrily) at the factories, or the events that might have led to his farm being for sale.

FIGURE 7

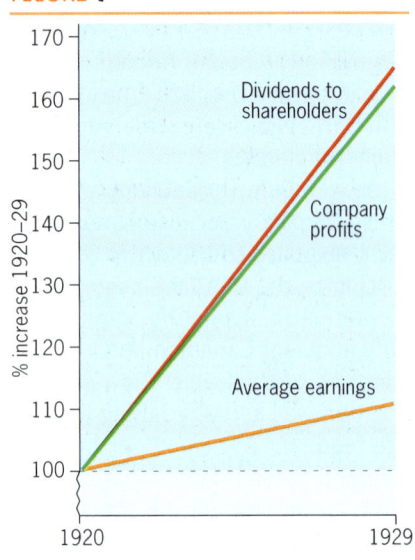

A comparison of the growth of profits and the growth of average earnings.
(Graph showing % increase 1920–29 from 1920 to 1929: Dividends to shareholders rising to ~165, Company profits rising to ~160, Average earnings rising to ~110.)

FIGURE 8

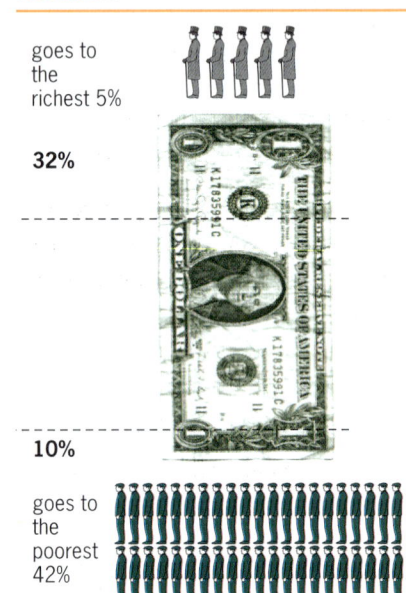

- 32% goes to the richest 5%
- 10% goes to the poorest 42%

The distribution of income in 1925.

Revision Tip
Ensure you know an example of industries that were harmed by each of: electrification; oil; declining sales; declining profits.

Why didn't traditional industries prosper?

You have already seen how the farmers – a very large group in American society – did not share in the prosperity of the 1920s. But they were not alone. Workers in many older industries did not benefit much either.

The coal industry was a big employer but it began to struggle. First, like farming there was over-production. This reduced the price of coal and therefore profits. At the same time coal power was losing out to new power sources like electricity and oil. Although electricity producers used coal to generate electricity, the new generating technology was highly efficient so it did not need much coal to produce a lot of energy. Manufacturers were either switching to electricity or oil, or used more efficient machinery which used less coal. The same pattern could be seen in homes where improved boilers gave users the same amount of heat with less coal.

Other industries such as leather, textiles and shoe-making also struggled. They were protected from competition with foreign imports by tariffs. However, they were not growth markets. They also suffered from competition from industries which used new man-made materials and were often mechanised. In the TRADITIONAL INDUSTRIES generally growth was slow and profits were gradually declining. Workers in these industries lost their jobs as processes became increasingly mechanised. Skilled workers struggled to compete against both machinery and cheap labour in the southern states. Even if workers in these industries did get a pay rise, their wages did not increase at the same rate as company profits or dividends paid to shareholders (see Figure 7).

In 1928 there was a strike in the coal industry in North Carolina, where the male workers were paid only $18 and women $9 for a 70-hour week, at a time when $48 per week was considered to be the minimum required for a decent life. In fact, for the majority of Americans wages remained well below that figure. It has been estimated that 42 per cent of Americans lived below the poverty line – they did not have the money needed to pay for essentials such as food, clothing, housing and heating for their families.

SOURCE 9

A hunger march in Washington during the brief recession which hit some industries in 1921–22.

FOCUS TASK 9.3
Did all Americans benefit from the boom?

In 1928 a new Republican president, Herbert Hoover, was elected. He said:

SOURCE 9

One of the oldest and perhaps the noblest of human activities [aims] has been the abolition of poverty ... we in America today are nearer to the final triumph over poverty than ever before in the history of any land.

Herbert Hoover.

Gather evidence from pages 293–95 to contest Hoover's claim. Write a paper setting out in detail:
- how badly off some farmers have become since the war
- why farmers are poor and how Republican policies have contributed to this
- why workers in older industries are suffering and what has happened to their wages (give an example)
- why immigrant workers and African Americans are not well off.

Try to use specific examples such as Chicago in the 1920s.

Revision Tip
- Choose two points about Chicago which you could use in a question about whether all Americans shared in the boom.
- Explain to someone else how you would use those points.

Unemployment

What's more, throughout this period unemployment remained a problem. The growth in industry in the 1920s did not create many new jobs. Industries were growing by electrifying or mechanising production. The same number of people (around 5 per cent) were unemployed at the peak of the boom in 1929 as in 1920. Yet the amount of goods produced had doubled. These millions of unemployed Americans were not sharing in the boom. They included many poor whites, but an even greater proportion of African American and Hispanic people and other members of the USA's large immigrant communities.

The plight of the poor was desperate for the individuals concerned. But it was also damaging to American industry. The boom of the 1920s was a consumer-led boom, which means that it was led by ordinary families buying things for their homes. But with so many families too poor to buy such goods, the demand for them was likely to begin to tail off. However, Republican policy remained not to interfere, and this included doing nothing about unemployment or poverty.

Case study: Chicago in the 1920s

Chicago was one of America's biggest cities. It was the centre of the steel, meat and clothing industries, which employed many unskilled workers. Such industries had busy and slack periods. In slack periods the workers would be 'seasonally unemployed'. Many of these workers were Polish or Italian immigrants, or African American migrants from the southern United States. How far did they share in the prosperity of the 1920s?

- Only 3 per cent of semi-skilled workers owned a car. Compare that with richer areas where 29 per cent owned a car.
- Workers in Chicago didn't like to buy large items on credit. They preferred to save for when they might not have a job. Many bought smaller items on credit, such as radios.
- The poor white Americans did not use the new chain stores which had revolutionised shopping in the 1920s. Nearly all of them were in middle-class districts. Poorer white industrial workers preferred to shop at the local grocer's where the owner was more flexible and gave them credit.

Key Question Summary

How far did the US economy boom in the 1920s?

1. The 1920s saw unprecedented growth in mass consumption in the USA. People bought a vast range of new products which changed the way people lived their lives.
2. The period saw dynamic business growth and prosperity with the creation of vast new cities, characterised by skyscrapers, and new systems of transport to link towns and cities.
3. The boom was encouraged by the policies of the Republican Party which believed in laissez-faire, low taxes and protective tariffs.
4. It was also underpinned by the development of new industries using new materials and innovative production techniques, especially mass production.
5. The motor car was particularly important, changing the American way of life and stimulating other industries.
6. Large sections of American society did not benefit to the same degree from prosperity including farmers and farm labourers – farming in the 1920s was very depressed through a combination of over-production and environmental problems.
7. Older industries such as coal or leather suffered because of competition from new materials such as oil and plastics and because their methods and machinery became outdated.

FOCUS

The 1920s are often called the Roaring Twenties. For some it was a time of riotous fun, loud music and wild enjoyment. However, for others it was a time of hardship, intolerance and fear of moral decline. In this section you will examine these contrasts and the conflicts that resulted from them.

Focus Points

- What were the 'Roaring Twenties'?
- How widespread was intolerance in US society?
- Why was Prohibition introduced, and then later repealed?
- How far did the roles of women change during the 1920s?

Source Analysis

Study Source 1. Is the artist positive or negative about the building boom taking place in US cities? How can you tell?

FIGURE 2

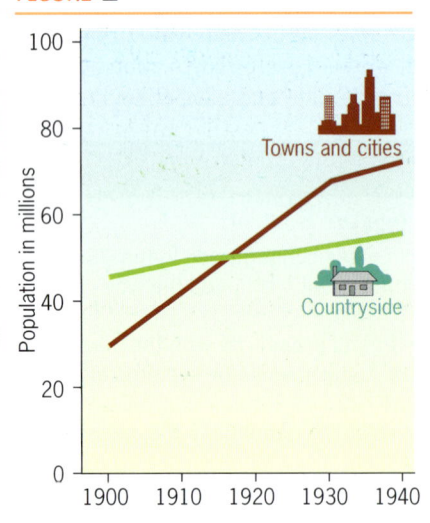

The change in the USA's urban and rural populations, 1900–40.

9B How far did US society change in the 1920s?

The USA in the Roaring Twenties

Town v. country

In 1920, for the first time in American history, more Americans lived in towns and cities than in the country. People flocked to them from all over the USA. The growing city with its imposing skyline of skyscrapers was one of the most powerful symbols of 1920s USA.

Throughout the 1920s there was tension between rural USA and urban USA. Certain rural states, particularly in the South, fought a rearguard action against the 'evil' effects of the city throughout the 1920s, as you will see on page 298.

SOURCE 1

The Builder, painted by Gerrit A Beneker in the 1920s. Beneker had worked for the US Government producing propaganda posters in the First World War.

Entertainment

The term 'ROARING TWENTIES' is particularly associated with entertainment and changing morality. During the 1920s working wages hours fell and wages rose for most Americans. A lot of this spare time and money was channelled into entertainment, creating a huge leisure industry.

Radio

Almost everyone in the USA listened to the radio. Most households had their own set. In poorer districts where not all people could afford a radio, they shared. By 1930 there was one radio for every two to three households in the poorer districts of Chicago. The choice of programmes grew quickly. In August 1921 there was only one licensed radio station in America. By the end of 1922 there were 508 of them. By 1929 the new network NBC was making $150 million a year.

SOURCE 3

(i) *Jazz employs primitive rhythms which excite the baser human instincts.*

(ii) *Jazz music causes drunkenness. Reason and reflection are lost and the actions of the persons are directed by the stronger animal passions.*

Comments on jazz music in articles in the 1920s.

Source Analysis

What do you think the writers in Source 3 mean by 'the baser human instincts' and 'the stronger animal passions'?

Source Analysis

Study Source 4. Do you think it is more useful as evidence about movies, jazz or morals? Make sure you can explain your answer.

SOURCE 4

An advertisement for *The Jazz Bride*, a movie released in 1928.

Jazz

The radio gave much greater access to new music. Jazz music became an obsession among young people. African Americans who moved from the country to the cities had brought jazz and blues music with them. Blues music was particularly popular among African Americans, while jazz captured the imagination of both white and African American youth.

Such was the power of jazz music that the 1920s became known as the Jazz Age. Along with jazz went new dances such as the Charleston, and new styles of behaviour which were summed up in the image of the FLAPPER, a woman who wore short dresses and make-up and who smoked in public. One writer said that the ideal flapper was 'expensive and about nineteen'.

The older generation saw jazz and everything associated with it as a corrupting influence on the young people of the USA. The newspapers and magazines printed articles analysing the influence of jazz (see Source 3).

Sport

Sport was another boom area. Baseball became a big money sport with legendary teams like the New York Yankees and Boston Red Sox. Baseball stars like Babe Ruth became national figures. Boxing was also a very popular sport, with heroes like world heavyweight champion Jack Dempsey. Millions of Americans listened to sporting events on the radio.

Cinema

In a small suburb outside Los Angeles, called HOLLYWOOD, a major film industry was developing. All-year-round sunshine meant that the studios could produce large numbers of films or 'movies'. New stars like Charlie Chaplin and Buster Keaton made audiences roar with laughter, while Douglas Fairbanks thrilled them in daring adventure films. Until 1927 all movies were silent. In 1927 the first 'talkie' was made.

During the 1920s movies became a multi-billion dollar business and it was estimated that, by the end of the decade, a hundred million cinema tickets were being sold each week. Even the poor joined the movie craze. Working people in Chicago spent more than half of their leisure budget on movies. Even those who were so poor that they were getting Mothers' Aid Assistance went often. It only cost ten or twenty cents to see a movie.

Morals

Source 5 reflects the gulf which many people felt had opened up in moral attitudes. In the generation before the war, sex had still been a taboo subject. After the war it became a major concern of tabloid newspapers, Hollywood films, and everyday conversation. Scott Fitzgerald, one of a celebrated new group of young American writers who had served in the First World War, said: 'None of the mothers had any idea how casually their daughters were accustomed to be kissed.'

The cinema quickly discovered the selling power of sex. The first cinema star to be sold on sex appeal was Theda Bara who, without any acting talent, made a string of wildly successful films with titles like *Forbidden Path* and *When a Woman Sins*. Clara Bow was sold as the 'It' girl. Everybody knew that 'It' meant 'sex'. Hollywood turned out dozens of films a month about 'It', such as *Up in Mabel's Room, Her Purchase Price* and *A Shocking Night*. Male stars too, such as Rudolph Valentino, were presented as sex symbols. Women were said to faint at the very sight of him as a half-naked Arab prince in *The Sheik* (1921).

Today these films would be considered very tame indeed, but at the time they were considered very daring. The more conservative rural states were worried by the deluge of sex-obsessed films, and 36 states threatened to introduce CENSORSHIP legislation. Hollywood responded with its own censorship code which ensured that, while films might still be full of sex, at least the sinful characters were not allowed to get away with it!

Meanwhile, in the real world, contraceptive advice was openly available for the first time. Sex outside marriage was much more common than in the past, although probably more people talked about it and went to films about it than actually did it!

SOURCE 5

It seems to be accepted nowadays that our young people are going to the devil. Press, pulpit, and publicist are agreed that youth is wild and getting wilder. The college boy and his flapper friend, it is charged, drink, pet, and are disrespectful to their elders, while the neighbourhood gangster, aided by his youthful sweetie and stimulated by the false courage of heroin or cocaine, robs and murders with casual calmness long before he is out of his teens. Most of this lamentation, of course, is based on theory and not on fact. Those who indulge in it have read in the papers of a few sensational cases … The Children's Bureau of the United States Bureau of Labour recently undertook to throw a little light, of a really scientific character, on this question. If youth is as wild as is represented, and the wildness extends through all classes, the results certainly ought to be reflected in the records of the juvenile courts and the institutions in which delinquents are detained. Accordingly, a careful study was made of the statistics dealing with the subject. The figures investigated included delinquency rates in fourteen of the leading cities of the United States. … In nearly all these fourteen cities, the delinquency rates per 1,000 children of "delinquency age" were decidedly lower in 1924 or 1925 than in 1915. Youth may really be wild, in a fashion which does not get itself reflected in the delinquency and prison statistics. In so far, however, as the complaint has been made of youthful criminals as a new phenomenon, it is clearly without foundation.

Extract from the New-York-based liberal journal *The New Republic*, 1926.

Revision Tip
- Make sure you can describe at least two features of the Roaring Twenties.
- Ideally, try to make sure you can also explain why each feature was new to America.

The car

The motor car was one factor that tended to make all the other features of the 1920s mentioned above more possible. Cars helped the cities to grow by opening up the suburbs. They carried their owners to and from their entertainments. Cars carried boyfriends and girlfriends beyond the moral gaze of their parents and they took Americans to an increasing range of sporting events, beach holidays, shopping trips, picnics in the country, or simply on visits to their family and friends.

ACTIVITY

1. Draw a mind map to summarise the features of the Roaring Twenties. You can get lots of ideas from the text on pages 296–313, but remember that other factors may also be relevant; for example, material on the economy (pages 287–92). You can also add to your mind map as you find out about the period, particularly women (pages 299–300) and Prohibition (pages 309–12).
2. Think about the way these new developments in the 1920s affected people's lives. Choose three aspects of the Roaring Twenties that you think would have had the greatest impact and explain why. Compare your choices with others in your class.

SOURCE 6

A school teacher in 1905.

Think!
1 Compare the clothes of the women in Sources 6 and 7. Write a detailed description of the differences between them.
2 Flappers were controversial figures in the 1920s. List as many reasons as possible for this.

SOURCE 7

Flappers, identified by short skirts, bobbed hair, bright clothes and lots of make-up, were the extreme example of liberated urban women.

Women in 1920s USA

Women formed half of the population of the USA and their lives were as varied as those of men. It is therefore difficult to generalise. However, before the First World War middle-class women in the USA, like those in Britain, were expected to lead restricted lives. They had to wear very restrictive clothes and behave politely. They were expected not to wear make-up. Their relationships with men were strictly controlled. They had to have a chaperone with them when they went out with a boyfriend. They were expected not to take part in sport or to smoke in public. In most states they could not vote. Most women were expected to be housewives. Very few paid jobs were open to women. Most working women were in lower-paid jobs such as cleaning, dressmaking and secretarial work. In rural USA there were particularly tight restrictions owing to the Churches' traditional attitude to the role of women.

In the 1920s, many of these things began to change, especially for urban and middle-class women, for a range of reasons.

- **Impact of war** When the USA joined the war in 1917, some women were taken into the war industries, giving them experience of skilled factory work for the first time.
- **The vote** In 1920 they got the vote in all states.
- **The car** Through the 1920s, they shared the liberating effects of the car.
- **Housework** Their domestic work was made easier (in theory) by new electrical goods such as vacuum cleaners and washing machines.
- **Behaviour** For younger urban women many of the traditional roles of behaviour were eased as well. Women wore more daring clothes. They smoked in public and drank with men, in public. They went out with men, in cars, without a chaperone. They kissed in public.

Employment

In urban areas more women took on jobs – particularly middle-class women. Typically, these jobs were created by the new industries. There were 10 million women in jobs in 1929, 24 per cent more than in 1920. With money of their own, working women became the particular target of advertising. Even women who did not earn their own money were increasingly seen as the ones who took decisions about whether to buy new items for the home. There is evidence that women's role in choosing cars triggered Ford, in 1925, to make them available in colours other than black.

Choices

Films and novels also exposed women to a much wider range of role models. Millions of women a week saw films with sexy or daring heroines as well as other films that showed women in a more traditional role. The newspaper, magazine and film industries found that sex sold much better than anything else.

Women were less likely to stay in unhappy marriages. In 1914 there were 100,000 divorces; in 1929 there were twice as many.

Limitations

It might seem to you as if everything was changing, and for young, middle-class women living in cities a lot was changing in the 1920s. However, this is only part of the story.

Take work, for example. Women were still paid less than men, even when they did the same job. One of the reasons women's employment increased when men's did not was that women were cheaper employees.

SOURCE 8

It is wholly confusing to read the advertisements [for] ... devices which should lighten the chores of women in the home. On the whole the middle classes do their own housework ...

Women who live on farms ... besides caring for their children, washing the clothes, caring for the home and cooking ... [also] labour in the fields ... help milk the cows ...

The largest group of American women are the families of ... the vast army of unskilled, semi-skilled and skilled workers. The wages of these men are on the whole so small [that] wives must do double duty – caring for the children and the home and toiling on the outside as wage earners.

Doris E. Fleischman, *America as Americans See It*, F.J. Ringel (ed.), 1932.

Source Analysis

How does Source 9 contrast with the image of women given by Source 7?

Profile

Eleanor Roosevelt

- Born 1884 into a wealthy family.
- Married Franklin D. Roosevelt in 1905.
- Heavily involved in:
  - League of Women Voters
  - Women's Trade Union League
  - Women's City Club (New York)
  - New York State Democratic Party (Women's Division).
- Work concentrated on:
  - uniting New York Democrats
  - public housing for low-income workers
  - birth control information
  - better conditions for women workers.

In politics as well, women in no way achieved equality with men. They may have been given the vote but it did not give them access to political power. Political parties wanted women's votes, but they didn't particularly want women as political candidates as they considered them 'unelectable'. Although many women, such as Eleanor Roosevelt (see Profile), had a high public standing, only a handful of women had been elected by 1929.

How did women respond?

From films of the 1920s such as *Forbidden Path* (see page 297) you would think that all American women were living passionate lives full of steamy romance. However, novels and films of the period can be misleading. Women certainly did watch such films, in great numbers. But there is no evidence that the majority of women began to copy what they saw in the 1920s. In fact, the evidence suggests that the reaction of many women was one of opposition and outrage. There was a strong conservative element in American society. A combination of traditional religion and old country values kept most American women in a much more restricted role than young urban women enjoyed. For most, raising a family and maintaining a good home for their husbands were their main priorities.

SOURCE 9

Though a few young upper middle-class women in the cities talked about throwing off the older conventions – they were the flappers – most women stuck to more traditional attitudes concerning 'their place' ... most middle-class women concentrated on managing the home ... Their daughters, far from taking to the streets against sexual discrimination, were more likely to prepare for careers as mothers and housewives. Millions of immigrant women and their daughters ... also clung to traditions that placed men firmly in control of the family ... Most American women concentrated on making ends meet or setting aside money to purchase the new gadgets that offered some release from household drudgery.

J.T. Patterson, *America in the Twentieth Century*, 1999.

FOCUS TASK 9.4

How far did the roles of women change during the 1920s?

It's the Roaring Twenties – life's one big party!

It might be roaring for you, but life's not so great for me!

You are going to write a script to continue this conversation. Aim for six more scenes: three for each woman. To get you started, draw up a table with two columns headed:

- Roaring Twenties
- Not so Roaring Twenties.

In each column summarise the points each speaker might make to support their view of the 1920s.

Revision Tip

Select two changes for women in this period. Make sure you can describe both of them fully. Then select two ways in which life did not change for women and describe those.

FIGURE 9

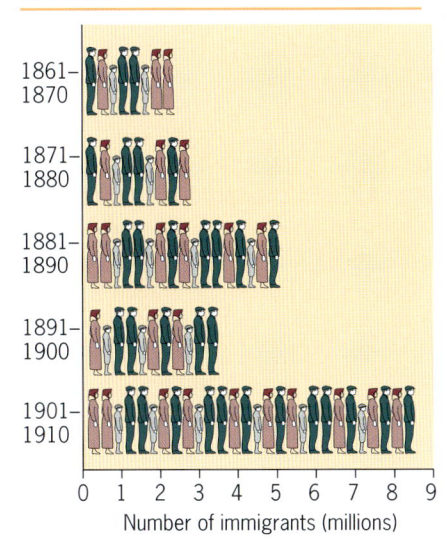

1861–1870
1871–1880
1881–1890
1891–1900
1901–1910

0 1 2 3 4 5 6 7 8 9
Number of immigrants (millions)

Immigration to the USA, 1861–1910.

Intolerance towards immigrants

At the same time as some young Americans were experiencing liberation, others were facing intolerance and racism.

The vast majority of Americans were either immigrants or descendants of recent immigrants. Figure 11 shows you the ethnic background of the main groups. As you can see from Figure 10, IMMIGRATION to the USA was at an all-time high from 1901 to 1910. Many Jewish immigrants arrived from eastern Europe and Russia who were fleeing persecution. Many Italians arrived who were fleeing poverty. Many Italian immigrants did not intend to settle in the USA, but hoped to make money to take back to their families in Italy.

The United States had always prided itself on being a 'melting pot'. In theory, individual groups lost their ethnic identity and blended together with other groups to become just 'Americans'. In practice, however, this wasn't always the case. In the USA's big cities the more established immigrant groups – Irish Americans, French Canadians and German Americans – competed for the best jobs and the best available housing. These groups tended to look down on the more recent eastern European and Italian immigrants. These in turn had nothing but contempt for African Americans and Mexicans, who were almost at the bottom of the scale.

FIGURE 11

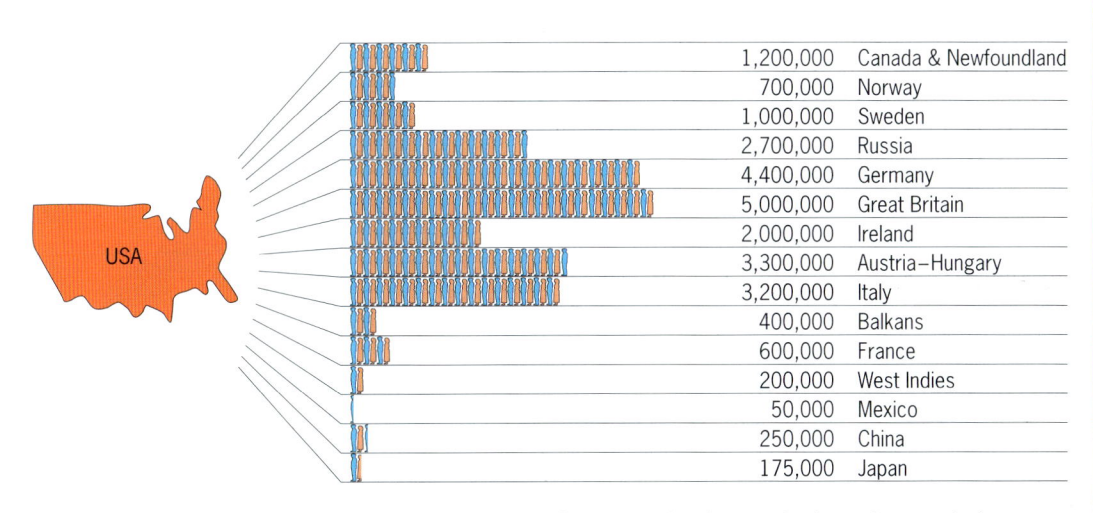

Number	Origin
1,200,000	Canada & Newfoundland
700,000	Norway
1,000,000	Sweden
2,700,000	Russia
4,400,000	Germany
5,000,000	Great Britain
2,000,000	Ireland
3,300,000	Austria–Hungary
3,200,000	Italy
400,000	Balkans
600,000	France
200,000	West Indies
50,000	Mexico
250,000	China
175,000	Japan

The ethnic background of American immigrants in the early twentieth century.

SOURCE 12

The blaze of revolution is eating its way into the homes of the American workman, licking at the altars of the churches, leaping into the belfry of the school house, crawling into the sacred corners of American homes, seeking to replace the marriage vows with libertine laws, burning up the foundations of society.

Mitchell Palmer, US Attorney General, speaking in 1920.

The Red Scare

In the 1920s these racist attitudes towards immigrants were made worse by an increased fear of Bolshevism or COMMUNISM. The USA watched with alarm as Russia became communist after the Russian Revolution of 1917. It feared that many of the more recent immigrants from eastern Europe and Russia were bringing similar RADICAL ideas with them to the USA. This reaction was called the RED SCARE.

In 1919 Americans saw evidence all around them to confirm their fears. There was a wave of disturbances. Some 400,000 American workers went on strike. Even the police in Boston went on strike and looters and thieves roamed the city. There were race riots in 25 towns.

SOURCE 13

The steamship companies haul them over to America and as soon as they step off the ships the problem of the steamship companies is settled, but our problem has only begun – Bolshevism, red anarchy, black-handers and kidnappers, challenging the authority and integrity of our flag … Thousands come here who will never take the oath to support our constitution and become citizens of the USA. They pay allegiance to some other country while they live upon the substance of our own. They fill places that belong to the wage earning citizens of America … They are of no service whatever to our people … They constitute a menace and a danger to us every day.

Republican Senator Heflin speaking in 1921 in a debate over whether to limit immigration.

Source Analysis

Look at Sources 12–14. Do they tell historians more about communists or the enemies of communism? Explain your answer.

Think!

Work in pairs.
1 One of you collect evidence to show that the Red Scare was the result of the fear of communism.
2 The other collect evidence to show that the Red Scare was the result of prejudice and intolerance.
3 Now try to come up with a definition of the Red Scare that combines both of your views.

Revision Tip

- Make sure you can describe two attacks that sparked off the Red Scare 1919–20.
- Make sure you can explain at least one reason for Palmer's downfall.

Today, most historians argue that the strikes were caused by economic hardship. However, many prominent Americans in the 1920s saw the strikes as the dangerous signs of communist interference. Fear of communism combined with prejudice against immigrants was a powerful mix.

The fears were not totally unjustified. Many immigrants in the USA did hold radical political beliefs. Anarchists published pamphlets and distributed them widely in American cities, calling for the overthrow of the government. In April 1919 a bomb planted in a church in Milwaukee killed ten people. In May, bombs were posted to 36 prominent Americans. In June more bombs went off in seven US cities, and one almost succeeded in killing Mitchell Palmer, the US Attorney General. All those known to have radical political beliefs were rounded up in what were called the 'Palmer Raids'. They were generally immigrants and the evidence against them was often flimsy. J. Edgar Hoover, a clerk appointed by Palmer, built up files on 60,000 suspects and in 1919–20 around 10,000 individuals were informed that they were to be deported from the USA.

SOURCE 14

A 1919 cartoon entitled 'Come On!' showing attitudes to communism in the USA. The character in the black suit looks like Trotsky and has 'Revolution maker' written on his chest. The piece of paper says 'Propaganda for US'.

Palmer discovered that these purges were popular, so he tried to use the fear of revolution to build up his own political support and run for president. Trade unionists, African Americans, Jewish people, Catholics and almost all minority groups found themselves accused of being communists. In the end, however, Palmer caused his own downfall. He predicted that a Red Revolution would begin in May 1920. When nothing happened, the papers began to make fun of him and officials in the Justice Department who were sickened by Palmer's actions undermined him. Secretary of Labor Louis Post examined Palmer's case files and found that only 556 out of the thousands of cases brought had any basis in fact.

> **Revision Tip**
> - Practise explaining to someone else why the Sacco and Vanzetti case received so much publicity.

Sacco and Vanzetti

Two high-profile victims of the Red Scare were Italian Americans Nicola Sacco and Bartolomeo Vanzetti. They were arrested in 1920 on suspicion of armed robbery and murder. It quickly emerged that they were self-confessed anarchists. Anarchists hated the American system of government and believed in destroying it by creating social disorder. Their trial became less a trial for murder, more a trial of their radical ideas. The prosecution relied heavily on racist slurs about their Italian origins, and on stirring up fears about their radical beliefs. The judge at the trial said that although Vanzetti 'may not actually have committed the crime attributed to him he is nevertheless morally culpable [to blame] because he is the enemy of our existing institutions'.

Sacco and Vanzetti were convicted on flimsy evidence. A leading lawyer of the time said: 'Judge Thayer is ... full of prejudice. He has been carried away by fear of Reds which has captured about 90 per cent of the American people.' After six years of legal appeals, Sacco and Vanzetti were executed in 1927, to a storm of protest around the world from both radicals and moderates who saw how unjustly the trial had been conducted. Fifty years later, they were pardoned.

Immigration quotas

By 1910, nearly 14 million immigrants were living in the USA. The government had already banned immigrants from China in 1917, but in the 1920s, two further laws were passed:

- The Emergency Quota Act, 1921 – was passed in response to the influx of immigrants from eastern and southern Europe. A quota system was introduced. This limited total immigration to three per cent of a country's foreign-born population living in the USA. This meant it was harder for eastern and southern Europeans to move to the USA compared to those from northern and western Europe.
- The National Origins Act, 1924 – which limited total immigration to just 150,000 per year. The Act also effectively banned Asian immigrants. The government said that it was 'to preserve US homogeneity' meaning it wanted most Americans to be White, Anglo-Saxon and Protestant (sometimes called WASPs).

The experience of African Americans

African Americans had long been part of America's history. The first Africans had been brought to the USA as slaves by white settlers in the seventeenth century. By the time slavery was ended in the nineteenth century, there were more African Americans than white people in the southern United States. White governments, fearing the power of African Americans, introduced many laws to control their freedom. They could not vote. They were denied access to good jobs and to worthwhile education, and well into the twentieth century they suffered great poverty.

The Ku Klux Klan

The KU KLUX KLAN was a white supremacy movement. It used violence to intimidate African Americans. It had been in decline, but was revived after the release of the film *The Birth of a Nation* in 1915. The film was set in the 1860s, just after the Civil War. It glorified the Klan as defenders of decent American values against renegade African Americans and corrupt white businessmen. President Wilson had it shown in the White House. He said: 'It is like writing history with lightning. And my only regret is that it is all so terribly true.' With such support from prominent figures, the Klan became a powerful political force in the early 1920s.

SOURCE 15

A lad whipped with branches until his back was ribboned flesh ... a white girl, divorcee, beaten into unconsciousness in her home; a naturalised foreigner flogged until his back was pulp because he married an American woman; a negro lashed until he sold his land to a white man for a fraction of its value.

R.A. Patton, writing in *Current History* in 1929, describes the victims of Klan violence in Alabama.

> **Source Analysis**
> What does Source 15 tell you about the motives of Klan violence?

Jim Crow

African Americans throughout the South faced fierce racism. In theory, they became free in 1865 when the end of the American Civil War ended slavery. In reality, however, white supremacy remained through the discriminatory set of laws and practices which became known as 'Jim Crow'. African Americans were prevented from voting by literacy tests, intimidation and violence. They were discriminated against in employment and education. Even their streets were rebuilt to remind them that they were second-class citizens. During the 1920s thousands of monuments were erected to white Confederate Civil War soldiers and commanders. This was 60 years after the war had ended and it was a clear attempt to remind African Americans who was in charge. Some states are beginning to address this issue. Since 2018, over 120 Confederate statues and memorials have been taken down.

'Strange Fruit'

African Americans faced violence if they stood up for themselves and they often faced violence even when they had done nothing at all. For example, in 1930 James Cameron, aged sixteen, was arrested with two other African American men on suspicion of the murder of a white man and the rape of a white woman. They were in prison in Marion, Indiana. A mob arrived intending to LYNCH them (hang them without trial). The mob broke down the doors of the jail, dragged out the two other men and hanged them. Miraculously Cameron was spared. He still does not know what saved him. The crowd had the rope round his neck before they suddenly stopped and let him limp back to the door of the jail. He called it 'a miraculous intervention'. A photograph of the lynchings became very well known and inspired a New York writer, Abel Meeropol, to write a poem he called 'Bitter Fruit' (referring to the lynched men), later changed to 'Strange Fruit'.

Factfile

The Ku Klux Klan

- Formed in the 1850s by former soldiers after the American CIVIL WAR with the aim of keeping whites in control.
- It used parades, beatings, lynchings and other violent methods to intimidate African Americans. It also attacked Jewish people, Catholics and foreign immigrants.
- It was strongest in the Midwest and rural South, where working-class whites competed with African Americans for unskilled jobs.
- It was strongly anti-communist and was even supported by some of the Protestant churches in the South. It had also supported Prohibition.
- It declined in the late nineteenth century but was started up again in 1915. It spread rapidly in the early 1920s, managing to get Klansmen elected into positions of political power.
- By 1924 it had 4.5 million members.
- Oregon and Oklahoma had governors who belonged to the Klan. The Klan was especially dominant in Indiana.
- The Klan declined after 1925. One of its leaders, Grand Wizard David Stephenson, was convicted of a vicious sexually motivated murder. He turned informer and the corruption of the Klan became common knowledge.

FOCUS TASK 9.5

What caused prejudice and intolerance in the 1920s?

On pages 301–05 you have seen several different causes of prejudice and intolerance: politics; race; religion.
1. Create some cards and put one of these headings on each card. Now add some examples of each factor from what you have read on pages 301–05. Add other cards if you think there are factors that we have not included.
2. Arrange the cards in what you think is their order of importance for causing prejudice or intolerance. See if others in your class agree with you.

Profile

Paul Robeson

- Born 1898, son of a church minister who had been a former slave.
- Went to Columbia University and passed his law exams with honours in 1923.
- As a black lawyer, it was almost impossible for him to find work, so he became an actor – his big break was in the hit musical 'Showboat'.
- Visited Moscow in 1934 on a world tour and declared his approval of communism saying 'Here, for the first time in my life, I walk in dignity.'
- As a communist sympathiser, Robeson suffered in the USA – he was banned from performing, suffered death threats and had his passport confiscated.
- He left the USA in 1958 to live in Europe, but returned in 1963.

Cameron's experience was not unusual. Thousands of African Americans were murdered by lynching in this period. Many reports describe appalling atrocities at which whole families, including young children, clapped and cheered. It is one of the most shameful aspects of the USA at this time.

Faced by such intimidation, discrimination and poverty, many African Americans left the rural South and moved to the cities of the northern USA. Through the 1920s the African American population of both Chicago and New York doubled: New York's from 150,000 to 330,000 and Chicago's from 110,000 to 230,000.

Improvements

In the north, African Americans had a better chance of getting good jobs and a good education. For example, Howard University was an exclusively African American institution for higher education.

In both Chicago and New York, there was a small but growing African American middle class. There was a successful 'black CAPITALIST' movement, encouraging African Americans to set up businesses. In Chicago they ran a successful BOYCOTT of the city's chain stores, protesting that they would not shop there unless African American staff were employed. By 1930 almost all the shops in the South Side belt where African Americans lived had black employees.

There were internationally famous African Americans, such as the singer and actor Paul Robeson (see Profile). The popularity of jazz made many African American musicians into high-profile media figures. The African American neighbourhood of Harlem in New York became the centre of the Harlem Renaissance. Here musicians and singers made Harlem a centre of creativity and a magnet for white customers in the bars and clubs. African American artists flourished in this atmosphere, as did African American writers. The poet Langston Hughes wrote about the lives of ordinary working-class African Americans and the poverty and problems they suffered. Countee Cullen was another prominent poet who tried to tackle racism and poverty. In one famous poem ('For A Lady I Know') he tried to sum up attitudes of wealthy white employees to their African American servants:

> *She even thinks that up in heaven,*
> *Her class lies late and snores*
>
> *While poor black cherubs rise at seven,*
> *To do celestial chores.*

Revision Tip

Racial prejudice is a major part of the course. You need to be able to describe:
- two examples of intolerance which African Americans faced
- at least two ways African Americans responded (look at page XXX as well).

ACTIVITY

Read the profile of Paul Robeson. Imagine you are interviewing him on the radio as he looks back on his life in the 1920s. Write three questions you'd like to ask him.

SOURCE 16

If I die in Atlanta my work shall only then begin ... Look for me in the whirlwind or the storm, look for me all around you, for, with God's grace, I shall come and bring with me countless millions of black slaves who have died in America and the West Indies and the millions in Africa to aid you in the fight for Liberty, Freedom and Life.

Marcus Garvey's last word's before going to jail in 1925.

SOURCE 17

Marcus Garvey after his arrest.

Revision Tip
Prepare your ideas ready for a question about how far life changed for African Americans in the 1920s. Choose:
- two points to help you explain how life improved
- two points to help explain how it did not change or got worse.

Think!
James Cameron went on to found America's Black Holocaust Museum, which records the suffering of black African Americans through American history. Write a 100-word summary for the museum handbook of the ways in which the 1920s were a time of change for African Americans.

The beginnings of the Civil Rights movement

African Americans also entered politics. W.E.B DuBois founded the National Association for the Advancement of Colored People (NAACP). In 1919 it had 300 branches and around 90,000 members. It campaigned to end racial segregation laws and to get laws passed against lynching.

Another important figure was Marcus Garvey. He founded the Universal Negro Improvement Association (UNIA). Garvey urged African Americans to be proud of their race and colour. The UNIA helped African Americans to set up their own businesses. By the mid-1920s there were UNIA grocery stores, laundries and restaurants.

Garvey set up a shipping line to support both UNIA businesses and his scheme of helping African Americans to emigrate to Africa away from white racism. Eventually, his businesses collapsed, partly as a result of the hostility of the authorities, particularly FBI director. J. Edgar Hoover. Garvey's movement attracted over 1 million members at its height in 1921. One of these was the Reverend Earl Little. He was beaten to death by Klan thugs in the late 1920s, but his son went on to be the civil rights leader Malcolm X.

Continuing inequality

Although important, these movements failed to change the USA dramatically. Life expectancy for African Americans increased from 45 to 48 between 1900 and 1930, but for whites it increased from 54 to 59. Many African Americans in the northern cities lived in great poverty. In Harlem in New York they lived in poorer housing than white people, yet paid higher rents. They had poorer education and health services than white people. Large numbers of black women worked as low-paid domestic servants. Factories making cars employed few black people or operated a white people-only policy.

In Chicago African Americans suffered great prejudice from longer-established white residents (see Source 18).

SOURCE 18

There is nothing in the make up of a negro, physically or mentally, that should induce anyone to welcome him as a neighbour. The best of them are unsanitary ... ruin follows in their path. They are as proud as peacocks, but have nothing of the peacock's beauty ...

From the *Chicago Property Owners' Journal*, 1920.

In Chicago when African Americans attempted to use parks, playgrounds and beaches in the Irish and Polish districts, they were set upon by gangs of white people calling themselves 'athletic clubs'. The result was that African American communities in northern areas often became isolated ghettos.

Within the African American communities prejudice was also evident. Middle-class African Americans who were restless in the ghettos tended to blame newly arrived migrants from the South for intensifying white racism. In Harlem, the presence of some 50,000 West Indians was a source of inter-racial tension. Many of them were better educated, more militant and prouder of their colour than the newly arrived African Americans from the South.

'The vanishing Americans'

The Native Americans were the original settlers of the North American continent. They almost disappeared as an ethnic group during the rapid expansion of the USA during the nineteenth century – declining from 1.5 million to around 250,000 in 1920. Those who survived or who chose not to leave their traditional way of life were forced to move to RESERVATIONS in the Midwest.

SOURCE 19

Photograph of a Native American, Charlie Guardipee, and his family taken for a US Government report of 1921. According to the report Charlie Guardipee had twenty horses, ten cattle, no chickens, no wheat, oats or garden, and no sickness in the family.

In the 1920s the Government became concerned about the treatment of Native Americans. Twelve thousand had served in the armed forces in the First World War, which helped to change white attitudes to them. The Government did a census in the 1920s and a major survey in the late 1920s which revealed that most lived in extreme poverty, with much lower life expectancy than white people, that they were in worse health and had poorer education and poorly paid jobs (if they were able to get a job at all). They suffered extreme discrimination. They were quickly losing their land. Mining companies were legally able to seize large areas of Native American land. Many Native Americans who owned land were giving up the struggle to survive in their traditional way and selling up.

They were also losing their culture. Their children were sent to special boarding schools. The aim of the schools was to 'assimilate' them into white American culture. This involved trying to destroy the Native Americans' beliefs, traditions, dances and languages. In the 1920s the Native Americans were referred to as 'the vanishing Americans'.

However, the 1920s were in some ways a turning point. In 1924 Native Americans were granted US citizenship and allowed to vote for the first time. In 1928 the Merriam Report proposed widespread improvement to the laws relating to Native Americans, and these reforms were finally introduced under Roosevelt's New Deal in 1934.

Think!
Make two lists:
a) evidence of prejudice and discrimination towards Native Americans
b) evidence that the treatment of Native Americans was improving in the 1920s.

Revision Tip
Make sure you can describe:
- at least two ways in which Native Americans suffered in the 1920s
- one improvement.

SOURCE 20

For nearly two hours ... Mr Darrow [lawyer for the defendant] goaded his opponent. [He] asked Mr Bryan if he really believed that the serpent had always crawled on its belly because it tempted Eve, and if he believed Eve was made from Adam's rib ... [Bryan's] face flushed under Mr Darrow's searching words, and ... when one [question] stumped him he took refuge in his faith and either refused to answer directly or said in effect: 'The Bible states it; it must be so.'

From the report of the Monkey Trial in the *Baltimore Evening Sun*, July 1925.

Think!
1. Why do you think the trial became known as the Monkey Trial?
2. In what ways did the trial show American intolerance of other points of view?

Revision Tip
Try to summarise this page in three points:
- a reason for the Monkey Trial
- a description of the trial
- the results of the trial.

Religious intolerance

There was an increasing divide between urban and rural America in the 1920s. Many younger people and professionals in the growing towns and cities indulged in the consumerism and partying associated with the Roaring Twenties. They held liberal and progressive views about race relations and religion. In many parts of rural America, especially in some states in the South and Midwest known as the 'Bible Belt', many people still went to church regularly. They held more traditional and conservative opinions. Some Protestant churches preached that city life was increasingly immoral and threatened the fabric of American society.

The Monkey Trial

In 1925, these opposite opinions on religion would result in a showdown between evolutionists and creationists. Evolutionists believed in Charles Darwin's theory of evolution – the belief that humans are descended from a common, ape-like ancestor. Anti-evolutionists or creationists believed in the literal truth of the biblical story of creation. This showdown would become known as the Monkey Trial.

In 1925 the Butler Act was passed in Tennessee. This prohibited schools from teaching Darwin's theory of evolution because it contradicted the Bible. Six other states followed suit and passed similar laws. The American Civil Liberties Union (ALCU) was an organisation set up to defend civil liberties. They promised to defend anyone who broke this law in Tennessee. A science teacher, called John Scopes, agreed to do this and he was put on trial in July for teaching the theory of evolution.

The ACLU brought in their best lawyer, Clarence Darrow, to defend Scopes. The leader of the anti-evolutionists, William Jennings Bryan, led the prosecution. The trial was a spectacle. The courtroom was packed every day and journalists from all over the South and around the world reported on the proceedings. It was the first trial to be broadcast on national radio and hooked families across the USA. There was no doubt that Scopes was guilty of breaking the law, but that was not the real aim of the trial. Darrow wanted America to see how censorship of free speech was being attacked in the South. As the trial reached a climax, Darrow called Bryan to the witness stand and posed question after question about his beliefs in the literal truth of the story of creation. Bryan was unable to defend himself (see Source 21) and the courtroom erupted when Darrow had finished.

Scopes was convicted of breaking the law and fined $100, but it was really American fundamentalism itself which was on trial – and it lost! At the trial the anti-evolutionists were subjected to great mockery. Their arguments were publicly ridiculed and their spokesman Bryan, who claimed to be an expert on religion and science, was shown to be ignorant and confused. After the trial, the anti-evolution lobby was weakened.

FOCUS TASK 9.6
How widespread was intolerance in US society in the 1920s?

You have looked at various examples of intolerance and prejudice in the 1920s. Draw a table with all the different groups that faced intolerance in the first column – Immigrants; Communists; African Americans; Native Americans; Evolutionists. In the second column, find some evidence from pages 301–08 to explain how intolerance affected each group, using examples to support your comments. In the final column, explain how the different groups reacted and comment on whether their situation improved, stayed the same or got worse.

SOURCE 21

Our nation can only be saved by turning the pure stream of country sentiment and township morals to flush out the cesspools of cities and so save civilisation from pollution.

A temperance campaigner speaking in 1917.

FOCUS TASK 9.7
Why was Prohibition introduced?
1 Make some cards to summarise the reasons why Prohibition was introduced. You could include:
- race
- politics
- religion
- economics
- values
- patriotism
- health.

Note down examples of how each of these factors contributed to the passing of Prohibition.

2 Decide which was most important and then compare your top factor with your top factor for causing prejudice and intolerance (see page 305).

Why was Prohibition introduced?

In the nineteenth century, in rural areas of the USA there was a very strong 'TEMPERANCE' movement. Members of temperance movements agreed not to drink alcohol and also campaigned to get others to give up alcohol. Most members of these movements were devout Christians who saw the damage alcohol did to family life. They wanted to stop that damage.

In the nineteenth century the two main movements were the Anti-Saloon League and the Women's Christian Temperance Union (see Sources 22 and 23). The temperance movements were so strong in some of the rural areas that they persuaded their state governments to prohibit the sale of alcohol within the state. Through the early twentieth century the campaign gathered pace. It became a national campaign to prohibit (ban) alcohol throughout the country. It acquired some very powerful supporters. Leading industrialists backed the movement, believing that workers would be more reliable if they did not drink. Politicians backed it because it got them votes in rural areas. By 1916, 21 states had banned saloons.

Supporters of PROHIBITION became known as 'dries'. The dries brought some powerful arguments to their case. They claimed that '3000 infants are smothered yearly in bed, by drunken parents'. The USA's entry into the First World War in 1917 boosted the dries. Drinkers were accused of being unpatriotic cowards. Most of the big breweries were run by German immigrants who were portrayed as the enemy. Drink was linked to other evils as well. After the Russian Revolution, the dries claimed that Bolshevism thrived on drink and that alcohol led to lawlessness in the cities, particularly in immigrant communities. Saloons were seen as dens of vice that destroyed family life. The campaign became one of country values against city values.

In 1917 the movement had enough states on its side to propose the Eighteenth Amendment to the Constitution. This 'prohibited the manufacture, sale or transportation of intoxicating liquors'. It became law in January 1920 and is known as the Volstead Act.

SOURCE 22

A poster issued by the Anti-Saloon League in 1915.

SOURCE 23

A poster issued by the Women's Christian Temperance Union.

Think!
1. Prohibition did not actually make it illegal to drink alcohol, only to make or supply it. Why?
2. Is it possible to enforce any law when the population refuses to obey it? Try to think of laws that affect you today.

What was the impact of Prohibition?

Prohibition lasted from 1920 until 1933. It is often said that Prohibition was a total failure. This is not entirely correct. Levels of alcohol consumption fell by about 30 per cent in the early 1920s (see Figure 24). Prohibition gained widespread approval in some states, particularly the rural areas in the Midwest, although in urban states it was not popular (Maryland never even introduced Prohibition). The Government ran information campaigns and Prohibition agents arrested offenders (see Figure 25). Two of the most famous agents were Isadore Einstein and his deputy Moe Smith. They made 4392 arrests. Their raids were always low key. They would enter speakeasies (illegal bars) and simply order a drink. Einstein had a special flask hidden inside his waistcoat with a funnel attached. He preserved the evidence by pouring his drink down the funnel and the criminals were caught!

FIGURE 24

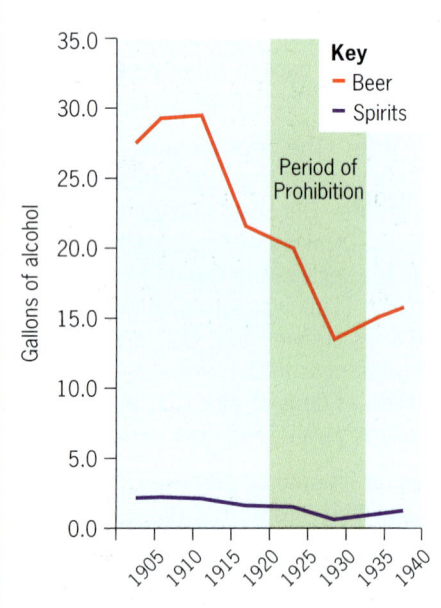

Average alcohol consumption of Americans (in US gallons) per year, 1905–40.

FIGURE 25

	1921	1925	1929
Illegal distilleries seized	9,746	12,023	15,794
Gallons (US) of spirit seized	414,000	11,030,000	11,860,000
Arrests	34,175	62,747	66,878

Activities of federal prohibition agents.

Supply and demand

Despite the work of the agents, Prohibition proved impossible to enforce effectively in the cities. Enforcement was underfinanced. There were not enough agents – each agent was poorly paid and was responsible for a huge area. By far the biggest problem was that millions of Americans, particularly in urban areas, were simply not prepared to obey this law. So a vast network of suppliers stepped in to meet the demand for illegal alcohol.

Bootleggers

The suppliers of illegal alcohol were called 'bootleggers'. Some made vast fortunes. About two-thirds of the illegal alcohol came from Canada. The vast border between the USA and Canada was virtually impossible to patrol. Other bootleggers brought in alcohol by sea. They would simply wait in the waters outside US control until an opportunity to land their cargo presented itself. One of the most famous was Captain McCoy, who specialised in the finest Scotch whisky. This is where the phrase 'the real McCoy' comes from.

Stills

Illegal stills (short for distilleries) sprang up all over the USA as people made their own illegal whisky – moonshine. The stills were a major fire hazard and the alcohol they produced was frequently poisonous. Agents seized over 280,000 of these stills, but we have no clear way of knowing how many were not seized.

Speakeasies

Most Americans had no need for their own still. They simply went to their favourite speakeasy. By 1925 there were more speakeasies in American cities than there had been saloons in 1919. Izzy Einstein filed a report to

Source Analysis
Which source or figure on pages 309–11 is most useful to the historian investigating the impact of Prohibition, or are they more useful when taken together? Explain your answer.

Revision Tip
The main debate about Prohibition is why it failed. Even so it is worth remembering one or two examples of its success.

SOURCE 26

Alcohol being tipped down the drain. Vast quantities of bootleg (illegal) liquor were seized, but were only a fraction of the total.

SOURCE 27

A visit to a speakeasy.

SOURCE 29

'The National Gesture': a cartoon from the Prohibition era.

his superiors on how easy it was to find alcohol after arriving in a new city. Here are the results:

- Chicago: 21 minutes
- Atlanta: 17 minutes
- Pittsburg: 11 minutes
- New Orleans: 35 seconds (he was offered a bottle of whisky by his taxi driver when he asked where he could get a drink!)

The speakeasies were well supplied by bootleggers. Al Capone (see page XXX) made around $60 million a year from his bootlegging and speakeasies. His view was that 'Prohibition is a business. All I do is supply a public demand.' And the demand was huge.

Corruption

Prohibition led to massive corruption. Many of the law enforcement officers were themselves involved with the liquor trade. Big breweries stayed in business throughout the Prohibition era. This is not an easy business to hide! But the breweries stayed in operation by bribing local government officials, Prohibition agents and the police to leave them alone.

In some cities, police officers were quite prepared to direct people to speakeasies. Even when arrests were made, it was difficult to get convictions because more senior officers or even judges were in the pay of the criminals. One in twelve Prohibition agents was dismissed for corruption. The New York FBI boss, Don Chaplin, once ordered his 200 agents: 'Put your hands on the table, both of them. Every son of a bitch wearing a diamond is fired.'

SOURCE 28

Statistics in the Detroit police court of 1924 show 7391 arrests for violations of the prohibition law, but only 458 convictions. Ten years ago a dishonest policeman was a rarity … Now the honest ones are pointed out as rarities … Their relationship with the bootleggers is perfectly friendly. They have to pinch two out of five once in a while, but they choose the ones who are least willing to pay bribes.

E. Mandeville, in *Outlook* magazine, 1925.

Source Analysis

1. Explain the message of Source 29.
2. Read Source 28. How has Prohibition affected the police in Detroit?
3. Which of Sources 28 and 29 do you most trust to give you accurate information about corruption during the Prohibition era?

Revision Tip

Make sure you can use these key terms correctly in an answer about why Prohibition failed: bootlegger, speakeasy, demand, corruption.

SOURCE 30

A photo of Al Capone from 1930.

ACTIVITY

In other chapters of this book, you have seen profiles of important historical figures. Use the information and sources to produce two different profiles of Al Capone.
- The first profile is the kind of profile that might appear in this book.
- The second profile is one that might have appeared inside a news magazine of the time in 1930 after the St Valentine's Day Massacre.

Make sure you can explain (to your teacher) why the two profiles are different.

This information about Capone will get you started:
- Born 1889 in New York.
- Arrived in Chicago in 1919.
- Took over from Johnny Torio in 1925.
- Jailed in 1931 for not paying taxes.
- Released in January 1939.
- Died in 1947 from syphilis.

Revision Tip

Add these to your list of terms you should know how to explain in relation to Prohibition: gangster, Chicago.

Gangsters

The most common image people have of the Prohibition era is the GANGSTER. Estimates suggest that organised gangs made about $2 billion out of the sale of illegal alcohol. The bootlegger George Remus certainly did well from the trade. He had a huge network of paid officials that allowed him to escape charge after charge against him. At one party he gave a car to each of the women guests, while all the men received diamond cuff links worth $25,000.

The rise of the gangsters tells us a lot about American society at this time. The gangsters generally came from immigrant backgrounds. In the early 1920s the main gangs were Jewish, Polish, Irish and Italian. Gangsters generally came from poorer backgrounds within these communities. They were often poorly educated, but they were also clever and ruthless. Dan O'Banion (Irish gang leader murdered by Capone), Pete and Vince Guizenberg (hired killers who worked for Bugsy Moran and died in the St Valentine's Day Massacre), and Lucky Luciano (Italian killer who spent ten years in prison) were some of the most powerful gangsters. The gangs fought viciously with each other to control the liquor trade and also the prostitution, gambling and protection rackets that were centred on the speakeasies. They made use of new technology, especially automobiles and the Thompson sub-machine gun, which was devastatingly powerful but could be carried around and hidden under an overcoat. In Chicago alone, there were 130 gangland murders in 1926 and 1927 and not one arrest. By the late 1920s fear and bribery made law enforcement ineffective.

Chicago and Al Capone

The gangsters operated all over the USA, but they were most closely associated with Chicago. Perhaps the best example of the power of the gangsters is Chicago gangster boss Al Capone. He arrived in Chicago in 1919, on the run from a murder investigation in New York. He ran a drinking club for his boss Johnny Torio. In 1925 Torio retired after an assassination attempt by one of his rivals, Bugsy Moran. Capone took over and proved to be a formidable gangland boss. He built up a huge network of corrupt officials among Chicago's police, local government workers, judges, lawyers and Prohibition agents. He even controlled Chicago's mayor, William Hale Thompson. Surprisingly, he was a high-profile and even popular figure in the city. He was a regular at baseball and American football games and was cheered by the crowd when he took his seat. He was well known for giving generous tips (over $100) to waiters and shop girls and spent $30,000 on a soup kitchen for the unemployed.

Capone was supported by a ruthless gang, handpicked for their loyalty to him. He killed two of his own men whom he suspected of plotting against him by beating their brains out with a baseball bat. By 1929 he had destroyed the power of the other Chicago gangs, committing at least 300 murders in the process. The peak of his violent reign came with the St Valentine's Day Massacre in 1929. Capone's men murdered seven of his rival Bugsy Moran's gang, using a false police car and two gangsters in police uniform to put Moran's men off their guard.

The end of Prohibition

The St Valentine's Day Massacre was a turning point. The papers screamed that the gangsters had graduated from murder to massacre. It seemed that Prohibition, often called 'the Noble Experiment', had failed. It had made the USA lawless, the police corrupt and the gangsters rich and powerful. When the Wall Street Crash was followed by the Depression in the early 1930s, there were also sound economic arguments for getting rid of it. Legalising alcohol would create jobs, raise tax revenue and free up resources tied up in the impossible task of enforcing Prohibition. The Democrat president Franklin D Roosevelt was elected in 1932 and Prohibition was REPEALED in December 1933.

FOCUS TASK 9.8
Why did Prohibition fail?
In the end Prohibition failed. Here are four groups who could be blamed for the failure of Prohibition.

a) **the American people** who carried on going to illegal speakeasies making Prohibition difficult to enforce

b) **the law enforcers** who were corrupt and ignored the law breakers

c) **the bootleggers** who continued supplying and selling alcohol

d) **the gangsters** who controlled the trade through violence and made huge profits

1. For each of the above groups find evidence on pages 309–12 to show that it contributed to the failure of Prohibition.
2. Say which group you think played the most important role in the failure. Explain your choice.
3. Draw a diagram to show links between the groups.

FOCUS TASK 9.9
Why was Prohibition repealed in 1933?

Many people who were convinced of the case for Prohibition before 1920 were equally convinced that it should be abolished in 1933.

Write two letters.
- The first should be from a supporter of Prohibition to his or her Congressman in 1919 explaining why the Congressman should vote for Prohibition. In your letter, explain how Prohibition could help to solve problems in America.
- The second should be from the same person to the Congressman in 1933 explaining why the Congressman should vote against Prohibition. In your letter, explain why Prohibition has failed.

Key Question Summary
How far did US society change in the 1920s?
1. The 'Roaring Twenties' is a name given to this period to get across the sense of vibrancy, excitement and change.
2. The 1920s saw enormous social and cultural change in the cities with new attitudes to behaviour, entertainment, dress styles and morals. This was not shared by many in traditional, conservative rural communities.
3. There was also a growth in prejudice and intolerance, particularly towards new immigrants. This was highlighted by the Sacco and Vanzetti case.
4. The divide between the urban and rural USA was evident in different attitudes to the role of women in society, views on morality and religious values (as shown in the Monkey Trial).
5. In 1920 the manufacture and sale of alcohol was prohibited. But Prohibition was difficult to enforce and had disastrous effects, leading to the growth of organised crime, lawlessness and corruption in politics and business.

9C What were the causes and consequences of the Wall Street Crash?

FOCUS

In 1928 there was a presidential election. Not surprisingly, with the booming economy, the Republican Herbert Hoover won. But within a year he was being cursed by many Americans as the economy collapsed and a long depression destroyed much of the prosperity of the 1920s. What went wrong?

Focus Points
- How far was speculation responsible for the Wall Street Crash?
- What impact did the Crash have on the economy?
- What were the social consequences of the Crash?
- Why did Roosevelt win the election of 1932?

Causes of the Wall Street Crash

To understand the Wall Street Crash you first need to understand how the stock market is supposed to work (see Factfile).

Factfile

Investment and the stock market
- To set up a company you need money to pay staff, rent premises, buy equipment, etc.
- Most companies raise this money from investors. In return, these investors own a share in the company. They become 'shareholders'.
- These shareholders can get a return on their money in two ways:
  - by receiving a dividend – a share of the profits made by the company
  - by selling their shares.
- If the company is successful, the value of the shares is usually higher than the price originally paid for them.
- Investors buy and sell their shares on the stock market. The American stock market was known as Wall Street.
- The price of shares varies from day to day. If more people are buying than selling, then the price goes up. If more are selling than buying, the price goes down.
- For much of the 1920s the price of shares on the Wall Street stock market went steadily upwards.

Speculation

You can see that investment on the stock market would be quite attractive during an economic boom. The American economy was doing well throughout the 1920s. Because the economy kept doing well, there were more share buyers than sellers and the value of shares rose.

It seemed to many Americans that the stock market was an easy and quick way to get rich. Anyone could buy shares, watch their value rise and then sell the shares later at a higher price. Many Americans decided to join the stock market. In 1920 there had been only 4 million share owners in America. By 1929 there were 20 million, out of a population of 120 million (although only about 1.5 million were big investors).

Around 600,000 new investors were speculators. SPECULATION is a form of gambling. Speculators don't intend to keep their shares for long. They

> **Revision Tip**
> Speculation sounds simple but it is not easy to explain.
> - Make sure you can describe two examples which show how speculation worked.
> - Practise explaining why speculation was attractive to Americans.
> - Also practise explaining why it was risky to the US economy.

borrow money to buy some shares, then sell them again as soon as the price has risen. They pay off their loan and still have a quick profit to show for it. In the 1920s speculators didn't even have to pay the full value of the shares. They could buy 'on the margin', which meant they only had to put down 10 per cent of the cash needed to buy shares and could borrow the rest.

Women became heavily involved in speculation. Women speculators owned over 50 per cent of the Pennsylvania Railroad, which became known as the 'petticoat line'. It was not only individuals who speculated. Banks themselves got involved in speculation. And certainly they did nothing to hold it back. American banks lent $9 billion for speculating in 1929.

Through most of the 1920s the rise in share prices was quite steady. There were even some downturns. But in 1928 speculation really took hold. Demand for shares was at an all-time high, and prices were rising at an unheard-of rate. In March, Union Carbide shares stood at $145. By September 1928 they had risen to $413.

One vital ingredient in all this was confidence. If people were confident that prices would keep rising, there would be more buyers than sellers. However, if they thought prices might stop rising, all of a sudden there would be more sellers and ... crash, the whole structure would come down. This is exactly what happened in 1929.

SOURCE 1

The stock market hysteria reached its apex that year [1929] ... Everyone was playing the market ... On my last day in New York, I went down to the barber. As he removed the sheet he said softly, 'Buy Standard Gas. I've doubled ... It's good for another double.' As I walked upstairs, I reflected that if the hysteria had reached the barber level, something must soon happen.

Cecil Roberts, *The Bright Twenties*, 1938.

Weaknesses in the US economy

The construction industry (one of the leading signs of health in any economy) had actually started its downturn as far back as 1926. You have already seen how farming was in trouble in the 1920s. You have also seen the decline in coal, textile and other traditional trades. There were other concerns, such as the unequal distribution of wealth and the precarious state of some banks. In the decade before the Crash, over 500 banks had failed each year. These were mainly small banks that lent too much.

By 1929 other sectors of the economy were showing signs of strain after the boom years of the 1920s. The boom was based on the increased sale of consumer goods such as cars and electrical appliances. There were signs that American industries were producing more of these goods than they could sell. The market for these goods was largely the rich and the middle classes. By 1929 those who could afford consumer goods had already bought them. The majority of Americans who were poor could not afford to buy them, even on the generous hire purchase and credit schemes on offer.

Companies tried high-pressure advertising. In 1929 American industry spent a staggering $3 billion on magazine advertising. But with workers' wages not rising and prices not falling, demand decreased.

In the past, American industry would have tried to export its surplus goods. But people in Europe could not afford American goods either. In addition, after nine years of American tariffs, Europe had put up its own tariffs to protect its industries.

FIGURE 2

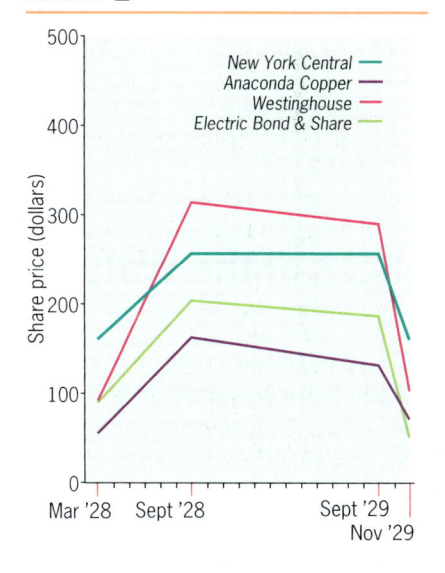

Selected share prices, 1928–29.

> **Factfile**
>
> ### The Wall Street Crash, 1929
>
> - **June** Factory output starts declining. Steel production starts declining.
> - **3 Sept** The hottest day of the year. The last day of rising prices.
> - **5 Sept** 'The Babson Break': Roger Babson, economic forecaster, says 'Sooner or later a crash is coming and it may be terrific.' The index of share prices drops ten points.
> - **6 Sept** Market recovers.
> - **Mon 21 Oct** Busy trading. Much selling. So much trading that the 'ticker' which tells people of changes in price falls behind by 1½ hours. Some people don't know they are ruined until after the exchange closes. By then it is too late to do anything about it.
> - **Thu 24 Oct** Busiest trading yet. Big falls. Banks intervene to buy stock. Confidence returns. Prices stabilise.
> - **Mon 28 Oct** Massive fall. Index loses 43 points. It is clear that the banks have stopped supporting share prices.
> - **Tue 29 Oct** Massive fall. People sell for whatever they can get.

The Wall Street Crash, October 1929

By the summer of 1929 these weaknesses were beginning to show. Even car sales were slowing, and in June 1929 the official figures for industrial output showed a fall for the first time for four years. Speculators on the American stock exchange became nervous about the value of their shares and began to sell.

As you can see from the Factfile, the slide in share values started slowly. But throughout September and October it gathered pace. Many investors had borrowed money to buy their shares and could not afford to be stuck with shares worth less than the value of their loan. Soon other investors sold their shares and within days panic set in. On Tuesday 29 October 1929 it became clear to the speculators that the banks were not going to intervene to support the price of shares, and so Wall Street had its busiest and its worst day in history as speculators desperately tried to dump 13 million shares at a fraction of the price they had paid for them.

> **Revision Tip**
>
> Make sure you can describe:
> - two weaknesses in the US economy in the late 1920s
> - two events leading up to the Crash.

> **FOCUS TASK 9.10**
>
> **How far was speculation responsible for the Wall Street Crash?**
>
> Work in groups.
> 1. Here are five factors that led to the Wall Street Crash. For each one explain how it helped to cause the Crash:
>   - poor distribution of income between rich and poor
>   - over-production by American industries
>   - the actions of speculators
>   - no export market for US goods
>   - decision by the banks not to support share prices.
> 2. If you think other factors are also important, add them to your list and explain why they helped to cause the Crash.
> 3. Decide whether there is one factor that is more important than any of the others. Explain your choice.

The economic consequences of the Wall Street Crash

At first, it was not clear what the impact of the Crash would be. In the short term, the large speculators were ruined. The rich lost most because they had invested most. For example:
- The Vanderbilt family lost $40 million.
- Rockefeller lost 80 per cent of his wealth – but he still had $40 million left.
- The British politician Winston Churchill lost $500,000.
- The singer Fanny Brice lost $500,000.
- Groucho and Harpo Marx (two of the Marx Brothers comedy team) lost $240,000 each.

The rich had always been the main buyers of American goods, so there was also an immediate downturn in spending. Many others had borrowed money in order to buy shares that were now worthless. They were unable to pay back their loans to the banks and insurance companies, so they went bankrupt. Some banks themselves also went bankrupt if they had lent too much.

SOURCE 3

An attempt to make some cash after the Wall Street Crash, 1929.

At first, however, these seemed like tragic but isolated incidents. President Hoover reassured the nation that prosperity was 'just around the corner'. He cut taxes to encourage people to buy more goods and by mid-1931 production was rising again slightly and there was hope that the situation was more settled.

In fact, it was the worst of the Depression that was 'just around the corner', because the Crash had destroyed the one thing that was crucial to the prosperity of the 1920s: confidence.

Banking crisis

This was most marked in the banking crisis. In 1929, 659 banks failed. As banks failed people stopped trusting them and many withdrew their savings. In 1930 another 1352 went bankrupt. The biggest of these was the Bank of the United States in New York, which went bankrupt in December 1930. It had 400,000 depositors – many of them recent immigrants. Almost one-third of New Yorkers saved with it. This was the worst failure in American history. To make matters worse, 1931 saw escalating problems in European banks, which had a knock-on effect in the USA. Panic set in. Around the country a billion dollars was withdrawn from banks and put in safe deposit boxes, or stored at home. People felt that hard currency was the only security. Another 2294 banks went under in 1931.

> **Revision Tip**
> The impact of the Crash is a big theme. There are so many examples to choose from it is helpful to narrow it down.
> - Choose four examples and make sure you can describe them thoroughly.
> - Make sure at least one of your examples is about the collapse of banks and one is about unemployment.

SOURCE 4

A cartoon by American cartoonist John McCutcheon, 1932. The man on the bench has lost all his savings because of a bank failure.

Speech/labels in cartoon: "VICTIM OF BANK FAILURE", "I DID", "BUT WHY DIDN'T YOU SAVE SOME MONEY FOR THE FUTURE, WHEN TIMES WERE GOOD?"

Source Analysis

Look at Source 4. Do you think the cartoonist is sympathetic or critical of the man on the bench? Explain your opinion.

Downward spiral

So while Hoover talked optimistically about the return of prosperity, Americans were showing their true feelings. They now kept their money instead of buying new goods or shares. Of course, this meant that banks had less money to give out in loans to businesses or to people as mortgages on homes. To make matters worse banks started to demand businesses repay loans. Businesses that could not afford to do so went bankrupt. Others cut production further, laid off workers or reduced the wages of those who still worked for them. A downward spiral was firmly established. Between 1928 and 1933 both industrial and farm production fell by 40 per cent, and average wages by 60 per cent.

As workers were laid off or were paid less, they bought less. This reduction in spending was devastating. The American economy had been geared up for mass consumption and relied on continued high spending. Fewer goods bought meant fewer people employed. By 1932 the USA was in the grip of the most serious economic depression the world had ever seen. By 1933 there were 14 million unemployed, and 5000 banks had gone bankrupt.

The problems in the urban areas soon had an impact on the countryside. Farm prices were already low before the Crash for the reasons we saw on page 293. Now people in the towns could not afford to buy so much food so prices went into freefall. Soon they were so low that the cost of transporting animals to market was higher than the price of the animals themselves. Total farm income had slipped to just $5 billion.

To complete the mess international trade had collapsed. Other countries were suffering from the Depression too so bought less American goods. To protect American business the US Government put tariffs on imports so other countries sold less goods to America. The USA's international trade was drastically reduced from $10 billion in 1929 to $3 billion in 1932.

FOCUS TASK 9.11

What impact did the Crash have on the American economy?

You can see how a downward spiral was started by the Crash. Draw your own copy of this diagram and add explanations and examples to each heading.

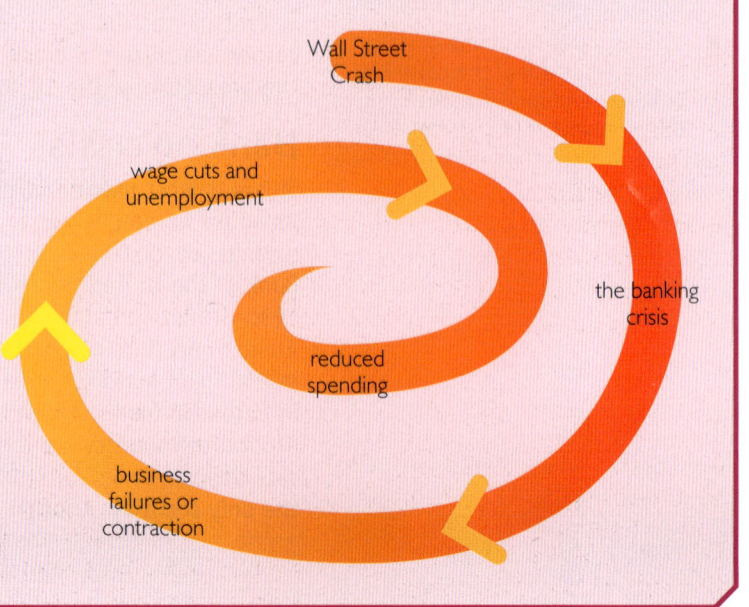

Diagram labels: Wall Street Crash → the banking crisis → reduced spending → business failures or contraction → wage cuts and unemployment

SOURCE 5

During the last three months I have visited ... some 20 states of this wonderfully rich and beautiful country. A number of Montana citizens told me of thousands of bushels of wheat left in the fields uncut on account of its low price that hardly paid for the harvesting. In Oregon I saw thousands of bushels of apples rotting in the orchards. At the same time there are millions of children who, on account of the poverty of their parents, will not eat one apple this winter.

... I saw men picking for meat scraps in the garbage cans of the cities of New York and Chicago. One man said that he had killed 3,000 sheep this fall and thrown them down the canyon because it cost $1.10 to ship a sheep and then he would get less than a dollar for it.

The farmers are being pauperised [made poor] by the poverty of industrial populations and the industrial populations are being pauperised by the poverty of the farmers. Neither has the money to buy the product of the other; hence we have overproduction and under-consumption at the same time.

Evidence of Oscar Ameringer to a US Government committee in 1932.

SOURCE 7

Last summer, in the hot weather, when the smell was sickening and the flies were thick, there were a hundred people a day coming to the dumps ... a widow who used to do housework and laundry, but now had no work at all, fed herself and her fourteen-year-old son on garbage. Before she picked up the meat she would always take off her glasses so that she couldn't see the maggots.

From *New Republic* magazine, February 1933.

Revision Tip

As with the economic effects of the Crash, the key here is to focus. Choose three examples of hardship and make sure you can describe those thoroughly. Make sure you include Hoovervilles.

The human cost of the Depression

In the countryside

People in agricultural areas were hardest hit by the Depression, because the 1920s had not been kind to them anyway. As farm income fell, huge numbers of farmers were unable to pay their mortgages. Some farmers organised themselves to resist banks seizing their homes. When sheriffs came to seize their property, bands of farmers holding pitch forks and hangman's nooses persuaded the sheriffs to retreat. Others barricaded highways. Most farmers, however, had no choice but to pack their belongings into their trucks and live on the road. They picked up work where they could.

Black farmers and labourers were often worse off than their white neighbours. They lost their land and their farms first. Hunger stalked the countryside and children fell ill and died from malnutrition. Yet this was happening while wheat and fruit were left to rot and animals killed because farmers could not afford to take them to market.

But worse was to come in the Southern and Midwest states where over-farming and drought caused the topsoil to turn to dust. This was whipped up by the wind to create an area known as the dustbowl. The dust covered everything, as Source 6 shows; it got into every crack and crevice making life unbearable. Many packed up all their belongings and headed for California to look for work. The plight of these migrants is one of the enduring impressions of the Depression.

SOURCE 6

A dustbowl farm. Over-farming, drought and poor conservation turned farmland into desert.

In the towns

In the towns, the story was not much better. Unemployment rose rapidly. For example, in 1932 in the steel city of Cleveland, 50 per cent of workers were unemployed and in Toledo 80 per cent. Forced to sell their homes or kicked out because they could not pay the rent, city workers joined the army of unemployed searching for work of any kind. Thousands were taken in by relatives but many ended up on the streets. At night the parks were full of the homeless and unemployed. In every city, workers who had contributed to the prosperity of the 1920s now queued for bread and soup dished out by charity workers. A large number of men (estimated at 2 million in 1932) travelled from place to place on railway freight wagons seeking work.

FIGURE 8

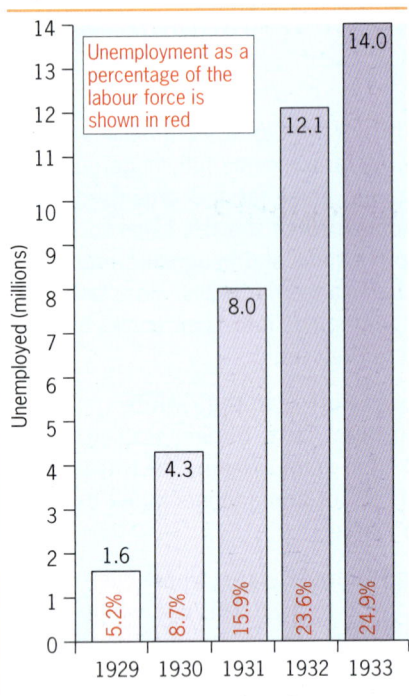

Unemployment as a percentage of the labour force is shown in red

Year	Unemployed (millions)	%
1929	1.6	5.2%
1930	4.3	8.7%
1931	8.0	15.9%
1932	12.1	23.6%
1933	14.0	24.9%

Unemployment in the USA, 1929–33.

Thousands of children lived in wagons or tents next to the tracks. Every town had a so-called HOOVERVILLE. This was a shanty town of ramshackle huts where the migrants lived while they searched for work. The rubbish tips were crowded with families hoping to scrape a meal from the leftovers of more fortunate people. Through 1931, 238 people were admitted to hospital in New York suffering from malnutrition or starvation, 45 of whom died.

SOURCE 9

A Hooverville shanty town on wasteland in Seattle, Washington.

SOURCE 10

There is not an unemployed man in the country that hasn't contributed to the wealth of every millionaire in America. The working classes didn't bring this on, it was the big boys … We've got more wheat, more corn, more food, more cotton, more money in the banks, more everything in the world than any nation that ever lived ever had, yet we are starving to death. We are the first nation in the history of the world to go to the poorhouse in an automobile.

Will Rogers, an American writer, 1931. Rogers had a regular humorous column in an American magazine which was popular with ordinary people.

SOURCE 11

A migrant family.

Source Analysis

1 Read Source 10. What do you think Will Rogers means by 'the big boys'?
2 Explain how a writer such as Rogers can be useful to a historian studying the impact of the Depression in the 1930s.

FOCUS TASK 9.12

What were the social consequences of the Crash?

1 You have been asked to prepare an exhibition of photos which compares the life of Americans during the boom times of the 1920s with the depressed years of the 1930s. Choose two pictures from the 1920s and two from the 1930s which you think present the greatest contrast. Explain your choice.
2 Do you think everyone suffered equally from the Depression? Explain your answer by referring to Sources 5–11. In particular, think about how the effects of the Depression in the countryside were different/similar to those in the towns and cities.

The 1932 presidential election

In the 1932 election President Hoover paid the price for the Depression. It was partly his own fault. Until 1932 he insisted that 'prosperity is just around the corner'. This left him open to bitter criticisms such as Source 14 (on page 322).

Hoover – the 'do-nothing' president?

Hoover was criticised by many at the time for not doing enough for people who were hit hard by the Depression. At first he believed the Depression would be short-lived. But as the scale of the problem became clear, his inaction damaged his reputation. As a Republican, Hoover believed in 'rugged individualism'. This meant he was opposed to the government providing welfare support for people without jobs. He believed that instead of government, charities and families should help the poor. However, as banks failed and unemployment rose rapidly, charities became unable to cope. More and more Americans fell into desperate poverty.

However, the view that he was a 'do-nothing president' was not entirely fair. When he realised the economic downturn was a long-term issue he did take action. The following measures were enforced, but as you can see, they were regarded by many as too little too late:

- In 1930 and 1931 he tried to restart the economy with tax cuts worth nearly $130 million...
  BUT they did little to restore confidence and consumer spending.
- In 1930 he introduced the Hawley-Smoot Act which put further tariffs on imported goods to protect American business...
  BUT this led to other countries increasing their tariffs. As a result, selling surplus goods and produce overseas was made even more difficult for businesses and the farming industry. Trade fell to many countries by almost 30 per cent. Even Henry Ford called it 'economic stupidity'!
- In 1930, Hoover tried to encourage businesses to not cut wages or dismiss workers...
  BUT this was voluntary and not set in law.
- In 1931, he set up the National Credit Corporation to help failing banks...
  BUT many bankers refused to invest in other failing banks as it was too risky.
- Hoover did put money into public works programmes such as the Hoover Dam on the Colorado River. This did create thousands of jobs...
  BUT it was not enough to tackle the huge unemployment issue across the USA.
- In 1932 Hoover set up the Reconstruction Finance Corporation to provide nearly $2 billion in loans for failing banks and businesses...
  BUT by this point it was not enough money to stop the bank closures.
- In 1932 he also tried to help farmers using the Federal Farm Board which used $500,000 to buy up surplus grain and cotton from farmers to stabilise prices...
  BUT food prices continued to drop due to continued overproduction and tariff wars with other countries.

SOURCE 12

Farmers are just ready to do anything to get even with the situation. I almost hate to express it, but I honestly believe that if some of them could buy airplanes they would come down here to Washington to blow you fellows up … The farmer is a naturally conservative individual, but you cannot find a conservative farmer today. Any economic system that has in its power to set me and my wife in the streets, at my age what can I see but red?

President of the Farmers' Union of Wisconsin, A.N. Young, speaking to a Senate committee in 1932.

Source Analysis
Source 13 had a very powerful effect on Americans. Explain why.

SOURCE 14

Never before in this country has a government fallen … so low … in popular estimation or been [such] an object of cynical contempt. Never before has [a president] given his name so freely to latrines and offal dumps, or had his face banished from the [cinema] screen to avoid the hoots and jeers of children.

Written by a political commentator.

Think!
From Sources 12 and 14 make a list of criticisms of Hoover and his Government.

The Bonus Marchers

In June 1932, over 40,000 demonstrators, including over 17,000 First World War veterans, marched on Washington. They demanded their war bonuses (a kind of pension) be paid early. The Bonus Army, as it was known by the media, peacefully camped outside the White House. While waiting for Hoover's response they sang patriotic songs with journalists.

At first police were sent in to deal with the demonstrators. Two people were injured by gunfire in the clash that followed. Hoover then ordered General Douglas MacArthur (Chief of Staff of the army) to handle the situation. MacArthur believed that the demonstration was organised by communist agitators. He ignored Hoover's instructions to treat the marchers with respect. Infantry, cavalry and six tanks were sent in to clear the camp. Tear gas was used on the demonstrators and their camp was burned down. This was a political disaster for Hoover, particularly as the new presidential elections were just around the corner.

SOURCE 13

Smile away the Depression!

Smile us into Prosperity! wear a SMILETTE!

This wonderful little gadget will solve the problems of the Nation!

APPLY NOW AT YOUR CHAMBER OF COMMERCE OR THE REPUBLICAN NATIONAL COMMITTEE

WARNING—Do not risk Federal arrest by looking glum!

A 1932 Democrat election poster.

Roosevelt's characteristics

There could be no greater contrast to Hoover than his opponent in the 1932 election, the Democrat candidate, Franklin D. Roosevelt. Roosevelt's main characteristics as a politician were:
- He was not a radical, but he believed in **'active government'** to improve the lives of ordinary people.
- He promised a New Deal for the American people focusing on the 3 Rs: Recovery of the economy; Relief for the unemployed and those in poverty; Reform of the financial system to make the USA a **fairer society** and to prevent another Depression from taking place.
- He had plans to **spend public money** on getting people back to work. As Governor of New York, he had already started doing this in his own state.
- He was not afraid to **ask for advice** from experts, such as factory owners, union leaders and economists.

SOURCE 15

Millions of our citizens cherish the hope that their old standards of living have not gone forever. Those millions shall not hope in vain … I pledge myself, to a New Deal for the American people. This is more than a political campaign; it is a call to arms. Give me your help, not to win votes alone, but to win this crusade to restore America … I am waging a war against Destruction, Delay, Deceit and Despair.

Roosevelt's pre-election speech, 1932.

Revision Tip

Make sure you can describe:
- two actions taken by Hoover
- two factors which damaged Hoover
- two reasons why people supported Roosevelt.

FOCUS TASK 9.13

Why did Roosevelt win the election of 1932?

In many ways Roosevelt's victory needs no explanation. Indeed, it would have been very surprising if any president could have been re-elected after the sufferings of 1929–32. But it is important to recognise the range of factors that helped Roosevelt and damaged Hoover.

Write your own account of Roosevelt's success under the following headings:
- The experiences of ordinary people, 1929–32
- The policies of the Republicans
- Actions taken by the Republicans
- Roosevelt's election campaign and personality.

The campaign

Both the Republicans and Democrats spent vast sums of money on their campaigns. However, while Roosevelt could be criticised for being vague, Hoover was criticised for his inaction. Republican policies were seen as one of the main causes of the Crash and Hoover's perceived lack of action meant many blamed him for the Depression. Even many Republicans in Congress did not support Hoover, some even openly supporting Roosevelt. Most damaging of all for Hoover was the open hostility Hoover received during his campaign tour where on many occasions he had objects thrown at him or his vehicle as he rode through the streets. With such ill-feeling towards Hoover being expressed throughout the country, Roosevelt was confident of victory, but he took no chances. He went on a train tour of the USA in the weeks before the election and mercilessly attacked the attitude of Hoover and the Republicans.

Roosevelt's own plans were rather vague and general. But he realised people wanted action, whatever that action was. In a 20,800-km campaign trip he made sixteen major speeches and another 60 from the back of his train. He promised the American people a 'New Deal' (see Source 15). It was not only his policies that attracted support; it was also his personality. He radiated warmth and inspired confidence. He made personal contact with the American people and seemed to offer hope and a way out of the terrible situation they were in. He also inspired many people. Roosevelt had been diagnosed with polio at the age of 39. As a result of the disease he was virtually paralysed from the waist down. To the surprise of the crowds, he used a walking stick and metal braces to ensure he could stand during his speeches.

The election was a landslide victory for Roosevelt. He won by 7 million votes and the Democrats won a majority of seats in Congress. It was the worst defeat the Republicans had ever suffered.

Key Question Summary

What were the causes and consequences of the Wall Street Crash?

1 In October 1929 the Wall Street stock market crashed with a devastating impact on America and the rest of the world.
2 The Crash was partly to do with uncontrolled speculation but it was also the result of underlying weaknesses in the American economy; in particular, industry was over-producing goods which it could not sell.
3 The main consequences for the economy were huge losses for investors, bank failures, factories closing, mass unemployment, the collapse of farm prices and a drastic reduction in foreign trade.
4 The human cost was devastating: unemployment, homelessness, poverty and hunger. Families were split and 'Hoovervilles' appeared on the edges of cities.
5 Farmers lost their land and were dispossessed. Poverty was rampant in rural areas. Matters were made even worse by the dustbowl, which led to mass migration from central southern America to California.
6 President Hoover was unable to deal with the crisis. He believed that government should not interfere too much: the system would repair itself. The measures he undertook were too little too late and he did not do enough to provide relief to those who were suffering.
7 In 1932, Americans elected Franklin D Roosevelt as president. He promised a New Deal to help people and get America back to work.

FOCUS

During his election campaign Roosevelt had promised the American people a New Deal. He planned to use the full power of the government to get the USA out of depression. In 10.4 you will examine how far he succeeded.

Focus Points

- What was the New Deal as introduced in 1933?
- How far did the character of the New Deal change after 1933?
- Why did the New Deal encounter opposition?
- Why did unemployment persist despite the New Deal?
- Did the fact that the New Deal did not solve unemployment mean that it was a failure?

SOURCE 1

This is the time to speak the truth frankly and boldly ... So let me assert my firm belief that the only thing we have to fear is fear itself ... This nation calls for action and action now ... Our greatest primary task is to put people to work ... We must act and act quickly.

Roosevelt's inauguration speech, 4 March 1933.

9D How successful was the New Deal?

The Hundred Days

In the first hundred days of his presidency, Roosevelt worked round the clock with his advisers (who became known as the 'Brains Trust') to produce an enormous range of sweeping measures.

One of Roosevelt's advisers at this time said, 'During the whole Hundred Days Congress, people didn't know what was going on, but they knew something was happening, something good for them.' In the HUNDRED DAYS, Roosevelt sent fifteen proposals to Congress and all fifteen were adopted. Just as importantly, he took time to explain to the American people what he was doing and why he was doing it. Every Sunday he would broadcast on radio to the nation. An estimated 60 million Americans tuned in to these '**fireside chats**'. Nowadays, we are used to politicians doing this. At that time it was a new development.

Two of the most pressing issues affecting the USA were its loss of confidence in the banks and in the stock market. Two measures were introduced to tackle these problems.

- The **Emergency Banking Act** was passed by Congress the day after Roosevelt's inauguration. All banks in the USA were closed for a four-day bank holiday while government officials checked them over to see if they were stable enough to run. A few days later 5000 trustworthy banks were allowed to reopen with the promise of government loans to support them. About five per cent of banks were permanently closed down. As a result, confidence was quickly restored. In 1933 over $1 billion was redeposited by customers.
- In 1934, the **Securities Exchange Commission (SEC)** was set up to help restore investor confidence in the stock market. Government officials tightened up rules and regulations to stop the reckless speculation that had caused the Crash in 1929. This initiative became very popular with the American business community as confidence slowly returned.

Next Roosevelt turned his attention to the issues of poverty and unemployment.

- The **Civilian Conservation Corps** (CCC) was aimed at unemployed young men. They could sign on for periods of six months, which could be renewed if they could still not find work. Most of the work done by the CCC was on environmental projects in national parks. The money earned generally went back to the men's families. Around 2.5 million were helped by this scheme.
- The **Federal Emergency Relief Administration (FERA)** was set up in 1933. Its purpose was to help state and local governments create temporary work for the unemployed and provide help for those in desperate need. Roosevelt hoped that it would restore some self-esteem to those out of work and living in poverty. Nearly 20 million temporary and part-time jobs were created by FERA between 1933 and 1935. $500 million was spent on soup kitchens, clothing and employment schemes.
- This was accompanied by the **Civil Works Administration (CWA)** which was set up in late 1933 to help unemployed Americans during the winter of 1933–34. The CWA provided a further four million short-term jobs.

SOURCE 2

The bank rescue of 1933 was probably the turning point of the Depression. When people were able to survive the shock of having all the banks closed, and then see the banks open up again, with their money protected, there began to be confidence. Good times were coming. It marked the revival of hope.

Raymond Moley, one of Roosevelt's advisers during the Hundred Days Congress session.

Roosevelt also took action to help the many Americans at risk of losing their home due to unemployment and falling wages. In 1933 he created the **Home Owners Loan Corporation (HOLC)**. Over one million families received loans by 1935, but it stopped offering help after this date and instead focused on repayments.

- The **Agricultural Adjustment Administration** (AAA) tried to take a long-term view of the problems facing farmers. It set quotas to reduce farm production in order to force prices gradually upwards. At the same time, the AAA helped farmers to modernise and to use farming methods that would conserve and protect the soil. In cases of extreme hardship, farmers could also receive help with their mortgages. Over 90 per cent of the large landowners and farmers were helped by the AAA and prices of agricultural produce rose by 50 per cent between 1933 and 1936. However, the AAA failed to help smaller tenant farmers, farm labourers and the many African-American sharecroppers. Modernisation within farming also had the effect of putting more farm labourers out of work.

The final measure of the Hundred Days passed on 18 June was the **National Industrial Recovery Act** (NIRA). It set up two important organisations:

- The **Public Works Administration** (PWA) used government money to build schools, roads, dams, bridges and airports. It spent $7 billion in total on job creations schemes and built 70 per cent of US schools and 35 per cent of hospitals in the 1930s. This would be vital once the USA had recovered but required a huge amount of public money in the form of taxes to pay for it all.
- The **National Recovery Administration** (NRA) improved working conditions in industry and outlawed child labour. It also set out fair wages and sensible levels of production. The idea was to stimulate the economy by giving workers money to spend, without over-producing. It was voluntary, but firms that joined used the blue eagle as a symbol of presidential approval. Over two million employers joined the scheme.

Source Analysis

Look carefully at the two cartoons – Sources 3A and 3B.
1. Use the text on pages 324–25 to help you to understand all the details. You could annotate your own copy.
2. Put the message of each cartoon into your own words.

SOURCE 3

Two 1933 American cartoons.

The Tennessee Valley Authority

As you can see from Figure 4, the Tennessee Valley was a huge area that cut across seven states. The area had great physical problems. In the wet season, the Tennessee river would flood. In the dry it would reduce to a trickle. The farming land around the river was a dust bowl. The soil was eroding and turning the land into desert. The area also had great social problems. Within the valley people lived in poverty. The majority of households had no electricity. The problems of the Tennessee Valley were far too large for one state to deal with and it was very difficult for states to co-operate.

Roosevelt therefore set up an independent organisation called the TENNESSEE VALLEY AUTHORITY (TVA), which cut across the powers of the local state governments. The main focus of the TVA's work was the construction of 33 dams on the Tennessee River. This transformed the area. Land could be irrigated and electricity could be provided to homes and businesses. Over 9000 jobs were created, including the hiring of some African Americans. Many new industries were formed as a result. In the 1930s new textile mills opened which employed thousands of women in the area.

Despite its successes, the TVA also led to the displacement of nearly 15,000 families. Some Native American archaeological sites and cemeteries were also destroyed. However, the TVA was considered one of the most successful of the new agencies created under the New Deal. It still exists today.

FIGURE 4

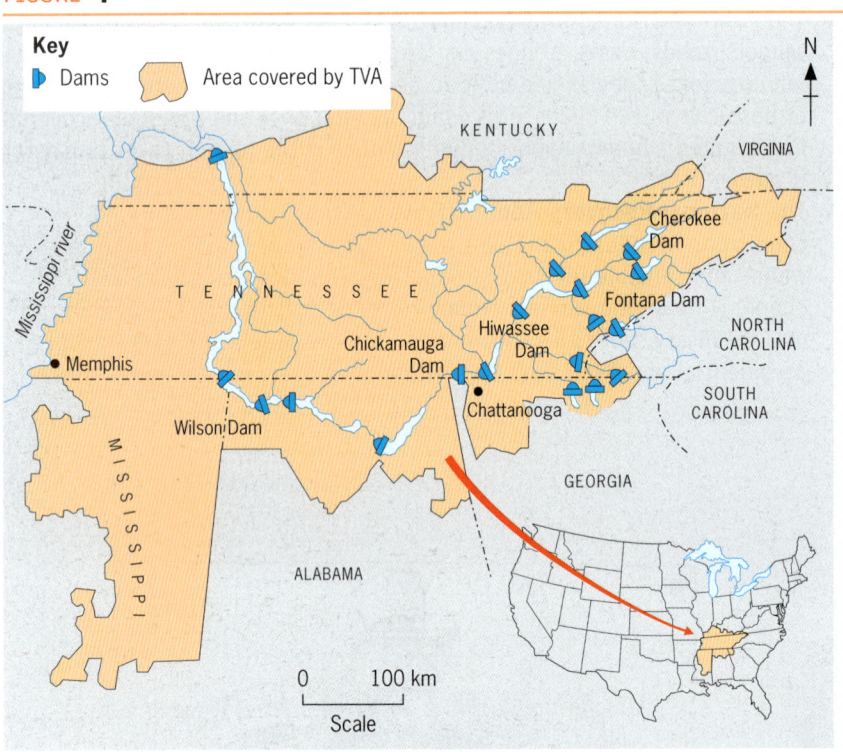

The Tennessee Valley and the work of the TVA.

FOCUS TASK 9.14

What was the New Deal, as introduced in 1933?

Through pages 324–26 all the New Deal measures and agencies are **highlighted like this**. Use the text to complete your own copy of this table.

New Deal measure/agency	Issue/problem it aimed to tackle	Actions taken/powers of agency	Evidence it was/was not effective

Factfile

Main events of the Hundred Days

- **4 March** Roosevelt inaugurated.
- **5 March** Closed banks.
- **9 March** Selected banks reopened.
- **12 March** Roosevelt's first radio 'fireside chat'. Encouraged Americans to put their money back into the banks. Many did so.
- **31 March** The Civilian Conservation Corps set up.
- **12 May** The Agricultural Adjustment Act passed.
- **18 May** The Tennessee Valley Authority created.
- **18 June** The National Industrial Recovery Act passed.

Achievements of the Hundred Days

- It restored confidence and stopped investors pulling money out of the banks.
- Banking measures saved 20 per cent of home owners and farmers from repossession.
- Farmers were 50 per cent better off under AAA by 1936.
- TVA brought electrical power to underdeveloped areas.
- Public Works Administration created 600,000 jobs and built landmarks like San Francisco's Golden Gate Bridge.

Source Analysis

1. What do Sources 5–7 agree about?
2. What do they disagree about?

Revision Tip

- The various New Deal agencies can be a bit confusing. Make sure you can describe the aims and the work of at least the National Industrial Recovery Act and the Tennessee Valley Authority.
- There was a lot of activity in the Hundred Days but you need to focus on effects. Make sure you can give examples of at least three ways the Hundred Days had an impact on Americans.

Impact of the Hundred Days

The measures introduced during the Hundred Days had an immediate effect. They restored confidence in government. Reporters who travelled the country brought back reports of the new spirit to be seen around the USA. Historians, too, agree that Roosevelt's bold and decisive action did have a marked effect on the American people.

SOURCE 5

Wandering around the country with one of New York's baseball teams, I find that [what was] the national road to ruin is now a thriving thoroughfare. It has been redecorated. People have come out of the shell holes. They are working and playing and seem content to let a tribe of professional worriers do their worrying for them.

Rudd Rennie, an American journalist, on the early days of the New Deal. From *Changing the Tune from Gloom to Cheer*, 1934.

SOURCE 6

The CCC, the PWA, and similar government bodies (the alphabet agencies as Americans called them) made work for millions of people. The money they earned began to bring back life to the nation's trade and businesses. More customers appeared in the shops … As people started to buy again, shopkeepers, farmers and manufacturers began to benefit from the money the government was spending on work for the unemployed. This process was described by Roosevelt as 'priming the pump'. By this he meant that the money the Federal Government was spending was like a fuel, flowing into the nation's economic machinery and starting it moving again.

D.B. O'Callaghan, *Roosevelt and the USA*, published in 1966.

SOURCE 7

As Roosevelt described it, the 'New Deal' meant that the forgotten man, the little man, the man nobody knew much about, was going to be dealt better cards to play with … He understood that the suffering of the Depression had fallen with terrific impact upon the people least able to bear it. He knew that the rich had been hit hard too, but at least they had something left. But the little merchant, the small householder and home owner, the farmer, the man who worked for himself – these people were desperate. And Roosevelt saw them as principal citizens of the United States, numerically and in their importance to the maintenance of the ideals of American democracy.

Frances Perkins, *The Roosevelt I Knew*, 1947. Perkins was Labour Secretary under Roosevelt from 1933.

It is clear that the policies of the New Deal led to the creation of jobs and help for the poor. However, the creation of the alphabet agencies came at a huge cost. Public spending and debt increased significantly. In 1933 the US government debt was $22 billion. By 1936 it had reached $33 billion. Investing public money into the economy to create jobs is often called 'pump priming'. This strategy was opposed by many Republicans and industrialists who felt that taxpayers' money was being wasted.

Roosevelt did try to balance the federal budget by cutting government spending elsewhere. Salaries and pensions for some government employees were cut by 15 per cent. Military spending was reduced. Taxes were raised on the rich. Prohibition was repealed in 1933 and the Beer Act passed the same year put taxes on alcoholic beverages. Overall, the first New Deal had failed to end the Depression and many critics remained.

The Second New Deal

Despite his achievements, by May 1935 Roosevelt was facing a barrage of criticism. Roosevelt was unsure what to do. He had hoped to transform the USA, but it didn't seem to be working as he had hoped.

Tuesday, 14 May 1935 turned out to be a key date. Roosevelt met with a group of senators and close advisers who shared his views and aims. They persuaded him to take radical steps to achieve his vision and make the USA a fairer place for all Americans (see Source 7). One month later, he presented the leaders of Congress with a huge range of laws that he wanted passed. This became known as the SECOND NEW DEAL and was aimed at areas that affected ordinary people – for example strengthening unions to fight for the members' rights, financial security in old age – as well as continuing to tackle unemployment. The most significant aspects were:

- The **Resettlement Administration (RA)** helped smallholders and tenant farmers who had not been helped by the AAA. This organisation moved over 500,000 families to better-quality land and housing. The **Farm Security Administration (FSA)** replaced the RA in 1937. It gave special loans to small farmers to help them buy their land. It also built camps to provide decent living conditions and work for migrant workers.
- The **Works Progress Administration (WPA)**, later renamed the Works Project Administration, brought together all the organisations whose aim was to create jobs. It also extended this work beyond building projects to create jobs for office workers and even unemployed actors, artists and photographers. The photograph in Source 8 was taken by a photographer working for a New Deal agency. Opponents of the New Deal coined these jobs and work creation schemes 'boondoggles' in the newspapers. They claimed over $3 million of taxpayers' money was wasted on pointless jobs that did not contribute to economic growth. Over $1 billion was spent helping the poorest farmers.

SOURCE 8

Source Analysis

1 What feelings do you think the photographer has tried to capture in Source 8?
2 Why do you think the photographer published this photo?

Migrant Mother (number 6) by Dorothea Lange, taken in Nipomo, California, March 1936. Many farmers migrated to California where farming had been less badly hit by the Depression.

- The **Wagner Act** forced employers to allow TRADE UNIONS in their companies and to let them negotiate pay and conditions. It made it illegal to sack workers for being in a union. It also set up a National Labour board to oversee disputes between trade unions and employers.
- The **Social Security Act** provided state pensions for the elderly and for widows. It also allowed state governments to work with the federal government to provide help for sick and disabled people. Most importantly, the Act set up a scheme for unemployment insurance. Employers and workers made a small contribution to a special fund each week. If workers became unemployed, they would receive a small amount to help them out until they could find work.

SOURCE 9

Steel Industry by Howard Cook, painted for the steel-making town of Pittsburgh, Pennsylvania.

Revision Tip
For the Second New Deal the key measures are the Wagner Act and the Social Security Act. Make sure you can describe them.

Source Analysis
1 What impression of the New Deal does Source 9 attempt to convey?
2 Why do you think Roosevelt wanted artists and photographers to be employed under the New Deal?

FOCUS TASK 9.15
How far did the character of the New Deal change after 1933?

Draw up two spider diagrams to compare the objectives and measures of the New Deal and the Second New Deal. Then explain how the measures of the Second New Deal were different from those in 1933.

Opposition to the New Deal

A programme such as Roosevelt's New Deal was unheard of in American history. It was bound to attract opposition and it did.

Not enough!

A number of high-profile figures raised the complaint that the New Deal was not doing enough to help the poor. Despite the New Deal measures, many Americans remained desperately poor. The hardest hit were African Americans and the poor in farming areas.

A key figure was Huey Long. He became Governor of Louisiana in 1928 and a senator in 1932. His methods of gaining power were unusual and sometimes illegal (they included intimidation and bribery). However, once he had power he used it to help the poor. He taxed big corporations and businesses in Louisiana and used the money to build roads, schools and hospitals. He employed African Americans on the same terms as white people and clashed with the Ku Klux Klan.

He supported the New Deal at first, but by 1934 he was criticising it for being too complicated and not doing enough. He put forward a scheme called Share Our Wealth. All personal fortunes would be reduced to $3 million maximum, and maximum income would be $1 million a year. Government taxes would be shared between all Americans. He also proposed pensions for everyone over 60, and free washing machines and radios. Long was an aggressive and forceful character with many friends and many enemies. Roosevelt regarded him as one of the two most dangerous men in the USA. Long was assassinated in 1935.

Dr Francis Townsend founded a number of Townsend Clubs to campaign for a pension of $200 per month for people over 60, providing that they spent it that month, which would stimulate the economy in the process. A Catholic priest, Father Coughlin, used his own radio programme to attack Roosevelt. He set up the National Union for Social Justice and it had a large membership.

Too much!

The New Deal soon came under fire from sections of the business community and from Republicans for doing too much. There was a long list of criticisms:

- The New Deal was complicated and there were too many codes and regulations.
- Government should not support trade unions and it should not support calls for higher wages – the market should deal with these issues.
- Some business leaders set up the Liberty League in 1934 and claimed the New Deal was destroying free enterprise in the USA.
- Schemes such as the TVA created unfair competition with private companies.
- The New Deal schemes were like the economic plans being carried out in the communist USSR and unsuitable for the democratic, free-market USA.
- Roosevelt was behaving like a DICTATOR.
- High taxes discouraged people from working hard and gave money to people for doing nothing or doing unnecessary jobs (see Source 10).

SOURCE 11

A cartoon published in an American newspaper in the mid-1930s.

SOURCE 10

The New Deal is nothing more or less than an effort to take away from the thrifty what the thrifty and their ancestors have accumulated, or may accumulate, and give it to others who have not earned it and never will earn it, and thus to destroy the incentive for future accumulation. Such a purpose is in defiance of all the ideas upon which our civilisation has been founded.

A Republican opponent of the New Deal speaking in 1935.

Think!

Look at the criticisms of the New Deal. Roosevelt's opponents were often accused of being selfish. How far do the criticisms support or contradict that view?

Profile

Franklin D. Roosevelt (FDR)

- Born 1882 into a rich New York family.
- Went to university and became a successful lawyer.
- Entered politics in 1910 as a Democratic senator for New York.
- Paralysed by polio in 1921 and spent the rest of his life in a wheelchair.
- Became president in 1933, in the middle of the economic crisis.
- Roosevelt was an excellent public speaker, an optimist and a believer in the 'American Dream' – that anyone who worked hard enough could become rich.
- His 'New Deal' policies made him extremely popular.
- Elected president four times.
- Led the USA through the Second World War until his death in April 1945.
- Often referred to simply as FDR.

Roosevelt fights back

Roosevelt was upset by the criticisms, but also by the tactics used against him by big business and the Republicans. They used a smear campaign against him and all connected to him. They said that he was disabled because of a sexually transmitted disease rather than polio. Employers put messages into their workers' pay packets saying that New Deal Schemes would never happen. Roosevelt turned on these enemies bitterly (see Source 12). And it seemed the American people were with him. In the 1936 election, he won 27 million votes – with the highest margin of victory ever achieved by a US president. He was then able to joke triumphantly, 'Everyone is against the New Deal except the voters.'

SOURCE 12

For twelve years this nation was afflicted with hear-nothing, see-nothing, do-nothing government. The nation looked to government but government looked away. Nine crazy years at the stock market and three long years in the bread-lines! Nine mad years of mirage and three long years of despair! Powerful influences strive today to restore that kind of government with its doctrine that government is best which is most indifferent ... We know now that government by organised money is just as dangerous as government by organised mob. Never before in all our history have these forces been so united against one candidate – me – as they stand today. They are unanimous in their hate of me – and I welcome their hatred.

A speech by Roosevelt in the 1936 presidential election campaign.

SOURCE 13

A 1930s cartoon attacking critics of the New Deal.

Source Analysis

Study Sources 10–13.
1. How would the author of Source 10 react to Source 11?
2. How would they react to Sources 12 and 13? Make sure you can explain your answer.

SOURCE 14

THE ILLEGAL ACT.
PRESIDENT ROOSEVELT. "I'M SORRY, BUT THE SUPREME COURT SAYS I MUST CHUCK YOU BACK AGAIN."

A *Punch* cartoon, June 1935.

SOURCE 15

"I DID NOT VOTE FOR THAT!"

A cartoon from the *Brooklyn Daily Eagle*, February 1937.

Opposition from the Supreme Court

Roosevelt's problems were not over with the 1936 election. In fact, he now faced the most powerful opponent of the New Deal – the American Supreme Court. This Court was dominated by Republicans who were opposed to the New Deal. It could overturn laws if those laws were against the terms of the Constitution. In May 1935 a strange case had come before the US Supreme Court. The Schechter Poultry Corporation had been found guilty of breaking NRA regulations because it had: sold diseased chickens for human consumption; filed false sales claims (to make the company worth more); exploited workers; and threatened government inspectors. It appealed to the Supreme Court. The Court ruled that the Government had no right to prosecute the company. This was because the NRA was unconstitutional. It undermined too much of the power of the local states. The AAA was also declared unconstitutional in 1936 and shutdown for the same reason.

Roosevelt was angry that this group of old Republicans should deny DEMOCRACY by throwing out laws that he had been elected to pass. He asked Congress to give him the power to appoint six more Supreme Court judges who were more sympathetic to the New Deal. This was known as his 'court-packing plan'. But Roosevelt misjudged the mood of the American public. They were alarmed at what they saw as Roosevelt attacking the American system of government. Roosevelt had to back down and his plan was rejected. Even so, his actions were not completely pointless. The Supreme Court had been shaken by Roosevelt's actions and was less obstructive in the future. Most of the main measures in Roosevelt's Second New Deal were approved by the Court from 1937 onwards.

Source Analysis

Look at Sources 14 and 15. One supports Roosevelt's actions and the other one doesn't. Explain which is which, and how you made your decision.

FOCUS TASK 9.16

Why did the New Deal encounter opposition?
The thought bubbles below show some of the reasons why people opposed the New Deal. Use the text and sources on pages 330–32 to find examples of individuals who held each belief. Try to find two more reasons why people opposed the New Deal.

- It won't work.
- It'll harm me.
- It'll harm the USA.

The end of the New Deal

The events of 1936 took their toll on Roosevelt and he became more cautious after that. Early in 1937 prosperity seemed to be returning and Roosevelt did what all conservatives had wanted: he cut the New Deal BUDGET. He laid off many workers who had been employed by the New Deal's own organisations and the cut in spending triggered other cuts throughout the economy. This meant that unemployment spiralled upwards once more.

FIGURE 16

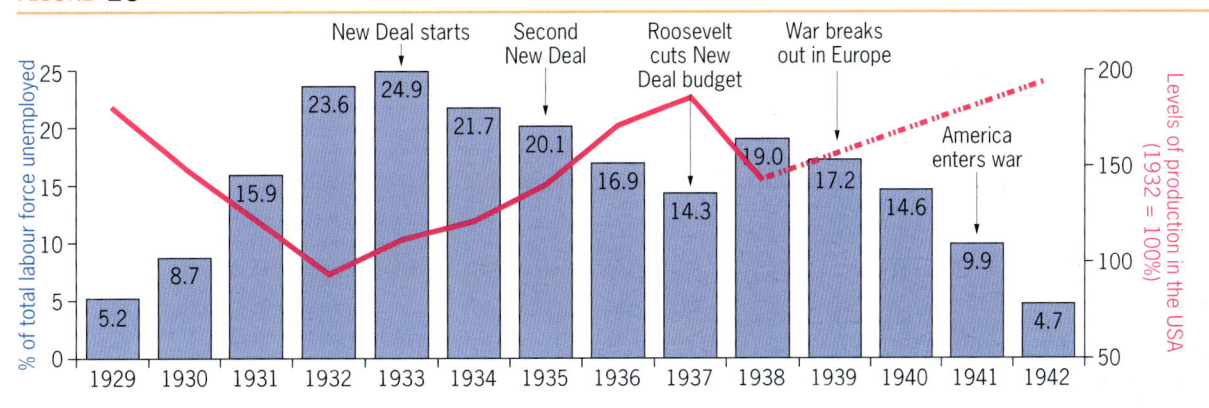

Year	% of total labour force unemployed
1929	5.2
1930	8.7
1931	15.9
1932	23.6
1933	24.9
1934	21.7
1935	20.1
1936	16.9
1937	14.3
1938	19.0
1939	17.2
1940	14.6
1941	9.9
1942	4.7

Key events marked on chart: New Deal starts (1933), Second New Deal (1935), Roosevelt cuts New Deal budget (1937), War breaks out in Europe (1939), America enters war (1941). Red line shows Levels of production in the USA (1932 = 100%).

Unemployment, and the performance of the US economy during the 1930s.

SOURCE 17

A 1937 cartoon from the *Portland Press Herald* showing Harold Ickes in conflict with big business. Ickes was Secretary of the Interior and in charge of the PWA.

The 1937 recession damaged Roosevelt badly. Middle-class voters lost some confidence in him. As a result, in 1938 the Republicans once again did well in the congressional elections. Now it was much harder for Roosevelt to push his reforms through Congress. However, he was still enormously popular with most ordinary Americans (he was elected again with a big majority in 1940). The problem was that the USA was no longer as united behind his New Deal as it had been in 1933. Indeed, by 1940 Roosevelt and most Americans were focusing more on the outbreak of war in Europe and on Japan's exploits in the Far East.

FOCUS TASK 9.17

Study the sources and the material on this page. Write a short, 200-word explanation of why unemployment continued to be an issue up until the outbreak of the Second World War.

Source Analysis

Do you think Source 17 is praising or criticising Ickes? Explain your answer.

Did the fact that the New Deal did not solve unemployment mean that it was a failure?

> **FOCUS TASK 9.18**
>
> **What was the impact of the New Deal?**
> Pages 334–35 summarise the impact of the New Deal on various aspects of 1930s America.
>
> 1 For each of the six aspects, decide where you would place this aspect of the New Deal on the scale. Explain your score and support it with evidence from Chapter 10D.
>
> –5 –4 –3 –2 –1 0 1 2 3 4 5
>
> Negative impact is –5. Positive impact is +5.
>
> 2 Compare your six 'marks' on the scale with those of someone else in your class.
>
> 3 Working together, try to come up with an agreed mark for the impact of the whole New Deal. You will have to think about the relative importance of different issues. For example, you might give more weight to a low mark in an important area than to a high mark in a less important area.

Impact on... confidence in government

- The New Deal restored the faith of the American people in their Government.
- The New Deal was a huge social and economic programme. Government help on this scale would never have been possible before Roosevelt's time. It set the tone for future policies for government to help people.
- The New Deal handled billions of dollars of public money, but there were no corruption scandals. For example, the head of the Civil Works Administration, Harold Hopkins, distributed $10 billion in schemes and programmes, but never earned more than his salary of $15,000. The Secretary of the Interior, Harold Ickes, actually tapped the phones of his own employees to ensure there was no corruption. He also employed African Americans, campaigned against ANTISEMITISM and supported the cause of Native Americans.
- The New Deal divided the USA. Roosevelt and his officials were often accused of being communists and of undermining American values. Ickes and Hopkins were both accused of being antibusiness because they supported trade unions.
- The New Deal undermined local government.

Impact on... industrial workers

- The NRA and Second New Deal strengthened the position of labour unions.
- Roosevelt's Government generally tried to support unions and make large corporations negotiate with them.
- Some unions combined as the Committee for Industrial Organisation (CIO) in 1935 – large enough to bargain with big corporations.
- The Union of Automobile Workers (UAW) was recognised by the two most anti-union corporations: General Motors (after a major sit-in strike in 1936) and Ford (after a ballot in 1941).
- Big business remained immensely powerful in the USA despite being challenged by the Government.
- Unions were still treated with suspicion by employers.
- Many strikes were broken up with brutal violence in the 1930s.
- Companies such as Ford, Republic Steel and Chrysler employed their own thugs or controlled local police forces.
- By the end of the 1930s there were over 7 million union members and unions became powerful after the Second World War.

Impact on... unemployment and the economy

- The New Deal created millions of jobs.
- It stabilised the American banking system.
- It cut the number of business failures.
- Projects such as the TVA brought work and an improved standard of living to deprived parts of the USA.
- New Deal projects provided the USA with valuable resources such as schools, roads and power stations.
- The New Deal never solved the underlying economic problems.
- The US economy took longer to recover than that of most European countries.
- Confidence remained low – throughout the 1930s Americans only spent and invested about 75 per cent of what they had before 1929.
- When Roosevelt cut the New Deal budget in 1937, the country went back into recession.
- There were 6 million unemployed in 1941.
- Only the USA's entry into the war brought an end to unemployment.

Impact on... African Americans

- Around 200,000 African Americans gained benefits from the Civilian Conservation Corps, other New Deal agencies, and relief programmes.
- Many African Americans benefited from New Deal slum clearance and housing projects.
- Some New Deal agencies discriminated against African Americans. There was racial segregation in the CCC. Mortgages were not given to black families in white neighbourhoods.
- More black workers were unemployed (35 per cent living on relief in 1935) but they were much less likely to be given jobs and the ones they did get were often menial.
- Domestic workers (the area in which many black women were employed) were not included in the Social Security Act.
- Roosevelt failed to put through any civil rights legislation, particularly laws against the lynching of African Americans. He feared that Democrat senators in the Southern states would not support him.

SOURCE 18

African Americans queuing for government relief in 1937 in front of a famous government poster.

Impact on... women

- The New Deal saw some women achieve prominent positions. Eleanor Roosevelt became an important campaigner on social issues.
- Mary Macleod Bethune, an African-American woman, headed the National Youth Administration.
- Frances Perkins was the Secretary of Labor. She removed 59 corrupt officials from the Labor Department and was a key figure in making the Second New Deal work in practice.
- Most of the New Deal programmes were aimed to help male manual workers rather than women (only about 8000 women were involved in the CCC).
- Local governments tried to avoid paying out social security payments to women by introducing special qualifications and conditions.
- Frances Perkins was viciously attacked in the press as being Jewish and a Soviet spy. Even her cabinet colleagues tended to ignore her at social gatherings.

Impact on... Native Americans

- The Indian Reorganisation Act 1934 provided money to help Native Americans to buy and improve land and control their own tribal areas.
- The Indian Reservation Act 1934 helped Native Americans to preserve and practise their traditions, laws and culture and develop their land as they chose.
- Native Americans remained a poor and excluded section of society.

Revision Tip

There is a lot happening on this spread! When it comes to revision, choose two points from each panel, one positive and one negative, and try to remember those.

SOURCE 19

Many of Roosevelt's experiments were failures, but that is what experimentation entails. He would be satisfied he said if 75 per cent of them produced beneficial results. Experimentation depended on one of his distinctive characteristics: receptivity to new and untried methods and ideas.

Written by historian Samuel Rosemann.

Verdicts on the New Deal

So was the New Deal a success? One of the reasons why this question is hard to answer is that you need to decide what Roosevelt was trying to achieve. We know that by 1940, unemployment was still high and the economy was certainly not booming. On the other hand, economic recovery was not Roosevelt's only aim. In fact it may not have been his main aim. Roosevelt and many of his advisers wanted to reform the USA's economy and society. So when you decide whether the New Deal was a success or not, you will have to decide what you think the aims of the New Deal were, as well as whether you think the aims were achieved.

FOCUS TASK 9.19

How successful was the New Deal?

This is a complicated question. You have already spent time thinking about it; now you are going to prepare to write an essay.

1 First recap some key points by answering these questions.

A Roosevelt's aims
What were Roosevelt's aims for the First New Deal? (see pages 324–25)
What new aims did the Second New Deal have? (see pages 328–29)
Which of these aims did Roosevelt succeed in?
How far do you agree with Source 19 about Roosevelt's successes and failures?
B Unemployment and the economy
Why did unemployment remain high throughout the 1930s? (see page 333)
Does this mean that Roosevelt's New Deal was not a success?
C Opposition
Why did some people oppose Roosevelt? (see page pages 330–32)
How far do you think opposition to the New Deal made it hard for the New Deal to work?
D Criticisms and achievements
Which criticism of the New Deal do you think is most serious? Why?
Which achievement do you think is the most important? Why?
Would Roosevelt have agreed with your choice? Why?

2 Now write your own balanced account of the successes and failures of the New Deal, reaching your own conclusion as to whether it was a success or not. Consider:
- the nature and scale of the problem facing Roosevelt
- the action he took through the 1930s
- the impact of the New Deal on Americans
- the reasons for opposition to the New Deal
- your own judgement on its success.

Include evidence to back up your judgements.

Keywords

Make sure you know these terms, people or events and are able to use them or describe them confidently.

- Boom
- Capitalism
- Communism
- Competition
- Credit
- Democrat
- Depression
- Flapper
- Gangster
- Hire purchase
- Hollywood
- Hooverville
- Hundred Days
- Immigration
- Isolationism
- Jazz
- Ku Klux Klan
- Laissez-faire
- Lynch
- Mail order
- Mass consumption
- Mass production
- Monkey Trial
- NAACP
- New Deal
- Normalcy
- Over-production
- Production line
- Prohibition
- Radical
- Red Scare
- Republican
- Reservation (Native American)
- Roaring Twenties
- Second New Deal
- Shares
- Speculation
- Stock market
- Supreme Court
- Tariff
- Temperance
- Tennessee Valley Authority
- Traditional industries
- Trusts
- Wall Street Crash

Key Question Summary

How successful was the New Deal?

1. Roosevelt's New Deal promised action to get industry and agriculture working, get Americans back to work and provide relief for those suffering from the Depression.
2. The first Hundred Days was a whirlwind of activity, putting into place a number of New Deal agencies to achieve Roosevelt's aims. These involved huge public works programmes, schemes to boost employment and measures to put agriculture and industry on a more sustainable basis. Millions of dollars were set aside for relief.
3. Roosevelt restored confidence in the banks and put financial bodies in America on a more stable footing.
4. He explained his actions to Americans and gave hope and optimism through his radio talks, 'fireside chats', to the nation.
5. The Tennessee Valley Authority was a special example of government planning across several states.
6. In 1935 Roosevelt introduced a Second New Deal, which was focused more on reform and creating a better life for ordinary Americans.
7. There was a lot of opposition to his policies from those who thought he was not doing enough to help and those who thought he was doing too much. Many thought that the New Deal was a huge waste of money and resources and was wrong in principle – it involved too much government interference and undermined American individualism and self-reliance.
8. The Supreme Court ruled some parts of the New Deal to be unconstitutional.
9. The American people re-elected Roosevelt in 1936 in a landslide victory.
10. The New Deal did not solve the underlying problems of the American economy or conquer unemployment. It was the Second World War that got it going again. Some groups in society did not do as well out of it as they might have hoped.
11. It did save the banking system, create millions of jobs and relieve the suffering of millions of Americans. It left much of lasting value, for example in roads, public buildings and schools. It set the tone for future government action in the USA.

PRACTICE QUESTIONS

Structured questions

1. (a) What was the Tennessee Valley Authority? **[4]**
   (b) Why did Roosevelt introduce the Emergency Banking Act in 1933? **[6]**
   (c) 'The New Deal was a failure.' How far do you agree with this statement? Explain your answer. **[10]**

Alternative to Coursework questions

1. a) Write an account of the US government's economic policies in the 1920s. **[15]**
   b) Discuss the impact of new methods of production used in US industry in the 1920s. **[25]**

See pages 338–55 for advice on the different types of questions.

Focus on: Structured Questions

The information in this section is based on the Cambridge International syllabus. You should always refer to the appropriate syllabus document for the year of examination to confirm the details and for more information. The syllabus document is available on the Cambridge International website at www.cambridgeinternational.org.

The Depth Study you have studied in Chapters 7, 8 or 9 will be examined in the second part (Section B) of Paper 1 Structured Questions.

Note: If you are doing Cambridge IGCSE History and not doing Coursework then you will be doing Paper 4 Alternative to Coursework instead which will also be based on your Depth Study. This Exam Focus deals with Structured questions. Alternative to Coursework questions are dealt with on pages 343–53.

Structured essay questions

Depth Study and Core Content structured essay questions rely upon the same skills, so make sure you read all of the advice again on pages 148–54.

Think before you write

It is a common mistake to launch straight into writing as soon as your teacher gives you questions or assessments begin, but our advice is that you spend some time thinking before you do so.

1 Choose your questions carefully

- When answering practice questions or using practice papers, make sure you choose the correct Depth Study, of course – the one you have actually studied!
- Whenever you have a choice of questions make sure you have read all of them before you decide which to answer. You should have revised enough to mean you could do any of the questions but don't simply opt for your favourite topic. Possibly your less favoured topic might have a question that suits you better.

2 Read the questions carefully

This might sound obvious but there is a skill to it.
- Look for the **command words** such as 'describe' and 'explain', which let you know what type of skills you have to use.
- Identify **the topic** and the sub-topic. Questions will often focus on an event, individual or historical issue.
- Look for **dates**. If dates are given they will be important – this is History after all!

3 Plan your answer

If you think through your answer first, then writing it is easy. If you skip the thinking and just start writing the risks are:
- Your writing will be muddled.
- You will write in an illogical order.
- Your points won't lead to your conclusion.
- Even more likely, you will keep thinking of something more to say and will run out of time.

4 Plan your time

Managing your time while studying the History syllabus is really important. It is important that you practise your timings in lessons, assessments and at home when answering practice questions.
- Make sure you know how long an assessment or a set of practice questions should take. You can use the Specimen Exam Papers from the Cambridge International website to help you with this.
- The marks for each sub-question guide you as to how long to spend as well.

5 Avoid the most common mistakes

- The structured essay questions contain a different number of marks for each part, so make sure you don't spend too much time on questions with lower marks. Poor time management could mean you don't end up answering all of the questions!
- Make sure you are applying the correct skills for the relevant question. If it is asking you to describe, then don't explain. If the question is asking you to make a judgement, make sure you use your own knowledge to support the judgement. Remember, the skill of making a judgement means you need to compare and contrast different factors to reach your conclusion, so make sure you always examine a variety of factors to give a more balanced response.
- Questions that ask you to explain are not just asking you to make lists or give an account of an event. Use connectives and phrases like 'because', 'this meant that' and 'therefore' to develop your answer fully.

Pages 339–42 give you example answers with comments to show how to approach these kinds of questions. Read them all through – not just your Depth Study topic – so you can see the different types of question and possible approaches in an answer.

Worked example: Germany, 1918-45

(a) What methods did the Nazis use to control the population? **[4]**

> The SS under Himmler were used to intimidate and terrorise people into obedience. There was also the Gestapo who were the secret police. They tapped telephones and spied on people. Political opponents were taken to concentration camps. Propaganda was also used to prevent opposition. This was the job of Goebbels who controlled what people read and heard. Newspapers were taken over or their content strictly controlled. Cheap radio sets were sold so people could hear Hitler's speeches.

There is nothing wrong with this response but for some students it might take too much time to write – remember to be aware of your timings for description-based questions. There is plenty of accurate knowledge in this answer to give a full account of Nazi methods of control.

(b) Why were some Germans opposed to Nazi rule? **[6]**

> The Communists opposed Nazi rule because of their political beliefs.
>
> Some youth groups such as the Edelweiss Pirates were anti-Nazi. They liked to listen to music and many gangs went looking for the Hitler Youth to beat them up. They sang songs but changed the lyrics to mock Germany.

This part of the answer correctly identifies a group who opposed the Nazis, but it is quite vague. To develop the answer, remember to add relevant examples.

*The second part of this answer is only **describing** the youth opposition, rather than saying **why** people opposed the Nazis. To develop the answer you would need to explain how the popularity of youth groups fell as the war progressed because the activities were more focused on military drill and the war effort.*

(c) 'The success of Nazi economic policy was more important than the police state in controlling opposition to the Nazis.' How far do you agree with this statement? Explain your answer. **[10]**

> The Nazis' economic policies did help. They promised employment and did this through the development of public works such as building autobahns. Schemes like 'Strength Through Joy' gave workers cheap theatre and cinema tickets. So some workers were won over by economic improvements and popular policies and this stopped opposition arising in the first place.
>
> From 1935 conscription was applied and rearmament meant thousands of jobs in armament factories. So some people were scared of losing their jobs if they spoke out. Germany had been hit hard by the Depression and many were terrified of being out of work again.
>
> However, the police state was also important. The Nazis were very successful at getting rid of opposition. The SS went round terrorising people into obedience. It could arrest people without trial and put them into concentration camps where people were tortured or indoctrinated. The Gestapo spied on people. It had informers and encouraged people to inform on their neighbours and children on their families. It also tapped phones. The Germans thought the Gestapo was much more powerful than it actually was, so lots of people informed on each other purely because they thought the Gestapo would find out anyway.

*This answer starts well by addressing the question. It states clearly **why** economic policy helped to control opposition.*

*This is the clinching bit that makes all the above supporting detail into an excellent **explanation**.*

This paragraph goes further by offering more evidence of economic policy stifling opposition.

There are two factors mentioned in the question. This paragraph shows the student has developed a more balanced answer by also examining the second factor as well.

> This is a very good example of reaching a judgement that **links** the two factors together. The answer distinguishes between two types of opposition and shows how a different method was more successful for each.

In conclusion, I would say that economic successes were vital in controlling opposition amongst ordinary citizens but that the police state was also vital for dealing with the opposition when it did arise; the two actually worked together. The Nazis' main political opponents had been dealt with swiftly with the help of the SS and Gestapo, which left smaller pockets of opposition. Ordinary people with weaker political motivation were more easily won over by the Nazis' successes and the fear of losing their jobs.

Worked example: Russia, 1905-41

> The questions, example answers and comments that appear on pages 339–42 were written by the author. In an examination, the way marks would be allocated to questions like these may be different.

(a) Describe the problems facing the Provisional Government after March 1917. [4]

> This is a very succinct response which is accurate and to the point. It contains a well-developed account of the problems facing the Provisional Government.

The war effort was failing and some soldiers were deserting. The peasants were demanding land and some were starting to take it. The Bolsheviks had also started rioting after Lenin returned from exile. Workers in the cities were starving.

(b) Why was Lenin able to secure Bolshevik control in Russia soon after the November Revolution of 1917? [6]

> These are all precise things that Lenin did, but haven't been explained to show how they were helping the Bolsheviks hold on to their power.

Lenin banned non-Bolshevik papers and set up the 'Cheka' secret police. The banks were placed under Bolshevik control.

> This is better because it is a much fuller explanation of how Lenin's actions were leading to the Bolsheviks' retention of power.

Lenin had promised free elections and these were held in late 1917. However, under the first democratic elections to the new Constituent Assembly, the Socialist Revolutionaries beat the Bolsheviks. This could have been the end of the Bolsheviks' power. However, Lenin simply sent the Red Guards to close down the assembly and to put down the protests against him.

> Another sound explanation, showing how Lenin was attempting to secure power through popularity with the people.

Finally, Lenin had to negotiate a peace treaty to end the war because he had promised the people 'bread, peace and land'. He hoped that this would increase the popularity of the Bolsheviks and they would stay in power.

(c) 'The main reason that the Reds won the Civil War was because the Whites were not unified.' How far do you agree with this statement? Explain your answer. [10]

> This is a full explanation of how the disunity of the Whites led to Red success.

The success of the Reds was definitely helped by the lack of unity in their opposition. The Whites were made up of lots of different elements such as the Czech Legion, moderate socialists and ex-tsarists. This meant they had different leaders and different objectives and therefore were not able to work together effectively. This allowed Trotsky to defeat them one by one.

This paragraph goes on to examine an alternative factor which is going to help develop a much more balanced response. It explains how War Communism was also a factor in the Reds' victory.	However, other things helped the Reds win the Civil War as well. For example, Lenin introduced War Communism. This system allowed Reds total control over people's lives and possessions in order to win the war. Ruthless discipline was introduced into the factories. Food was taken from peasant farmers by force in order to feed the Red Army and the workers in the cities. Strict rationing was introduced and the Cheka was used to terrify opponents. This policy ensured the Red Army was kept supplied and could continue to fight.
The answer attempts a conclusion, but this is more of a summary than a judgement. What you need to do here is to actively **compare** the factors, or to draw them together to show how they are **linked**. For example, you might say that 'although it was always going to be difficult for the Whites to win because they were such a broad alliance, it was the ruthless and harsh policy of War Communism, which determined their defeat by 1920 and meant that the Bolsheviks held onto their power so firmly.'	I think that overall the Reds won because the Whites were not unified, which helped the Reds pick them off, and also because of War Communism, which allowed the Red Army to keep fighting.

Worked example: USA, 1919-41

(a) What problems were faced by farmers in the USA in the 1920s? **[4]**

This is a really strong response which shows a strong factual knowledge of the problems faced by farmers. However, this answer might be too long for some students to write, so be aware of time management for description-based questions.	Many farmers did not share in the prosperity that other groups experienced in the boom. Farmers had been over-producing since the end of the First World War and after the European markets had recovered from the war, they could not sell the extra produce. Due to this, prices for farming produce fell rapidly in the 1920s. This was made worse due to high tariffs imposed by overseas nations and the competition from other countries like Canada who were able to sell their wheat at a cheaper price than the USA.

(b) Why was Prohibition introduced in the USA? **[6]**

The first paragraph doesn't answer the question why Prohibition was introduced but how it was introduced – you must be very careful here and read the question properly.	Prohibition was introduced in 1920 due to the passing of the Volstead Act in 1919 which banned the sale and manufacture of alcohol in the USA.
This part of the answer is focused on the question and is a very convincing explanation of how temperance movements helped the introduction of Prohibition. It is well-supported by valid evidence.	There was a strong temperance movement in the USA in the nineteenth and early twentieth centuries such as the Anti-Saloon League and the Women's Christian Temperance Movement. These devout Christians wanted to stop the damage that alcohol did to family life such as causing poverty and violence. This led to a lot of support for Prohibition, especially in the Southern states of the USA.
The last part of the answer describes some other valid reasons for the introduction of Prohibition, but it would be better if it had been developed into an explanation to give a fuller response.	Also, some industrialists and doctors supported the idea of Prohibition. Politicians also backed it as it helped them win votes from many Christians. These are all reasons why Prohibition was introduced.

(c) 'The most successful aspect of the New Deal was the help it gave to farmers.' How far do you agree with this statement? Explain your answer. **[10]**

> The first paragraph is clearly focused on the question here and introduces one of the key alphabet agencies that dealt with problems faced by the agricultural sector.

The New Deal was a massive help to farmers in the 1930s. Farmers had been suffering since the 1920s and Roosevelt introduced the Agricultural Adjustment Administration (AAA) to help solve some of the problems that they faced.

> Here the point made in the first paragraph is developed into an explanation and is supported by some strong evidence about its success.

AAA set quotas on farm production. This would help push food prices up as in the 1920s prices had been dropping rapidly due to over-production and the impact of tariffs. The AAA also helped farmers modernise their production methods which successfully increased efficiency on farms and protected the quality of the soil. This was a successful aspect of the New Deal.

> The answer has now been developed to give it balance by examining another aspect of the New Deal – in this case, dealing with the unemployed.

However, other aspects of the New Deal were also successful such as dealing with the problem of the unemployed during the Depression of the 1930s.

> There is a wide variety of good examples of how the New Deal dealt with the unemployed – the CCC, PWA and WPA. A strong explanation of the New Deal's success is provided here by using statistical data on unemployment to support the argument.

The Civilian Conservation Corps targeted young, unemployed men for six months at a time, often providing low-paid work in national parks and forests. The Public Works Administration created jobs by using government money to build schools, bridges and roads. Later, the Works Progress Administration united all of the job creation agencies of the New Deal to provide work for office workers, actors and artists. Due to these agencies, unemployment was reduced from 25 per cent in 1933 to 14 per cent in 1937 proving it was successful.

> Another valid aspect of the New Deal is explained here, banking. It lacks the depth of the last paragraph, but is a valid explanation.

Also, the New Deal dealt with the banking crisis with the Emergency Banking Act. This closed down all banks and only allowed trustworthy ones to reopen – 5000 in total. This successfully helped people regain confidence in the banking system after the Crash in 1929.

> The conclusion is only a simple statement containing an unsupported judgement. This could have been improved by comparing this aspect of the New Deal against the success of the others discussed in this answer.

Overall, I think that the most successful aspect of the New Deal was how it helped the unemployed.

Focus on: Alternative to Coursework

> Your teacher will decide whether you are going to do Coursework Component 3 or Paper 4 Alternative to Coursework. The approach towards answering the questions in the Coursework and Alternative to Coursework is very different and the advice that follows is NOT applicable to the Coursework.
>
> Cambridge O Level History students do not take Coursework or Alternative to Coursework.

> The information in this section is based on the Cambridge International syllabus. You should always refer to the appropriate syllabus document for the year of examination to confirm the details and for more information. The syllabus document is available on the Cambridge International website at www.cambridgeinternational.org.

Structure

The Alternative to Coursework paper is a one-hour examination focusing on your chosen Depth Study. Make sure you use the Specimen Papers on the Cambridge International website to familiarise yourself with the format of the exam paper so you can practise in lessons and at home. It takes the form of a single structured question which is split into two parts, a) and b). The a) part of the question requires you to use your own knowledge to write a logical account on an event or topic linked to your chosen Depth Study. The b) part of the question typically requires you to write an extended answer to assess the importance or impact of an individual, group, event or idea.

Part a) is worth 15 marks and part b) is worth 25 marks, so the total marks available in the paper is 40.

Example questions

The questions usually draw from some aspect of the Key Questions and Focus Points for each of the Depth Studies. For example:

Germany, 1918–45 has the following Key Questions:
1. Was the Weimar Republic doomed from the start?
2. Why was Hitler able to dominate Germany by 1934?
3. How effectively did the Nazis control Germany, 1933–45?
4. What was it like to live in Nazi Germany?

An example of a structured question that draws from Key Question 1 might be:

> **a)** Write an account of the Spartacist Uprising in 1919. **[15]**
> **b)** Discuss the impact of political violence in the early Weimar Republic, 1919–23. **[25]**

Russia, 1905–41 has the following Key Questions:
1. Why did the tsarist regime collapse in 1917?
2. How did the Bolsheviks gain power, and how did they consolidate their rule?
3. How did Stalin gain and hold on to power?
4. What was the impact of Stalin's economic policies?

An example of a structured question that draws from Key Question 3 might be:

a) Write an account of the First Five-Year Plan. [15]
b) Discuss the importance of industrial modernisation in the USSR after 1928. [25]

USA, 1919–41 has the following Key Questions:
1 How far did the US economy boom in the 1920s?
2 How far did US society change in the 1920s?
3 What were the causes and consequences of the Wall Street Crash?
4 How successful was the New Deal?

An example of a structured question that draws from Key Question 4 might be:

a) Write an account of Roosevelt's first 'Hundred Days'. [15]
b) Discuss the importance of the alphabet agencies as part of the first New Deal. [25]

When writing an account, it is vital to use in-depth knowledge and order your information logically in paragraphs. For the extended answer, make sure you assess (weigh up) the importance or impact in different ways and explain your arguments using good examples.

Mark scheme

The Alternative to Coursework paper has a generic mark scheme which can be used to mark any question from any of the Depth Studies that you choose to answer. Your teacher can help you understand this mark scheme. You can find the mark scheme on the Cambridge Assessment International Education website in the Cambridge IGCSE History Syllabus along with Specimen Papers and mark schemes.

Think before you write

The Alternative to Coursework paper contains two structured questions on each of the five Depth Studies. You will answer two questions on one Depth Study.
- The questions all follow the same style.
- They are all worth 40 marks in total, split into a **part a)** worth 15 marks and **part b)** worth 25 marks.
- They all require a descriptive and sequenced account for **part a)** and an extended answer for **part b)**.

1 Read questions carefully

When answering exam-style questions or using practice papers, make sure you choose the correct Depth Study, of course – the one you have actually studied!

Whenever you have a choice of questions make sure you have read all of them before you decide which to answer. You should have revised enough so that you could do any of the questions, but don't simply opt for your favourite topic.

Read the question to identify precisely the focus of the account for **part a)** and the focus for the discussion in **part b)**.

> **b)** Discuss the impact of political violence in the early Weimar Republic, 1919–23. **[25]**

*The **impact of political violence** is the focus.*

1919–23 is the date range.

2 Choose your question carefully

Remember you have two questions to answer! Choose the questions where:
- you know the content best and
- where you already have a clear view on the different features of the question focus for **part b)**.

3 Plan your answer

This is always an important aspect for developing your skills, especially if you are writing an extended answer. Assessments and exam papers have time limits, so make sure you don't spend too long doing this. This may seem like a waste of time or a luxury, but you will be surprised how much it will help you.

If you think through your answer first, then writing it is easy. If you skip the thinking and just start writing the risks are:
- Your writing will be muddled – it won't be an argument, it will just be a collection of paragraphs.
- You will write in an illogical order – and you never have time to rewrite things in an exam.
- Your points won't lead to your conclusion – and the conclusion is very important in the part b) question.
- Even more likely, you will keep thinking of something more to say and you will run out of time to even write your conclusion.

4 Organise your thinking

We have given advice on how to plan an extended answer on page XXX. That was to allow you to practise before an assessment or the exams. In an actual assessment or test, you will have to use something much more streamlined.

For example, for a **part b)** question:

> **b)** Discuss the impact of political violence in the early Weimar Republic, 1919–23. **[25]**

Focus of question	Main points to include
Impact on stability	Political extremist groups from left and right; Spartacist Uprising; Kapp Putsch, etc.
Impact on the economy	Example
Impact on Ebert's ability to govern	Example
Conclusion	

5 Decide on a structure

There are many ways to structure an extended answer for **part b)**. Here is a common structure taught by many teachers:
- Start with a short introduction which sets out your argument by examining the different aspects of the question focus you could discuss.
- Then explain how each aspect was important or had impact in separate paragraphs which include supporting examples from your own knowledge.
- Finish by writing a conclusion to show the relative importance/impact of the different factors by comparing them and using some good evidence to support your judgement.

The next three pages offer you worked examples from each topic. These are not perfect answers. They could all be developed to produce even stronger responses.

Planning answers for part a) questions

The Alternative to Coursework paper is only a one-hour exam, so time management is crucial. This can often tempt many learners to start writing the answer straight away without any planning or preparation. However, it is always worth at least noting down the main points you are going to describe for **part a)** questions. Below is a simple but effective approach based on a flow diagram.

Using a flow diagram

A flow diagram is used to put ideas or factors into a logical order or sequence. This is exactly what you want to achieve when writing an account. You can order the flow diagram horizontally or vertically – whatever works best for you.
- Put the title at the top just to help you keep focused on the question. This can just be the main focus of the question, for example 'the Spartacist Uprising in 1919'.
- Then, in each box, write the events or factors you are going to describe in a logical sequence or chronological order. You can use the spaces or arrows in between the boxes to show the connections or links.

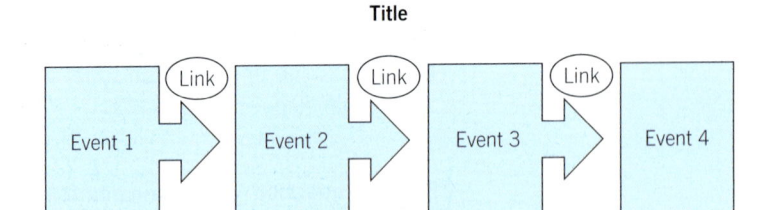

Title

Event 1 → [Link] → Event 2 → [Link] → Event 3 → [Link] → Event 4

On the next page, you can see how the flow diagram might look in planning an answer to this question:

a) Write an account of the Spartacist Uprising in 1919. [15]

Spartacist Uprising, 1919

```
[Communists led by Luxemburg and Liebknecht – wanted a Soviet style system] →(Overthrow Republic)→ [Strike action by workers and some soldiers; seizing control of newspapers] →(Government reactions)→ [Ebert's use of the army and the Freikorps] →(Consequences)→ [Brutal fighting; 170 killed; leaders murdered; led to further left-wing uprisings]
```

Planning answers for part b) questions

Part b) questions will require you to write an extended answer and need a bit more planning before you start writing but as always, keep an eye on your time management in an actual exam or assessment.

Below are two different approaches to planning an extended answer.
- The first uses a table comparing the different feature or aspects of the focus of the question. This should help you assess and explain importance or impact.
- The second uses a factor map. This approach is useful where you need to show links between features or aspects of the focus in the question.

We are not suggesting you use anything as complex as this in an assessment or when answering an exam-style question – there won't be time. But it is precisely because it is so hard to give time to planning in an actual exam that it is so important to practise it before, without the time pressures, so that it becomes almost instinctive.

Approach 1: Using a table

In the table like the one below:
- make notes about the content in Column 1, then
- explain how that factor caused the thing in the question in Column 2.

Column 2 is where you do the thinking and analysis. In your essay you won't just be listing the factors, you will be evaluating their importance.

Focus of the question for discussion	Importance/impact, etc.
Aspect 1:	This was an important aspect because...
Aspect 2:	
Aspect 3:	
Aspect 4:	

You can see below how the table might look in planning an answer to this question:

b) Discuss the importance of industrial modernisation in the USSR after 1928. **[25]**

Industrial modernisation in the USSR after 1928	Importance/impact, etc.
Aspect 1: Defence of the USSR	This was an important because the USSR had been invaded from the West in the First World War and Stalin believed that Hitler wanted to expand eastwards in the near future.
Aspect 2: Create a communist system	This was an important because Stalin wanted to apply Marxist ideas and rapidly turn the USSR into a model communist state by increasing the number of industrial workers.
Aspect 3: Replace the NEP	This was an important because many Communist Party leaders, including Stalin, viewed Lenin's NEP as a return to capitalism which went against communist ideology.
Aspect 4: Compete with the West/ capitalism	This was an important because Stalin wanted to increase production so it did not have to rely on imports and could become an industrial superpower like the USA.

Approach 2: Using a factor map

In a diagram like the one below you:
- write the different aspects and any details/facts about them in the boxes, then
- explain the links between them on arrows between the boxes.

The arrow links are where you do your thinking and analysis. These links will help you decide on relative importance – if everything links back to a single aspect, that suggests it is the most important factor. They will also give you an angle to your paragraphs. Showing links between factors is one way of improving your essays.

To keep your diagram neat you could number or letter the links and write about them on a separate sheet (see below left).

Below right is how the factor map might look in planning an answer to this question:

b) Discuss the importance of the alphabet agencies as part of the first New Deal. **[25]**

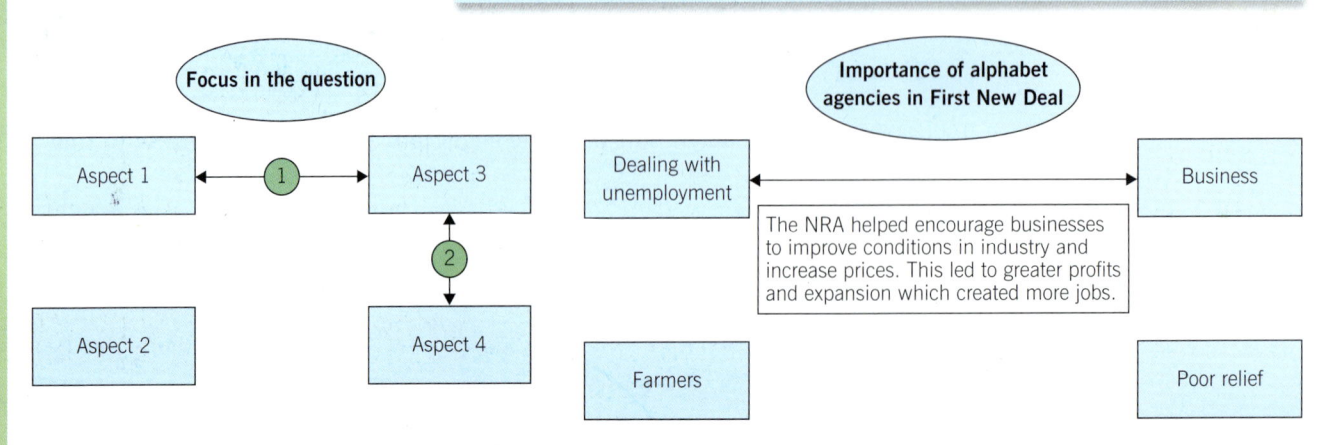

Focus in the question

Aspect 1 ↔ (1) ↔ Aspect 3
Aspect 2
Aspect 4
(2)

Importance of alphabet agencies in First New Deal

Dealing with unemployment ↔ Business

The NRA helped encourage businesses to improve conditions in industry and increase prices. This led to greater profits and expansion which created more jobs.

Farmers
Poor relief

Worked example: Germany 1918–45

The questions, example answers and comments that appear on pages 343–53 were written by the author. In an examination, the way marks would be awarded to questions like these may be different.

The focus of the account.

The date range.

a) Write an account of the Spartacist Uprising in 1919. **[15]**

The first two paragraphs contain a lot of background narrative and though there is some relevant knowledge on the Spartacists in the first paragraph that does add to the quality of the answer, much of it does not focus on the Uprising in 1919.

This paragraph is more focused on the Uprising and examines how the Spartacists tried to seize control of the cities and towns. The detail is accurate and relevant.

Some good examples and in-depth knowledge add necessary detail to the description.

The final paragraph logically continues where the last paragraph left off. A good level of detail is included on the consequences of the uprising.

> The Spartacists were a revolutionary communist organisation that wanted to create a soviet-style system in Germany by overthrowing the German Republic. They had support from some of the workers, soldiers and sailors at the end of the First World War and were led by Liebknecht and Luxemburg.
>
> In January 1919, the German Republic had many issues such as political instability and economic problems caused by the shortages created by the British blockade of Germany's ports and the huge amount of debt built up by the Kaiser's government. Germany had signed an Armistice in November 1918 which the Allies agreed to only if the Kaiser abdicated and Germany became a Republic with a democratic system. The government agreed to avoid invasion by the Allies.
>
> The Spartacists began their uprising by seizing control of the newspapers, building barricades and setting up soviets in the towns and cities across Germany. They also called for the workers to go on strike – many were armed. The government, under Ebert, made a deal with the army as well as ex-soldiers who formed themselves into anti-communist Freikorps units. This resulted in near civil war and over 150 Spartacists were killed.
>
> The Freikorps and the army crushed the uprising and the leaders were murdered when the fighting ended. The communists never forgave the ruling Socialist Party under Ebert for using the military and Freikorps brigades against them. It led to further uprisings in 1919 in Bavaria and in the Ruhr in 1920.

The focus of the discussion is the impact of political violence in the Weimar Republic.

1919–23 is the date range.

b) Discuss the impact of political violence in the early Weimar Republic, 1919–23. **[25]**

The introduction is nicely focused and begins by considering a number of different aspects of how political violence impacted the Weimar Republic. It lacks any kind of judgement at this point, however.

> The early Weimar Republic faced many problems and some say it was doomed from the beginning because of the social, political and economic issues it faced between 1919 and 1923. Political violence from both the left and the right impacted how the Weimar Republic was viewed by the German people; it also resulted in a massive amount of instability for Ebert's new government. Finally, political violence impacted the way in which the authorities would react to threats from extremists.

Focus on: Alternative to Coursework

349

The first aspect is considered here and the explanation given is focused on impact. There is some good use of contextual knowledge though it lacks specific examples to support.	One impact of political violence that was important was how it affected ordinary Germans and their opinion of the new Weimar government. In January 1919, the Spartacist Uprising showed many Germans that extreme left-wing groups were a threat to the new democracy and would even try to overthrow the regime by revolution. This especially worried the middle-classes and the elites in Germany who did not want a communist system like in Russia where private property had been taken over by the state and capitalism crushed by the Bolsheviks under Lenin.
The explanation is developed further which adds depth and breadth to the paragraph.	Furthermore, the Kapp Putsch by the right-wing nationalist Freikorps in 1920 demonstrated to many Germans that the new Weimar Republic did not have the support of the army or ex-soldiers and that some Germans opposed the military restrictions imposed by the Treaty of Versailles. This added to the nationalist concept of the stab in the back myth propagated by some right-wing groups. However, Ebert's government also clearly had some support and the Kapp Putsch impacted the workers in Berlin who went on a general strike to end the putsch.
The next paragraph examines a different aspect linked to the question focus and gives convincing explanations of how it impacted early Weimar Germany using more precise examples to support compared to the first aspect.	Another impact of political violence was the instability it caused for the Weimar Republic. Communist uprisings occurred throughout Germany such as in 1919 in Bavaria and 1920 in the Ruhr region. Ebert was forced to use emergency powers (Article 48) to order the army and the Freikorps units to crush these rebellions using force which resulted in thousands of deaths. This led to instability as it demonstrated how close to revolution early Weimar Germany was. This was further demonstrated in the Kapp Putsch where the army refused to stop the Freikorps uprising. The government looked weak and did not have the loyalty of the army and so was powerless to stop the uprising until the Berlin workers reacted. Right-wing extremists even assassinated key politicians such as Walther Rathenau- he, like others, was blamed for stabbing Germany in the back by signing the Armistice and the Treaty of Versailles. The Munich Putsch led by Hitler and the Nazis in 1923 also demonstrated that there was a lot of resentment about the terms of the Treaty of Versailles and particularly the economic impact the reparations had. The Nazis wanted to overthrow the Weimar government and abolish the Treaty.
This response shows a clear structure and logic to the arguments. A third and final aspect of how political violence impacted the early Weimar Republic is stated. It lacks some of the depth of the other two paragraphs but is very focused in terms of the discussion.	A final impact political violence had on early Weimar Germany was the effect it had on Ebert and his government. Ebert was prepared to defend the new Weimar democracy using all means necessary- especially when the threat of communist revolution was present in the Spartacist Uprising. Ebert used Article 48 over 130 times in the early years of the Republic which effectively side-lined democracy and empowered the President to use the army and the Freikorps to crush their opposition. It seemed that the only was the early government survived the political extremism in its early years was to make deals with opposing extremist groups like the Freikorps.
A short but focused conclusion attempts to prioritise the most important impact. The explanation could have been developed further by comparing or more explicitly developing the links between this aspect and the others discussed in the essay.	In conclusion, political violence had the biggest impact on stability of early Weimar Germany more than anything else. It meant the democracy was constantly under threat and even led some citizens to support radical groups during the elections where they won a number of seats in the Reichstag.

Worked example: Russia, 1905–41

The First Five-Year Plan is the focus of the account. There is no date range given in the question, but you are expected to know that this started in 1928 and ended in 1932.	**a)** Write an account of the First Five-Year Plan. **[15]**

A very focused start to the account. It logically begins by describing the reasons behind the First Five-Year Plan.	Stalin was desperate to modernise the Soviet Union rapidly, particularly industry. He, like other Bolsheviks in the Party, opposed the New Economic Policy introduced by Lenin in 1921. He viewed the NEP as a betrayal of communist principles as it allowed limited capitalism back into the USSR after it had been initially swept away by the revolution and during the Civil War.
The next paragraph in the account follows logically on from the first. Some detailed description is given on how the plan was implemented and what it tried to achieve.	Stalin wanted to focus on heavy industry first. When he introduced the plan in 1928, he used GOSPLAN to set targets for each industry such as coal, iron, steel and oil. Stalin needed to increase production in these areas as quickly as possible to lay the foundation for further development in the second and third Five-Year Plans. Targets were then set for each region, each city and each factory manager.
This next section is shorter but factually rich in terms of the detail given in the description. It makes sense as it now examines the achievements of the plan.	The First Five-Year Plan did have some success. Huge steel mills were built, such as the one at Magnitogorsk and 1500 new industrial plants were constructed across Russia. This resulted in a doubling of coal and iron output. Electrification also brought power to many areas of Russia that previously had none.
The final paragraph loses focus and starts to describe the aims of the later plans which is not the aim of the account. Be careful to keep within the parameters set out in the question so as to not waste time. For example, the student could have given a short account of the failures associated with the First Five-Year Plan instead.	The Second and Third Five-Year Plans focused on further increasing output from these primary industries but also expanding secondary industries such as chemicals, metals, railways and later farm machinery and even some consumer goods.

The importance of industrial modernisation in the USSR is the focus for the discussion.	**b)** Discuss the importance of industrial modernisation in the USSR after 1928. **[25]**
After 1928 is the date range.	

The introduction here is a great start. Different aspects are listed for the discussion and a judgement about the most important aspect is stated.	The modernisation and expansion of industry in the USSR was vitally important for Stalin for many different reasons. Firstly, it would allow Stalin to increase his personal control over the workforce by setting targets for industry. Secondly, it was important because it would allow Stalin to compete with its main rival in the West, the USA. Finally, and most importantly, modernisation was crucial in allowing the USSR to defend itself from invasion in the future by increasing the power of its military.

The first aspect is discussed here and shows a good level of understanding. Explanations are focused on the question and on addressing importance. It does lack specific examples to support the explanations, however.	Stalin wanted to leave his mark on the Soviet Union when he became leader and create a cult of personality around himself as a worthy successor to Lenin who had led the revolution in 1917. His Five-Year Plans represented a major undertaking which would transform the USSR into an industrial superpower and increase the size of the workforce. In Marxism, the industrial workers were considered the main revolutionary class who the Communist Party drew the most support from. Stalin wanted to be viewed as the leader who helped create a communist system and modernised the USSR away from its mainly agrarian past. This would help him increase his personal control over the Communist Party because he would be seen as building on Lenin's legacy and continuing the revolution but also because it would allow him to use the state to set the targets and rules, thus controlling the workforce across the USSR.
There is less depth in this explanation but it does add another valid aspect to the overall discussion.	Perhaps more importantly than this was the fact that Stalin and many other communists wanted the Soviet Union to become a model communist state which would inspire other countries to have revolutions of their own. This could only be achieved if the Soviet Union was seen to be modern and advanced like the capitalist countries in the West, such as the UK and the USA. Stalin wanted the industrial system in the USSR to match and even exceed that of its main competitors in the capitalist West.
The final aspect of the discussion is well explained and focused on addressing importance. There is better detail included in the explanations which adds depth to the judgement given in the introduction.	Finally, and most importantly, industrial modernisation would allow the USSR to defend itself against invasion from the West. The First World War and the Civil War in Russia had seen foreign nations successfully invade the country. This had led to a huge number of casualties and damage to Russia's economy leading to food and fuel shortages and even famine. Stalin wanted to ensure that the Five-Year Plans focused first on building up primary industries such as coal, iron and steel so that they could help develop secondary industries needed for war and defence, such as chemicals and munitions. Only with mass production methods could Stalin hope to survive an invasion from the West. This was especially vital after Hitler came to power in Germany in 1933 and began rearming Germany and then reintroducing conscription in 1936.
The conclusion is succinct but to the point. The judgement is fleshed out and a comparison is made with the other aspects discussed to reinforce the argument.	Defence was the most important reason for the modernisation of Soviet industry. Stalin had to ensure the survival of communism in the face of capitalism and the threat of fascism and Nazism in Germany. Whilst control and competition with the West were important, Stalin knew that if the USSR could not resist invasion, then his legacy would be destroyed and the USSR crushed in a war as it had been in the First World War.

Worked example: USA, 1919–41

a) Write an account of Roosevelt's first 'Hundred Days'. **[15]**

> Roosevelt's first 'Hundred Days' is the focus of the account.

> Roosevelt campaigned in 1932 against President Hoover. He promised the American people a New Deal to help the huge numbers of unemployed and impoverished during the economic Depression. This was something that the public could get behind after Hoover had failed to try to solve the problems.

> Again, there is no specific date stated in the question, but you are expected to know that the first Hundred Days of his Presidency was in 1933.

> The account begins with the background to the Hundred Days and focuses on Roosevelt's election campaign against Hoover. This is not the focus of the question and should be avoided.

> Roosevelt's first Hundred Days in office was him use his 'Brains Trust' to introduce a wide range of reforms often called the first New Deal. Roosevelt communicated his ideas and aims to the public via radio broadcast every Sunday to millions of Americans in what were called his 'fireside chats' – this was very popular.

> The account then examines the beginnings of the Hundred Days. This is more focused and contains some good, detailed description.

> Roosevelt dealt with the banks first by passing a law. This was a pressing issue as thousands of banks had collapsed since the Wall Street Crash leaving businesses without loans and losing billions of dollars in people's savings. He then dealt with other areas.

> The account then logically examines some of the different areas focused on in the Hundred Days legislation such as the banking crisis and the creation of alphabet agencies. These paragraphs are well-sequenced but some lack specific examples such as the name of the banking act passed or the agency set up to help farmers.

> He tried to help the poor and the unemployed by setting up the FERA which spent over $500 million on relief and job creation schemes. The CCC helped provide 2.5 million jobs to young Americans on environmental projects and the PWA employed millions on public works projects like road building and constructing new hospitals across the USA.

> Roosevelt also helped farmers by encouraging them to destroy crops and slaughter livestock so prices would increase – in fact, their income doubled over the 1930s. He helped businesses with the NRA and tried to improve wages for the workers.

b) Discuss the importance of the alphabet agencies as part of the first New Deal. **[25]**

> The importance of the alphabet agencies as part of the first New Deal is the focus of the discussion.

> The alphabet agencies created in the first New Deal were important in many different ways. Firstly, they provided relief from the Depression by creating jobs, helping farmers and industry. This was probably the most important aspect of the alphabet agencies. However, they were also important because they restored confidence in the government and its policies after the Crash of 1929. Finally, they were important because they demonstrated a radical change in many Americans' view of the role of government.

> There is no explicit date stated in the question, but you are expected to know that the first New Deal took place between 1933 and 1935.

> The introduction effectively lists the different aspects of the discussion and provides a partial judgement about the most important aspect. A wide variety of different angles are explored here.

The first paragraph demonstrates excellent contextual knowledge and is full of meaningful and well-selected examples. There is some explanation provided, but much of it is description.	The Depression had caused many social and economic problems in the USA in the early 1930s. Most significantly, unemployment was close to 14 million by 1933 and this had led to homelessness as people were unable to pay their mortgages. It had also resulted in a sharp drop in production – almost a third since 1928 – and this caused a constant cycle of depression in the economy. The alphabet agencies were created as part of the first New Deal with the aim of using government money to create jobs for the unemployed, provide help for the poor and homeless and support farmers and industry to increase their prices and with it their profit.
A common error is made here to include the Emergency Banking Act as an alphabet agency. It was a law passed by the government, but it did not see the creation of a government agency.	The first agency was the Emergency Banking Act which closed down the unstable banks and only allowed strong ones to reopen. This was crucial for the economy to rebuild and for businesses to borrow money to invest. Roosevelt then set up the CWA and PWA to provide jobs for millions of unemployed Americans in public works projects across the country. The PWA alone spent nearly $7 billion of taxpayers' money on building hospitals, schools and roads. Farmers were helped with the AAA which set quotas on food production. It helped about 99 per cent of farmers increase their income. The NRA focused on industry and improved working conditions for workers, and the poor were given relief by the FERA. These agencies were important as they tackled the problems caused by the Depression.
An interesting second aspect is discussed here in some depth. Good examples are used to explain the importance of the agencies in restoring confidence in the USA after the Crash.	However, the restoring of consumer confidence and confidence in the stock market was also important as it would encourage spending and investment. The NRA allowed members to fly the Blue Eagle symbol which encouraged consumers to buy their products and this helped boost production by over 20 per cent in 1933 alone. The more people with jobs would also increase spending and the CWA, PWA and FERA all helped provide short-term work for many – in fact, the FERA gave temporary jobs to over 20 million Americans by 1935. Roosevelt knew this was important to boost morale in the USA and encourage consumer spending again after the Crash. The SEC was set up to restore faith in the stock market after the Crash. Many investors had lost confidence after the reckless speculation of the 1920s and the SEC was designed to stop this from happening again by introducing rules and codes about buying and selling shares.
This is also an interesting and valid angle to discuss for this question. The paragraph elaborates this aspect convincingly through the use of well chosen examples and a very balanced assessment of the importance of the agencies on people's opinions about the role of government.	Lastly, the alphabet agencies were important because they represented a change in American values due to the effects of the Depression. Most Americans would have believed in the Republican principle of laissez-faire in the 1920s while the economy was booming for many. They did not want to see the government interfere with people's livelihoods or businesses. However, the Crash had shifted the opinion of many as they now viewed Hoover's perceived lack of help as shameful while many suffered on the streets living in Hoovervilles without food or jobs and reliant on charities. Roosevelt had won a landslide victory in 1933 with his promises of 'action and action now' and the alphabet agencies saw the government for the first time using massive amounts of public money to directly intervene in people's lives and businesses. However, it is also important to not

overstate this point as many business leaders and Republicans opposed these un-American actions and saw the agencies as threatening the American way of life. The Supreme Court even shut down the NRA and AAA after they were declared unconstitutional.

Overall, the most important aspect of the agencies was their impact on the effects of the Depression. This is why most Americans had voted against the Republicans and for the Democratic Party in 1932. Although the agencies never solved the Depression in the first New Deal, they did relieve the symptoms for millions of Americans and even saw the economy recover slightly and unemployment drop.

> The concluding argument is quite convincing and is supported by explanation, but a comparison with the other aspects discussed in the answer would have added extra weight.

Glossary

Agent Orange Poisonous chemical used by US forces in Vietnam to defoliate (remove leaves) from forest areas to deprive enemy of cover.

Alliance Arrangement between two countries to help or defend each other, usually in trade or war.

Anschluss Joining of Austria and Germany as one state – forbidden by the Treaty of Versailles 1919 but carried out by Hitler in 1938.

Anti-Comintern Pact Alliance between Germany, Italy and Japan in 1936 to combat spread of communism.

Antisemitism Prejudice against Jewish people.

Appeasement Policy of Britain and France in the 1930s allowing Hitler to break the terms of the Treaty of Versailles.

Armistice End to fighting.

Arms race Competition to build stockpiles of weapons

Article 10 Article of League of Nations Covenant which promised security to League members from attack by other states.

Assembly Main forum of the League of Nations for discussing important issues.

Assembly line System of producing cars in which each worker had only one job.

Atomic bomb/H bomb Nuclear weapons, only used in Second World War by USA against Japan but a constant threat in the Cold War.

Autobahns High-speed motorways built by the Nazis in Germany in the 1930s to create jobs.

Autocracy Rule by one individual with total power.

Bauhaus German design movement incorporating sleek lines and modern materials.

Bay of Pigs Bay in Cuba, scene of disastrous attempt by Cuban exiles to overthrow Fidel Castro. Caused humiliation for USA, which backed the attack.

Beauty of Labour Nazi movement to improve conditions for industrial workers and try to win their support.

Berlin airlift Operation in 1948–49 using aircraft to transport supplies to West Berlin which had been cut off by USSR.

Berlin Blockade Action by USSR to cut road, rail and canal links between West Berlin and the rest of Germany. Aim was to force USA and allies to withdraw from West Berlin.

Berlin Wall Barrier constructed by communist East German Government to block movement between East and West Berlin. As well as a wall there were fences, dogs and armed guards.

Big Three 1) Three main leaders at Versailles Peace Conference 1919 – Lloyd George (Britain), Wilson (USA), Clemenceau (France); 2) Leaders at Yalta and Potsdam Conferences 1945 – Roosevelt/Truman (USA), Churchill/Atlee (Britain), Stalin (USSR).

Blitzkrieg An intense military campaign aimed at achieving a quick victory.

Blockade Tactic involving cutting off supplies to a city or country. Usually by sea but can also be land or air blockade.

Bolshevik/Bolshevism Russian political movement led by Lenin and following communist ideas developed by Karl Marx and further developed by Lenin.

Boom Period of high economic prosperity.

Boycott Refusing to have anything to do with a person or group.

Brezhnev Doctrine Policy of USSR from 1968 which effectively meant no Eastern European states would be allowed to have a non-communist government.

Budget The spending plans of a government. Can refer to a particular policy or the whole government spending plan.

Capitalism/Capitalist Political, social and economic system centred on democracy and individual freedoms such as free speech, political beliefs and freedom to do business.

Censorship System of controlling information to the public, usually employed by governments. Can refer to paper, radio, TV or online information.

CENTO Central Treaty Organisation – alliance of countries including Britain, Turkey and Pakistan designed to resist the spread of communism.

Chancellor Head of the government.

Checkpoint Charlie Most famous point where travel between communist East Berlin and US-controlled West Berlin was possible.

Chemical weapons Usually refers to weapons which employ poisonous gas to kill enemies.

CIA The Central Intelligence Agency is a US government department, formed in 1947, which gathers information (intelligence) about threats to the USA but which also funds direct action (such as the Bay of Pigs invasion) to support American foreign policy.

Civil war War between two sides within the same nation or group. Examples in Russia 1919–21 and Spain 1936–37.

Coalition A government made up of two or more political parties.

Co-existence Living side by side without threatening the other side. Most famously put forward by Soviet leader Khrushchev when he proposed East and West could live in peaceful co-existence.

co-operation Working together – could be political, economic or legal.

Cold War Conflict that ran from c.1946 to 1989 between the USA and the USSR and their various allies. They never fought each other but used propaganda, spying and similar methods against other. Also sponsored other countries in regional wars.

Collective security Key principle of the League of Nations that all members could expect to be secure because the other members of the League would defend them from attack.

Collectivisation Policy to modernise agriculture in the USSR 1928–40. Succeeded in modernising farming to some extent but with terrible human cost.

Comecon Organisation to control economic planning in communist countries of eastern Europe.

Cominform Organisation to spread communist ideas and also make sure communist states followed ideas of communism practised in USSR.

Commissions Organisations set up by the League of Nations to tackle economic, social and health problems.

Communism/Communist Political, economic and social system involving state control of economy and less emphasis on individual rights than capitalism.

Communist bloc Eastern European states controlled by communist governments from the end of the Second World War to 1989.

Competition Pressure from rivals, usually in business and often rivals in other countries.

Concentration camps Camps used by Nazis to hold political opponents in Germany.

Concordat A deal between the state and the Catholic Church.

Conference of Ambassadors Organisation involving Britain, France, Italy and Japan which met to sort out international disputes. Worked alongside League of Nations.

Conscription Compulsory service in the armed forces.

Consolidation Making a position more secure, usually when a political party has just taken power.

Constitution A system of government.

Containment US policy in Cold War to stop the spread of communism.

Conventional weapons Non-nuclear weapons. Can refer to ground, air or sea including missiles.

Cossacks Elite troops of the Russian tsars.

Council Influential body within the League of Nations which contained the most powerful members of the League.

Coup Revolution.

Covenant Agreement or set of rules.

Crash Collapse in value of US economy in 1929 which led to economic depression in the 1930s.

Credit Borrowing money, usually from a bank.

Dawes Plan Financial aid package provided by the USA to Germany in 1924.

De-Stalinisation Policy of Soviet leader Khrushchev in the 1950s to move away from the policies of Stalin.

Demilitarised zone Area of land where troops cannot be stationed, e.g. Rhineland area of Germany after the First World War.

Democracy Political system in which the population votes for its government in elections held on a regular basis.

Democrat Member of one of the main US political parties.

Depression Period of economic hardship in which trade is poor and usually leading to problems such as unemployment and possibly political unrest.

Dictator Leader of a state who has total control and does not have to listen to opponents or face elections.

Dictatorship System in which one person runs a country.

Diktat Term used in Germany to describe the Treaty of Versailles because Germany had no say in the terms of the Treaty.

Diplomatic relations How countries discuss issues with each other. Breaking off diplomatic relations can sometimes be a first step towards war.

Disarmament Process of scrapping land, sea or air weapons.

Domino theory Policy in which the USA believed it had to stop countries becoming communist otherwise they would fall to communism like dominoes.

Draft US term for compulsory military service.

Duma Russian Parliament established after 1905 revolution in Russia and a source of opposition to the tsar 1905–17.

Ebert President of Germany 1919–25. He was the first democratically elected president.

Economic depression Period of economic downturn where trade between countries and inside countries declines, often leading to unemployment.

Edelweiss Pirates Youth groups in Germany who opposed the Nazis, especially in the war years.

Enabling Act Law passed in 1933 which gave the government powers to arrest opponents.

Federal A system where power is shared between central and state governments.

Final Solution Nazi plan to exterminate Jewish people and other races in Europe. Generally thought to have begun in 1942.

Five-Year Plan Programme of economic development in the USSR from 1928 onwards. Achieved considerable progress in industry but with heavy human cost.

Flappers Young women in the 1920s, especially in the USA, who had greater freedom than previously because of job opportunities and changing attitudes.

Freedom of speech Ability to publish or speak any religious or political view without being arrested.

Freikorps Ex-soldiers in Germany after the First World War.

Führer Leader (German).

Gangster A criminal.

General strike Large-scale co-ordinated strike by workers designed to stop essential services like power, transport etc.

Gestapo Secret police in Nazi Germany.
Glasnost Openness and transparency – policy of Soviet leader Mikhail Gorbachev in the 1980s designed to allow people to have their views heard and criticise the government.
Gleichschaltung Process of making sure that all organisations were controlled by Nazis.
Guerrilla warfare Type of warfare which avoids large-scale battles and relies on hit-and-run raids.
Gulag Prison camp in remote area where prisoners were put to work.
Hindsight Looking back on historical events with the ability to see what happened since.
Hire purchase System of paying for goods in instalments so they could be enjoyed straight away.
Hitler Youth Youth organisation in Nazi Germany designed to prepare young people for war and make them loyal Nazis.
Ho Chi Minh Trail Route in Cambodia used by North Vietnamese and Viet Cong forces to supply forces fighting South Vietnamese and US forces.
Hollywood Suburb of Los Angeles, home of the US film industry.
Holocaust The mass murder of Jewish people and other racial groups by the Nazis in the Second World War.
Hooverville Shanty town made up of temporary shacks, common in the economic depression of the 1930s in the USA and named after President Hoover.
Hundred Days The initial period of President F.D. Roosevelt in 1933 in which he passed a huge range of measures to help bring economic recovery.
Hyperinflation Process of money becoming worthless, most notable instance was in Germany in 1923.
ICBM Inter Continental Ballistic Missile – nuclear missiles capable of travelling through space and almost impossible to stop.
idealist Person motivated by particular beliefs, e.g. commitment to right of peoples to rule themselves.

Immigration Entry into a country with the purpose of settling.
Indochina Former name for Vietnam.
Industrialisation Building up factories, coal, electricity etc.
Inflation Rising prices.
Intelligence (as in CIA) Secret services of states, e.g. CIA in USA or KGB in USSR.
Iron curtain Term used by Churchill in 1946 to describe separation of eastern and western Europe into communist and non-communist blocs.
Isolationism Policy in the USA in the 1920s which argued that the USA should not get involved in international disputes.
Jazz Type of music which became extremely popular from the 1920s, generally associated with African American musicians.
Kaiser Ruler of Germany.
Kapp Putsch Attempt to overthrow democratically elected government in Germany in 1920.
Kerensky Leader of the Provisional Government which governed Russia after first revolution in 1917.
Kolkhoz Large farms created by merging smaller farms under policy of collectivisation.
Kristallnacht Night of Broken Glass – attack on Jewish properties across Germany in November 1938.
Ku Klux Klan Secret Society in USA which aimed to keep white supremacy in USA and terrorised African Americans and other groups.
Kulak Prosperous peasant farmer.
Laissez-faire Philosophy based on the idea that governments should not get involved in economy, business or people's lives.
Landlord/peasant Key figures in farming, particularly in Russia c.1900. Landlords owned land but also maintained Tsar's authority. Peasants worked for the landlords.
League of German Maidens Organisation in Nazi Germany for girls designed to get girls to embrace Nazi beliefs and values.

League of Nations Organisation set up to manage international disputes and prevent wars after the First World War. Brainchild of US President Woodrow Wilson.
Lebensraum Living Space – became part of Hitler's plans to conquer an empire for Germany in the 1930s.
Left-wing Groups or individuals whose political beliefs are rooted in socialism or communism.
Lenin Leader of the Bolshevik/Communist Party in Russia and a key figure in bringing them to power in 1917 and keeping power until his death in 1924.
Lynch Murder, usually by a mob and carried out on African Americans.
MAD Mutually Assured Destruction – the idea that no state would ever use nuclear weapons because they would themselves be destroyed by retaliation.
Mail order Popular type of shopping in the USA in the 1920s in which customers ordered from catalogues.
Manchurian crisis International crisis sparked off when Japan invaded the Chinese province of Manchuria in 1931. Despite investigating, the League of Nations failed to stop Japanese aggression.
Mandates System by which Britain and France took control of territories ruled by Germany and Turkey which had been on the losing side in the First World War.
Marshall Aid Programme of US economic aid to western Europe 1947–51. Aim was to aid economic recovery but also to prevent more states becoming communist.
Marshall Plan The plan behind Marshall Aid. Although it was an economic programme it was also political. Some commentators argued it was an economic form of imperialism designed to allow the USA to dominate western Europe.
Martial law Rule by the military rather than a civil police force.
Martyr Person who dies for a cause they believe in.

Marxist Person who follows the ideas of Karl Marx, a political commentator who believed that societies would eventually become communist as workers overthrew bosses and took control of wealth and power.

Mass consumption Buying of goods by large proportion of the population.

Mass production System of producing goods in factories using production lines in which workers specialised in one task. Made production quick, efficient and relatively cheap.

Mein Kampf 'My Struggle': the autobiography of Adolf Hitler in which he set out his theories about power and racial superiority.

Mensheviks Opposition party in Russia in early 1900s, part of the Social Democratic Party before it split into Bolsheviks and Mensheviks.

Military force Use of armed force (e.g. troops, bombing by aircraft) as opposed to political or economic methods.

Missile gap Term to describe the alleged advantage of the USSR over the USA in nuclear missiles. Historians doubt whether the missile gap was as real as was claimed.

Mobilised Armed forces told to prepare for war.

Monkey Trial Trial of teacher John Scopes for teaching about evolution in Tennessee in 1925.

Moral condemnation Criticism of a state for actions against another state – prelude to stronger action such as economic sanctions or military force.

Munich Agreement Agreement in October 1938 in which Britain and France agreed to Hitler's demands to control the Sudetenland area of Czechoslovakia. This is generally seen as the final stage of the policy of Appeasement.

Munich Putsch Attempted revolt by Hitler and Nazis in 1923, aiming to overthrow the government.

NAACP National Association for the Advancement of Colored People – organisation whose aim was to promote and support the cause of African Americans in the USA in the 1920s and 1930s.

Napalm Highly explosive chemical weapon which spread a fireball over a large area. Used extensively in the Vietnam War.

National Community Key idea of Nazis in Germany in the 1930s – they wanted people to become part of and promote a 'National Community'.

Nationalism Strong sense of pride in your own country, sometimes directed aggressively towards other countries or minority groups.

Nationalities Racial groups within larger states, e.g. Poles in the Russian Empire or Hungarians in the Austrian Empire.

NATO North Atlantic Treaty Organisation: Alliance formed by USA and other Western states which promised to defend members against any attack, particularly from the USSR.

Nazism National Socialism, the political belief of Adolf Hitler and the Nazi Party based on aggressive expansion of German lands and the superiority of the Aryan race.

Nazi–Soviet Pact Agreement in 1939 between Hitler and Stalin to not attack each other and to divide Poland between them.

Negative cohesion Term coined by historian Gordon Craig to describe the way different groups in Germany supported the Nazis because they feared the opponents of the Nazis (particularly the Communists).

NEPmen Traders and small businessmen who took advantage of the private trade established by the NEP.

New Deal Policies introduced by US President Roosevelt from 1933 onwards to try to tackle US economic problems.

New Economic Policy Policy introduced by Lenin in the USSR after the Russian Civil War. Basically allowed limited amounts of private enterprise, which went against communist theory but was an emergency measure to help the economy recover from war.

Night of the Long Knives Attack on Ernst Rohm and other leading figures in the SA in June 1934.

NKVD Secret police in USSR, later becoming the KGB.

Nobel Peace Prize Prize awarded to politicians who have made major contribution to bringing an end to a conflict.

Normalcy Term used by US President Warren Harding in the 1920s to describe the return to normal life after the First World War.

November Criminals The German politicians who signed the Treaty of Versailles. This was a term of abuse exploited by extreme parties in Germany, especially the Nazis, to undermine democracy.

Nuclear deterrent Term which referred to the nuclear weapons owned by each side in the Cold War. The fact that each side had these weapons stopped the other side from using theirs.

Nuremberg Laws Series of laws passed in Germany in 1935 discriminating against Jewish people and other racial groups in Germany.

Nuremberg rally Huge political meeting held every June from 1923 to 1938.

Okhrana Secret police force of the Russian Tsars.

One-party state State where only one political party is permitted by law such as Nazi Germany or the USSR under communism.

Operation Rolling Thunder Huge-scale bombing campaign by USA against North Vietnam during the Vietnam War.

Over-production Usually in agriculture – growing too much food so that demand is filled and prices fall.

Paris Peace Conference Conference which ran 1919–23 to decide how to officially end the First World War. Resulted in Treaty of Versailles with Germany and three other treaties.

Peasants Poor farmers who worked their own small plots of land and usually had to work the lands of landlords as well.

People power Term to describe the rise of popular action against communist regimes in 1989 which contributed to the fall of communism.

Perestroika Restructuring – the idea of Soviet leader Mikhail Gorbachev in the later 1980s that the USSR needed to reform.

Polish Corridor Strip of land which under the Treaty of Versailles 1919 gave Poland access to the sea but separated East Prussia from the rest of Germany.

Politburo Main decision-making group of the Communist Party in the USSR, similar to British Cabinet.

Potsdam Conference Conference held in August 1945 between President Truman (USA), Stalin (USSR) and Churchill, then Atlee (Britain). Discussed major issues including the atomic bomb and Soviet take-over of eastern Europe.

Prague Spring Reform movement in Czechoslovakia to change communist rule in Czechoslovakia, eventually crushed by Soviet forces.

Prohibition Amendment to US Constitution passed in 1919 to ban production of alcohol.

Propaganda Method of winning over a population to a particular idea or set of beliefs. Also used in wartime to raise morale.

Provisional Government Government headed by Alexander Kerensky which took control of Russia after the March 1917 revolution which overthrew the Tsar.

Public opinion View of majority or large section of population on an issue, most important in democracies where politicians often have to win over public opinion.

Purges Policy pursued by Stalin in the USSR in the 1930s to remove potential opponents. Involved arrests, torture, show trials, deportations to labour camps and executions.

Putsch Revolt designed to overthrow the existing government, most commonly associated with the Kapp Putsch in 1920 and the Nazis' attempted Munich Putsch in 1923.

Radical Term used to describe extreme political views.

Realist Politician who accepts a particular course of action even though it is not what they would prefer to do.

Rearmament Building up arms and armed forces, used as a means to fight unemployment by many states in the 1930s, including Nazi Germany and Britain.

Red Army Armed forces of the Communists in the Russian Civil War 1918–21 and then the official forces of the Soviet Union.

Red Scare Wave of fear about communist infiltration of American political and social life to undermine it. Seen in the 1920s and also the 1940s and 1950s.

Reichstag German parliament.

Remilitarisation Reintroduction of armed forces into the Rhineland area of Germany in 1936 even though this was banned by the Treaty of Versailles.

Reparations Compensation to be paid by Germany to France, Belgium, Britain and other states as a result of the First World War.

Repeal The overturning of a law.

Republic System of government which does not have a monarch.

Republican One of the two main political parties in the USA.

Reservation Area of land set aside for Native Americans.

Reunification The bringing back together of Germany in 1990 after the division of 1945.

Rhineland Area of Germany that bordered France. Under Treaty of Versailles it was demilitarised – no German forces were allowed there.

Right-wing Political groups or individuals with beliefs usually in national pride, authoritarian government and opposed to communism.

Roaring Twenties Refers to the 1920s in the USA, a period of major social and economic change for many Americans.

Ruhr Main industrial area of Germany.

SA The Brownshirts – Stormtroopers of the Nazi Party.

Saar Region on the border between France and Germany. Run by League of Nations from 1920 to 1935 when its people voted to become part of Germany.

Sanctions Actions taken against states which break international law, most commonly economic sanctions, e.g. refusing to supply oil.

Satellite state State that is controlled by a larger state, e.g. eastern European states controlled by USSR after the Second World War.

Search and destroy Type of tactic used by US military in Vietnam to locate Viet Cong fighters and kill them.

SEATO South East Asia Treaty Organisation – alliance formed in 1954 designed mainly to block the spread of communism.

Second New Deal Set of policies introduced by US President Roosevelt in 1935–36.

Secret police Police force specialising in dealing with threats to the state, e.g. political opponents rather than normal crimes.

Secretariat The section of the League of Nations which carried out administrative tasks and also the agencies of the League.

Shares System which allows large or small investors to own part of a company and get a share of its profits.

Show trials Trials of political opponents which were given great publicity – most prominent in the USSR under Stalin in the 1930s.

Social Democratic Party Main left-wing (and generally most popular) political party in Germany in the 1920s and 1930s. Eventually banned by the Nazis when they came to power in 1933.

Socialism Political system in which government takes strong control of economic and social life. In theory socialist societies would eventually become communist societies.

Socialist Revolutionaries Opposition group in tsarist Russia, the most well-supported as they had the support of the peasants.

Solidarity Polish trade union which emerged in the 1980s and opposed the communist government there.

Soviet republics The various smaller states which made up the USSR.

Soviet sphere of influence Terms agreed at Yalta Conference in 1945 – Western powers agreed that Poland and other parts of eastern Europe would be under Soviet influence.

Soviet Union The former Russian empire after it became a communist state in the 1920s.

Soviets Councils of workers.

Spanish Civil War Conflict in Spain which was seen as a rehearsal for the Second World War when German and Italian forces intervened to support General Franco.

Spartacists Communists in Germany in 1919 who wanted a revolution in Germany similar to the 1917 revolution in Russia.

Speculation Buying shares in the hope that their price will rise when they can be sold at a profit.

SS Organisation within the Nazi Party which began as Hitler's bodyguard but expanded to become a state within a state.

Stakhanovite A very hard and committed Soviet worker.

Stalin Leader of the USSR from 1929 to his death in 1953.

Stock market Trading arena where investors can buy and sell shares in companies.

Stolypin Minister of the Tsar in imperial Russia.

Strength Through Joy Leisure programme run by the Nazis in Germany to improve the lives of ordinary people.

Sudetenland Area of Czechoslovakia which bordered Germany and contained many German speakers. Taken over by Hitler in 1938 as part of the Munich Agreement.

Summit meeting Meeting of leaders to discuss key issues, e.g. US President Reagan and Soviet leader Gorbachev's meetings in the 1980s.

Sunni One of the main branches of the Muslim faith.

Superpower A country in a dominant international position that is able to influence events.

Supreme Court Highest court in the USA, whose job was to rule if laws passed by the government were challenged as being unconstitutional.

Surveillance Watching, usually by intelligence agencies or secret police.

Tariffs Taxes on imported goods which made them more expensive – often designed to protect makers of home-produced goods.

Temperance Movement that opposed alcohol.

Tennessee Valley Authority Organisation set up by President Roosevelt to help provide economic development in the Tennessee Valley. Most famous projects were giant hydroelectric dams.

Tet Offensive Attack launched by Viet Cong and North Vietnamese forces in 1968. Seen by many as the turning point in the Vietnam War as US public turned against the war.

Totalitarian Complete control.

Trade sanctions Restricting sale of goods to a nation or sales from a nation.

Trade union Organisation that represents workers.

Traditional industries Well-established industries such as textiles, coal, agriculture.

Treaty of Brest-Litovsk Treaty between Germany and Russia in 1918 which ended war between the two. Germany took massive amounts of land and reparations.

Treaty of Versailles Treaty that officially ended war between Allies and Germany in 1919. Controversial because of the terms, which Germany claimed to be excessively harsh.

Trotsky Leading figure in the Bolshevik Party, especially in the Russian Civil War 1918–21.

Truman Doctrine Policy of US President Truman from 1947 to promise help to any state threatened by communism.

Trusts Groups of businesses working together illegally to reduce competition.

Tsar Ruler of Russia up until revolution in 1917.

Tsarina Wife of tsar.

Unanimous Agreed by all.

United Nations Organisation that succeeded the League of Nations in 1945 and whose aim was to solve international disputes and promote humanitarian causes.

Universal suffrage Equal voting rights for all adults.

US sphere of influence Areas seen as under the control or political or economic influence of the USA.

USSR The former Russian empire after it became a communist state in the 1920s.

Viet Cong/Viet Minh Underground army fighting against French rule in the 1950s and then government of South Vietnam and its US allies in Vietnam War.

Vietnamisation Policy of handing over Vietnam War to South Vietnam forces.

Volk People (German).

Wall Street Crash Collapse in value of US companies in October 1929 which led to widespread economic collapse.

War Communism Policy pursued by communist leader Lenin 1918–21 to try to build communist society in Russia and also fight against his opponents. Caused major hardships and had to be temporarily replaced with New Economic Policy.

War guilt Clause in Treaty of Versailles which forced Germany to accept blame for the First World War.

Warsaw Pact Alliance of USSR and eastern European states to defend against attack and preserve communist control in eastern Europe.

Weimar Small town in Germany, home of the German government in the 1920s.

West/Western Powers Term generally used to refer to USA and its allies in the Cold War.

WMD (Weapons of Mass Destruction) Missiles, bombs or shells which were armed with chemical, biological or nuclear weapons.

Yalta Conference Conference between USA, USSR and Britain in 1945 to decide the shape of the world after the Second World War ended.

Young Plan American economic plan in 1929 to reorganise reparations payments to make it easier for Germany to pay.

Zemstva Local councils in tsarist Russia.

Index

Aaland Islands dispute 34, 35
Abyssinian crisis 42, 48–51, 75
advertising 292, 315
African Americans 303–6, 334, 335
agriculture 209–11, 218, 240, 272, 287, 289, 293
Ali, Muhammad 121
Andropov, Yuri 140
Anglo-German Naval Agreement 47, 58
Anglo-German Pact 54
Anschluss 12, 15, 63
Anti-Comintern Pact 62
antisemitism 259–61, 279, 334
appeasement 55, 64–5, 67, 68–9, 72–3, 75, 83
April Theses 189
arms race 105
Atlee, Clement 86
autocracy 173
Bauhaus 233, 234
Bay of Pigs 107
Beck, Gad 278
Beneš, Edvard 45, 66, 68
Berlin airlift 94
Berlin Blockade 93–5
Berlin Wall 135–7, 142
Big Three 6–11, 18, 84–5
Blitzkrieg tactics 62
Bolsheviks 176, 180, 187, 188, 189, 190, 191, 192, 194–6
Bonhoeffer, Dietrich 258, 280
Bonus Army 322
Bradley, Omar 102
Brest-Litovsk, Treaty of 9, 19, 194
Brezhnev, Leonid 132, 139
Brezhnev Doctrine 133
Bukharin, Nikolai 202, 203, 204, 212
Bulgarian crisis 34, 36–7
capitalism 83, 135, 175, 183, 199, 225
Capone, Al 311, 312
Castro, Fidel 106–8, 112, 113
censorship 173
    Czechoslovakia 132, 133
    Germany 233, 255, 274, 281
    USA 102, 298, 308
    USSR 128, 213
CENTO 104, 105
Central Intelligence Agency (CIA) 106, 107
Chamberlain, Neville 54, 55, 62, 63, 66, 69, 70, 77
    and appeasement 64, 67, 68, 72, 73
Cheka 194, 195, 197
chemical weapons 46, 119

Chicago 295, 305, 306, 312
Churchill, Winston 68, 72, 84–6, 90, 91, 274
cinema
    Germany 233, 255, 271, 274
    USA 297–8, 299, 300
Civil Rights movement 306
Clemenceau, Georges 7, 9, 10, 11
Cold War 82–145
collective security 30, 49, 50
collectivisation 209–11, 218
Comecon (Council for Mutual Economic Assistance) 128
Cominform (Communist Information Bureau) 89, 128, 129
Comintern 62
communism 56, 83, 99–100
    collapse of 142–3
    fear of 64, 244, 301–2
    Germany 225, 228, 244
    war communism 198, 199
concentration camps
    Germany and 84, 248, 251, 252, 253, 259, 261
    USSR 217
Conference of Ambassadors 26, 34, 35–6
conscription 13, 58, 249, 270
containment 91, 99, 104, 116, 124
Coolidge, Calvin 289
Corfu crisis 34, 35–6
Cronkite, Walter 105, 120
Cuban Missile Crisis 105–8, 110–13
Czechoslovakia 66, 69, 91, 132–3
DAF (German Labour Front) 247, 271
Dawes Plan 38, 39, 231, 232
death camps 274, 278, 279
Death's Head battalions 252, 253, 279
dekulakisation 210
Depression 41–51, 75, 77, 319–20
Diem, Ngo Dinh 115
disarmament 7, 13, 15, 38, 46
Disarmament Conference 42, 46–7, 58
domino theory 114, 116, 124
Dresden bombing 275
Drexler, Anton 235
Dubček, Alexander 132
Dulles, J. F. 104, 114, 115
eastern Europe 6, 7, 11, 84, 87
    communism, collapse of 142–3
    USSR and 88–9, 127–45
Ebert, Friedrich 14, 16, 222, 224, 228, 229, 230
Edelweiss Pirates 276
Einsatzgruppen 277, 279

Eisenhower, Dwight 102, 106, 107, 114, 116, 130
eugenics 260
euthanasia programme 259, 260
famines 174, 198, 210–11
Final Solution 274, 278, 279
Five-Year Plans 205–9, 215
Fourteen Points 7, 15
Freikorps 16, 228
Galen, Clemens 258, 280
Gapon, Father Georgi 178, 179, 180
Garvey, Marcus 306
Geneva Protocol 36
Germany
    agriculture 240
    and Depression 43
    economic recovery 270–1
    hyperinflation 16, 17, 231
    impact of WW1 222–3
    impact of WW2 274–5
    political parties 232
    reactions to Versailles Treaty 14–15
    religion 258
    reunification of 143
    strikes 16, 228, 230
    territories and colonies 12–13, 15
Gerö, Ernö 130
Gestapo 252, 255, 262, 276
glasnost (openness) 141
Goebbels, Joseph 59, 237, 238, 241, 247, 254–6, 274
Goering, Hermann 239, 247, 248, 270
Gomulka, Wladyslaw 129
Gorbachev, Mikhail 127, 140–1, 142, 143, 144, 145
GOSPLAN 205
Greece 35, 90–1
Harding, Warren 29, 288, 289
Henlein, Konrad 66
Hess, Rudolf 239
Heydrich, Reinhard 239, 252
Himmler, Heinrich 239, 248, 252, 274, 278
Hindenburg, Paul von 234, 245, 246, 247, 248, 249
Hitler, Adolf 16, 17, 20, 43, 50, 54, 56–61, 64, 75, 82, 235–49
    and *Anschluss* 63
    as Chancellor 46, 245
    consolidation of power 246–9
    Enabling Act 247, 249
    henchmen 238–9
    invasion of Czechoslovakia 69
    invasion of Poland 71
    Mein Kampf 56, 76, 229, 237, 255, 259

and Nazi–Soviet Pact 70–1
and Spanish Civil War 62
and Sudetenland 66–8
Hitler myth 281
Hitler Youth 237, 265–7
Ho Chi Minh 114, 118
Ho Chi Minh Trail 115, 116
Hoare–Laval Pact 50
Honecker, Erich 142
Hoover, Herbert 289, 295, 317, 321–2, 323
Hundred Days 324–7
Hungarian uprising 130–1
hyperinflation 16, 17, 231
ICBMs 105
industry
    USA 287, 290–1, 294
    USSR 204–8, 217
International Labour Organization (ILO) 32, 40
internationalism 39
iron curtain 88
isolationism 29, 64, 83
Jaruzelski, General 139
jazz 297
Jim Crow 304
Johnson, Lyndon B. 115–16, 121, 123
July Bomb Plot 280
July Days 190
Kádár, János 131
Kadets 187, 188, 194
Kamenev, Lev 202, 203, 212
Kapp, Wolfgang 16, 228
Kapp Putsch 16, 228
Kennedy, John F. 105, 107, 108, 110, 113, 115, 136, 137
Kerensky, Alexander 187, 190–1, 192
Keynes, John Maynard 18
Khrushchev, Nikita 95, 106, 107, 110–11, 113, 129, 137, 213
Kim Il Sung 100
King, Martin Luther 121
Kirov, Sergei 212
Kissinger, Henry 123
Kohl, Helmut 143
Korean War 100–4
Kornilov, General 190, 191
Kristallnacht 260–1
Kronstadt naval base 192, 198
Ku Klux Klan 303, 304, 306
kulaks 174, 182, 206, 209, 210
labour camps 198, 204, 212, 274, 278, 279
laissez-faire 288, 289, 292
League of Nations 13, 15, 24–51, 233
    Assembly 32
    Council 30, 32, 35
    Covenant 26, 30, 49

Depression and 41–51
Health Committee 33, 40
International Labour Organization (ILO) 32, 40
Mandates Commission 33
membership 31
organisation of 2–3
peacekeeping attempts 34–9
Permanent Court of International Justice 32
Refugees Committee 33, 40
Secretariat 32
Slavery Commission 33
weaknesses in 25–33
Lebensborn 269
Lebensraum 56, 75, 237
Lenin, Vladimir Ilyich 176, 180, 187, 192, 193–5
    death of 200, 202
    in power 194–5, 198–9
    and rise of Bolsheviks 189
Liebknecht, Karl 228
Lloyd George, David 7, 8–9, 10, 11
Locarno treaties 38, 60, 233
Long, Huey 330
Low, David 45, 47, 65, 101
Ludendorff, Erich 236, 237
Luxemburg, Rosa 228
Lytton Report 45
MacArthur, Douglas 100, 102, 322
McNamara, Robert 116
MAD (Mutually Assured Destruction) 105
Manchurian crisis 42, 43, 44–5, 75
Mao Tse-tung 102
Marshall Aid 92
Marshall Plan 91
Marxist theory 176
Mensheviks 176, 187, 188, 189
militarism 62
Monkey Trial 308
Morgenthau Plan 93
Moscow Soviet 180, 181, 189, 192
Moscow uprising 180
Mukden Incident 44, 45
Munich Agreement 67–8, 70
Munich Putsch 16, 236–7, 238
Mussolini, Benito 35–6, 43, 48–50, 51, 62–3, 67
My Lai massacre 122
Nagy, Imre 130, 133
Nation of Islam 121
Native Americans 307, 326, 334, 335
NATO (North Atlantic Treaty Organization) 95, 113
Nazi Party 16, 21, 43, 58, 235, 237–41, 243, 272
    antisemitism 259–61

in Austria 63
consolidation of power 246–9
Depression and rise of 242, 244
election successes 237, 242–4
eugenics 260
euthanasia programme 259, 260
main beliefs 237, 259
minorities, persecution of 259–61
opposition to 262, 269, 280–1
police state 252–3
and religion 258
seizure of power 250–1
Twenty-Five Points 235, 242
and *Volksgemeinschaft* 273
Nazi Women's League 267
Nazi–Soviet Pact 70–1, 75
negative cohesion 244
New Deal 324–34
    opposition to 330–2
    Second New Deal 328–9
New Economic Policy (NEP) 199, 209
Nicholas II, tsar 172, 173, 178–85, 195
Niemöller, Martin 258
Night of the Long Knives 248
Nixon, Richard 123
November Criminals 16, 56, 222
Nuclear Test Ban Treaty 113
nuclear weapons 104, 141
    Cuban Missile Crisis 105–8, 110–13
Nuremberg Laws 259, 260
Nuremberg Rallies 239, 254
Oberdorfer, Don 120
October Manifesto 181
Octobrists 187
Okhrana 173, 176
Olympic Games: Berlin (1936) 257
Operation Rolling Thunder 116
Owens, Jesse 257
Palmer, Mitchell 301, 302
Papen, Franz von 245
Paris Peace Conference 7, 10–11
peace treaties 22
perestroika (restructuring) 141
Petrograd Soviet 180, 181, 185, 187, 188, 189, 192
Pioneers, USSR 215
Poincaré, Raymond 9
Poland 71, 84, 86, 128, 129
    Solidarity 138–9, 142
    Warsaw ghetto 277, 278
Polish Corridor 16, 70
Potemkin mutiny 180
Potsdam Conference 86–7
Prague Spring 132–3
Progressive Party, Russia 187
Prohibition 293, 309–12
propaganda

Germany 251, 254–6, 281
   USSR 213
pump priming 327
racism, USA 303–6
Rákosi, Mátyás 130
Rapallo Treaty 38
Rasputin, Gregory Yefimovich 183, 185
Rathenau, Walther 16, 228
rationing 274
Reagan, Ronald 141
rearmament 42, 43, 46, 48, 58, 75, 249, 270
Red Army 89, 139, 141, 195–6
Red Scare 301–3
Red Terror 195, 196
Reichstag Fire 246
reparations 12, 15, 16–17, 19, 20, 38, 56, 87, 230, 231, 232
Rhee, Syngman 100
Rhineland 11, 13, 50, 60–1
Ribbentrop, Joachim von 70
Ridenhour, Ronald 122
Roaring Twenties 296–8
Robeson, Paul 305
Röhm, Ernst 236, 238, 248
Rome–Berlin Axis 50, 62
Roosevelt, Eleanor 300, 335
Roosevelt, Franklin D. 83, 84–6, 312, 322–36
rugged individualism 288, 289, 321
Ruhr 16–17, 35, 228, 230
Russia
   Bloody Sunday 178–80
   Civil War 195–8
   March 1917 revolution 185
   New Economic Policy (NEP) 199, 209
   1905 revolution 178–81
   November Revolution 192–3
   political parties 187
   Provisional Government 187, 188, 190–1, 192
   Red Army 89, 139, 141, 195–6
   Red Guards 191, 192, 194
   Russian empire 172, 174–5, 198
   strikes 180, 183, 185
   Whites 195–7
   and WW1 184–5
Russo–Japanese War 178
SA (Stormtroopers/Brownshirts) 235, 236, 238, 241, 244, 248
Saarland 11, 12, 15, 59
Sacco, Nikola 303
St Valentine's Day Massacre 312
sanctions 28, 31, 32, 43, 49, 50
Schacht, Hjalmar 270
Schindler, Oskar 278
Schleicher, Kurt von 245, 248
Schuschnigg, Kurt 63

SD 239, 252
SEATO 104
Second New Deal 328–9
slavery 33, 40
Social Democrats, Germany 244
Socialism in One Country 202, 203, 204
Socialist Realism 214
Socialist Revolutionaries (SRs) 176, 180, 187, 188, 194
Solidarity, Poland 138–9, 142
Soviet Union, see USSR (Union of Soviet Socialist Republics)
soviets
   Germany 228
   USSR 180, 181, 185, 189, 191
Sovnarkom (Council of People's Commissars) 194
Spanish Civil War 62
Spartacists 228
speculation 314–15, 316
Speer, Albert 243, 269, 274
SS 239, 241, 244, 248, 252, 253, 255, 260–1
   in WW2 274, 279
Stakhanov, Alexei 206
Stalin, Joseph 84–7, 88, 89, 92, 93, 94, 202–8
   collectivisation 209–11
   control of USSR 212–13, 217–18
   cult of personality 213, 217
   death of 102
   industrialisation of USSR 204–8
   and Nazi-Soviet Pact 70–1
   purges 212, 217
   rivalry with Trotsky 202–3
   and Soviet sphere of influence 128
stock markets 314
Stolypin, Peter 182
Stresa Pact 48
Stresemann, Gustav 231, 232–4, 236
Sudetenland 66–8
Suez Canal 49
Swing movement 276
tariffs 43, 44, 288, 289, 318
temperance movements 309
Tennessee Valley Authority (TVA) 326
Tet Offensive 120
Tito, Marshal 89
Tolstoy, Leo 178
Tonkin Gulf Resolution 115–16
Trotsky, Leon 180, 191, 192, 193, 194, 212
   and Red Army 195, 196
   rivalry with Stalin 202–3
Truman, Harry 86, 90–1, 92, 93, 94, 100, 102
Truman Doctrine 91
tsarist system 172, 176
Ulbricht, Walter 133, 135, 137

United Nations 84, 90, 100
United States of America (USA) 285–95
   and appeasement 64
   and Depression 43
   economic boom 286–95, 315
   government system 288
   ideology 82, 83
   and isolationism 64
   and League of Nations 26–9, 30
   mass production/mass consumption 290–2, 318
   1920s society changes 296–312
   1932 presidential election 321–3
   peace movement 121
   political parties 29
   reaction to Soviet expansion 90–2
   Republican policies 288
   strikes 301–2
   unemployment 295
USSR (Union of Soviet Socialist Republics) 64, 70
   agriculture 209–11, 218
   collapse of 144
   collectivisation 209–11, 218
   creation of 200
   and eastern Europe 88–9, 127–45
   Great Retreat 215
   ideology 83
   industrialisation 204–8, 217
   modernisation of 204–11
   nationalities 174, 216
   society and culture 214–16
   and Spanish Civil War 62
Vaculik, Ludvik 132
Vanzetti, Bartolomeo 303
Versailles, Treaty of 5–21, 56, 75, 228, 229
   assessments of 18–21
   Big Three and 6–11, 18
   consequences of 16–17
   German reactions to 14–15
   terms of 12–13
Viet Cong 115, 118–20
Viet Minh 114
Vietnam War 114–24
Vilna: Polish–Lithuanian dispute 34, 35
Volksgemeinschaft 273
Waffen-SS 252
Walesa, Lech 138–9
Wall Street Crash 314–18
Wallenberg, Raoul 278
Wandervogel movement 234
war communism 198, 199
war guilt 12, 15
Warsaw Pact 95, 104
Washington Conference 38
Weimar Republic 224–34
   Constitution 224–5

culture 233, 234
economy 232, 233
foreign policy 233, 234
Hitler and 235–6
political parties 225–7, 232, 234
under Stresemann 232–4
threats to 228–31
White Rose 280
White Terror 197
Wilson, Woodrow 6–7, 8, 10, 11, 288
  Fourteen Points 7, 15
  and League of Nations 26–9
women
  Nazi Germany 267–9
  USA 299–300, 335
  USSR 215

Yalta Conference 84–5
Yeltsin, Boris 144
Young Plan 12, 38, 233
youth organisations, Germany 237, 265–7, 276
Zinoviev, Grigory 202, 203, 212